ANCIENT RECORDS OF EGYPT

I0320523

HISTORICAL DOCUMENTS

FROM THE EARLIEST TIMES TO THE PERSIAN CONQUEST, COLLECTED
EDITED AND TRANSLATED WITH COMMENTARY

BY

JAMES HENRY BREASTED, Ph.D.

PROFESSOR OF EGYPTOLOGY AND ORIENTAL HISTORY
IN THE UNIVERSITY OF CHICAGO

VOLUME II

THE EIGHTEENTH DYNASTY

ISBN: 978-1-63923-643-5

All Rights reserved. No part of this book maybe reproduced without written permission from the publishers, except by a reviewer who may quote brief passages in a review to be printed in a newspaper or magazine.

Printed: January 2023

Published and Distributed By:
Lushena Books
607 Country Club Drive, Unit E
Bensenville, IL 60106
www.lushenabks.com

ISBN: 978-1-63923-643-5

ANCIENT RECORDS OF EGYPT

TABLE OF CONTENTS

VOLUME I

	§§
THE DOCUMENTARY SOURCES OF EGYPTIAN HISTORY	1–37
CHRONOLOGY	38–57
CHRONOLOGICAL TABLE	58–75
THE PALERMO STONE: THE FIRST TO THE FIFTH DYNASTIES	76–167
I. Predynastic Kings	90
II. First Dynasty	91–116
III. Second Dynasty	117–144
IV. Third Dynasty	145–148
V. Fourth Dynasty	149–152
VI. Fifth Dynasty	153–167
THE THIRD DYNASTY	168–175
Reign of Snefru	168–175
Sinai Inscriptions	168–169
Biography of Methen	170–175
THE FOURTH DYNASTY	176–212
Reign of Khufu	176–187
Sinai Inscriptions	176
Inventory Stela	177–180
Examples of Dedication Inscriptions by Sons	181–187
Reign of Khafre	188–209
Stela of Mertityôtes	188–189
Will of Prince Nekure, Son of King Khafre	190–199
Testamentary Enactment of an Unknown Official, Establishing the Endowment of His Tomb by the Pyramid of Khafre	200–209
Reign of Menkure	210–212
Debhen's Inscription, Recounting King Menkure's Erection of a Tomb for Him	210–212
THE FIFTH DYNASTY	213–281
Reign of Userkaf	213–235

	§§
Testamentary Enactment of Nekonekh	213–215
I. The Priesthood of Hathor	216–219
II. The Mortuary Priesthood of Khenuka	220–222
III. Nekonekh's Will	223–225
IV. Nekonekh's Mortuary Priesthood	226–227
V. Nekonekh's Mortuary Statue	228–230
Testamentary Enactment of Senuonekh, Regulating His Mortuary Priesthood	231–235
Reign of Sahure	236–241
Sinai Inscriptions	236
Tomb Stela of Nenekhsekhmet	237–240
Tomb Inscription of Persen	241
Reign of Neferirkere	242–249
Tomb Inscriptions of the Vizier, Chief Judge, and Chief Architect Weshptah	242–249
Reign of Nuserre	250–262
Sinai Inscription	250
Tomb Inscriptions of Hotephiryakhet	251–253
Inscription of Ptahshepses	254–262
Reign of Menkuhor	263
Sinai Inscription	263
Reign of Dedkere-Isesi	264–281
Sinai Inscriptions	264–267
Tomb Inscriptions of Senezemib, Chief Judge, Vizier, and Chief Architect	268–277
Mortuary Inscription of Nezemib	278–279
Tomb Inscription of the Nomarch Henku	280–281
THE SIXTH DYNASTY	282–390
Reign of Teti	282–294
Inscriptions of Sabu, Also Called Ibebi	282–286
Inscription of Sabu, Also Called Thety	287–288
Inscription of an Unknown Builder	289–290
Inscription of Uni	291–294
I. Career under Teti (l. 1)	292–294
II. Career under Pepi I (ll. 2–32)	306–315
III. Career under Mernere (ll. 32–50)	319–324
Reign of Pepi I	295–315
Hammamat Inscriptions	295–301

TABLE OF CONTENTS

	§§
I. The King's Inscriptions	296
II. The Expedition's Inscription	297–298
III. Chief Architect's Inscription	299
IV. Inscription of the Treasurer of the God Ikhi	300–301
Sinai Inscription	302–303
Inscription in the Hatnub Quarry	304–305
Inscription of Uni: II Career under Pepi I	306–315
Reign of Mernere	316–336
Inscriptions at the First Cataract	316–318
I. Northern Inscription	317
II. Southern Inscription	318
Inscription of Uni: III Career under Mernere	319–324
Inscriptions of Harkhuf	325–336
Inscriptions of Harkhuf (continued)	350–354
Reign of Pepi II	337–385
Conveyance of Land by Idu, Called Also Seneni	337–338
Sinai Inscription	339–343
Stela of the Two Queens, Enekhnes-Merire	344–349
Inscriptions of Harkhuf (continued from § 336)	350–354
Letter of Pepi II	350–354
I. Dates and Introduction	351
II. Acknowledgment of Harkhuf's Letter	351
III. Harkhuf's Rewards	352
IV. King's Instructions	353–354
Inscriptions of Pepi-Nakht	355–360
Inscriptions of Khui	361
Inscriptions of Sebni	362–374
Inscriptions of Ibi	375–379
Inscription of Zau	380–385
Reign of Ity	386–387
Hammamat Inscription	386–387
Reign of Imhotep	388–390
THE NINTH AND TENTH DYNASTIES	391–414
Inscriptions of Siut	391–414
I. Inscription of Tefibi	393–397
II. Inscription of Kheti I	398–404
III. Inscription of Kheti II	405–414

	§§
THE ELEVENTH DYNASTY	415–459
The Nomarch, Intef	419–420
Mortuary Stela	419–420
Reign of Hòrus-Wahenekh-Intef I	421–423
Royal Tomb Stela	421–423
Reign of Horus-Nakhtneb-Tepnefer-Intef II	423A–423G
Stela of Thethi	423A–423G
Reign of Nibhotep-Mentuhotep I	423H
Temple Fragments from Gebelen	423H
Reigns of Intef III and Nibkhrure-Mentuhotep II	424–426
Relief near Assuan	424–426
Reign of Senekhkere-Mentuhotep III	427–433
Hammamat Inscription of Henu	427–433
Reign of Nibtowere-Mentuhotep IV	434–459
Hammamat Inscriptions	434–459
I. The First Wonder	435–438
II. The Official Tablet	439–443
III. The Commander's Tablet	444–448
IV. The Second Wonder	449–451
V. Completion of the Work	452–456
Stela of Eti	457–459
THE TWELFTH DYNASTY	460–750
Chronology of Twelfth Dynasty	460–462
Reign of Amenemhet I	463–497
Inscription of Khnumhotep I	463–465
Hammamat Inscription of Intef	466–468
Inscription of Nessumontu	469–471
Inscription of Korusko	472–473
The Teaching of Amenemhet	474–483
Dedication Inscription	484–485
The Tale of Sinuhe	486–497
Reign of Sesostris I	498–593
The Building Inscription of the Temple of Heliopolis	498–506
Inscription of Meri	507–509
Wadi Halfa Inscription of Mentuhotep	510–514
Inscription of Amenemhet (Ameni)	515–523
Stela of Ikudidi	524–528
Inscription of Intefyoker	529

Inscriptions of Mentuhotep	530–534
The Contracts of Hepzefi	535–538
I. First Contract	539–543
II. Second Contract	544–548
III. Third Contract	549–553
IV. Fourth Contract	554–558
V. Fifth Contract	559–567
VI. Sixth Contract	568–571
VII. Seventh Contract	572–575
VIII. Eighth Contract	576–581
IX. Ninth Contract	582–588
X. Tenth Contract	589–593
Reign of Amenemhet II	594–613
Inscription of Simontu	594–598
Inscription of Sihathor	599–605
Sinai Inscription	606
Stela of Khentemsemeti	607–613
Reign of Sesostris II	614–639
Inscription of Hapu	614–618
Inscription of Khnumhotep II	619–639
Reign of Sesostris III	640–748
The Conquest of Nubia	640–672
I. The Canal Inscriptions	642–649
I. First Inscription	643–645
II. Second Inscription	646–648
II. The Elephantine Inscription	649–650
III. The First Semneh Stela	651–652
IV. The Second Semneh Stela	653–660
V. Inscription of Ikhernofret	661–670
VI. Inscription of Sisatet	671–673
See also	676 ff. and 687
Hammamat Inscription	674–675
Stela of Sebek-Khu, called Zaa	676–687
Inscriptions of Thuthotep	688–706
Hammamat Inscriptions	707–712
Inscriptions of Sinai	713–738
I. Wadi Maghara	713–723
I. Inscriptions of Khenemsu	714–716

	§§
II. Inscription of Harnakht	717–718
III. Inscription of Sebekdidi	719–720
IV. Inscription of Ameni	721–723
II. Sarbût el-Khadem	724–738
I. Inscription of Sebek-hir-hab	725–727
II. Inscription of Ptahwer	728–729
III. Inscription of Amenemhet	730–732
IV. Inscription of Harurre	733–738
Turra Inscription	739–742
Inscription of Sehetepibre	743–748
Reign of Amenemhet IV	749–750
Kummeh Inscription	749
Sinai Inscriptions	750
FROM THE THIRTEENTH DYNASTY TO THE HYKSOS	751–787
Reign of Sekhemre-Khutowe	751–752
Records of Nile-Levels	751–752
Reign of Neferhotep	753–772
Great Abydos Stela	753–765
Boundary Stela	766–772
Reign of Nubkheprure-Intef	773–780
Coptos Decree	773–780
Reign of Khenzer	781–787
Inscriptions of Ameniseneb	781–787

VOLUME II

	§§
THE EIGHTEENTH DYNASTY	1–1043
Reign of Ahmose I	1–37
Biography of Ahmose, Son of Ebana	1–3
I. Career under Ahmose I (ll. 1–24)	4–16
II. Career under Amenhotep I (ll. 24–29)	38–39
III. Career under Thutmose I (ll. 29–39)	78–82
Biography of Ahmose-Pen-Nekhbet	17–25
I. Ahmose's Campaigns [Continued § 40]	18–20
II. Ahmose's Rewards	21–24
III. Ahmose's Summary	25

TABLE OF CONTENTS

	§§
Quarry Inscription	26–28
Karnak Stela	29–32
Building Inscription	33–37
Reign of Amenhotep I	38–53
Biography of Ahmose, Son of Ebana	38–39
II. Career under Amenhotep I (ll. 24–29)	38–53
Biography of Ahmose-Pen-Nekhbet	40–42
Career under Amenhotep I	40–42
Biography of Ineni	43–46
I. Career under Amenhotep I	44–46
II. Career under Thutmose I	99–108
III. Career under Thutmose II	115–118
IV. Career under Thutmose III and Hatshepsut	340–343
Stela of Harmini	47–48
Stela of Keres	49–52
Reign of Thutmose I	54–114
Coronation Decree	54–60
Biographical Inscription of Thure	61–66
Tombos Stela	67–73
Inscriptions at the First Cataract	74–77
I. Sehel Inscription	75
II. Sehel Inscription	76
III. Assuan Inscription	77
Inscription of Ahmose, Son of Ebana	78–82
III. Career under Thutmose I (ll. 29–39)	78–82
Biography of Ahmose-Pen-Nekhbet	83–85
Career under Thutmose I	83–85
Karnak Obelisks	86–89
Abydos Stela	90–98
Biography of Ineni	99–108
II. Career under Thutmose I (ll. 4–14)	99–108
Stela of Yuf	109–114
Reign of Thutmose II	115–127
Biography of Ineni	115–118
III. Career under Thutmose II	115–118
Assuan Inscription	119–122
Biography of Ahmose-Pen-Nekbet	123–124
IV. Career under Thutmose II	123–124

	§§
Campaign in Syria	125
The Ebony Shrine of Der el-Bahri	126–127
Reign of Thutmose III and Hatshepsut	128–390
Introduction	128–130
Inscription of the Coronation; Buildings and Offerings	131–166
Semneh Temple Inscriptions	167
I. Renewal of Sesostris III's List of Offerings	168–172
II. Dedication to Dedun and Sesostris III	173–176
Biography of Nebwawi	177
I. The Statue Inscription	178–183
II. Abydos Stela	184–186
The Birth of Queen Hatshepsut	187–191
I. The Council of the Gods	192
II. Interviews Between Amon and Thoth	193–194
III. Amon with Queen Ahmose	195–198
IV. Interview Between Amon and Khnum	199–201
V. Khnum Fashions the Child	202–203
VI. Interview Between Thoth and Queen Ahmose	204
VII. Queen Ahmose is Led to Confinement	205
VIII. The Birth	206–207
IX. Presentation of the Child to Amon	208
X. Council of Amon and Hathor	209
XI. The Nursing of the Child	210
XII. Second Interview of Amon and Thoth	211
XIII. The Final Scene	212
Statue of Enebni	213
Vase Inscription	214
The Coronation of Queen Hatshepsut	215
I. The Purification	216
II. Amon presents the Child to All the Gods	217–220
III. The Northern Journey	221–225
IV. Coronation by Atum	226–227
V. Reception of the Crowns and the Names	228–230
VI. Proclamation as King before Amon	231
VII. Coronation before the Court	232–239
VIII. Second Purification	240–241
IX. Concluding Ceremonies	242
Southern Pylon Inscription at Karnak	243–245

TABLE OF CONTENTS xiii

	§§
The Punt Reliefs	246–295
I. Departure of the Fleet	252–253
II. Reception in Punt	254–258
III. The Traffic	259–262
IV. Loading the Vessels	263–265
V. The Return Voyage	266
VI. Presentation of the Tribute to the Queen by the Chiefs of Punt, Irem and Nemyew	267–269
VII. The Queen Offers the Gifts to Amon	270–272
VIII. Weighing and Measuring the Gifts to Amon	273–282
IX. Formal Announcement of the Success of the Expedition before Amon	283–288
X. Formal Announcement of the Success of the Expedition to the Court	289–295
Inscription of the Speos Artemidos	296–303
The Karnak Obelisks	304–307
I. Shaft Inscriptions; Middle Columns	308–311
II. Shaft Inscriptions; Side Columns	312–313
III. Base Inscription	314–321
Reliefs of Transportation of Obelisks	322
I. Transport	323–329
II. Reception in Thebes	330–335
III. Dedication of the Obelisks	336
Rock Inscription in Wadi Maghara	337
Building Inscription of Western Thebes	338–339
Biography of Ineni	340–343
IV. Career under Thutmose III and Hatshepsut	340–343
Biography of Ahmose-Pen-Nekhbet	344
Conclusion of Summary	344
Inscriptions of Senmut	345–368
I. Inscriptions on the Karnak Statue	349–358
II. Assuan Inscription	359–362
III. Inscriptions on the Berlin Statue	363–368
Inscription of Thutiy	369–378
Inscriptions of Puemre	379
I. Statue of Inscription	380–381
II. Tomb Inscriptions	382–387
Inscriptions of Hapuseneb	388–390

TABLE OF CONTENTS

	§§
Reign of Thutmose III	391–779
The Annals	391–405
The Annals: Conspectus of Campaigns	406
I. Introduction	407
II. First Campaign (Year 23)	408–443
Wadi Halfa Inscription	411–437
Fragment on the Siege of Megiddo	438–443
III. Second Campaign (Year 24)	444–449
IV. Third Campaign (Year 25)	450–452
V. Fourth Campaign	453
VI. Fifth Campaign (Year 29)	454–462
VII. Sixth Campaign (Year 30)	463–467
VIII. Seventh Campaign (Year 31)	468–475
IX. Eighth Campaign (Year 33)	476–487
X. Ninth Campaign (Year 34)	488–495
XI. Tenth Campaign (Year 35)	496–503
XII. Eleventh Campaign (Year 36)	504
XIII. Twelfth Campaign (Year 37)	505
XIV. Thirteenth Campaign (Year 38)	506–515
XV. Fourteenth Campaign (Year 39)	516–519
XVI. Fifteenth Campaign	520–523
XVII. Sixteenth Campaign	524–527
XVIII. Seventeenth Campaign	528–539
XIX. Conclusion	540
Feasts and Offerings from the Conquests	541–573
Biography of Amenemhab	574–592
Fragments of Karnak Pylon VII	593–598
Great Karnak Building Inscription	599–608
Building Inscription of the Karnak Ptah-Temple	609–622
Obelisks	623
I. Karnak Obelisks	624–625
II. Lateran Obelisks	626–628
III. Constantinople Obelisk	629–631
IV. London Obelisk	632–633
V. New York Obelisk	634–636
Medinet Habu Building Inscriptions	637–641
Heliopolis Building Inscriptions	642–643
Nubian Wars	644–654

TABLE OF CONTENTS

§§

- I. Canal Inscription 649–650
- II. Inscriptions of Nehi, Viceroy of Kush . . . 651–652
- III. Offerings from the South Countries . . 653–654
- Hymn of Victory 655–662
- Tomb of Rekhmire 663–759
  - I. Appointment of Rekhmire as Vizier . . . 665–670
  - II. Duties of the Vizier 671–711
  - III. The Sitting of the Vizier 712–713
  - IV. Reception of Petitions 714–715
  - V. Inspection of Taxes of Upper Egypt . . . 716
    - A. Above Thebes 717–728
    - B. Below Thebes 729–745
  - VI. Reception of Dues to the Amon-Temple . . 746–751
  - VII. Inspection of Daily Offerings and of Monuments 752
  - VIII. Inspection of Craftsmen 753–755
  - IX. Inspection of Sculptors and Builders . . . 756–759
  - X. Reception of Foreign Tribute 760–761
  - XI. Accession of Amenhotep II 762
- Stela of Intef the Herald 763–771
- Tomb of Menkheperreseneb 772–776
- Stela of Nibamon 777–779
- Reign of Amenhotep II 780
- Asiatic Campaign 780–798
  - I. Karnak Stela 781–790
  - II. Amâda and Elephantine Stelæ . . . 791–798
  - III. Karnak Chapel 798A
- Turra Inscription 799–800
- Tomb of Amenken 801–802
- Karnak Building Inscription 803–806
- Biography of Amenemhab 807–809
- Reign of Thutmose IV 810–840
  - Sphinx Stela 810–815
  - Asiatic Campaign 816–822
  - Konosso Inscription 823–829
  - Lateran Obelisk 830–838
  - Stela of Pe'aoke 839–840
- Reign of Amenhotep III 841–931
  - Birth and Coronation 841

TABLE OF CONTENTS

	§§
Nubian War	842–855
I. Stela at First Cataract	843–844
II. Stela of Konosso	845
III. Bubastis Inscription	846–850
IV. Semneh Inscription	851–855
Tablet of Victory	856–859
The Commemorative Scarabs	860–869
I. Marriage with Tiy	861–862
II. Wild Cattle Hunt	863–864
III. Ten Years Lion-Hunting	865
IV. Marriage with Kirgipa	866–867
V. Construction of a Pleasure Lake	868–869
Jubilee Celebrations	870–874
Quarry and Mine Inscriptions	875–877
Building Inscription	878–892
I. Introduction (ll. 1–2)	882
II. Temple of the (Memnon) Colossi (ll. 2–10)	883–885
III. Luxor Temple and Connected Buildings	886–887
IV. Sacred Barge of Amon (ll. 16–20)	888
V. Third Pylon of Karnak (ll. 20–23)	889
VI. Temple of Soleb (ll. 23–26)	890
VII. Hymn of Amon to the King (ll. 26–31)	891–892
Building Inscriptions of the Soleb Temple	893–898
Great Inscription of the Third Karnak Pylon	899–903
Dedication Stela	904–910
I. Speech of the King (ll. 1–13)	905–908
II. Speech of Amon (ll. 14–20)	909
III. Speech of the Divine Ennead (ll. 20–24)	910
Inscriptions of Amenhotep, Son of Hapi	911–927
I. Statue Inscription	913–920
II. Mortuary Temple Edict	921–927
Statue of Nebnefer	928–931
Reign of Ikhnaton	932–1018
Quarry Inscription at Silsileh	932–935
Tomb of the Vizier Ramose	936–948
The Tell El-Amarna Landmarks	949–972
Assuan Tablet of the Architect Bek	973–976
The Tell El-Amarna Tombs	977–1018

TABLE OF CONTENTS

	§§
Tomb of Merire II	981
Tomb of Merire I	982–988
Tomb of Eye	989–996
Tomb of Mai	997–1003
Tomb of Ahmose	1004–1008
Tomb of Tutu	1009–1013
Tomb of Huy	1014–1018
Reign of Tutenkhamon	1019–1041
Tomb of Huy	1019–1041
I. Investiture of the Viceroy of Kush	1020–1026
II. Tribute of the North	1027–1033
III. Tribute of the South	1034–1041
Reign of Eye	1042–1043

LIST OF FIGURES

	PAGE
Plan of Punt Reliefs	105

VOLUME III

	§§
THE NINETEENTH DYNASTY	1–651
Reign of Harmhab	1–73
Tomb of Harmhab	1–21
I. Leyden Fragments	2–9
I. Stela with Adoration Scene	2–5
II. Reward of Gold	6–9
II. Vienna Fragment	10–12
III. Alexandria Fragments	13
IV. British Museum Fragments	14–19
I. Doorposts	14–17
II. Stela with Three Hymns	18–19
V. Cairo Fragments	20–21
Coronation Inscription	22–32
Graffiti in the Theban Necropolis	32A–32C
The Wars of Harmhab	33–44
I. In the North	34–36
II. In the South	37–44
Edict of Harmhab	45–67

TABLE OF CONTENTS

		§§
I.	Introduction (ll. 1-10)	49
II.	Introduction: The King's Zeal for the Relief of the People (ll. 10-14)	50
III.	Enactment Against Robbing the Poor of Dues for the Royal Breweries and Kitchens (ll. 14-17)	51
IV.	Enactment Against Robbing the Poor of Wood Due the Pharaoh (ll. 17-18)	52
V.	Enactment Against Exacting Dues from a Poor Man Thus Robbed (ll. 18-20)	53
VI.	Against Robbing the Poor of Dues for the Harem or the Gods by the Soldiers (ll. 20-24)	54
VII.	Enactments Against Unlawful Appropriation of Slave Service (ll. 22-24)	55
VIII.	Enactment Against Stealing of Hides by the Soldiers (ll. 25-28)	56-57
IX.	Against Connivance of Dishonest Inspectors with Thievish Tax-Collectors, for a Share of the Booty (ll. 28-32)	58
X.	Enactment Against Stealing Vegetables Under Pretense of Collecting Taxes (ll. 32-35)	59
XI.	Enactments too Fragmentary for Analysis (ll. 35-39) and Right Side (ll. 1, 2)	60-62
XII.	Narrative of the King's Reforms, Containing Also an Enactment Against Corrupt Judges (ll. 3-7)	63-65
XIII.	Narrative of the King's Monthly Audiences and Largesses (ll. 7-10)	66
XIV.	Laudation of the King, and Conclusion (Left Side)	67
Tomb of Neferhotep		68-73
Reign of Ramses I		74-79
Wadi Halfa Stela		74-79
Reign of Seti I		80-250
Karnak Reliefs		80-156
Scene 1. March through Southern Palestine		83-84
Scene 2. Battle with the Shasu		85-86
Scene 3. Capture of Pekanan		87-88
Scene 4. Capture of Yenoam		89-90

TABLE OF CONTENTS xix

	§§
Scene 5. Submission of the Chiefs of Lebanon	91–94
Scenes 6 and 7. Binding and Carrying Away Prisoners	95–97
Scene 8. Reception in Egypt	98–103
Scene 9. Presentation of Shasu Prisoners and Precious Vessels to Amon	104–108
Scene 10. Presentation of Syrian Prisoners and Precious Vessels to Amon	109–112
Scene 11. Slaying Prisoners Before Amon	113–119
Scene 12. First Battle with the Libyans	120–122
Scene 13. Second Battle with the Libyans	123–132
Scene 14. Return from Libyan War	133–134
Scene 15. Presentation of Libyan Prisoners and Spoil to Amon	135–139
Scene 16. Capture of Kadesh	140–141
Scene 17. Battle with the Hittites	142–144
Scene 18. Carrying off Hittite Prisoners	145–148
Scene 19. Presentation of Hittite Spoil and Prisoners to Amon	149–152
Scene 20. Slaying Prisoners before Amon	153–156
Wadi Halfa Stela	157–161
Inscriptions of Redesiyeh	162–198
I. First Inscription	169–174
II. Second Inscription	175–194
III. Third Inscription	195–198
Building Inscriptions	199–250
I. First Cataract Inscription	201–204
1. Assuan Inscription	201–202
2. Elephantine Stela	203–204
II. Silsileh Quarry Stela	205–208
III. Gebelên Quarry Inscription	209–210
IV. Mortuary Temple at Thebes (Kurna)	211–221
V. Temple of Karnak	222–224
VI. Mortuary Temple at Abydos	225–243
VII. Temple Model of Heliopolis	244–246
VIII. Miscellaneous	247–250
Reign of Ramses II	251–568
Great Abydos Inscription	251–281
Kubbân Stela	282–293

	§§
The Asiatic War	294–391
I. Beginning of the Hittite War	296–351
I. First Campaign	297
II. Second Campaign: The Battle of Kadesh	298–351
a. Poem of the Battle of Kadesh	305–315
b. Official Record of the Battle of Kadesh	316–327
c. The Reliefs of the Battle of Kadesh.	328
I. The Council of War	329–330
II. The Camp	331–332
III. Ramses' Messengers	333–334
IV. The Battle	335–338
V. The Defense of the Camp	339–340
VI. After the Battle	341–347
VII. Presentation of Captives to Amon	348–351
III. Palestinian Revolt	352–362
I. Reconquest of Southern Palestine	353–355
II. Reconquest of Northern Palestine	356–362
IV. Campaign in Naharin	363–391
I. Conquest of Naharin	364–366
II. Treaty with the Hittites	367–391
Relations of Egypt with the Hittites after the War	392–491
I. The Blessing of Ptah	394–414
II. Marriage Stela	415–424
III. Message of the Chief of Kheta to the Chief of Kode	425–426
IV. Coptos Stela	427–428
V. Bentresh Stela	429–447
Nubian Wars and References to Northern Wars	448–491
I. Abu Simbel Temple	449–457
II. Bet el-Walli Temple	458–477
III. Assuan Stela	478–479
IV. Luxor Temple	480–484
V. Abydos Temple	485–486
VI. Tanis Stelæ	487–491
Building Inscriptions	492–537
I. Great Temple of Abu Simbel	495–499
II. Small Temple of Abu Simbel	500–501
III. Temple of Serreh	502

TABLE OF CONTENTS

		§§
IV.	Temple of Derr	503
V.	Temple of Sebûᶜa	504
VI.	Temple of el Kab	505
VII.	Temple of Luxor	506–508
VIII.	Temple of Karnak	509–513
IX.	The Ramesseum	514–515
X.	Temple of Kurna	516–522
XI.	Seti I's Temple at Abydos and Great Abydos Inscription	262–267
XII.	Ramses II's Temple at Abydos	524–529
XIII.	Memphis Temples	530–537
	1. Great Abydos Inscription (l. 22)	260
	2. Blessing of Ptah (ll. 32, 35)	412–413
XIV.	City of Tanis (Blessing of Ptah (ll. 16–18))	406

Stela of the Year 400 538–542
Royal Jubilee Inscriptions 543–560

I.	First Gebel Silsileh Inscription	552
II.	Bigeh Inscription	553
III.	Second Gebel Silsileh Inscription	554
IV.	Third Gebel Silsileh Inscription	555
V.	Fourth Gebel Silsileh Inscription	556
VI.	Sehel Inscription	557
VII.	El Kab Inscription	558
VIII.	Fifth Gebel Silsileh Inscription	559
IX.	Sixth Gebel Silsileh Inscription	560

Inscription of Beknekhonsu 561–568
Reign of Merneptah 569–638
  The Invasion of Libyans and Mediterranean Peoples . 569–617

I.	The Great Karnak Inscription	572–592
II.	The Cairo Column	593–595
III.	The Athribis Stela	596–601
IV.	The Hymn of Victory	602–617

Inscriptions of the High Priest of Amon, Roy . . 618–628
Daybook of a Frontier Official 629–635
Letter of a Frontier Official 636–638
Reign of Siptah 639–650
  Nubian Graffiti 639–650

LIST OF FIGURES

	PAGE
Fig. 1. Plan of the Reliefs of Seti I, on the North Wall of the Great Hall of Karnak	39
Fig. 2. Seti I on the Route through Southern Palestine (Scene 1)	44
Fig. 3. Showing Two Superimposed Figures	61
Fig. 4. Inserted Figure of "First King's-Son"	61
Fig. 5. An Unknown Prince Following the Chariot of Seti I (Scene 14)	66
Fig. 6. Figure of an Unknown Prince Inserted in a Fragmentary Scene (§ 130)	66
Fig. 7. Map of the Orontes Valley in the Vicinity of Kadesh	126
Fig. 8. March to Kadesh: First Positions	128
Fig. 9. Battle of Kadesh: Second Positions	130
Fig. 10. Battle of Kadesh: Third Positions	130
Fig. 11. Battle of Kadesh: Fourth Positions	130
Fig. 12. Battle of Kadesh: Fifth Positions	130
Fig. 13. The Modern Mound of Kadesh	152

VOLUME IV

	§§
THE TWENTIETH DYNASTY	1–603
Reign of Ramses III	1–456
Medinet Habu Temple	1–150
Building and Dedication Inscriptions	1–20
Historical Inscriptions	21–138
I. Treasury of Medinet Habu Temple	25–34
II. First Libyan War, Year 5	35–58
1. Great Inscription in the Second Court (Year 5)	36–58
III. Northern War, Year 8	59–82
1. Great Inscription on the Second Pylon, Year 8	61–68
2. Relief Scenes Outside North Wall and in Second Court, Year 8	69–82
IV. Second Libyan War	83–114

TABLE OF CONTENTS

§§
- 1. Great Inscription on the First Pylon (Medinet Habu) 85–92
- 2. Poem on Second Libyan War . . . 93–99
- 3. Relief Scenes on First Pylon and Outside North Wall (Medinet Habu) . . 100–114
- 4. Papyrus Harris . . . 405
- V. The Syrian War . 115–135
- VI. The Nubian War . 136–138
- Medinet Habu Temple Calendar . . . 139–145
- Act of Endowment of the Temples of Khnum 146–150
- Papyrus Harris 151–412
  - Discussion of 151–181
  - Content:
    - I. Introduction 182–183
    - II. Theban Section 184–246
    - III. Heliopolitan Section 247–304
    - IV. Memphite Section 305–351
    - V. General Section (Small Temples) . . 352–382
    - VI. Summary 383–396
    - VII. Historical Section . . 397–412
- Record of the Royal Jubilee . . . 413–415
- Records of the Harem Conspiracy . . . 416–456
  - I. Appointment of the Court . . 423–424
  - II. The Condemned of the First Prosecution . 425–443
  - III. The Condemned of the Second Prosecution 444–445
  - IV. The Condemned of the Third Prosecution . 446–450
  - V. The Condemned of the Fourth Prosecution 451–452
  - VI. The Acquitted 453
  - VII. The Practicers of Magic . 454–456
- Reign of Ramses IV 457–472
  - Hammamat Stela . . . 457–468
    - I. The First Stela . . 457–460
    - II. The Second Stela . . 461–468
  - Abydos Stela 469–471
  - Building Inscription of the Khonsu Temple . . . 472
- Reign of Ramses V 473
  - Tomb Dedication 473
- Reign of Ramses VI 474–483

	§§
Tomb of Penno	474–483
Reign of Ramses VII	484–485
Stela of Hori	484–485
Reign of Ramses IX	486–556
Inscriptions of the High Priest of Amon, Amenhotep	486–498
I. Building Inscriptions	488–491
II. Records of Rewards	492–498
The Records of the Royal Tomb-Robberies	499–556
I. Papyrus Abbott	509–535
II. Papyrus Amherst	536–541
III. Turin Fragment	542–543
IV. Mayer Papyri	544–556
Reign of Ramses XII	557–603
The Report of Wenamon	557–591
Records of the Restoration of the Royal Mummies	592–594
Letter to the Viceroy of Kush	595–600
Building Inscriptions in the Temple of Khonsu	601–603
THE TWENTY-FIRST DYNASTY	604–692
The Twenty-First Dynasty	604–607
Reign of Hrihor	608–626
Inscriptions of the Temple of Khonsu	608–626
Reign of Nesubenebded	627–630
Gebelên Inscription	627–630
Reign of the High Priest and King Paynozem I	631–649
I. Paynozem I as High Priest	631–635
Building Inscriptions	631–635
Records on the Royal Mummies	636–642
II. Paynozem I as King	643 ff.
Records on the Royal Mummies	643–647
Building Inscriptions	648–649
High Priesthood of Menkheperre	650–661
Stela of the Banishment	650–658
Record of Restoration	659
Karnak Graffito	660
Records on the Royal Mummies	661
High Priesthood of Paynozem II	662–687
Records on the Priestly Mummies	662–663
Records on the Royal Mummies	664–667

TABLE OF CONTENTS

	§§
Record of Paynozem II's Burial	668
Stela of the "Great Chief of Me," Sheshonk	669–687
High Priesthood of Pesibkhenno	688–692
Records on Mummy-Wrappings	688
Burial of Nesikhonsu	689
Records on the Royal Mummies	690–692
The Twenty-Second Dynasty	693–792
Records of Nile-Levels at Karnak	693–698
Reign of Sheshonk I	699–728
Records on Mummy-Bandages of Zeptahefonekh	699–700
Building Inscription	701–708
Great Karnak Relief	709–722
Presentation of Tribute	723–724
Karnak Stela	724A
Dakhel Stela	725–728
Reign of Osorkon I	729–737
Record of Temple Gifts	729–737
Reign of Takelot I	738–740
Statue of the Nile-God Dedicated by the High Priest, Sheshonk	738–740
Reign of Osorkon II	742–751
Flood Inscription	742–744
Statue Inscription	745–747
Jubilee Inscriptions	748–751
Reign of Takelot II	752–755
Graffito of Harsiese	752–754
Stela of Kerome	755
Reign of Sheshonk III	756–777
Annals of the High Priest of Amon, Osorkon	756–770
I. East of Door	760–761
II. West of Door	762–770
First Serapeum Stela of Pediese	771–774
Record of Installation	775–777
Reign of Pemou	778–781
Second Serapeum Stela of Pediese	778–781
Reign of Sheshonk IV	782–792
Stela of Weshtehet	782–784

	§§
Serapeum Stela of Harpeson	785–792
THE TWENTY-THIRD DYNASTY.	793–883
Records of Nile-Levels at Karnak	793–794
Reign of Osorkon III	795
Will of Yewelot	795
Reign of Piankhi	796–883
The Piankhi Stela.	796–883
THE TWENTY-FOURTH DYNASTY	884
Reign of Bocchoris	884
Serapeum Stelæ	884
THE TWENTY-FIFTH DYNASTY	885–934
Records of the Nile-Levels at Karnak	885–888
Reign of Shabaka	889
Building Inscription	889
Reign of Taharka	892–918
Tanis Stela	892–896
Building Inscription in Large Cliff-Temple of Napata	897–900
Inscription of Mentemhet	901–916
Serapeum Stela	917–918
Reign of Tanutamon	919–934
Stela of Tanutamon	919–934
THE TWENTY-SIXTH DYNASTY	935–1029
Reign of Psamtik I	935–973
Adoption Stela of Nitocris	935–958
Statue Inscription of the Chief Steward, Ibe	958A–958M
First Serapeum Stela	959–962
Second Serapeum Stela	963–966
Statue Inscription of Hor	967–973
Reign of Necho.	974–980
Serapeum Stela	974–979
Building Inscription	980
Reign of Psamtik II.	981–983
Statue Inscription of Neferibre-Nofer	981–983
Reign of Apries.	984–995
Serapeum Stela	984–988
Stela of the Divine Consort Enekhnesneferibre	988A–988J
Inscription of Nesuhor	989–995

TABLE OF CONTENTS xxvii

§§
Reign of Amasis (Ahmose II). 996–1029
   Elephantine Stela 996–1007
   Serapeum Stela 1008–1012
   Statue Inscription of the General Ahmose . . 1013–1014
   Statue Inscription of Pefnefdineit 1015–1025
   Mortuary Stelæ of the Priest Psamtik . . . 1026–1029

LIST OF FIGURES

PAGE
Plan of Scenes and Inscriptions in Medinet Habu Temple . . 5

INDEX 521

EXPLANATION OF TYPOGRAPHICAL SIGNS AND SPECIAL CHARACTERS

1. The introductions to the documents are in twelve-point type, like these lines.

2. All of the translations are in ten-point type, like this line.

3. In the footnotes and introductions all quotations from the documents in the original words of the translation are in *italics*, inclosed in quotation marks. *Italics* are not employed in the text of the volumes for any other purpose except for titles.

4. The lines of the original document are indicated in the translation by superior numbers.

5. The loss of a word in the original is indicated by —, two words by — —, three words by — — —, four words by — — — —, five words by — — — — —, and more than five by —————. A word in the original is estimated at a "square" as known to Egyptologists, and the estimate can be but a very rough one.

6. When any of the dashes, like those of No. 5, are inclosed in half-brackets, the dashes so inclosed indicate not lost, but uncertain words. Thus ⌜—⌝ represents one uncertain word, ⌜— —⌝ two uncertain words, and ⌜—————⌝ more than five uncertain words.

7. When a word or group of words are inclosed in half-brackets, the words so inclosed are uncertain in meaning; that is, the translation is not above question.

8. Roman numerals I, II, III, and IV, not preceded by the title of any book or journal, refer to these four volumes of Historical Documents. The Arabic numerals following such Romans refer to the numbered paragraphs of these volumes. All paragraph marks (§ and §§, without a Roman) refer to paragraphs of the same volume.

9. For signs used in transliteration, see Vol. I, p. xv.

THE EIGHTEENTH DYNASTY

REIGN OF AHMOSE I

BIOGRAPHY OF AHMOSE, SON OF EBANA[a]

1. This inscription contains the biography of a naval officer, Ahmose, a nobleman of El Kab, who served with distinction under three successive kings: Ahmose I, Amenhotep I, and Thutmose I, his father having served under the predecessor of Ahmose I, Sekenenre. It is especially important, because it is our only contemporary source for the expulsion of the Hyksos, and forms, with the biography of Ahmose-Pen-Nekhbet (§§ 17 ff.), our only source for the wars of the early Eighteenth Dynasty; for the royal records of this critical period have totally perished. The family of nomarchs at El Kab[b] were strong supporters of the rising dynasty, and it is clear that such loyalty was liberally rewarded with the gifts of slaves and land,[c] of which both the El Kab Ahmoses boast. It was by thus cementing a firm friendship with such local nobility that the first kings

---

[a]On the wall of Ahmose's cliff-tomb at El Kab; in two parts: the first, of 31 lines on the right-hand wall, and the second, of 8 lines, on the door-wall at the left of door. Text: Champollion, *Notices descriptives*, I, 655–57, only 26 lines, and very inaccurate; first completely published by Lepsius, *Denkmäler*, III, 12, *a* and *d;* thence inaccurately copied by Rheinisch, *Chrestomathie*, Pl. 6, omitting *d;* and equally incorrectly, Lemm, *Lesestücke*, 67; Bunsen, *Egypt's Place*, 2d ed., V, 732, 733 (beginning only). I have collated the excellent Berlin squeeze (No. 172), which mostly sustains Lepsius, *Denkmäler*, but furnishes some important corrections. Valuable discussion of difficult passages by Piehl, *Proceedings of the Society of Biblical Archæology*, XV, 256–58, and *Sphinx*, III, 7–12.

[b]The family is far older than the Empire, and already under the Thirteenth Dynasty enjoyed the favor of the king (Lepsius, *Denkmäler*, III, 14, *b*); but it is impossible to trace the line back of Ahmose, son of Ebana's grandmother.

[c]A boundary stone marking one limit of such a gift by Thutmose I was acquired by the Berlin Museum in 1899. It reads: "*Southern boundary of the fields given as a favor of the royal presence, to the orderly (snn) of his majesty, Nekri (Nkry); 150 stat,*" See a similar tablet in Mariette, *Monuments divers*, 47A, under Thutmose IV.

of the Eighteenth Dynasty maintained themselves during their long and exhausting wars. The royal children were even intrusted to these El Kab princes, to be reared under their charge,[a] and they finally ruled from El Kab to Esneh.[b]

2. The ten campaigns in which Ahmose took part are treated in the respective reigns under which they fall, as follows:

I. Career under Ahmose I, ll. 1-24 (§§ 4 ff.).
II. Career under Amenhotep I, ll. 24-29 (§§ 38 ff.).
III. Career under Thutmose I, ll. 29-39 (§§ 78 ff.).

3. The immediate authorship of the inscription is established by the neighboring relief. Ahmose is represented as standing at the left, and before him is his grandson, Pahri ($P^{\circ}\text{-}hry$), accompanied by the following words:

> By the son of his daughter the conductor of the works in this tomb, perpetuating the name of the father of his mother, the draughtsman[c] of Amon, Pahri,[d] triumphant.

The long inscription was therefore executed by Ahmose's grandson, Pahri, who was a draughtsman.

I. CAREER UNDER AHMOSE I
[Ll. 1-24; continued §§ 38 ff.]

4. After an introduction and a few words about his youth and parentage, Ahmose plunges directly into his first

---

[a]See *Tomb of Pahri*, "Eleventh Memoir," Egyptian Exploration Fund, and Lepsius, *Denkmäler*, III, 10, *b* and 11, *b*.

[b]Pahri, grandson of Ahmose, son of Ebana, was "*prince of Esneh (Yny·t), governor of the southern lands (? ḥ·t), satisfying the excellent heart of his lord from the House of Hathor to El Kab.*" Tylor, *Tomb of Pahri*, Pl. III.

[c]See Goodwin, *Zeitschrift für ägyptische Sprache*, 1872, 21.

[d]His tomb is the most interesting one at El Kab; see *The Tomb of Pahri at El Kab*, by Griffith and Tylor, "Eleventh Memoir," of Egyptian Exploration Fund.

campaign, with an account of a siege of the city of Hatwaret ($ḥt$-$w^cr·t$). This can be no other than the city called Avaris by Manetho (Josephus, *Contra Apion*, I, 14), where, according to him, the Hyksos make their last stand in Egypt.[a] It is also mentioned as the residence of the Asiatics ($^c{}^{\supset}mw$, § 303, l. 37) by Hatshepsut, and by a papyrus of the late Nineteenth Dynasty,[b] as the residence of an Apophis; so that there is no doubt about the identification with Avaris. The siege, which must have lasted many years, was interrupted by the rebellion of some disaffected noble in Upper Egypt; but the city was finally captured, and the Hyksos, fleeing into Asia, were pursued to the city of Sharuhen (Josh. 19:6). Here they were besieged for six years by Ahmose·I, and this stronghold was also captured. It was probably at the conclusion of this siege that Ahmose I pushed northward and invaded Syria, as narrated by Ahmose-Pen-Nekhbet (§ 20), probably still in pursuit of the last remnants of the Hyksos.

5. The king now returned, and carried his army to the other extreme of his domain, invading Nubia. He was recalled from a successful campaign there, to quell two successive rebellions, the last of the internal dissensions which had distracted the country since the fall of the Middle Kingdom. At this point the wars, and probably the reign, of Ahmose I closed, Ahmose, son of Ebana, having gained distinction in all his campaigns.

---

[a]According to *Egypt Exploration Fund Archæological Report* (1900–1901, 13), there is in Cairo a stela containing a reference to this war with the Hyksos, but I have been unable to gain any information concerning it. It is probably § 30.

[b]Sallier I, 1–3; it contains a folk-tale narrating the cause of the war between a Hyksos king, Apophis in Avaris, and a Sekenenre, who was ruler ($ḥḳ^{\supset}$) in Thebes. Unfortunately, only the beginning is preserved. Most of the current translations and interpretations of this document are largely the products of a vivid imagination.

Introductory Address

6. ¹Chief of the sailors, Ahmose ($Y^c\d{h}$-$m\acute{s}$), son of Ebana ($^{\jmath}$-$b^{\jmath}$-$n^{\jmath}$), triumphant; ²he says: "I will tell you, O all ye people; I will cause you to know the honors which came to me. I was presented with gold seven times[a] in the presence ³of the whole land; male and female slaves likewise. I was endowed with very many fields." The fame of one valiant in his achievements shall not perish ⁴in this land forever.[b]

His Youth

7. He speaks as follows: "I spent my youth in the city of Nekheb[c] ($N\d{h}b$), my father being an officer of the king of Upper and Lower Egypt, Sekenenre ($S\d{k}nyn\ R^c$-), triumphant, Baba ($B^{\jmath}b^{\jmath}$), ⁵son of Royenet, ($R^{\jmath}$-$yn\cdot t$), was his name. Then I served as an officer in his stead, in the ship 'The Offering' in the time of the Lord of the Two Lands, Nebpehtire (Nb-$phty$-R^c, Ahmose I), triumphant, ⁶while I was (still) young, not having taken a wife,[d] and while I was still sleeping in the ⌜—⌝ garment.[e] Then after I set up a household, I was transferred ⁷to the northern fleet, because of my valor. I followed the king on foot[f] when he rode abroad in his ⁸chariot.

Campaign against the Hyksos; Siege of Avaris

8. One besieged the city of Avaris ($\d{H}t$-$w^c r\cdot t$); I showed valor on foot[f] before his majesty; then I was appointed ⁹to (the ship) 'Shining-in-Memphis.'[g]

---

[a] Ahmose has recorded elsewhere in his tomb (Lepsius, *Denkmäler*, III, 12, *c*) a list of the gifts he received, making a total of 9 men and 10 women; the total of land is lost. This does not agree with his narrative, which does not summarize, but in different gifts mentions in all 9 men and 7 women received from the king, and 8 men and 7 women captured.

[b] This last statement is probably a proverbial phrase; see Spiegelberg, *Recueil*, XXVI, 41, 42.

[c] El Kab.   [d] See Müller, *Liebespoesie*, 3.

[e] This is, of course, some garment worn by a youth; cf. the girdle of Uni's youth (I, 294, l. 1).

[f] Lit., "*on my two feet;*" this is emphasized as land service, Ahmose being a naval officer.

[g] Reward after the first battle at Avaris.

Second Battle of Avaris

9. One fought on the water in the canal: Pezedku ($P\ni\text{-}\underline{d}dkw$) of Avaris. Then I fought hand to hand, ¹⁰I brought away a hand.[a] It was reported to the royal herald. One gave to me the gold of valor.[b]

Third Battle of Avaris

10. Then there was again fighting in this place; I again fought hand to hand ¹¹there; I brought away a hand. One gave to me the gold of bravery in the second place.[c]

First Rebellion, Interrupting Siege of Avaris

11. One fought in this Egypt,[d] south of this city; ¹²then I brought away a living captive, a man; I descended into the water; behold, he was brought[e] as a seizure upon the road of this ¹³city,[e] (⌜although¹⌝) I crossed with him over the water. It was announced to the royal herald. Then one presented[f] me with gold in double measure.[g]

Capture of Avaris

12. One ¹⁴captured Avaris; I took captive there one man and three women, total four heads, his majesty gave them to me for slaves.[h]

---

[a]Cut off as a trophy, from a slain enemy.
[b]Reward after the second battle.   [c]Reward after the third battle.
[d]There can be no doubt that the word ($km\cdot t$) means here, as always elsewhere, "*Egypt;*" "*this city*" is then El Kab, for the word "*south*" is an adjective feminine agreeing with "*Egypt.*" The phrase can only be translated into a language like Greek or German, thus: "in diesem südlich von dieser Stadt befindlichen Aegypten." The siege of Avaris is therefore interrupted by a rebellion in upper Egypt, similar to the two later ones (§§ 15, 16), and for this reason the narrative particularly specifies "*this Egypt, south, etc.*" See also § 13, l. 15.

[e]Contrast with this the two men "*captured as a seizure upon the ship of the enemy*" (l. 21). There is no ground for the fanciful rendering, indicating that he lost his way! Ahmose means that, although obliged to descend to and cross over the water (of some canal) with his prisoner, he brought him away as safely as one seized upon the road of the city.

[f]Read $\d{hr}$ for myk (confusion from hieratic?), as in l. 28.
[g]Reward after the fourth battle.
[h]Reward after the fifth battle; apparently Avaris was captured on the fourth assault; but these brief references to fighting may each one indicate a whole season of the siege, which would then have lasted four years, as that of Sharuhen lasted six. See § 13.

Siege of Sharuhen

13. ¹⁵One besieged Sharuhenª (*Šʾ-rʾ-ḥʾ-nʾ*) for 6 years,ᵇ (and) his majesty took it. Then I took captive there two women and one hand. ¹⁶One gave me the gold of bravery, ⌜besides⌝ giving me the captives for slaves.

Campaign against Nubia

14. Now, after his majesty had slain the Asiatics (*Mntyw Stt*), ¹⁷he ascended the river to Khenthennofer (*Ḫnt-ḥn-nfr*), to destroy the Nubian Troglodytes;ᶜ his majesty made a great slaughter among them. ¹⁸Then I took captive there, two living men, and three hands. One presented me with gold in double measure, ⌜besides⌝ giving to me two female slaves.ᵈ ¹⁹His majesty sailed down-stream, his heart joyous with the might of victory, (for) he had seized Southerners and Northerners.

Second Rebellion

15. ²⁰There came an enemy of the South; his fate, his destruction approached; the gods of the South seized him, and his majesty found him in Tintto-emu (*Tynt-tʾ-ʿ mw*).ᵉ His majesty carried him off ²¹a living prisoner, and all his people carried captive. I carried away two

---

ªCf. Josh. 19:6.

ᵇLepsius, *Denkmäler*, has "5," which has been generally accepted; Champollion's text and Brugsch's translation have "6." I repeatedly examined the squeeze for this point with especial care; it has a clear "6." The correctness of the rendering "*for 6 years*" rather than "*in the year 6*" has been clearly demonstrated by Piehl (*Proceedings of the Society of Biblical Archæology*, XV, 258). Another proof is that *m*, the preposition here, is used all through the Beknekhonsu inscription (Munich) for "*during*" or "*for*" a period of years. This throws a new light on the whole Asiatic campaign, for the stubbornness of the besieged and the persistence of Ahmose are almost certainly an indication that the siege is an extension of the campaign against the Hyksos, who, having retreated to Sharuhen, are here making their last stand. We may suppose, therefore, that the siege of Avaris itself also lasted many years, allowing opportunity for a rebellion in Upper Egypt. See § 11, l. 11.

ᶜCf. Müller, *Asien und Europa*, 21.

ᵈThese slaves being women, are not the two captives just taken, as the translations of Renouf and Petrie indicate.

ᵉLit., "*She of the land of the water-supply*" (ʿ-*mw*, "*water-supply*," occurs at Siut, I, 407, l. 6, and in Rekhmire, § 698, l. 25); possibly the district of the first cataract is meant, as the rebellion was in the South. The name is elsewhere unknown.

archers[a] as a seizure in the ship of the enemy;[b] one [22]gave to me five heads besides pieces of land (amounting to) five stat (*st ꜣ·t*)[c] in my city.[d] It was done to all the sailors likewise.

Third Rebellion

16. Then came that fallen one,[e] [23]whose name was Teti-en (*Tty-ꜥ n*);[f] he had gathered to himself rebels.[g] His majesty slew him and his servants,[h] annihilating[i] them. There were given [24]to me three heads, and fields (amounting to) five stat[j] in my city.

[Continued §§ 38 ff.]

BIOGRAPHY OF AHMOSE-PEN-NEKHBET

17. This El Kab nobleman, like Ahmose, son of Ebana (§§ 1-16), served under the first kings of the Eighteenth Dynasty, but he lived to a greater age. Beginning his career under Ahmose I, he continued under Amenhotep I, Thutmose I, II, and III, and died enjoying the favor of Thutmose III and Hatshepsut. He has separated his

---

[a]This hitherto uncertain word (*myg ꜣ*) is rendered tolerably certain by a scene in the tomb of Harmhab (*Mémoires de la mission française au Caire*, V, Pl. III, foll. p. 434; see also 420), where it bears the determinative of shooting, and stands over a man with a bow, with the title "*chief archer (myg ꜣ) of his majesty.*"

[b]The determinative indicates an enemy, not a proper name, but the meaning of the word (ꜣ ꜣ t ꜣ) is unknown. The rendering "fiévreux" from Chabas is based on an impossible etymology. See Piehl, *Sphinx*, III, 11.

[c]A land measure containing about seven-tenths acres, here in apposition with "*pieces of land.*"

[d]El Kab. [e]Term of contempt for a foe.

[f]There is no reason for supposing that this is not the rebel's real name. On the contrary, this very name was especially common at this period; see the ushebtis published by Borchardt (*Zeitschrift für ägyptische Sprache*, 32, pp. 113 f.).

[g]Lit., "*the wicked of heart.*"

[h]Written feminine(!) in the text.

[i]Lit., "*as that which exists not.*"

[j]A land measure containing about seven-tenths of an acre, here in apposition with "*pieces of land.*"

biography into three parts: his campaigns,[a] his rewards,[b] and a summary.[c]

I. AHMOSE'S CAMPAIGNS[d]

[Continued § 40]

18. He enumerates his campaigns and his captures under Ahmose I, Amenhotep I, Thutmose I and II.

I. Career under Ahmose I

19. His meager reference to a campaign of Ahmose I in Zahi is our sole source of knowledge for that event. It probably followed the capture of Sharuhen.

Campaign in Syria

20. [1]"Hereditary prince, count, wearer of the royal seal,[e] chief treasurer, herald ʳof his Lord,[f] —¹, ²ᵍAhmose, called Pen-Nekhbet (*Pn-Nḫb·t*), triumphant; he says: "I followed King Nebpehtire (*Nb-pḥty-Rˁ*, Ahmose I), triumphant. ³I captured for him in Zahi (*Ḏ ꜣ-ḥy*) a living prisoner and a hand."

[Continued § 40]

---

[a]Campaigns, three originals: (1) statue-base belonging to Mr. Finlay, *Zeitschrift für ägyptische Sprache*, 1883, 77, 78; (2) statue-base in the Louvre, Lepsius, *Auswahl der wichtigsten Urkunden*, XIV A; Prisse, *Monuments égyptiens*, IV; (3) Ahmose's tomb-wall at El Kab, Lepsius, *Denkmäler*, III, 43, *a* (lower left-hand corner), and Sethe, *Untersuchungen*, I, 85. All sources have been collated.

[b]Rewards, two originals: (1) statue-base belonging to Mr. Finlay, *Zeitschrift für ägyptische Sprache*, 1883, 78; (2) statue-base in the Louvre, Lepsius, *Auswahl der wichtigsten Urkunden*, XIV B; Prisse, *Monuments égyptiens*, IV.

[c]Summary, Ahmose's tomb-wall in El Kab, Lepsius, *Denkmäler*, III, 43, *a*, ll. 10–20; Sethe, *Untersuchungen*, I, 85, corrected and revised; and partially, Lepsius, *Denkmäler*, Text, IV, 46.

[d]The translation of the campaigns is distributed under the different reigns, under which he lived, because they furnish very important historical events, but his rewards and the summary, being more purely personal, are given in this reign.

[e]All except the Finlay text insert other titles here, but, except the first, "*sole companion*," they are illegible.

[f]All the other texts have *whm kfˁ*, which would mean "*repeating captures.*" This unusual title was also in the rewards (l. 4).

[g]Lines numbered from the Finlay statue text.

II. AHMOSE'S REWARDS

21. ^{1}......^{2}......^{3}......^{4}...^{a} Ahmose, called Pen-Nekhbet; he says: "By the ^{5}sovereign, who lives forever! I was not separated from the king upon the battlefield, from (the time of) ^{6}King Nebpehtire (Ahmose I), triumphant, to King Okhepernere (Thutmose II), triumphant; I was in the favor ^{7}of the king's presence, until King Menkheperre (Thutmose III), living forever.^{b}

22. King Zeserkere (Amenhotep I), triumphant, gave to me, ^{8}of gold: two bracelets, two necklaces, an armlet, a dagger, a headdress, a fan, and a mekhtebet.

23. ^{9}King Okheperkere (Thutmose I), triumphant, gave to me, of gold: two bracelets, four necklaces, one armlet, six flies,^{c} ^{10}three lions;^{d} two golden axes.

24. King Okhepernere (Thutmose II),^{e} triumphant, gave to me of gold: three bracelets, six necklaces, three armlets, a mekhtebet; a silver axe."

III. AHMOSE'S SUMMARY^f

25. $^{10\,g}$He says, "I followed the Kings ^{11}of Upper and Lower Egypt, the gods; I was with ^{12}their majesties when they went to the South and North country, in every place where they went; [from] ^{13}King Nebpehtire (Ahmose I), triumphant, King Zeserkere (Amenhotep I) [triumphant], King ^{14}Okheperkere (Thutmose I), triumphant, King

---

^{a}Unimportant titles of Ahmose (see § 20, l. 1) very fragmentary; lines are numbered according to text in Lepsius, *Auswahl der wichtigsten Urkunden*.

^{b}This phrase shows that Thutmose III is still alive at this time, but Ahmose is now too old to be *"upon the battlefield,"* under him.

^{c}These are golden flies, like those among Ahhotep's jewelry at Cairo. They were a decoration of honor. The word has been mistranslated "helmets." See Breasted, *Proceedings of the Society of Biblical Archæology*, 1900, pp. 94, 95.

^{d}Cf. inscription of Amenemhab, § 585.

^{e}Finlay text, according to Maspero's copy, has Thutmose I; corrected by Maspero, *Struggle of the Nations*, 239, n. 1, as above.

^{f}Ahmose's tomb-wall in El Kab; published by Lepsius, *Denkmäler*, III, 43, *a*, ll. 10–20; *ibid.*, Text, IV, 46; Sethe, *Untersuchungen*, I, 85, corrected and revised, most of the lacunæ restored from Lepsius' papers and his squeeze.

^{g}The summary does not begin until l. 10; ll. 1 and 2 contain an adoration of Re by Ahmose, and his titles occupy ll. 3–9. These 9 lines lack half their length.

Okhepernere (Thutmose II), triumphant, until this Good God, King Menkheperre (Thutmose III) ¹⁵who is given life forever.ᵃ

I have attained a good old age, having ¹⁶had a lifeᵇ of royal favor, having hadᵇ honor under their majesties and the love of me having been in the court."

[Concluded in § 344]

QUARRY INSCRIPTIONᶜ

26. The inscription records the work of Neferperet, an official of Ahmose I, who, in the latter's twenty-second year, took out stone from the Ma ᶜ sara quarry, for the temples of Ptah and of Amon. The inscription is important, because it is the last dated document of Ahmose I, because it records the first resumption of building after the expulsion of the Hyksos, and for its reference to the Fenkhu, whose cattle were captured on some Asiatic campaign.

Above, in a position of significant prominence in the queen's case, are the names and titles of Ahmose I, and his queen, Ahmose-Nefretiri (Y ᶜh-$m\acute{s}$, $n\acute{j}r$·t-yry).

27. ¹Year 22 under the majesty of the king, Son of Re, Ahmose, who is given life. ²The quarry-chambers were opened a[ne]w; good limestone ³of Ayan (ᶜ nw) was taken out for his temples of myriads of [years],ᵈ the temple of Ptah, the temple of Amon in southern Opet (Yp·t, Luxor), and all the monuments which his majesty made ⌜for him⌝.

ᵃThis phrase after Thutmose III's name shows that he was living at the time of this inscription; all the others were at this time *"triumphant"* (deceased). Hence Ahmose, now an old man, died under Thutmose III.

ᵇLit., *"having been in a life,"* and *"having been in honor."*

ᶜOn the wall of the limestone quarry of Ma ᶜ sara, just southeast of Cairo. Published by Vyse, *Operations*, III, 99; Young, *Hieroglyphics*, 88; Lepsius, *Denkmäler*, III, 3, a = Champollion, *Notices descriptives*, II, 488 = Rosellini, *Monumenti Storici*, I, 15; and Lepsius, *Denkmäler*, III, 3, b; the text of the last is the same as the preceding, but it represents a second inscription. Both are badly broken, but they supplement each other, so that practically nothing is lost.

ᵈA conventional phrase applied to all temples, and referring, of course, to their durability.

The stone was dragged with oxen[a] which his m[ajesty] captured [in his] victories [among][b] the Fenkhu (*Fnḫw*).

28. The assistant, the hereditary prince ———, ⌜vigilant⌝[c] one of the Lord of the Two Lands in restoring the monuments of e[⌜ternity⌝], greatly [satisfying] the heart of the Good God; the wearer of the royal seal, sole companion, chief treasurer, Neferperet (*Nfr-pr·t*).

KARNAK STELA[d]

29. Among Ahmose's pious works for the temples was the restoration of the furniture, utensils, and the like, belonging to the ritual of the Karnak temple of Amon. He recorded this work upon a splendid stela, containing thirty-two lines of inscription, of which only the last six are devoted to the record of his benefactions, while the other twenty-six contain only conventional eulogy of himself. In the course of this tedious succession of phrases, there is a vague reference to his wars:

30. The Asiatics approach with fearful step together, standing at his judgment-hall; his sword is in Khenthennofer, his terror is in the Fenkhu-lands, the fear of his majesty is in this land like Min (l. 12).

31. He was thus as much feared in Egypt as in Nubia or Asia. The introduction closes with the names of Ahmose I and the queen Ahhotep, after which follows the record of the work in Karnak (ll. 27–32):

---

[a]It is not the Fenkhu themselves who are employed in the quarry (as sometimes stated, e. g., Maspero, *Struggle of the Nations*, 93; also Petrie, *History of Egypt*, II, 36), but only the oxen captured.

[b]The horizontal lines in Lepsius, *Denkmäler*, III, *a*, l. 5, indicate an *m* = "*in*," or "*among;*" indeed, the entire phrase, "*which his majesty captured in his victories in* —," is so common that the restorations are probable.

[c][*Rš*]-*ḏ'ḏ'*, lit., "*of watchful head.*"

[d]A white limestone stela over 7½ feet high and nearly 3½ feet wide; found by Legrain by Pylon VII at Karnak. It was below the pavement of Thutmose III, and had been buried before Ikhnaton's time. Published in *Annales*, IV, 27–29.

32. Now, his majesty commanded to make monuments for his father Amon-Re, being: great chaplets of gold with rosettes of genuine lapis lazuli; seals[a] of gold; large vases (*ḥs·t*) of gold; jars (*nms·t*) and vases (*ḥs·t*) of silver; tables (*wḏḥ·w*) of gold, offering-tables (*dbḥ·t ḥtp*) of gold and silver; necklaces of gold and silver combined with lapis lazuli and malachite; a drinking-vessel for the ka, of gold, its standard of silver; a drinking-vessel for the ka, of silver rimmed with gold, its standard of silver; a flat dish (*ṯnyw*) of gold; jars (*nms·t*) of pink granite, filled with ointment; great pails (*wšmw*)[b] of silver rimmed with gold, the ⌜handles⌝ thereon of silver; a harp of ebony,[c] of gold and silver; sphinxes of silver; a ⌜—⌝[d] with gold; a barge of the "Beginning-of-the-River" called "Userhetamon,"[e] of new cedar of the best of the terraces, in order to make his voyage ⌜therein⌝. I erected columns of ⌜cedar — —⌝ likewise; I gave ———.

BUILDING INSCRIPTION[f]

33. This document discloses to us the name of the mother of Ahmose I's father and mother. She was a queen Tetisheri, and although she is called a *"king's-mother and great king's-wife,"* she is not designated as king's daughter. She was doubtless the wife of the last Sekenenre, and her daughter Ahmose I's mother, was, of course, the famous Queen Ahhotep. The latter's brother-husband, the father of Ahmose I, was probably Kemose.

---

[a]Or: "*seal rings.*"

[b]These are the ceremonial pails with bucket handles, swelling or bulbous below, with more or less pointed bottom. Schaefer calls my attention to the example on the Ethiopian stela in the Louvre, l. 11 (*Zeitschrift für ägyptische Sprache*, 1895, Pl. V). There are many examples in bronze in the museums.

[c]I suspect that a word has been omitted at this point, as the repetition of the preposition indicates.

[d]*Špt*, Schaefer suggests the *spd* which appears in the Mentuhotep coffin at Berlin.

[e]Meaning "*mighty is the front of Amon.*" This is the usual name of the sacred barge of Amon.

[f]Stela about 6½ feet high and 3 feet wide, found by Petrie at Abydos; published by him in *Abydos*, III, Pl. LII.

BUILDING INSCRIPTION

The inscription is so picturesque, and unconventional in form, as to be unique. In content it records the king's determination to erect further mortuary buildings for his grandmother, Queen Tetisheri.

Introduction

34. ¹Now, it came to pass that his majesty sat in the audience-hall, (even) the King of Upper and Lower Egypt, Nebpehtire, Son of Re, Ahmose (I), given life; ²while the hereditary princess, great in favor, great in amiability, king's-daughter, king's-sister, divine consort, great king's-wife, Ahmose-Nefretiri, who liveth, was with his majesty.

The Conversation

35. One spoke ³with the other, seeking benefactions for[a] the departed (dead), to present libations of water, to offer upon the altar, ⁴to enrich the offering-tablet at the first of every season, at the monthly feast of the first of the month, the feast of the coming forth of the sem, ⁵the feast of the night-offerings on the fifth of the month, the feast of the sixth of the month, the feast of Hakro[b] ($H \, ꜣ \, k\text{-}r \, ꜣ$), the feast of Wag ($W \, ꜣ \, g$), the feast of Thoth, and at the first ⁶of every season of heaven, and of earth. His sister spake and answered him: "Wherefore has this been remembered? ⁷And why has this word been spoken? What has come into thy heart?"

Ahmose's Purpose

36. The king himself spake to her: "I, ⁸it is, who have remembered the mother of my mother, and the mother of my father, great king's-wife and king's-mother, Tetisheri ($Tty\text{-}šry$), triumphant. ⁹(Although) she already has a tomb ($yš$) and a mortuary chapel[c] ($m \, ꜥ \, ḥ \, ꜥ \cdot t$) on the soil of Thebes and Abydos, I have said this to thee, in that ¹⁰my majesty has desired to have made for her (also) a pyramid and a house ($ḥ \cdot t$) in

---

[a]The negative n is to be read as the preposition n; see the converse confusion in l. 14.

[b]The $r \, ꜣ$ has been overlooked in the publication?

[c]Lit., "*Her tomb and her chapel are at this moment* ($m \, ty$ (sic!) $ꜣ \, t$) *on the soil, etc.*" I can only understand this clause as concessive, and that the new buildings planned by Ahmose are in addition to the ones in l. 9.

Tazeser, as a monumental donation of my majesty. Its lake shall be dug, its trees shall be planted, [11]its offerings shall be founded, equipped with people, endowed with lands, presented [12]with herds, mortuary priests and ritual priests having their duties, every man knowing his stipulation."

37. [13]Lo, his majesty spake this word, while this was in process of construction. His majesty did [14]this because he so greatly loved her, beyond everything. Never did former kings the like of it for [15]their mothers. Lo, his majesty extended his arm, and bent his hand;[a] he pronounced for her a mortuary prayer. . . . .[b]

---

[a]A posture of prayer.

[b]Here follow three fragmentary lines, giving the names of the gods appealed to, and the usual objects in such an offering.

REIGN OF AMENHOTEP I

BIOGRAPHY OF AHMOSE, SON OF EBANA[a]

[Ll. 24-29, continued from § 16; concluded §§ 78 ff.]

II. CAREER UNDER AMENHOTEP I

38. Under this king Ahmose commands the royal transports in a campaign against Kush. The enemy is defeated, Ahmose fighting at the head of the Egyptian troops. He brings the king back to Egypt in two days, and is given *"the gold,"* and a title of honor: *"Warrior of the Ruler."* The campaign extended to the Middle Kingdom frontier, for a rock inscription of Amenhotep's eighth year has been found on the island of Uronarti, just below Semneh.[b]

39. I sailed the King Zeserkere ($Dsr-k^{3}-R^{c}$, Amenhotep I), triumphant, when he ascended the river to Kush (Ks), in order to extend [25]the borders of Egypt. His majesty captured that Nubian Troglodyte in the midst of his army, ——————— who were brought away as prisoners, none of them missing. [— —] thrust [26]aside[c] like those who are annihilated. Meanwhile I was at the head of our[d] army; I fought incredibly;[e] his majesty beheld my bravery. I brought off two hands, [27]and took (them) to his majesty. One pursued his people and his cattle. Then I brought off a living prisoner, and took (him) to his majesty. I brought his majesty in two days to

---

[a]Bibliography, etc., p. 3, n. a.

[b]Steindorff, *Berichte der Philologisch-historischen Classe der Königlichen Sächsischen Gesellschaft der Wissenschaft*, Leipzig, Sitzung vom 18. Juni, 1900, p. 233.

[c]Same phrase, Tombos Inscription (§ 71, l. 7).

[d]This and § 81 are the only places in all the historical texts of Egypt, where *"our troops"* are spoken of. It is a real touch of patriotism.

[e]Lit., *"I fought more than what is true."*

Egypt ²⁸from the upper well;ᵃ one presented me with gold. Then I brought away two female slaves, in addition to those which I had taken ²⁹to his majesty. One appointed me 'Warrior of the Ruler.'

BIOGRAPHY OF AHMOSE-PEN-NEKHBETᵇ

[Continued from § 20; continued §§ 83 ff., and 344]

II. CAREER UNDER AMENHOTEP I

40. Ahmose-Pen-Nekhbet accompanied the king on two campaigns: one against the Nubians, of which we have a fuller account in the biography of Ahmose, son of Ebana (§ 39); and the other against the Libyans; this biography being our only source for this war of Amenhotep I in Libya. For his valor on these occasions he was rewarded by the king.

Campaign in Kush

41. I ⁴followed King Zeserkere ($Dsr-k^{\mathrm{?}}-R^{c}$, Amenhotep I), triumphant; I captured for him ⁵in Kush, a living prisoner.

Campaign in Libya

42. Again I served for King Zeserkere, triumphant; ⁶I captured for him on the north of Imukehek ($Y^{\mathrm{?}} mw-khk$), three hands.

[Continued §§ 83 ff., and 344]

BIOGRAPHY OF INENIᶜ

43. This official served under four kings: Amenhotep I, Thutmose I, Thutmose II, and Thutmose III, reigning with

---

ᵃIn view of Amenhotep I's inscription at the second cataract, we are probably correct in concluding that the second cataract is meant here.

ᵇBibliography on p. 10, n. a.

ᶜFrom a Theban tomb at Abd el-Kurna, first noted by Champollion (*Notices descriptives*, I, 492–94), and then by Brugsch, who published some fragments (*Recueil de monuments*, I, 36, 1–3, tree list, etc., and Pl. 65, 4–5); also Piehl. *Inscriptions*, I, Pls. 129 Q–130 and pp. 105, 106. The long text is found in *Recueil*,

Hatshepsut. He evidently died under this joint reign; his biography was composed at this time, and is the most important of all sources for the history of the succession of the Thutmosids. Ineni was:

> Hereditary prince, count, chief of all works in Karnak; the double silver-house was under his charge; the double gold-house was on his seal; sealer of all contracts in the House of Amon; excellency, overseer of the double granary of Amon.[a]

These offices brought him the superintendence of many of the most important works executed in Thebes by the kings whom he served. His career is divided as follows:

I. Career under Amenhotep I (§§ 44-46).
II. Career under Thutmose I (§§ 99-108).
III. Career under Thutmose II (§§ 115-18).
IV. Career under Thutmose III and Hatshepsut (§§ 340-43).

I. CAREER UNDER AMENHOTEP I

44. The beginning, containing the name of the king, is lost, and the narrative begins in the middle of the account of a building probably Amenhotep I's gate on the south of the Karnak temple, found below the later pavement, of which the two dedications read:[b]

> 1. "Amenhotep I; he made (it) as his monument for his father Amon, lord of Thebes (ns·wt-t ꜣ wy), erecting for him a great gate of 20 cubits (in height) at the double façade of the temple, of fine limestone of Ayan, which the Son of Re, Amenhotep, living forever, made for him."

XII, 106, 107, where it is inaccurately published by Bouriant. (See also, *ibid.*, XIV, 73, 74.) The first "7 or 8 lines" are wanting, according to Bouriant, and also the ends of the first 14 remaining lines; following these are 6 complete lines. The wall scenes and plans of the tomb (also the long inscription) have been published by an architect, H. Boussac (*Mémoires de la mission française au Caire*, XVIII). To the Egyptologist the publication is little more than worthless, and the work must be done again. But the long inscription has now disappeared.

[a]One of Boussac's plates; he has not numbered them!
[b]Legrain, *Annales*, IV, 15 ff.

2. [Amenhotep I]; .... .ᵃ building his house, establishing his temple, erecting the southern gate, made high, even 20 cubits, of fine white limestone ⸺.

It is important to note that this gate was erected in celebration of the king's first Sed Jubilee. Turning again to Ineni, his inscription begins:

*Buildings*ᵇ

45. ⸺ ¹Hatnub (*Ḥt-nb*), its doors were erected of copper made in one sheet; the parts thereof were of electrum. I inspected that which his majesty made ⸺ ²bronze, Asiatic copper, collars, vessels, necklaces. I was foreman of every work, all offices were under my command. ⸺ ³at the feasts of the beginning of the seasons; likewise for his father Amon, lord of Thebes; they were under my control. Inspection was made for me, I was the reckoner. ⸺ ⁴⸢—⸣.

Death of Amenhotep I

46. His majesty having spent life in happiness and the years in peace, went forth to heaven; he joined the sun, he associated (with him) and went forth ⸺.

[Continued §§ 99–108]

STELA OF HARMINIᶜ

47. Harmini (*ḥr-myny*) prefixes no other title to his name than "*scribe*," but he was no less a man than the chief magistrate of Nekhen-Hieraconpolis. This impor-

---

ᵃAs in the first, as far as "*Thebes*."

ᵇPossibly also the mortuary temple of Amenhotep I, found by Spiegelberg in 1896 at Drah abu-'n-Neggah on the west side at Thebes (see Spiegelberg, *Zwei Beiträge zur Geschichte und Topographie der thebanischen Nekropolis im Neuen Reich* (Strassburg, 1898; and Sethe, *Götting'sche Gelehrte Anzeigen*, 1902, No. 1, 29–31). The temple is referred to as "*House of Zeserkere (Amenhotep I) on the west of Thebes*" (Lepsius, *Denkmäler*, Text, III, 238). See also Sethe, *loc. cit.*, 30.

ᶜMortuary stela of unknown provenience (probably Abydos), now in the Florence Museum, No. 1567; published in *Catalogue*, 288–90; Piehl, *Recueil*, II, 122–24. I had also my own photograph of the original.

tant post on the original Nubian frontier either resulted in his promotion to the governorship of Wawat in lower Nubia, or his Nekhen appointment involved jurisdiction in Wawat, in view of the fact that earlier Nubia began in the vicinity of Nekhen. In any case, he had charge of the *"tribute"* from Wawat, which was later in the hands of the *"king's-son of Kush"* (§§ 1034 ff.). Although the inscription mentions no king, it clearly belongs to the Eighteenth Dynasty before the first appointment of a *"governor of the south countries, and king's-son of Kush,"* by Thutmose I (§§ 61 ff.). Hence we are not far wrong in placing it under Amenhotep I, though Harmini must of course have served under Ahmose I, also.

48. After the usual mortuary prayer, the inscription continues, in Harmini's own words:

I passed many years as mayor ($h^\jmath ty$-^{c}) of Nekhen (Hieraconpolis). I brought in its tribute to the Lord of the Two Lands; I was praised, and no occasion was found against me. I attained old age in Wawat, being a favorite of my lord. I went north with its tribute for the king, each year; I came forth thence justified; there was not found a balance against me.

STELA OF KERES[a]

49. Keres, like his contemporary, Yuf (§§ 109 ff.), was in the service of one of the queen-mothers. The question arises here whether the *"king's-mother Ahhotep,"* whom Keres served, was Ahhotep (II), wife of Amenhotep I, in whose tenth year her command was issued, or Ahhotep (I), mother of King Ahmose. As Ahhotep II was never the mother of a king, it must have been Ahhotep I, who had a tomb

---

[a]Limestone stela, 0.82 m. high, from Drah abu-'n-Neggah, now in Cairo, without a number. Published by Bouriant, *Recueil*, IX, 94 f., No. 74 (his text is excessively incorrect); much better by Piehl, *Zeitschrift für ägyptische Sprache*, 1888, 117 f. I am also indebted to Schaefer for a carefully collated copy made from the original.

erected at Abydos for Keres. We thus see this queen, from whom the Eighteenth Dynasty sprang, still living in the tenth year of the second king of the dynasty.

50. Keres, who was her herald, has not only preserved for us the old queen's command, honoring him with a tomb and a statue at Abydos, but has also added a loose enumeration of his duties as her herald, which resembles that of the herald, Intef (§§ 763–71).

51. [1]Year 10, first month of the third season (ninth month), first day, under the majesty of the King of Upper and Lower Egypt: Zeserkere, Son of Re, of his body: Amenhotep (I), beloved of Osiris, given life.

52. [2]Command of the king's-mother to the hereditary prince, count, wearer of the royal seal, sole companion, overseer of the gold-house, overseer of the silver-house, chief steward of the king's-mother, [3]Ahhotep, who liveth; the herald ($whm \cdot w$), Keres ($K^{\jmath} rs$). The king's-mother has commanded to have made for thee a tomb [4]at the stairway of the great god, lord of Abydos, confirming thy every office and every favor. There shall be made for thee thy [5]statues, abiding in the temple, among the followers of ———[a] their virtues in writing [6]in — — —.[a] There shall be made for thee mortuary offerings ($htp\ dy\ \check{s}tny$), as the king's-wife does for the one whom she has loved, for the hereditary prince, count, wearer of the royal seal, the steward, the herald, Keres (Krs), only favorite united [7]with the limbs of Sekhmet, following his queen ($hnw \cdot t$) at her going. He ⌜—⌝ before the people, the real ⌜confidant⌝ of his queen, to whom secret things are told, [8]⌜experienced⌝ in the plans of his queen, transmitting affairs to the palace, finding [9]solutions, making agreeable unpleasant matters, one upon whose word his queen depends, approaching the truth, knowing the affairs of the mind, profitable in speech to his queen, [10]great in respect in the house of the king's-mother, weighty in affairs, excellent in speech, secretive in mind, administering the palace, [11]sealing (his) mouth concerning that which he hears, official who solves knotty problems, chief steward, Keres (Krs), vigilant administrator for the king's-mother, [12]not more lax[b] by night than by day, the herald, Keres (Krs).

---

[a]Cut out.   [b]Read wsf.

53. He says: "O ye mayors, scribes, ritual priests, ¹³attendants, citizens (ᶜnḫ·w) of the army, as your city-gods favor you, and love you, as ye would bequeath your office(s) to your children ¹⁴after old age; verily so shall ye say: 'An offering which the king gives; ─────,ᵃ king, of the two lofty plumes, lord of life, giver of that which is desired, ¹⁵lord of burial after old age. May he give bread, beer, oxen, geese, everything good and pure, that comes forth upon the table of ¹⁶the All Lord, for the ka of . . . . .ᵇ Keres, a man of truth, before the Two Lands, really honest, free ¹⁷from lying, ⌜─⌝ in deciding matters, protecting the weak, defending him who is without ¹⁸him (sic!), sending forth two men, reconciled by the utterance of his mouth, accurate like a pair of balances, ¹⁹the like [⌜of Thoth⌝] in ⌜─⌝ the name, inclining the heart to hear matters, the likeness of a god in his hour, real ⌜confidant⌝ ²⁰of his queen, whom the queen of the Two Lands has advanced. . . . Keres."

ᵃName of Amon cut out in time of Ikhnaton.
ᵇHis titles.

REIGN OF THUTMOSE I

CORONATION DECREE[a]

54. This unique document is a royal decree issued on the king's coronation day to the viceroy of Nubia, Thure, informing him of the king's accession, fixing the full titulary, the royal name to be used in offering oblations, and the royal name to be used in the oath. Thure's official residence was doubtless Elephantine, for he is charged to offer oblations to the gods of that city, and it was he who put up the records of Thutmose I's return from his Nubian campaign, at the first cataract (§§ 74 ff.). He then caused the decree to be cut on stelæ and set up in Wadi Halfa,[b] Kubbân, and probably also Elephantine.

Superscription

55. Royal[c] command to the king's-son, the governor of the south countries, Thure (*Tw-r*ʾ) triumphant.

Announcement of Accession

Behold, there is brought to thee this [command][d] of the[d] king in order to inform thee that my majesty has appeared[e] as King of Upper

---

[a]In two copies: (1) a sandstone (?) stela, 72 by 84 cm., found at Wadi Halfa, now in Cairo, published from a copy of Brugsch by Erman (*Zeitschrift für ägyptische Sprache*, 29, 117 = Erman, *Aegyptische Grammatik*, 37*–38*); (2) a sandstone stela, 67 by 76 cm., found by Borchardt at Kubbân (*Zeitschrift für ägyptische Sprache*, 36, 26, n. 1), now in Berlin (No. 13725, *Ausführliches Verzeichniss des Berliner Museums*, 131), unpublished. The beginning is lost on the Cairo stela, and the end on the Berlin stela; the two thus furnish a practically complete text. The relief at the top is lost on both. I used my own copy of the Berlin text.

[b]Not Elephantine, as stated (*Zeitschrift für ägyptische Sprache*, 29, 117). See *ibid.*, 36, 3, n. 1.

[c]See the similar introduction to Pepi II's letter to Harkhuf (I, 351, l. 2).

[d]Supplied from the Story of Sinuhe, 180, 181.

[e]Lit., "*dawned;*" the same word is used for the rising sun, and is transferred without change to the king. It is regularly used also of his appearance in public.

and Lower Egypt upon the Horus-throne of the living, without his like forever.

Titulary

56. Make my titulary as follows:
Horus:[a] "Mighty Bull, Beloved of Mat;"
Favorite of the Two Goddesses:[a] "Shining in the Serpent-diadem, Great in Strength;"
Golden Horus:[a] "Goodly in Years, Making Hearts Live;"
King of Upper and Lower Egypt:[a] "Okheperkere;"
Son of Re:[a] "[Thutmose], Living forever, and ever."

Name to be Used in the Cultus

57. Cause thou oblations to be offered to the gods of Elephantine of the South,[b] as follows:[c] "Performance of the pleasing ceremonies[d] on behalf of the King of Upper and Lower Egypt, Okheperkere, who is given life."

Name to be Used in the Oath

58. Cause thou that the oath be established in the name of my majesty, born of the king's-mother, Seniseneb, who is in health.

Conclusion

59. This is a communication to inform thee of it; and of the fact that the royal house is well and prosperous — —.

Date

60. Year 1, third month of the second season (seventh month) twenty-first day; the day of the feast of coronation.

---

[a]These five titles are common to all Middle Kingdom and Empire kings; only the names following each title are individual.

[b]Cf. Erman (*Zeitschrift für ägyptische Sprache*, 29, 117).

[c]This preposition (*m*) introduces the title or designation of the ceremony of presenting oblations by the priest on the king's behalf.

[d]Lit., "*doing of the pleasing things.*"

BIOGRAPHICAL INSCRIPTION OF THURE[a]

61. In this inscription the name of the author is lost. He served under Ahmose, Amenhotep I, Thutmose I, by whom he was appointed viceroy of Kush (l. 6), Thutmose II, and Thutmose III (l. 14, note). He is supposed by Brugsch (*Egypt under the Pharaohs*, 135), and by Maspero (*Struggle of the Nations*, 230, n. 2) to be the same as Nehi, the viceroy of Kush, who also served under Thutmose III, and has also placed his inscription on the façade of the Semneh temple (§§ 651 ff.).

Now, Nehi was still in office in Thutmose III's fifty-second year, and if he began his official career under Ahmose, he would have been over 117 years old[b] at that time! The identity with Nehi, which was at best an assumption, is therefore impossible. Another identification is, however, certain. This unknown was appointed viceroy of Kush by Thutmose I, at whose accession he was in his prime. He is therefore the same as the viceroy, Thure, whom we find at Elephantine in Thutmose I's first year (§ 55), being the earliest viceroy of Kush whom we know. That he survived into Thutmose III's reign is shown by a tomb at Silsileh, where he is mentioned under Hatshepsut.[c]

Service under Ahmose I

62. ¹———— under the King of Upper and Lower Egypt, Nebpehtire (Ahmose I); he made me overseer of the — ²———— of very good character in his heart, not careless in — ³———— his court.

---

[a]Inscribed on the south wall (façade) of Thutmose III's Semneh temple; text: Young, *Hieroglyphics*, 91; Lepsius, *Denkmäler*, III, 47, c. The upper half of all the lines has been cut away for a later relief of Thutmose III. I am indebted to Steindorff for the use of his collation of the original.

[b]If he was 25 at Ahmose I's death, we must then add 10 for Amenhotep I, 30 for Thutmose I, and 51 for Thutmose III—a total of 117 years.

[c]Griffith, *Proceedings of the Society of Biblical Archæology*, XII, 104. See also note on l. 14 in the translation, *infra*.

Service under Amenhotep I

63. Favor was repeated by his son, King of Upper and Lower Egypt [Zeserke]re (Amenhotep I) [4]———— the granary of Amon, to conduct the works in Karnak —— [5]———— [ΓI did⁷] for him the excellent things of (his)[a] heart; he favored me for doing his[a] truth —— [6]————.

Service under Thutmose I

64. The King of Upper and Lower Egypt, Okheperkere (Thutmose I); he appointed me to be king's-son of [Kush] ——— [7]———— of gold; an armlet the second time —————— [8]———— gave me of gold: a vase, two bracelets ————— [9]———— he — me more than the magnates of the palace, he recognized the excellence of —— ——— [10]———— Γ————⁷b [11]———— in the place of satisfying the heart. He attained old age ———— [12]————.

Service under Thutmose II

65. The first of the repetition of the favor of the King of Upper and Lower Egypt, Okhepernere (Thutmose II); he made [Γme⁷] ———— [13]———— with a royal message, recording ———— [14]————.[c]

Service under Thutmose III

66. [King Thutmose III]; he magnified me in the midst ————.

TOMBOS STELA[d]

67. Three important facts are preserved to us in this inscription:

---

[a]Both these pronouns refer to Amon; the same thought occurs in Suti and Hor's tablet (British Museum, 826), ll. 16, 17.

[b]The portion preserved is hopelessly obscure.

[c]Here are the remains of a royal oval, which certainly contained the name of Thutmose III; in this king's second year, a viceroy of Kush is mentioned in this same temple (§ 170, l. 2), but the name is unfortunately broken out. He is doubtless the same as our viceroy.

[d]Engraved on the rocks on the island of Tombos, just above the third cataract of the Nile; published by Lepsius, *Denkmäler*, III, 5, *a*, and thence Piehl, *Petites études égyptologiques*. The Berlin squeeze (No. 284) permitted some important corrections, but the publication (Lepsius, *Denkmäler*) is a brilliant example of correctness in the form of the signs, as drawn by M. Weidenbach.

1. In the second year Thutmose I defeated the Nubians and conquered the country as far as the third cataract[a] (cf. ll. 6 and 7, and the location of the inscription);

2. He then built a fortified station for his troops at Tombos, remains of which still survive, and thus established his southern frontier at this point (cf. l. 10).[b]

3. His empire extended from this point on the south to the Euphrates on the north (cf. l. 13); the Asiatic peoples are already subdued (cf. ll. 3, 4, and 16), but his Asiatic campaign did not take place until after this Nubian expedition (see § 81, l. 35). Hence we must suppose, either that he had already made an Asiatic campaign of which no account has survived; or that his predecessors had already made the conquest of the country as far as Euphrates, and thus he could refer to it as in his domain. The latter is the more probable supposition.

68. Other interesting data are the fact that the oath, even in the foreign provinces, is made in the name of the king (l. 14), according to the instructions in his coronation announcement (cf. § 58); and the curious reference to the Euphrates as "*that inverted water which goes down-stream in going up-stream*" (cf. l. 13, note).

Unfortunately, this important inscription offers no sober narrative of the events which it commemorates, but is written in that fulsome style so often found in victorious hymns of the Pharaohs. This is a style so overloaded with far-fetched figures and unfamiliar words that it is often quite unintel-

---

[a]An unpublished inscription of his, on the Island of Arko (Wilkinson, *Thebes*, 472, note) shows that he pushed some forty miles south of the third cataract.

[b]This expedition left another inscription at Tangûr, about seventy-five miles above the second cataract, but we possess only a partial copy by a layman, from which it is impossible to make out much. It is dated "*Year 2, first month of third season*," which shows that it was made on the way out (Sethe, *Untersuchungen*, I, 41), about five months before the Tombos inscription.

ligible.ᵃ It is at its worst in ll. 5–9, where some phrases containing only exaggerated epithets applied to the king have necessarily been left untranslated.

Introduction

69. ¹Year 2, second month of the first season, fifteenth day, under the majesty of Horus: Mighty Bull, Beloved of Mat (M ⁾ ᶜ· t); Favorite of the Two Goddesses: Shining in the Serpent-diadem, Mightyᵇ in Strength; Golden Horus: Goodly in Years, Making hearts live; King of Upper and Lower Egypt: Okheperkere, who is given life; Son of Re: Thutmose (I, living) forever, eternally.ᶜ

Hymn of Victory

70. ⸢— —⸣ of his induction ²his coronation as Lord ($ḥry-ḏ$ ⸢ $ḏ$ ⸣) of the Two Lands, to rule the circuit of the sun; South and North land as ruler of the portions of Horus and Set,ᵈ the Uniter of the Two Lands. He has seated himself upon the throne of Keb, wearing ³the radiance of the double crown, the staffᵉ of his majesty; he hath taken his inheritance, he hath assumed the seat of Horus, in order to extend the boundaries of Thebes and the territory of Khaftet-hir-nebes;ᶠ so that the Sand-dwellers and the barbarians shall labor for her.ᵍ ⁴ᶠAn abomination⸣ of the god are the Haunebu; bound are the Ekbet (⸢ $kb·t$); the Southerners come downʰ·river, the Northerners come upʰ·river, and all lands are together bringing their tribute ⁵to the Good God, the primordial, Okheperkere (Thutmose I), who liveth forever, the mighty one,

---

ᵃThere is a good example on the second Semneh stela (I, 657).

ᵇThe coronation letter has "*great in strength*," the usual form.

ᶜCf. the titulary given by the king himself in the coronation letter (§ 56).

ᵈThe myth of Horus and Set states that they divided the Nile country between them; over both these domains the Pharaoh rules, and hence follow the words: "*uniter, etc.*," It is possible that "*Horus and Set*" should be translated only "*the two lords;*" see Piehl, *Proceedings of the Society of Biblical Archæology*, XX, 199, 200.

ᵉFor the same phrase applied to a successor, see I, 692.

ᶠThe goddess of western Thebes.

ᵍThe pronoun refers to Thebes; the foreign captives are to be employed on her buildings.

ʰTo Thebes, the royal residence.

Horus, Lord of the Two Lands, ⌜— — —⌝. The [Sand]-dwellers, chiefs of their tribes ⌜—⌝ to him, bowing down; the ⌜interior⌝[a] peoples[b] ⁶send to his majesty, doing obeisance to that which is on his front.[c]

Victory in Nubia

71. He hath overthrown the chief of the ⌜Nubians⌝; the Negro is ⌜helpless, defenseless⌝ in his grasp. He hath united the boundaries ⁷of his two[d] sides, there is not a remnant among the Curly-Haired,[e] who come to attack him; there is not a single survivor among them. The Nubian Troglodytes fall by the sword, and are thrust aside in their lands; ⁸their foulness, it floods their valleys; the ⌜—⌝ of their mouths is like a violent flood. The fragments cut from them are too much for the birds,[f] carrying off the prey to another place. ⁹ᵍ . . . . the sole staff of Amon; Keb, divine begetter, whose name is hidden, ¹⁰reproducer, Bull of the divine ennead, chosen emanation of the divine members who doeth the pleasure of the Spirits of Heliopolis.

Tombos Fortress Built

72. The lords of the palace have made a fortress for his army, (called) "None-Faces-Him-¹¹Among-the-Nine-Bows-Together;"[h] like a young panther among the fleeing cattle; the fame of his majesty blinded them.

Universal Triumph

73. (He) brought the ends of the earth into his domain; (he) trod its two extremities ¹²with his mighty sword, seeking battle; (but) he

---

[a]*Ḥnwtyw*, with a hide as the first determinative.

[b]The interior peoples of the neighboring lands.

[c]This means the sacred uraeus serpent on his forehead, as the determinative shows.

[d]See I, 311, l. 14.

[e]An epithet for the Negro, used also by Amenhotep II (Lepsius, *Denkmaler*, III, 61), by Seti I (III, 155, l. 4); and again in the Nineteenth Dynasty, *Recueil*, XXII, 107, ll. 7, 8. See Piehl, *Proceedings of the Society of Biblical Archæology*, XV, 261 f., and *Sphinx*, VI, 19 f.

[f]Determinative is an eagle.

[g]The first half of line 9 is a series of obscure epithets of praise applied to the king.

[h]It is doubtful whether this is the name of the fortress. It is probably the same fortress which is referred to by Thutmose II in his Assuan inscription (§ 121, l. 7).

found no one who faced him.ᵃ (He) penetrated valleys which ¹³the (royal) ancestors knew not, which the wearers of the double diadem had not seen. His southern boundary is as far as the frontier of this land,ᵇ (his) northern as far as that inverted waterᶜ which goes downstream in going up-stream.ᵈ ¹⁴The like has not happened to other kings; his name has reached as far as the circuit of heaven, it has penetrated the Two Lands as far as the nether world;ᵉ the oath is takenᶠ by it (viz., his name) in all lands, because of the greatness of the fame of his majesty. ¹⁵They (viz., the lands) were not seen in the archives of the ancestors since the Worshipers of Horus,ᵍ who gives his breath to the one that follows him, his offerings to the one that treads ¹⁶his way. His majesty is Horus, assuming his (Horus's) kingdom of myriads of years, ⌈subject⌉ to him are the isles of the Great Circle ($šn[w]$-wr, Okeanos), the entire earth is under his two feet; ¹⁷bodily son of Re, his beloved, Thutmose (I), living forever and ever. Amon-Re, king of gods is his father, the creator of his beauty, ¹⁸beloved of the gods of Thebes, who is given life, stability, satisfaction, health, joy of his heart upon the throne of Horus, ⌈leading⌉ all the living like Re, forever.

INSCRIPTIONS AT THE FIRST CATARACT

74. Some eight months after the preceding expedition passed Tangur, about seventy-five miles above the second cataract, on the way out, they had reached Assuan on the return—a fact which was recorded by Thure, the viceroy of Kush, in two inscriptions on the island of Sehel and one at Assuan.

ᵃSee Sethe, *Verbum*, II, § 967.
ᵇNubia. ᶜThe Euphrates.

ᵈFor the Egyptian on the Nile north was "*down-stream*," and south was "*up-stream*." It seemed very curious to him that in another country as here on the Euphrates, one went south in going down-stream; hence the anomaly of the text, which becomes clear, if we substitute "south" for "*up-stream*." See also IV, 407.

ᵉHeaven, earth, and the nether world, include the entire Egyptian universe.

ᶠIn the coronation announcement the form of the king's title to be used in the oath is given (see § 58).

ᵍThe pre-dynastic kings, now mythical demigods.

I. SEHEL INSCRIPTION[a]

75. On arriving at the first cataract, the king found the canal of Sesostris III (see I, 642 ff.) stopped up. He cleared it, and the viceroy made the following records:

Year 3, first month of the third season, day 22, under the majesty of the King of Upper and Lower Egypt, Okheperkere (Thutmose I), who is given life. His majesty commanded to dig this canal, after he found it [stopped up] with stones, (so that) no [ship sailed upon it]. He [sail]ed [down-stream] upon it, his heart [glad, having slain his enemies].[b] The king's-son, [Thure].[c]

II. SEHEL INSCRIPTION[d]

76. Above are the Horus-, throne- and personal-names of Thutmose I; and below, the following:

Year 3, first month of the third season, day 22. His majesty sailed this canal in victory and in power, at his return from overthrowing the wretched Kush.

The king's-son, Thure.

III. ASSUAN INSCRIPTION[e]

77. On the same day the king arrived at Assuan, where he left a similar record:

Year 3, first month of the third season, day 22, under the majesty of Thutmose (I).[f] His majesty arrived from Kush, having overthrown the enemy.

---

[a]De Morgan, *Catalogue des monuments*, 85, No. 13.

[b]The preceding restorations are from Thutmose III's copy of this inscription (see §§ 649 f.).

[c]Restored from the following inscription. Thure, also § 55.

[d]Discovered by Wilbour, and published in *Recueil*, XIII, 202; better, de Morgan, *Catalogue des monuments*, 85, No. 19.

[e]De Morgan, *Catalogue des monuments*, 41, No. 185.

[f] Full titulary.

INSCRIPTION OF AHMOSE, SON OF EBANA[a]

[Ll. 29-39; concluded from § 39]

III. CAREER UNDER THUTMOSE I

78. Ahmose's career under Thutmose I is still one of active service in campaigning. He first sails the royal transport in the campaign against Nubia (§ 80), resulting in his appointment to the head of the naval forces. They returned in triumph with the Nubian foe hanged head downward at the bow of the royal barge.

79. It was not until after this Nubian campaign that the famous expedition to Naharin set out. Our only sources for this event are the biographies of the two El Kab Ahmoses. Thutmose III states that he set up his boundary tablet beside that of his father (§ 478), and it must have been on this campaign that this first boundary tablet was set up by Thutmose I.[b] For it is always supposed that this campaign was the only Asiatic expedition of Thutmose I; but as the Tombos inscription (§§ 67 ff.) speaks of the conquest of Asia as far as the Euphrates, before the Asiatic campaign narrated by the two Ahmoses, we must suppose either that Thutmose I had already made a still earlier campaign in Syria; or that his predecessors, Ahmose I and Amenhotep I, had achieved greater conquests in Asia than our scanty sources for their reigns would indicate.

Campaign against Nubia

80. I sailed the King Okheperkere (Thutmose I), triumphant, when he ascended the river to Khenthennofer ($Hnt-hn-nfr$), ³⁰in order to cast

---

[a]For bibliography, see p. 3, note a.

[b]The inscription of Hatshepsut's childhood (§ 225, l. 11) mentions her father's (Thutmose I's) survivals among the chiefs of Retenu, meaning those he had left.

out violence in the highlands, in order to suppress the raiding[a] of the hill region. I showed bravery in his presence in the bad water, in the ⌜passage⌝ of ³¹the ship by the bend. One appointed me chief of the sailors. His majesty was ———————.[b]

³²His majesty was furious thereat, like a panther;[c] his majesty cast his first lance, which remained in the body of that fallen one.[d] This was — — — —[e] ³³⌜—⌝ powerless before his flaming uraeus,[f] made ⌜so⌝ in an instant of destruction; their people were brought off as living prisoners. ³⁴His majesty sailed down-river, with all countries in his grasp, that wretched Nubian Troglodyte being hanged head downward at the [prow][g] of the ba[rge] of his majesty, and landed ³⁵at Karnak.

Asiatic Campaign

81. After these things[h] one journeyed to Retenu (*Rṯnw*) to [i]wash his heart[i] among the foreign countries.

His majesty arrived at Naharin (*N ꜣ-h ꜣ-ry-n ꜣ*) ³⁶his majesty found that foe when he was ⌜planning⌝ destruction; his majesty made a great slaughter[j] among them. ³⁷Numberless were the living prisoners, which his majesty brought off from his victories. Meanwhile I was at

---

[a]The flying raids into the valley of the Nile made by the barbarians inhabiting the desert behind the hills on either side of the valley. The account of the battle is very obscure, but the weakness of the enemy makes the result certain.

[b]The text ends here in the middle of a sentence, and proceeds around the corner of the wall with what seems to be the account of another incident in the same Nubian campaign.

[c]This is precisely what is said of Thutmose II in his Nubian war (Assuan Inscription, l. 9, II, 121) when the announcement of revolt was brought to him, hence a similar incident probably should precede here.

[d]Cf. Sinuhe's weapon which *"remained in his (his foe's) neck."*

[e]It is possible that there is no lacuna here, as the squeeze shows not a trace of a sign in the last 9 inches of the line.

[f] The sacred serpent which crowns the royal forehead.

[g]The restoration is from the Amâda tablet of Amenhotep II, II, 797, l. 17, where the same phrase occurs.

[h]This phrase shows clearly that the Nubian campaign took place before the Asiatic campaign. The same order is observed in the biography of Ahmose-Pen-Nekhbet (§§ 84, 85). The usual supposition that the Asiatic preceded the Nubian campaign is based on a false conclusion from the Tombos inscription (§§ 67 ff.).

[i] An idiom for taking revenge or obtaining satisfaction.

[j] From the squeeze; cf. also l. 17.

the head of our troops,[a] and his majesty beheld my bravery. ³⁸I brought off a chariot, its horses, and him who was upon it as a living prisoner, and took them to [b]his majesty.[b] One presented me with gold in double measure.

His Old Age

82. ³⁹When I grew old, and had attained old age, my honors were as at their beginning.[c] ———[d] a tomb, which I myself made.

BIOGRAPHY OF AHMOSE-PEN-NEKHBET[e]
[Continued from § 42; concluded §§ 123-4, 344]

III. CAREER UNDER THUTMOSE I

83. In this reign Ahmose-Pen-Nekhbet took part in the campaign in Nubia; and also accompanied the Asiatic campaign to Naharin, of which Ahmose, son of Ebana, furnishes a fuller account (§ 81). He was then richly rewarded for his valor by the king.

Campaign in Kush

84. I ⁷followed the King Okheperkere (Thutmose I), triumphant; I captured for him ⁸in Kush, two living prisoners, beside three living prisoners, whom I brought off ⁹in Kush, without counting them.[f]

Campaign in Naharin

85. Again[g] I served ¹⁰for King Okheperkere (Thutmose I), triumphant; I captured for him in the country of Naharin ($N^{\jmath}\text{-}h\text{-}ry\text{-}n^{\jmath}$), ¹¹21 hands, one horse, and one chariot.

---

[a]See note on l. 26, § 39.
[b]From the squeeze; cf. also l. 27.
[c]He continued to receive rewards as at the beginning.
[d]Nearly one-third line is lacking.
[e]Bibliography, p. 10, note a.
[f] Perhaps meaning that they were not included in the official count.
[g]Showing clearly that the Asiatic campaign took place after the Nubian campaign.

KARNAK OBELISKS[a]

86. This pair stood before the pylon (IV) of Thutmose I in the great Karnak temple; the northern obelisk, which Pococke saw still standing, has since fallen. Their erection by Thutmose I is narrated by the chief architect in charge, Ineni (see § 105). Both Ineni and the standing obelisk refer to "*two great obelisks,*" so that there can be no doubt that Thutmose I erected both.[b] The work must have been done just before his demission of the crown—an event which left the northern obelisk still uninscribed. It is certainly very significant that it was later inscribed by Thutmose III! If he did not reach the throne until after the reigns of Thutmose II and Hatshepsut, the northern obelisk remained uninscribed for some twenty-three years at least! This is improbable, and the fact that the northern obelisk was not usurped by Thutmose II or Hatshepsut would indicate that they had no opportunity to do so, because Thutmose III, having succeeded Thutmose I for a few years, had already taken possession of it himself (see Sethe, *Zeitschrift für ägyptische Sprache*, 36, 39 f.).

Only the middle columns of the standing obelisk are the inscriptions of Thutmose I; the side columns are later additions by Ramses IV and Ramses VI of the Twentieth Dynasty. The middle columns of the north and south sides contain only the elaborate titulary of Thutmose I; those of the east and west, his dedication, as follows:

---

[a]Text: Lepsius, *Denkmäler*, III, 6; Champollion, *Notices descriptives*, II, 127 f.; Champollion, *Monuments*, IV, 312–313; Rougé, *Album photographique*, 50, 53, 54, 68. See also Pococke, *Description of the East*, I, 95; and Brugsch, *Reiseberichte*, 159.

[b]See Breasted, *Proceedings of the Society of Biblical Archæology*, XXII, 90. The two additional bases noted in Baedeker (1902, 253) probably belong to some other king, perhaps Amenhotep III, who mentions obelisks (§ 903, l. 57); or to Thutmose III.

87. ᵃHorus: Mighty bull, beloved of Truth; King of Upper and Lower Egypt; Favorite of the Two Goddesses: Shining with the Serpent-diadem, great in strength; Okheperkere, Setepnere; Golden Horus: Beautiful in years, who makes hearts live; Bodily Son of Re, Thutmose (I), Shining-in-Beauty.

He made (it), as his monument for his father Amon, Lord of Thebes, Presider over Karnak, that he might be given life like Re, forever.

88. ᵇHorus: Mighty bull, beloved of Truth, King of Upper and Lower Egypt: Okheperkere, Setep-Amon (Thutmose I).

He made (it) as his monument for his father Amon-Re, chief of the Two Lands, erecting for himᶜ two great obelisksᶜ at the double façade of the temple. The pyramidions were of ———.ᵈ

89. A fragment of an obeliskᵉ on the island of Elephantine also refers to Thutmose I's jubilee. It still bears the words:

——— Thutmose (I); Shining-in-Beauty; he made (it) as his monument to his father, Khnum; making for him two obelisks of granite. First occurrence.ᶠ That he may be given life forever.

ABYDOS STELAᵍ

90. This stela recorded the king's works in the Abydos temple of Osiris. In the lost introduction he has apparently held an audience and declared his intention of exe-

---

ᵃMiddle column, east side.

ᵇMiddle column, west side.

ᶜSee Ineni, ll. 9–11, § 105.

ᵈAbout one-third of the line is flaked off; the material of the pyramidions crowning the obelisks was usually copper or bronze.

ᵉBrugsch, *Thesaurus*, V, 1220. The epithet, "*Shining-in-Beauty*," is found on Thutmose I's Karnak obelisk, and is not used by other Thutmosids. Hence the obelisk certainly belongs to Thutmose I.

ᶠReferring, of course, to the royal jubilee.

ᵍSandstone stela from Abydos, now in Cairo; published by Mariette (*Abydos*, II, 31) and by de Rougé (*Inscriptions hiéroglyphiques*, 19–22). Only the lower portion is preserved, the relief above being broken off, and probably a considerable fraction of the text.

cuting certain works for the god; whereupon the priests reply in the words with which the preserved portion begins. The chief treasurer is then instructed to execute the said works, which, he states, he did. On their completion the king delivers an address to the priests like that of Thutmose III (§§ 571 ff.).

Address of the Priests

91. [a]—[a] "How pleasant is this in the hearts of the people! How beautiful is this in the sight of the gods! Thou makest a monument for Osiris, thou beautifiest the First of the Westerners, the great god of the beginning, whose place Atum advanced, whom he magnified before ³his — — his heart, for whom kings have labored since this land was founded. As for thee, thou wast born to him; he made thee in the uprightness of his heart, to do that which he did in the earth, to restore ⁴the sanctuaries of the gods, [to] — their temples. Thou art gold, thine is the silver, Keb[b] has opened for thee that which is in him, Tatenen[c] has given to thee his things. All the countries labor for thee, all the lands are under thy rule. ⁵Every costly stone is ⌜collected⌝ — in thy house; ⌜if there is⌝ a wish in thee, it must be done; it is that which thy ka desires which happens.

Royal Instructions to the Chief Treasurer

92. His majesty commanded the chief treasurer: "Conduct the work, causing to come ⁶— — — — — every prepared one of his workmen, the best of his lay priests, who knows the directions and is skilful in that which he knows, who does not transgress what was commanded him, ⁷⌜to erect⌝ the monument of his father [Osiris], to equip his everlasting statue. Execute the very secret things, no one seeing, no one beholding, no one knowing his body. Make for him the portable chapel-barque (wts-$nfr\cdot w$) of silver, gold, lapis lazuli, black copper, ⁸every splendid costly stone."

Words of the Chief Treasurer

93. I executed for him the offering-tables, — ($sḫm$-) sistrums and ($šsy\cdot t$-) sistrums, necklace-rattles ($mny\cdot wt$), censers, ⌜a flat dish⌝ ($inyw$),

---

[a]The number of lines lost before this point is uncertain.
[b]The earth-god.   [c]Ptah.

a great oblation there. I did not ⌜remove⌝ them. I did not discontinue them.

The Sacred Barge

94. I built[a] ⁹the august [barge] of new cedar of the best of the terraces; its bow and its stern being of electrum, making festive the lake;[b] to make his voyage therein at his feast of the "District of Peker" (*Pḳy*).

Statues of the Gods

95. Furthermore, ¹⁰[his majesty] commanded to shape[c] (statues of) the great ennead of gods dwelling in Abydos; (each) one of them is mentioned by his name; Khnum, lord of Hirur, dwelling in Abydos; Khnum, lord of the cataract, dwelling in Abydos; Thoth, leader of the great gods, ¹¹presider over Hesret; Horus, presider over Letopolis; Harendotes; Upwawet of the South, and Upwawet of the North; mysterious and splendid were their bodies. The standards[d] thereof were of ¹²electrum, more excellent than their predecessors; more splendid were they than that which is in heaven; more secret were they than the fashion of the nether world; more — were they than the dwellers in Nun.

Words of the King

96. ¹³My majesty did these things for my father Osiris, because I loved him so much more than all gods, in order that my name might abide and my monuments endure in the house of my father, Osiris, First of the Westerners, ¹⁴lord of Abydos, forever and ever.

Address to the Priests

97. [I say to] you, divine fathers[e] of this temple, priests (*w ᶜ b· w*), ritual priests, dwellers in the place of the hand,[f] ¹⁵all the lay priests of the temple; offer ye to my tomb, present ye to my oblation-tablet; maintain ye the monuments of my majesty; mention ye my name;

---

[a]Read: ꜣ *ḳh* as in Ineni (§ 105, l. 10).
[b]Meaning it was reflected in the water; see same idea more clearly (§ 888, l. 20).
[c]*Ms*, "*to shape*," with a following name of a god, is not uncommon (cf. I, 672).
[d]These are the standards upon which the statues were borne.
[e]Priestly title.
[f]An order of priests of whom we know nothing.

remember ye my titulary; give ye ¹⁶praises to my likeness; praise ye the statue of my majesty; set my name in the mouth of your servants, my memory among your children. For ¹⁷I am a king excellent because of what he has done; the unique in might through the (mere) mention of his name ⌜— —⌝ᵃ which I made in this land, till ye know it. There is no lie before you, nor exaggeration ¹⁸therein. I have made monuments for the gods; I have beautified their sanctuaries for the future; I have maintained their temples, I have restored that which was ruinous, I have surpassed ¹⁹that which was done before. I have informed the priests ($w^c b \cdot w$) of their duties, I have led the ignorant to that which he did not know. I have increased the work of others, the kings ²⁰who have been before me; the gods had joy in my time, their temples were in festivity.

Universal Triumph

98. I made the boundaries of Egypt ($t^{\circ}\text{-}mry$) as far as that which the sun encircles. I made ²¹strong those who were in fear; I repelled the evil from them. I made Egypt the superior of every land ⌜— — — —⌝ favorite of Amon, ²²Son of Re, of his body, his beloved Thutmose (I), Shining like Re, beloved of Osiris, First of the Westerners; Great God, lord of Abydos, ruler of eternity; given life, stability, satisfaction, and health, while shining as King upon the Horus-throne of the living; and joy of his heart, together with his ka, like Re, forever.

BIOGRAPHY OF INENIᵇ

[Continued from § 46; continued § 115]

II. CAREER UNDER THUTMOSE I (LL. 4–14)

99. The career of Ineni, which began under Amenhotep I, continues here under Thutmose I. The king's name and the narrative of his accession unfortunately fall in the lacunæ at the ends of the lines (probably l. 4). The biography then narrates the wide dominion of the king, and the rich tribute therefrom (§ 101); Ineni's advancement to

---

ᵃRead $r\underline{d}\supset \cdot t$.   ᵇBibliography on p. 18, note c.

superintendence of the king's building projects (§ 102) especially the construction of the Karnak pylons of Thutmose I, and the erection before them of his two obelisks, one of which still stands (§§ 103-5); also the excavation of the king's cliff-tomb and improvements in the necropolis of Thebes (§ 106); Ineni's rewards in serfs and treasury dues (§ 107); and the death of the king (§ 108).

100. The Karnak hall, which Ineni constructed, is of great historic interest, as it was the first hall on entering the building, and served as the chief hypostyle, or colonnaded hall, of the temple throughout the reign of Thutmose I. It was in this hall that Thutmose III was proclaimed king by the priests of Amon (§§ 131 ff.), thus putting aside either its builder, Thutmose I, or the weakling Thutmose II, and in this hall Hatshepsut erected her two great obelisks. The description of the erection of the hall itself is unfortunately lost in the lacuna at the end of l. 7, and l. 8 begins with a reference to the "*great pylons on its either side,*" the erection of which follows. But Thutmose III informs us of the interesting fact that he replaced with stone columns the cedar columns erected by Thutmose I in this hall (§ 601). Indeed, Thutmose I himself was obliged to replace the northernmost two of his cedar columns by stone ones before the end of his reign.[a] The fact is recorded by him on one of the new columns (see Piehl, *Actes du 6me congrès des orientalistes à Leide*, 1883, IVme partie, section 3, 203-19). This inscription is unfortunately now only a series of disconnected fragments, of which little is intelligible. The dedication on one of the columns is as follows: "*Thutmose I, he made (it) as his monument for his father Amon-Re, chief of the Two Lands,*

---

[a]This is a hint as to the length of his reign; he must have reigned long enough for the wooden colonnade to begin to decay.

making for him an august colonnade, which adorns the Two Lands with its beauty." (Brugsch, *Thesaurus*, VI, 1311, and Rougé, *Inscriptions hiéroglyphiques*, 163.) On the further career of this historic hall, only begun here, see §§ 599 ff.; 803 ff.

Accession and Power of Thutmose I

101. ———— ⁵the Good God, who smites the Nubians, lord of might, who overthrows the Asiatics. He made his boundary as far as the ªHorns of the Earth,ª and the marshes in Kebeh (Kbh) ———— ⁶——¹ Elephantine. The Sand-dwellers bore their tribute like the impost of the South and the North; his majesty forwarded them to Thebes, for his father Amon, each year. Everything was made to prosper[b] for me under ————.

Ineni's Promotion

102. ⁷He filled his heart with me,[c] I was brought to be a dignitary, overseer of the granary; the fields of divine offerings were under my authority; all[d] the excellent works together were under my administration.

Karnak Pylons

103. I inspected the great monuments[e] which he made ———— ⁸great pylons on its either side of fine limestone of Ayan (ᶜ *nw*); august flagstaves were erected at the double façade of the temple of new cedar of the best of the Terraces;[f] their tops were of electrum.[g] I inspected ———— ⁹wrought with electrum.

---

[a]The same phrase occurs in Assuan inscription of Thutmose II (§ 120, l. 4), where it refers to the south; the marshes above must therefore be those of the Euphrates in the north, also used by Thutmose II, *loc. cit.*

[b]Such a passive is often a respectful circumlocution to indicate an act of the king.

[c]An idiom signifying favor with the king.

[d]Read: *nb·t*.

[e]The following is the description of the erection and adornment by Ineni of the hall and two pylons of Thutmose I at Karnak (IV and V), and the two obelisks before them, of which one still stands.

[f]Meaning the slopes of Lebanon; cf. the *"Myrrh-terraces."*

[g]Four such flagstaves, set in channels cut for them in the faces of the pylons, usually adorned the temple façade.

Karnak Portal

104. I inspected the erection of the great doorway (named): "Amon-Mighty-in-Wealth;"[a] its huge door was of Asiatic copper whereon was the Divine Shadow,[b] inlaid with gold.

Karnak Obelisks

105. I inspected the erection of two[c] obelisks ——— ¹⁰[d]built the august boat[d] of 120 cubits in its length, 40 cubits in its width,[e] in order to transport these obelisks. (They) came in peace, safety[f] and prosperity, and landed at Karnak ——— ¹¹of the city. Its ⌜track⌝ was laid with every pleasant wood.

Thutmose I's Cliff-tomb

106. I inspected the excavation of the cliff-tomb of his majesty, alone, no one seeing, no one hearing.[g] I sought out the excellent [h]things upon ——— ¹²⌜—⌝ [i]I was vigilant[i] in seeking that which is excellent. I made fields of clay, in order to plaster their tombs of the necropolis; it was a work such as the ancestors had not done which I was obliged to do there ⌜— — —⌝ ——— ¹³I sought out for those

---

[a]The name is not among the ten gates given by Mariette, *Karnak*, 38.

[b]Explained § 889, note.

[c]Hence Petrie, depending on Mariette's plan (*Karnak*, 2) is under misapprehension in attributing one of these obelisks to Thutmose III (Petrie, *History of Egypt*, II, 67). The standing obelisk of this pair distinctly refers to the erection of "*two great obelisks*" (§ 88); hence Thutmose III must have appropriated the now fallen obelisk after it was up, and before the inscriptions were cut.

[d]The same words are used of the transport of Hatshepsut's obelisks; see § 326, note.

[e]*Egypt Exploration Fund Archæological Report*, 1895–96, 9 and 10, where Naville gives the equivalents of the above dimensions rather inaccurately. One hundred and twenty royal cubits = 206.6 feet, and 40 royal cubits = 68.86 feet.

[f] Read ḥtp, ᶜ nḏ, wḏ ͗.

[g]The same phrase: "*no one seeing, no one hearing*," occurs on the statue of Sennefer, British Museum, 48. See also § 92. This remarkable statement indicates the secrecy with which the vast rock-cut tombs of the Emperors were excavated, in order to avoid the tomb-robberies, which finally forced the removal of the royal mummies to Der el-Bahri. Another officer, Hapuseneb (§ 389, ll. 7, 8), also states that he worked on the king's "*cliff-tomb*" (ḥrˑt), see Piehl, *Zeitschrift für ägyptische Sprache*, 23, 59. See Breasted, *Proceedings of the Society of Biblical Archæology*, XXII, 90–94. The construction of such a tomb is described in the last twelve lines of Sinuhe; see Goodwin, *Zeitschrift für ägyptische Sprache*, 1872, 21 ff.

[h]The various supplies for the tomb. [i] Lit., "*My head was watchful.*"

who should be after me. It was a work of my heart, my virtue was wisdom; there was not given to me a command by an elder. I shall be praised because of my wisdom after years, by those who shall imitate that which I have done, ———— [14]while I was chief ($r^{\jmath}$-ḥry) of all works.

Ineni's Rewards

107. My praise endured in the palace, my love among the court. His majesty endowed me[a] with peasant-serfs, and my income was from the granary of the king's estate on each day.

Death of Thutmose I

108. The king rested from life, going forth to heaven, having completed his years in gladness of heart.

[Continued §§ 115-18]

STELA OF YUF[b]

109. This official served under Queen Ahhotep, the mother of King Ahmose I, and administered her property in Edfu. He also repaired for her there a ruined tomb belonging to her ancestor, the queen Sebekemsaf, who was the wife of one of the Thirteenth Dynasty Intefs.[c] He says nothing of any subsequent connection with the royal house under the following reign of Amenhotep I, but he was later in the service of Queen Ahmose, the favorite wife of Thutmose I, and mother of Hatshepsut. His career therefore extended through at least part of four generations of the royal house.

---

[a]The same rare phrase in Ahmose, son of Ebana (§ 6, l. 3).

[b]Sandstone stela, 0.62 m. high, from Edfu, now in Cairo, old No. 238; published by Bouriant, *Recueil*, IX, 92, 93, No. 72. I had also a carefully revised copy, kindly loaned me by Schaefer.

[c]See Newberry, *Proceedings of the Society of Biblical Archæology*, XXIV, 285-89. Maspero supposed (*Momies royales*, 625-28) that Sebekemsaf was a deceased daughter of Ahhotep, but Newberry has clearly shown that she was an ancestor of Ahhotep.

Relief

110. In the middle is an offering-table, before which on the left are two women sitting, and on the right a man, standing, accompanied by his son. Before the first woman are the words: "*Divine consort, great king's-wife, Ahhotep, triumphant;* before the second: "*King's-wife, king's-sister [Sebek]emsaf*[a] —.*"

Before the first man is a mortuary prayer for "*thy (fem.) ka,*" but his name is illegible; before the son: "*His son, prophet of the dues ($š^{\supset}w$), Harhotep, triumphant.*" Below is the following inscription:

Mortuary Prayer

111. ¹An offering which the king gives; Horus of Edfu, Osiris and Isis; may they give bread, beer, oxen, geese, everything good and pure for the ka of the great king's-wife, ²the king's-mother, Ahhotep, triumphant; and her son Nebpehtire (Ahmose I), triumphant.

Restoration of Sebekemsaf's Tomb

112. She gave to me.[b] The ⌈second⌉[c] prophet of the dues ($š^{\supset}w$) of the altar, ³the door-keeper of the temple, the priest, Yuf ($Yw\cdot f$), son of Iritset ($Yry\cdot t\text{-}s\cdot t$), he says: "I repaired this tomb (ysy) of ⁴the king's-daughter, Sebekemsaf, after finding it beginning to go to ruin."

Favor under Queen Ahhotep

113. Then this priest said: "⁵O ye who pass by this stela, I will tell you, and I will cause you to hear my favor with the great king's-wife, Ahhotep. She appointed ⁶me to offer to her; she intrusted me with the statue of her majesty. She gave to me bread: ⁷100 ($by\cdot t$-) loaves, and 10 persen loaves; 2 (ds-) jars of beer, and a joint ($pnsw$) from every ox. I was endowed[d] [with] ⁸upland, and with lowland.

---

[a]Of course, Sebekemsas is meant.

[b]The connection of this phrase is not clear; the following list of titles terminating with the name of the owner of the stela can hardly be connected with the preceding. Perhaps the stela is the gift meant.

[c]Two strokes, perhaps misunderstood from hieratic determinative for a man.

[d]$S^{\supset}h\cdot kwy$, as in Ahmose, § 6, l. 3.

She repeated to me another favor, she gave to me all her property in Edfu, ⁹to administer[a] it for her majesty.

Favor under Queen Ahmose

114. Another favor of the great king's-wife, Ahmose, triumphant, whom king ¹⁰Okheperkere (Thutmose I), triumphant, loves. She appointed me to be scribe of the assistant treasurer. She intrusted me with ¹¹the statue of her majesty, she gave to me 100 loaves of bread, 2 (*ds*-) jars of beer, and a joint (*w ᶜ b · t*) from every ox. ¹²I was endowed with upland, and with lowland.

Field-scribe[b] of Horus of Edfu, Denereg (*Dnrg*).

---

[a] *Ḥrp;* hence we may possibly render: "*to present it (the income?) to her majesty.*"

[b] Evidently the subscript of the scribe who made the document.

REIGN OF THUTMOSE II
BIOGRAPHY OF INENI[a]
[Continued from 108; concluded §§ 340 ff.]

III. CAREER UNDER THUTMOSE II

115. According to this biography, Thutmose II succeeded directly at the death of Thutmose I;[b] under the new reign, Ineni enjoyed the greatest favor, until the death of Thutmose II.

Succession of Thutmose II

116. The Hawk[c] in the nest[c] [appeared as][d] the [15]King of Upper and Lower Egypt, Okhepernere (^{c} $^?$-$ḥpr$-n-R ^{c}, Thutmose II), he became king of the Black Land[e] and ruler of the Red Land,[e] having taken possession of the Two Regions in triumph.

Ineni's Favor

117. I was a favorite of the king[f] in his every place; greater was that which he did for me than[g] those who preceded (me). I attained the old age of the revered, I possessed the favor of his majesty every day. I was supplied from the table of the king [16]with bread of oblations for

---

[a]Bibliography on p. 18, note c.

[b]This seems unfavorable to Sethe's theory that Thutmose III succeeded Thutmose I and reigned for a short time before the accession of Thutmose II. But Sethe offers very cogent arguments in explanation of Ineni's silence on this point. See Sethe, *Untersuchungen*, I, 19, § 29, and 39, § 52; and *Zeitschrift für ägyptische Sprache*, 36.

[c]This is a poetical designation of the crown prince as Horus, who also succeeded his father, Osiris.

[d]Erman's restoration. Sethe, *Untersuchungen*, I, 40, ll. 1.

[e]The cultivable land and the desert.

[f] Lit., "*one who filled the heart of the king.*"

[g]Supply of course: "*than that which he did for those who, etc.;*" or "*than that which those did who, etc.,*" meaning he received greater favor than from preceding kings.

the king, beer likewise, meat, fat-meat, vegetables, various fruits, honey, cakes, wine, oil. My necessities were apportioned in health and life, as his majesty himself said, for love of me.

Death of Thutmose II

118. (He) went forth to heaven, having mingled with the gods.[a]
[Concluded §§ 340–43]

ASSUAN INSCRIPTION[b]

119. This inscription narrates: (1) the arrival of a messenger who announces to his majesty a rebellion in Kush, and mentions a frontier fortress of the king's father, Thutmose I (see § 72) (ll. 5–9); (2) the anger of the king (ll. 9–11); (3) his dispatch of an army thither (ll. 11, 12); (4) the overthrow of Kush, and the capture of one of the chief's children with some other prisoners (ll. 12–15); (4) the complete pacification of the country (ll. 15–17). The inscription is dated on the day of the king's accession, and, according to l. 7, his father, Thutmose I, was living at the time, thus proving the coregency of the two.

Protocol

120. ¹Year 1, second month of the first season, day 8, coronation day[c] under the majesty of Horus: Mighty Bull, Powerful in Strength; Favorite of the Two Goddesses: Divine in kingship; Golden Horus: Powerful in Being; ²King of Upper and Lower Egypt: Okhepernere, Son of Re: Thutmose (II), Beautiful in diadems, upon the Horus-

---

[a]See also Senmut's reference to his death (§ 368, ll. 7, 8).

[b]Cut into the rock on the road from Assuan to Philæ; text in Lepsius, *Denkmäler*, III, 16, a; de Morgan, *Catalogue des monuments*, I, 3, 4, and Rougé, *Inscriptions hiéroglyphiques*, 250, 251; but the best text is revised from a squeeze by Sethe, *Untersuchungen*, I, 81; translation, 38.

[c]The "*appearance*" (lit., *dawning*) of a king is his coronation; it is to be construed with "*upon, etc.,*" after the names of the king. As this is the king's first year, the coronation is not an anniversary, but the very first day of the reign.

throne of the living; his father, Re, is his protection, and Amon, lord of Thebes; ³they smite for him his enemies. Lo, his majesty is in the palace, (⸢but⸣) his fame is mighty; the fear of him is in the land, [his] terror in the lands of the Haunebu; ⁴the two divisions of Horus and Set[a] are under his charge; the Nine Bows together are beneath his feet. The Asiatics come to him bearing tribute, and the Nubian Troglodytes bearing baskets. His southern boundary is as far as the Horns of the Earth[b] (his) ⁵northern as far as the ends; [c]the marshes of Asia[c] are the dominion of his majesty, the arm of his messenger is not repulsed among the lands of the Fe[n]khu.

Announcement of Rebellion

121. One came to inform[d] his majesty as follows: " The wretched Kush ⁶has begun to rebel, those who were under the dominion of the Lord of the Two Lands purpose hostility, beginning to smite him. The inhabitants of Egypt are about to bring away the cattle behind this ⁷fortress[e] which thy father built in his campaigns, the King of Upper and Lower Egypt, Okheperkere (Thutmose I), living forever,[f] in order to repulse the rebellious barbarians, the Nubian Troglodytes of Khenthennofer, for those who are ⁸there on the north of the wretched Kush ⸢— — —⸣[g] with the two Nubian Troglodytes among the children of the chief of the wretched Kush who ⸢—⸣ before the Lord of the Two Lands ⁹— ⸢———⸣." His majesty was furious thereat, like a panther, when he ¹⁰heard it. Said his majesty, "I swear,[h] as Re loves me, as my father, lord of gods, Amon, lord of Thebes, favors me, I will not let live anyone among their males ⸢—⸣ ¹¹among them."

---

[a]Cf. § 70, l. 2.

[b]Cf. § 101, l. 5; and Index V.

[c]See Index V, s. v.

[d]Lit., "*to make prosperous the heart of his majesty,*" which is the conventional form for introducing a matter to a superior in letter-writing.

[e]These are the cattle of Egyptians who have settled in Nubia beyond the frontier military station, and are thus in danger of being pillaged by the rebellious Nubians.

[f] This epithet indicates that Thutmose I is still living.

[g]Sethe: "neigen zum Bündniss?"

[h]Compare the same royal oath in the obelisk inscription of Hatshepsut (§ 318, l. 2, north side) and in the Megiddo campaign of Thutmose III (§ 422, l. 40).

The Campaign

122. Then his majesty dispatched a numerous army into Nubia (*T ꜣ-pd·t*) on his first occasion of a campaign, in order to overthrow all those who were rebellious against his majesty or hostile to the Lord of the Two Lands. ¹²Then this army of his majesty arrived at wretched Kush [————].ᵃ This army ¹³of his majesty overthrew those barbarians; they did [not]ᵇ let live anyone among their males, according to all the command of his majesty, except one of those children of the ¹⁴chief of wretched Kush, who was taken away alive as a living prisoner with their people toᶜ his majesty. They were placed under the feet of the Good God; for his majesty had appeared upon his throne when ¹⁵the living prisoners were brought in, which this army of his majesty had captured. This land was made a subject of his majesty as formerly, the people ¹⁶rejoiced, the chiefs were joyful; they gave praise to the Lord of the Two Lands, they lauded this god, excellent in examples of his divinity. It came to pass on account of the fame of his majesty, ¹⁷because his father Amon loved him so much more than any king who has been since the beginning. The King of Upper and Lower Egypt: Okhepernere, Son of Re: Thutmose (II), Beautiful in Diadems, given life, stability, satisfaction, like Re, forever.

BIOGRAPHY OF AHMOSE-PEN-NEKHBETᵈ

[Concluded from § 85; see also § 344]

IV. CAREER UNDER THUTMOSE II

123. The conclusion of the long military career of this officer, at least in so far as he has recorded it, was a campaign of Thutmose II against the Shasu-Bedwin, of which this is our only record. It is probable that this defeat of the Shasu was only an incident in the northward march

---

ᵃPartially broken away.

ᵇThe negative is broken out in the text, but may certainly be supplied from l. 10.

ᶜLit., "*to a place under his majesty*" = the place where his majesty was.

ᵈBibliography on p. 10, note a.

against Niy (§ 125).[a] This last campaign also brought its reward of valor from the king (§ 24).

Campaign against the Shasu

124. I followed King Okhepernere[b] (Thutmose II), triumphant; there were brought off for me in Shasu (Šꜣ-sw) very many living prisoners; I did not count them.

[See also § 344]

CAMPAIGN IN SYRIA[c]

125. The great importance of this fragment has been overlooked in all the histories, and was first noticed by Sethe.[d] It records a campaign of Thutmose II in "*Retenu, the Upper*" and as far probably as Niy.

¹ᵉ[Gifts which were brought to]ᵉ the fame of the king, Okhepernere (Thutmose II)[f] [from his vic]²tories ——— ³elephant[s]ᵍ ——— ⁴horse[s] ——— [Retenu] ⁵the Upper ——— [the land] ⁶of Niy ——— ⁷kings ——— ⁸his majesty in ——— ⁹[when] he came out of ———.

---

[a] The reign of Thutmose II was so short that we can hardly suppose that he made more than one campaign into Asia, in addition to his Nubian campaign (§§ 119–22).

[b] Published by Maspero (*Zeitschrift für ägyptische Sprache*, 1883, 78) as "Thutmose I;" corrected as above, Maspero, *Struggle of the Nations*, 239, n. 1.

[c] Fragment from the Der el-Bahri temple, middle colonnade, toward the right end of the Punt reliefs (§ 272). Only the extreme tops of nine lines are preserved. Text: Mariette, *Deir-el-Bahari*, 7; Dümichen, *Historische Inschriften*, II, 17; Sethe, *Untersuchungen*, I, 102 and 40. Naville, *Deir-el-Bahari*, III, 80. Besides this inscription, there is a short building inscription of Thutmose II in the Der el-Bahri temple, giving the usual dedication of a doorway which he erected there (Brugsch, *Recueil de monuments*, 69, 1).

[d] Sethe, *Untersuchungen*, I, 40.

[e] As the inscription accompanies a relief representing gifts, the beginning is undoubtedly to be restored according to numerous analogies, as Sethe has done, *Untersuchungen*, I, 40.

[f] In Naville's text the end of the name is lost; hence Naville, not having collated the old publications, is unable to identify the name, but says "it seems to be that of Thothmes I" (Naville, *Deir-el-Bahari*, III, 17). Both Mariette and Dümichen give Thutmose II.

[g] Cf. the elephant hunt in the same region here mentioned, in Amenemhab (ll. 22–25, § 588) under Thutmose III.

THE EBONY SHRINE OF DER EL-BAHRI[a]

126. The left side-panel of an ebony shrine, unearthed by Naville in the temple of Der el-Bahri, contains the following dedication written thrice on the outside. It is in the name of Thutmose I and II, but the feminine pronoun occurs thrice, and the feminine verbal ending four times;[b] hence Hatshepsut was certainly the author of the monument. Moreover, one of Hatshepsut's partisans, Thutiy, states that he made just such an ebony shrine in her time (§ 375, l. 24). It was therefore later usurped by the two Thutmoses, showing that Hatshepsut reigned for a time before them.

127. The Good God, Lord of the Two Lands, lord of offering, lord of diadems, who hath taken the crown of the Two Lands, King of Upper and Lower Egypt, Okhepernere, Bodily Son of Re, Thutmose (II)[c]; he made (it) as his monument for his[d] father, Amon-Re, making for him an august shrine of ebony of the best of the highlands, that she[e] might live and abide[f] ⌜for him⌝[g] like Re, forever.

---

[a]Naville, *Deir-el-Bahari*, II, xxv–xxix.

[b]The feminine occurs continually in the other inscriptions on the shrine also, as Sethe has shown (*Zeitschrift für ägyptische Sprache*, 8, 9).

[c]Right-hand column has Thutmose I!

[d]The column on the edge has "*her!*"

[e]Naville has not noted this feminine, which occurs in two of the three texts; he offers an impossible masculine in his translation.

[f]"*Live*" and "*abide*" are both feminine forms. They are ignored by Naville; Pl. XXVII is very inaccurate in reproducing the alterations evident in the original.

[g]Or: "*through him.*"

REIGN OF THUTMOSE III AND HATSHEPSUT
INTRODUCTION

128. The close of Thutmose I's independent reign was followed by years of conflict and strife among the Thutmosids, in which the parties of Thutmose I (not yet deceased), Thutmose II, Thutmose III, and Hatshepsut were all pushing the claims of their respective candidates for the throne at the same time. As they all succeeded for longer or shorter periods, there is the greatest confusion of royal names on the monuments dating from this period. It seems to the author that Sethe's explanation of the problem is the first correctly to solve the difficulty. It is the first, and thus far the only, scientific study of the problem employing and reckoning with all the materials. Sethe maintains the following propositions:

1. The instigator of the insertion of a royal name over another royal name is the king bearing the inserted name; hence

2. The systematic insertion of the names of Thutmose I and Thutmose II together, over the name of Hatshepsut on buildings erected by her together with Thutmose III, shows that Thutmose I and II reigned for a short time together, after the joint reign of Hatshepsut and Thutmose III had begun.

3. The earliest monuments of Thutmose III show that he at first reigned alone, Hatshepsut being called merely "*great king's-wife*," until she later became king coregent with him.

129. The real succession on the first fall of Thutmose I was therefore probably thus:

1. Thutmose III reigns for a time alone.

2. Hatshepsut's party forces her upon Thutmose III as coregent.

3. About year 6 of Thutmose III, Thutmose I and II together gain the throne, for a brief coregency, but are not able to suppress Thutmose III, who, on the disappearance (probably death) of Thutmose I, regains the throne, and rules as coregent with Thutmose II, till the latter's death,[a] which followed shortly, about year 8 of Thutmose III's reign (numbered from his first accession).

4. Thutmose III, with Hatshepsut now associated with him permanently, holds the throne, and they rule together at least twelve years more, till the death of the queen, when Thutmose III finally holds undivided possession. He numbered his years from his first accession, ruling at least thirty-four years more, till the year 54.[b]

130. It will be seen that in this readjustment of the reigns practically all of the reign of Thutmose I falls before, and the bulk of Thutmose III's reign after, the period of the family conflict; while the reign of Thutmose II falls in the midst of this period of conflict that lies between. Hence the old numbering of these three kings need not be changed, and for this reason also their inscriptions are taken up in the old order. It should be noted that a number of difficulties

---

[a]Fragments of a statue from the temple of Wazmose at Thebes, as published by Daressy (*Annales du service*, I, 99) bear the date: year 18 of Thutmose II! In view of Daressy's numerous errors in publishing the short inscription, this is not to be accepted without examination of the original which, according to Borchardt, is stated by Daressy to be missing at Cairo. The date is probably year 18 of Thutmose I.

[b]It is impossible here to discuss the large mass of evidence which favors the above conclusions. Some of it will be found in the following translations. For the rest, the student is referred to Sethe's first treatise (*Untersuchungen*, I), his discussion with Naville (*Zeitschrift für ägyptische Sprache*, 35, 36, and 37), and Breasted, *A New Chapter in the Life of Thutmose III* (Leipzig, 1900, or *Untersuchungen*, II). For year 20 of Hatshepsut, see Petrie, *Catalogne* .... *Sinai*, p. 19.

beset any theory of the Thutmosid struggle. The above reconstruction, in view of recent discoveries, is perhaps not to be regarded as finally demonstrated, but it at least deals with and attempts to solve the otherwise insuperable difficulties of the current traditional theory.

INSCRIPTION OF THE CORONATION; BUILDINGS AND OFFERINGS[a]

131. This inscription contains historical material of the highest importance, which has been overlooked in all the histories. On the occasion of the completion of one of his numerous additions to the Karnak temple, sometime between the years 15 and 22 (l. 17), Thutmose III held an audience and addressed his court, informing them that he owed his crown to Amon, and that he had shown his gratitude by great buildings and sumptuous offerings (ll. 1-22). The court replied, acknowledging his divine call to the throne (ll. 22-24). All this is now recorded as an intro-

---

[a]In the Karnak temple of Amon, on the exterior of the south wall of the chambers south of the sanctuary; three fragments were first published in 1863 by Brugsch (*Recueil de Monuments*, I, Pl. XXVI), then entire by Mariette (*Karnak*, 14-16) in 1875, with lines numbered backward and incorrect arrangement of fragments; then more accurately, but less completely and without the fragments, by de Rougé (*Inscriptions hiéroglyphiques*, 165-74) in 1879, with lines numbered correctly; then much better than either, with correct arrangement of fragments, by Brugsch (*Thesaurus*, 1281-90); finally I published the coronation portion alone, based on the old publications (*New Chapter*, 6-9). But I have since secured much better materials, especially a careful copy of the original by my friend, Mr. Alan Gardiner, which he kindly placed at my disposal; also, through the kindness of Mr. Newberry, two large photographs made by Dr. Page May; and finally two more, which I owe to the thoughtfulness of Borchardt. These materials add much to the publications, and show that Brugsch made numerous restorations in the lacunæ, without indication that the added signs were not found on the original. The inscription is in forty-nine vertical lines, and as the upper courses of masonry have perished, the upper half of all the lines has been lost, except ll. 36-49, where fragments with the tops of these lines have survived, though with lacunæ below them.

duction to a three-fold list of the king's benefactions to the god: first, his buildings (ll. 25-36); second, his offerings of the field, and the herds, besides gifts of lands (ll. 36-41); third, temple utensils and the like (ll. 42-48). A short peroration concludes the record (ll. 48-49).

132. The introductory speech of the king begins with an account of his youth and of how he was named king. In the course of these reminiscences, the king in one phrase only (l. 3) compares himself to the youthful Horus in the Delta marshes. This very common comparison of the king with Horus[a] in the Delta, together with the following context,[b] was misunderstood by Brugsch as literal.[c] This error was exposed by Maspero[d] in 1880, and since then the inscription was left for twenty years untouched, as if its significance and content had been finally settled. This conclusion, however, is hardly to be justified if we notice that the inscription as used in all the histories now current, is translated backward![e]

133. Translating the king's speech in the proper direction, it becomes coherent in spite of the loss of the first half of each line, and tells a remarkable story. The king states, with protestations of his truthfulness, that he was a lad in the temple of Amon, before he had received his appointment as priest (*ḥn-nṯr*, "*prophet*,"[f] l. 2); and that he later

---

[a]See, for example, the identical statement with reference to Amenmeses, III, 642, note (Lepsius, *Denkmäler*, III, 201, *c*).

[b]It was the following context which misled Brugsch, for he remarks that such comparisons were an "oft wiederkehrende Redensart *junger Könige*" (365).

[c]*Geschichte*, 365, and 288, 289; for the same error recently repeated, see *Proceedings of the Society of Biblical Archæology*, 1904, 37.

[d]*Revue critique*, 1880, I, 107, n. 1; and *Zeitschrift für ägyptische Sprache*, 1882, 133.

[e]Brugsch, the entire inscription, beginning with the last line, and ending with the first. . As far back as 1879 the publication of the admirable de Rougé had added the proper numbering to the lines; Brugsch has it in his *Thesaurus* (1891).

[f]Of course, this appointment must have followed later.

occupied the priestly office of "*Pillar of his Mother*" (l. 3). On the occasion of a great feast the young priest was stationed by the god in the northern hypostyle (l. 3). The splendid procession of the god appeared (l. 4), with the then king (who is unfortunately not named) offering incense and conducting the ceremonies (l. 5). The procession passed around the hall where the young priest was, while the god[a] sought for him (l. 6). As he stopped before the young priest the latter fell down before him in adoration, but was raised up and placed before the god (l. 7).

134. Then followed the oracle[b] of the god, proclaiming him king; it is unfortunately lost in the lacuna, but immediately following is a reference to the "*secrets in the hearts of the gods*" now revealed, namely, their intention to make him king (l. 8).[c] At this juncture in their coronation by the gods, Hatshepsut and Amenhotep III proceed to Heliopolis to be crowned by the sun-god, as was the immemorial custom (cf. §§ 221 ff.). But the young priest, Thutmose, is more highly favored; for him the gates of heaven are opened, he flies thither to be received by the sun-god (l. 9), who then crowned him (ll. 10, 11), and fixed his four royal names[d] (in addition to the fifth, Thutmose, which he already bore), in accordance with divinely conferred qualities (ll. 12–14). Thus he is installed in the kingship, and his authority established at home and abroad (ll. 15, 16), in

---

[a]Or possibly the then king.

[b]This oracle is referred to by the court in their reply (l. 23), and by Thutmose III himself in his inscription of year 23 at Halfa: "*He (the god) hath assigned to him his inheritance as a body which he begat; he uttered an oracle concerning him (nḏ·f rꜣ ḥr·f) that his coronation might be established for him (as) king upon the Horus-throne of the living*" (ll. 3, 4, from a photograph by Steindorff).

[c]Compare the designation of Hatshepsut and Amenhotep III as king by the gods before their coronation (§ 231).

[d]Harmhab's names are declared at his divine coronation at precisely the same juncture (III, 29, l. 19).

order that he may offer the wealth of the earth to Amon (ll. 16, 17), erect him buildings, and present him offerings like the present ones (ll. 17–22).

135. This remarkable narrative, under a cloak of alleged divine interposition, like that in the life of Harmhab (III, 22 ff.), records the elevation of Thutmose III from a position of humble rank in the priesthood of the Karnak temple of Amon to the throne of Egypt. This is unquestionable fact. The only difference between this elevation of Thutmose III and that of Harmhab is that Harmhab reached it after a long official career, culminating in great political power, while Thutmose III rose to it directly from his priestly rank in the temple. Any attempt to explain this is to pass distinctly from fact to theory. Suppose that Thutmose III was the oldest son of Thutmose I, born before the latter's accession; his mother being, as we know, a lady not of royal blood, named Isis. This would explain why we find him as a priest in the Amon temple. When his father, Thutmose I, after marrying the royal princess Ahmose, gained the throne, and Hatshepsut, his daughter by her, grew up, she (Hatshepsut) was given in marriage to the king's eldest son, still a priest in the temple. Thus was the young priest immediately invested with a future claim upon the throne—a claim which a young man of the ability which we know he possessed, would surely make effective. Queen Ahmose dies, and with her perishes Thutmose I's right to the throne. The young priest immediately claims his right to reign, through his wife, precisely as his father, Thutmose I, had done.ᵃ And now we pass from theory to fact again.

ᵃHarmhab also gained his right to the throne through his wife, a royal princess, who is referred to in his coronation inscription (III, 28, l. 15).

136. On the occasion of a great feast, when the god appears in procession, the future Thutmose III has all arranged so that the god shall stop before him as he stands in his place among the ranks of priests in the colonnaded hall, and shall indicate him as the future king. The plan is carried out successfully, and a superb stroke of imagination adds also the visit to the celestial realm there to be crowned and named by Re, the sun-god himself. Thus Thutmose III succeeded his father; and of his wife, the royal heiress, Hatshepsut, in whose right he ruled, we hear not a word in the whole transaction.[a] The later buildings and gifts are also all in his own name.

137. The inscription refers to offerings of the fifteenth year; it is important to note that already at this time, between this date and the beginning of his great campaigns (year 22), Thutmose III possessed forest domains in Syria (l. 34), from which he drew cedar for his temple doors. He was also receiving captives and the children of native princes from Syria at this time. These facts indicate that he was still holding his father's conquests, at least as far north as Lebanon;[b] and it was to suppress a widespread and persistent revolt that he began his campaigns in Syria at the close of the year 22.[c]

Birth and Youth of Thutmose III

138. [1]————[d] my — is he; I am his[e] son, whom he commanded that I should be upon his throne, while I was one dwelling in his

---

[a] This coincides with Sethe's conclusion that Thutmose III succeeded Thutmose I for a time alone, before the legitimists forced Hatshepsut upon him as coregent.

[b] Where his forest domains of cedar must have been located.

[c] For a full exposition of the historical and other data in this remarkable inscription, see the author's *A New Chapter in the Life of Thutmose III* (in Sethe's *Untersuchungen*), Hinrichs, Leipzig, 1900.

[d] The king in the relief is represented enthroned at the left, holding audience. There is little doubt that l. 1 began "*year x, month x, day x, occurred the sitting* (ḫpr ḥms't")," as, e. g., at Der el-Bahri (§ 292). The audience now begins with a speech from the throne.

[e] The god's; see "*his temple*" (l. 2).

nest;[a] he begat me in uprightness of heart [2]———— there is no lie therein; since my majesty was a stripling, while I was a youth in his temple, before occurred my installation to be prophet [3]———— my majesty. I was in the capacity[b] of the "Pillar of his Mother,"[c] like the youth Horus in Khemmis. I was standing in the northern hypostyle[d] [4]————.

The Feast

139. ———— the splendors of his horizon.[e] He made festive heaven and earth with his beauty; he received the great marvels;[f] his rays were in the eyes of the people like the "Coming forth of Harakhte." The people, they gave to him [5][praise] ———— the ⌜altar⌝ of his temple. His majesty placed for him incense upon the fire, and offered to him a great oblation consisting of oxen, calves, mountain goats, [6]————.

Search and Discovery

140. ———— [the god][g] made the circuit of the hypostyle[h] on both sides[i] of it, the heart of those who were in front did not comprehend his actions, while searching for my majesty in every place. On recognizing me, lo, he halted [7]———— [I threw myself on] the pave-

---

[a] A common figure for the young king, conceived as the young Horus-hawk; see § 116.

[b] Or: "*rôle*."

[c] A title of the god Horus, and then of a priest; (see *New Chapter*, 12 and 30) as it was an office which could be held by a high priest (*ibid.*, 30), this indicates promotion of Prince Thutmose from the rank of "*prophet*."

[d] This is the northern half of the colonnaded hall built by Thutmose I in the Karnak temple between his two Pylons (IV and V, see § 99 and my *New Chapter*, 12–14, 30, 31). As it was later dismantled by Hatshepsut for the erection of her obelisks in it, we have here also a terminus ad quem for the date of Thutmose III's coup d'état. On the later history of the hall, see §§ 600, 601, and 803 ff.

[e] A common poetic designation for the temple of a god; to or from the temple at this juncture the sacred procession is moving, as the following three sentences show. In the lacuna opening the next line, he reaches "*his temple*," these being the first words of the line which are preserved.

[f] Doubtless the things offered to him.

[g] Or the procession.

[h] Where Prince Thutmose has already been stationed by the god (l. 3).

[i] Meaning the colonnades on either side of the central aisle; Prince Thutmose is standing in the left, or "*northern*," colonnade.

ment, I prostrated myself in his presence. He set me before his majesty;ᵃ I was stationed at the "Station of the King."ᵇ He was astonished at me ⁸────── without untruth. Then they ⌜revealed⌝ before the people the secrets in the hearts of the gods, who know these his —; there was none who knew them, there was none who revealed them ⁹⌜beside him⌝].

Ascent to Heaven

141. [⌜He opened ⌝for] me the doors of heaven; he opened the portals of the horizon of Re. I flew to heavenᶜ as a divine hawk, beholdingᵈ his form in heaven; I adored his majesty ¹⁰────── feast. I saw the glorious forms of the Horizon-God upon his mysterious ways in heaven.

Coronation in Heaven

142. Re himself established me, I was dignified with the diadems which [we]re upon his head, his serpent-diadem, rested upon ¹¹[my forehead] ────── [he satisfied] me with all his glories; I was sated with the counselsᵉ of the gods, like Horus, when he counted his body at the house of my father, Amon-Re. I was [⌜present⌝]ed with the dignities of a god, with ¹²────── my diadems.

Fixing Titularyᶠ

143. His own titulary was affixed for me.

ᵃProbably "*his majesty*" = "himself;" viz., he raised me up and set me before himself.

ᵇThe "*Station of the King*" is the place in the holy of holies where the king stood in the performance of the prescribed state ritual. One is known in Amâda, in Elephantine, in Thebes (temple of Memnon colossi), and, as above, at Karnak. (See Spiegelberg, *Recueil*, XX, 50, and my *New Chapter*, 16, 17.) I have since found another at Memphis (III, 532). The placing of Prince Thutmose at this official "*Station of the King*" is a public recognition of him as king.

ᶜThe usual meaning of this phrase applied to a king is that he died, but this is clearly not its meaning here, where the king on the throne uses the phrase himself in addressing his courtiers.

ᵈSo Brugsch, but Gardiner and photographs have only a lacuna for "*beholding.*"

ᵉ$S \supset r \cdot t$," see Piehl, *Zeitschrift für ägyptische Sprache*, 24, 83–85; it occurs also in Harmhab's coronation, ll. 3 and 11.

ᶠCompare the fixing of the titulary by the gods in the coronation of Hatshepsut and that of Amenhotep III (§§ 230, 239).

First Name

He fixed my Horus upon the standard;[a] he made me mighty as a mighty bull. He caused that I should shine in the midst of Thebes [13][in this my name, Horus: "Mighty Bull, Shining in Thebes"].[b]

Second Name

144. [He made my kingship enduring, like Re in heaven, in][c] this my [name], Favorite of the Two Goddesses: "Enduring in Kingship, like Re in Heaven."

Third Name

145. He formed me as a Horus-hawk of gold, he gave to me his might and his strength and I was splendid with these his diadems, in this my name, [14][Golden Horus: "Mighty in Strength, Splendid in Diadems"].

Fourth Name

146. ——— [in this my name], King of Upper and Lower Egypt, Lord of the Two Lands: "Menkheperre" (the being of Re abides).

Fifth Name

147. I am his son who came forth from him, a likeness fashioned like the presider over Hesret;[d] he beautified all my forms, in this my name, Son of Re: "Thutmose, Beautiful of Form," living forever and ever.

Recognition of His Authority

148. [15]——— my —; he caused that [the princes of] all [coun]tries [should come], doing obeisance because of[e] the fame of my majesty; my terror was in the hearts of the Nine Bows; all lands were under my sandals. He gave victory by my arms, in order to widen [16][the boundaries of Egypt] ——— because — so much — — — him. He

---

[a]This is the Horus-hawk which surmounts the so-called standard or banner (really the façade of a building) containing the Horus-name of the king.

[b]Restored from the name of the king, as it occurs elsewhere.

[c]This restoration is not literally certain, but something similar must have occupied the lacuna.

[d]That is, Thoth, with whose name "*Thutmose*" (or Thothmose) is compounded.

[e]Or: "*to.*"

rejoiced in me, more than (in) any king who had been in the earth since it was loosened.ᵃ

Purpose of His Choice

149. I am his son, beloved of his majesty, whom his double desires ⌜to cause⌝ that I should present this land at the place, where he is. I cause to encompass ¹⁷——— which he established, to make a monument abiding in Karnak. I requited his beauty with something greater than it by magnifying him more than the gods. The recompense of him who does excellent things is a reward for him of things more excellent than they. I have built his house as an eternal work. ¹⁸——— my [⌜father⌝] caused that I should be divine, that I might extend the throne of him who made me; that I might supply with food his altars upon earth; that I might make to flourish for him the sacred slaughtering-block with great slaughters in his temple, consisting of oxen and calves without limit. ¹⁹——— descending ⌜for⌝ things, of those which were paid anew, — the dues therefor. I filled for him his granaries with barley and spelt without limit. I increased for him the divine offerings, I gave to him increase, ²⁰——— for this temple of my father Amon, at all feasts; ᵇof the sixth day (of the month)ᵇ satisfied with that which he desired should be. I know that it is forever; that Thebes is eternal. Amon, Lord of Karnak, Re of Heliopolis of the South (Hermonthis), his glorious eye which is in this land ²¹———.

Erection of This Monument

150. I made my monument, I recorded my commands at the stairway of the lord of Karnak, of the fashioner of all that is or exists. Everything shall remain forever, that is therein ⌜———⌝ ²²——— a libation, together with the things of his gods, when the god is satisfied with his things. The monument is a work in the temple for a memorial of my beauty in his house, and I shall endure in the mouthᶜ forever.

ᵃThat is, loosened (*wḥ ꜥ*) and separated from the heavens at the beginning, as in the Pyramid Texts.

ᵇSo Brugsch; it is not now visible on the wall.

ᶜOf the people.

Reply of the Court

151. These companions, they said: [23]"——— this [word] which has been spoken to us; which we have heard in the court, L. P. H. May thy nostrils be rejuvenated with satisfying life; may thy majesty endure upon the great throne. The oracle of the god himself,[a] is like the word of Re at the first beginning. Thoth is he who makes the writing speak,[b] [24]——— rejoicing. His kingship is assigned to thee; established is thy coronation upon the Horus-throne, and recorded are thy annals as King of Upper and Lower Egypt. He has united for thee the Two Lands in peace, all countries in subjection."

A New Chapel[c]

152. [25]——— anew, together with a "Divine Abode," a monument of fine white sandstone. The king himself performed with his two hands the stretching of the cord and the extension of the line, putting (it) upon the ground, and furnishing on this monument the exaction of work, according to the command of [26]——— enduring work of their hands.

A Holy of Holies

153. Behold, my majesty erected for him an august Holy of Holies,[d] the favorite place of Amon (named): "His-Great-Seat-is-Like-the-Horizon-of-Heaven," of sandstone of the Red Mountain.[e] Its interior was wrought with electrum [27]———.

Three Portals

154. I [erected] the first portal, (named:) "Menkheperre-is-Splendid-in-the-Opulence-of-Amon;" the second portal, (named:) "Menkhe-

---

[a]Evidently a reference to the oracle which decreed Thutmose III king. Compare the "*oracle of the god himself*" in the Punt reliefs (§ 285, l. 5).

[b]See Papyrus Ebers, I, 8.

[c]Here the audience of the court seems to have been concluded, and the list of buildings and offerings begins.

[d]The form of the determinative is like the shrine of Saft-el-Henneh.

[e]Near Cairo (cf. Baedeker's *Egypt*, 1902, 77; wrongly stated to be near Syene in *Egypt under the Pharaohs*, 176), about two miles east of the city. It yields a reddish, sandy conglomerate called "gritstone." This passage shows the elastic character of the word rendered "*sandstone*" (*rwd·t*); it indicated only gritty, hard stone, and usually sandstone. See also Erman, *Life in Ancient Egypt*, 478, n. 1.

perre-is-Abiding-in-Favor-with-Amon;" [the third[a] portal, (named:) "Menkheperre,][b]-is-the-Great-One-of-the-Souls-of-Amon;" wrought with real electrum, through which Mat[c] enters for him ²⁸——— making festive the monument. He rejoiced in his praise, he did that which he desired, he united his (sic) majesty with satisfying life, and joy of heart forever.

Pylon VI

155. My majesty [erect]ed an august pylon[d] of the interior in front of ²⁹[ʳthe holy of holiesʴ] ——— I erected for him a great door, fashioned of new cedar, wrought with gold, mounted with real black copper, — with copper. The great name upon it was of electrum, doubly ʳrefinedʴ gold and black copper ³⁰——— the ʳ—ʴ thereof were of doubly ʳrefinedʴ gold made in the likeness of the horizon of heaven. It was more beautiful than [ʳanythingʴ] that has (ever) been.

My majesty further made for him these three portals[e] ³¹———.

Shrines and Statues

156. ——— the northern —; shrines of stone, (with) doors of new cedar thereto; ʳthe statues ofʴ [my majesty] belonging thereto, and the statues[g] of my fathers, the kings ³²[of Egypt who were before me].

---

[a]Mariette found six gates bearing the name of Thutmose III in Karnak; but of the three above named he could only find the last (see Mariette, *Karnak*, Textes, 58, and Brugsch, *Thesaurus*, VI, 1311, 1312, 1315. The first was found by Legrain in 1901 (*Annales du service*, II, 227); the second has never been found.

[b]Inserted by Brugsch, but no longer visible on original.

[c]Goddess of truth.

[d]This pylon of the interior is, of course, the pylon (VI) of Thutmose III, behind the two pylons (IV and V) of his father, Thutmose I, and just in front of the holy of holies. The back of this pylon is occupied by the conclusion of the Annals and the record of feasts and offerings (§§ 541 ff.), and the front by Nubian lists.

[e]Apparently a further reference to the three portals mentioned before (§ 154).

[f]So Brugsch, but it is probably one of his tacit restorations, as there is no trace of it on the wall.

[g]These statues were those of his ancestors mentioned in the list in one of the rear chambers of the Karnak temple and now in Paris (see §§ 604 f.).

A Restoration[a]

157. ———— [for] my father Amon-Re in Karnak, by making for him a monument anew, — upon — the ancestors, by beautifying for him his temple which built[b] for him ³³[my majesty] ————. Behold, my majesty found this (made) of brick,[c] very ruinous, of the work of the ancestors. My majesty himself wrought with his two hands, at the feast of "Stretching-the-Cord," upon this monument ³⁴————. Its beautiful name which my majesty made was: "Menkheperre-(Thutmose-III)-Adored-of-the-People-is-Great-in-the-Strength-of-Amon." Its great door was of cedar of the royal domain,[d] wrought with [copper; the great name upon it][e] was of electrum. ³⁵————.

Conclusion of Buildings

158. He [⌈did⌉] more than any king who has been since the beginning. There was none beyond his majesty in knowledge of everything in every handicraft, exacting ⌈— — — — —⌉ ³⁶ ᶠ— ⌈when⌉ there was an "Appearance"[g] at ———— of very great monuments, excellent in work according to the desire of his majesty concerning them, because he so much loved his father Amon [⌈lord of Thebes⌉].

---

[a]It is impossible to identify this structure, but it must have been a considerable building, as a special ceremony of laying out the plan was held. It may have been the chambers attributed to Hatshepsut, on the south wall of which the inscription stands. As this is the last building in the list, its conclusion or dedication is doubtless the occasion of the audience of the court and the introductory speech of the king.

[b]Egyptian order preserved, to indicate division of lines.

[c]In contrast with his restoration of it in stone (which here falls into the following lacuna); cf. Thutmose III's Ptah-temple at Karnak, which bears the inscription: "*His majesty found this temple of brick — — he made this temple of sandstone*" (Brugsch, *Thesaurus*, V, 1188).

[d]This domain must have been in Syria, for cedar did not grow in Egypt. This indicates that Thutmose III maintained his authority there before the beginning of his great campaigns (see my *New Chapter*, 28, 29).

[e]So Brugsch; evidently another tacit restoration.

[f] At this point begins a part of the lost upper portions of the lines, preserved on two blocks at the top of the wall. They have been set on wrong by Mariette, and should be shifted two lines to the right. From here to the end, the average loss is from one-quarter to one-half line.

[g]Of the god, in procession.

New Offerings

159. The king himself commanded to make divine offerings, [37]anew for his father Amon-Re, lord of Thebes, ———— 30 jars of —, 100 bundles of vegetables, 3 (*hbn·t-*) jars of wine, (*ḥt-ᶜᵓ-*) fowl, fruit, white loaves, [a]1 *nḏᵓ* of (ᵓ *ḥ-*) herb and 1 *nḏᵓ* of dates.[a]

Live Offerings

160. My majesty furthermore commanded [38]to present an offering, consisting of oxen, calves, of bulls, of gazelles, ————.

Vegetable Garden and Lands

161. My majesty made for him a garden anew, in order to present to him vegetables and all beautiful flowers. My majesty furthermore gave lands, [39]2800 stat[b] to be fields of divine offerings; many lands in South and North, —[c] ⌈stat⌉.

Foreign Slaves

162. ———— supplied with people. I filled it with [captives] from the south and north countries, being children [40][of] the chiefs of Retenu[d] and children [of the chiefs] of Khenthennofer, according as my father [Amon] commanded ———— milk therein, each day for these vessels[e] (*m[hr]w*) of silver, gold, and bronze, which my majesty made for him [41]anew.

Another New Offering

163. Year 15, first (month) of the third season, day 27; my majesty commanded to found a great divine offering anew ———— [⌈in the year⌉][f] for the sake of the life, prosperity, and health of my majesty, in order that the altars of my father Amon may be supplied for all eternity.

---

[a]See same two items together in feasts and offerings (§ 571, l. 30, and note).
[b]See Griffith, *Proceedings of the Society of Biblical Archæology*, XIV, 412.
[c]Numeral is lost.
[d]See *New Chapter*, 28.
[e]They are mentioned from l. 42 on, § 164.
[f]So Brugsch, but there is now no trace of it.

Small Monuments,[a] Utensils, Etc.

164. [42]My majesty furthermore presented to him [very many][b] monuments: a great vase ($ḥs·t$) of electrum, of 7 cubits[c] ——— of silver, gold, bronze, and copper, they shone over the (sacred) lake; the Two Lands were flooded with their brightness, [43]like the stars in the body of Nut, while my statue followed. Offering-tables of electrum of ——— real —, which my majesty exacted anew. I made it for him out of the conceptions of my heart,[d] by the guidance of the god himself, [44]being the work of the hands of "Him-Who-is-South-of-His-Wall."[e] Never was made the like in this land since the time of the an[cestors] ——— ⌜beyond everything⌝. My majesty furthermore presented to him 2 great ($ḥbn·t$-) jars, as the first of this great oblation, [45]which my majesty founded anew, for my father Amon, lord of Thebes, ——— at all his feasts forever. My majesty furthermore [made] many ⌜chambers⌝[f] wrought with electrum and black copper,[g] erecting an ⌜enclosure⌝, a seat [46]———.

A Harp, Etc.

165. [My majesty made][h] a splendid harp wrought with silver, gold, lapis lazuli, malachite, and every splendid costly stone, [47]for the praise of the beauty of his majesty[i] at his appearances in the names ——— gold, bronze, and every costly stone, a hall as in the beginning; ($mnḫ·t$-) linen, made anew, supplied with all that belongs thereto; [48]two chambers ($yšwy$) containing splendid ointment for [⌜my father Amon⌝] ——— [⌜which⌝] I [⌜exact⌝]ed for it.

Conclusion

166. My majesty did this for my father Amon, ⌜lord [of Thebes]⌝, as recompense for the permanence of [49]the statues of my majesty which are in [this] temple ——— the limbs, as an everlasting work, to make his voyage therein, at his great feasts of the New Year.

---

[a]The Egyptian uses the word *"monument"* also for smaller works, vessels, utensils, etc., of which a list begins here.

[b]So Brugsch, but Gardiner has the $mḥ$-sign and a lacuna.

[c]If this refers to the height, as seems certain, it was of the astonishing height of twelve feet!

[d]The same phrase ($km ꜣ-n-yb$) occurs in Papyrus Harris (IV, 308, l. 4).

[e]An epithet of Ptah, patron of handicrafts.   [f]$Sbḫ·t$.

[g]See Building Inscription of Amenhotep III, ll. 3, 11, and 22 (§§ 883, 886, and 889).

[h]So Brugsch; no trace on original.   [i]The god.

SEMNEH TEMPLE INSCRIPTIONS[a]

167. The temple of Semneh was rebuilt of stone from the ground up, by Thutmose III, with the pious intention of restoring the brick sanctuary of his great ancestor (at least officially so), Sesostris III, in whose fortress of Semneh the temple stands. Of Sesostris III's original temple nothing has ever been found, unless the "Second Semneh Tablet" (I, 653–60) was a part of it. This tablet Thutmose III piously set up in the wall of his new temple; and also had recorded on the new walls the old list of feasts and offerings which he found among the inscriptions of Sesostris III. More than this the old temple was sacred to Khnum and Dedun; but Thutmose III adds to them Sesostris III, now apotheosized as the hero who conquered Nubia[b] (see I, 640 ff.). There is here a noble regard for the greatest king of the Middle Kingdom, which contrasts very strikingly with the shameful desecration of which the Nineteenth Dynasty was guilty.

Thutmose III completed his new temple early in his second year, and the original sculptures show not a trace of Queen Hatshepsut's regnancy.[c]

I. RENEWAL OF SESOSTRIS III'S LIST OF OFFERINGS[d]

Scenes

168. On the right Sesostris III is enthroned under a baldachin. Before him at the extreme left stands Thutmose III.

---

[a]Lepsius, *Denkmäler*, III, 47, *a*–56, *b;* Young, *Hieroglyphics*, 91–95. Steindorff's collation of Lepsius with the original shows that the latter's plates are very accurate.

[b]This apotheosis of Sesostris III doubtless took place earlier than this, but we have no earlier evidence.

[c]On later traces of her in the reliefs, see Sethe, *Zeitschrift für ägyptische Sprache*, 36, 59–63, and Pls. VI–X.

[d]On the east wall, outside (Lepsius, *Denkmäler*, III, 55, *a*–*b*).

Inscription

169. ¹Year 2, second month of the third season (tenth month), day 7 under the majesty of . . . . . . .ᵃ ²Thutmose (III), given life.

Decree of Renewal

170. That which was spoken byᵇ the majesty of the Court, L. P. H., to the wearer of the royal seal, sole companion, king's-son, governor of the southern countries —ᶜ: ³"Cause that there be engraved the divine offerings, which the King of Upper and Lower Egypt, Lord of the Two Lands, Lord of Offering, Khekure (Sesostris III)ᵈ . . . . . . made— — — ⁴in the temple of his father Dedun, presider over Nubia, the avenging son; that he might do excellent things for his fathers who begat him; and the festal offerings, that [his name might be mentioned in the house ofᶠᵉ his father] ⁵Khnum, binder of the (Nine) Bows, smiter of the Shasu ($\check{S}s$ ᵓ· w); while the king, Khekure (Sesostris III) was among the living, while he lived ———— ⁶the gods; causing that there be offered divine offerings to the gods and the mortuary offering to the dead by his majesty. Divine offerings were made anew — — — — ⁷in the house of his father Dedun, that his name might be mentioned in the house of his father Khnum, binder of the (Nine) Bows, smiter of the Shasu.

Sesostris III's List

171. There shall be given: southern grain and speltᶠ for them, and the water of Wawat — — — — — ⁸for his father Dedun, presider over Nubia, a festal offering of the beginning of the seasons: of southern grain, 15 heket;ᵍ for his father Dedun, presider over Nubia: of southern grain, 645 heket; of spelt, 20; — — — — [for his father], ⁹Khnum, binder of the (Nine) Bows: a festal offering of the beginning of the seasons: southern grain, 50 heket; southern grain, 425 heket; of spelt, 20; each year for his father Khnum, binder of the (Nine) Bows: a bull of the herd for the New Year (wp-rnp·t); for his father

---

ᵃFull titulary.   ᵇLit., "*from*" (*m*).
ᶜThe name of the official is lost, but it is almost certainly the viceroy of Kush, who was appointed by Thutmose I (§§ 61 ff.), whose name was probably Thure.
ᵈHis Horus-name follows.   ᵉRestored after l. 7.
ᶠSee Griffith (*Proceedings of the Society of Biblical Archæology*, XIV, 430).
ᵍThe offerings are separated by a semicolon.

Dedun: a bull — — — — — ¹⁰a bull of the herd for the feast, (named:) "Repulse-of-the-Troglodytes,"ᵃ which occurs in the fourth month of the second season, on the twenty-first day, ᵇa festal offering of the beginning of the seasons;ᵇ southern grain, 50 heket; southern grain, 202ᶜ heket; of spelt, 15; each year at (the feast) "Repulse-of-the-Troglodytes:" royal linen, 8 — — — — — [for] ¹¹the feast, which occurs in the first of the third seasonᵈ (ninth month): a bull of the herd; for his father Khnum, binder of the (Nine) Bows, smiter of the Shasu: southern grain, 26 heket; each year for the king's-wife: ————, ¹²southern grain, 26 heket; each year for the great king's-wife, Merseger (*Mr-sgr*), at (the feast) "Binding-of-the-Barbarians:"ᵉ southern grain, 135 heket; of spelt, 10; each year for the king, Khekure (Sesostris III): ————.

172. ¹³His majesty enjoined them upon the chiefs, and governors of the fortresses of Elephantine of the South, as dues of each year to abide and to endure: ————.

II. DEDICATION TO DEDUN AND SESOSTRIS III

*Scene*ᶠ

173. Sacred barque, containing a shrine with statue of Sesostris III; behind this Thutmose III and Dedun standing, the god embracing the king.

Words of Dedun

174. My beloved son, Menkheperre, how beautiful is this beautiful monument, which thou hast made for my beloved son, King of Upper and Lower Egypt, Khekure (Sesostris III). Thou hast perpetuated his name forever, that thou mayest live.

ᵃSee I, 654.

ᵇThe season feast and the feast of victory seem to have fallen together.

ᶜThere is a small lacuna after the units; the number is probably 205.

ᵈProbably Thutmose III's coronation feast, which occurred on the fourth of this month.

ᵉThere is no doubt that this is another feast introduced by *r*, "*at*," as in l. 10.

ᶠInside, on the west wall (Lepsius, *Denkmäler*, III, 48, *b*–49, *a*). There is a similar scene on the newer portion of the same wall, farther north.

175. On the opposite wall in a similar scene[a] Dedun adds:

Thou hast renewed his birth[b] a second time in a monument in memoriam.[c] Thou hast presented to him many offering-tables of silver and gold, bronze, and Asiatic copper. The reward thereof for thee is satisfying life, like Re, forever.

176. The dedication inscription in full is as follows:[d]

¹The Good God, Menkheperre (Thutmose III). He made (it) as his monument for his father Dedun, presider over Nubia (T ᵓ-$pd˙t$), and for the King of Upper and Lower Egypt, Khekure (Sesostris III); making for them a temple ²of fine white stone of Nubia (T ᵓ-$pd˙t$) although my majesty found (it) of ruinous brick; as a son does, ⌜according to⌝ the desire which his father desired, ³who assigned to him the Two Regions, who brought him up to be Horus, lord of this land. I have set it in my divine heart that I should make his monument; that I should make him mighty according as he gave ⁴—; that I should perpetuate his house forever, according as he has become greater than any god. He hath given to me all life, stability and satisfaction like Re, forever.

BIOGRAPHY OF NEBWAWI

177. This official enjoyed a long career, beginning early in the reign of Thutmose III and continuing under Amenhotep II. The narrative of his career was evidently distributed upon a number of monuments,[e] some of which are lost, so that we now possess only the story of his earliest and latest years, the former on a statue, the latter on a stela, both of which were gifts from the king.

---

[a]Lepsius, *Denkmäler*, III, 50, *b*.
[b]Lit., "*repeated birth for him.*"
[c]Lit., "*a monument of putting the heart*," that is, of putting in mind, reminding. Compare Hebrew, סִים לֵב.
[d]On the outside of the west wall; Lepsius, *Denkmäler*, III, 52, *b*; see also Young, *Hieroglyphics*, 93.
[e]Perhaps four (see Spiegelberg, *Recueil*, XIX, 99).

I. THE STATUE INSCRIPTION[a]

178. This text narrates the career of Nebwawi during the first nine years of Thutmose III; during which he rises to be High Priest of Osiris at Abydos. It is significant that Hatshepsut is not referred to until the ninth year, and even then not by name.

At this point the narrative is abruptly concluded, as if to be continued on another monument.

Introduction

179. ¹Given as a favor of the king, the King of Upper and Lower Egypt, Menkheperre (Thutmose III), living forever, to the High Priest of Osiris, Nebwawi (*Nb-w* ᶜ˙ *wy*). He saith: "I was a servant, useful to his lord, zealously serving[b] him who favored him.

First Period

180. I filled the first office in the house of my father, Osiris; I was made chief in the — of the temple. A royal command came before me every day ————[c] in the secret of the lord of Abydos. I ————.[c] This period was until the year ⌈3⌉.[d] My lord, the King of Upper and Lower Egypt, Menkheperre (Thutmose III), praised me for it.

Second Period

181. I was appointed to be High Priest of my father Osiris; every office of this house was placed under the authority of the king's-servant. Another time it was commanded me, that I should go, to [e]bring forth in procession[e] his father, Harendotes, in the house of Min, lord of

---

[a]On a statue in the hands of a native dealer in Luxor; seen and copied by Spiegelberg and published, *Recueil*, XIX, 97, 98; thence by Révillout, *Revue égyptologique*, VIII, 132. Unfortunately, the dealer allowed Spiegelberg only a few moments to copy it, and he was unable to secure a reliable text. See the translation and full discussion by Sethe, *Zeitschrift für ägyptische Sprache*, 36, 71 ff.

[b]Lit., "*pressing (i. e., following) the way of*, etc."

[c]An entire line is lost; its length is not given as published.

[d]It is almost certain that Spiegelberg's 10 is to be read 2; giving 3.

[e]Lit., "*to cause to dawn.*"

Panopolis, at all his feasts in Panopolis, I being there as chief of the prophets and all the workmen of the entire temple. This period was until the year 6. It was the occasion —————— in the Thinite nome. The majesty of my lord praised me.

Third Period

182. I was appointed to be chief in the —— of his father, the King of Upper and Lower Egypt, Nebpehtire (Ahmose I); his treasuries were upon my seals; I came forth therefrom, safe and prosperous, until the year 9.

183. I conducted the work on the ship.[a] I repulsed him that rebelled against her majesty[b] (fem.).

II. ABYDOS STELA[c]

184. This monument takes up the life of Nebwawi after a long interruption at the close of Thutmose III's reign, after the coregency of Amenhotep II had begun, for it carries the narrative into the reign of Amenhotep II, although the monument is a gift of Thutmose III.[d] This conclusion is corroborated by the epithet *"living forever"* after the name of Thutmose III, in the reign of Amenhotep II. Nebwawi was called to the court, and probably died there during the coregency.

---

[a]This is the sacred barge used in the drama of the Osiris-myth; see the same connection in the inscription of Pefnefdineit (IV, 1023).

[b]Read *"his majesty;"* the feminine was doubtless inserted by Spiegelberg as consistent with the rest of the inscription. Osiris is referred to.

[c]Stela found at Abydos, now in Cairo; Mariette, *Abydos*, II, 33, = Birch, *Zeitschrift für ägyptische Sprache*, 1876, 5, 6 (very bad) = Rougé, *Album photographique*, No. 151. I have not seen the last, but used Berlin squeeze (A 1628). Translated by Spiegelberg, *Recueil*, XIX, 99.

[d]On the coregency, see Sethe, *Untersuchungen*, I, 55. It must have begun late in the year 53, or early in 54, for we find Thutmose III still alone in year 52 (Lepsius, *Denkmäler*, III, 45, e; Sethe, *Untersuchungen*, I, 23, n. 1), and Amenhotep II already alone in his third year. As the campaign in Asia was already over by Amenhotep II's third year, and it was certainly made necessary by Thutmose III's death, it is clear that Amenhotep II reigned his first year with Thutmose III, fought out his war in Asia in his second year, and went to Nubia in his third (§§ 780 ff.).

Reign of Thutmose III

185. ¹Given as a favor of the king's presence, the King Menkheperre, living forever, ²to the High Priest of Osiris, Nebwawi.

He saith: "I conducted many works in ³the house of my father Osiris, of silver, gold, lapis lazuli, malachite, and every splendid costly stone. ⁴All these were upon my seal, (for) he knew that I was excellent of heart ⁵toward him. I administered the ⌈affairs⌉ of my lord, as protector of the house of my father. ⁶I attained reverence[a] under the favor of the king's presence. I was summoned ⁷to his house of gold, and my place was made among his princes. ⁸My feet strode in the splendid place;[b] I was anointed with the best ointment, ⁹a wreath ($w^{\circ} h$) was at my throat, as the king does to him whom he has favored.

Reign of Amenhotep II

186. His son repeated to me favor, ¹⁰the King of Upper and Lower Egypt, Okheprure (Amenhotep II), living forever. He gave to me a statue of his father, the King of Upper and Lower Egypt, ¹¹Menkheperre (Thutmose III), living forever; his likeness of millions of years in the house of his father Osiris; divine offerings; ¹²lands of the royal domain. Every writing remained ⌈in force⌉ for the L. P. H. of the Son of Re, his beloved ¹³Amenhotep (II), beloved of Osiris, First of the Westerners, lord of Abydos, given life, like Re, forever."[c]

THE BIRTH OF QUEEN HATSHEPSUT[d]

187. Beginning with the Fourth Dynasty, every Egyptian king might bear the title, "*Son of Re*," the sun-god. It is not an accident therefore, that the interesting folktale preserved to us in the Papyrus Westcar narrates

---

[a]Old age.
[b]The halls of the palace.
[c]Here follow seven lines containing the usual mortuary prayer.
[d]A series of reliefs and inscriptions in the Der el-Bahri temple, occupying the north half of the middle colonnade (corresponding to the Punt reliefs on the south half, §§ 246 ff.). They were uncovered by the excavations of the Egypt Exploration Fund under Naville, which began excavating the temple in 1894. Published in Naville, *Deir-el-Bahari*, II, 46–55.

that the three children of a priest's wife, begotten by Re, and born among astonishing prodigies, became the first three kings of the Fifth Dynasty.[a] The rise of the title, "*Son of Re*," on the Fifth Dynasty monuments thus corresponds remarkably with the legendary tale current a thousand years later among the common people.[b] As Re had once ruled as king of Egypt, lineal descent from him through intervening kings was claimed by all Pharaohs from this time on, and was sufficient to justify the assumption of the title; but in its strictest sense the title indicated that the king was immediately and physically the offspring of the god and a mortal mother. It is probable that this interpretation was pressed at first only by kings whose claims to the throne through their mortal parents were questionable. Naturally, there gradually grew up around so fruitful a theme a literary version of the story, as well as pictures of the various incidents in the drama. These finally took stereotyped form, and the pictures,[c] accompanied by explanatory text, made up of fragmentary quotations from the story in poetic form, have been preserved to us by Hatshepsut at Der el-Bahri and by Amenhotep III at Luxor.

188. The Papyrus Westcar,[b] dating from the rise of the Eighteenth Dynasty, has preserved to us the charming

---

[a]See Petrie, *History of Egypt*, I, 69 f.

[b]The Papyrus Westcar (see Erman, *Die Märchen des Papyrus Westcar*, Berlin, 1890; Erman, *Life in Ancient Egypt*, 373 ff., and *Aus den Papyrus des königlichen Museums zu Berlin*, 38, 39) is from 700 to 1,000 years later than the birth of the three kings which it narrates.

[c]That these pictures are composed of conventionally current scenes is shown by the fact (1) that both Hatshepsut and Amenhotep III used almost identically the same scenes in their birth reliefs; (2) that the sculptor of Hatshepsut's scenes, copied his traditional models in every detail, including the sex of the child (of course, a boy! This was not to conceal the child's sex, for all the pronouns in the accompanying texts are feminine!); had he been sketching something new, prompted by this particular occasion, his sketches would have been made to suit the occasion.

folk-tale in which the state fiction found expression and circulated among the common people. The explanatory texts, accompanying the reliefs of Hatshepsut and Amenhotep III, unfortunately furnish us only the merest fragments of the fine poem in which the court and the higher classes heard the story of the monarch's divine paternity. The meagerness of the surviving fragments of the court poem makes a comparison with the folk-tale a very brief matter, but enough of the former is preserved to show that one quotes from the other, or both quote from a common source in traditional stock phrases long orally current. For the same gods figure at the birth in both, and at least in two incidents the same words are employed by both.

189. Later every king claimed Amon (successor of Re) as his physical father, and in Ptolemaic times the incidents in the divine birth of the king were regularly depicted in the temple reliefs.[a] The most notable example in late times, Alexander the Great, who journeyed to the Oasis of Amon that he might be recognized as the god's son, was therefore merely acting in harmony with a state fiction as old as the Fifth Dynasty. He thus became the legitimate king of Egypt by the only possible means.

190. In the case of Hatshepsut, it was, of course, a violent wrenching of the traditional details to apply the fiction to a woman, for the entire legend was fitted only to a man. The result was in some cases startling inconsistency (e. g., § 202). Undoubtedly, this tale of Hatshepsut's divine

---

[a]For example, Lepsius, *Denkmäler*, II, 59–61; Champollion, *Monuments*, II, 145 sext. ff.; these late representations have not been collected and published; to put them all, early and late, together would be a very useful piece of work. Much material, especially with reference to Alexander the Great, has been collected by Maspero (*Comment Alexandre devint dieu en Egypte*, Ecole des hautes études, annuaire 1897).

[b]See Mahaffy, *The Ptolemic Dynasty*, 15, 16.

paternity, designing her before her birth for the throne, was intended by her supporters to enforce her claims to the kingship. The whole was therefore sculptured in a series of magnificent reliefs at Der el-Bahri, which have suffered sadly from a twofold attack: by the triumphant Thutmose III, who erased the figure and inscriptions of the queen; and by the Amon-hating Amenhotep IV, who did likewise for those of Amon. Hence it has been necessary to employ also the duplicate by Amenhotep III in Luxor.[a]

191. The reliefs begin at the south end of the colonnade, proceed northward (lower row) without interruption, and conclude at the north end.

I. THE COUNCIL OF THE GODS[b]

Scene

192. Amon enthroned at the right, before twelve gods[c] in two rows at the left.

Inscription

The long inscription of probably twenty-one lines[d] between Amon and the gods contained the words of the gods (three lines at the left) and those of Amon (all the rest) in which he has evidently prophesied the birth of Hatshepsut and promises her great power; for we can still read:

I will unite for her the Two Lands in peace......... I will give to her all lands, all countries.[e]

---

[a]See §§ 841 ff. I have arranged the Der el-Bahri and Luxor texts in parallel columns, and find that they largely supplement each other. They are practically identical.

[b]Naville, *Deir-el-Bahari*, II, 46 (Luxor, Gayet, 73 (66), fig. 189).

[c]Osiris, Isis, Harsiese, Nephthys, Anubis, Hathor, Montu, Tum, Shu, Tefnut, Keb, and Nut.

[d]Including two lines behind Amon; all have been carefully hacked away, and only the tops of the lines have escaped destruction. In front of Amon is Ramses II's clumsy note: "*Restoration of the monument which King Usermare-Setepnere (Ramses II) made, for his father Amon.*" The note has been cut directly over the old inscription!

[e]Amenhotep III has Thoth before this council of gods at Luxor.

II. INTERVIEW BETWEEN AMON AND THOTH[a]

Scene

193. Amon stands at the left before Thoth on the right.[b]

Inscriptions[c]

The words of Amon are almost totally illegible, the record of Ramses II's restoration being placed over the lower half. Without them, it is difficult to discern the exact purpose of the interview. The words of Thoth are better preserved:

Words of Thoth[d]

194. ——— thou[e] maiden whom thou hast mentioned. Lo, [— —] an old man.[f] Ahmose is her name, the beneficent, mistress of ——— in this whole land, She is the wife of the king [O]kheperkere (Thutmose I), given life forever. While his majesty is in [—], go thou ——— to her.

Amon and Thoth are now seen[g] proceeding to the queen.

III. AMON WITH QUEEN AHMOSE[h]

Scene

195. Amon and Queen Ahmose are seated facing each other; the god extends to her the symbols of life. They

---

[a]Naville, *Deir-el-Bahari*, II, 47 (Luxor, Gayet, 62 (72)).

[b]The Luxor scene shows one feature omitted in Der el-Bahri, viz., the queen and Hathor standing between Amon and Thoth. Hathor embraces the queen, and the fragmentary inscription would indicate that the goddess is informing the queen of what is to befall her.

[c]Between and over the gods.

[d]By combining Der el-Bahri and Luxor.

[e]End of an optative imperative?

[f]Possibly a reference to the fact that the king is old as a reason that Amon should become the father of Hatshepsut?

[g]On the right of the preceding scene (Naville, *Deir-el-Bahari*, II, 47; Luxor, 63 (71)).

[h]Naville, *Deir-el-Bahari*, II, 47, Luxor, Gayet, 63 (71); a much better text than Gayet's, although with impossible conjectures in the lacunæ, is by Bouriant, *Recueil*, IX, 84, 85.

are sitting upon the heavens,[a] symbolic of the exalted character of the interview, supported by two female divinities who are seated upon a couch.[b] The inscriptions are as follows:

The Interview[c]

196. Utterance of Amon-Re, lord of Thebes, presider over Karnak.[d] He made his form like the majesty of this husband, the King Okheperkere (Thutmose I). He found her as she slept in the beauty of her palace. She waked at the fragrance of the god, which she smelled in the presence of his majesty. He went to her immediately, coivit cum ea, he imposed his desire upon her, he caused that she should see him in his form of a god. When he came before her, she rejoiced at the sight of his beauty, his love passed into her limbs, which the fragrance of the god flooded; all his odors were from Punt.

Words of the Queen[e]

197. Utterance by the king's-wife and king's-mother Ahmose, in the presence of the majesty of this august god, Amon, Lord of Thebes: "How great is thy fame![f] It is splendid to see thy front; thou hast united my majesty (fem.) with thy favors,[f] thy dew is in all my limbs." After this, the majesty of this god did all that he desired with her.

Words of Amon[g]

198. Utterance of Amon, Lord of the Two Lands, before her: 'Khnemet-Amon-Hatshepsut shall be the name of this my daughter, whom I have placed[h] in thy body, [i] this saying which comes out of thy mouth.[i] She shall exercise the excellent kingship in this whole land.[j]

---

[a]Plainer in Luxor.   [b]Upon which the interview really took place.
[c]Text behind Amon.   [d]The following is not really the words of Amon.
[e]Behind the queen.

[f]Luxor has a different text here: "— — — — *the plans which thou hast made; thy [heart] is satisfied with my majesty*" (feminine).

[g]Next to the right; four lines.   [h]Read *wd·ny*.

[i]The connection is not clear.

[j]This announcement of the god to Hatshepsut's mother is strikingly like the announcement of Re to Rededet, the mortal mother of his three unborn children in Papyrus Westcar (IX, 10, 11): "*He (Re) hath said to her: 'They shall exercise this excellent office in this whole land.'*"

My soul is hers, my ⌜bounty⌝ is hers, my crown ⌜is hers,⌝ that she may rule the Two Lands,[a] that she may lead all the living ———.[b]

IV. INTERVIEW BETWEEN AMON AND KHNUM[c]

199. Amon now calls in the aid of the god Khnum, who created man.

Scene

Amon stands on the left before Khnum on the right. The following inscriptions accompany them:

Instructions of Amon[d]

200. Utterance of Amon, presider over Karnak: "Go, to make her, together with her ka, from these limbs which are in me; go, to fashion her better than all gods; ⌜shape for me,⌝[e] this my daughter, whom I have begotten. I have given to her all life and satisfaction, all stability, all joy of heart from me, all offerings, and all bread, like Re, forever."

Reply of Khnum

201. "I will form this [thy] daughter [Makere] (Hatshepsut),[f] for life, prosperity and health; for offerings ——— for love of the beautiful mistress. Her form shall be more exalted than the gods, in her great dignity of King of Upper and Lower Egypt."

V. KHNUM FASHIONS THE CHILD[g]

Scene

202. Khnum is seated before a potter's wheel, upon which he is fashioning two male (!) children,[h] the first being

---

[a]Luxor adds: "*like Re, forever*" and ends here.

[b]Nearly two lines of conventional promises, in a very fragmentary state, follow here.

[c]Naville, *Deir-el-Bahari*, II, 48 (=Luxor, 63 (71), Fig. 203).

[d]They have all disappeared but one line. The rendering is partially from Luxor, with corresponding changes of gender. In fashioning the child (at Der el-Bahri, Pl. 48), Khnum repeats the instructions he has received from Amon, which can thus be reconstructed from this source, also. I have arranged the three sources in parallel columns, and employed all.

[e]Read *twt ny*?

[f]Luxor adds: "*together with all his (Amenhotep III's) ka's.*"

[g]Naville, *Deir-el-Bahari*, II, 48 (=Luxor, 63 (71), Fig. 202).

[h]This would indicate that the reliefs were made according to old and traditional sketches in which, of course, a female child had no place. All the pronouns used by Khnum in addressing the child are feminine!

Hatshepsut and the second her ka. The frog-headed goddess Heket,[a] kneeling on the right, extends the symbol of life to the two children.

Inscription

203. Khnum repeats the instructions he has received from Amon, putting them now in the first person.

Utterance of Khnum, the potter, lord of Hirur ($Ḥr$-wr): "I have formed thee of these limbs of Amon, presider over Karnak. I have come to thee (fem.), to fashion thee better than all gods.[b] I have given to thee (fem.) all life and satisfaction, all stability, all joy of heart with me; I have given to thee (fem.) [c]all health, all lands; I have given to thee (fem.) all countries, all people;[c] I have given to thee (fem.) all offerings, all food; I have given to thee (fem.) to appear upon the throne of Horus like Re, forever; ———[d] I have given to thee (fem.) to be before the ka's of all the living, while thou (fem.) shinest as King of Upper and Lower Egypt, of South and North, according as thy (fem.) father who loves thee (fem.) has commanded.

VI. INTERVIEW BETWEEN THOTH AND QUEEN AHMOSE[e]

Scene

204. Queen Ahmose standing on the right is saluted by Thoth, who stands with outstretched arm at the left.

Inscriptions

They unfortunately contain only titles and epithets of praise, so that the purpose of the interview is not clear.

VII. QUEEN AHMOSE IS LED TO CONFINEMENT[f]

Scene

205. Khnum and Heket appear on each side of the queen leading her by either hand. Before them nine divinities in three rows of three. All are led by Amon.

---

[a]At Luxor it is Hathor.
[b]In Papyrus Westcar (X, 14) Khnum *"makes sound his limbs."*
[c]Unimportant variants in Luxor.   [d]Two short lines lost.
[e]Naville, *Deir-el-Bahari*, II, 48 (=Luxor, 64 (69), Fig. 197).
[f]Naville, *Deir-el-Bahari*, II, 49 (=Luxor 64 (69), Fig. 198).

Inscriptions

They again offer only titles and epithets of praise; the inscription of Heket,[a] however, did contain some references to the scene; we can discern: "*Thou didst conceive immediately after this, thou ⌐—⌐ a child ——— [⌐Go⌐] with him*[b] *to the court, to* ———;" but the bulk of her speech is hacked out or covered by Ramses II's renewals. Before Amon a long inscription of thirteen lines, now completely hacked out, doubtless contained the description of the scene.

VIII. THE BIRTH[c]

Scene

206. The queen[d] sits enthroned in the middle of the upper row, holding the child; before her are four female divinities, acting as midwives and extending their arms for the child.[e] Behind her are five goddesses;[f] the foremost, extending to the queen the sign of life. The entire row rests upon a couch. In the middle row, which also rests upon a couch, we see directly under the queen two genii of myriads of years; and on either side of them the genii of the east and west.[g] The bottom row shows: on the left, the genii of the north and south; on the right, Bes and

---

[a]Her titles are also interesting: "*Heket, mistress of Hirur, White One of Nekhen, deliverer*" (at births), in which she is identified with Eileithuia because of similar functions.

[b]Khnum or Amon?

[c]Naville, *Deir-el-Bahari*, II, 51 (=Luxor, 65 (70), Fig. 199).

[d]She bears the name of Hatshepsut! But in Luxor the corresponding position is occupied by the mother of the child, and there can be no doubt of the identity here.

[e]In Luxor, one of these midwives is passing the child to the next.

[f]Among them Isis and Nephthys; these two, together with Khnum and Heket who led in the queen, and Meskhenet, who sits at the right, are the same five divinities who figure at the birth of the children of Re in Papyrus Westcar (IX, 23).

[g]Naville, *Deir-el-Bahari*, II, 16.

Teweret, with a blank space which contained an inscription now totally gone.[a] At the extreme right sits Meskhenet, the goddess of births, directing the midwives.

Inscriptions

207. The divinities on the right in the upper row and Meskhenet all utter the conventional promises, as in the speech of Khnum[b] (§ 203).

IX. PRESENTATION OF THE CHILD TO AMON[c]

208. The child is now presented to her father by Hathor.

Scene

1. Hathor, enthroned on the right, extends the child to Amon, who is standing on the left.

Inscriptions

2. The brief words of Hathor have almost disappeared; one can still read: "*she extends her arm before his majesty.*"

Words of Amon

3. Utterance of [Amon] .... [d] ——— to see his daughter, his beloved, the king, Makere (Hatshepsut), living, after she was born, [e]while his heart was exceedingly happy.[e]

Utterance[f] of [Amon to] his bodily daughter [Hatshepsut]: "Glorious part which has come forth from me; king, taking the Two Lands, upon the Horus-throne forever."

---

[a]It is better preserved at Luxor, but I can see no connection with chap. 137 of the *Book of the Dead*, to which Naville finds a resemblance (*Deir-el-Bahari*, II, 16).

[b]In Papyrus Westcar (X, 13, 14). Meskhenet says: "*A king, who shall exercise the kingship in this whole land.*"

[c]Naville, *Deir-el-Bahari*, II, 52 (=Luxor, 65 (70), Fig. 200).

[d]The usual promises.

[e]Exactly the same phrase (*nḏm yb*) is used by the divinities in Papyrus Westcar (XI, 5), as they announce the birth of his children to Rawoser, saying: "*Let thy heart be happy, Rawoser; behold three children are born to thee.*"

[f]Under his extended arm.

X. COUNCIL OF AMON AND HATHOR

Scene

209. Amon is enthroned at the left holding the child before Hathor, enthroned at the right. Behind the latter is the goddess Serek,[a] who is perhaps summoning the child to its nourishment in the following scene.

Inscriptions

They are unfortunately so defaced that little more than the conventional promises can be made out.[b]

XI. THE NURSING OF THE CHILD[c]

Scene

210. On a couch at the left (above) sits Queen Ahmose, supported by a goddess, and before her the child and its ka are nursed by two cow-headed Hathors. Below the couch are two Hathor cows, suckling the child and its ka.[d] On the right are the ka's, twelve in number, which have already been suckled and are being passed on to the Nile-god and an obscure deity named Heku ($hk^{\supset}w$), who present them to three enthroned divinities.

Inscription

It has almost all been hacked out, but we can discern the words: "*Nursing her majesty* (fem.) *together with all her ka's.*"

---

[a]She is lacking at Luxor.

[b]Luxor is no better.

[c]Naville, *Deir-el-Bahari*, II, 53 (=Luxor, 66 (67), Figs. 192 and 193, and 67 (68), Fig. 194).

[d]The children have been hacked out, but they are clear in Luxor. There is a splendid granite statue of such a Hathor cow in Florence, suckling the infant King Harmhab.

XII. SECOND INTERVIEW OF AMON AND THOTH

Scene

211. Amon and Thoth stand facing each other, and hold between them the child[a] and its ka.[a]

Inscriptions

Only the conventional promises; the purpose of the interview is perhaps the arrangement of the child's future.

XIII. THE FINAL SCENE[b]

Scene

212. At the left Khnum and Anubis advance, the latter rolling a large disk before him. Before them two female divinities in the upper row present the child and its ka to a kneeling god (the Nile-god?), and in the lower row the same scene appears before another unknown divinity. Behind (at the right) stands Sefkhet, keeping record, accompanied by an attendant god.

Inscriptions

Only the conventional promises; it is therefore impossible to explain the purpose of this scene. The child is now launched upon its career.

STATUE OF ENEBNI[c]

213. A statue upon which the nobleman Enebni refers to Thutmose III as "*her* (Hatshepsut's) *brother.*"

---

[a]Hacked out.

[b]Naville, *Deir-el-Bahari*, II, 55 (=Luxor, 67 (68), Fig. 195, and 64 (69), Fig. 196.

[c]Statue in the British Museum. Inscription: Lepsius, *Auswahl der wichtigsten Urkunden*, 11; Sethe, *Untersuchungen*, I, 123, e, and cf. also 6, 7, and 51; also Maspero, *Proceedings of the Society of Biblical Archæology*, XIV, 170 ff.

Made as a favor[a] of the Good Goddess, Mistress of the Two Lands, Makere (Hatshepsut), living and abiding like Re, and her brother the Good God, Lord of Offering, Menkheperre (Thutmose III), who is given life like Re, forever.

An "offering-which-the-king-gives" ———[b] for the ka of the only excellent one, the favored of his god, the beloved of his lord, because of his excellence; the follower of his lord on his journeys in the South country and the North country,[c] the king's-son, chief of the archers, master of the royal weapons, Enebni (ᵓnbny), triumphant before the great ennead of gods.

VASE INSCRIPTION[d]

214. A small jar, presented by Hatshepsut to her mother, Ahmose, bears the words:

Divine Consort, Great King's-Wife,[e] Hatshepsut; she made (it) for her mother, Great King's-Wife, Ahmose, triumphant before Osiris.

THE CORONATION OF QUEEN HATSHEPSUT[f]

215. The scenes and inscriptions in this series are in uninterrupted continuation of the birth series (§§ 187–212).

---

[a] The usual formula has: "*Given as a favor, etc.,*" see, e. g., Senmut statue (§ 366).

[b] The usual formulary—in the name of Amon, Osiris, and Anubis—is omitted.

[c] This suggests unknown campaigns of Thutmose III, while he was still hampered by the association with Hatshepsut.

[d] In Gizeh; text in Mariette, *Monuments divers*, 48, *d* 1; Maspero, *Momies royales*, 633, n. 4; Brugsch, *Recueil de monuments*, I, Pl. 36, 4, and p. 49; Sethe, *Untersuchungen*, I, 122, 6, 20.

[e] Showing clearly that the queen for a time after her accession bore the usual titles of the king's legitimate wife, with no pretense of being king herself. See Sethe, *Untersuchungen*, I, § 31 and § 36, where another vase inscription shows the same fact.

[f] Reliefs and inscriptions on the wall of the northern half of the middle colonnade in the Der el-Bahri temple; they begin on the south end-wall (directly over the first scene of the birth series, which they continue), proceed northward along the west wall, and conclude on the north end-wall (directly over the last scene of the birth series). They were uncovered by the Fund excavations under Naville, and published by Naville, *Deir-el-Bahari*, III, 56–64.

They represent the child consecrated to the kingship by the gods; then grown to maidenhood and crowned by them; and finally crowned by her father, Thutmose I, before the assembled court. This is followed by some concluding ceremonies by the gods. The birth series of Amenhotep III at Luxor continues to furnish a parallel as far as the coronation by Atum (III) and the reception of names and crowns (IV). The entire series has been more or less defaced and systematically hacked out by the queen's political enemies. The historical value of the different sections is discussed as they are taken up.

I. THE PURIFICATION[a]

Scene

216. The child[b] stands between Amon on the right and Khonsu on the left, who are pouring water over her head.

Inscriptions

Both the gods utter the following words:[c]

Thou art pure, together with thy ka, [for] thy great dignity of King of Upper and Lower Egypt, living.

II. AMON PRESENTS THE CHILD TO ALL THE GODS[d]

Scene

217. Amon, enthroned at the left, fondles the child upon his knees; before him stand six figures: three (above) representing "*all the gods of the South,*" and three (below) representing "*all the gods of the North.*"

---

[a]Middle terrace, northern half, on the south end-wall, upper row, over the first scene in the birth series; published by Naville, *Deir-el-Bahari*, III, 56 (=Luxor, 75 (64), Fig. 186).

[b]The figure has totally disappeared at Der el-Bahri, but is preserved at Luxor.
[c]Same in Luxor.

[d]Naville, *Deir-el-Bahari*, III, 56 (=Luxor 73 (66), Fig. 190).

Inscriptions

218. They have as usual been hacked out and further obscured by the barbarous restorations of Amon's name where it did not belong, by Ramses II.

Words of Amon

219. Utterance of Amon-Re, lord of ᵃ[heaven to] the gods:ᵃ "Behold ye, my daughter [Hatshepsut]ᵇ living; be ye loving toward her, and be ye satisfied with her."

He showsᶜ her to all the gods of South and North, who come to look upon her, ⌜doing obeisance before her⌝.

Words of the Gods

220. ¹Utterance of all the gods, [to] Amon-[Re]: "This thy daughter [Hatshepsut], who liveth, we are satisfied with her in life and peace. ²She is now thy daughter of thy form, whom thou hast begotten, prepared. Thou hast given to her thy soul, thy ⌜—⌝, thy ⌜bounty⌝, the magic powers of the diadem.ᵈ ³While she was in the body of her that bare her, the lands were hers, the countries were hers;ᵉ all that the heavens cover, all that the sea encircles. Thou hast now done ⁴this with her, for thou knowest the two æons.ᶠ Thou hast given to her the share of Horus in life, the years of Set in satisfaction. We have given to herᵍ . . . .

III. THE NORTHERN JOURNEYʰ

221. With this incident in the queen's childhood we pass out of pure fiction into a narrative which possibly contains

---

ᵃRamses II's restoration renders this uncertain.

ᵇIn the blank where the name of the queen had been cut out, Ramses II has inserted "*Amon.*"

ᶜLit., "*he causes them to see her.*"

ᵈSee the same statement by Amon himself in the birth scenes (§ 198).

ᵉRead $ḥ \circ s\cdot t$ (or nt) and $ns\ ymy$ = "*belonging to.*"

ᶠPeriods of 60 years.

ᵍRamses II has again put in a restoration of Amon in the wrong place. After that follow the conventional promises of life, satisfaction, etc.

ʰText first published by Naville, *Recueil*, 18, Pl. 1, and corrections, *ibid.*, 19, 209–11. Later and much more correctly Naville, *Deir-el-Bahari*, III, 57.

a kernel of fact. Having actually, during her father's lifetime, made a journey with him to the north, she now slightly warps its purpose (of which we really know nothing) and represents the journey as the occasion of an acknowledgment of her coming kingship by all the gods of Egypt as she proceeds to Heliopolis to be crowned by Atum. According to the date of her jubilee (year 15), she must have spent fifteen years as crown prince (being nominated thirty years before the jubilee).[a] After references to her godlike appearance and blooming beauty, having grown from childhood to maidenhood, the journey is barely mentioned, but it is stated that all the gods came to her as she journeyed northward. Following this, over half of the inscription (ll. 8–15) is occupied with the splendid promises of the gods regarding the greatness of her future kingdom. That this journey northward is represented as primarily in order to visit Heliopolis, and there be acknowledged and crowned by Atum, is shown by the accompanying scene, in which she is crowned in his presence.

222. The same incident occurs in the coronation of Amenhotep III. This was undoubtedly an old custom, for Atum was the solar deity, who was always associated with the kingship; and, as we noticed in the preceding birth series, Atum's successor at Heliopolis, Re, became the father of all mortal kings of Egypt. In accordance with this old custom, Amenhotep III also visited Atum, and was crowned by him, before his accession. The visit of Piankhi (IV, 871) was due to the same custom, and Thutmose III's ascension to heaven (§ 141) to be crowned and receive his royal names is but a splendid variation of the customary fiction.

---

[a]See Sethe, *Zeitschrift für ägyptische Sprache*, 36, 65.

The Queen's Growth and Beauty

223. ¹Her majesty saw all this thing[a] herself, which she told to the people, who heard, falling down for terror among them. ²Her majesty grew beyond everything; to look upon her was more beautiful than anything; her ⌜—⌝ was like a god, her form was like a god, she did ³everything as a god, her splendor was like a god; her majesty (fem.) was a maiden, beautiful, blooming, Buto in her time. ⁴She made her divine form to flourish, a ⌜favor of⌝ him that fashioned her.

The Journey

224. Her majesty (fem.) journeyed ⁵to the North country after her father, the King of Upper and Lower Egypt, Okheperkere, who liveth forever. There came[b] her mother, Hathor, patroness of Thebes; Buto, mistress of Dep; Amon, lord of Thebes; ⁶Atum, lord of Heliopolis; Montu, lord of Thebes; Khnum, lord of the Cataract; all the gods that are in Thebes, all the gods of the South and North, and approached ⁷her. They traversed for her, pleasant ways, (they) came, and they brought all life and satisfaction with them, they exerted their protection behind her; one proceeded ⁸after another of them, they passed on behind her every day.

Promises of the Gods

225. They said, "Welcome, daughter of Amon-Re; thou hast seen thy administration in the land, thou shall set ⁹it in order, thou shalt restore that which has gone to its ruin,[c] thou shalt make thy monuments in this house, thou shalt victual the offering-tables of him who begat thee, thou shalt pass through the land[d] and thou shalt embrace ¹⁰many countries. Thou shalt strike among the Tehenu, thou shalt smite with the mace the Troglodytes; thou shalt cut off the heads of the soldiers, thou shalt seize ¹¹the chiefs of Retenu, bearing the sword, the survivals[e]

---

[a]What thing is meant is not clear; possibly it refers to the preceding presentation to the gods, which she narrates now to the people. Then follow her growth into youth and beauty, and the journey.

[b]$Yw\cdot hr$ is a $sdm\cdot hr\cdot f$-form.

[c]This is a clear reference to the queen's restoration of the temples recorded at Benihasan (§§ 296 ff.), and plainly indicates the late date of the coronation reliefs, which are thus evidently later than the temple restorations.

[d]Read $hns\cdot t\ t$ ⸱ (t for two land-signs).

[e]Meaning those whom her father Thutmose I had left; hence this is further evidence of his Asiatic campaign.

of thy father. Thy tribute is myriads of men, the captives of thy valor; thy ⌜reward⌝ is [12]thousands of men for the temples of the ⌜Two Lands⌝. Thou givest offerings in Thebes, the steps of the king, Amon-Re, lord of Thebes. [13]The gods have [endowed] thee with years, they ⌜present⌝ thee with life and satisfaction, they praise thee, for their heart hath given understanding to the egg[a] which [14][they] have fashioned. They shall set thy boundary as far as the breadth of heaven, as far as the limits of the twelfth hour of the night; the Two Lands shall be filled with children —, thy numerous children [15]are (as) the number of thy grain, ⌜which⌝ thou ⌜—⌝ in the hearts of thy people; it is the daughter of the bull of his mother,[b] — beloved.

IV. CORONATION BY ATUM[c]

226. The queen on the left is led by Hathor[d] into the presence of Atum standing on the right. In Luxor, after being led in by Sekhmet, the king (corresponding to the queen in Der el-Bahri) kneels before Atum enthroned.[e] Before them stands Thoth, of whose inscription only the following has survived:

Words of Thoth

227. Set his diadem upon his head; put — — — — — titulary — — — — before the gods. . . . .[f]

V. RECEPTION OF THE CROWNS AND THE NAMES[g]

228. The coronation before Atum is followed by a similar ceremony before Amon.[h]

---

[a]Meaning the queen.   [b]Amon-Kamephis.

[c]Naville, *Deir-el-Bahari*, III, 57, 58 (=Luxor, 73 (66), Fig. 191, and 74 (65), Fig. 188).

[d]There is another divinity before the queen, and there were others behind Hathor, but all have disappeared.

[e]It is probable that this scene was also in the Der el-Bahri series in the erased space immediately following the above introduction to Atum.

[f]The conventional phrases.

[g]Naville, *Deir-el-Bahari*, III, 4, where only an account of the scene is given with a few sentences of text, as the whole is almost completely hacked out. At Luxor the scene of the crowns is well preserved (Gayet, 75 (64), Fig. 184 incomplete; better Lepsius, *Denkmäler*, III, 75, c), but the scene of names is omitted.

[h]This is of course a later custom, as Amon himself is a later god.

Scene

The queen,[a] standing, is embraced by Amon, enthroned at the left; from the right approach two goddesses,[b] one bearing the crown of Upper and the other the crown of Lower Egypt, and behind them are the genii of the cardinal points.

Inscriptions

229. Presented to thee is this red crown, which is upon the head of Re; thou shalt wear the double crown, and thou shalt take the Two Lands by this its name

Presented to thee is this white crown, mighty upon thy head; thou shalt take the lands by its diadem, by this its name.

Reception of Names

230. There was here a scene (wanting in Luxor), representing the reception by the queen of her new royal names, conferred by the gods.[c] The scene is totally destroyed, with the exception of the figures[d] of Sefkhet and Thoth (?) on the right accompanied by the words:

Writing the name, Golden Horus: Divine of Diadems. Writing the name, King of Upper and Lower Egypt, Makere.

VI. PROCLAMATION AS KING BEFORE AMON[e]

Scene

231. The queen, in king's costume, with the double crown of Upper and Lower Egypt, stands before Amon, enthroned on the left. Behind the queen are the genii of the cardinal points, and behind these again Sefkhet and Thoth are keeping record.

---

[a]From Luxor, where, of course, it is the king.

[b]From the Der el-Bahri inscription it is evident that they are Nekhbet and Buto, the goddesses of South and North, as we should expect.

[c]See the conferring of names upon Thutmose III (§§ 143 ff.) by the gods. Later, when the queen's names are really conferred by the officials, it is naïvely explained that they have been revealed to the officials by the god (§ 239).

[d]Naville, *Deir-el-Bahari*, III, 59.   [e]Naville, *Deir-el-Bahari*, III, 59, 60.

Inscriptions

The accompanying inscriptions are either destroyed or, where preserved, show only conventional phrases. That the coronation before the gods is complete is seen from the fragmentary words of Thoth: *"Thou hast set these thy diadems [upon thy head]."*

VII. CORONATION BEFORE THE COURT[a]

232. We now reach the alleged real coronation of the queen, which is represented as taking place before the court, at the command of Thutmose I, who retires from the throne in Hatshepsut's favor. As she bore the title "*great king's-wife,*" for some time after her accession,[b] it is clear that she did not immediately succeed her father in the kingship as here represented.

233. This fact alone shakes one's confidence in the truth of the coronation inscription; but to this fact we must add another still more decisive. The date of the coronation is given as the first of Thoth, New Year's Day, of itself a remarkable coincidence. The selection of this date is explained as intentional on the part of Thutmose I in a passage, which states:[c]

---

[a]First published by Naville in *Recueil*, 18, Pl. III; corrections, *ibid.*, 19, 211, 212; finally, much better (but not without errors) in Naville, *Deir-el-Bahari*, III, 60–63.

[b]See Sethe, *Untersuchungen*, I, § 31 and § 36, and *Zeitschrift für ägyptische Sprache*, 36, 67.

[c]Naville's rendering is as follows: "at (*r*) the festival day (*ḫ*-disk) of her coronation; when the first day of the year and the beginning of the seasons should be united, etc." (Naville, *Deir-el-Bahari*, III, 7, l. 33). The *ḫ*-disk cannot be read as the sun-disk ("*day*"), for it lacks the stroke, never lacking with the sun-disk in this inscription (e. g., in the neighboring lines twice, l. 27 and l. 29). We must read *rḫ-f*, "*he knew, recognized.*" *Nfr* follows in the usual construction with *n*. There is not a shadow of doubt as to the correct rendering. Later: Naville's later altered rendering, in a recent number of *Sphinx*, is grammatically impossible.

THE CORONATION OF QUEEN HATSHEPSUT

"He (Thutmose I) recognized the auspiciousness of a coronation on[a] New Year's Day as the beginning of the peaceful years and of the spending of myriads (of years) of very many jubilees."[b]

Thutmose I therefore ostensibly selected New Year's Day as the most auspicious day for his daughter's coronation. But if we examine her obelisk inscription (§ 318, l. 8), we find that, as she actually reckoned, the beginning of her regnal year fell somewhere between the first of the sixth and the thirtieth of the twelfth month, and not on New Year's Day. Finally, this account of the coronation in the Der el-Bahri temple, is taken verbatim from the account of the coronation of Amenemhet III in the Middle Kingdom temple at Arsinoe,[c] and deserves no more credence than the geographical lists of Ramses III at Medinet Habu, which have been copied from the lists of the Eighteenth and Nineteenth Dynasties. It is clear that this entire coronation of Hatshepsut, like the supernatural birth, is an artificial creation, a fiction of later origin, prompted by political necessity. As such it is closely paralleled by the similar representations of Ramses II in his great Abydos inscription (III, 251–81), with the sole difference that his father is stated to have remained as coregent on the throne.

Scene

234. Thutmose I is enthroned at the left, with his daughter standing before him; in their presence three rows of courtiers standing on the right.

---

[a] Lit., "*of*," making the phrase, "*New Year's coronation*."

[b] § 239, ll. 33, 34.

[c] Fragments in Berlin (Nos. 15801–4; see *Aegyptische Inschriften aus den Königlichen Museen zu Berlin*, Heft III, 138). I owe the knowledge of the character of these fragments to my friend, Mr. Alan Gardiner, who kindly called my attention to them.

Inscriptions[a]

They furnish the only surviving account of such a coronation, in the presence of the superseded monarch and the court.

Thutmose I Summons His Daughter to be Crowned

235. ¹There saw her[b] the majesty of her father, this Horus;[c] how divine is her great fashioner! Her heart is glad, (for) great is her crown; ²she advocates her cause ⌜in⌝ truth, ⌜exalter⌝ of her royal dignity, and of that which her ka does. ᵈThe living were set before her[d] ³in his palace[e] of ⌜—⌝. Said his majesty to her: "Come, glorious one;[f] I have placed (thee) before me; that ⁴thou mayest see thy administration[g] in the palace, and the excellent deeds of thy ka's[h] that thou mayest assume thy royal dignity, glorious ⁵in thy magic, mighty in thy strength. Thou shalt be powerful in the Two Lands; thou shalt seize the rebellious; ⁶thou shalt appear in the palace, thy forehead shall be adorned with the double diadem, resting upon the head of the heiress of Horus, whom I begat, ⁷daughter of the white crown, beloved of Buto. The diadems are given to thee by him who presides over the thrones of the gods.

Thutmose I Summons the Court

236. ⁸My majesty caused that there be brought to him the dignitaries of the king, the nobles, the companions, ⁹the officers of the court,[i] and the chief of the people,[j] that they may do homage,[k] to set the maj-

---

[a]They are in vertical lines, divided into three groups by the king's throne and the group of courtiers. The language is in many respects unusual, the whole is difficult and sometimes uncertain.

[b]Hatshepsut.

[c]Meaning King Thutmose I, to whom all the following epithets are applied.

[d]Referring to the court spectators.

[e]Of course, read: $ᶜḥᶜ-j-n-ys·t$ as in l. 10.

[f]Addressed to his daughter, the queen.

[g]She has already seen it in the land at large on the northern journey (§ 224, l. 8).

[h]That which the ka does, is to reign; the phrase is not uncommon.

[i]Of course, correct to $šny·t$.

[j]$Rḥy·t$, a class of people not yet closely defined.

[k]$Nḏ·t-ḥr$.

esty of ¹⁰the daughter of this Horus[a] before him in his palace of ⌜—⌝.[b] There was a sitting[c] of the king himself, ¹¹in the audience-hall of the right of the ⌜court⌝, while these people prostrated themselves[d] in the court.

Thutmose I's Address to the Court

237. Said[e] his majesty before them: "This my daughter, Khnemet-Amon, Hatshepsut, who liveth, I have appointed [her] — —; she is my successor[f] ¹³upon my throne, she it assuredly is who shall sit upon my wonderful seat.¹⁴ She shall command the people[g] in every place of the palace; she it is who shall lead you; ¹⁵ye shall proclaim her word, ye shall be united at her command. He who shall do her homage shall live, he who shall speak evil in ¹⁶blasphemy of her majesty shall die. Whosoever proclaims with unanimity the name of her majesty (fem.), ¹⁷shall enter immediately into the royal chamber, just as it was done by the name of this Horus (viz., by my name).[h] For ¹⁸thou art divine, O daughter of a god, for whom even the gods fight; behind whom they exert their protection every day according to the command of her father, the lord of the gods.[i]

The Court and People Acknowledge the New Queen

238. ¹⁹The dignitaries of the king, the nobles and the chief of the people[j] hear ²⁰this command for the advancement of the dignity of

---

[a]Meaning the king, Thutmose I.

[b]See l. 3 (note). Possibly referring to the tomb-temple of Der el-Bahri, where the scene is engraved. In this case, the events narrated took place in the Der el-Bahri temple itself.

[c]See sitting of year 9, Punt relief (§ 292, l. 1).

[d]Lit., "*were upon their bellies.*"

[e]At this point the inscription is interrupted by the scene representing the king seated in a pavilion, etc.

[f]This word (*ys·ty*) is very important; for it indicates, not association as coregent, but accession as successor. It is used in the same sense, precisely, by the nomarch Key (I, 692).

[g]Lit., "*She shall command matters to the people (r̄ḫy·t).*"

[h]That is, the name of the new queen is to be as effective in securing entrance as had been that of the king, her father.

[i]Here the text is interrupted by the bas-relief of the three rows of officials named in ll. 8, 9.

[j]See § 236, l. 9, n. f.

his daughter, the king of Upper and Lower Egypt, Makere (Hatshepsut) living forever. They kissed the earth at his feet, when the ²¹royal word fell among them; they praised all the gods for the King of Upper and Lower Egypt, Okheperkere (Thutmose I), living forever. They went forth, their mouths ²²rejoiced, they published his proclamation [to] them. All the people[a] of all the dwellings ²³of the court heard; they came, their mouths rejoicing, they proclaimed (it) beyond everything, dwelling on dwelling ²⁴therein was announcing (it) in his name; soldiers on soldiers ⌜—⌝,[b] they leaped and they danced ²⁵for the double joy of their hearts. They ⌜proclaimed⌝, they ⌜proclaimed⌝[c] the name of her majesty (fem.) as king; while her majesty (fem.) was a youth, while the great god was ²⁶⌜turning⌝ their hearts to his daughter, Makere (Hatshepsut), living forever, when they recognized that it was the fa[ther] of the divine daughter, and ²⁷thus they were excellent in her great soul beyond everything. As for any man who shall love her in his heart, and shall do her homage every day, ²⁸he shall shine, and he shall flourish exceedingly; [but] as for any man who shall speak against the name of her majesty, the god shall determine his death immediately, ²⁹even by the gods who exercise protection behind her every day. The majesty of this her father hath published this, all the people[d] have united upon ³⁰the name of this his daughter for king. While her majesty was a youth, the heart of his majesty inclined to [her] exceedingly.

Proclamation of the Queen's Names

239. ³¹His majesty commanded that the ritual priests be brought to ⌜proclaim⌝ her great names that belonged to the assumption of the dignities of her royal crown and for insertion in (every) work and every seal of the ³²Favorite of the Two Goddesses, who makes the circuit north of the wall,[e] who clothes all the gods of the Favorite of the Two Goddesses. ³³He has recognized the auspiciousness of the coronation on New Year's Day as the beginning of the peaceful years and of the

---

[a]See § 236, l. 9, n. f.

[b]A verb of shouting is lacking, as it is construed with *ḥr*.

[c]Written twice, cf. note a.

[d]See § 236, ll.

[e]Some ceremony unknown to us. The whole line refers to ceremonies in which the official name of the monarch must be used (see § 57).

spending of myriads (of years) of ³⁴very many jubilees. They proclaimed her royal names, for ³⁵the god caused that it should be in their hearts to make her names according to the form with which he had made them before:ᵃ

³⁶Her great name, Horus: [Wosretkew (*wsr·t-k ꜣ w*)],ᵇ forever;

³⁷Her great name, Favorite of the Two Goddesses: "Fresh in Years,"ᶜ good goddess, mistress of offering;

³⁸Her great name, Golden Horus: "Divine of diadems;"ᵈ

³⁹Her great name of King of Upper and Lower Egypt: "Makere, who liveth forever."ᵉ

It is her real name which the god made beforehand.

VIII. SECOND PURIFICATIONᶠ

240. After the public coronation, further ceremonies of the gods follow.

First Scene

The queen is led away by the god Kheseti.

Inscriptions

ᵍThe first (day) of the first season, New Year's Day, the first of the peaceful years of the King of Upper and Lower Egypt, Favorite of the Two Goddesses, who makes the circuit north of the wall, the Feast of Shed . . . . . . .ʰ

ⁱThe leading away to enter the "Great House" (⌜by⌝) the "Pillar of his Mother,"ʲ of the "Great House" (⌜for the⌝) purification of the "Great House."

ᵃThey were inspired to announce the same names which the god had already conferred upon her before (§ 230). This is to explain how the officials knew the same names already conferred by the god.

ᵇ"*Mighty of doubles.*"

ᶜ*W ꜣ ḏ·t rnp·wt.*   ᵈ*Nṭr·t-ḫ ꜣ w.*

ᵉThe complete titulary should contain five names of which the last is here lacking. This last fifth name was her personal name, Hatshepsut, which she had already received in childhood.

ᶠNaville, *Deir-el-Bahari*, III, 63.

ᵍOver the queen.   ⁱOver the god.

ʰCf. I, 150. Titulary of the queen.   ʲA priestly title.

Second Scene

241. The god Kheseti, standing at the right, holds over the queen, who stands at the left, a vessel in the form of the sign of life.

Inscription

Over the queen, merely her name with epitheta; over the god, the following:

I have purified thee with these waters of all satisfying life, all stability, all health, all joy of heart, to celebrate very many jubilees, like Re, forever.

IX. CONCLUDING CEREMONIES[a]

242. The queen is now led away by Horus, and several ceremonies follow, which are too nearly destroyed to be clear, but one of them was the "*making of the circuit north of the wall,*" in accordance with the title of the queen used above.[b] The coronation is now regarded as complete, for Horus says: "*Thou hast established thy dignity as king, and appeared upon the Horus-throne.*"

SOUTHERN PYLON INSCRIPTION AT KARNAK[c]

243. There is a distinct tendency on the part of Hatshepsut to show especial respect to her father, Thutmose I. The evident purpose of the following inscription is to make clear that her father recognizes her right to rule as king. It represents him shortly after her accession, as praying for

---

[a]Naville, *Deir-el-Bahari*, III, 63, 64.

[b]In § 240, and elsewhere.

[c]On the north side of the third southern pylon, left wing, below; text: Lepsius, *Denkmäler*, III, 18; Sethe, *Untersuchungen*, I, 113, 114; translated by de Rougé, *Mélanges d'archéologie égyptienne*, I, 46 f.; Sethe, *ibid*, I, 27, 28 (cf. also p. 1). The inscription is very mutilated, and some omissions have been necessary.

the blessing and favor of the gods upon her reign,[a] and the entire document is of course, the work of the queen herself.

244. The accompanying scene shows Thutmose I standing on the right before Amon, Mut, and Khonsu, the Theban triad on the left; the inscription of twenty lines occupies the space between. Over half of it is occupied with the names, titles, and fulsome epithets of Thutmose I, and the translation omits these, beginning in the middle of l. 11, with the king's address to the three divinities.

245. ¹¹.........I come to thee, lord of gods; I do obeisance[b] [before] thee, in return for this that [thou hast put][c] ¹²the Black and the Red Land[d] under (the dominion of) my daughter, the King of Upper and Lower Egypt, Makere[e] (Hatshepsut), who lives forever, just as thou didst put (it) under (the dominion of) my majesty..........¹³.... Thou hast given to me the kingdom of every land in the presence of the Two Lands, exalting my beauty while I was a youth.... [the Black Land] ¹⁴and the Red Land are under my dominion. I am satisfied with victories, thou hast placed every rebellious land under my sandals which thy serpent-diadem has bound, bearing their gifts; thou hast strengthened the fear [of me] ———— ¹⁵their limbs tremble, I have seized them in victory according to thy command; they are made my subjects; [they come to me] doing obeisance, and all countries with bowed head. Tribute ———— ¹⁶......ᶠ ¹⁷..... the heart of my majesty is glad because of her.......¹⁸⌈the petition⌉ concerning my daughter Wosretkew,[g] King of Upper and Lower Egypt, of whom thou hast desired, that she be associated with [thee][h] — ⌈that⌉ thou mightest

---

[a]Sethe has shown (*Untersuchungen*, I, 28) that it does not record the installation of Hatshepsut as coregent.
[b]Lit., "*smell the ground.*"
[c]Sethe's emendation, *Untersuchungen*, I, 113.
[d]The black land of the valley and the red of the desert hills.
[e]The name has been changed to that of Thutmose II, but the queen's name can still be read.
[f]The conventional praise of the king; in the following lines which are very fragmentary, only the references to the queen are translated.
[g]Horus-name of Hatshepsut.
[h]Apparently a play on her name, "*Associate of Amon*" (Khnemet-Amon).

assign [this] land [to] her grasp. Make her prosperous as King ———
¹⁹mayest thou [ˈgrantᵀ] for me the prayer of the first time, my petitions concerning [my] beloved (fem.) ——— ²⁰........ under her majesty (fem.).

THE PUNT RELIEFS[a]

246. These are undoubtedly the most interesting series of reliefs in Egypt, and form almost our only early source of information for the land of Punt. They are as beautiful in execution as they are important in content. They record an important expedition of the queen thither, which was successfully concluded just before her ninth year (§ 292, l. 1).

247. The only earlier evidences of intercourse with Punt are as follows: In the Fourth Dynasty a Puntite negro appears as the slave of one of the sons of King Khufu;[b] in the Fifth, King Sahure sent an expedition thither (I, 161, 8),

---

[a]In the Der el-Bahri temple, occupying the south half of the middle terrace (corresponding to the Birth and Youth on the north half, §§ 187 ff.). See accompanying plan (p. 105). First copied by Dümichen and published by Dümichen, *Historische Inschriften*, II, 8–20, and *Fleet*, 1–3, and 18, *a;* then by Mariette, *Deir - el - Bahari*, 5–10. The excavations of the Egypt Exploration Fund since 1894 have for the first time uncovered all the Punt reliefs, and they have all now appeared in the superb publication of the Egypt Exploration Fund (Naville, *The Temple of Deir-el-Bahari*, Introductory Memoir, Pls. 7–10, and Vol. III, Pls. 69–86). Unfortunately, the old publications have not been collated and the portions since lost, added. It is therefore still necessary to collate Mariette and Dümichen; I have placed all copies in parallel columns as a basis for the present translation. The inscriptions and reliefs have suffered, not merely from the hand of time and modern vandalism, but the inscriptions and figures of Hatshepsut were hacked out by her political enemies after her fall, and the figure and neighboring inscriptions of Amon, wherever occurring, were later erased by Amenhotep IV. The faint traces remaining on the wall are difficult to read; hence the numerous errors in the old publications. The most useful treatments are Erman (*Life in Ancient Egypt*, 505 ff.), Maspero (*Struggle of the Nations*, 247–53, with very full citation of the older bibliography); and for Punt especially see Müller (*Mittheilungen der Vorderasiatischen Gesellschaft*, III, 42; also *Orientalistische Litteraturzeitung*, II, 416) and Krall (*Beiträge zur Geschichte der Blemyer und Nubier*, "Denkschriften der Wiener Akademie," Philologisch-historische Classe, Vol. XLVI, 4te Abhandlung) to which is added an excursus on Punt).

[b]Lepsius, *Denkmäler*, II, 23; see Erman, *Aegypten*, 670.

and King Isesi sent another, which brought back a dancing dwarf (I, 351); in the Sixth, an officer of Pepi II, named Enenkhet, was killed by the Sand-dwellers on the coast, while building a ship for the Punt voyage (I, 360), and another expedition thither under the same king was led by the assistant treasurer, Thethy (I, 361); in the Eleventh Dynasty, Henu, chief treasurer of King Senekhkere-Mentuhotep III, dispatched an expedition to Punt, which he accompanied only to the coast of the Red Sea (I, 430); in the Twelfth Dynasty, an officer of Amenemhet II, named Khentkhetwer, records his safe return from Punt (I, 604–6);[a] and finally there was also an expedition under Sesostris II (I, 618). None of these sources contains more than the meagerest reference to the fact of the expedition.

248. The reliefs illustrating her expedition, which Hatshepsut had carved in her beautiful Der el-Bahri temple, are therefore, as stated, the first and only full source for a study of ancient Punt and the voyage thither. The expedition, like those of Henu[b] and of Khentkhetwer, may have left the Nile at Koptos, and proceeded by caravan to Wadi Gasûs on the Red Sea, where the ships may have been built.[c] But as no shift of cargo is mentioned, and the same ships depicted as sailing the Red Sea are afterward shown on the Nile, it is possible that the canal through the Wadi Tumilât connecting the Nile and the Red Sea had existed from the Twelfth Dynasty, having been made by one of the Sesostrises.[d] The question of the location of Punt is too large for dis-

---

[a] A fairy-tale in a St. Petersburg papyrus of the Middle Kingdom, in possession of M. Golénischeff, narrates the adventures of a shipwrecked sailor on a voyage to Punt.

[b] As Henu returned by way of Hammamat, he must have sent his expedition from the Red Sea terminus of the Koptos-Hammamat road.

[c] Cf. the ship of Enenkhet (I, 360).

[d] Strabo, XVII, 1, 26.

cussion here, but it was certainly in Africa, and probably was the Somali coast.

249. The successive scenes and the accompanying inscriptions tell the story of the expedition so clearly that no introductory outline is necessary.

250. Historically, it is important to note that Thutmose III appears only once in the Punt reliefs, and that in a subordinate position, so that, as far as this source is concerned, the queen is the author of the expedition, which she undertakes in accordance with an oracle of Amon (§ 284).

251. The arrangement of the reliefs on the wall is interesting; Punt is at the extreme south (left) on the end wall of the colonnade (see plan), and the fleet bound thither is placed by the artist with prows literally toward the south, while the returning fleet is correspondingly represented with stern toward Punt in the south and bows to the north. The successive scenes then proceed northward (to the right) and conclude on the north end-wall.

I. DEPARTURE OF THE FLEET[a]

Scene

252. Five vessels, two of which are still moored, the rest already under sail. The last vessel bearing over its stern the pilot's command, "*Steer*[b] *to port.*" A small boat lashed to a tree has above it the words: "(*An offering*) *for the life, prosperity, and health of her majesty* (fem.), *to Hathor, mistress of Punt* ⌜————⌝ *that she may bring wind;*"

---

[a]First scene on the west wall, lower row; Mariette, *Deir-el-Bahari*, 6 below; Mariette, *Voyage dans la haute Egypte*, II, 63; Dümichen, *Historische Inschriften*, II, 11; Dümichen, *Fleet of an Egyptian Queen*, 1; Naville, *Deir-el-Bahari*, III, 72, 73.

[b]Lit., "*make.*"

West Wall	West Wall	West Wall
Chests,Panthers Electrum &c ----- ueen Offers the	Balances ----- Weighing (81)	IX Formal Announcement of the Success of the Expedition Before Amon (82-84)
Gifts to Amon (77 Figure Three L of Queen Trees	Measuring (82) ----- Myrrh Heaps	Thutmose III offers Myrrh before the Sacred Barque Borne by Priests (82-83)	Queen standing (83)	Long Inscription (84)	Amon Enthroned(

South Wall

PLAN OF THE PUNT RELIEFS AT DER EL-BAHRI

They begin at the left with Scene I, and the vessels face southward, as they should for the voyage out. On the return voyage, however (Scene V), they have bows to the north, that is, toward Egypt. The scenes are numbered with Roman numerals, corresponding to the Roman numerals in the text (pp. 104 ff.); the Arabic numerals indicate the plates of the Egypt Exploration Fund Publication.

showing that a propitiatory offering is being made ashore as they leave.[a]

Inscriptions

253. [1]Sailing in the sea, [2]beginning[b] the goodly way toward God's-Land, journeying [3]in peace to the land of Punt, by [4]the army of the Lord of the Two Lands, according to the command[c] [5]of the Lord of Gods, Amon, lord of Thebes, presider over Karnak, [6]in order to bring for him the marvels of [7]every country, because he so much loves [8]the King of Upper and Lower Egypt, [Makere (Hatshepsut)],[d] [9]for his father Amon-Re, lord of heaven, lord of earth, [10]more than the other kings [11]who have been [12]in this land [13]forever.

II. RECEPTION IN PUNT[e]

254. The voyage has been safely made, and the expedition has landed.

Scene[f]

On the right the *"king's-messenger"* advances at the head of his soldiers. A pile of necklaces, hatchets, daggers, etc., before him, ostensibly an offering to Hathor, are for trade with the Puntites, whose chief, *"Perehu,"* advances from the left to meet the Egyptians. Behind him follow his abnormally fleshy wife,[g] *"Eti,"* their children — two sons[g]

---

[a]Cf. Erman, *Aegypten*, 675. Henu in the Eleventh Dynasty made a similar offering as he dispatched his Punt expedition (I, 432; see also III, 423).

[b]Lit., *"taking the head of the way."*

[c]See Oracle, § 285.

[d]The queen's name has been cut out; later Ramses II inserted his name over the old erasure; the following clause, to the word *"earth,"* is also due to him; hence *"his father"* and the entire loss of connection with l. 10.

[e]On the south wall, lowest two rows; Mariette, *Deir-el-Bahari*, 5; Dümichen, *Historische Inschriften*, II, 8 and 10; Naville, *Deir-el-Bahari*, III, 69. As Naville has unfortunately not added the now lacking portions contained in the old publications, it is necessary here to employ them also.

[f]Lowest row.

[g]Only in the old publications, as this block has been stolen from the wall; see Dümichen, *Resultate*, LVII; photograph in Mariette, *Voyage dans la haute Egypte*, II, 62.

and a daughter[a]—and three Puntites[a] driving the "*ass which bears his wife.*" Behind these is a landscape in Punt, showing among the trees the houses of the Puntites set on poles (*Pfahlbauten*). Below the whole is a line of water, showing that the scene is near the sea or the haven in which the Egyptians have landed. The inscriptions are these:

Over the Egyptians

255. [The arrival] of the king's-messenger in God's-Land, together with the army which is behind him, before the chiefs of Punt; dispatched with every good thing from the court, L. P. H., for Hathor, mistress of Punt; for the sake of the life, prosperity, and health of her majesty.

Before the Puntites

256. The coming of[b] the chiefs of Punt, doing obeisance, with bowed head, to receive this army of the king; they give praise to the lord of gods, Amon-Re ————.[c]

Over the Puntites

257. They say, as they pray for peace: "Why have ye come thither[d] unto this land, which the people[e] know not? Did ye come down upon the ways of heaven, or did ye sail upon the waters, upon the sea of God's-Land? Have ye trodden (⌈the way of⌉)[f] Re? Lo, as for the King of Egypt, is there no way to his majesty, that we may live by the breath which he gives?

Before the Leader of the Puntites

258. The chief of Punt, Perehu (*P ꜣ -r ꜣ -hw*).

---

[a]Only in the old publications. [b]Egyptian "*by.*"

[c]Here evidently the name of the queen originally stood; it was then erased by Thutmose III, and in the time of Ramses II the blank was mistaken for an erasure of Amon's name by Amenhotep IV, which name was then inserted. Traces of the old inscription are visible at the end.

[d]Lit., "*Why have ye reached this?*"

[e]The people of Egypt (*rmṯ*). See the oracle, § 285, l. 10.

[f]The text has "*Re*" as the direct object of "*trodden;*" something must be supplied.

Before His Wife

His wife, Eti (ˀty).[a]

Over the Ass

The ass which bears his wife.

III. THE TRAFFIC[b]

Scene[c]

259. At the right is the tent of the "*king's-messenger*," who stands before it. Before him are the products of Punt, and approaching from the left is a long line of Puntites, bearing similar products; at their head, as before, the chief and his enormous wife. At the extreme left the Puntite landscape, as in II.

In the Tent

260. Pitching the tent of the king's-messenger and his army, in the myrrh-terraces of Punt on the side[d] of the sea, in order to receive the chiefs of this country. There are offered to them bread, beer, wine, meat, fruit, everything found in Egypt, according to that which was commanded in the court, L. P. H.

Before the Egyptian

261. Reception of the tribute of the chief of Punt, by the king's-messenger.

Before the Puntites

262. The coming of[e] the chief of Punt bearing tribute at the side of [f]the sea before the king's-[messenger][f] ———.

---

[a]Before the two sons who follow her: "*His son;*" before the daughter: "*His daughter.*"

[b]South wall; references as for II.   [c]Second row from below.

[d]The Egyptian has a dual, "*on the two sides of,*" from which Dümichen (*Geschichte*, 120) would locate Punt on both sides of the Red Sea, but this dual is a common idiom, meaning no more than a singular. See § 262, where it is absurd to suppose that the chief of Punt is bringing his gifts "*at both sides of the sea!*" Dümichen's translation "von beiden Seiten" is, moreover, impossible, for the text has "*upon,*" not "von."

[e]Egyptian "*by.*"

[f]These words extend over the Puntites; it is uncertain how much has been lost at the end.

IV. LOADING THE VESSELS[a]

Scene

263. Two vessels heavily laden with myrrh trees, sacks of myrrh, ivory, woods, apes; on shore[b] and ascending the gang-planks, men carrying sacks and trees.

Over Men with Trees on Shore

264. (⌜Look to⌝)[c] your feet, ye people! Behold! the load is very heavy!

[d]Prosperity ⌜be⌝ with ⌜us,⌝ for the sake of the myrrh tree in the midst of God's-Land, for the house of Amon; there is the place ⌜where⌝ it shall be made to grow for Makere, in his temple, according to command.

Over the Vessels

265. ¹The loading of the ships very heavily with marvels of ²the country of Punt; all goodly fragrant woods of God's-Land, heaps of ³myrrh-resin, with fresh myrrh trees, ⁴with ebony[e] and pure ivory, with green gold ⁵of Emu, (ᶜ mw), with cinnamon wood, ⁶khesyt wood,[f] with ihmut-incense, ⁷sonter-incense, eye-cosmetic, ⁸with apes, ⁹monkeys, ¹⁰dogs, ¹¹and ¹²with skins ¹³of the southern panther, ¹⁴with natives and ¹⁵their children. Never was brought ¹⁶the like of this for any king who has been since the beginning.

---

[a]South wall, uppermost row; first scene on the west wall, upper row; Mariette, *Deir-el-Bahari*, 5 and 6; Dümichen, *Historische Inschriften*, II, 9 and 12; *Fleet of an Egyptian Queen*, 2; Naville, *Deir-el-Bahari*, III, 69 above, and 74 below.

[b]At the left, over the scene of the traffic.

[c]A guess; the words are broken away, and some similar exclamation on the part of the men carrying the trees is to be expected. Note the Puntites represented as speaking Egyptian!

[d]Words of a second man.

[e]Fragments of the Punt wall show the felling of the ebony trees, with the inscription: "*Cutting the ebony in great quantities*" (Naville, *Deir-el-Bahari*, III, 70).

[f]Sweet wood, used in making incense.

V. THE RETURN VOYAGE^a

Scene^b

266. Three vessels under full sail, with the cargo enumerated in § 265.

Inscriptions^c *over the Vessel*

Sailing, arriving in peace, journeying to Thebes^d with joy of heart, by the army of the Lord of the Two Lands, with the chiefs of this country^e behind them. They have brought that, the like of which was not brought for other kings, being marvels of Punt, because of the greatness of the fame of this ^frevered god, Amon-Re, Lord of Thebes.^f

VI. PRESENTATION OF THE TRIBUTE TO THE QUEEN BY THE CHIEFS OF PUNT, IREM, AND NEMYEW^g

Scene^h

267. At the right the cartouches of the queen, badly defaced; approaching from the left, two lines of men with gifts, led by four lines of kneeling chiefs, being the chiefs of Punt (two lower lines), "*the chiefs of Irem*"ⁱ (upper middle line) and "*the chiefs of Nemyew*"ⁱ (*Nm⸱yw*, upper line, negroes). Behind them approach Egyptians and Puntites with myrrh trees and other products of Punt.

---

^aMariette, *Deir-el-Bahari*, 6; *Voyage dans la haute Egypte*, II, 63; Dümichen, *Historische Inschriften*, 13; *Fleet of an Egyptian Queen*, 3; Naville, *Deir-el-Bahari*, III, 75.

^bAt the right of the vessels loading.   ^cBeginning at the right.

^dThis scene is therefore upon the Nile, not upon the Red Sea.

^ePunt.

^fRestored by Ramses II, supposing that the name of Amon had been here erased by Amenhotep IV. In reality, it was the name of Hatshepsut which had been erased.

^gMariette, *Deir-el-Bahari*, 6; Dümichen, *Historische Inschriften*, 14, 15; Naville, *Deir-el-Bahari*, III, 74 and 76.

^hOver the loading of the ships and the return voyage.

ⁱThe location of these two countries is uncertain; Nemyew is entirely unknown, and it is a question whether Irem is one of the inland Nubian countries or on the Red Sea coast north of Punt.

Inscriptions[a]

268. ¹———— [Kis]sing the earth to Wosretkew[b] (Hatshepsut) by the chiefs of Punt ²———— the Nubian Troglodytes of Khenthennofer, every country — of ³———— doing obeisance with bowed head, bearing their tribute to the place where her majesty (fem.) is ⁴———— ways not trodden by others ⁵———— every country is dominion of her majesty and counted ⁶———— lord of Thebes, as tribute each year ⁷ᶜwhich her father Amon [ˈappointedˈ] for her, ᵈwho hath set all the lands beneath her sandals, living forever.

Over the Chiefs of Punt[e]

269. They say as they pray for peace from her majesty (fem.): "Hail to thee, king (*sic*) of Egypt, Re (fem.),[f] who shines like the sun, your sovereign, mistress of heaven ————. Thy name reaches as far as the circuit of heaven, the fame of [Makere (Hatshepsut)][g] encircles the [ˈseaˈ] ————.

VII. THE QUEEN OFFERS THE GIFTS TO AMON[h]

Scene

270. The queen stands at the left; before her the products of Punt and Irem (lower row), brought back by the expedition, mingled with those of Nubia (upper row).

Before the Queen

271. The King himself, the King of Upper and Lower Egypt, Makere (Hatshepsut); presentation[i] of the marvels of Punt, the treasures

---

ᵃBy the queen's cartouches.
ᵇThe queen's Horus-name: *"Mighty in ka's."*
ᶜMore probably a short lacuna here.   ᵈReferring to Amon.
ᵉThe remains of a similar inscription are visible over the chiefs of Nemyew.
ᶠFeminine; cf. the similar *"female Horus"* (obelisk-base, south, l. 1, § 314; Senmut statue, § 354; etc.).
ᵍTraces of the cartouche in Naville, (Pl. 74); the determinative for "*sea*" is also probable, and suits the context admirably.
ʰMariette, *Deir-el-Bahari*, 7, 8; Dümichen, *Historische Inschriften*, II, 16, 17; Naville, *Deir-el-Bahari*, III, 77, 78, and 80.
ⁱAn absolute infinitive used as the title of the scene, the preceding royal name being the date.

of God's-Land, together with the gifts of the countries of the South, with the impost of the wretched Kush,[a] the baskets of the Negro-land, to[b] Amon, lord of Thebes, presider over Karnak, for the sake of the life, prosperity, and health of the King of Upper and Lower Egypt, Makere (Hatshepsut), that she may live, abide, and her heart be joyful; that she may rule the Two Lands like Re, forever.

By the Trees[c]

272. Thirty-one fresh myrrh trees, brought as marvels of Punt for the majesty of this god, Amon, lord of Thebes; never was seen the like since the beginning.

Under the Trees[c]

Electrum; eye-cosmetic; throw-sticks of the Puntites; ebony; ivory, ⌈shells⌉ ($k\ni \check{s}$).

With Panther[d]

A southern panther alive, captured[e] for her majesty (fem.) in the [south] countries.

Miscellaneous Objects

Electrum;[f] many panther-skins; 3,300 (small cattle).[g]

VIII. WEIGHING AND MEASURING THE OFFERINGS[h]

273. This scene is closely connected with the preceding presentation scene, of which it forms the unbroken continuation. It is accompanied by the following descriptive text:[i]

---

[a]By an evident emendation. [c]Lower row.
[b]Construe with "*presentation.*" [d]Upper row.

[e]Lit., "*brought*" (*ynyy*); it is regularly used of prisoners and apparently also of wild beasts, e. g., also the lions captured by Amenhotep III (§ 865). Two more panthers show fragments of a similar inscription.

[f]With four chests, probably made by Thutiy (§ 376, l. 31).

[g]Over a gap among these offerings is the inscription recording the Asiatic campaign of Thutmose II (§ 125).

[h]On the right of the preceding scene in two rows; Mariette, *Deir-el-Bahari*, 8; Dümichen, *Historische Inschriften*, II, 18, 19; Naville, *Deir-el-Bahari*, III, 79, 81, 82.

[i]At the extreme right in five columns, behind the figure of Thutmose III offering incense (Naville, *Deir-el-Bahari*, III, 82).

274. ¹The king himself, the King of Upper and Lower Egypt, Makere (Hatshepsut).ᵃ Taking the measure (ḥḳ·t) of the electrum, laying the hand on the ⌜—⌝ of the heaps, first instance of doing the good things. Measuring of the fresh myrrh unto Amon, lord of Thebes, lord of heaven, the first of the harvest ²— — — of the marvels of the countries of Punt. The lord of Khmunu (Thoth) records them in writing; Sefkhet counts the numbers. Herᵇ majesty (fem.) ³herself, is acting with her two hands, the best of myrrh is upon all her limbs, her fragrance is divine dew, her odor is mingled with Punt, her skin is gildedᶜ with electrum, ⁴shining as do the starsᵈ in the midst of the festival-hall, before the whole land. There is rejoicing by all the people; they give praise to the lord of gods, ⁵they laud Makere (Hatshepsut) in her divine qualities, because of the greatness of the marvels which have happened for her. Never did the like happen under any godsᵉ who were before, since the beginning. May she be given life, like Re, forever.

*Measuring Scene*ᶠ

275. Two huge heaps of myrrh are being scooped into measures by four men; a fifth, whose figure has been carefully erased, is Hatshepsut's favorite, "*the scribe and steward, Thutiy*" (§§ 369 ff.), who is keeping record of the measure for the queen; while the god Thoth at the extreme right performs a similar office for Amon.

Over the Myrrh Heaps

276. Heaps of myrrh in great quantities.

Over the Men Measuring

277. Measuring the fresh myrrh, in great quantities, for Amon, lord of Thebes; marvels of the countries of Punt, treasures of God's-Land, for the sake of the life, prosperity and health ———.ᵍ

ᵃThe date.   ᵇRead -*s* for -/.

ᶜA bold figure referring to the yellow hue of the women of ancient Egypt.

ᵈYellow stars painted on a blue field form a common ceiling decoration. For comparison of the king with a star, not so common as with the sun, see I, 510 ff., l. 2.

ᵉThat is, "*kings*."   ᶠLower row (Naville, *Deir-el-Bahari*, III, 79).

ᵍThe queen's name has been erased.

Before Thoth

278. Recording in writing, reckoning the numbers, summing up in millions, hundreds of thousands, tens of thousands, thousands and hundreds; reception of the marvels of Punt, [a]for Amon-Re, lord of Thebes, lord of heaven.[a]

Weighing Scene[b]

279. A huge pair of balances piled on one side with commercial gold in large rings, against weights in the form of cows on the other side, is presided over by the gods Horus and Dedun of Nubia,[c] standing at the left. At the right is Sefkhet, the goddess of letters, keeping record. Round and cow "*weights*," and quantities of "*electrum*" in bars and rings, are piled up beside the balances.

Over the Balances

280. The balances, accurate and true, of Thoth, which the King of Upper and Lower Egypt, [Make]re (Hatshepsut), made for her father, Amon, lord of Thebes, in order to weigh the silver, gold, lapis lazuli, malachite, and every splendid costly stone, for the sake of the life, prosperity, and health of her majesty (fem.) ———.[d]

Under the Balances

281. Weighing the gold and electrum, — the impost of the southern countries, for Amon-Re, lord of Thebes, ———, presider over Karnak ———.[d]

Before Sefkhet

282. Recording in writing, reckoning the numbers, summing up in millions, hundreds of thousands, tens of thousands, thousands, and hundreds. Reception of the marvels of the South countries, for Amon, lord of Thebes, presider over Karnak.

---

[a]Amon is here not properly restored by Ramses II; see end of 9.
[b]Upper row (Naville, *Deir-el-Bahari*, III, 81).
[c]Because the gold comes from Nubia.
[d]The name of the queen has been erased.

IX. FORMAL ANNOUNCEMENT OF THE SUCCESS OF THE EXPEDITION BEFORE AMON[a]

Scene

283. The queen stands at the extreme left, staff in hand, before Amon, enthroned at the extreme right. Behind the queen is the sacred barque of Amon borne by priests,[b] before which Thutmose III[c] offers "*of the best of fresh myrrh.*"

Inscription

284. This long text in vertical lines between the queen and Amon falls into two parts. The first contains the titulary and encomium of the queen (ll. 1–4), followed by the oracle of Amon (ll. 4–6), in accordance with which the expedition was made. It is here repeated, in order to enforce the statement that all that was commanded has been done (l. 6). To this favorable statement Amon replies with praise (ll. 7–9), and reverts to a description of former times when the "*myrrh-terraces*" were not visited by Egyptians, but their products were obtained only through intermediaries (ll. 10–12). The success of future expeditions is promised, and his guidance of the expedition just successfully carried out is mentioned. The inscription closes with further praise of the queen, which gradually becomes too mutilated for translation.

---

[a]At the extreme right; Mariette, *Deir-el-Bahari*, 10; Dümichen, *Historische Inschriften*, II, 20; through some confusion in Dümichen's papers his l. 10 and l. 11 have exchanged places, and Mariette has the same mistake! It is clear, therefore, that Mariette's text is drawn from Dümichen, an astonishing number of errors having crept in during the process. From these sources Sethe constructed a skilfully emended text (Sethe, *Untersuchungen*, I, 103, 104), which is sustained in almost all cases by the last and best text (Naville, *Deir-el-Bahari*, III, 84), which is undoubtedly very nearly correct. The entire inscription has been carefully hacked away; hence the numerous errors in the old publications, a collation of which demonstrates the superiority of Naville's texts.

[b]Naville, *Deir-el-Bahari*, III, 83.   [c]*Ibid.*, 82.

Titles and Encomium of Hatshepsut

285. [a][1]Horus: Mighty in Ka's; Favorite of the Two Goddesses: Fresh in Years; Golden Horus: Divine in Diadems; King of Upper and Lower Egypt: Makere (Hatshepsut), — of Amon, whom he loves, who is upon his throne, for whom he has made to flourish the inheritance of the Two Lands, the kingdom of the South and North, [2]to whom he hath given that which the sun encompasses, that which Keb and Nut inclose. She hath no enemies among the Southerns, she hath no foes among the Northerns; the heavens and every country which the god hath created, they all labor for her. [3]They come to her with fearful heart, their chiefs with bowed head, their gifts upon their back. They present to her their children that there may be[b] [4]given to them the breath of life, because of the greatness of the fame of her father, Amon, who hath set all lands beneath her sandals.

The Oracle

The king himself, the King of Upper and Lower Egypt, Makere (Hatshepsut). The majesty of the court made supplication at the steps[c] of the [5]lord of [gods]; a command was heard from the great throne, an oracle of the god himself, that the ways to Punt should be searched out, that the highways to the Myrrh-terraces should be penetrated: [6]"I[d] will lead the army on water and on land, to bring marvels from God's-Land for this god, for the fashioner of her beauty." It was done, according to all that the majesty of this revered god commanded, according to the desire of her majesty (fem.), in order that she might be given life, stability, and satisfaction, like Re, forever.

Promises of Amon

286. [7]Utterance of Amon-Re, lord of Thebes: "Welcome![e] my sweet daughter, my favorite, the King of Upper and Lower Egypt,

---

[a]The first line at the left before the queen. This first part comprises six lines.

[b]Read [m] yswt? Compare § 804, l. 3.

[c]The steps leading up to his throne, which have been hacked away in the relief, but are shown to have existed by the lower ends of the lines of text which shorten by steps in front of the throne (Naville, *Deir-el-Bahari*, III, 84).

[d]The first person in the same sentence where the god occurs in the third person is of course very strange.

[e]Lit., "*Come! Come! in peace.*"

Makere (Hatshepsut), who makes my beautiful monuments, who purifies the seat of the great ennead of gods for my dwelling, as a memorial of her love. ⁸Thou art the king, taking possession of the Two Lands, Khnemet-Amon, Hatshepsut, great in oblations, pure in food-offerings. Thou satisfiest my heart at all times; I have given thee all life and satisfaction from me, all stability from me, all health from me, all joy ⁹from me, I have given to thee all lands and all countries, wherein thy heart is glad. I have long intended them for thee, and the æons shall behold them until those myriads of years ⌈of usefulness which I have thought to spend⌉. ¹⁰I have given to thee all Punt as far as the lands of the gods of God's-Land."

Punt in Former Time

287. "No one trod the Myrrh-terraces, which the people (*rmṭ*) knew not; it was heard of from mouth to mouth ¹¹by hearsay of the ancestors —. The marvels brought thence under thy fathers, the Kings of Lower Egypt, were brought from one to another, and since the time of ¹²the ancestors of the Kings of Upper Egypt, who were of old, as a return for many payments;ᵃ none reaching themᵇ except thy carriers."

Punt under the Queen

288. "But I will cause thy army to tread them,ᵇ ¹³I have led them on water and on land, to exploreᶜ the waters of inaccessible channels, and I have reached the Myrrh-terraces."

"It is a glorious region of God's-Land; it is indeed my place of delight. I have made it for myself, in order toᵈ ⌈divert⌉ ¹⁴my heart, together with Mut, Hathor, Wereret, mistress of Punt, the mistress, 'Great in Sorcery,'ᵉ mistress of all gods. Theyᶠ took myrrh as they wished, they loaded the vessels to their hearts' content, ¹⁵with fresh myrrh trees, every good gift of this country, Puntites whom the people (*rmṭ*) know not, Southerns of God's-Land. I conciliated them byᵍ love

---

ᵃMeaning that in going from hand to hand many successive prices were paid.

ᵇThe Myrrh-terraces.

ᶜThis is the word (*wbꜣ*) used long before of exploring unknown countries in the Old Kingdom by Harkhuf (I, 333, 334) and employed again by the queen in her speech (§ 294, l. 11).

ᵈRead *r* for *yr*.　　ᶠHatshepsut's people.

ᵉIsis.　　ᵍLit., "*because of.*"

that they might give ¹⁶to thee praise, because thou art a god, because of thy fame in the countries. I know ⌜them⌝, I am their wise lord, ⌜—⌝ I am the begetter, Amon-Re; my daughter, who binds the lords, is the king [Makere] (Hatshepsut). I have begotten her for myself. I am thy father, who sets thy fear ¹⁷among the Nine Bows, while they come in peace to all gods. They have brought all the marvels, every beautiful thing of God's-Land, for which thy majesty[a] sent them: heaps of ¹⁸gum of myrrh, and enduring trees bearing fresh myrrh, united in the festival-hall, to be seen of the lord of the gods. May thy majesty cause them to grow.[b] ———— my temple, ¹⁹in order to delight my heart among them. My name is before the gods, thy name[c] is before all the living, forever. Heaven and earth are flooded with incense; odors are in the Great House. Mayest thou offer them to me, pure ²⁰and cleansed, in order to express the ointment for the divine limbs, to offer myrrh, to make ointment, to make festive my statue with necklaces, while I am making ²¹libations for thee. My heart is glad because of seeing thee." ....[d]

X. FORMAL ANNOUNCEMENT OF THE SUCCESS OF THE EXPEDITION TO THE COURT[e]

Scene

289. The queen is enthroned at the left in a splendid kiosk, and before her are the figures of three noblemen (see § 348). All the figures have been hacked out.

---

[a]Feminine! The *t* of the second feminine singular suffix is visible under the scourge; the *t* of "*majesty*" (*ḥn·t*) should be over the scourge, as in l. 18.

[b]The verb is *s·rwd·k* ᵓ with nominal subject (*sdm·k* ᵓ form, Sethe, *Verbum*, II, § 434).

[c]Read: *rn·t pw*. That this is the proper emendation is shown by the Semneh inscription of Thutmose III (Lepsius, *Denkmäler*, III, 52, *b*, line before goddess).

[d]The remainder, consisting of four short and two long lines, is very fragmentary and contains only the conventional promises of the gods.

[e]On the south side of the causeway which ascends through the center of the middle terrace. The date and a few random words were published by Dümichen (*Fleet of an Egyptian Queen*, 18, *a*); but the first complete text by Naville (*Recueil*, 18, Pl. III, corrections, *ibid.*, 19, 212, 213; much better, Naville, *Deir-el-Bahari*, III, 85, 86.

THE PUNT RELIEFS

Inscriptions

290. The texts with the noblemen are as follows:

With the First Man

Behold, it was commanded, as follows: "They shall give the court,[a] L. P. H., to the hereditary prince, count, wearer of the royal seal, sole companion, chief treasurer, Nehsi,[b] to dispatch the army [to] Punt."

With the Two Other Men

Over both are the words: "*The king's-dignitaries, the companions of the court, L. P. H.*," and over the man in the middle: "*Steward of Amon, Senmut*," the well-known favorite of the queen (see §§ 345 ff.). The third man bears no individual inscription.[c] All three figures have been hacked out by political enemies after the triumph of Thutmose III.

The Long Inscription[d]

291. This is perhaps the most interesting inscription in the Punt series. It furnishes the date ("*year 9*") when the expedition had already safely returned. The queen, having publicly exhibited the results of the expedition (VIII), and having announced its success to Amon himself (IX), now holds ceremonious court, to announce in a speech from the

---

[a] The meaning of the phrase is not clear, but it seems as if "*court*" were here used for "decree of the court."

[b] This man has therefore been identified as "*the king's-messenger*" (§§ 260, 261) who commanded the Punt expedition. But this conclusion does not follow; the word "*dispatch*" (*sby*) does not mean to conduct, as we may see in the exactly parallel case of Henu (I, 427 ff.; especially § 432, ll. 13, 14), who conducted the expedition only to the sea and then dispatched (*sby*) it to Punt, returning then, not from Punt, but merely "*from the sea.*" Hence we have no evidence that Nehsi did more than accompany the expedition to the sea, and the "*king's-messenger*" is probably a different man.

[c] He is supposed by Spiegelberg (*Recueil*, 22, 115–25) to be Thutiy (§§ 369 ff.).

[d] In 22 columns before the queen; it has all been more or less hacked out, the last six lines (excluding one phrase) and the upper fourth of lines 6–16 completely so.

throne to her nobles the unprecedented success of the expedition. She glorifies herself as having made a Punt for Amon in Egypt[a] (ll. 14 and 16), and exhorts them to maintain in the future the increased offerings which she has established (ll. 8 and 15). This last was apparently the practical purpose of the session.

Introduction

292. [1]Year 9, occurred the sitting in the audience-hall,[b] the king's-appearance with the etef-crown, upon the great throne of electrum, in the midst of the splendors of his[c] palace. The grandees, the companions of the court, came to hear; a command was brought, a [2]royal edict to his[c] dignitaries, the divine fathers, the companions of the king, the grandees:

Queen's Speech

293. "I shine forever in your faces through that which my father hath desired.[d] Truly, it was greatly my desire in doing, that I should make [3]great him that begat me; and in assigning to my father, that I should make splendid for him all his offerings; that which my fathers, the ancestors knew not, I am doing as the Great One[e] (did) [4]to the Lord of Eternity; I am adding increase to that which was formerly done. I will cause it to be said to posterity: 'How beautiful is she,

---

[a]In the weighing and measuring scene the trees, of which there were three, appear planted in tubs; and again they appear planted in the ground, and thus a "*Punt*" was made for the god. It is possible that not only the trees, but also the terraces of the temple are a part of this "*Punt*," and that the terraced structure of the temple planted with myrrh trees thus reproduced the "*myrrh-terraces.*" This could not be better described in the text than by calling it "*a Punt.*" The fact that the temple is a reproduction of the small terraced temple of Mentuhotep III does not prohibit us from supposing that the queen was conscious of the resemblance above noted. The service and equipment of the temple receive some light from the mention of its High Priest, with twelve subordinate priests in four orders (see note, § 679).

[b]See I, 239, and note.

[c]These masculine pronouns simply represent the word "*king*" here, ($ḥ\ ꜥ$-stny and šps῾ w-stny is what is meant), and do not refer personally to the queen.

[d]"I shine as king, because my father Amon willed it so."

[e]"*Great One*" is feminine and means Isis, referring to that which Isis did for the deceased Osiris, "*the Lord of Eternity.*"

through whom this has happened,' because I have been so very excellent to him, and the heart[a] ⁵of my heart[a] has been replete with that which is due to him. I am his splendor ⌜on high, and in the nether world⌝. I have entered into the qualities of the august god, he hath opened ⁶⸺. He hath recognized my excellence, that I speak a great thing ⌜which⌝ I set among you; it shall shine for you upon the land of the living ⁷⸺ ye may grasp my virtues. I am the god, the beginning of being, nothing fails that goes out of my mouth, beloved ⁸⸺ that which he desired. Ye shall fulfil according to that which I have exacted. Your lifetime is the life ⌜that is⌝ in my mouth[b] ⌜⸺⸺⌝⁹⸺ for the future. I have given a command of my majesty that the offerings of him who begat me should be made splendid, that the ointment should be increased ¹⁰⸺ of prime ointment of the pure ox, in order to supply with offerings ¹¹⸺."

Punt Expedition Commanded

294. '⸺' ⌜[a decree of]⌝ my majesty commanding to send to the Myrrh-terraces, to explore his ways ⌜for him,⌝ to learn his circuit, to open his highways, according to the command of my father, Amon. ¹²⸺ for choice ointment, in order to express ointment for the divine limbs, which I owed to the lord of gods, in order to establish the laws of his house. Trees were taken up in God's-Land, and set in the ground in ¹³[Egypt][c] ⸺ for the king of the gods. They were brought[d] bearing myrrh therein for expressing ointment for the divine limbs, which I owed to the lord of Gods."

Punt in Egypt

295. Said my majesty (fem.): "I will cause you to know that which is commanded me, I have hearkened to my father ¹⁴⸺ that which he hath — commanding me to establish for him a Punt in his

---

[a]Two different words in Egyptian, but the distinction between them, if any, is not clear; see the thirtieth chapter of the "Book of the Dead." One expects "for his heart."

[b]My words control your lives?

[c]The pits in which certain trees had been planted were found by the Fund excavations before the lower terrace at the inner end of the dromos. They contained earth and tree stumps which proved to be of the Mimusops, that is, the Persea (Naville, *Zeitschrift für ägyptische Sprache*, 37, 52).

[d]Read: *yn·tw*.

house, to plant the trees of God's-Land beside his temple, in his garden, according as he commanded. It was done, in order to endow the offerings which I owed. ¹⁵——— I was [not] neglectful of that which he needed. Ye shall fulfil according to my regulations without transgression of that which my mouth hath given. He hath desired me as his favorite; I know all that he loveth; he is a god ¹⁶——— his desire and that which he loveth ⌜—⌝. I have made for him a Punt in his garden, just as he commanded me, for Thebes. It is large for him, he walks abroad in it."ᵃ ¹⁷———ᵇ . . . . ²²——— Hathor, mistress of myrrh; she hath opened to thee (fem.) her two arms with resin — — — — —.

INSCRIPTION OF THE SPEOS ARTEMIDOSᶜ

296. In this remarkable document the energetic queen has left a record of her systematic restorations in the temples which had been desolated by the barbarities of the Hyksos, and had remained so down to her reign. There is a reference to the Punt expedition (l. 13), so that the inscription dates from some time after the ninth year. Its references to the Hyksos coincide remarkably with the account of their treatment of the temples as recorded by Manetho. The Hyksos are called *"Asiatics"* (ʿ ᵓ *mw*), and their city is *"Avaris (ḥ·t-wʿr·t) of the Northland."* The building of the cliff-temple of Pakht, on whose front the inscription is cut, is mentioned only incidentally with the queen's other pious works. The language is often unusual, and the whole is so badly preserved that there are necessarily many omissions in the translation.

ᵃLit., *"under it,"* referring to the trees.

ᵇLl. 17–21 are so completely hacked out that not a sign can be read.

ᶜCut high up on the front of the cliff-temple of Pakht, excavated at Benihasan by Hatshepsut and Thutmose III, called Speos Artemidos by the Greeks, Stabl Antar by the modern natives. The inscription was discovered and published by Golénischeff (*Recueil*, VI, 20; see also *ibid.*, III, 1–7). It is in a bad state of preservation, and the copy is evidently a hurried one.

The Queen's Power

297. ¹.......... ²He hath established her great name like the heavens. She hath made excellent the ⌜records⌝ of her might over the Red Land of the Goddess of the Mountain[a] as far as the rising ³⌞— — —⌟ set his flame behind the two hill-countries.

Restoration of the Temples

298. The altars are opened, the sanctuaries ⁴are enlarged — the desire of all gods; every one is in possession of the dwelling which he has loved, his ka rests upon his throne ... ⁵......... their colonnades .... ⁶..... [b] Every [statue] is overlaid on its body with electrum of Emu.[c] Their feasts are permanent at the division of the time, ⁷the festival offering [⌜is made⌝] at its time by the ⌜authority⌝ of the command of my[d] maker; the regulations of the commandant are perpetuated, which he made in this ⁸— —. My divine heart searches for the sake of the future; [my] heart — that which it had not known forever, because of the command which the hidden persea tree, lord of myriads (of years), communicates.

The Queen's Piety and Power

299. ⁹I have made bright the truth which he loved, [I] know that he liveth by it (the truth);[e] it is my bread, I eat of its brightness,[f] I am ¹⁰a likeness from [his] limbs, one with him. He hath begotten me, to make strong his might in this land. — ⌜lord⌝ — Atum ¹¹in —; Khepri doing that which Re exacted at the foundation (of the world). The lands together are under my authority, the Black and the Red are under my authority. ¹²My fame makes the great ones of the countries to bow down, while the uraeus upon my forehead —ᵍ all lands. The

---

[a]See Sinuhe, I, 493, l. 15.

[b]The passage refers to rebuilding the temples.

[c]Written here ᶜ m ᵓ mw; cf. Müller, *Asien und Europa*, 119.

[d]Beginning with l. 7, the first person appears and continues to the end of the inscription, the queen being the speaker.

[e]In the sun-hymn of Sute and Hor (British Museum, 826, l. 16), Sute says to the sun-god, "*I acted as an effective leader among thy monuments, performing the truth of thy heart, I know thou restest in truth.*"

[f]An extraordinary idea, but clearly in the text.

[g]Doubtless a verb of subjugating or the like.

land of ¹³Reshu,ᵃ and the land of Yu,ᵇ they cannot ⌈hide⌉ from my majesty; Punt is mine, and the fields of ¹⁴sycamore bearing fresh myrrh, the highways which were closed up, and the two ways. ¹⁵My soldiers smote that which was ⌈— — —⌉ since my appearance as king.

Restoration of the Temple of Cusae

300. The temple of the Mistress of Cusaeᶜ which had begun to fall to ruin, the ground had swallowed up its august sanctuary, so that the children played upon its house; ¹⁷the serpent,ᵈ it caused no fear; the poor counted the ⌈—⌉ in the ⌈covering⌉,ᵉ ¹⁸no processions ⌈marched⌉. I adorned it, having been built anew, I overlaid its image with gold; ¹⁹in order to protect its city . . . .

Building of the Temple of Pakht

301. Pakht the great, who traverses the valleys in the midst of the eastland, ²⁰whose ways are ⌈storm-beaten⌉ . . . . I made her temple with that which was due ²¹to her ennead of gods. The doors were of acacia wood, fitted with: bronze. ———————ᶠ ²²at the seasons. The priests knew this; her city ⌈— — —⌉ ———————ᶠ ²³I made divine their temples, furnished with that which comes forth ⌈—⌉ ———————ᶠ . . . ²⁴ . . . . . ——————— the offering-table [⌈was wrought⌉] with ²⁵silver, and gold, chests of linen, every vessel that abides in the place. . . . . . .

Restoration of an Unknown Templeᵍ

302. . . . . . . ²⁶. . . . . . in whose house there was no understanding; the divine fathers . . . . ²⁷. . . . . . . He gave readiness to the arms of the god.ʰ I built his great temple of limestone of Ayan, its ⌈—⌉ were ²⁸of alabaster of Hatnub, the doors were of copper, the ⌈—⌉

ᵃR ꜣ-š ꜣ w probably for R ꜣ-š ꜣ-ty; see Müller, *Asien und Europa*, 133.

ᵇYww.

ᶜFourteenth nome of Upper Egypt, whose goddess was a local Hathor.

ᵈPerhaps referring to the serpent of the goddess.

ᵉPossibly: "*The poor counted the breaches in the wall;*" but this is a mere guess.

ᶠNearly one-half line.

ᵍThe paragraph deals with another divinity and his temple; it is not clear who he may be.

ʰThis must refer to the queen herself.

thereon were of electrum, splendid with "Him-of-the-Two-Lofty-Feathers."[a] ⌜— —⌝ ————. I [honor]ed [29]the majesty of this god with feasts ⌜— —⌝ the feast of Thoth; I added to him [⌜offerings⌝] anew [30]....... I doubled for him the offerings, an [31]increase upon that which had been previously; as I did for the Eight, for Khnum in [all] his forms, for Heket, Renenet and [32]Meskhenet together, in order to build ——— [Neh]emewi and Nehebkew, ... [33]. .... great in [34]walls, and in foundation. I equipped it; I made it festive, I gave houses to the lord .... [35]whom Amon has made to appear as king himself upon the throne of Horus.

Restoration of the Desolation of the Hyksos

303. Hear ye, all persons! ye people as many as ye are! I have done this according to the design of my [36]heart.[b] .... I have restored that which was ruins, I have raised up that which was unfinished[c] [37]since the Asiatics (ꜥꜣmw) were in the midst of Avaris of the Northland, and the barbarians[d] were in the midst of them, [38]overthrow-

---

[a]Lit., "*the lofty of two feathers*," a title of Min, a figure of whom was therefore on the door. The "*shadow*," which was often put on the door, has the determinative of Min's figure; hence there is no doubt that it is such a "*shadow*," which is meant here.

[b]This rare phrase (*m k[ꜣ]t yb·y*) occurs also on the statue of Senmut (Lepsius, *Denkmäler*, III, 25, *i*, correct *nb* to *k*), and in a clear passage over vases "*of costly stone, which his majesty made according to the design (k ꜣ·t) of his own heart*" (Brugsch, *Thesaurus*, V, 1187) among offerings of Thutmose III. See Breasted, *Proceedings of the Biblical Society of Archæology*, May, 1901, 237.

[c]*Stp-ḥ ꜣ ty-ꜥ*, lit., "*begun;*" cf. use of *stp* in beginning a journey.

[d]The same term is applied by Thutmose III to his foes in Lebanon (II, 548). W. M. Müller (*Mittheilungen der Vorderasiatischen Gesellschaft*, 1898, Heft 3, p. 7), would recognize in this term (*šm ꜣ mw* or *š ꜣ mw*) a class or nationality different from the Hyksos; but if the word means simply strangers (Coptic "shemmo"), as Müller thinks, it indicates no distinction at all, for the Hyksos were also "strangers." The construction of the whole context shows that it is one of those poetic passages common in such inscriptions, the parallelism is evident:

"*I have restored that which was ruins,
I have raised up that which was unfinished,
Since the Asiatics were in the midst of Avaris of the Northland,
And the barbarians were in the midst of them.*"

"*Them*" is therefore parallel with the "*Northland*," and does not refer to the "*Asiatics*." That a land or a part of it should be resumed by a plural pronoun is very common in the inscriptions of Egypt.

ing that which was made, while they ruled in ignorance[a] of Re. He[b] did not do according to the divine command until my majesty (fem.). When I was 39firm upon the throne of Re, I was ennobled until the two periods of years[c] ⌜— — —⌝ I came as Hor-watit[d] .40flaming against my enemies. I removed the abomination of the great god, [I] captured the land of their sandals.[e] It is a regulation of the 41fathers .... I have commanded that my [titulary] abide like the mountains; when the sun 42shines, (its) rays are bright upon the titulary of my majesty; my Horus is high upon the standard ⌜—⌝ forever.

THE KARNAK OBELISKS[f]

304. Of the queen's four obelisks at Karnak, one pair has entirely disappeared from the temple; their position is unknown, and only the summit of one is now preserved in Cairo (§ 320 and *Zeitschrift für ägyptische Sprache*, 30, Pl. II); of the surviving pair one still stands behind the great Nineteenth Dynasty hypostyle hall, and the summit of its fallen companion lies near by.

Standing Obelisk

The standing survivor is now the largest obelisk in Egypt, being 97½ feet high.[g] The history of these two important monuments can be followed for a long period. Work upon them was begun on the first of Mechir (sixth month) in the

---

[a]*M ḥm*, or it may mean "*without.*"
[b]A sudden change of number; the individual ruler of the Hyksos is meant.
[c]Each sixty years long.
[d]Meaning: "*the only Horus,*" and of the feminine gender.
[e]The land which they trod.
[f]Inscriptions on standing obelisk: Lepsius, *Denkmäler*, III, 22–24, d; Champollion, *Monuments*, IV, 314; *Notices descriptives*, II, 133 ff.; Rosellini, *Monumenti Storici*, I, 31 ff. Fallen obelisk: Lepsius, *Denkmäler*, III, 24, a–c; *Recueil*, X, 142; 23, 195 f.; Champollion, *Notices descriptives*, II, 136.
[g]Petrie, *History of Egypt*, II, 131 (Naville's statement that they are the largest known (*Zeitschrift für ägyptische Sprache*, 37, 52) is an error; the obelisk of Thutmose III, before the Lateran in Rome, is the highest known; see § 626).

queen's fifteenth year[a] by Senmut, the queen's favorite (§§ 345 ff.). The quarry work of clearing the enormous shafts from the granite at Assuan was completed on the last of Mesore (twelfth month) of the queen's sixteenth year, seven months after beginning. Transported to Thebes on a huge barge, drawn by a large fleet of galleys (see §§ 322 ff.), they were destined for erection, not before a temple, as is customary, but in the historic hall built between his two Karnak pylons,[b] by the queen's father, Thutmose I, the hall where, fifteen years before, her father had been supplanted by Thutmose III. Whether this fact influenced her in the following procedure is, of course, purely conjectural, but in order to introduce her obelisks into this hall, she broke away the southern wall, removed all the cedar columns of Thutmose I on the southern side and four on the northern, of course unroofing all but the northern quarter of the hall,[c] and thus totally dismantling the place, which could no longer be employed for religious ceremonial.

305. A relief[d] on a few fragmentary blocks at Karnak shows the queen presenting two obelisks to Amon of Karnak; these may be the pair with which we are now dealing. Before the queen is the following inscription:

The king himself;[e] erection of two great obelisks for her (sic!) father, Amon-Re, in front of the august colonnade, wrought with exceedingly plentiful electrum. Their height pierces to heaven, illuminating the Two Lands like the sun-disk. Never was done the like since the beginning; that she might be given life.

---

[a]Base, north side, § 318, l. 8.   [b]IV and V. See § 317, ll. 7–8.

[c]Thutmose III restored the northern half (§§ 600–2), and Amenhotep II, the southern (§§ 803 ff.).

[d]Found by Legrain, and reported by Naville at the Congress at Rome (see *Revue égyptologique*, IX, 108–10); partially published by Naville (*Zeitschrift für ägyptische Sprache*, 37, 53) and fully by Naville and Legrain (*Annales du Musée Guimet*, XXX, Pl. XII, A).

[e]The relation of this phrase to the following is difficult.

306. On erection, the obelisks were supplied with the usual single, central column of inscription on each face. Later, side columns were added. Some time before the completion of the side-column inscriptions, the obelisks were surrounded by masonry up to the fifth scene from the top, and the inscriptions never were finished (see Sethe, *Untersuchungen*, I, 54, 55). During the extermination of the Amon cult by Amenhotep IV, he had the name of Amon erased from them,[a] and two or three generations afterward the name of the dishonored god was recut by Seti I.[b]

307. The inscriptions on the shaft will be clear from the translation below; those of the base are of unusual interest. They furnish the date of the obelisks, viz., the end of the fifteenth and the beginning of the sixteenth year of the queen's reign. Their erection celebrates "*the first occurrence*" of the queen's jubilee, a feast marking the thirtieth anniversary of the sovereign's appointment as crown prince. This would place the queen's appointment fifteen years before her accession to the throne.

I. SHAFT INSCRIPTIONS; MIDDLE COLUMNS

South Side

308. Horus: Wosretkew, King of Upper and Lower Egypt, Lord of the Two Lands, Makere, brilliant emanation of Amon, whom he has caused to appear as king upon the throne of Horus before the splendors[c] of the Great House, whom the great ennead of gods have brought up to be mistress of the circuit of the sun. They have united her with life, satisfaction, and joy of heart before the living; Son of Re, Khnemet-Amon, Hatshepsut, beloved of Amon-Re, king of gods, who is given life, like Re, forever.

---

[a]Only down to the surrounding masonry on the standing obelisk (see Lepsius, *Denkmäler*, Text, III, 21 f.).

[b]Side columns of the shaft inscriptions, south and west sides (§ 312).

[c]The meaning of this phrase is clear from the last scene in the Punt reliefs (§ 292, l. 1).

West Side

309. Horus: Wosretkew; Favorite of the Two Goddesses; Fresh in Years; Golden Horus; Divine of Diadems; King of Upper and Lower Egypt: Lord of the Two Lands, Makere. She made (it[a]) as her monument for her father Amon, lord of Thebes, erecting for him two great obelisks at the august gate (named): "Amon-is-Great-in-Terror,"[b] wrought with very much electrum; which illuminate the Two Lands like the sun; never was the like made since the beginning. May the Son of Re, Khnemet-Amon, Hatshepsut, be given life through him, like Re, forever.

North Side

310. Like the west side as far as Makere, then:

Her father Amon hath established her great name; Makere upon the august Ished tree; her annals are myriads of years, possessing life, stability, and satisfaction. Son of Re, Khnemet-Amon, Hatshepsut, beloved of Amon-Re, king of gods— — — — —. (⌈When⌉) she celebrated [⌈for⌉] him the first occurrence of the royal jubilee, in order that she may be given life forever.

East Side

311. Like the south side as far as Makere, then:

Beloved of Amon. Her majesty (fem.) made the name of her father established upon this monument, and abiding, when favor was shown to the King of Upper and Lower Egypt, the Lord of the Two Lands, Okheperkere (Thutmose I), by the majesty of this god,[c] when the two great obelisks were erected by her majesty (fem.) on the first occurrence;[d] the lord of the gods said: "Thy father, King of Upper and Lower Egypt, gave command to erect obelisks,[e] and thy majesty (fem.) will repeat[f] the monuments, in order that thou mayest live forever."

---

[a]The obelisk.   [b]This is the gate of Pylon V.

[c]The "*favor*" shown to her father consisted in the honor paid him in that the following oracle of Amon came to the queen regarding her father.

[d]Of the jubilee.

[e]These are the two obelisks before the Karnak pylon of Thutmose I (see §§ 86 ff.).

[f]That is, she will build obelisks as her father had done.

II. SHAFT INSCRIPTIONS; SIDE COLUMNS[a]

312. These represent thirty-two oblation scenes, eight on each side of the shaft; of each eight (beginning at the top), the second and seventh represent Thutmose III, the fourth Thutmose I, and the rest the queen, all offering to Amon, with the exception that on the west and south sides Seti I has cut out the queen's name in the fifth scene and inserted the inscription: "*Son of Re, Seti-Merneptah, who restored the monument of his father Amon-Re, lord of heaven.*"[b]

313. The pyramidion at the top contains a fourfold representation of Amon blessing and crowning the queen.[c]

III. BASE INSCRIPTION

Titulary and Encomium of the Queen

314. [d]¹Live the female Horus ....[e] daughter of Amon-Re, his favorite, ²his only one, who exists by him, the splendid part of the All-Lord, whose beauty the spirits of Heliopolis fashioned; who hath taken the land like Irsu,[f] whom he hath created to wear his diadem, ³who exists like Khepri[g] ($Hpry$), who shines with crowns like "Him-of-the-Horizon," the pure egg, the excellent seed, whom the two Sorceresses[h] reared, whom Amon himself caused to appear ⁴upon his

---

[a]These are later additions.

[b]This is on the south side; the west side has: "*Renewal of the monument, which the lord of diadems, Seti-Merneptah, made.*" This is the restoration by Seti I of the name of Amon, erased by Amenhotep IV. This erasure is found only in the five upper scenes, showing that the obelisk was surrounded by masonry up to that point; cf. Sethe, *Untersuchungen*, I, 54, 55. Cf. similar restoration by Seti I, § 878.

[c]See Sethe's plate (*Zeitschrift für ägyptische Sprache*, 36, Pl. II).

[d]South side.

[e]Here follows the full titulary of the queen; cf. coronation inscription (§ 239).

[f]A god's name, lit., "*He who made him*" (*yr-sw*), a common term for "his father." See also § 985.

[g]God of continued existence; this and the following phrase show threefold paronomasia: $hpr·t\ hprw\ my\ hpry$, $h^c·t\ h^cw\ my\ y^ɔ\ h·wty$.

[h]A divine name, lit., "*two great in sorcery*," here referring to Isis and Nephthys; it is more often applied to Isis alone; the reference is to their similar rearing of Horus in the mythology.

throne in Hermonthis, whom he chose to protect Egypt, to ⌜defend⌝ the people; the female Horus, avengeress of her father, the oldest (daughter)[a] of the "Bull-of-his-Mother,"[b] ⁵whom Re[c] begat to make for himself excellent seed upon earth for the well-being of the people; his living portrait, King of Upper and Lower Egypt, Makere (Hatshepsut), the electrum of kings.[d]

Queen's Dedication

315. ⁶She made (them)[e] as her monument for her father, Amon, lord of Thebes, presider over Karnak, making for him two great obelisks of enduring granite of the South,[f] (their) summit[s] being of electrum ⁷of the best of every country, which are seen on both ⌜sides⌝ of the river. Their rays flood the Two Lands when the sun rises between them,[g] as he dawns in the horizon of heaven.

Speech of the Queen

316. [h]⁸"I have done this from a loving heart[i] for my father Amon; I have entered upon his ⌜project⌝ of the first occurrence,[j] I was wise by his excellent spirit, I did not forget anything of that which he exacted. [k]¹My majesty (fem.) knoweth that he is divine. I did (it) under his command, he it was who led me; I conceived not any works without his do⌜ing⌝, ²he it was who gave the directions. I slept not because of his temple, I erred not from that which he commanded, my heart was

---

[a]Sethe, *Untersuchungen*, I, 46.

[b]An old title of the self-begetting sun-god, Kamephis.

[c]These are old conventional phrases; of course, Amon is the father of the queen (see §§ 187 ff.), but he has gradually been identified with Re.

[d]See a similar epithet applied to the queen in the Punt reliefs (§ 274, l. 3). The long list of epitheta is here ended, and the real matter now begins.

[e]The obelisks; this is the usual form of dedication in which the object dedicated is not represented by a pronoun, being regarded as a matter of course; cf. "fecit."

[f]The quarries at Assuan.

[g]This simply shows that the obelisks stood in a general north-and-south line.

[h]The queen herself begins to speak, and continues to l. 4, west side.

[i]See similar phrase in Speos Artemidos inscription (§ 303, l. 35).

[j]The first occurrence of the jubilee; or the beginning of time, the primeval plan.

[k]West side begins.

wise[a] before my father, I entered ³upon[b] the affairs of his heart, I did not turn my back upon the city of the All-Lord, but turned to it the face. I know that Karnak is the horizon[c] on earth, ⁴the August Ascent of the beginning, the sacred eye of the All-Lord, the place of his heart, which wears his beauty,[d] and encompasses those who follow him."

Origin of the Obelisks

317. The king himself, he saith, ⁵"I set (it) before the people, who shall be ⌜after⌝ two æons,[e] those whose heart shall consider[f] this monument, and that which I have made for my father, ⁶those who shall speak ⌜—⌝ and who shall look to the future.[g] I sat in the palace, I remembered him who fashioned me, ⁷my heart led me to make for him two obelisks of electrum, whose point[s][h] mingled with heaven, in the august colonnade between ⁸the two great pylons[i] of the king, the mighty bull, the King of Upper and Lower Egypt, Okheperkere (Thutmose I), the deceased Horus. Now, my heart took —————— words."

Oath to Posterity

318. "O ye people, ʲ¹who shall see my monument after years, those who shall speak of that which I have made, beware (lest) ye say, 'I know not, I know not ²why this was made, (and) a mountain fashioned entirely from gold like anything ⌜which happens⌝.[k] I swear[l] as Re

---

[a]Lit., "*my heart was the god Esye (Sy ᵓ);*" a divinity whose name means the "*wise one.*"

[b]Same construction as in § 316, l. 8.

[c]The word (*y ᵓ ḥw-t*) usually translated "*horizon*" is not yet fully understood. It indicates the abiding-place of the solar gods, a region of light or something similar.

[d]This phrase, "*Bearer of his beauty*" (*wṯs·t-nfrwf*), is usually the appellation of the sacred barque, in which the image of the god was borne.

[e]Two periods of sixty years each are meant.

[f] Lit., "*whose heart shall be behind this monument.*"

[g]Rather the opposite, the past is to be expected here.

[h]The word indicates the pyramidal top of the shaft, the pyramidion.

[i] These are Pylons IV and V, between the ruins of which the obelisk stands, surrounded by the fallen columns of the colonnade.

[j] North side begins.

[k]As if it were an everyday occurrence.

[l]Compare the same royal oath in the Assuan inscription of Thutmose II (§ 121, l. 10), or Megiddo campaign of Thutmose III (§ 422, l. 40).

loves me, as ³my father Amon favors me, as my nostrils are filled with satisfying life, as I wear the white crown, as I appear in the red crown, as Horus[a] and Set have united for me ⁴their halves, as I rule this land like the son of Isis,[b] as I have become strong like the son of Nut,[c] as Re sets in the evening-barque, as he rises[d] in ⁵the morning-barque, as he joins his two mothers[e] in the divine barque, as heaven abides, as that which he hath made endures, as I shall be unto eternity like an 'Imperishable,'[f] as I shall go down ⁶in the west like Atum,[g] [h](so surely) these two great obelisks which my majesty hath wrought with electrum for my father, Amon, in order that ⁷my name may abide, enduring in this temple forever and ever, (so surely) they are of one block of enduring granite without seam or ⁸joining ⌜—⌝. My majesty exacted work[i] thereon from the year 15, the first of Mechir (sixth month), until[j] the year 16, the last of Mesore (twelfth month) making seven months of exaction in the mountain.

History

319. [k]¹"I did (it) for him in ⌜fidelity⌝ of heart, ⌜as⌝ a king to every god. It was my desire to make them for him, gilded with electrum; I laid ²their side upon their ⌜—⌝; I thought how the people would say my mouth was excellent by reason of that which issued from it, (for) I did not turn back from that which I had said. ³Hear ye! I gave for them of the finest electrum, which I had measured by the heket[l] like sacks (of grain). My majesty appointed the numbers[m] more than ⁴the entire Two Lands had (ever) seen. The ignorant like the wise knoweth it."

---

[a]The text has two Horus birds; the reference is explained in the note on l. 2 of the Tombos inscription of Thutmose I (§ 70, l. 2).
[b]Horus.   [c]Osiris.
[d]Lit., "*visit or approach*" (s·w ᵓ ḥ). See Papyrus Prisse, 9, 7.
[e]Isis and Nephthys, by a confusion and mingling of the solar and Osirian myths.
[f]Name of a star.   [g]Sun-god.
[h]Here the long introduction to the oath closes and the real asseveration begins.
[i]See Breasted, *Proceedings of the Society of Biblical Archæology*, XXII, 92.
[j]Meaning it continued "*until*," etc.   [k]East side begins.
[l]A grain measure (nearly 5 liters); this is literally true, for Thutiy records the measurement of electrum by the heket under his supervision, and gives the total between 13 and 14 bushels! (§ 377, l. 38).
[m]The quantity of precious metals, but cf. Sethe, *Untersuchungen*, I, 48.

Conclusion

"Let not him who shall hear this say it is a lie which I have said, ⁵but say, 'How like her it is! ⌜who is⌝ truth⌜ful⌝ in the sight of her father!' The god knew it in me,ᵃ Amon, lord of Thebes; he caused that I should reign over ⁶the Black and the Red Land as a requital therefor. I have no enemy in any land, all countries are my subjects, he has made my boundary ⁷to the extremities of heaven, the circuit of the sun has labored for me, which he has given to the one who is with himᵇ (for) he knew that I would offer it to him. I am his daughter ⁸of a truth, who glorifies him, — that which he exacted; my ⌜—⌝ is with my father; life, stability, and satisfaction, upon the Horus-throne of all the living, like Re, forever.

320. The shaft of the fallen obelisk, of which only the uppermost section has survived,ᶜ bears only fragments of the queen's titulary,ᵈ which has been altered into that of Thutmose III. The base, however, carried an interesting inscription, of which the following fragmentsᵉ are still visible:

321. ¹———ᶠ excellent —, beloved of his majesty.ᵍ He hath made my kingdom, the Black Land, and the Red Lands are united under my feet. My southern boundary is as far as the lands of Punt, ²and ———; my eastern boundary is as far as the marshes of Asia, and the Asiatics are in my grasp; my western boundary is as far as the mountain of Manu, and I rule ³— — —; [my northern boundary is as far as —], and my fame is among the Sand-dwellers altogether.ʰ

ᵃViz., knew that I would erect these obelisks.

ᵇMeaning the queen herself.

ᶜA fragment has been found at Abutig (*Recueil*, X, 142; see *Zeitschrift für ägyptische Sprache*, 30, Pl. II).

ᵈLepsius, *Denkmäler*, III, 24, *a–c; Recueil*, X, 142; Champollion, *Notices descriptives*, II, 136.

ᵉ*Recueil*, 23, 195 f.

ᶠThe amount of loss at the beginning of each line varies from one-fifth to one-eighth of the total length of the line, increasing gradually from beginning to end.

ᵍAmon?

ʰIt looks as if the scribe had here confused the northern and eastern boundaries.

The myrrh of Punt has been brought to me ⌜— — —⌝ 4——— all the luxurious marvels of this country were brought to my palace in one collection, which the Asiatics presented 5——— malachite in the country of Reshet. They have brought to me the choicest products of ⌜—⌝a consisting of cedar, of juniper, and of meru wood. 6——— all the good sweet woods of God's-Land. I brought the tribute of Tehenu, consisting of ivory and 700 tusks ⌜which were there⌝. 7——— numerous panther-skins of 5 cubits along the back and 4 cubits in his girth,[b] of the southern panther; besides all the tribute of this country 8——— . . . .[c]

RELIEFS OF TRANSPORTATION OF OBELISKS[d]

322. The queen had reliefs representing the transportation and dedication of two obelisks carved on the wall of the lower colonnade; and, as in the Punt reliefs, the vessels of the transport are actually represented with bows to the north, as they should be in sailing from Assuan; while farther northward is the dedication in Thebes. The identity of these obelisks is uncertain; Wilkinson[e] says that he saw the bases of two obelisks at the termination of the long avenue of sphinxes leading to the temple door, and one would think that the representation in Der el-Bahri

---

[a]A country.

[b]Lit., circumference = the girth of the beast before the skin was removed?

[c]The usual wishes for the monarch's welfare follow, with all pronouns and endings in the feminine.

[d]Scenes and inscriptions in the Der el-Bahri temple on the west wall of the lower colonnade, in the south half; the transportation published by Naville (in *Egypt Exploration Fund Archæological Report*, 1895–96, Pl. and pp. 6–13).

[e]*Thebes and General View*, 90, published in 1831. Naville denies the existence of obelisks at Der el-Bahri; but he once unreservedly accepted their existence. (*Deir-el-Bahari, Introductory Memoir*, 10) on Wilkinson's testimony. It is difficult to suppose that so good an observer as Wilkinson mistook the pits in which trees were planted for obelisk-bases, as Naville states (*Zeitschrift für ägyptische Sprache*, 37, 52). It is possible that they have either been broken up since Wilkinson's day, or that Naville's search has missed them. The map of the French expedition in the *Description* shows a block of granite on the very spot where the right-hand obelisk would have stood.

would concern the obelisks of that temple. But Naville's excavations on the spot failed to turn up the bases seen by Wilkinson; and the transport inscriptions speak of landing on the east side (§ 329). This last datum would indicate Karnak as the destination of the transports, and in this case it is impossible to say which of the queen's two pairs in Karnak is meant (§§ 304 ff.).[a]

I. TRANSPORT

Scene[b]

323. A large tow-boat with the obelisks[c] lying trussed upon it, is being towed by three rows of oared barges,[d] nine in a row; each row headed by a pilot-boat. The tow-boat is accompanied by an escort of three boats, in which religious ceremonies are being performed.

Inscriptions[e]

324. The following is the long text in the upper row; it contains:

a) Titulary and encomium of the queen (ll. 1–?).

b) The command to gather material and build the vessel needed in the transport (three lines).

c) The command to muster men and troops for the transport (four lines).

d) The transport (ten lines).

---

[a]It is difficult to understand how Naville can maintain that the queen erected only two obelisks at Karnak (*Zeitschrift für ägyptische Sprache*, 37, 52), when three obelisk-summits of hers are still in existence.

[b]The whole scene is very fragmentary, and as it was put together from squeezes, there is no doubt that some blocks are put together in questionable places.

[c]Only one can be seen, but the inscription refers to two.

[d]Of these three rows of barges the lowest is still in situ (cf. Mariette, *Deir-el-Bahari*, 11, Dümichen, *Fleet of an Egyptian Queen*, IV); below this in one long row are the marines (on the right) and the offering scene (on the left), with priests and officials approaching (§§ 333–35).

[e]The texts are badly mutilated.

Titulary and Encomium of Queen

325. [Live] the Horus: Wosretkew; Favorite of the Two Goddesses; Fresh in Years; Golden Horus: Divine of Diadems; ²splendid part of [her] father, Amon-Re, lord of [heaven], who has not been far removed from the father of all gods, ³shining in brightness like "The-Horizon-God" (Yᵓḫwty); Rayet (Rᶜy·t)[a] she illuminates ⁴like the sun, vivifying the hearts of the people, who is exalted in name (so that) it hath reached ⁵heaven. Her fame has encompassed the 'Great Circle' (Okeanos) ———— ᵇ⁶their tribute presented to the palace ———— ⁷chief ————ᶜ.

Building the Tow-Boat

326. Give ye ————| sycamores from the whole land ————| the work of building a very great boat;[d] finished ————.

Muster of Men[e] and Troops

327. ————| orders the whole army before ————|, in order to load the two obelisks in Elephantine[f] ————| the people in Aphroditopolis and the entire Two Lands were gathered in [one] place ————| in every way; the young men were mustered ————.

The Transport

328. ————| sailed down-stream with gladness of heart ————| took the ⌜tow-rope⌝, rejoicing ————| ⌜rejoiced⌝ the marines and the crew ————| —— jubilee, the Two Lands |———— in peace.

---

[a]Feminine of Re, the sun-god.   [b]Half a line is lost.

[c]An uncertain number of lines is now lacking, and numbering is impossible from this point. Lines are separated by |, the second half of each line being gone.

[d]The wanting end of the line is not long enough for the dimensions of the boat; but we find Ineni (§ 105) giving the size of the boat on which he moved the Karnak obelisks of Thutmose I. His boat was 206.6 feet long and 68.86 feet wide for an obelisk about 75 feet (Murray) high; hence the boat of the queen (if these are the large Karnak pair) on the same proportion would have been about 268¼ feet long and 89½ feet wide. The proportion between width and length is 1 to 3. See *Egypt Exploration Fund Archæological Report*, 1895–96, 9, 10.

[e]Confer the muster of men for the el-Bersheh colossus (I, 697 ff.).

[f]Referring to the embarkation of the obelisks at the granite quarries of Assuan. They were dragged on board the barges on sledges. The sledge is still under the obelisk on the barge—a fact which has been overlooked in the explanation of the reliefs (*ibid.*).

The king himself, he took the lead[a] ——————| Amon-Re with praise, Khnum. ——————| of Amon ——————| in this monument, which they have established[b] ——————| they have increased years at the jubilee of the King of Upper and Lower Egypt ——————|·······

Over the Pilot-Boats[c]

329. Landing in peace at "Victorious Thebes,"[d] heaven is in festival, earth in rejoicing; — ⌈they⌉ receive joy of heart (when) they behold this monument which [Makere] has established for her father [Amon].[e]

II. RECEPTION IN THEBES

Scene[f]

330. On shore appear the marines and the recruits (on the right), mustered to unload the obelisks. At the opposite end (the left) is an offering scene in celebration of the arrival of the obelisks, with priests and officials approaching.

---

[a]This may also be "*the bow-rope*," but the determinative is broken off.

[b]Possibly: "[*Her name is established*], *in this monument, and fixed; which she has given to thee.*" Cf. east side, middle line (§ 311).

[c]The lowermost boat; the other two bore similar inscriptions, but they have now perished.

[d]Thebes on the east bank.

[e]Over the three escort-boats in the lower right-hand corner is a fragment of text, mentioning the bow and stern cables (as in Ineni, l. 17, § 341) and "*sailing from Elephantine to* ——————." Other fragments of interest are: over the three men in the bow of the obelisk-barge, three names: "*Steward of the King's-Wife, the scribe, Tetem-Re* (*Tty-m-R* [c]); *overseer of the granary, Minmose* (*Mn-ms*); *count of Thinis* (*Tny*), *Sitepeh* (*S ꜣ-tp-yh*)." The last person, Sitepeh, is known on a tablet of Abydos, where he appears with the same titles; cf. Mariette, *Catalogue général d'Abydos*, 393. These names are not original, but are cut over others now illegible. The original names are very likely to have been those of Senmut, the queen's favorite, in charge of the obelisks (§§ 345 ff.), and the other two partisans of the queen, Thutiy and Nehsi, who already appear in Der el-Bahri (§§ 275, 289), and have been erased in the Punt reliefs.

[f]In one long row immediately below the transport scene; published by Mariette, *Deir-el-Bahari*, 11; Dümichen, *Historische Inschriften*, II, 21, and *Fleet of an Egyptian Queen*, 4, 7, 8; see also Sethe, *Untersuchungen*, I, 104, 105, where both the texts are combined.

Inscriptions

331. They record the rejoicing of the troops mustered from the North, South, and Upper Nubia, to assist in the work of the obelisks.[a] It is important to note that their acclamations also mention Thutmose III, but after the queen.

Rejoicing of Marines and Recruits

332. The rejoicing by the royal marines of the ship of the king —.[b]
[c]They say, "Hark the acclamation! Heaven is in [joy, the earth] hath rejoicing. [Amon] [d]increased the years of his daughter who maketh his monuments, upon the Horus-throne of the living, like Re, forever.[d]

[e]The acclamation by the recruits of the South and North, the young men of Thebes, the youths of Khenthennofer (Hnt-hn-nfr), for the sake of the life, prosperity and health of the King of Upper and Lower Egypt ———,[f] (and) for the sake of the life, prosperity and health of the King of Upper and Lower Egypt, Menkheperre (Thutmose III), who giveth life; that their heart may be glad, like Re, forever."

With the Offering

333. An offering for thy ka, O lord of gods, that thou mayest make healthy ———[g] at this (feast) of "Myriad-of-Years"[h] of her who liveth forever.[i]

---

[a]See the mustering at Elephantine, to load the obelisks (§ 327).
[b]Cartouche cut out; undoubtedly that of the queen.
[c]Over the troops marching toward the left.
[d]The same phrase occurs on the Berlin block (No. 1636, Lepsius, *Denkmäler*, III, 17, a; Dümichen, *Historische Inschriften*, II, 21; and *Fleet of an Egyptian Queen*, IV, top row). Its inscriptions are as follows: (over the forward ship) "*Landing at 'The West' with joy of heart, the whole land is in rejoicing at this beautiful feast of this god; they acclaim, they give praise, they celebrate the king, the Lord of the Two Lands.*" The titles have been inserted in place of the queen's name. Then follows: "*Rejoicing by the marines of the ship of the king, Okhepernere (Thutmose II), 'Star-of-the-Two-Lands;' they say: 'This beautiful feast of —* (queen's cartouche cut out) *whereon Amon appears, increasing the years of his son, King of Upper and Lower Egypt, Menkheperre (Thutmose III), upon the Horus-throne of the living, like Re, forever.*'" It is possible that all this belongs to the same feast, at the landing of the obelisks. The block was found on the upper terrace.
[e]Over the soldiers marching toward the right.
[f]Cartouche of the queen cut out.
[g]A name is cut out, undoubtedly that of Hatshepsut.
[h]Name of royal jubilee or feast.
[i]Words of two other priests in the same place are too mutilated for translation.

Rejoicing of the Priests

334. That which the priests of Karnak say: "O king, beautiful[a] of monuments —. As she is, so they are for eternity."

Rejoicing of the Court

335. The companions, the dignitaries, the officials, the soldiers of the whole land, say: "Happy is thy heart ——— thy heart; this thy desire, it has come to pass."

III. DEDICATION OF THE OBELISKS[b]

336. "On the corresponding wall of the northeast side[c] two obelisks are dedicated to Amunre, by the monarch who founded this building and who erected the great obelisks of Karnak; but from the following translation of the little that remains of their hieroglyphics, it is evident they differ widely from those of the great temple of Diospolis[d] and will probably have stood on the pedestals of the dromos above alluded to.[e] The inscription after the name of Pharaoh Amunneitgori[f] continues: "— She has made (this) *her* work for *her* father Amunre, lord of the regions, (and) erected to him two fine obelisks of granite . . . . . *she* did this (who is) the giver of life, like the sun."[g]

---

[a]Should be feminine to suit the context.

[b]Not yet published, and probably partially lost since seen by Wilkinson. Hence I can only offer Wilkinson's remarks (*Thebes and General View*, 92).

[c]The right-hand end of the colonnade on the northeast (practically north) side of the ascent to the next terrace.

[d]The Karnak temple. So good an observer as Wilkinson is to be trusted in a remark like this; there must have been some striking difference in the inscription, distinguishing it from those of Hatshepsut's standing obelisk at Karnak; it is therefore improbable that these obelisk reliefs refer to the said Karnak pair.

[e]The obelisk-pedestals which he saw before the temple portal.

[f]This is Khnemet-Amon, Hatshepsut; Wilkinson adds the following note: "I am uncertain as to the precise reading of this name, but cannot adopt the Amenthe of M. Champollion. I suppose her to have been a queen." This was written seventy-five years ago.

[g]This old translation is without a flaw, except in the last sentence, which should be "*that she may be given life, etc.*," and even this change, with the exception of the "final" construction, was suspected by Wilkinson (p. 94, n. 1).

ROCK INSCRIPTION IN WADI MAGHARA[a]

337. Above is a bas-relief in which Thutmose III worships Hathor, and Hatshepsut worships Soped; over this is the inscription: "*Year 16 under the majesty of,*" which is to be connected with the names in the relief. Below is a much-mutilated inscription of three short lines:

[Came][b] the king's[-messenger] at the head of his army, to traverse the [inaccessible[c]] valley[s,] [to please[d]] Horus who is in the palace, by bringing that which exists to his majesty ———,[e] living again, revered.

BUILDING INSCRIPTION OF WESTERN THEBES[f]

338. Above is a relief showing Hatshepsut worshiping before Amon-Re, with Thutmose III standing behind her. An inscription of five lines below records repairs in the fortress of the necropolis by Hatshepsut. Hence the goddess of western Thebes, Khaftet-hir-nebes, stands behind Thutmose.

339. ¹Live the Horus: Wosretkew; Favorite of the Two Goddesses: Fresh in Years; Golden Horus: Divine of Diadems, Ruler of South and North; King of Upper and Lower Egypt, Makere; ²Son of Re, of his body, his beloved Khnemet-Amon, Hatshepsut. She made (it) as her monument for her father, Amon, lord of Thebes; erecting for him ³the fortress of Khaftet-hir-nebes anew as a work for eternity. Its

---

[a]Lepsius, *Denkmäler*, III, 28, 2; Sethe, *Untersuchungen*, I, 122; Brugsch, *Thesaurus*, VI, 1491; Laborde, *Voyage de l'Arabie Pétrée*, Pl. 8, No. 4; Laval, *La Péninsule Arabique*, Pl. 2, No. 4,; Weill, *Sinai*, 152.

[b]Restored from Senmut's Assuan inscription, see § 362.

[c]Restored from I, 728.

[d]Cf. Sethe, *Untersuchungen*, I, 122 and 51.

[e]Fragments, among them the determinative belonging to the lost name of the messenger.

[f]Stela in the Vatican (No. 130); published by Champollion, *Notices descriptives*, II, 700, 701; Piehl, *Recueil*, II, 129; Sethe, *Untersuchungen*, I, 110. I had also my own copy of the original, a collation of which furnished some corrections.

⌈——⌉a was ⌈built⌉ 4of beautiful stone of Ayan (ᶜ nw).b It was according to the ancient plan; never was done the like since the beginning. 5Her majesty (fem.) did this, because she loved her father Amon so much more than all gods, in order that she might be given life, like Re, forever.

BIOGRAPHY OF INENIc
[Concluded from § 118]

IV. CAREER UNDER THUTMOSE III AND HATSHEPSUT

340. After outliving three kings, Ineni himself dies under the joint reign of Thutmose III and Hatshepsut. His account of their accession upon the death of Thutmose II unfortunately does not refer to Thutmose III by name, although there can be no doubt that he is meant by *"his son"* (l. 16). The position of Hatshepsut is described in such a way as to give the impression that she is really the ruling power, and *"his son"* merely a figurehead.

Accession of Thutmose III and Hatshepsut

341. Hisd son stood in his place as king of the Two Lands, having become ruler upon the throne of the one who begat him. 17His sister the Divine Consort, Hatshepsut, settled the ⌈affairs⌉e of the Two Lands by reason of her plans. Egypt was made to labor with bowed head for

---

aOriginal has ᶜ ḥm·t, with wedge determinative of land, a rare word occurring also in similar connection in Piehl, *Inscriptions*, I, cxxix, *Q* B; it doubtless designates some inclosure or wall.

bThe original shows ynr nfr n ᶜ nw (heretofore misread), though it is very faint and confused with the paint of a modern incorrect restoration.

cBibliography on p. 18, note c.

dThutmose II's son; this passage would prove that Thutmose III was the son (and not the brother) of Thutmose II, but see Sethe, *Untersuchungen*, I, 7 ff. Cf. also Maspero, *Proceedings of the Society of Biblical Archæology*, XIV, 178, and Petrie, *History of Egypt*, II, 78, and Sethe, *Untersuchungen*, I, 42, 43.

eLit., *"made the land-affairs (mḫr) of the Two Lands."* This rare phrase occurs in the Annals on the eve before the battle of Megiddo: *"the affairs (mḫr-w) of the chiefs were settled (yr-tw)."* (§ 429, l. 2). The *"mḫr·w of the Two Lands"* is also found in Rekhmire's tomb (Newberry, Pl. VII, l. 13) applied to Thutmose III. Ramses II also *"made the mḫr of the land"* (Blessing of Ptah, III, 411, l. 31).

her, the excellent seed of the god, which came forth from him. The bow-rope[a] of the South, the mooring-stake of the Southerners; the excellent stern-rope[a] of the Northland is she; the mistress of command, whose plans are excellent, who satisfies the Two Regions, when she speaks.

Ineni's Favor and Rewards

342. Her majesty praised me, she loved me, she recognized my worth at the court, she presented me with things, she magnified me, she filled my house with silver and gold, with all beautiful stuffs of the royal house.

Ineni's Good Character

343. I (can) not tell (it), I increased beyond everything, I will tell you, ye people; hear ye, do ye the good that I did; [19]do ye likewise. I continued powerful in peace, I met no misfortune,[b] my years were (passed) in gladness of heart, I showed no treachery, I did not inform against, I did no evil, I did no wrong. I was the foreman of the foremen, I did not fail; an excellent one for the heart of his lord, devoid of hesitancy, I was one who hearkened to that which his superior said. My heart was not deceitful toward the great ones in the palace. I did that which the god of the city loved. I was devoid of blasphemy toward sacred things. As for the one who ⌜passes⌝ the years as a favorite, his soul shall live ⌜with⌝ the All-Lord, his good name shall be in the mouth of the living, his memory and his excellence shall be forever. The revered dignitary, the overseer of the granary of Amon, the scribe, Ineni ($Y^{\jmath} nn(y)$), triumphant.

BIOGRAPHY OF AHMOSE-PEN-NEKHBET[c]

[Concluded from § 25]

Conclusion of Summary

344. [18]The Divine Consort, the Great King's-Wife, Makere ($M^{\jmath c \cdot} t\text{-}k^{\jmath}\text{-}R^c$, Hatshepsut), triumphant, repeated honors to me. [19]I

---

[a]These strange epithets will be quite clear to one who has seen a Nile boat, moored at bow and stern, with a fierce current holding both ropes taut. The ship is of course the state, of which the queen is the mooring-lines. Note that the vessel faces southward, the usual position in determining directions.

[b]Lit., "*my misfortune was not;*" all the following negative clauses show the same construction.

[c]Bibliography on p. 10, note c.

reared her eldest daughter, the Royal Daughter, Nefrure (*Nfrw-R ͨ*), triumphant, while she was a ²⁰child upon the breast.........ᵃ

INSCRIPTIONS OF SENMUT

345. Senmut was the most powerful noble among the group of influential state officials who supported Hatshepsut. He was her architect in Karnak, Luxor, Der el-Bahri, and Hermonthis; and in Karnakᵇ and Der el-Bahri statues of him have been found. In the latter temple, also, he appears in an adoration scene on the wall of the Southern Speos,ᶜ with the inscription: "*Giving praise to Hathor, for the sake of the life, prosperity, and health of Makere (Hatshepsut), by the steward of Amon, Senmut.*"ᵈ This is a remarkable evidence of his power. Among his works in Karnak he erected the queen's great obelisks (§§ 304 ff.), the largest now in Egypt, and went personally to the granite quarries at Assuan to secure the two vast blocks, leaving on the rocks a record of his visit there (§§ 359 ff.).

346. He was prominent in the Punt expedition; being overseer of the storehouse of Amon, he would naturally have much to do with the products of that expedition, which were

---

ᵃThe remainder of the line, and of several lines now broken away, contained titles of Ahmose, § 25, note.

ᵇThe base of a black granite statue, as yet unpublished (Naville, *Deir-el-Bahari*, "Preliminary Report," 19).

ᶜBenson and Gourlay, *The Temple of Mut in Asher*, 310. The building inscriptions or dedications of this temple have not survived. The fragmentary end of such an inscription was seen by Brugsch (*Recueil de monuments*, 69, 6), which is as follows: "———— *of fine white (lime)stone of Ayan; its splendid seat of the first time, which (former) kings knew not* ————." Still another, where the name of Thutmose II has been inserted over that of the queen, is preserved toward the end: "———— *making for him a great temple of myriads of years (named)* '*House-of-Amon-Most-Splendid;*' *of fine white limestone of Ayan, in his seat, etc.*," Sethe, *Untersuchungen*, I, 93.

ᵈDümichen, *Historische Inschriften*, II, 34 = Sethe, *Untersuchungen*, I, 109.

for the most part devoted to Amon. He therefore appears with Nehsi (§ 289), the commander of the expedition in the presence of the queen, praising her on the success of the enterprise.

347. He was selected by the queen to rear her daughter and heiress to the throne, the princess, Nefrure, sharing this honor with Ahmose-Pen-Nekhbet (§ 344). His statue, now in Berlin, shows him with the infant princess (§§ 363 ff.).

348. Judging from the titles on the Karnak statue (§§ 349 ff.), he controlled many of the functions of the vizier himself, and all but held that office. There is no doubt that the queen's remarkable career as king in opposition to Thutmose III was in some measure due to him, and in great measure to the coterie of legitimists, of which he was the most powerful member. It is only on this supposition that we can explain the fact that both he and they were exposed to the same persecution suffered by their queen. On Senmut's Berlin statue, on his Karnak statue, in his tomb,[a] on his tombstone,[b] and in the Punt reliefs, his name is everywhere chiseled out. In the Punt relief his entire figure, and those of his two companions, Nehsi and Thutiy (? see § 289), likewise ardent supporters of the queen, are chiseled out. The same persistent persecution is evident in the tomb of Thutiy (§§ 369 ff.), who was hardly second in power to Senmut; in that of Senmen,[c] Senmut's brother; in that of an unknown man,[c] next to the tomb of Senmut; and in that of a "*chief steward*"[d] of the queen at Silsileh. In all these the

---

[a]Discovered by Steindorff and Newberry at Thebes (Benson and Gourlay, *The Temple of Mut in Asher*, 310).

[b]Now in Berlin (No. 2066; *Ausführliches Verzeichniss des Berliner Museums*, 160); published by Lepsius, *Denkmäler*, III, 25 bis a; see also Sethe, *Untersuchungen*, I, 111.

[c]Sethe, *Untersuchungen*, I, 128 f.

[d]*Ibid.*, 84, § 11, e. His name cannot be read.

name of the owner is chiseled out, and this common persecution is quite sufficient to show that these men formed the queen's party of legitimists opposed to Thutmose III, who has therefore treated their monuments and their memory as he did hers.[a]

1. INSCRIPTIONS ON THE KARNAK STATUE[b]

349. This statue was presented to Senmut by Hatshepsut and Thutmose III (§ 350) as a token of honor, for the special purpose of being set up in the temple of Mut at Karnak. The inscriptions contain chiefly his many titles, and epithets of honor, showing clearly that he was little, if any, below the vizier himself in power.

Statue was Presented by Queen[c]

350. [1][Given as a fav]or of the king's-presence, the King of Upper and Lower Egypt, Makere (Hatshepsut), who is given [life, to [2]the hereditary prince, count], wearer of the royal seal, sole companion, steward of Amon, Senmut, triumphant; in order to be in the temple[d] of [3][I]shru; in order to receive the plenty that comes forth from before the presence of this great goddess.

[4][Given] as a favor of the king's-presence, extending the period of life to eternity, with a goodly memory among [5]the people after the years that shall come; to[e] the prince and count, overseer of the granary of Amon, Senmut, triumphant.

---

[a]Small objects from Senmut's tomb, see Spiegelberg, *Recueil*, 19, 91; and Newberry, *Proceedings of the Society of Biblical Archæology*, XXII, 63, 64; full list by Newberry, Benson and Gourlay, *The Temple of Mut in Asher*, 310.

[b]Discovered by Misses Benson and Gourlay in 1896 in the Temple of Mut at Karnak (M. 852). The inscriptions are published by Benson and Gourlay in *The Temple of Mut in Asher* (London, 1899), 299-309. I had also an excellent copy made for the Berlin Lexicon by Borchardt, the corrections and additions from this copy are inserted without remark in the translation below.

[c]On the back, Benson and Gourlay, *The Temple of Mut in Asher*, 301-3.

[d]The statue was found in this temple, and its purpose is here noted. The lacuna in Borchardt's copy is not large enough for "*Mut, mistress of,*" which we would expect.

[e]Construe with "*given.*"

His Duties as Architect

351. ⁶[ᵣIt wasᵣ]ᵃ the chief steward, Senmut, who conducted all the works of the king: in Karnak, in Hermonthis, [in] ⁷Der el-Bahri, of Amon, in the temple of Mut, in Ishru, in southern Opet of Amon (Luxor), in [the presence] ⁸of this august god, while maintaining the monuments of the Lord of the Two Lands, enlarging, restoring — ⁹works, without deafness, (but) according to all that was commanded at the court, L. P. H. It was commanded him that [ᵣheᵣ] should be — ¹⁰because he was so excellent for the heart (of the king). It came to pass in every respect,ᵇ as was commanded by doing according to the desire of his majesty concerning it. ¹¹His true servant, without his like;ᶜ strong-hearted, not lax concerning the monuments of the lord of gods; wearer of the royal seal, prophet of Amon, ¹²[Se]nmut.

His Praise of Himself; His Offices

352. He says: "I was the greatest of the great in the whole land; one who heard the hearing alone in the privy council, steward of [Amon], ¹³Senmut, triumphant."

"I was the real favorite of the king, acting as one praised of his lord every day, the overseer of the cattle of Amon, Senmut."

"I was ¹⁴— of truth, not showing partiality; with whose injunctions the Lord of the Two Lands was satisfied; attached to Nekhen, prophet of Mat, Senmut."

"I was one who entered in [love], ¹⁵and came forth in favor, making glad the heart of the king every day, the companion, and master of the palace, Senmut."

"I commanded ¹⁶in the storehouse of divine offerings of Amon every tenth day; the overseer of the storehouse of Amon, Senmut."

"I conducted — ¹⁷—ᵈ of the gods every day, for the sake of the life, prosperity, and health of the king; overseer of the ᵣ—ᵣ of Amon, Senmut."

"I was a foreman of foremen, superior of the great, ¹⁸[overseer] of all [works] of the house of silver, conductor of every handicraft, chief of the prophets of Montu in Hermonthis, Senmut."

ᵃRead *yn* (Sethe).
ᵇLit., "*very, very much*" (*wr wr mnḫ*).
ᶜLit., "*without one possessed of his qualities.*'
ᵈThe first word shows traces of the sign for ' *feast.*

"I was one [19]to whom the affairs of the Two Lands were [repor]ted; that which South and North contributed was on my seal, the labor of all countries [20]was [under] my charge."

"I was one, whose steps were known in the palace; a real confidant of the king, his beloved: overseer of the gardens of Amon, Senmut."

Address to the Living, and Prayer

353. [21]"O ye living upon earth, lay priests of the temple,[a] who shall see my statue, which I have formed as a likeness,[b] [22]that I may be remembered in the nether world; may your great goddess (Mut) praise you, because ye say: 'A royal offering, which Mut of I[shru] gives! [c][23]May she give the going in and out in the nether world ⌜in⌝ the following of the just; for the ka of Senmut,[d] who repeats the utterance of the king to the "companions;" the one useful to the king, [e][24]faithful to the god, without his ⌜blemish⌝ before the people; steward of Amon, Senmut. May he (Amon) grant to come forth [25]as a living soul; to breathe the sweet north wind, to the [ka of] the steward of Amon, [Senmut]; [26]to receive loaves (*sn·w*) from the table of Amon, at every feast of heaven and earth, [f][27]for the ka of the citizen, mighty in his arm; who followed the king in the South, North, East, and West countries, ⌜— — — —⌝,[g] to whom was given the gold of praise, [h][28]— Senmut. May he come forth as a living soul; may he follow the god, lord of gods; may he be presented with the two regions of Horus; may his name not perish forever; breath for the mouth, splendor for the dead; this is not a thing under which one should ⌜be lax⌝."

---

[a]The temple of Mut, in which the statue was set up.

[b]Lit., "*which I have likened.*"

[c]Newberry begins a new numbering here (Benson and Gourlay, *The Temple of Mut in Asher*, 309) as the inscription proceeds at this point to the left side of the top of the base, but there is no break.

[d]Title omitted.

[e]Goes to the front of the top of the base (Benson and Gourlay, *The Temple of Mut in Asher*, 308).

[f]Goes to the right side of the top of the base (Benson and Gourlay, *The Temple of Mut in Asher*, 309).

[g]"*Pure of limb between the two bows*" (?), Sethe.

[h]Goes to the front and sides of the base (Benson and Gourlay, *The Temple of Mut in Asher*, 309).

"I was a noble, to whom one hearkened; moreover, I had access to all the writings of the prophets; there was nothing which I did not know of that which had happened since the beginning.[a] ⌜————⌝.

Statue was Presented by Queen and King

354. [b]1[Given] as a favor of the king's-presence [to] the hereditary prince, count, steward of Amon, Sen[mut], triumphant, 2steward of the female Horus: Wosretkew,[c] favorite of Horus: "Shining-in-Thebes,"[d] when maintaining their monuments 3forever, firm in favor with them every day.

4Overseer of the fields of Amon, Senmut, triumphant.
5Overseer of the gardens of Amon, Senmut.
6Overseer of the cattle of 7Amon, Senmut, triumphant.
8Chief steward of 9Amon, Senmut, triumphant.
10Chief steward of the king, Senmut, triumphant.
11Chief of the peasant-serfs of Amon, Senmut, triumphant.

Prayers for Food-Offerings

355. [e]1The oblations in the South for the ka of the magnate of the South and North, Senmut. May she (Mut) give 2the food-offerings in the Northland to the ka of the greatest of the great, the noblest of the noble, 3[Se]nmut. May she (Mut) give all that comes forth from her table in Karnak, 4[in] the temples of the gods of the South and North, to the ka of the master of secret things in the temple, 5Senmut.

Prayers for Food-Offerings

356. May she (Mut) give the mortuary offering of bread, beer, oxen, geese; and to drink 6water at the living stream; to the ka of the

---

[a]In this connection it is interesting to note that on his tombstone Senmut placed an archaic text long forgotten, and no longer used in his day (*Ausführliches Verzeichniss des Berliner Museums*, 160).

[b]Above the knees and arms on the sistrum; Benson and Gourlay, *The Temple of Mut in Asher*, 300.

[c]Horus-name of Hatshepsut (read $Ḥr·t$, not t, as published).

[d]Horus-name of Thutmose III (read $ḫ^c$, not t, as published). This important correction is due to Sethe, who made it in Borchardt's manuscript (containing the same mistake), and it was afterward verified by Borchardt from the original.

[e]Left side of sistrum (Benson and Gourlay, *The Temple of Mut in Asher*, 305 f.); it is evidently to be connected with one of the verbs "to give" in the other texts.

chief steward of Amon, ⁷[Se]nmut, triumphant; ⁸overseer of the cattle of ⁹Amon, Senmut; ¹⁰filling the magazines, ¹¹⸢supplying⸣ the storehouses, ¹²overseer of the storehouse of ¹³Amon, ¹⁴Senmut, ¹⁵triumphant; ¹⁶overseer of the gardens of Amon, Senmut, triumphant.

He Carries the Goddess in Processions

357. ᵃ¹⸢Master⸣] of all people, chief of the whole land, steward of Amon, Senmut, triumphant, ²chief [steward] of the king, Senmut; revered by the great god. When he carries Hathor, ³sovereign of Thebes, and Mut, mistress of Ishru, he causes her to appear,ᵇ ⁴he bears her beauty, for the life, prosperity, and health of the King of Upper and Lower Egypt, Makere (Hatshepsut), living forever.

Prayer for Goodly Burial

358. ⁵May he (Osiris) give: goodly burial in the western highland, ⁶[as one revere]d by the great god; to the ka of the privy councilor of the right hand, Senmut; ⁷splendor in heaven, ⁸power on earth; ⁹to the ka of the overseer of the ⸢temples⸣ ($ḥ·wt$) ¹⁰of Neit, Senmut, ¹¹begotten of Ramose, ¹²born of ¹³Henofer ($Ḥ\ ?-nfr$).

II. ASSUAN INSCRIPTION ᶜ

359. Engraved on the rocks at Assuan by Senmut, to commemorate his commission by Queen Hatshepsut to cut out the two Karnak obelisks erected by her (§§ 304 ff.). He appears in relief doing reverence to the queen, with the following inscriptions:

Titles Accompanying the Queen

360. Hereditary princess, great in favor and kindness, great in love — — Re, the kingdom of heaven, who is true in the midst of the divine ennead, the King's-Daughter, the King's-Sister, the Divine Consort, the

---

ᵃRight side of the sistrum (Benson and Gourlay, *The Temple of Mut in Asher*, 307).

ᵇThe idiom for "*bring out in procession.*"

ᶜText: Lepsius, *Denkmäler*, III, 25 *bis q;* better, Lepsius, *Denkmäler*, Text, IV, 116; de Morgan, *Catalogue des monuments*, I, 41, No. 181 *bis* (copied from Lepsius, *Denkmäler*, with all mistakes!); corrected by Sethe, *Untersuchungen*, I, 82.

Great King's-Wife,[a] Hatshepsut, who liveth, the beloved of Satet, mistress of Elephantine, the beloved of Khnum, lord of the Cataract.

Accompanying Senmut

361. Ascription of [honor] to the Divine Consort, Sovereign of the entire Two Lands, by the wearer of the royal seal, companion, great in love, chief steward, Senmut (*Sn-Mw· t*).

Record beneath the Two Figures[b]

362. Came the hereditary prince,[c] count, who [greatly] satisfies the heart of the Divine Consort, who pleases the Mistress of the Two Lands by his injunction, chief steward of the Princess, Nefrure (*Nfrw-R ͨ*), who liveth, Senmut, in order to ⌜conduct⌝ the work of two great obelisks[d] of a [e]" Myriad-(of-Years ")·[e] It took place according to that which was commanded; everything was done; it took place because of the fame of her majesty (fem.).

III. INSCRIPTIONS ON THE BERLIN STATUE [f]

363. This statue, like the Karnak statue, was a royal gift (§ 350, l. 2). It represents Senmut in a squatting posture, holding between his knees the daughter and heir of the queen, the infant princess Nefrure, whom he reared. The inscriptions contain a most important reference to the death of Thutmose II (§ 368, ll. 7, 8).

---

[a]The same titles on an alabaster vase in Alnwick Castle, Birch catalogue 176, corrected by Sethe, *Untersuchungen*, I, 122 and 25.

[b]With corrections from M. Weidenbach's copy as given by Sethe, *Untersuchungen*, I, 82.

[c]Lit., "*The coming by the hereditary prince, etc.*"

[d]It is not entirely certain that these are the two Karnak obelisks, between Pylons IV and V.

[e]The name of a feast, see above, § 333.

[f]Certainly from Thebes, but probably not from his tomb; now in Berlin (No. 2296, *Ausführliches Verzeichniss des Berliner Museums*, 137-39); published by Sharpe (*Egyptian Inscriptions*, II, 107) and Lepsius (*Denkmäler*, III, 25); corrections by Sethe (*Untersuchungen*, I, 111); partial translation (*ibid.*, 50, 51).

Senmut, Tutor of the Princess

364. ᵃSenmut, triumphant, not found ⌜among the writings⌝ of the ancestors,ᵇ great father-tutor of the king's-daughter, Sovereign of the Two Lands, Divine Consort, Nefrure,ᶜ ⌜— —⌝ which I did according to the thoughtᵈ of my heart ⌜— — —⌝.

Mortuary Prayer

365. ᵉ¹A royal offering, which Amon-Re and the King of Upper and Lower Egypt, Makere, give; may theyᶠ grant the mortuary oblation of bread, beer, oxen, geese, linen, incense, ointment.

A Royal Gift

366. ²Given as a favor of the king's-presence [to] the hereditary prince, count, companion, great in love, steward of Amon, Senmut.

Mortuary Prayer

367. ³A royal offering which Osiris, lord of Abydos gives; may he grant all that cometh forth from his table every day ⁴for the ka of the hereditary prince — ⌜—⌝, who greatly satisfies the heart of the Lord of the Two Lands, the favorite of the Good God, the overseer of the granary of Amon, Senmut.

Senmut's Favor with King and Queen

368. ⁵He says, "I was a noble, beloved of his lord, who enteredᵍ upon the wonderful plans of the Mistress of the Two Lands. Heʰ exalted me before the Two Lands, he appointed me ⁶to be chief of his

---

ᵃBeside the princess.

ᵇThis very ambiguous phrase has been rendered: "[whose] ancestors were not found in writing," a rendering not at all certain; possibly the word "like" has been omitted, and we should translate: "*Whose like was not found among, etc.*," more nearly parallel to the common statement.

ᶜThe daughter of the queen, whom Senmut is holding between his knees.

ᵈSee Speos Artemidos Inscription, l. 35, § 303 and note.

ᵉOn the front.   ᶠCorrected from my own copy.

ᵍAn idiom meaning "*to support, be in sympathy with;*" cf. obelisk of Hatshepsut, base, south, § 316, l. 8.

ʰAccording to Sethe, the masculine pronoun refers to Thutmose III. Cf. Sethe, *Untersuchungen*, I, 50; this supposition is rendered very probable by the Karnak statue (§§ 349 ff.).

estate ⌜throughout⌝ the entire land. I was the superior of superiors, the chief of ⁷chiefs of works. I was in this land under his command since the occurrence of the death of his ⁸predecessor.ᵃ I was in life under the Mistress of the Two Lands, King of Upper and Lower Egypt, Makere (Hatshepsut), who liveth forever."ᵇ

INSCRIPTION OF THUTIYᶜ

369. Thutiy was a loyal supporter of Queen Hatshepsut (see § 348), and hence throughout his tomb his name and that of the queen have been entirely erased. He was the successor of Ineni (§§ 340 ff.) as "*overseer of the double gold- and silver-houses,*" and this brought him many monumental enterprises, for which he furnished the metals, at the same time having the construction of a large number of such monuments under his charge. He was probably the builder of the queen's ebony shrine (l. 24 and § 126 ff.); he furnished the metal-work on two great obelisks (l. 28), superintended many other monuments, and was charged with the measuring of the splendid returns in precious metal from the queen's southern expeditions, particularly the famous one to Punt (ll. 33–38). That Thutiy is strictly veracious in this statement is most strikingly shown by the scene of weighing and measuring in the Punt reliefs (§ 275), where the traces of his figure, busily engaged in taking his notes, is identifiable by means of his name and title, "*Scribe and*

ᵃThis probably refers to the death of Thutmose II, the predecessor of Thutmose III and Hatshepsut. See Sethe, *Untersuchungen*, I, 50.

ᵇOn the feet are engraved the titles of Senmut, and the two sides contain the one hundred and sixth and fifty-fourth chapters of the "Book of the Dead."

ᶜStela on the façade of Thutiy's tomb, in the southern part of Drah-abu-'n-Neggah on the west shore at Thebes. First seen by Lepsius, who published two lines (*Denkmäler*, III, 27, 10); later lost and rediscovered by the Marquis of Northampton, Newberry, and Spiegelberg, in 1898; published by Spiegelberg in *Recueil*, 22, 115–25, with translation.

steward, Thutiy," which accompany his figure.[a] Both figure and inscription have been carefully obliterated as in the tomb.

Prayer for the King and Queen

370. [1]Giving praise to Amon-[Re, king of] gods; adoring his majesty every day at his rising in the eastern heavens, for the sake of the life, prosperity, and health of King Makere (Hatshepsut), given life forever, and King Menkheperre (Thutmose III), given life, stability, satisfaction, health, like Re, forever.

Titles of Thutiy

371. [2]Hereditary prince, count, overseer of the double silver-house, overseer of the double gold-house, great favorite of the Lord of the Two Lands, Thutiy.

[3]Hereditary prince, count, chief of prophets in Hermopolis, Thutiy.

[4]Hereditary prince, count, sealing the treasures in the king's-house, Thutiy.

[5]Hereditary prince, count, who gives instruction to[b] the craftsmen how to work, Thutiy.

[6]Hereditary prince, count, who reveals [to][c] him who is skilled in work, Thutiy.

[7][Hereditary prince, count] —— who gives regulations, Thutiy.

[8][Hereditary prince, count], —— the head in indolence, Thutiy.

[9]Hereditary prince, count, [⌜vigilant⌝ when] commissions are commanded him, Thutiy.

[10][Hereditary prince, count], executing the plans that are commanded him, Thutiy.

[11][Hereditary prince, count], not forgetful of that which is commanded him, Thutiy.

---

[a]Naville, *Deir-el-Bahari*, III, 79.

[b]Spiegelberg "anleitet;" lit., "*who opens the face to, etc.*"

[c]The parallelism clearly demands "*to*" (*n*), thus:

(l. 5) . . . . *sbɜ ḥr n wb ɜ·w r yr·t*
(l. 6) *wn [ḥr n] sš ɜ m yrw·t*

Spiegelberg has supplied the *ḥr* ("*face*") in the lacuna, but overlooks the *n* ("*to*"), necessarily common to both lines: "*who opens the face to* (two different words for "*open*," *sbɜ* and *wn*). Compare *wb ɜ-yb* on Lateran obelisk (side lines, § 836).

[12]Hereditary prince, count, knowing the useful things that are established forever, Thutiy.

[13]Hereditary prince, count, favorite of Horus, lord of the palace, Thutiy.

[14]Hereditary prince, count, of sweeping step[a] in the court, Thutiy.

[15]Hereditary prince, count, wearer of the royal seal, overseer of every handicraft of the king, Thutiy.

[16]Hereditary prince, count, great companion of the Lord of the Two Lands, the excellent scribe, active with his hands, Thutiy.

List of Works

372. [17]He says: "I acted as chief (r°-$ḥr$), giving the directions; I led the craftsmen to work in[b] the works, in:[c]

Second Nile-Barge

373. [18]the great barge of the "Beginning-of-the-River" (named): "Userhet-Amon,"[d] wrought with gold of the best of the highlands; it illuminated the Two Lands with its rays.

Unknown Shrine

374. [19]a shrine, the horizon of the god, his great seat, of electrum of the best of the highlands, in work established for eternity.

[20]Seret-mat[e] ($s^{c} r \cdot t$-$m^{\circ c} \cdot t$); its august façade of electrum, great — — [Amon].

---

[a]Lit., "*jar of foot.*"

[b]That this is the proper rendering is shown by the words of Amenhotep, son of Hapi (§ 917, l. 38). Spiegelberg's rendering: "nach dem Vorbild der Arbeiten," demands a word ("Vorbild") not in the original, and makes Thutiy represent himself as merely working after the patterns of someone else.

[c]This line (17) is vertical, extending along the ends of ll. 18–32 like an embracing bracket, thus:

Before each of the fifteen works enumerated in ll. 18–32 we are to understand the last sentence of l. 17: "*I led the craftsmen to work, etc., on*" —. The preposition "*on*" must be changed to "*in*" according as a small monument or a temple follows, a difference not necessary in Egyptian.

[d]See § 32.

[e]Lit., "*sending up (exhibiting) truth,*" probably the name of a shrine.

Works in Der el-Bahri

375. ²¹"Most Splendid"[a] the temple of myriads of years; its great doors fashioned of black copper,[b] the inlaid figures of electrum.

²²Khikhet,[c] the great seat of Amon, his horizon in the west; all its doors of real cedar, wrought with bronze.

²³the house[d] of Amon, his enduring horizon of eternity; its floor wrought with gold and silver; its beauty was like the horizon of heaven.

²⁴a great shrine[e] of ebony of Nubia ($T^{\,\jmath}\text{-}pd\cdot t$); the stairs beneath it, high and wide, of pure alabaster of Hatnub.

²⁵a palace[f] of the god, wrought with gold and ⌜silver⌝; it illuminated the faces (of people) with its brightness.

Works in Karnak

376. ²⁶great doors, high and wide in Karnak; wrought with copper and bronze; the inlaid figures[g] of electrum.

²⁷magnificent necklaces, large amulets of the great seat, of electrum and every costly stone.

²⁸two great obelisks;[h] their height was 108 cubits; wrought throughout with electrum; which filled the Two Lands with their brightness.

²⁹an august gate (named): "Terror-of-Amon,"[i] fashioned of copper in one sheet; its likenesses likewise.

---

[a] Name of Der el-Bahri temple.

[b] The making of metal doors may be seen in the tomb of Rekhmire, ed. Newberry, Pl. XVIII.

[c] Meaning "*Shining of the horizon*" ($H^{\,c}\text{-}y^{\,\jmath}\,hwt$). According to Spiegelberg, this is another name for Der el-Bahri; it is, however, strange that the doors of this temple should be mentioned twice. Possibly the "*great doors*" of l. 21 are the huge entrance doors, and those of l. 22 the inner doors.

[d] Possibly some part of the Der el-Bahri temple.

[e] This is very probably the ebony shrine found in the Der el-Bahri temple (see § 126).

[f] A structure not met with elsewhere in the inscriptions. Its purpose and character are unknown.

[g] Read: hpw.

[h] There is no doubt that these obelisks were in Karnak, but the height given far exceeds that of Hatshepsut's surviving obelisk in Karnak. The theory that the height of the pair has been combined in one datum receives some confirmation from the discovery that the two obelisks on the barge in Hatshepsut's relief lie end to end; but the total is 10 feet less than twice the height of the Karnak obelisk.

[i] There is a Karnak gate called "*Amon-Great-in-Terror*" (Mariette, *Karnak*, 38, *a*, 8); but none is known of the above name.

³⁰many offering-tables of Amon in Karnak, of electrum without limit; of every costly stone —.

³¹magnificent chests,ᵃ wrought with copper and electrum; every vessel; linen; of every precious stone of the divine members.ᵇ

³²a great seat, a shrine, built of granite; its durability is like the pillars of heaven; its work is a thing of eternity.

Measuring of the Punt Tribute, Etc.

377. ³³Behold, all the marvels and all the tribute of all countries, the best of the marvels of Punt, were offeredᶜ to Amon, lord of Karnak [for the sake of the life, prosperity, and health of the King Makere (Hatshepsut), ⌈given life, stability, health.⌉] He (Amon) hath given the Two Lands, ³⁴(for) he knew that he (the king) would offer them to him. Now, I was the one who counted them, because I was so excellent in his heart; my praise was — with him; — — — — me more than his suite ³⁵— my ⌈integrity⌉ of heart for him. He recognized me, as one doing that which is spoken, concealing my speech concerning the affairs of his palace. He appointed me to be leader of the palace, knowing that I was instructed in work. ³⁶— — — the double silver-house; every splendid costly stone in the temple of Amon in Karnak, filled with his tribute to their roof. The like has not happened since the time of the ancestors. His majesty commanded to make ³⁷—ᵈ of electrum of the best of the highlands, in the midst of the festival-hall; measuredᵉ by the heket for Amon in the presence of the whole land.

ᵃA number of such chests are shown in the Punt reliefs (Naville, *Deir-el-Bahari*, III, 80).

ᵇThe line has been cut wrong, was filled with stucco, and cut again; the stucco has fallen out, revealing the old mistakes and producing confusion.

ᶜThis is the offering scene in the Punt reliefs (Naville, *Deir-el-Bahari*, III, 77), in which the inscription (§ 289) agrees strikingly with this. The official offering is "*for the sake of the life, prosperity, and health of the king,*" and is usually conducted by someone else (see § 57); hence the impersonal passive here.

ᵈIt is possible that the word "*balance*" should be supplied here, for the inscription over the balance in the scene of the weighing in the Punt reliefs (§ 280, although it does not mention electrum particularly) would indicate that the balance had been made especially for the purpose. In Papyrus Harris (IV, 256) the balance is also of electrum. Spiegelberg conjectures "eine grosse Haufe," but it is only the myrrh which appears in "*heaps*" in the Punt reliefs.

ᵉOne of the frequent pseudo-participles in building and similar inscriptions, referring back to nouns mentioned long before; it refers here to the tribute in l. 33.

Statement thereof: of electrum 88½ heket,[a] making: ³⁸— (x+) 57½ deben; for the life, prosperity, and health of the king [Makere (Hatshepsut), who is given] life forever.

Conclusion

378. I received (*snw-*) loaves from that which comes forth before Amon, lord of Karnak. All these things happened in truth; no deceitful utterance [came from my mouth]. ³⁹I — them; I was vigilant, my heart was excellent for my lord; that I might rest in the highland of the blessed who are in the necropolis; that my memory might abide on earth; that my soul might live with the lord of eternity; that he[b] may not be repelled ⁴⁰[by] the porters who guard the gates of the nether world; that he may come forth at the cry of the offerer[c] in my tomb of the necropolis; that he may ⌈abound⌉ in bread; that he may overflow with beer, that he may drink at the living water of the river. ⁴¹May I go in and out like the glorious ones, who do that which their gods praise; may my name be goodly among the people who shall come[d] after years; may they give to me praise at the two seasons with the praise ⌈— —⌉.

INSCRIPTIONS OF PUEMRE

379. One of the important architects under Hatshepsut, and later under Thutmose III, was Puemre, who has left some references to his building activity, in his tomb inscriptions and on his statue.

I. STATUE INSCRIPTION[e]

Construction of Ebony Shrine

380. I inspected the erection of a great shrine of ebony, wrought with electrum, by the King of Upper and Lower Egypt, Makere (Hatshepsut), for her mother Mut, mistress of Ishru.

---

[a] Eleven four-fifths bushels.
[b] His soul.
[c] Lit., "*the one who places the things.*"
[d] Read: *yw·ty·sn*.
[e] On a statue discovered in the temple of Mut, at Karnak; published by Benson and Gourlay, *The Temple of Mut in Asher*, 315, 316.

Uncertain Building

381. I inspected the erection of a —[a] of fine white (lime)stone of Ayan by . . . .[b]

II. TOMB INSCRIPTIONS[c]

Relief Scene

382. 1. At the left sits Puemre receiving reports from six "*overseers of workmen*," behind whom are two obelisks (see § 624). The inscriptions are as follows:

Over Puemre

383. 2. Inspection of the great and excellent monuments, which the King of Upper and Lower Egypt, Lord of the Two Lands, Menkheperre (Thutmose III) made for his father Amon, in Karnak,[d] of silver, gold, and every splendid, costly stone; by the hereditary prince, count, divine father, Puem[re].

Before the Overseers

384. 3. The approach of the officials, the chiefs of works; they say before this official, "Thy heart is glad because all the works have reached their positions for thee."

On the Obelisk[e]

4. . . . . . .[f] Thutmose (III); [he] made (it) [as] his monument for his father, Amon-Re, that he might be given life forever.

Relief Scene[g]

385. 5. Puemre stands at the left, staff and baton in hand, receiving three lines of chiefs bringing tribute, which three scribes are recording.

---

[a]Possibly a doorway. [b]Continued as in preceding paragraph.

[c]From his tomb at Abd el-Kurna; partially published by Lepsius, *Denkmäler*, III, 39, c, and *Denkmäler*, Text, III, 243, 244. It is stated by Newberry (Benson and Gourlay, *The Temple of Mut in Asher*, 315, note) to be a peculiarly fine tomb, and he promises its full publication, which has not yet appeared.

[d]This shows that the obelisks were erected in Karnak.

[e]Only the base of the second obelisk has survived, and its inscription is of course lost.

[f]Horus-, throne-, and $S\supset\text{-}R^c$-names.

[g]On the left wall; published by Dümichen, *Die Oasen der Libyschen Wüste*, Pl. I; see also pp. 22 f.

Inscription before Puemre

6. Reception of the tribute of the ⌈products⌉ of the marshes of Asia, of Watet-Hor[a] and the tribute of the southern and northern oases; presentation for the king, to the temple — — — — — by the hereditary prince, count, wearer of the royal seal, sole companion ——— Puemre, triumphant.

Upper Row

386. 7. ᵇ⌈—⌉ the tribute of the ends of Asia.

Middle Row

8. ᵇRecording the tribute of Watet-Hor.
9. ᶜThe chief of the vineyards of this god, Amon —.

Lower Row

10. ᵇRecording the tribute of the oasis-region.
11. ᶜThe chiefs of the southern and northern oases.

Fragment[d]

387. 12. Inspection of the weighing of great heaps of myrrh ———,ᵉ ivory, ebony, electrum of Emu (ꜥmꜣw), all sweet woods ———ᵉ living captives, which his majesty brought from his victories ———ᵉ Menkheperre (Thutmose III).

INSCRIPTIONS OF HAPUSENEB[f]

388. Hapuseneb, vizier under Hatshepsut, was architect of a royal tomb, probably that of Hatshepsut,[g] and super-

---

[a] *Wꜣt-Ḥr*, "*way of Horus*" (in Sinuhe, it is written *wꜣwt Ḥr*, "*ways of Horus*," but other texts write as above; read *Wꜣtyt*?). As used in Sinuhe it must be on or near the Asiatic frontier of the Delta; but as it sends tribute, it must be in Asia. There was an Egyptian governor there in the Eighteenth Dynasty. His title was *ymy-r ꜥ ysꜥt m Wꜣt-Ḥr* (Sharpe, *Egyptian Inscriptions*, I, 56, statue of ꜥ *nbniy*).

[b] With the scribe.   [c] With the man (lower row, men) before the scribe.

[d] Accompanying a weighing scene not given by Dümichen.

[e] Unknown amount lost.

[f] Statue in the Louvre, published by Newberry (*Proceedings of the Society of Biblical Archæology*, XXII, 31–36). I had also my own copy of the original, which added a few readings. Another statue, with unimportant inscriptions, Benson and Gourlay, *The Temple of Mut in Asher*, 312–15. A further record of his services on a statue in Bologna has been hacked out by Hapuseneb's enemies. I was unable to secure any important data from a study of the original.

[g] Against my own former opinion (*Proceedings of the Society of Biblical Archæology*, XXII, 94).

vised the construction of other royal monuments. His works are recorded on his Louvre statue, but the inscriptions are in a sadly fragmentary state, and the name of Thutmose II has been inserted over that of Hatshepsut, as the feminine endings show.[a]

Hapuseneb was the most powerful man in Hatshepsut's party, being not merely vizier, but also "*High Priest of Amon, and chief of the prophets of South and North,*"[b] besides a number of positions which he held in the treasury. He thus united in his person all the power of the administrative government with that of the strong sacerdotal party. The formation of the priesthood of the whole land into a coherent organization, with a single individual at its head, appears here for the first time. This new and great organization was thus through Hapuseneb enlisted on the side of Hatshepsut.

Introduction

389. ¹Made as a favor of the king's presence, the King of Upper and Lower Egypt [Okheperne]re ──── (Thutmose II), beloved of Amon-Re, king of all gods.

²The majesty (fem.!) of the King Okhepernere, given life, commanded ──── sandstone and with every splendid costly stone, ³..... ──── for the hereditary prince, count, ⁴great lord in the South, (*sm*-) priest of ⌈Heliopolis⌉, governor of the city, vizier, overseer of the tem[ples]. ⁵Lo, his majesty was in his palace ⌈── ── ──⌉ of the king's-house, ────[d] [whom] ⁶her (sic!) majesty — before millions; whom she magnified among the people, because of the greatness of the excellence of — over ────.

Cliff-Tomb

⁷He saith: "The good god, King Okhepernere, praised me ⌈──⌉ in the temple. [He appointed me] ⁸to conduct the work upon his cliff-

---

[a]I found the cartouches also sunken, showing the effect of cutting out the first name.

[b]Louvre statue.   [c]Down the front of the legs.

[d]Here the name of Hapuseneb, of course, occurred, to which belong the following two relative clauses.

tomb (ḥr·t), because of the great excellence of my plans. ⌜My⌝ lord appointed me, — ⁹King Okhepernere, and I was made chief (Ḥry) in Karnak, in the house of Amon,ᵃ in every ⌜—⌝ of Amon,ᵃ ¹⁰of gold. . . . . . ⌜I made⌝ ¹¹the mortuary offerings of Amon-Re, king of gods, before his temple in Karnak, in Hermonthis ———— ¹²—————— . . . . . . He commanded that I should be ———— ¹³———— should be appointed at the going out of ————.

Various Works

390. ᵇ¹⁴By the majesty (fem.) of the king, the Lord of the Two Lands, Okhepernere, the living.ᶜ Lo, I was leader (ḥrp) of the works [on] ¹⁵———— [in Kar]nak, wrought with gold; ¹⁶————chief, of silver, gold, and black copper; ¹⁷— — —ᵈ wrought of ⌜copper⌝, the great name upon it was of electrum;ᵉ

¹⁸— [a shrine] of —ᶠ and ebony, wrought with gold; ¹⁹— a ⌜chamber for⌝ everything and that which is in its inclosure; ²⁰— many offering-tables of gold, silver, and lapis lazuli, vessels, and necklaces; ²¹the making of two doors of copper, of a single stone; the great name upon them being of electrum; ²²the erection of a temple of fine limestone of Ayan (named): "Thutmose II-is-Divine-of-Monuments;" ²³— — —ᵍ of gold, silver, lapis lazuli, malachite, every splendid, costly stone, and every sweet wood.ʰ

ᵃAmon has been restored, and perhaps where it does not belong.

ᵇRight side; the arrangement of this and the following lines is the same as in the stela of Thutiy (§ 372, ll. 17 ff.; see note); l. 14 above is numbered 26 in the publication, and is to be understood before all the works enumerated, one in each of the following lines.

ᶜFeminine participle!　　　　　ᵉNot silver, as in the publication.
ᵈThis monument is a door.　　　ᶠA kind of wood is broken out.
ᵍThe last three words are lost.
ʰLl. 24 and 25 are broken off, and possibly still a third line.

REIGN OF THUTMOSE III

THE ANNALS[a]

391. This document, containing no less than 223 lines, is the longest and most important historical inscription in Egypt, and forms the most complete account of the military achievements of any Egyptian king. It demonstrates the injustice of the criticism that the Egyptians were incapable of giving a clear and succinct account of a military campaign, for it shows plainly that at least in this reign careful, systematic records were made and preserved in the royal archives,

---

[a]They occupy the inside of the walls inclosing the corridor which surrounds the granite holy of holies of the great Karnak temple of Amon. These walls were built by Thutmose III, forming a large sandstone chamber (into which the granite holy of holies was finally inserted by Phillip Arrhidæus) about 25 meters in length from east to west, and 12 meters wide. The east end was left bare. The Annals, beginning at the northeast corner, read westward along the north wall, and southward along the west wall, terminating at the door in the center of this wall. At the other side of this door terminate also the presentation scenes and inscriptions (§§ 541 ff.) which read from east to west along the south wall, and northward along the west wall to the said door. Or, as Mariette says: " . . . . . après avoir enjambé sur la paroi dans laquelle se trouve la porte d'entrée (in middle of east wall) vont se rejoindre en se terminant aux deux scènes d'adoration qui forment l'encadrement de cette porte" (in middle of west wall; scene, Lepsius, *Denkmäler*, III, 30, a. See Mariette, *Revue archéologique*, 1860², I, N. S., 30). Of the Annals walls, he further says: "Elle se décompose en trois parties qui sont les suivantes:

"1°. Un texte de 19 lignes qui se termine par: *comme le soleil à toujours*, ce qui prouve que l'inscription n'allait pas plus loin. (voy. Lepsius, *Denkmäler*, III, 31, b; M. Lepsius n'a connu que 11 lignes; voy. aussi Birch, *The Annals of Thothmes III*, dans les *Archaeologia*, Vol. XXXV, 121).

"2°. Un seconde chapitre de 110 lignes qu'une porte latérale (la porte nommée *Ra-men-Kheper Amen* (*ouer biou*) coupe en deux en laissant 67 lignes d'un côté (voy. Lepsius, *Denkmäler*, III, 31, 6, b; . . . . . .), et 43 de l'autre côté (M. Lepsius n'en donne que 39; voy. *ibid.*, 32; . . . . . .).

"3°. Un troisième chapitre de 94 lignes, dont 74 occupent la moitié ouest de la paroi nord à la suite des 110 lignes précédentes, et les 20 dernières sont gravées sur la paroi à gauche de la porte d'entrée. Ces 20 lignes sont publiées dans Lepsius, *Abth*, III, Bl. 30, a. . . . . Quant aux 74 premières lignes, elles se décomposent en 54 lignes qui sont à Paris et qui commencent le chapitre (Lepsius, *Auswahl*, taf. XII; . . . . .), en 6 lignes qui suivent celles-ci et qui sont perdues, et enfin en

giving a detailed account of each invasion in language indicating the strategic operations of the army in each of its many campaigns.

392. The existence of such records is indicated in the account of the first campaign (ll. 11, 12, § 433):

Now, all that his majesty did to this city, to that wretched foe and his wretched army, was recorded each day by its (the day's) name under the title of: ⌜—⌝ ——— recorded upon a roll of leather[a] in the temple of Amon to this day.

Elsewhere the king also speaks of *"recording for the future"* (§ 568, l. 22). We even know the official, named Thaneni, who kept these records. His tomb, on the west shore at Thebes, first noticed by Champollion, contains, among others, biographical inscriptions in which he states:[b]

---

14 autres lignes que M. Lepsius a publiées imparfaitement (Lepsius, *Denkmäler* III, 31, a; . . . . .).''

Mariette then appends the following table summarizing the above:

1er chapitre:	19 lignes	. . . . .	Lepsius, *Denkmäler*, III, 31, b
2e chapitre:	110 lignes {	67 lignes . . .	Lepsius, *Denkmäler*, III, 31, 6, b
		43 lignes . .	Lepsius, *Denkmäler*, III, 32
		6 lignes perdues	
3e chapitre:	94 lignes {	14 lignes . .	Lepsius, *Denkmäler*, III, 31, a
		20 lignes . .	Lepsius, *Denkmäler*, III, 30, a
Total:	223 lignes		

Mariette gives 233 as the total, but refers to 223 (*loc. cit.*, 32).

They are in a very bad state of preservation, the upper courses having mostly disappeared, and with them the upper parts of the vertical lines of the inscription. The translation begins at the extreme northeast corner on the north wall and proceeds to the left.

The complete text of the Annals has never been edited together; being scattered through several publications (see conspectus below) none of which is accurate except Bissing. These texts must be supplemented and corrected by fragments in Champollion, *Notices descriptives*, II, 154–58; Young, *Hieroglyphics*, 41–44; *Description de l'Egypte*, Pl. 38 (No. 26, 27, 29); Brugsch, *Recueil de monuments*, Pl. 56, Nos. 5–7; de Rougé, *Revue archéologique*, N. S., II, Pl. 16; Griffith, Corrections from an early copy (about 1825) by James Burton, *Zeitschrift für ägyptische Sprache*, XXXIII, 125.

[a]On the use of leather, which was very common, see Birch, *Zeitschrift für ägyptische Sprache*, 1871, 104 and 117; and Pietschmann, *Leder und Holz als Schreibmaterialien bei den Aegyptern* (from *Beiträge zur Theorie und Praxis des Buch- und Bibliothekswesens*, Heft 2).

[b]See Champollion, *Notices descriptives*, I, 487, 831, 832; Brugsch, *Thesaurus*, V, 1151.

"I followed [12]the Good God, Sovereign of Truth, King of Upper and Lower Egypt, Menkheperre (Thutmose III); I beheld the victories of the king which he won in every country. He brought the chiefs of Zahi as living prisoners to Egypt; he captured all their cities; he cut down their groves; no country remained — — —. I recorded the victories which he won in every land, putting (them) into writing according to the facts.

There is no doubt that we have here the author of some of the ephemerides referred to in the Annals.[a]

393. The character of these ephemerides space will not permit us to discuss here, further than to note that in the account of the first, or Megiddo, campaign (§§ 408 ff.) we have a somewhat full excerpt from them, in which the strategic details, like the line of march, the dispositions in battle, etc., are given with such clearness that it is possible to draw a plan of the field of battle. Unfortunately, this fulness in excerpting is confined to the Megiddo campaign, and even toward its end the abbreviation and omission[b] already begin. That the excerpts are much abbreviated is distinctly stated in the account of the seventh expedition (l. 13, § 472), with reference to the supplies furnished to the "*harbors:*"

---

[a]A comparison of the phrases and words used by Thaneni, above, with those of the accounts in the Annals makes this certain. This is evident even in the English. It is a question whether Thaneni could have been the author of the earliest campaign records, for he is still in active service under Thutmose IV (see *Recueil*, IV, 130), so that, supposing he began with the Megiddo campaign at twenty-five years of age, he would have been over eighty years old at the accession of Thutmose IV, under whom he completed a census of the people and live-stock in all Egypt (see Champollion, *Notices descriptives*, I, 487), which is recorded as follows: "*Mustering of the whole land before his majesty, making an inspection of everybody, knowing the soldiers, priests, ⸢royal serfs⸣, and all the craftsmen of the whole land, all the cattle, fowl, and small cattle, by the military scribe, beloved of his lord, Thaneni.*" On his wide powers, see also the inscription in Brugsch, *Recueil de monuments*, 66, 2, a. On his tomb, see Bouriant, *Recueil*, XI, 156–59; Champollion, *ibid.*, I, 484–87, 831, 832; further inscriptions also by Piehl, *Inscriptions*, I, CVII, D–CVIII, E.

[b]The omission in the later campaigns, evident anyway, may be clearly seen by a comparison with the narrative of Amenemhab (§§ 574 ff.).

"They (the supplies) remain in the daily register of the palace, the statemen of them not being given in this inscription, in order not to multiply words.[a]

394. The excerpting scribe, being a priest, is more interested in the booty than the strategic operations which led to its capture, because this booty was largely given to his temples; hence he pares down his extracts to the meagerest statement of the king's whereabouts, adding a tolerably full summary of the booty and tribute. Indeed, it may be said that, although the king did command that this permanent record of his campaigns should be made on the temple wall, yet the entire record which we call the Annals serves as little more than an introduction to the list of feasts and offerings (§§ 541 ff.) by which the Annals are continued. They merely explain whence came the magnificent offerings to Amon.[b] It is therefore frequently impossible to distinguish between a serious campaign[c] like that of Megiddo and mere expeditions for inspection.

395. The conquests recorded in the Annals involved the most serious military projects undertaken by any Egyptian king—projects so successfully carried out by Thutmose III that he is to be regarded as unquestionably the greatest military leader of ancient Egypt. Thutmose I had been able to march to the Euphrates without meeting any serious

---

[a]This register of daily supplies is, of course, not the ephemerides of Thaneni; but the fact of excerption is equally clear, nevertheless. This interesting statement finds a parallel in the tomb of Hui, where it is said concerning his praises: "*One mentions them (one) time (each) by its name, (for) they are too numerous to put them in writing*" (Lepsius, *Denkmäler*, III, 117 = *Denkmäler*, Text, III, 302).

[b]There is on this same wall a relief showing Thutmose III presenting to Amon a magnificent array of costly gifts in gold and silver. Many of the objects mentioned in the Annals may be seen here (Champollion, *Monuments*, IV, 316, 317; and Brugsch, *Thesaurus*, V, 1185 ff.). The whole scene is of the greatest interest (§§ 543 ff.); it also contains the two obelisks of § 624.

[c]The word regularly used ($w\underline{d}y \cdot t$) really means "*expedition*."

coalition of his foes, so far as we know. The results of his conquest had not been permanent; that is, they could not endure indefinitely without further campaigning, especially in the extreme north. This Hatshepsut had not done, although the Lebanon or a part of it was still held in the year 15. Then the kingdom and city of Kadesh, on the upper Orontes, quietly organized a formidable revolt, which united all Egypt's Asiatic enemies from Sharuhen on the south to the Euphrates on the north. It is clear also that the powerful kingdom of Mitanni assisted this general revolt with men and means. For the Mitannian king naturally feared to see the armies of the Pharaoh in Naharin at his very threshold. Early in the year 23, Thutmose III met and overthrew the allied Syrians at Megiddo, which he besieged and captured, and although he marched northward to the southern end of Lebanon, he was far from able to reach and punish Kadesh. But he established a fortress in the southern Lebanon, to prevent another southward advance by the king of Kadesh, and then returned home.

396. Of the next eighteen years the summers of sixteen were spent campaigning in Syria, making a total of seventeen campaigns. The next three campaigns (2, 3, and 4) are meagerly recorded,[b] but in the year 29, on the fifth campaign, we find the king plainly making preparations for the conquest of Kadesh, by first securing the coast and getting possession of the harbors of Phœnicia. He then returned to Egypt for the first time by water, and hereafter the army is regularly transported to Syria by the fleet.

397. The next year, therefore, the king disembarked his

---

[a]The decree of Harmhab incidentally shows that Thutmose III was back in Egypt each year by the time of the feast of Opet (I, 58, ll. 29–31), early in October. See Breasted, *Zeitschrift für ägyptische Sprache*, 39, 60, 61.

[b]The record of the fourth is lost.

army in some Phœnician harbor, and marched upon Kadesh, which he captured and chastised, returning then to the coast at Simyra, and going north to punish Arvad again. The foothold in north Syria necessary for an advance into the Euphrates country had now been gained, and Kadesh, the dangerous enemy who would have threatened his rear on such a march, had been subdued. The next year (31) was therefore spent in equipping the Phœnician harbors with supplies and quelling any smouldering embers of rebellion there.

398. It was not until the second year (33) after these preparations that the great king landed in Phœnicia for his march into the heart of Naharin. Already in the year 24, as a result of the great Megiddo victory, the king of Assur had sent presents, but now the Egyptians were again to plunder the Euphrates countries—a feat which had not been repeated since Thutmose I. The long and arduous march[a] was successfully made, the king of Mitanni, who had, with Kadesh, been the heart and soul of the Syrian resistance, was totally defeated, Carchemish[b] was reached and taken, the Euphrates was crossed, and at last Thutmose III sets up his boundary tablet, marking the northern limits of his empire, beside that of his father, Thutmose I. Before he has left the region the envoys from the king of Babylon and the king of the Hittites, having doubtless started at the news of his invasion, appear with their gifts. On his return to the coast the king arranges that the princes of Lebanon shall keep the harbors supplied with all provisions.

399. The conquest of all Syria has consumed exactly ten

---

[a]On the arrangements of Thutmose III's herald Intef, to provide the king with a dwelling, supplies, etc., on such marches, see the Stela of Intef (§§ 771, ll. 24–27).

[b]Amenemhab, § 583.

years, but revolt has still to be reckoned with. Only a voyage of inspection along the Phœnician coast was required in the next year (34), but the revolt of the king of Mitanni called Thutmose into Naharin in the following year, and after a decisive defeat the people of Naharin were again brought under the Egyptian yoke. The records of the next two years (36 and 37) are lost, but in the year 38 we find the king punishing the princes of the southern Lebanon region, in order to protect the road north between the Lebanons. On this occasion, for the first time, he receives gifts from the prince of Cyprus, and also Arrapachitis, the later Assyrian province.

400. The punishment of the raiding Bedwin of southern Palestine forms a preliminary to the usual journey of inspection in the next year (39), and the record of the next two years (39 and 40) is too fragmentary to show more than that the tribute was paid as usual.

401. Finally, the long series of revolts in Syria culminates in a last desperate rebellion, in which Thutmose's archenemy, the source of most of his trouble in Syria, Kadesh, is the leader. Naharin sends allies, and Tunip likewise, so that the whole of north Syria, at least inland, is again combined against Thutmose. In the year 42 he proceeded first against Tunip, and after its subjugation besieged Kadesh, which was finally captured. Thus the nearly twenty years of Syrian campaigning was concluded, as it had begun, by the humiliation of Kadesh, which during all that time had been Egypt's thorn in the flesh. This last downfall was final; Kadesh no longer stirred revolt in Syria,[a] and Thutmose III could relax his ceaseless efforts continued during seventeen campaigns.

---

[a]When the campaigns of the Nineteenth Dynasty begin in northern Syria, it is Tunip, the old ally of Kadesh, that plays the leading rôle.

402. The extent of these campaigns is further indicated by two lists of conquered Asiatic cities left by Thutmose III in the great Karnak temple. Those belonging to the first campaign, preserved in triplicate,[a] are 119 in number, and embrace, in general, the region from the northern limits of Palestine southward an uncertain distance into Judea (southern Judea being at that time already under Egyptian control; cf. Müller, *Asien und Europa*, 144, 154, 155), as well as Damascus and its district. Many Old Testament names have been recognized in it. It is introduced by the superscription:

List of the countries of Upper Retenu which his majesty shut up in the city of Megiddo (*My-k-ty*) the wretched, whose children his majesty brought as living prisoners to the city of Suhen-em-Opet,[b] on his first victorious campaign, according to the command of his father Amon, who led him to excellent ways.

The third copy of the list (Mariette, *Karnak*, 19) has the same superscription, with the variant:

to the city of Thebes, in order to fill the storehouse[c] of his father Amon, [presider over] Karnak, on his first, etc.

The second copy of the list has a different superscription:

---

[a]The first copy is on the west side of the Pylon VI, north end; the other two are, one on the north side and the other on the south side of the Pylon VIII, Baedeker's Karnak, or the VIIth, Mariette, *Karnak*). Text: *ibid.*, 17–20; important corrections by Golénischeff, *Zeitschrift für ägyptische Sprache*, XX, Pls. V and VI, and more fully by Maspero, *Recueil*, VII, 94–97. Treatments by Maspero, *Zeitschrift für ägyptische Sprache*, XXIX, 119–31, and Müller, *Asien und Europa*, 156–64, 144, and 154 f.; less critical Tomkins, *Transactions of the Society of Biblical Archæology*, IX, 257–80 (with text).

[b]*Swhn m Yp·t* means "*Castle (or Prison) in Thebes.*" a place of confinement or dwelling for the foreign princes residing in Thebes as hostages. In the sixth campaign (§ 467) the purpose of thus keeping them is given.

[c]It is not infrequently distinctly stated that such disposal was made of these children; cf. Building Stela of Amenhotep III, front, ll. 6, 7 (§ 884), and Papyrus of Capture of Joppa, III, ll. 11, 12, where, after the fall of the city, Thutiy says to Thutmose III: "*Let people come, to take them as captives; fill thou the house of thy father Amon-Re, ... with male and female slaves.*"

All inaccessible lands of the marshes of Asia,ᵃ which his majesty brought as living captives — — — they had never been trodden by the other kings, beside his majesty —,

a title which would indicate that some of the places belong farther north than the limits above indicated.

403. The second listᵇ embraced 248 names (of which many are lost) of cities in northern Syria and also perhaps as far east as the Chaboras River,ᶜ but our geographical knowledge of this region is too meager as yet to identify any number of the places included.

404. In addition to these materials the great list of "Feasts and Offerings from the Conquests" (§§ 547 ff.), the Building Inscription of the Karnak Ptah-Temple (§§ 609 ff.), the king's obelisks (§§ 629 ff.), and his "Hymn of Victory" (§§ 655 ff.), furnish important references to the campaigns. The great portal of Pylon VII at Karnak also bore a long recital of his wars, of which only scanty fragments have survived (§§ 593 ff.).

405. The tombs of the contemporary officials in the Theban cemetery also contain very valuable supplementary material. The career of Amenemhab, the most important of these, is translated below (§§ 574 ff.). Next to these are the representations in the tomb of Rekhmire (§§ 760 ff.), which show many of the objects mentioned in the tribute lists of the Annals, besides a reference to Thutmose III's campaigns (§ 755). The tomb of Menkheperreseneb shows

---

ᵃSee also the "Hymn of Victory" (§§ 655 ff.).

ᵇOn the Pylon VIII at Karnak as an appendix to the third copy of the first list (Baedeker's Karnak; seventh in Mariette, *Karnak;* cf. B, 252, Mariette). Text: Mariette, *Karnak,* 20, 21; Tomkins, *Transactions of the Society of Biblical Archæology,* IX, Pls. III, IV; the best treatment, Müller, *Asien und Europa,* 286-92; Tomkins, *ibid.,* IX, 227–54, depends too much on modern names for his identifications.

ᶜSee Müller, *Asien und Europa,* 287.

the tribute of Asia (§§ 772 ff.). The tomb of Puemere contains a relief showing the reception of tribute from "*the ends of Asia*" (§ 385), and that of Imnezeh[a] ($Y^{\text{?}}\ m\text{-}n\underline{d}h$) a similar scene of tribute from "*Retenu the wretched.*" Finally, among the most interesting of these contemporaries is the court herald, Intef, who tells how he preceded Thutmose III on the march and prepared the Syrian palaces for his reception (§§ 771, ll. 24-27).

CONSPECTUS OF CAMPAIGNS

406. FIRST CAMPAIGN, YEARS 22 AND 23 (§§ 408-43, 593 ff., 616)

(Lepsius, *Denkmäler*, III, 31, *b*, ll. 1-67; *ibid.*, III, 32, ll. 1-32= Brugsch, *Thesaurus*, 1153-66, ll. 1-79, and 1-21; Bissing's unpublished collation.[b])

Battle of Megiddo; captured: Megiddo, Yenoam, Nuges, Herenkeru; built fort in Lebanon; tribute and booty of these.

[SECOND CAMPAIGN] YEAR 24 (§§ 444-49)

(Lepsius, *Denkmäler*, III, 32, ll. 32-39=Brugsch, *Thesaurus*, 1166-68, ll. 21-28; Bissing's unpublished collation.)

Tribute of Assur and Retenu.

[THIRD CAMPAIGN] YEAR 25 (§§ 450-52)

(Mariette, *Karnak*, Pls. 28 and 31.)

Plants of Retenu.

[FOURTH CAMPAIGN, YEARS 26-28] (§ 453)

Lost.

---

[a]*Mémoires de la mission française au Caire*, V, 356 f.

[b]This is incorporated in the Berlin Dictionary, and I owe to von Bissing my sincere thanks for permission to use it.

FIFTH CAMPAIGN, YEAR 29 (§§ 454-62)

(Lepsius, *Auswahl der wichtigsten Urkunden*, XII, ll. 1-7; Mariette, *Karnak*, 13, ll. 1-6 = Brugsch, *Thesaurus*, 1168-70, ll. 1-7 = Bissing, *Statistische Tafel*, ll. 1-7.)

Second caption; campaign in Zahi; capture of "W⸺⸺"; sacrifice to Amon; spoil of city; capture of Arvad; list of tribute received *"on this expedition;"* sailed home.

SIXTH CAMPAIGN, YEAR 30 (§§ 463-67)

(Lepsius, *Auswahl der wichtigsten Urkunden*, XII, ll. 7-9; Mariette, *Karnak*, 13, ll. 7, 8 = Brugsch, *Thesaurus*, 1170, 1171, ll. 7-9 = Bissing, *Statistische Tafel*, ll. 7-9.)

Capture of Kadesh; tribute of Retenu; punishment of Arvad.

[SEVENTH CAMPAIGN], YEAR 31 (§§ 468-75)

(Lepsius, *Auswahl der wichtigsten Urkunden*, XII, ll. 9-17; Mariette, *Karnak*, 13, ll. 9-16 = Brugsch, *Thesaurus*, 1171-73, ll. 9-17 = Bissing, *Statistische Tafel*, ll. 9-17.)

Capture of Ullaza; tribute of Retenu; supplies for the harbors; harvest of Retenu; tribute of Genebteyew; impost of Wawat.

[EIGHTH CAMPAIGN], YEAR 33 (§§ 476-87)

(Lepsius, *Auswahl der wichtigsten Urkunden*, XII, ll. 17-29; Mariette, *Karnak*, 13, ll. 17-28 = Brugsch, *Thesaurus*, 1173-75, ll. 17-29 = Bissing, *Statistische Tafel*, ll. 17-29.)

Conquest of Naharin; battle in Naharin; the booty (capture of Carchemish); crossing of Euphrates; boundary tablets; tribute of Naharin, supplies for the harbors; tribute of Babylon; tribute of Hittites; Punt expedition; impost of Wawat.

[NINTH CAMPAIGN], YEAR 34 (§§ 488-95)

(Lepsius, *Auswahl der wichtigsten Urkunden*, XII, ll. 29-37; Mariette, *Karnak*, 13, ll. 29-35 = Brugsch, *Thesaurus*, 1175-77, ll. 29-37 = Bissing, *Statistische Tafel*, ll. 29-37.)

Surrender of Zahi towns; tribute of Retenu; supplies for the harbors; tribute of Cyprus; impost of Kush and Wawat.

TENTH CAMPAIGN, YEAR 35 (§§ 496–503)

(Lepsius, *Auswahl der wichtigsten Urkunden*, XII, ll. 37–41; Lepsius, *Denkmäler*, III, 31, a, ll. 1–3 = Brugsch, *Thesaurus*, 1177, 1178, ll. 37–44, and l. 2 = Bissing, *Statistische Tafel*, ll. 37–44.)

Revolt of Naharin; battle in Naharin, king's booty; army's booty; impost of Kush and Wawat.

[ELEVENTH CAMPAIGN, YEAR 36] (§ 504)

Lost.

[TWELFTH CAMPAIGN, YEAR 37] (§ 505)

Lost.

[THIRTEENTH CAMPAIGN, YEAR 38] (§§ 506–15)

(Lepsius, *Denkmäler*, III, 31, a, ll. 3–10 = Brugsch, *Thesaurus*, 1178–81, ll. 2–9.)

Capture of Nuges; booty of same; tribute of Syria; harbor supplies; tribute of Cyprus and Arrapakhitis; products of Punt; impost of Kush and Wawat.

FOURTEENTH CAMPAIGN, YEAR 39 (§§ 516–19)

(Lepsius, *Denkmäler*, III, 31, a, ll. 10–14 = Brugsch, *Thesaurus*, 1181–1182, ll. 9–13.)

Defeat of Shasu; Syrian tribute; harbor supplies.

[FIFTEENTH CAMPAIGN, YEAR 40] (§§ 520–23)

(Lepsius, *Denkmäler*, III, 30, a, ll. 1–4 = Brugsch, *Thesaurus*, 1182, ll. 1–4; photograph by Borchardt.)

Tribute of Cyprus; impost of Kush and Wawat.

[SIXTEENTH CAMPAIGN, YEAR 41] (§§ 524–27)

(Lepsius, *Denkmäler*, III, 30, a, ll. 4–10 = Brugsch, *Thesaurus*, 1182, 1183, ll. 4–10; photograph by Borchardt.)

Tribute of Retenu; tribute of Hittites; impost of Kush and Wawat.

[SEVENTEENTH CAMPAIGN, YEAR 42] (§§ 528-39)
(Lepsius, *Denkmäler*, III, 30, *a*, ll. 10-20 = Brugsch, *Thesaurus*, 1183-85, ll. 10-20; photograph by Borchardt.)

Campaign against Kadesh; overthrow of Erkatu, Tunip, Kadesh; booty of these; harbor supplies; tribute of unknown country; of Tinay; impost of Kush and Wawat.

I. INTRODUCTION

407. ¹Horus: ' Mighty Bull, Shining in Thebes; ———.
²King of Upper and Lower Egypt, ªLord of the the Two Lands:ª Menkheperre; Son of Re: [Thutmose (III)] ———.ᵇ ³His majesty commanded to cause to be recorded [his victories which his father, Amon, gave to him, uponᶜ] ⁴a tabletᵈ in the temple which his majesty made for [his father, Amon, ⌈setting forth each⌉]ᵉ ⁵expedition by its name, together with the plunder which [his majesty]ᶠ carried away [therein. It was done according to]ᶠ ⁶all [⌈the command⌉] which his father, Re, gave to him.

II. FIRST CAMPAIGN (YEAR 23)ᵍ

408. This, the most important of Thutmose III's campaigns in Asia, is fortunately the most fully recorded. The

---

ªOmitted by Brugsch's text.

ᵇThe lacking portion of the conventional fivefold titulary may be found *passim*.

ᶜRestored from Lepsius, *Auswahl der wichtigsten Urkunden*, XII, second horizontal line (§ 455).

ᵈReally temple wall; more often this word (*wḏ*) means a stela or slab of stone set up by itself.

ᵉThis line is unfortunately also broken away in Lepsius, *Auswahl der wichtigsten Urkunden*, XII; the restoration is probable, but conjectured.

ᶠRestored from Lepsius, *Auswahl der wichtigsten Urkunden*, XII, second horizontal line.

ᵍSeventy-nine short and 21 long vertical lines, beginning at the northeast corner of the passage. Text: Lepsius, *Denkmäler*, III, 31, *b*, ll. 167, and *ibid.*, III, 32, ll. 1-32 = Brugsch, *Thesaurus*, 1153-166, ll. 1-79 and 1-21. The short lines being next the base have almost all lost a portion of the lower ends, while a large part of the long lines lacks the upper ends and frequently the lower ends, also.

occasion of the campaign was a general revolt among his father's Syrian conquests from Sharuhen to the Euphrates. Fighting had already developed in Sharuhen, which was, of course, too near the Egyptian frontier to venture to make common cause with the revolters; and hence conflict resulted there. We are taken with the king and clearly shown his operations day by day till he overthrows a coalition of practically all Syria at Megiddo, headed by the king of Kadesh. He then besieges and captures Megiddo, but from the surrender of Megiddo on, the record degenerates, as in all the other campaigns, to little more than a list of spoils. Fortunately, this latter part of the campaign is supplemented and really continued by the introduction to the list of feasts and offerings[a] established on the king's return to Thebes from this campaign. The close of the campaign is there narrated, mentioning a fortress established in the Lebanon, whither the king had marched after the fall of Megiddo, capturing there the three cities at the seaward bend of the Litâny River, which we may call the Lebanon Tripolis:[b] Yenoam, Nuges, and Herenkeru, commanding the thoroughfare northward between the Lebanons. All this serves merely as an introduction to the splendid feasts of victory celebrated by the king, as is distinctly stated "*on his return from the first victorious campaign.*" The date of these celebrations is preserved, and enables us for the first and only time to determine the length of an Egyptian campaign in Syria.

409. The entire calendar of the campaign, as far as can be determined, is as follows:

---

[a] §§ 541 ff.

[b] Only the spoil of these cities is enumerated in the Annals, the march thither being entirely ignored. The record of feasts and offerings only mentions them later to say that they were given to Amon.

THE ANNALS: FIRST CAMPAIGN

Event	Approximate Distance (English Miles)	Egyptian Calendar			Modern Calendar
		Year of Reign	Calendar Month	Day	Approximate Date
In Tharu................	} 160	22d	8th	25th	April 19
In Gaza; Feast of Coronation...		23d	9th	4th	" 28
Departure from Gaza...........	} c. 80 to 90	"	"	5th	" 29
In Yehem................		"	"	16th	May 10
In Aruna................	?	"	"	19th	" 13
Departure from Aruna.........	} c. 4 or 5	"	"	20th	" 14
Arrival before Megiddo.........		"	"	20th	" 14
Battle of Megiddo.............		"	"	21st	" 15
Beginning of siege of Megiddo...		"	"	21st	" 15
Capture of Megiddo..........	} at least 75	"	"	?	? ?
March to Lebanon.............		"	?	?	? ?
Capture of Yenuam, Nuges, Herenkeru................		"	?	?	? ?
Construction of fort in Lebanon..	} over 900	"	?	?	? ?
Return to Thebes, not later than		"	2d	14th	Oct. 11

410. In less than 148 days, roughly five months, Thutmose III fought the Battle of Megiddo, completely invested with a wall the powerful fortress of Megiddo itself, and captured it; marched northward seventy-five miles to the Lebanon region, captured three cities, and built a fortress there; completed the return to the Delta coast and the voyage up-river to Thebes; and celebrated his first feast of victory there. The entire campaign from the departure from Tharu to the arrival in Thebes lasted a maximum of 175 days; that is, in five months and twenty-five days from the day on which he left Tharu he was celebrating his great Feast of Amon at Thebes. Fortunately, we are able to locate this period approximately in the astronomical calendar and tell in what month he went and returned.[a] (See § 409,

---

[a] For this purpose we have first the Elephantine calendar fragment, which gives the heliacal rising of Sothis in the reign of Thutmose III as the 28th of Epiphi (Young, *Hieroglyphics*, 59 = Brugsch, *Thesaurus*, II, 363 = Lepsius, *Denkmäler*, III, 43, e = de Morgan, *Catalogue des Monuments*, I, 121). Doubt has been cast upon this date, but I have examined the Berlin squeezes, and there is not a shadow of doubt that it belongs to the series of blocks from the reign of Thutmose III. In

last column). It is thus evident that the campaign falls exactly within the limits of the dry season in Palestine.[a]

411. Beside the celebration in Thebes, the victory was celebrated and recorded in a poetic inscription by the viceroy of Kush, Nehi (§§ 412, 413), at Wadi Halfa.[b] It refers to the first campaign, as follows:

412. ———— who (a god) stationed ¹⁰his majesty at the Horns of the Earth, in order to overthrow the Asiatics (*Mnṭ· w-Sṭṭ*). I am the Mighty Bull, Shining in Thebes, Son of Atum, beloved of Montu, ¹¹fighting for his army himself, that the Two Lands may see it; it is no lie. I came forth from the house of my father, the king of gods, Amon, who decrees me victory.

413. ¹²The king himself, he led the way of his army, mighty at its head, like a flame of fire, the king who wrought with his sword. He went forth, none ¹³like him, slaying the barbarians, smiting Retenu (*Rtnw· t, sic*!), bringing their princes as living captives, their chariots wrought ¹⁴with gold, bound to their horses. The countries of Tehenu do obeisance because of the fame of his majesty, with their tribute upon

---

width of column and height of corresponding signs it is identical with a block bearing the name of Thutmose III. Erman, with whom I examined it, was of the same opinion. Unfortunately, the regnal year is not given; but since my attempt to determine the season of the campaign (*Zeitschrift für ägyptische Sprache*, 37, 127 f.) on the basis of the Sothis date, the new moon dates have been finally established by Meyer, which modify my series of dates by two days, but corroborate entirely the season as I established it (Meyer, *Abhandlungen der Berliner Akademie*, 1904, *Aegyptische Chronologie*, 49 f.).

[a] Also shown by the fact that the army reaped the grain harvest about Megiddo, after having foraged upon it. From the king's Karnak building inscription (§ 608) we see that he was at home in February after the campaign of the year 24; and the Harmhab decree (III, 58) shows that Thutmose III was accustomed to be at home each year at the feast of Opet early in October after the summer's campaigning. The campaign of the year 31 also began in April (§ 469, l. 9); the Syrian campaign of Amenhotep II (§§ 780 ff.) and the Kadesh campaign of Ramses II (III, 298 ff.) also fell in the dry season (see *Zeitschrift für ägyptische Sprache*, 37, 129).

[b] On a pillar of the Empire temple. It is dated "*year 23.*" I am indebted for it to a photograph, kindly loaned me by Professor Steindorff, as it is still unpublished. There is in Cairo a fragment of a stela (unpublished, no number) recording the erection of this temple by Thutmose III ("*building for him a temple of white sandstone*"), and its endowment with offerings; but only the extreme ends of eight lines are preserved. I am indebted to Schaefer for a copy of it.

their backs, ¹⁵—— as do the dogs, that there might be given to them the breath of life.

414. Tnere is here further reference to the king's personal leading of his army through the mountains and in the Megiddo battle. Furthermore, we see that Libyans came with tribute on the king's return from the campaign. The Annals narrate the campaign as follows:

At the Frontier in Tharu

415. Year 22, fourth month of the second season (eighth month), on the twenty-fifth[a] day [his majesty was in] ⁷Tharu ($T^{\,\flat}$-rw) on the first victorious expedition to [extend] ⁸the boundaries of Egypt with might ———.

Revolt in Asia

416. ⁹Now, (at) that period[b] [ʳthe Asiatics had fallen into] ¹⁰disagreement,¹ each man [fighting[c]] against [ʳhis neighborˡ] ———. ¹¹Now, it happened ʳthat the tribesˡ —— the people, who were there ¹²in the city of Sharuhen ($\check{S}^{\,\flat}$-$r^{\,\flat}$-$h^{\,\flat}$-n); behold, from Yeraza[d] (Y-$r^{\,\flat}$-$\underline{d}^{\,\flat}$) ¹³to the marshes of the earth,[d] (they) had begun to revolt against his majesty.

Arrival in Gaza, Feast of Coronation

417. Year 23, first (month) of the third season (ninth month), on the fourth day,[e] the day of the feast of the king's coronation, (he arrived) ¹⁴at the city, ʳthe possession of the ruler,[f] Gaza[g] ($G^{\,\flat}$-$\underline{d}^{\,\flat}$-tw).

---

[a]The day is lacking in Lepsius and Brugsch, but is preserved by Champollion's early copy (Champollion, *Notices descriptives*, II, 154).

[b]Or: "*Now, at the time of these ʳevents, during yearsˡ;*" there are traces of the last two words ($m\ rnp\cdot wt$) at the end, before the lacuna.

[c]Restored from the determinative.

[d]That is, from northwestern Judea to beyond the Euphrates.

[e]Maspero (*Recueil*, II, 50, and *Struggle of the Nations*, 255 f.) has third day, but the text of Brugsch has fourth; moreover, the table of feasts on the south wall at Karnak (Mariette, *Karnak*, Pl. 14, b; Rougé, *Inscriptions hiéroglyphiques*, 164) has (l. 7): "*The first month of the third season, fourth day, the feast of the coronation of the king of Upper and Lower Egypt, Menkheperre (Thutmose III).*" Pylon VII (§ 594) gives the same date.

[f]This is possibly a proper name, made up of a verb (in relative form) and a noun, meaning: "*Which the ruler seized*" ($mh\cdot n\ p^{\,\flat}\ hk^{\,\flat}\ ?$).

[g]About 125 miles from the starting-point in nine days.

Departure from Gaza

418. [Year 23] ¹⁵first month of the third season (ninth month), on the fifth day; departure from this place in might, — — ¹⁶in power, and in triumph, to overthrow that wretched foe,ᵃ to extend ¹⁷the boundaries of Egypt, according as his father, Amon-Re, ⌜had commanded — —⌝ that he seize.

Arrival at Yehem

419. Year 23, first month of the third season (ninth month), on the sixteenth day, (he arrived) at the city of Yehem (*Y-ḥm*).

Council of War

420. [His majesty] ordered ¹⁹a consultation with his valiant troops, saying as follows: "That [wretched] enemy, [the chief] ²⁰of Kadesh (*Ḳd-šw*), has come and entered into Megiddo (*My-k-ty*); he [⌜is there⌝] ²¹at this moment. He has gathered to himself the chiefs of [all] the countries [which are] ²²on the water of Egypt,ᵇ and as far as Naharin (*N-h-ry-n*), consisting of [the countries] of ²³the Kharu (*Ḫ ꜣ-rw*), the Kode (*Ḳdw*), their horses, their troops, ——— ²⁴thus he speaks, 'I have arisen to [⌜fight against his majesty⌝] ²⁵in Megiddo (*My-k-ty*).' Tell ye me ———."ᶜ

Advice of the Officers

421. They spoke in the presence of his majesty, "How is it, that [we] should go upon this road, ²⁷which threatens to be narrow? While they [⌜come⌝] ²⁸and say that the enemy is there waiting, [⌜hold⌝]ing the ²⁹way against a multitude. Will not horse come behind [horseᵈ and man behindᵉ] ³⁰man likewise? Shall our [⌜advance-guard⌝] ³¹be fighting while our [⌜rear-guard⌝]ᶠ is yet standing yonder ³²in Aruna (*ꜥ ꜣ-rw-n ꜣ*) not having fought? There are yet two (other) roads: ³³one road, behold, it [will] — us, for it comes forth at ³⁴Taanach

---

ᵃThe king of Kadesh.

ᵇAn idiom for "*dependent upon*" or "*subject to.*"

ᶜThe king's demand upon his officers is for information concerning the road, as the subsequent developments show.

ᵈSee § 424, l. 55.

ᵉThe end is the restoration of Maspero (*Recueil*, II, 52) suggested probably by that of Brugsch (*Egypt under the Pharaohs*, 155).

ᶠMaspero, *Recueil*, II, 52; the determinative of men is still preserved after "*rear-guard.*"

($T^{\jmath\text{-}c\,\jmath}\text{-}n^{\,\jmath}\text{-}k^{\,\jmath}$), the other, [behol]d, it will [bring us upon] ³⁵the way north of Zefti ($Df\text{-}ty$), so that we shall come out to the north of Megiddo ($My\text{-}k\text{-}ty$). ³⁶Let our victorious lord proceed upon [the road] he desires; (but) cause us not to go by a difficult[a] road."

Decision of the King

422. Then —[b] ³⁸⌈messengers⌉ concerning [this] design ³⁹which they had uttered, in view of what had been said ⌈by⌉ the majesty of the Court, L. P. H.: "I [swear], as Re loves me, as my father Amon, favors me, as my [nostrils] are rejuvenated with satisfying life, my majesty will proceed upon this road of ⁴²Aruna ($^{c\,\jmath}\text{-}rw\text{-}n^{\,\jmath}$). Let him who will among you, go upon those ⁴³roads ye have mentioned, and let him who will ⁴⁴among you, come in the following of my majesty. Shall they think among those ⁴⁵enemies whom Re detests: 'Does his majesty proceed upon ⁴⁶another road? He begins to be fearful of us,' so will they think."

Submission of the Officers

423. ⁴⁷They spoke before his majesty: "May thy father Amon, lord of Thebes, presider over Karnak, ⌈grant thee life⌉. ⁴⁸Behold, we are the following of thy majesty in every place, whither [thy majesty] proceedeth; ⁴⁹as the servant is behind [his] master."

Departure from Yehem

424. ⁵⁰[⌈Then his majesty⌉] commanded the entire army [⌈to march⌉] ———— [upon] ⁵¹that road[c] which threatened to be [narrow.[d] His majesty] ⁵²swore, saying: "None shall go forth [⌈in the way⌉] ⁵³before my majesty, in ————." ⁵⁴He went forth at the head of his army himself, ⌈showing [the way]⌉ ⁵⁵by his (own) footsteps;[e] horse behind[f] [horse], [⌈his majesty⌉][g] being ⁵⁶at the head of his army.

---

[a]The same word ($\check{s}t^{\,\jmath}$) is applied to the road upon which the great block for the el-Bersheh colossus (I, 696, l. 1) was brought. It means *"inaccessible"* or *"difficult;"* it is also used by Thutmose III of the celestial road of the sun (§ 141).

[b]Verb lost.

[c]Text has an Amon wrongly restored here.

[d]Cf. l. 27, above.

[e]Lit., *"steps of marching."*

[f]The army here enters the mountain pass.

[g]Or possibly:"[⌈the vanguard,⌉] *being of the best of his army."*

Arrival at Aruna

425. Year 23, first month of the third season (ninth month), on the nineteenth day; the watch in [safety]ᵃ ⁵⁷in the royal tent was at the city of Aruna (ᶜᵓ-rw-nᵓ).ᵇ ⁵⁸"My majesty proceeded northward under (the protection of my) father, Amon-Re, lord of Thebes, [who went] ⁵⁹before me, while Harakhte [strengthened my arms]ᶜ ——— ⁶⁰(my) father, Amon-Re, lord of Thebes, victorious of the sword ——— ⁶¹over my majesty."

Battle in the Mountains

426. [The enemy] went forth ——— ⁶²in numerous battle array ———. ⁶³The southern wing was in Taa[nach] (Tᵓ-ᶜᵓ[-nᵓ-kᵓ]), ⁶⁴the northern wing was on the ground south of ———.ᵈ ⁶⁵His majesty cried out to them before ——— ⁶⁶they fell; behold, that wretched foeᵉ ——— ⁶⁷——— ⁶⁸——— of [the city of]ᶠ ⁶⁹Aruna (ᶜᵓ-rw-nᵓ).

ᵃPerhaps we should supply: *"life, prosperity, and health,"* as in Ramses II's march to Kadesh (l. 1); but above, the said phrase is used after *"tent,"* to express the adjective *"royal,"* and would hardly appear twice in the same phrase.

ᵇThree days after the arrival at Yehem, Aruna, lying in the midst of the mountains, is reached. Here they spent the night of the nineteenth and marched on the twentieth (l. 58).

ᶜRestored from § 430, l. 3.

ᵈMaspero (*Recueil*, II, 56) following Brugsch, supplies Megiddo here. This is quite possible, but only on a different supposition from that of Maspero and Brugsch, viz., that the position described here is that of the Asiatic forces, not of the Egyptians, for the latter do not arrive *"south of Megiddo"* until long after this (§ 428). Furthermore, it is quite impossible for the Egyptians to have had their southern wing at Taanach, while defiling through the Megiddo road. This seems to have been the view in the translation in Petrie's *History* (II, 106), but no mention is made of an encounter with the enemy in the mountains in the summary, p. 101. The passage is important, for it decisively determines (even without supplying Megiddo above) the location of Megiddo against Conder's identification with Mujeddaᶜ. An Asiatic army which, we know, fought before Megiddo, has its southern wing at Taanach, which is known to be Tannuk of today; it must follow that Megiddo is northward from Tannuk. See Breasted, *Proceedings of the Society of Biblical Archæology*, 22, 96.

ᵉThere was some encounter with the enemy here in the mountains, and this moves the officers to urge calling in the straggling rear as soon as possible. This encounter has escaped all the historians except Meyer (*Geschichte*, 239); cf. Maspero, *Struggle of the Nations*, 257; Wiedemann, *Aegyptische Geschichte*, 347; Petrie, *History of Egypt*, II, 101; etc.

ᶠThere is a loss of five lines here, before l. 69, but it is not indicated in the publications.

Danger of the Rear

427. Now, the rear of the victorious army of his majesty was at the city of ⁷⁰Aruna (ᶜᵓ-rw-nᵓ), the front was going forth to the valley of —;ᵃ ⁷¹they filled the opening of this valley. Then [they] said in the presence of his majesty, L. P. H.: ⁷²"Behold, his majesty goeth forth with his victorious army, and it has filled ⁷³the hollow of the valley; let our victorious lord hearken to us this timeᵇ and ⁷⁴let our lord protect for us the rear of his army and his people. ⁷⁵Let the rear of this army come forth to us behind; then shall they (also) fight against ⁷⁶these barbarians; then we shall not (need to) take thought for the rear of our ⁷⁷army." His majesty halted outside and waited ⁷⁸there, protecting the rear of his victorious army.

Exit from the Mountains

428. Behold, when the front had reached the exit upon this road, the shadow had turned,ᶜ and when ᵈ¹his majesty arrived at the south of Megiddo (My-k-ty) onᵉ the bank of the brook of Kina (Ky-nᵓ), the seventh hourᶠ was turning, (measured) by the sun.

Camp in Plain of Megiddo

429. Then was set up the camp of his majesty, and command was given to the whole army, saying: "Equip yourselves! Prepare your weapons! for weᵍ shall advance to fight with that wretched foe in the morning." ⌜Therefore⌝ the king ᵃrested in the royal tent, the ⌜affairs⌝ʰ of the chiefs were arranged, and the provisions of the attendants. The watch of the army went about, saying, "Steady of heart! Steady of heart! Watchful! Watchful!ⁱ Watch for life at the tent of the king." One came to say to his majesty, "The land is well, and the infantry of the South and North likewise."

ᵃProper name ending in *n*.
ᵇPetrie, *History of Egypt*, II, 106.   ᶜIt was past midday.
ᵈA new enumeration of twenty-eight longer lines begins here.
ᵉThe army here emerges in safety upon the plain in the afternoon of the twentieth, and camps unmolested that night, to go forth to battle in the morning of the twenty-first.
 ᶠAbout one o'clock P. M.   ᵍThe text has the impersonal "*one*."
 ʰSee § 341, l. 17, for the same rare phrase.
 ⁱLit., "*Watchful of head*," meaning "to be vigilant," e. g., of the king (Amenhotep III) on the architrave at Luxor: "*the Good God who is very vigilant* (lit., *watchful of head*) *over the house of his father, Amon*" (Lepsius, *Denkmäler*, III, 73, *b*; again *ibid., e*); and often of the vigilance of a faithful official.

Battle of Megiddo

430. Year 23, first (month) of the third season (ninth month), on the twenty-first day, the day of the feast of the new moon, ⌜corresponding to⌝ the royal coronation, early in the morning, behold, command was given to the entire army to move — —. ³His majesty went forth in a chariot of electrum, arrayed in his weapons of war, like Horus, the Smiter, lord of power; like Montu of Thebes, while his father, Amon, strengthened his arms. The southern wing of this army of his majesty was on a hill south of the [brook of]ᵃ Kina (*Ky-nˀ*), the northern wing was at the northwest of Megiddo (*My-k-ty*),ᵇ while his majesty was in their center, with Amon as the protection of his members, ⌜—⌝ the valor — ⁴of his limbs. Then his majesty prevailed against them at the head of his army, and when they saw his majesty prevailing against them they fled headlong to Megiddo (*My-k-ty*) in fear,ᶜ abandoning their horses and their chariots of gold and silver. The peopleᵈ hauled them (up), pulling (them) by their clothing, into this city; the people of this city having closed (it) against them [and ⌜lowered⌝] ⁵clothing to pull them up into this city. Now, if only the army of his majesty had not given their heart to plundering the things of the enemy, they would have [captured] Megiddo (*My-k-ty*) at this moment, when the wretched foe of (*Ḳd-š*) Kadesh and the wretched foe of this cityᵉ were hauled up in haste to bring them into this city.ᵉ The fear of his majesty had entered ⁶[⌜their hearts⌝], their arms were powerless, his serpent diadem was ⌜victorious⌝ among them.

The Spoil

431. Then were captured their horses, their chariots of gold and silver were made spoil;ᶠ their champions lay stretched out like fishes

---

ᵃRestored from § 428, l. 1.

ᵇThis shows that Thutmose has gone around Megiddo toward the west and, having his army partially on the north of the city, has intercepted the enemy's northern line of retreat; at the same time probably securing his own line of retreat along the Zefti road (see § 421, l. 35). This position corroborates the position of the Asiatics with their southern wing at Taanach on the day before the battle (see § 426, especially note). This move must have been made by Thutmose in the afternoon or during the night before the battle.

ᶜLit., "*with or in the faces of fear.*"   ᵈLit., "*one.*"

ᵉMegiddo. The two kings of Kadesh and Megiddo are meant.

ᶠRead *m ys-ḥˀ k* (Sethe, *Verbum*, II, § 700), and compare the same phrase year 31, l. 10 (§ 470).

on the ground. The victorious army of his majesty went around counting their portions. Behold, there was captured the tent of that wretched foe [in] which was [his] son —— ⁷ ———.ᵃ The whole army made jubilee, giving praise to Amon for the victory which he had granted to his son on [ʳthis day, ᵇgiving praiseᵇ¹] to his majesty, exalting his victories. They brought up the booty which they had taken, consisting of hands,ᶜ of living prisoners, of horses, chariots of gold and silver, of ——⁸ ———.ᵈ

The Rebuke

432. [Then spake his majesty ʳon hearing¹ the words of his army, saying: "Had ye captured [this city] afterward, behold, I would have given ———ᵉ Re this day; because every chief of every country that has revolted is within it; and because it is the capture of a thousand cities, this capture of Megiddo (My-k-ty). Capture ye ʳmightily, mightily¹ᶠ — —ᵍ ⁹———."

Siege of Megiddo

433. [ʳHis majesty commanded¹] the ʳofficers¹ of the troops to go — —, [ʳassigning to¹] each his place. They measured this city, [ʳsurrounding it¹] with an inclosure, walled about with green timber of all their pleasant trees.ʰ His majesty himself was upon the fortification east of this city, [ʳinspect]ing¹ ¹⁰———— ⁱ

It was [wa]lled about with a thick wall —— —ʲ with its thick wall.ᵏ Its name was made: "Menkheperre (Thutmose III)-is-the-Surrounder-

---

ᵃAbout a quarter of l. 7 is lacking.

ᵇOr: "*the — of his majesty were exalting, etc.*"

ᶜCut off from the slain.

ᵈAbout one-fourth of l. 8 is lacking.

ᵉThree or four words are lacking, probably: "[*very many offerings to*] Re this day," or something similar.

ᶠThe lacuna doubtless contained the exhortation to begin the siege.

ᵍLl. 9–19 generally lack about one-third their length at the beginning.

ʰThutmose III describes the trees in his own garden of Amon, in the same way (§ 567). Possibly fruit trees are meant, as the word rendered "*pleasant*" (*bnr*) literally means "*sweet*."

ⁱAbout one-third line lacking.

ʲFive or six words are lacking.

ᵏThe same thick wall is also referred to in the building inscription of the Ptah-temple (§ 616, l. 11) and the fragment on this campaign (§ 596, l. 7).

of-the-Asiatics." People were stationed to watch over the tent of his majesty; to whom it was said: "Steady of heart! Watch ———."[a] His majesty 11[commanded, saying: "Let not [b]on]e among them [come forth] outside, beyond this wall, except to come out in order to ⌜knock⌝ at the door of their fortification."[c]

Now, all that his majesty did to this city, to that wretched foe[d] and his wretched army, was recorded on (each) day by its (the day's) name, under the title of: "⌜—⌝ — — —[e]" 12———.[f] Then it was recorded upon a roll of leather in the temple of Amon this day.[g]

Surrender of Megiddo

434. Behold, the chiefs of this country came to render their portions, to do obeisance[h] to the fame of his majesty, to crave breath for their nostrils, because of the greatness of his power, because of the might of the fame of his majesty — — 13the country[i] ——— came to his fame, bearing their gifts, consisting of silver, gold, lapis lazuli, malachite; bringing clean grain, wine, large cattle, and small cattle — for the army of his majesty. ⌜Each of the Kode⌝ (Kd-(w))[j] among them bore the tribute southward. Behold, his majesty appointed the chiefs anew for 14———.[k]

---

[a]Cf. § 429, l. 2; but there is not room here to restore as there indicated. So Maspero, *Recueil*, II, 145.

[b]The lacuna is slightly longer than this.

[c]Probably meaning to offer themselves as prisoners (Petrie, *History of Egypt*, II, 108).

[d]The king of Kadesh.

[e]The first word without the following connection seems doubtful; it means "*to sail, travel*" and possibly refers to the fact that the king sailed each year to Syria in the later campaigns; hence the title may have been: "*Voyages, etc.*" The whole reminds one of the statement concluding the reign of each king in the Book of Kings (e. g., 1 Kings 15:23).

[f]Almost one-third line lacking.

[g]The royal secretary Thaneni was apparently the one who kept this record (see § 392).

[h]Lit., "*to smell the earth.*"

[i]Almost one-third line lacking.

[j]Cf. l. 23, § 420. The sentence is uncertain in the original, both as to text and meaning. As the Kode are coast-people, it may possibly refer to their shipping the spoil to Egypt for the soldiers.

[k]Almost one-third line lacking.

Spoil of Megiddo

435. ———[a] 340 living prisoners; 83 hands; 2,041 mares;[b] 191 foals; 6 stallions; — young —; a chariot, wrought with gold, (its) ⌜pole⌝ of gold, belonging to that foe;[c] a beautiful chariot, wrought with gold, belonging to the chief of ¹⁵[Megiddo];[d] ———[e] 892 chariot[s] of his wretched army; total, 924[f] (chariots); a beautiful ⌜suit⌝ of bronze armor, belonging to that foe;[g] a beautiful ⌜suit⌝ of bronze armor, belonging to the chief of Megiddo (M-k-ty); ———,[h] 200 suits of armor, belonging to his wretched army; 502 bows; 7 poles of (mry) wood, wrought with silver, belonging to the tent of that foe. Behold, the army of [his majesty]took ¹⁶———,[i] 297 —, 1,929 large cattle, 2,000 small cattle,[j] 20,500 white small cattle.[k]

Plunder of the Lebanon Tripolis, Megiddo, Etc.

436. List of that which was afterward taken by the king, of the household goods of that foe who was in [⌜the city of⌝] Yenoam (Y-nw-$ʿɔ$-mw), in Nuges (Yn-yw-g-s ɔ), and in Herenkeru ($Ḥw$-r-n-k ɔ-rw),[l]

---

[a]The determinative sign of a foreign country is the first sign at the end of the lacuna before the list.

[b]This word ($ssmw·t$) I have elsewhere translated "*horses*" for what seem to me sufficient reasons, but in this context we have a clear distinction between mares and stallions.

[c]The king of Kadesh.   [d]Restored from the list of armor following.

[e]About one-third line lacking.

[f]There must be 30 chariots therefore, mentioned in the lacuna, which would probably be those of the officers or other chiefs.

[g]The king of Kadesh.

[h]Here followed the armor of the officers, as in the case of the chariots above.

[i]Almost one-third line lacking.

[j]Sheep?   [k]Goats?

[l]These three cities lay close together at the southern end of Lebanon. That Thutmose III marched to Lebanon after the fall of Megiddo is shown by the fact that he built a fortress there (§ 548, l. 1) just before returning to Thebes. The three cities formed a political whole under a single ruler ("*that foe*"), and were given as a whole to Amon by Thutmose III (§ 557). The location of these cities in the plain of Megiddo (Petrie, *Syria and Egypt*, 14) is plainly due to overlooking the other evidence (see Müller, *Asien und Europa*, 200–3); though Petrie is undoubtedly right in denying the identity of Nuges and Nukhasse, already opposed by Müller (*ibid.*, 394). If "*that foe*" refers to the king of Kadesh here, as it does elsewhere throughout this inscription, we have an important indication of the extent southward of the territory of that king.

together with all the goods of those cities which submitted themselves, which were brought to [17][his majesty: 474] —;[a] 38[b] lords ([*m-r*ʾ*-y-*]*n*ʾ) of theirs, 87 children of that foe and of the chiefs who were with him, 5 lords of theirs, 1,796 male and female slaves with their children, non-combatants who surrendered because of famine with that foe, 103 men; total, 2,503.[c] Besides flat dishes of costly stone and gold, various vessels, [18]————,[d] a large (two-handled) vase[e] (ʾ*-k*ʾ*-n*ʾ) of the work of Kharu (*Ḫ*ʾ*-rw*), (— *b*-) vases, flat dishes, (*ḫntw-*) dishes, various drinking-vessels, 3 large kettles (*rhd· t*), [8]7 knives,[f] amounting to 784 deben.[g] Gold in rings found in the hands of the artificers, and silver in many rings, 966 deben and 1 kidet.[h] A silver statue in beaten work [19]————[i] the head of gold, the staff with human faces; 6 chairs[j] of that foe, of ivory, ebony and carob wood, wrought with gold; 6 footstools[k] belonging to them; 6 large tables of ivory and carob wood, a staff of carob wood, wrought with gold and all costly stones in the fashion of a scepter, belonging to that foe, all of it wrought with gold; [l20]a statue of that foe, of ebony wrought with gold, the head of which ⌈was inlaid⌉ with lapis lazuli ————;[m] vessels of bronze, much clothing of that foe.

Harvest of the Plain of Megiddo

437. Behold, the cultivable land was divided into fields, which the inspectors of the royal house, L. P. H., calculated, in order to reap their

---

[a]About one-third line lacking.

[b]Brugsch, 39.

[c]The prisoners enumerated foot up to 2,029; hence 474 must have been mentioned in the lacuna at the head of l. 17. These must have included "*that foe and the chiefs who were with him*," and probably others whom we cannot identify.

[d]About one-third line lacking; the numeral belonging to the preceding objects is lost in this lacuna.

[e]Hebrew, אַגָּן.

[f]Restored from the 87 in l. 17.

[g]191.1 pounds, total of gold in the preceding list of articles.

[h]235.46 pounds.

[i]About one-third line lacking.

[j]In Egyptian the word (*ḳny*) often means a kind of open sedan chair.

[k]*Ḥdmw*, Hebrew, הֲדֹם.

[l]From this point on, four lines are again nearly complete.

[m]About one-fifth of the line is lacking.

harvest. Statement of the harvest which was brought to his majesty from the fields of Megiddo (*My-k t*): 208,200(+*x*)[a] fourfold heket of grain, [21]besides that which was cut as forage by the army of his majesty ———.[b]

FRAGMENT ON THE SIEGE OF MEGIDDO[c]

438. The inscription to which this fragment belonged contained an account of the first campaign and apparently no more, so that it was doubtless recorded at the close of this campaign before the others took place. It is probably therefore, the oldest of Thutmose III's war records, and introduces an offering-list.

The Insurrection

439. [1]——— Amon-Re, lord of Thebes, at the overthrow[d] of Retenu, the wretched [2]——— anew for my father, Amon ——— [3]——— the lands of the Fenkhu, who had begun to invade my boundaries.[e] ——— [4]⌈arrayed, in⌉ hatred of my majesty. They fell upon their faces [5]——— of Megiddo.

---

[a]The possible uncertainty is not more than 200 more. This makes about 112,632 imperial bushels (of 2,218.19 cubic inches). It is impossible to say how much an acre would yield at this time, but at twenty bushels to the acre, this harvest covered a territory of nearly nine square miles. (Mr. Petrie's reckoning of 150,000 bushels is based on an error in the original number of fourfold heket; he has 280,500 (*History of Egypt*, II, 112), while the text gives only 208,200, or possibly 208,400.

[b]About one-fifth line lacking. For the continuation of the campaign, see the record of "Feasts and Offerings," §§ 541 ff.

[c]South (?) wall in the Eighteenth Dynasty Karnak temple. It has been partially published by Brugsch (*Recueil de monuments*, I, XXVII, and again, *Thesaurus*, V, 1187), and more fully by Dümichen (*Historische Inschriften*, II, 38). I had also a photograph by Borchardt. The inscription is in vertical lines, which have been numbered backward by Dümichen and Brugsch (in Brugsch, *Recueil de monuments; Thesaurus*, without numbers). An unknown amount is lost at the top, ll. 17–21 are entirely lost, and only a few words are preserved at the bottoms of ll. 13–16 and 22–24.

[d]This dates the offering to Amon as occurring after the defeat of Retenu, and as the following shows, on the first campaign.

[e]This is the insurrection referred to in § 416. The battle of Megiddo is then rapidly passed over, and l. 5 begins the siege of Megiddo.

Siege of Megiddo

440. Then my majesty surrounded it with a wall, made thick ⁶——— they tasted not the breath of life, surrounded in front of their ⌈wall⌉ ⁷——— the Asiatics of all countries came with bowed head, doing obeisance to the fame of my majesty. ⁸———.

Surrender of Megiddo

441. These Asiatics who were in the wretched Megiddo ⁹——— [⌈came forth⌉] to the fame of Menkheperre (Thutmose III), [⌈given life, saying⌉]: "Give us a chance,ᵃ that we may present to thy majesty [our] impost." ¹⁰——— all that my majesty did in this land forever.

The Inhabitants Shown Mercy

442. Then my majesty commanded to give to them the breath of life ¹¹——— all their goods, bearing ¹²———.

Further March

443. ——— led me to a goodly way ¹³——— inclosed in ¹⁴——— ⌈Tyre⌉ᵇ ¹⁵——— ᶜ ¹⁶——— these ¹⁷——— ᵈ ²² ——— with every fragrant wood ²³——— I did this ²⁴———. I was ²⁵——— victorious in all lands, shining upon the Horus-throne of the living — like Re, forever.

III. SECOND CAMPAIGN (YEAR 24)ᵉ

444. This campaign seems to have been only a circuitous march through Palestine and southern Syria (l. 25), to receive the submission and tribute of the dynasts. Far-off Assyria also, which had now heard of the great victory of the preceding year, sent gifts, which the scribe calls "*tribute*" (*ynw*) like that of Syria.

ᵃLit., "*Give our occasion.*"

ᵇThe line is broken just above this word; hence, although it spells Tyre ($D\ {}^{\flat}\text{-}r\ {}^{\flat}$), it may be the end of a longer word terminating in $d\ {}^{\flat}\text{-}r\ {}^{\flat}$, like $Sn\text{-}d\ {}^{\flat}\text{-}r\ {}^{\flat}$ (Amenemhab, l. 11, § 584). But see Müller, *Asien und Europa*, 185.

ᶜEnd shows determinative of foreigners.

ᵈLl. 17–21 are entirely lost.

ᵉLepsius, *Denkmäler*, III, 32, ll. 32–39 = Brugsch, *Thesaurus*, 1166–68, ll. 21–28.

445. [List of the tribute of Assur and of] the chiefs of Retenu in the year 24.[a]

Tribute of Assur

446. The tribute[b] of the chief of Assur (*Ys-sw-rꜣ*): genuine lapis lazuli, a large block, making 20 deben, 9 kidet; genuine lapis lazuli, 2 blocks; total, 3;[c] and pieces, [making] 30 deben; total, 50 deben and 9 kidet;[d] fine lapis lazuli from Babylon (*Bb-rꜣ*); vessels of Assur (*ys-sw-rꜣ*) of (*ḥrtt-*) stone in colors,[e] — — — — ²²very many.

Tribute of Retenu

447. The tribute of the chiefs of Retenu: the daughter of a chief, (with) ornaments of — gold, lapis luzuli of t[his] country;[f] 30 ⌈slaves⌉ belonging ⌈to her⌉; 65[g] male and female slaves of his tribute; 103 horses; 5 chariots, wrought with gold, (with) ⌈poles⌉ of gold; 5 chariots, wrought with electrum, (with) ⌈poles⌉ of ʿ *g·t*; total, 10; 45 bullocks[h] (⌈and⌉) calves; 749 bulls; 5,703 small cattle; flat dishes of gold[i] ²³which could not be weighed; flat dishes of silver, and fragments, (making) 104 deben, 5 kidet;[j] a gold ⌈horn⌉ (*mḳ-rꜣ-dy-nꜣ*), inlaid with lapis lazuli; a bronze corselet (*ḥꜣ-n-rw*), inlaid with gold, ⌈ornamented⌉ ———[k] many — of silver — in battle ———[k] ²⁴823 (*mn-*) jars of incense; 1,718 (*mn-*) jars of honeyed wine;[l] ⌈—⌉ ʿ *g·t*[m] and much two-colored

---

[a]Brugsch (with sic!), Champollion, Lepsius, and Bissing, all have 40, in which 4 units have unquestionably been miswritten by the ancient copyist, for 2 tens— an easy error. Griffith does not give Burton's reading. The emendation to 24 is certain from l. 25, dated year 24.

[b]These are, of course, only gifts, but the text uses the same word as in the case of the chiefs of Retenu. It is at the head of the list, for it reached him early as a result of the Megiddo victory in the preceding year.

[c]This total of "*blocks*" is thrust in between as a parenthesis.

[d]12.40 pounds.

[e]So the texts of Champollion and Bissing.

[f]Or: "*of the foreigners*" (*ḥꜣ Styw*).

[g]These 65 slaves are not among the tribute of Assur, as Müller indicates, being misled by Champollion *Notices descriptives*, 158 (Müller, *Asien und Europa*, 278).

[h]So Lepsius, Champollion, and Bissing; Brugsch, 55.

[i]There is possibly a lost word or even two at the end of the line (22).

[j]25.47 pounds.

[k]About one-third of the line.

[l]Or: "*wine and honey*."

[m]Two sorts of ʿ *g·t*.

ᶜg·t,[a] ivory, carob wood, mrw wood,[b] psgw wood, many ⌜bundles⌝ of fire wood, all the luxuries of this country ———[c] ²⁵to every place of his majesty's circuit, (where) the tent was pitched.[d]

Appendix

448. YEAR 24. List of the tribute brought to the fame of his majesty in the country of Retenu.

Second Tribute of Assur

449. Tribute of the chief of Assur (Ys-sw-r ʾ): h[⌜orses⌝] ———.[e] ²⁶A ⌜—⌝[f] of skin of the M-ḫ ʾ-w[g] as the ⌜protection⌝ of a chariot, of the finest[h] of — wood; 190(+x) wagons ———[e] ²⁷— wood, nḥb [i]wood, 343 pieces; carob wood, 50 pieces; mrw wood, 190 pieces; nby and k ʾ nk wood, 206 pieces; ⌜olive wood⌝, ———[e] ²⁸———.[j]

IV. THIRD CAMPAIGN (YEAR 25)[k]

450. The Annals contain no account of the third campaign, which was evidently a peaceful tour of inspection. The record of its results required more room than the wall of the Annals afforded, hence it was transferred to a chamber in the rear of the temple, and recorded in a long series of reliefs representing the flora and fauna of Syria, brought

---

[a]Two sorts of ᶜg·t.

[b]Same as "*mery wood.*"

[c]Ll. 24–28 lack considerably over half their length below.

[d]The statement undoubtedly was that the tribute was brought to the king wherever he was in his circuit.

[e]Over half the line is wanting.

[f]Mśwy, perhaps the leathern front of a chariot. See also Müller, *Asien und Europa*, 278, n. 3.

[g]An unknown animal.

[h]Or: "⌜with⌝ heads of — wood."

[i]So Lepsius; Brugsch, *neheb;* unknown.

[j]A few numerals and fragments of words are visible, in which "*3,000 various* ⌜*trees*⌝" (or objects of wood) appear.

[k]Reliefs and inscriptions on the walls of the first chamber north of the second (rear) sanctuary of Karnak (marked Y' on Mariette's plan, Pl. 5); published by Mariette, *Karnak*, 28–31.

back from this campaign. They are accompanied by the following inscriptions:[a]

451. [b]YEAR 25, under the majesty of the King of Upper and Lower Egypt, Menkheperre (Thutmose III), living, forever. Plants which his majesty found in the land of Retenu.

[c]¹All plants that ⌈grow⌉, all flowers that are in God's-Land[d] [which were found by] ²his majesty when his majesty proceeded to Upper Retenu, to subdue ⌈all⌉ the countrie[s,] ³according to the command of his father, Amon, who put them beneath his sandals, from [⌈the year 1⌉] ⁴to myriads of years.

452. His majesty said: "I swear, as Re [loves me] ⁵as my father, Amon, favors me, all these things happened in truth —. ⁶I have not written fiction as that which really happened to my majesty;[e] I have ⌈engraved⌉ the excellent [deeds] ⁷⌈—⌉. My majesty hath done this from desire to put them ⁸before my father Amon, in this great temple of Amon, (as) a memorial forever and ever."

V. FOURTH CAMPAIGN

453. The account of this campaign, if any existed, is lost; it was not recorded on the wall of the Annals, and may have been put elsewhere, like the third.

---

[a]The only other inscription of year 25 is a stela cut on the rocks of the Sarbût el-Khadem, and dated in the *"year 25."* Above is a relief showing Thutmose III offering a libation to *"Hathor, mistress of malachite;"* behind the king stands the *"chief treasurer, Ray"* ($R ˀ y$), who conducted the expedition hither. An inscription of eight horizontal lines contains only titulary and praise of Thutmose III. Below stands Ray again with an inscription in eight vertical lines, which has almost wholly disappeared. The following may be discerned: *"He appointed him at the head of his army, to bring that which his majesty desired, of products of the lands of the gods, malachite without number, ... he exceeded that which was commanded him, and that which was exacted. . . . . . .* A reference to *"the sea"* ($w ˀ \underline{d}\text{-}wr$) at the end doubtless indicates the way in which the journey was made.

[b]Vertical line on the east wall; text, Mariette, *Karnak*, 31.

[c]Eight vertical lines on the north wall, left of the door; numbered from right to left; text, Mariette, *Karnak*, 28.

[d]Showing that $T ˀ\text{-}ntr$ (*"God's-Land"*) is sometimes applied to Asia; same in inscription of Thaneni (§ 820), and in § 888.

[e]Text has: *"the souls of my majesty."*

VI. FIFTH CAMPAIGN (YEAR 29)[a]

454. The first campaign extended no farther northward than the Tripolis of the southern Lebanon, and this was inland. The second and third campaigns were not aggressive, and apparently did not push far north; the record of the fourth campaign is lost, and it is not until the fifth, in the year 29, that we have certain information of an advance beyond the northern limits of the first campaign, and along the coast. This fifth campaign begins with a new caption, as if a new period of the wars had begun here, and it is clear that the revolt suppressed in the south in the year 23 was after six years not yet subdued in the cities of Zahi, which the king had not yet visited. The wars in the Annals are thus divided into two great groups, the first group being in the south, and the second group, beginning in the year 29, being the wars in the north.

After the capture of a city the name of which is lost ($W^{\text{?}}$——), which was supported by troops from Tunip, contained a sanctuary of Amon, and yielded rich plunder, the king proceeded southward and captured Arvad. The rich gardens and fields, now in the season of fruitage, were plundered, and the army spent the days in rioting and feasting. The king seized some Phœnician ships, and the expedition returned by water. This had perhaps been done by earlier expeditions, but the fifth is the first in which it is certain.

---

[a]The text here returns to the main sanctuary, where the annals are resumed, beginning at the jog in the north wall (see Mariette, *Karnak*, Pl. 13). Only the lower ends of the lines are still in situ, the rest having been barbarously quarried out by Salt; this section is now in the Louvre. Text of Louvre section and part of lines *in situ*, Lepsius, *Auswahl der wichtigsten Urkunden*, XII, ll. 1-7; lower ends of same lines, Mariette, *Karnak*, 13, ll. 1-6; both, Brugsch, *Thesaurus*, V, 1168-70, ll. 1-7 = Bissing, *Statistische Tafel*, xxvii f., ll. 1-7.

THE ANNALS: FIFTH CAMPAIGN

Introduction

455. [a]His majesty commanded to cause that the victories which his father [Amon] had given him should be recorded upon the stone wall in the temple which his majesty made anew [ᵣfor his father Amon, setting forth each¹ expedition][b] by its name,[c] together with the plunder which his majesty brought therefrom. It was done according to [all the command which his father, Re, gave to him[d]] ———.

Campaign in Zahi

456. ¹YEAR 29. Behold, [his] majesty was [in Za]hi subduing the countries revolting against him, on the fifth victorious campaign.

Capture of Unknown City

457. Behold, his majesty captured the city of Wa —— (W ͻ——)[e] ————. This army offered acclamations to his majesty,[f] giving praise to ²[Amon] for the victories which [he gave to] his son. They were pleasing to the heart of his majesty above everything.

Sacrifices to Amon

458. After this his majesty proceeded to the storehouse of offering[s], to give a sacrifice to Amon and to Harakhte[g] consisting of oxen, calves, fowl, [ᵣfor the life, prosperity, and health of[h]] Menkheperre (Thutmose III), who giveth life forever.

---

[a]Horizontal line at the top; cf. same beginning in the introduction to the Megiddo campaign, § 407, l. 3 (=Lepsius, *Denkmäler*, III, 31, *b*, 3 ff.).

[b]Excepting the word "*expedition*," this part is also broken out in the Introduction (l. 5, § 407).

[c]Apparently this means by its number, for from now on the expeditions are numbered: see year 29.

[d]Restored from § 407, l. 6 (=Lepsius, *Denkmäler*, III, 31, *b*, l. 6).

[e]Young shows that the name ended in *t*. About five or six words are lacking.

[f]As after the battle of Megiddo.

[g]Bissing (*Statistische Tafel*, XV) makes the obvious comparison with the mention of the presence of the gods of Egypt in "Dunip" (*Amarna Letters*, ed. Winckler, 41, 9, 10) in the Amarna letters.

[h]Seven or eight words are lacking.

Spoil of the City

459. List of the plunder taken out of this city, from ³the infantry of that foe of Tunip (*Tw-np*), the chief of this city, 1; (*T-h-r-*)ᵃ warriors, 329; silver, 100 deben;ᵇ gold, 100 deben;ᵇ lapis lazuli, malachite, vessels of bronze and copper.

The Return Voyage

460. Behold, ships were taken — — — laden with everything, with slaves, male and female; copper, lead, ⌜emery⌝, (and) ⁴everything good. Afterward his majesty proceeded southwardᶜ to Egypt, to his father. Amon-Re, with joy of heart.

Capture of Arvad

461. Behold, his majesty overthrew the city of Arvad (*ʾ-r ʾ-ty-wt*), with its grain, cutting down all its pleasant trees.ᵈ Behold, there were found [⌜the products⌝] of all Zahi. Their gardens were filled with their fruit, ⁵their wines were found remaining in their presses as water flows,ᵉ their grain on the terracesᶠ ⌜upon —⌝; it was more plentiful than the sand of the shore. The army were overwhelmed with their portions.

Tribute on This Expedition

462. List of the tribute brought to his majesty on this expedition: 51 slaves, male and female; 30 horses; 10 flat dishes of silver; ⁶incense, oil, 470 (*mn-*) jars of honey, 6,428 (*mn-*) jars of wine, copper, lead, lapis lazuli, green felspar, 616 large cattle, 3,636 small cattle, loaves, various

---

ᵃText has only "— *hr;*" I am indebted for the restoration to Erman; see also Müller (*Asien und Europa*, 360, n. 5).

ᵇ24.37 pounds.

ᶜThe return of the king is here prematurely narrated. It was, of course, by water, as the preceding context shows that Phœnician ships were seized for the purpose.

ᵈSee § 433 (Lepsius, *Denkmäler*, III, 32, l. 20) where the same was done for Megiddo.

ᵉCf. Bissing, *Statistische Tafel*, 16 ff., who makes the passage too difficult; and Piehl, *Proceedings of the Society of Biblical Archæology*, 1889–90, 376, whose emendation is not necessary. Precisely the same figure, with the same grammatical construction occurs in Papyrus Harris (IV, 213 and 216 = 7, 11 and 8, 6).

ᶠThe sloping fields of the mountain side.

($n/r\cdot t$-) loaves, clean grain in kernel and ground — —. All good fruit of this country. Behold, the army of his majesty was drunk and anointed with oil ⁷every day as at a feast in Egypt.

VII. SIXTH CAMPAIGN (YEAR 30)[a]

463. This year the expedition went by water and landed at Simyra,[b] the most convenient port for reaching Kadesh. This city had been the leader in the great coalition of revolters, defeated at Megiddo in the first campaign seven years before. It was doubtless also constantly supporting revolt in the Phœnician coast cities, as Tunip had done in the preceding year (29), causing the king to direct his forces thither in that year. Finally in the year 30 the king succeeded in reaching the source of the disturbance, capturing and severely punishing Kadesh,[c] a feat in which Amenemhab assisted. He returned to his fleet at Simyra, proceeded to Arvad and punished it as in the preceding year. On his return to Egypt he took with him the children of the native princes to be educated in friendship toward Egypt, that they might be sent back gradually to replace the old hostile generation of Syrian princes.

464. YEAR 30. Behold, his majesty was in the land of Retenu on the sixth victorious expedition[d] of his majesty.

---

[a]Lepsius, *Auswahl der wichtigsten Urkunden*, XII, ll. 7-9, and Mariette, *Karnak*, 13, ll. 7, 8; Brugsch, *Thesaurus*, 1170, 1171, ll. 7-9; Bissing, *Statistische Tafel*, ll. 7-9.

[b]This is not stated in the Annals, but as he returned to the coast at Simyra, and as Simyra was the port nearest Kadesh, the objective of his campaign, there can be little doubt about the place of landing.

[c]Although it still remained the center of Syrian rebellion and revolted again in year 42 (§§ 531, 532). Amenemhab refers to both conquests (§ 585 and §§ 589 f.).

[d]The word is in this case determined with a ship indicating the manner in which the king proceeded to Syria (cf. Wiedemann, *Zeitschrift der Deutschen Morgenländischen Gesellschaft*, 32, 128; also Bissing, *Statistische Tafel*, 19).

Punishment of Kadesh and Arvad

465. (He) arrived at the city of Kadesh (*Ḳd-šw*), overthrew it,[a] cut down its groves, harvested its grain. (He) came to the land of *Š—y—wt*,[b] arrived at the city of Simyra (*Ḏ ʾ-my-r ʾ*), arrived at the city of Arvad (*ʾ-r ʾ-t-wt*), doing likewise[c] to it.

Tribute

466. List of the tribute ⁸brought to the souls of his majesty by the chiefs of Retenu in this year.

Capture of Children of Chiefs

467. Behold, the children of the chiefs (and) their brothers were brought to be in strongholds in Egypt.[d] Now, whosoever died among these chiefs, his majesty would cause his son to stand in his place. List of the children of chiefs brought in this year: $(x+)2$[e] persons; 181 slaves, male and female; 188 horses; 40 chariots, ⁹wrought with gold and silver (and) painted.

VIII. SEVENTH CAMPAIGN (YEAR 31)[f]

468. The king again directs his attention to the coast cities of Phœnicia, and it is clear that he proceeds thither by water, first capturing Ullaza, a coast city in the vicinity of Simyra, when he receives the tribute and homage of the submissive Syrian kinglets. He then sailed along the coast from harbor to harbor, forcing submission, and laying up

---

[a]The language does not unequivocally state the capture of the city, but its capture is clearly stated by Amenemhab (§ 585, ll. 13, 14).

[b]This fragmentary name must indicate the country north of Kadesh, for, according to Amenemhab (§ 584), Thutmose went to Senzar on this Kadesh campaign.

[c]As he had done to Kadesh.

[d]They were kept in a special place of confinement or dwelling at Thebes, explained in § 402; cf. also Müller, *Asien und Europa*, 268.

[e]The first part of the number is broken out.

[f]Lepsius, *Auswahl der wichtigsten Urkunden*, XII, ll. 9–17, and Mariette, *Karnak*, 13, ll. 9–16 = Brugsch, *Thesaurus*, 1171–73, ll. 9–17 = Bissing, *Statistische Tafel*, ll. 9–17.

in each the necessary supplies for his garrisons and his future operations. After receiving reports on the harvest of Retenu, he returned to Egypt, where he found messengers bringing tribute from the southern tribe of the Genebteyew. The record here appends the annual taxes of the Nubian Wawat.

469. YEAR 31, first (month) of the third season, day 3. List of that which his majesty captured in this year.

Capture of Ullaza

470. Booty brought from the city of Ullaza (ʾ *n-r* ʾ-*tw*), which is upon the shore of Zeren (⸢*Dʾr-n* ʾ⸣),[a] 490 living captives; [3] ⸢—⸣[b] of the son of that foe of Tunip (⸢*Tʾw-n*[*p*]⸣); chief of the ⸢—⸣, who was there, 1; total, 494 persons. Twenty-six horses; 13 chariots, ¹⁰and their equipment of all the weapons of war. Verily, his majesty captured this city in a short hour, and all its property was spoil.[c]

Tribute of Submissive Princes

471. Tribute of the princes of Retenu, who came to do obeisance to the [souls] of his majesty in this year: — [d]slaves, male and female; 72 ———— of this country; silver, 761 deben, 2 kidet;[e] 19 chariots, wrought with silver; ¹¹the equipment of their weapons of war; 104 oxen with bullocks;[f] 172 calves and cows; total, 276; 4,622 small cattle; native copper, 40 blocks; lead, ————[g] 41 golden bracelets, figured with ⸢—⸣; together with all their produce and all the fine fragrant ¹²woods of this country.

---

[a]As corrected by Bissing, *Statistische Tafel*, 22. It has the determinative of a body of water.

[b]*Ḥnty*.

[c]Compare a similar phrase in year 23, l. 6 (§ 431), and "Hymn of Victory," l. 9 (§ 657); the identical phrase in Ahmose-si-Ebana, l. 21 (§ 15). Cf. Sethe, *Verbum*, II, § 70.

[d]Numeral lost.

[e]185.5 pounds.

[f]Cf. Lepsius, *Denkmäler*, III, 32, l. 33.

[g]Not more than five words lacking, and about the same in l. 12.

The Harbors

472. Now, every harbor[a] at which his majesty arrived was supplied with (*n/r-*) loaves and with assorted loaves, with oil, incense, wine, honey, f[ruit] — — — — abundant were they beyond everything, beyond the knowledge of his majesty's army; (it) is no fiction, [13]they remain in the daily register[b] of the palace, L. P. H., the list of them not being given in this inscription, in order not to multiply words, and in order to furnish ⌈their circumstances⌉ in this place[c] ——————— [d]

Harvest of Retenu

473. The harvest of the land of Retenu was reported, consisting of much clean grain, [14]grain in the kernel,[e] barley, incense, green oil, wine, fruit, every pleasing thing of the country; they shall[f] apportion it to the treasury, according as the impost of the — is counted ——————— 33 various —, together with green ⌈stone⌉, every costly stone of this country, and many stones [15]of ⌈sparkle⌉;[g] [all the] good [things] of this country.

---

[a]That these are the harbors on the Phœnician coast, there is no doubt. The word is a feminine noun (*mny·wt*) from *mny*, "to land," and sometimes has a ship as determinative (Papyrus Anast., IV, 15, 4). Some of the supplies with which these *mny·wt* were equipped were ships and spars (§ 492). These cannot apply to inland stations! When we notice that it is always Lebanon chiefs who furnish the supplies, the conclusion is clear. A new meaning is thus given the words of Abdkhiba of Jerusalem: "As long as ships were upon the sea, the strong arm of the king occupied Nahrima (Naharin) and Kas" (Babylonia) (*Amarna Letters*, ed. Winckler, 182, 32 f.). This observation throws a flood of light on Thutmose III's campaigns, and shows that his military operations were later regularly conducted from some harbor as a base. He therefore employed his navy in these campaigns to a far greater extent than we had supposed, regularly transporting his army to Syria by water, and even probably conducting the above campaign by water, sailing from harbor to harbor. See note, § 483, l. 24.

[b]*Hrwy·t*. The word is rare, but occurs also in the Decree of Harmhab (III, 63, l. 4), indicating a writing containing laws.

[c]Meaning, perhaps, that there is room on the wall only for offering the circumstances under which the spoil was taken, without enumerating the same.

[d]Over one-third of the line is broken out, and this is the case with each line as far as l. 35.

[e]Not ground.

[f]The tense shows that we have here the very words of the government scribe's books.

[g]The word has the fire determinative; same word in forty-second year, l. 14, § 533; and Papyrus Harris three times (not four, as given in Piehl's *Dictionnaire*, 21, 22), each time referring to costly stones. Hence Bissing's conjecture that it means a founder's mould of stone is impossible (Bissing, *Statistische Tafel*, 28).

Tribute of the Genebteyew

474. When his majesty arrived in Egypt, the messengers of the Genebteyew (*Gnb·tyw*) came bearing their tribute, consisting of myrrh, ⌜gum⌝ —————— 6 —; 10 male negroes for attendants; 113 oxen ¹⁶(and) calves; 230 bulls; total, 343; besides vessels laden with ivory, ebony, skins of the panther, products ————.

Impost of Wawat

475. [List of the impost of Wawat (*W ꜣ-w ꜣ· t*)]: 5 — of Wawat; 31 oxen and calves; 61 bulls; total, 92; ¹⁷besides vessels laden with all things of this country; the harvest of Wawat, likewise.

IX. EIGHTH CAMPAIGN (YEAR 33)[a]

476. In this year the king carries out the greatest campaign of his Asiatic wars, viz., the conquest of the Euphrates country. He has been long preparing for it, in the preceding campaigns, overthrowing Kadesh in the Orontes valley, subduing the coast cities, and filling them with provisions for his garrisons and his future operations. The story is unfortunately briefly told, and not always chronological. The voyage to Simyra,[b] and the long march thence down the Orontes and to the Euphrates, are entirely omitted. The crowning act of the campaign, the erection of his boundary tablet east of the Euphrates, and another in the vicinity beside that of his father, Thutmose I, is immediately narrated. The operations which led to this culmination are then recorded in the meagerest words. While marching northward, plundering as he went, probably not far from the Euphrates, he meets the king of Mitanni, defeats and

---

[a]Lepsius, *Auswahl der wichtigsten Urkunden*, XII, ll. 17-29; Mariette, *Karnak*, 13, ll. 17-28 = Brugsch, *Thesaurus*, 1173-75, ll. 17-29 = Bissing, *Statistische Tafel*, ll. 17-29.

[b]He must have landed at Simyra, for, according to the fragment of Pylon VII (§ 598) he conquered Ketne on this campaign. Ketne was in the Orontes valley behind Simyra (Meyer, *Aegyptiaca*, 68; Petrie's location of it by Damascus seems to me impossible. See *Syria and Egypt, s. v.*).

drives him in flight, capturing a great booty on the battlefield. Amenemhab mentions three battles on this campaign, of which the last, that at Carchemish, is probably, the one here mentioned in the Annals. Probably Carchemish marks the northern limit of the advance in this campaign, and the two other battles mentioned by Amenemhab occurred on the march thither (§§ 581, 582). The king then crossed the Euphrates, set up his boundary tablets, and, as he marched southward to Niy on his return, he was met by the subordinate princes, who immediately submitted and brought their tribute. Even far-off Babylon sends gifts, which, of course, the king calls tribute, and also the Hittites, who here make their first appearance in history. It is now arranged that the Lebanon princes shall keep the king's harbors supplied with provisions [a]

On the king's return, an expedition of his to Punt arrives with magnificent returns from *"God's-Land."* The impost of Wawat is paid as usual.

477. YEAR 33. Behold, his majesty was in the land of Retenu; [he] arrived ———.

Boundary Tablet on the Euphrates

478. [He set up a tablet] east of this water;[b] he set up another beside the tablet of his father, ¹⁸the king of Upper and Lower Egypt, Okheperkere (Thutmose I).

Battle in Naharin

479. Behold, his majesty went north[c] capturing the towns and laying waste the settlements of that foe[d] of wretched Naharin (*N-h-ry-n*ᵓ)

---

[a]This is narrated out of its place before the tribute of Babylon and the Hittites.

[b]This is the Euphrates; see also note on pursuit, ll. 18, 19.

[c]See Amenemhab, § 583, ll. 8, 9.

[d]The king of Mitanni.

―――― he [⌈pursu⌉]ed after them an iter (*ytr*)[a] of sailing; not one looked [19]behind him, but (they) fled, [b]forsooth,[b] like a ⌈herd⌉ of mountain goats; yea, the horses fled ――――.

The Booty

480. [⌈List of the booty taken⌉] among the whole army, consisting of: princes, 3; [20]their wives, 30; men taken, 80; 606 slaves, male and female, with their children; those who surrendered (and) their wives, ―――― (he) harvested their grain.

Arrival at Niy

481. His majesty arrived at the city [21]of Niy (*Nyy*), going southward, when his majesty returned, having set up his tablet in Naharin (*N-h-ry-n ʾ*),[c] extending the boundaries of Egypt.[d] ――――.

Tribute of Naharin

482. [List] of the tribute brought to his majesty by the chiefs of this country: [22]513 slaves, male and female; 260 horses; gold, 45 deben, ¼ kidet;[e] silver vessels of the workmanship of Zahi (*Ḏ ʾ-hy*) ―――― [chariots] with all their weapons of war; 28 oxen, [23]calves, and bullocks; 564 bulls; 5,323 small cattle; incense, 828 (*mn-*) jars; sweet oil and [green oil] ―――― every pleasing [thing] of this country; all fruits in quantity.

―――――――

[a]In view of the parallel passage in the Semneh stela of Amenhotep III, where the words, "*ytr of sailing*," are followed by a numeral, the word must be the linear measure, *ytr*, and not the word *ytr*, "*river*." Hence the rendering of Müller (*Asien und Europa*, 254): "er (überschritt) den Fluss des Rundfahrens (?)" must be given up. There is no statement of a crossing of the Euphrates here, but that Thutmose III really crossed this river is stated on his Constantinople obelisk (Lepsius, *Denkmäler*, III, 60, W,): "*Thutmose (III) who crossed the Great Bend of Naharin (N-h-r-n) with might and with victory at the head of his army*" (§ 631). That this crossing of the river was on this campaign is not to be doubted, and the second tablet of l. 17 was therefore set up on the "*east*" of the Euphrates. A further striking corroboration of the crossing is in the "Hymn of Victory" (§ 656, ll. 7, 8).

[b]A rare New Egyptian particle, *m-dwn*; cf. Erman, *Neuägyptische Grammatik* (§ 94, 2).

[c]As above narrated.

[d]The remainder of the campaign must have been very brief, as it occupied only the lacuna (about one-third of the line).

[e]Nearly eleven pounds, troy.

The Harbors

483. Behold, ²⁴these harbors were supplied with everything according to their dues, according to their contract of each year, together with the impost of Lebanon[a] (R ᵓ-mn-n) according to their contract of each year with the chiefs of Lebanon (R ᵓ-mn-n) ———— 2 unknown ⌈birds⌉; 4 wild fowl ²⁵of this country, which ⌈—⌉ every day.

Tribute of Babylon

484. The tribute of the chief of Shinar (S ᵓ-n-g-r ᵓ);[b] real lapis lazuli, 4(+x) deben; artificial lapis lazuli, 24 deben; lapis lazuli of Babylon (B-b-r ᵓ) ———— of real lapis lazuli; a ram's head[c] of real lapis lazuli; ²⁶15 kidet; and vessels ————.

Tribute of the Hittites

485. The tribute of Kheta ($Ḫ$-t ᵓ) the Great, in this year: 8 silver rings, making 401 deben;[d] of white precious stone, a great block; (t ᵓ-gw-) wood ———— ⌈returning⌉ to Egypt, at his coming from ²⁷Naharin (N-h-ry-n ᵓ), extending the boundaries of Egypt.

Products of Punt

486. Marvels brought to his majesty in[e] the land of Punt in this year: dried myrrh, 1,685 heket;[f] gold ———— gold, 155 deben, 2 kidet; 134 slaves, male and female; 114 oxen, ²⁸and calves; 305 bulls; total, 419 cattle; beside vessels laden with ivory, ebony, (skins) of the panther; every good thing of [this] country ————.

---

[a]The harbors lying at the foot of the Lebanon along the Phœnician coast would naturally be supplied by the Lebanon princes. It is to be noted that these supplies were collected as "*impost*" (not "*tribute*"), and probably by an Egyptian officer, as was the "*impost*" of Nubia.

[b]Identified long ago by Brugsch (*Gr. Oase*, 91) with the biblical Shinar ($Šn$ ᶜ r), an identification which was overlooked in favor of Meyer's identification with Singara. Meyer (*Aegyptiaca*, 63) now sees in S ᵓ-n-g-r ᵓ the Sanhar of the Amarna letters (*Amarna Letters*, ed. Winckler, 25, 49), which also leads him to recognize Shinar in both, although Brugsch's identification of S ᵓ-n-g-r ᵓ with Shinar seems not to have been noticed.

[c]Text really has "*face*," but the wall paintings show complete heads in such cases.

[d]97.74 pounds.

[e]Or possibly "*from*" (hr); it is noticeable that in the year 38 (§ 513) the preposition is m, "*from*." Hence perhaps an expedition here; but see § 616, l. 9.

[f]About 223⅞ bushels.

Impost of Wawat

487. [Impost of Wawat]: ———— 13 male [negro] slaves; total, 20;[a] 44 oxen and calves; ²⁹60 bulls; total, 104; beside vessels laden with every good thing of this country; the harvest of this place likewise.

X. NINTH CAMPAIGN (YEAR 34)[b]

488. The king confines himself this year to little more than a voyage of inspection to Zahi, receiving the surrender of submissive towns, and the tribute of Retenu, and Cyprus. The harbors are stocked with supplies as usual, including a fleet of foreign vessels laden with timber.

The annual impost of Kush and Wawat is recorded as usual.

489. YEAR 34. Behold, his majesty was in the land of Zahi (D°-hy).

Surrender of Zahi Towns

490. ———— he surrendered fully to his majesty with ⌜fear⌝. List of ³⁰the towns captured in this year: 2 towns, (and) a town which surrendered in the district of Nuges ($^{\circ}n$-yw-g-s°); total, 3. Captives brought to his majesty ———— taken captive 90, those who surrendered, their wives ³¹and their children ————;[c] 40 horses; 15 chariots, wrought with silver and gold; golden vessels and gold in rings, 50[d] deben, 8 kidet;[d] ⌜silver⌝ vessels of this country and rings, 153 deben;[e] copper ————;[f] 326 heifers; 40 white goats; 50 small goats; 70 asses; a quantity of (t°-gw-) wood; ³²⌜many⌝[g] chairs of black wood (and) carob wood; together with 6 tent-poles, wrought with bronze and set with costly stones; together with every fine wood of this country.

---

[a]Seven other persons therefore were mentioned in the lacuna.

[b]Lepsius, *Auswahl der wichtigsten Urkunden*, XII, 29–37; Mariette, *Karnak*, 13, ll. 29–35 = Brugsch, *Thesaurus*, 1175–77, ll. 29–27 = Bissing, *Statistische Tafel*, ll. 29–37.

[c]Only the number is lost; von Bissing gives no lacuna.

[d]About twelve and one-quarter pounds, troy.

[e]About thirty-seven and three-tenths pounds.

[f]The fragment marked ll. 55–62 (in Lepsius, *Auswahl der wichtigsten Urkunden*, XII) nearly fills out completely the gap between Lepsius' text and Mariette's (see Mariette, *Karnak*, 13).

[g]Possibly "*many*" belongs here, which might then give "*many tree-trunks*."

Tribute of Retenu

491. Tribute of the chiefs of Retenu in this year: —[a] horses; 31 (+x) [chariots,] wrought with silver and gold, and painted; 70[⌐+3⌐] slaves, male and female; gold, 55 deben, 8 kidet; various silver vessels ³³of the workmanship of the country, — deben, 6 kidet; gold and silver; (mnw-) stone; vessels of every costly stone; native copper, 80 blocks; lead, 11 blocks; colors, 100 deben; dry myrrh, ⌐feldspar⌐; green ⌐stone⌐ ⌐—⌐ — 13 oxen and calves; 530 bulls; 84 asses; bronze —; a quantity of wood; numerous vessels of copper; incense, 693 (mn-) jars; ³⁴sweet oil and green oil, 2,080 (mn-) jars; wine, 608 (mn-) jars; 3[b] chariots of ($t^{\jmath}$-gw-) wood, carob wood, ⌐logs⌐ of every wood of this country.

The Harbors Supplied

492. Behold, all the harbors of his majesty were supplied with every good thing of that ⌐which⌐ [his] majesty received [in] Zahi ($\underline{D}^{\jmath}$-hy), consisting of Keftyew ships, Byblos ships, and Sektu (Sk-tw) ships[c] of cedar laden with poles, and masts, together ³⁵with great trees for the ⌐—⌐[d] of his majesty.

Tribute of Cyprus

493. Tribute of the chief of Isy (Ysy) in [this year]: 108 blocks of pure copper (or) 2,040 deben;[e] 5(+x) blocks of lead; 1,200 ⌐pigs⌐[f] of lead; lapis lazuli, 110 deben; ivory, 1 tusk; 2 staves of — wood.

Impost of Kush

494. Impost of Kush the wretched: gold, 300 (+x) deben; 60 negroes;[g] the son[h] of the chief of Irem (Yrm) [i]— — ³⁶total, 64; oxen,

---

[a]Only the number is lacking.

[b]The three strokes may, of course, be the plural strokes.

[c]W. M. Müller (Asien und Europa, 339) inserts a lacuna between the initial S of this word and the end; but a glance at the neighboring lines (Lepsius, Auswahl der wichtigsten Urkunden, XII; and Mariette, Karnak, 13), especially 56 (=32), will show that there is room for only the sk-sign in the lacuna. The place is unknown. See also Bissing, Statistische Tafel, l. 34.

[d]Some construction of wood.   [f]Nws; see Papyrus Harris, passim.

[e]About 408 pounds.   [g]Persons of some sort.

[h]Maspero has daughter (Struggle of the Nations, 267; so also Petrie, History of Egypt, II, 118).

[i]Three persons must have been mentioned in this lacuna; but Bissing, Statistische Tafel, has no lacuna.

[95; calves,] 180; total, 275; besides [vessels] laden with ivory, ebony and all products of this country; the harvest of Kush likewise.

Impost of Wawat

495. The [impost] of Wawat; gold, 254[a] deben; 10 negro slaves, male and female; — oxen, and calves [besides vessels laden with] ³⁷every good thing of [this country].

XI. TENTH CAMPAIGN (YEAR 35)[b]

496. It was now the second year since the invasion of Naharin, and the kings of that region had revolted. Thutmose marched thither from the Phœnician coast, defeated the rebels who had united under some prince who is called the "*foe of Naharin.*" This may have been the king of Aleppo. The allies were defeated in a battle at Araina, possibly in the land of Tikhsi, as mentioned by Amenemhab (§ 587, l. 19), and Thutmose took great spoil. The tribute of the Syrian princes is not mentioned; it was doubtless paid as usual; the impost of Kush and Wawat are noted.

497. YEAR 35. Behold, his majesty was in the land of Zahi ($Ḏ\,{}^{\supset}\text{-}hy$) on the tenth victorious expedition.

Revolt in Naharin

498. When his majesty arrived at the city of Araina (${}^{\supset}\text{-}r\,{}^{\supset}\text{-}y\,{}^{\supset}\text{-}n\,{}^{\supset}$),[c] behold, that wretched foe [of Nahar]in ([$N\text{-}h\text{-}r$]$y\text{-}n\,{}^{\supset}$) had collected horses and people; [his] majesty — — — — ³⁸of the ends[d] of the earth. They were numerous — — they were about to fight with his majesty.

---

[a]The numeral may have contained more hundreds; as it is, it amounts to 61.91 pounds.

[b]Lepsius, *Auswahl der wichtigsten Urkunden*, XII, ll. 37–41; *Denkmäler*, III, 31, *a*, ll. 1–3 = Brugsch, *Thesaurus*, 1177–79, ll. 37–44, and l. 2 = Bissing, *Statistische Tafel*, ll. 37–44.

[c]Not Aruna, as sometimes supposed; it is an unidentified city, but was perhaps situated in the land of Tikhsi, where Amenemhab (§ 587) mentions a battle.

[d]Lit., "*hinder parts;*" see Thutmose III's "Hymn of Victory" (§ 661, l. 20).

Battle in Naharin

499. Then his majesty advanced [to fight][a] with them; then the army of his majesty furnished an example of attack,[b] in the matter[c] of seizing and taking.[b] Then his majesty prevailed against [these] barbarians by the souls of [his] f[ather] A[mon] ——— ³⁹of Naharin (*N-h-r-n*ᵓ). They fled headlong, falling one over another, before his majesty.

Booty of the King

500. List of booty which his majesty himself brought away from these barbarians of Naharin (*N-h-ry-n*ᵓ·): ——— 2 [⌈suits of⌉] armor; bronze —[d] deben —

Booty of the Army

501. List of booty which the army of his majesty brought away from [these foreigner]s: 10 living prisoners; 180 horses; 60 chariots; ——— ⁴¹——— 13 inlaid corselets; 13 bronze ⌈suits⌉ of armor —; 5 bronze helmets for the head; 5 bows of Kharu (Palestine); captures made in other [⌈countries⌉] ——— ᵉ⁴²——— ᶠ 226 —; a chariot, wrought with gold; 20(+x) chariots, wrought with gold and silver, ——— together with ——— ⁴³——— 21 (*mn*-) jars ———; sweet oil, 954[+x] (*mn*-) jars ——— ⁴⁴——— work of ———.[g]
ʰ¹——— gold ——— ²⌈rings⌉, bracelets, (*ybht·y*-) stone, eye cosmetic — wild goats, fire wood.

Impost of Kush

502. Impost of the wretched Kush: gold, 70 deben, 1 kidet; slaves, male and female, — — — — — oxen, calves, ——— [besides vessels

---

[a]This seems to have been omitted here. Cf. the Megiddo battle (l. 1, § 429).
[b]Piehl suggests: "pendant une suspension du pillage" (*Sphinx*, II, 109).
[c]*Ḥn* as in *ḥn-n-mdw·t*.
[d]Numeral lost.
[e]The block containing the tops of ll. 42–54 in Lepsius, *Auswahl der wichtigsten Urkunden*, XII, should be pushed to the left at least the width of three lines. This is evident from the text in Lepsius, *Denkmäler*, III, 31, *a*, and Brugsch, *Thesaurus*, 1178–84, with which we begin a new numbering of the above block.
[f]After the transfer of above block as above noted, the tops of ll. 42–44 are of course wanting.
[g]Probably several lines are wanting here.
[h]Numbered according to Lepsius, *Denkmäler*, III, 31, *a*.

laden] ³with ebony, ivory, all the good products of this country, together with the harvest of [Kush, likewise].ᵃ

Impost of Wawat

503. [Impost of Wawat] ———— 34 negro slaves, male and female; 94 oxen, calves, and bulls; besides ships laden with every good thing; the harvest of Wawat, [likewise].

XII. ELEVENTH CAMPAIGN (YEAR 36)

504. Lost.

XIII. TWELFTH CAMPAIGN (YEAR 37)

505. Lost.

XIV. THIRTEENTH CAMPAIGN (YEAR 38)ᵇ

506. The king directs his attention to the southern Lebanon region of Nuges again, where he is obliged to subjugate the local princes, who controlled the road northward between the two Lebanons at the seaward bend of the Litâny River. The regular Syrian tribute and the supplying of the harbors are mentioned, as usual; followed for the first time by the tribute of Cyprus and Arrapachitis, later known as an Assyrian province. The products of Punt are then followed by the usual impost of Kush and Wawat.

507. [YEAR 38. Behold, his majesty was in ————] ⁴on the thirteenth victorious expedition. Behold, his majesty was overthrowing ————ᶜ [in] the district of Nuges (ʾ n-yw-g-s ʾ).

Booty of Nuges District

508. List of booty which the army of his majesty brought away from the district of Nuges: 50 living captives; — horses; — 3 chariots; — — — with [their weapons] ⁵of war; — people who surrendered of the region of Nuges — — — —.

ᵃBrugsch's restoration (*Thesaurus*, 1179) to Wawat is an error, as the harvest of Wawat is mentioned in the next paragraph.

ᵇLepsius, *Denkmäler*, III, 31, a, ll. 3–10 = Brugsch, *Thesaurus*, 1178–81, ll. 2–9.

ᶜNearly one-quarter line lacking.

Syrian Tribute

509. Tribute which was brought to the fame of his majesty in this year: 328 horses; 522 slaves, male and female; 9 chariots, wrought with silver and gold; 61 painted (chariots); total, 70; a necklace of real lapis lazuli —————— a (two-handled ʾ-k ʾ-n ʾ-) — vase; 3 flat dishes; heads[a] of goats, head of a lion, vessels of all the work of Zahi ———— copper, 2,821 [deben], 3½ kidet; of crude copper, 276 blocks; lead, 26 blocks; incense, 656 (hbn· t)-jars; sweet oil and green oil, (sf· t-) oil, 1,752 (mn-) jars; wine, 156 (jars);[b] 12 oxen; ——— 46 asses; 5 heads of [7]tooth ivory; tables of ivory (and) of carob wood; white (mnw-) stone, 68 deben ————— bronze spears, shields, bows, — all weapons of war; sweet wood of this country, all the good product(s) of this country.

The Harbors Supplied

510. Behold, every harbor was supplied with every good thing according to their agreement of each year, in going [northward or][c] southward; the impost of Lebanon (R ʾ-mn-n)[d] [8]likewise; the harvest of Zahi, consisting of clean grain, green oil, incense, [win]e.

Tribute of Cyprus

511. Tribute of the prince of Isy (Ysy): crude copper —; horses.[e]

Tribute of Arrapachitis

512. Tribute of the country of Arrapachitis (ʾ-r ʾ-rḫ)[f] in this year: slaves, male and female; crude copper, 2 blocks; carob trees, 65 logs; and all sweet woods of his country.

Product of Punt

513. [Marvels] brought[g] to the fame of his majesty from Punt: [9]dried myrrh, 240 heket.

---

[a]The word hnn (written out phonetically at end of l. 6) means "*head*," not "*face*," as the graphic writing might indicate.

[b]Text has omitted the word.

[c]Restored from l. 13, fourteenth expedition.

[d]From which the harbors were supplied.   [e]Lit., "*spans*."

[f]Probably ʾ-r ʾ-r-p-ḫ = Arrapachitis, is meant. See Müller, *Asien und Europa*, 279.

[g]In the year 33 the gifts of Punt are introduced by the words: "*Marvels brought to his majesty, etc.*, (see § 486); hence restoration. There is no expedition this time, as the preposition is "*from*," not "*in*," as in § 486.

Impost of Kush

514. Impost of the wretched Kush: gold, 100 [+x]^a deben, 6 kidet; 36 negro slaves, male and female; 111 oxen, and calves; 185 bulls; total, 306 (sic!),^{b} besides vessels laden with ivory, ebony, all the good products of this country, together with the harvest of this country.

Impost of Wawat

515. Impost of Wawat: [gold], 2,844 [deben, — kidet]; 16 negro slaves, male and female; ^{10}77 oxen and calves; besides [vessels] laden with every good product of this country.

XV. FOURTEENTH CAMPAIGN (YEAR 39)^c

516. This campaign was introduced by an excursion to punish the raiding Bedwin on the northeastern frontier of Egypt, also referred to by Amenemhab (§ 580), after which the king proceeded northward, to receive the usual Syrian tribute and ensure supplies for the harbors.

Defeat of Shasu

517. YEAR 39. Behold, his majesty was in the land of Retenu on the fourteenth victorious expedition, after [his] going [to defeat] the fallen ones of Shasu ($\check{S}$ $^{\circ}$-sw).

Syrian Tribute

518. List of [the tribute of] — — — — 197 slaves, male and female; ^{11}229 horses; 2 flat dishes of gold; together with rings (of gold), 12 deben, 1 kidet; — real lapis lazuli, 30 deben; a flat dish of silver; a (two-handled) vase ($^{\circ}$-k $^{\circ}$-n $^{\circ}$) of silver; a vessel with the head of an ox; 325 various vessels (of silver): together with silver in rings, making 1,495 deben, 1 kidet;^{d} a chariot ——— made [with] ^{12}white costly stone, white (mnw-) stone; natron, (mnw-) stone, all the various costly stones of [this] country; incense, sweet oil, green oil, ($sf \cdot t$-) oil, honey 264^e [+x jars]; wine, 1,405 (mn-) jars; 84 bulls; 1,183 small cattle;^{f}

---

^{a}There is room for several hundreds more.
^{b}The total should be 296, the scribe has made an error of 10.
^{c}Lepsius, *Denkmäler*, 31, a, ll. 10–14 = Brugsch, *Thesaurus*, 1181, 1182, ll. 9–13.
^{d}364.43 pounds. ^{e}The hundreds may be increased indefinitely.
^{f}So Lepsius; Brugsch, 1193.

bronze ———;ᵃ ¹³the pleasant — and the perfume of this country, together with all good products of this country.

The Harbors Supplied

519. Behold, every harbor was supplied with every good thing according to their agreement of each [year];ᵇ in going northward [or sou]th[ward]ᶜ — — likewise; the harvest of [Lebanon]ᵈ ———ᵃ [the harvest] ¹⁴of Zahi, consisting of clean grain, incense, oil, — w[ine] ———.ᵉ

XVI. FIFTEENTH CAMPAIGN ᶠ

520. The fragments of the wall at this place show only the tribute-list of Cyprus and the impost of Kush and Wawat.

¹[YEAR 40] ———.ᵍ

Tribute of Cyprus

521. [Tribute of the chief] of Isy (*Ysy*): ivory, 2 tusks; copper, 40 bricks; lead, 1 brick.

ᵃNearly half a line is wanting.

ᵇThe scribe has omitted the word "*year;*" restored from l. 7, p. 210.

ᶜRestored from l. 7, thirteenth expedition.

ᵈLebanon and Zahi are regularly mentioned together in connection with the harbors. .

ᵉAll the rest (about nine-tenths) of the line is wanting; it is the last line on the north wall, and the inscription here turns to the left, to follow the west wall (the back of Pylon VI) southward to the door. It doubtless concluded with the impost of Kush and Wawat, which could not have occupied more than the rest of this line.

ᶠThe Annals are now continued on the back of Pylon VI. The visitor on the spot will notice that only the lower third (or less) of these twenty vertical lines on the pylon (north of door) is preserved; hence the first date is lost, and unfortunately also all the others on this wall section. The text in Lepsius, *Denkmäler*, III, 30, *a* =Brugsch, *Thesaurus*, V, 1182–85. The fragment certainly contains data from three different expeditions; it must remain somewhat uncertain whether the first of the three is the conclusion of the fourteenth expedition in year 39 or part of a fifteenth in year 40. It seems probable that the long lacuna (nearly the whole l. 1, west wall) contains the conclusion of the fourteenth expedition, which must otherwise have occupied more space than either of the campaigns before or after it. Line 1 of the west wall, therefore, begins the fifteenth expedition. Müller (*Asien und Europa*, 54) sees difficulties in this arrangement, which are not apparent to me. See further notes on text.

ᵍContained the tribute of some unknown country, probably Retenu; the restored date is almost certain.

Impost of Kush

522. Tribute of ²⸺.ᵃ [Impost of the wretched Kush in] this year: gold, 144 deben, 3 kidet; 101 negro slaves, male and female; oxen ³⸺.ᵇ

Impost of Wawat

523. [Impost of Wawat]: ⸺ 35 calves; 54 bulls; total, 89; besides vessels laden ⁴[with ebony, ivory, and all the good products of this countryᶜ] ⸺.ᵇ

XVII. SIXTEENTH CAMPAIGN

524. The record contains only tribute-lists.

[YEAR 41.ᵈ Tribute of] ⸺ 2ᵉ rings.

Tribute of Retenu

525. List of the tribute of the chiefs of Retenu, brought to the fame of his majesty in ⁵[this year]ᶠ ⸺ 40[+x] blocks ⸺ a sword of ⸢flint⸣, bronze spears — ⁶⸺.ᵇ

[Tribute of — in] this [yea]r: ivory, 18ᵍ tusks; carob wood, 242 logs; 184 large cattle; — small cattle ⁷⸺ᵇ ʰincense likewise.

Tribute of the Hittites

Tribute of the chief of Kheta ($\underline{H}$-t ?) the Great, in this year: gold — ⁸⸺.

ᵃContained the tribute of some unknown country followed by the impost of Kush, for *"tribute of"* at end of l. 1 cannot refer to Kush, for which $bk\cdot w$, *"impost,"* is always used. Kush is certain from the negroes in the list.

ᵇSee note f, p. 212.

ᶜAt least this is the usual continuation. Possibly, the tribute of some other country intervenes in the following lacuna.

ᵈAs the impost of Kush and Wawat usually concludes the year's list, it is evident that we should begin another year at this point, as usual, with Retenu; probably year 41.

ᵉSo Lepsius; Brugsch has *"second time."*

ᶠBrugsch's restoration, *"this land,"* is not according to the parallels.

ᵍSo Lepsius; Brugsch, 26.

ʰProbably the tribute of another country, also, is lost in the lacuna.

Impost of Kush

526. [Impost of Kush[a] the wretched in this year; gold, $x+$] 94[b] deben, 2 kidet; 8 negro slaves, male and female; 13 male (negroes), brought for following;[c] total, 21; oxen, 9⸺.[d]

Impost of Wawat

527. [Impost of Wawat]:[e] gold, 3,144[f] deben, 3 kidet; 35 oxen and calves; 79 bulls; total, 114; besides vessels laden with ivory 10⸺.[d]

XVIII. SEVENTEENTH CAMPAIGN[g]

528. The last campaign, which happened not later than the year 42, shows the old king, now probably over seventy years of age, suppressing a revolt of Tunip and Kadesh, who are supported by auxiliaries from Naharin. He marched from the northern coast of Syria, after capturing the coast city of Erkatu,[h] directly against Tunip. Having subjugated it, he then marched up the Orontes against his old enemy, Kadesh, whose prince led the allied forces, which Thutmose III had routed at Megiddo on the first campaign, nearly twenty years before. There was a stubborn defense, but, according to the narrative of Amenemhab, the walls of the city were breached, and it was taken by storm (§ 590). From it and surrounding towns great plunder was secured, among which were the Naharin auxiliaries and their horses.

---

[a]Restored from the character of the tribute.

[b]Lepsius, 83. Brugsch, 86; the photograph indicates 94 as probable.

[c]As *pedesequii*.   [e]Restored after § 539.

[d]See note f, p. 212.   [f]766.35 pounds.

[g]Lepsius, *Denkmäler*, III, 30, *u*, ll. 10–20 = Brugsch, *Thesaurus*, 1183–85, ll. 10–20.

[h]Erkatu (⸺*r-k*ꜣ-*tw*) must have been on the coast somewhere between the mouth of the Orontes and the Nahr el-Kebir. As it is the same as Irkata of the *Amarna Letters* (see § 529, note), it was not far from Simyra. Thutmose may have landed at Simyra, as he had evidently often done before, and hence he marched upon the "*coast road*" against Erkatu.

Long tribute-lists, the harbor supplies, and the impost of Kush and Wawat conclude the Annals.

Overthrow of Erkatu

529. [YEAR 42.]ᵃ ———— the Fenkhu ([F]nḥ·w). Behold,ᵇ his majesty was upon the coast road, in order to overthrow the city of Erkatuᶜ (ᶜr-ḳ ⸗-tw) and the cities of ¹¹ᵈ———— Kana (K ⸗-n ⸗) ————; this city was overthrown, together with its districts.

Overthrow of Tunip

530. (His majesty) arrived at Tunip (Tw-npᵉ), overthrew that city, harvested its grain, and cut down its groves ¹²———— the citizens of the army.

Overthrow of Cities of Kadesh District

531. Behold, (he) came in safety, arrived at the district of Kadesh (Ḳd-šw),ᶠ captured the citiesᵍ therein.

Booty of Kadesh District

532. List of the booty brought from there — ¹³————ᵈ of the wretched Naharin (N-h-ry-n ⸗) who were as auxiliaries among them,

---

ᵃHere a new year should begin for the same reason as in l. 4; see note. That its number should be 42 is clear from the date in the last line of this section; see note, § 540.

ᵇRead yst instead of "Amon," incorrectly restored by Harmhab.

ᶜThis important name is given by Lepsius as ᶜr-ḳ ⸗-n-tw, inserting an n before tw; in this he is followed by Brugsch, who evidently published (*Thesaurus*, V, 1183) an old copy of his made from Lepsius; for the original (in the photograph) shows no trace of n and no room for it. The signs are perfectly preserved, and the feet of the eagle in ḳ ⸗ practically touch the head of the w-bird in tw, leaving absolutely no room for n in the vertical column between ḳ ⸗ and tw. Neither is there any trace on the back of the eagle of n (horizontal). This makes the identity of our word, with Irkata of the *Amarna Letters* a certainty. See also Eduard Meyer, *Festschrift für Georg Ebers*, 69, n. 2; and compare above § 528, note.

ᵈSee note f, p. 212.

ᵉTo strike Tunip on turning inland, Erkatu must have been well to the north of Arvad, unless, of course, Thutmose's northward march is lost in the lacuna.

ᶠHe is therefore marching up the Orontes.

ᵍIncluding, of course, Kadesh itself.

together with their horses; 691 people;[a] 29 hands;[b] 44 horses;[c] 14————.[d]

Tribute of Unknown Coun.ry

533. [List of the tribute of —] in this year: 295 slaves, male and female;[e] 68 horses; 3 golden flat dishes;[f] 3 silver flat dishes;[f] (two-handled ⸢-k⸢-n⸢-) vases, 3;[f] ⸢sparkling⸣ stones,[g] together with silver 15————.[d]

Tribute of Tunip?

534. [List of the tribute (or booty) of ⸢Tunip⸣[h]]: ———— lead, 47 bricks; lead, 1,100 deben; colors, ⸢emery⸣, all beautiful costly stones of this country; bronze ⸢suits⸣ of armor; weapons of war 16————[i] [all the] pleasant [things] of this country.

The Harbors Supplied

535. Behold, every harbor was supplied with every good thing according to their agreement of each year; the harvest of this country 17[likewise] ————.[d]

Tribute of Unknown Country

536. [The tribute of —] ———— together with flat dishes, heads of bulls,[j] making 341 deben, 2 kidet; genuine lapis lazuli, 1 block, making 33[k] kidet, a fine (t⸢-gw-) wood staff, native copper 18————.

---

[a]So Lepsius; Brugsch, 690; photograph, 691.
[b]Of the slain, as usual.
[c]So Lepsius; Brugsch, 48; photo shows room for a much larger number.
[d]See note f, p. 212.
[e]So Lepsius; Brugsch, 195.
[f]It is possible that these are simply plurals without numerals.
[g]Same word ($wḏḥ$) in § 473, l. 15, *q. v.* and note.
[h]Above (l. 12) some captives were taken from Tunip, but the spoil of Tunip is perhaps not yet enumerated. Among the following list the rare emery occurs, which is found in the spoil taken from the Tunip auxiliaries in the unknown city of "Wa————" (year 29, § 461); hence this list may here belong to Tunip.
[i] Possibly another nation has been introduced in the lacuna; see note f, p. 212.
[j]Meaning that the bulls' heads were a decoration upon the vessels, as depicted in the reliefs.
[k]Lepsius, 41; Brugsch, 33; he is sustained by the photograph.

Tribute of Tinay

537. [The tribute of the chief] of Tinay (Ty-n ᵓ-y):[a] a silver ($š$ ᵓ-w ᵓ-b-ty)[b] vessel of the work of Keftyew (Kf-tyw), together with vessels of iron,[c] 4 hands of silver, making 56 deben, 1 kidet; ———.

Impost of Kush

538. [The impost of the wretched Kush in this year]: ———
[besides vessels laden] with every good thing of this country; the harvest of the wretched Kush, likewise.

Impost of Wawat

539. The impost of Wawat[d] in this year: gold, 2,374 deben,[e] 1 kidet, ²⁰———[f] [the harvest of Wa]wat.

XIX. CONCLUSION

540. Behold, his majesty commanded to record the victories which he won from the year 23[g] until the year 42, when this inscription was recorded upon this sanctuary;[h] that he might be given life forever.

---

[a]So Lepsius; Brugsch, Ty-n-my.

[b]See Bissing, *Zeitschrift für ägyptische Sprache*, 34, 166, who identifies this vessel with the suibdu (of stone) mentioned in an Amarna letter (Winckler, *Amarna Letters*, 393, 1. 61).

[c]By ᵓ.   [e]Over 578 pounds.

[d]One *wa* has been omitted in Lepsius' text.   [f]See note f, p. 212.

[g]Of course, 22 or 23 is to be read, the reading is based on: (1) our knowledge of the date when the campaigns began; (2) the fact that 22 is clear and there is only room in the possible lacuna for one unit more; (3) the fact that the list of offerings from the Asiatic wars (§§ 541 ff.) also begins in the year 23. This date, as well as the terminal date "*year 42*" (for which both Lepsius and Brugsch give 32), has been the subject of much discussion. The following remarks of Mariette in a letter to de Rougé which have been mostly overlooked, should settle the question (*Revue archéologique*, 1860², N. S., I, 32):

"La première de ces deux dates, à la vérité, est un peu détruite; mais la planche de M. Lepsius rapporte fidèlement l'arrangement des chiffres, et vous voyez qu'il n'y a place là que pour l'an 22, ou l'an 23; ...... Quant à la date donnée pour la dernière de ces campagnes, elle est celle de la quarante-deuxième année du règne de Thouthmès. Comme cela arrive fréquemment pour les textes gravés en relief très-mince sur le grès, l'un des chiffres *dix* a presque disparu par une sorte de dissolution spontanée de la pierre et il est évident que si M. Lepsius a fait sa publication sur un estampage, il a dû lire 32. Mais le chiffre qui tend à s'effacer est encore parfaitement clair, et c'est sans contredit l'an 42 qu'il faut voir, ..." These statements are confirmed by the photograph, although the space for the fourth ten (in 42) is absolutely smooth.

[h]Sh-ntr, with masculine demonstrative.

FEASTS AND OFFERINGS FROM THE CONQUESTS[a]

541. In this inscription Thutmose III records the new feasts and additional offerings which he established during the period of his splendid conquests in Asia. The record, therefore, begins with his return from the first campaign in the year 23, and continues till the year 42, when his campaigning ceased.[b] In order to connect the record with the occurrence of the first campaign, it goes back to the march to Lebanon after the fall of Megiddo, refers to a fortress which he built there, and proceeds then to his return and landing at Thebes. All this leads up to the establishment of three great "Feasts of Victory," for which it furnishes the motive. After fixing the calendar of these three feasts, with the lists of oblations to be offered at their celebration, the king proceeds to the gifts which he made to Amon at the feast of his voyage to southern Opet, which are exceedingly rich and numerous, including the three cities just captured in the Lebanon, fields and gardens, slaves, precious metals and stones, and the doubling of some of the old offerings (ll. 5–14). It would seem as if this feast was the first celebrated by the king after his return from the first campaign, for it is among its gifts that the acquisitions of that campaign appear.

---

[a]Wall inscription in the Karnak temple on the back of the south half of Pylon VI (Baedeker, plan opp. p. 239). It therefore by its position (as well as by its content) shows that it is really a continuation of the Annals, which are concluded at the door on the back of the north half of the same pylon. It is in vertical lines, and as a considerable amount of the pylon is lost at the top clear across, the tops of all the lines are lacking. Published by Lepsius, (*Denkmäler*, III, 30, b) and Brugsch (*Recueil des monuments*, I, 43, 44; last five lines omitted). Lepsius offers a more accurate text, but not so full in indistinct places. I collated the Berlin squeeze for the important historical portion (ll. 1–6) and a photograph by Borchardt for the whole.

[b]The date of the beginning is clearly shown in several places; that of the end by the list of Asiatic and Nubian slaves, which continues "*till the recording of this tablet,*" which is stated at the end of the Annals (§ 540) to be "*year 42.*"

542. The other offerings due to Amon, now richly increased, are then successively enumerated (ll. 14–25), and the long inscription closes with the king's exhortation to the priests, like that to the priests of Abydos (§§ 97 ff.) to be true to their duties and to offer the mortuary oblations due him, a list of which follows.

543. A splendid array of these gifts is depicted in a wall relief[a] in the corridor of the Annals. Chief among them are the two Karnak obelisks, one of which is now at Constantinople (§§ 629 ff.),[b] and two pairs of flagstaves for the temple façade, of course of cedar, tipped with electrum. But the relief shows the widest range of temple furniture: chests, a varied array of exquisite vessels; altars, and temple doors; besides ornaments for the divine statue, chiefly elaborate necklaces; the whole series being of gold, silver, bronze, and costly stones, especially lapis lazuli. The vessels bear the general inscription:

Very numerous; from the yearly dues (*ḥtr*).

544. The purpose of the gifts is indicated by such accompanying inscriptions as the following:

Over a jar:

(Of) alabaster; filled with pure ointment of the divine things.

By rich necklaces:

Ornaments of the "Appearance Festival;"[c] amulets upon the divine limbs.

---

[a]On the south wall of the passage south of the sanctuary; published by Champollion, *Monuments*, IV, 316, 317; partially by Rosellini, *Monumenti*, Text, III, 1, plate opp. p. 125; and Rosellini, *Monumenti Civili*, 57; partially by Burton, *Excerpta hieroglyphica*, 29; and Brugsch, *Thesaurus*, V, 1185 ff.; and see Birch, *Archæologia*, XXXV, 155.

[b]In the relief, this obelisk bears the complete dedication, of which only the first half is preserved on the original in Constantinople. See Breasted, *Zeitschrift für ägyptische Sprache*, 39, 55 ff., and *infra*, § 630, where the entire dedication will be found.

[c]When the god appears in procession.

545. The source of the gifts also appears thus:

Over armlet, necklace, etc.:

(Of) gold, and much costly stone; ornaments of his majesty.

Over a vase:

(Of) costly stone, which his majesty made according to the design of his own heart.[a]

546. Before these gifts, on the right, Amon sits enthroned, receiving them from Thutmose III on the left, before whom are the words:

Presentation of monuments by the king — — —, that he may be given life like Re, forever.[b]

547. It is clear from this and the following document that the beginning of Thutmose III's conquests in Asia marks a sudden and profound change in the cultus of Amon, occasioned by the enormous and entirely disproportionate wealth which from now on is poured into his treasury. We see here the beginning of that power and wealth to which the most remarkable witness is the Papyrus Harris (IV, 182–412).

Fortress in Lebanon

548. [1]——— in the land of Retenu ($R\underline{t}nw$) as a fortress which his[c] majesty built in his victories[d] among the chiefs of Lebanon (R-mn-n), the name of which is: "Menkheperre (Thutmose III)-is-the-Binder-of-the-Barbarians."

---

[a]The making of these vessels is depicted in the tomb of Menkheperreseneb, accompanied by the same remark (§ 775), showing that they were really designed by Thutmose III himself, and that the fact was thought worthy of remark there as well as here. He says the same thing in § 164, l. 43.

[b]There are other such short inscriptions of a single word or more, but they are as yet inadequately published. One is of especial interest. Over an offering-table made of four $ḥtp$-signs, precisely like the great alabaster altar recently found at Abusir, are the words: "(Of) ⌈shining⌉ alabaster of Hatnub."

[c]The text has "*my*."

[d]These victories in the Lebanon must have been won on first the expedition after the Megiddo victory, for they are here referred to as preceding the king's return to Egypt from that expedition (l. 2). The three cities which he captured in the Lebanon are enumerated in the First Campaign, l. 16 (§ 436). Of the historians only Brugsch (*Geschichte*, 328) and Meyer (240) have noted this march to Lebanon.

Arrival in Thebes

549. Behold, he landed at Thebes,[a] his father, Amon, being ²————. My majesty established for him a "Feast of Victory"[b] for the first time, when my majesty arrived from the first victorious expedition,[c] overthrowing wretched Retenu ($R\underline{t}nw$) and widening the borders of Egypt in the year 23,[d] by the victories which he[e] decreed to me, leading — ³————.

First Feast of Victory

550. [The first "Feast of Victory" was celebrated at (the feast) ————[f]] the first feast of Amon, in order to make it of five days' duration.[g]

Second Feast of Victory

551. The second "Feast of Victory" was celebrated at (the feast): "Day-of-Bringing-in-the-God,"[h] the second feast of Amon, in order to make it of five days' duration.

Third Feast of Victory

552. The third "Feast of Victory" was celebrated at the fifth feast of Amon in (the temple): "Gift-of-Life,"[i] the day of [j]— ⁴———— [in order to make it of ⌜five days'⌝ duration].

---

[a]Squeeze and photograph.

[b]As the next line shows, there were three *"Feasts of Victory;"* but the first is here referred to as celebrated on his arrival. On these feasts, see Breasted, *Zeitschrift für ägyptische Sprache*, 37, 123 ff.

[c]§§ 408 ff.   [d]Brugsch has "22," which is, of course, an error.

[e]Amon.

[f]The restoration is certain from the other feasts; only the name of the Feast of Amon, with which the first feast of victory coincided, being unknown.

[g]Lit., *"in order to cause that it take place during (m) 5 days."*

[h]This is the feast mentioned by Piankhi (IV, 836, 1. 26), who gives the date as the second of Hathor, which thus determines the date of the second Feast of Victory.

[i]This is the name ($hnk\cdot t$-$^c n\underline{h}$) of the mortuary temple (Memnonium) of Thutmose III on the west shore at Thebes (cf. *Recueil*, XIX, 86–89). It stood at the northeast end of the line of temples (see Baedeker, "Necropolis of Thebes," opp. p. 254); as the earliest known reference to this building, it is particularly interesting, because it shows that already in his twenty-third year, Thutmose III's mortuary temple was complete and in use (see also Lepsius, *Denkmäler*, Text, III, 139).

[j]The name of the Amon Feast here followed, the order being different from that in the first two feasts.

Offerings for the Feasts of Victory

553. [My[a] majesty established] a great oblation for the "Feast of Victory," which my majesty made for the first time, consisting of bread, beer, bull-calves, bulls, fowl, antelopes, gazelles, ibexes, incense, wine, fruit, white bread, offerings of everything good ⁵———.

Amon's Voyage to Luxor

554. [Year 23, second[b] month] of the first season, (day) 14, when the majesty of this august god proceeded, to make his voyage[c] in his southern Opet (Luxor); my majesty established for him a great oblation for this day at the entrance into Luxor, consisting of bread, bull-calves, bulls, fowl, incense, wine, ⁶———[d] from the first of the victories which he (Amon) gave me, in order to fill his storehouse, ⌜—⌝ peasant-serfs, in order to make for him royal linen ($šs$), white ($pḳ·t$-) linen, ($šhr·w$-) linen, ($wm·t$-) linen; — peasants performed the work of the fields, in order to make the harvest, to fill the storehouse of my father [Amon] ⁷——— to the goodly way.

Gifts of Slaves

555. Statement of the Asiatics, male and female, the negroes and negresses, which my majesty gave to my father Amon, from the year 23 until the recording of this tablet upon this sanctuary:[e] 1,578 Syrians ($Ḫ᾽-rw$) ⁸———.

---

[a]Having enumerated the three feasts, with their dates, he now proceeds to the celebration and the oblations to be offered.

[b]The numeral is partially broken out; but it can be clearly proven to be two. See Breasted, *Zeitschrift für ägyptische Sprache*, 37, 125 f. This date is very important, as it shows at what time Thutmose III was already in Thebes on his return from the first campaign, the length of which is thus determined. See the calendar of the campaign in § 409.

[c]This is the beautiful ceremony of the god's voyage in his sacred barge, called at Thebes "Userhetamon" (for a description of the barge made for this purpose by Ramses III, see IV, 209). It was probably on the above occasion that the officer Amenemhab officiated (see his inscription, § 809, ll. 33, 34). It was on the day of the return to Karnak from this voyage, called the "*Day-of-Bringing-in-the-God*," that the Second "*Feast of Victory*" began. It therefore continued for five days after the return, during which the Second Amon Feast also continued (see *Zeitschrift für ägyptische Sprache*, 37, 126).

[d]The "[*spoil*] *from the first, etc.*," was probably mentioned as part of the oblation.

[e]The concluding words of the annals are: "*from the year XXI*[*II*] *until the year* [*X*]*XXII, when this tablet was recorded upon this sanctuary;*" hence the year 42 was probably also the year when the feast inscription was recorded.

Gifts of Cattle

556. ———— of the south and north: 3 loan-cows of the cattle of Zahi; 1 loan-cow of the cattle of Kush; total, 4 loan-cows; in order to draw the milk thereof into jars of electrum each day, and to cause (it) to be offered [to] my father [9][Amon].

Gift of Three Cities

557. My majesty gave to him[a] three cities in Retenu the Upper: Nuges (ʾn-yw-g-sʾ) was the name of one, Yenoam (Y-nw-ᶜʾ-mw) was the name of another, Herenkeru (Ḥw-r-n-kʾ-rw) was the name of another. The dues consisting of the [b]impost of the fiscal year,[b] the divine offerings, [of] my father Amon —.

Gifts of Precious Metals and Stones

558. [10]———— all ⌈things⌉ of silver, gold, lapis lazuli, malachite. My majesty presented to him gold, silver, lapis lazuli, malachite, copper, bronze, lead, colors, ⌈emery,⌉ in great quantity, in order to make every monument of my father, Amon. — [11]————.

Gifts of Poultry

559. My majesty formed for him flocks of geese to fill the (sacred) pool, for the offerings of every day. Behold, my majesty gave to him 2[c] fattened geese each day, as fixed dues forever, for my father, Amon. — [12]———— ⌈the former offering to Amon consisted⌉ of various loaves, 1,000.

Ancient Offerings Increased

560. My majesty commanded to multiply this offering of 1,000 various loaves after the arrival of my majesty from smiting Retenu on the first victorious expedition, in order to gain favor[d] in the great house (called): "Menkheperre[e] (Thutmose III)-is-Glorious-in-Monuments." [13]———— various —; 632 — from the daily income of every day, as an increase of that which was formerly.

---

[a]Amon.
[b]Lit., "*the work (impost) of the affairs of the year.*"
[c]Brugsch, 3; photograph, 2.
[d]Of the god.
[e]This is the name of Thutmose III's Karnak halls; see § 599, note, and IV, 754, note.

Gifts of Lands

561. I took for him numerous fields, gardens, and plowed lands, of the choicest of the South and North,[a] to make fields, in order to offer him clean grain[b] — [14]————.

Further Offerings

562. ———— yearly; consisting of loaves, bull-calves, bulls, fowl, incense, wine, fruit, every good thing of the dues of each year. My majesty established divine offerings, in order to gain the favor of (my) father, Harakhte, when he rises [15]———— my majesty [established for] him a divine offering of barley, in order to perform the ceremonies therewith, at the feast of the new moon, at the feast of the sixth day (of the month); and as a daily (income) of each day, according to that which was done in Heliopolis. Behold, my majesty found it very good to plow the barley in — — [16]————.

Offerings for Obelisks

563. ———— divine offerings for four great obelisks[c] which my majesty made for the first time, for my father [Amon], consisting of various loaves, and 4 (ds-) jars of beer, which were for each one of these obelisks; 25 (loaves) of bread, 1 (ds-) jar of beer.

Offerings for Statues

564. My majesty added divine offerings for the statues[d] of [17]———— the opening[e] of this portal.

Evening Offering

565. My majesty founded for him an evening offering of bread, beer, fowl, incense, wine, loaves, white loaves, offerings of every good thing each day. My majesty added for him increase of things in [18]————.

---

[a]Sinuhe's land in Palestine is described in the same words (I, 496, l. 80).

[b]The gifts connected with the Southern Opet festival continue to this point. The gifts of slaves (ll. 7, 8) are brought down to the end of the campaigns (year 42), but he goes back again after that to the return from the first campaign, mentioning the three cities in Lebanon captured on that campaign (l. 9) and mentioning the return (l. 12).

[c]See §§ 623 ff.; also Legrain, *Annales*, V, which arrived too late for use here.

[d]In l. 27 it is written phonetically. These are the statues of the older Pharaohs, preserved in the temple (see § 604).

[e]*Tpḥ·t*?

Feast of Peret-Min

566. My majesty founded an offering for the feast of the "Going-Forth-of-Min" consisting of oxen, fowl, incense, wine, loaves, everything good; 120 "heaps[a] of offerings supplied with everything;" for the sake of the life, prosperity, and health of my majesty. I commanded the addition of 6 great jars ($hbn\cdot t$) of wine [19]——— [⌈each⌉] year as an increase of that which was formerly.

A New Garden

567. My majesty made for him a garden for the first time, planted with every pleasant tree, in order to offer vegetables therefrom for divine offerings of every day, which my majesty founded anew as increase of that which was formerly [20]——— with maidens[b] of the whole land.

Wise Administration

568. Behold, my majesty made every monument, every law, (and) every regulation which I made, for my father, Amon-Re, lord of Thebes, presider over Karnak, because I so well knew his fame. I was wise in his excellence, resting in the midst of the body;[c] while I knew [21]——— that which he commanded to do, of the things which he desired should be, of all things which his ka desired that I do them for him, according as he commanded. My heart led me, my hand performed (it) for my father, who fashioned me, performing every excellent thing for my father [22][Amon] ———. My majesty found all excellent things, while enlarging monuments, as a record for the future; by enactments,[d] by purifying, by regulations, by supplying with offerings this house of my father, Amon, lord of Thebes, presider over Karnak; ⌈when⌉ passing by [23]——— his desire every day.

Feasts of the Seasons

569. Behold, my majesty supplied with offerings the feasts of the beginning of the seasons yearly, and of the appearance (of the god)

---

[a]These are the heaps so often seen in the reliefs. See I, 785 and note h.

[b]Lit., "*beauties*" ($nfr\cdot wt$).

[c]Meaning where the most secret affairs of the god were, as it is frequently said of the king, "*he knows the bodies*," or that which is in the bodies of men, that is, their thoughts.

[d]Or possibly: "*by recording for the future in documents.*"

therein in the midst of the house of my father, Amon, presider over Karnak, after[a] my majesty found that offerings were made there, consisting of libation, incense, [24]——— the dues of each year.

Truth of the Record

570. I have not uttered exaggeration, in order to boast of that which I did, saying: "I have done something," although my majesty had not done it. I have not done (anything) to people, against which contradiction might be uttered. I have done this for my father [25][Amon] ——— saying something which was not done; because he[b] knoweth heaven, and knoweth earth, he seeth the whole earth hourly. I swear[c] as Re loves me, as my father [Amon] praises me, as my nostrils are filled with satisfying life, I have done this — [26]———.

Instructions to Priests

571. ———[d] Be ye vigilant concerning your duty, be ye not careless concerning any of your rules; be ye pure, be ye clean concerning divine things, ⌜take heed⌝ concerning matters of transgression, guard your heart lest your speech ⌜—⌝, every man ⌜looking to his own steps therein⌝. [27]——— to my statues, for the ⌜well-being⌝ of the monuments which I have made. Bring ye up for me that which came forth[e] before, for I made festive his house; put on the garments of my statues, consisting of ($šs$-) linen, for I filled the mortuary oblations of ($pḳ·t$-) linen — [28]——— offer ye to me of all fruit, for I consecrated a garden anew; give ye me — shoulders of beef, for I endowed the beginning of the seasons with bulls; fill ye for me the altar with milk, let incense be [29]——— tables of silver and gold —; give ye to my statues according as I supplied those who were before me;[f] bring forth my statues on the day when your hands row,[g] giving praise ⌜to⌝ my father.

---

[a]In addition to that which he found already being offered.

[b]This must be Amon, who, says the king, sees and knows everything and would detect a lie.

[c]Compare the oath on Hatshepsut's obelisk (§ 318).

[d]Compare similar instructions to the priests of Abydos (§§ 97 ff.). The lists which follow are the mortuary offerings for the king, to which he exhorts the priests.

[e]The offerings.

[f]The statues of the earlier kings, set up in the temple.

[g]In the periodic voyage of the god upon the Nile or sacred lake.

He will count it for the ⌈well-being⌉ of that which I have made in —ᵃ ³⁰————— anew daily as an increase of that which was before: 3,305ᵇ various loaves of the divine offering; 132 (*ds-*) jars of beer; of grain, two white loaves; 2 *nd*ᶜ of (? *ḥ-*) herb; 2 *nd*ᶜ of dates; — fattened (*ḥt-*ᶜ-) fowl ³¹————— manyᵈ (*ḥt-*ᶜ-) fowl; 5 vesselfuls of incense; 2 (*mn-*) jars of wine; 4 (*pg-*) vessels of honey; 2 (*mn-*) jars of ⌈—⌉; 1 (ᶜ*ḥ*ᶜ-) jar of beer; 2 white loaves of *dk*, 15 white loaves in oblations; — roasts of fresh fat; ³²————— 2 —; 6 ibexes; 9 gazelles; 125 fattened (*ḥt-*ᶜ-) fowl; 1,100 ⌈mated⌉ (*ḥt-*ᶜ-) fowl; 258 flocks of (*šd-*) birds; 5,237 flocks of ⌈mated⌉ birds; 1,440 (jars) of wine; incense.

Offerings for Four Obelisks

572. (For the) four obelisks: incense, 318 white loaves; — incense ³³————— 104 heket of [in]cense, making 334 *pd·t* of incense; 21 (*mn-*) jars of green incense; 5 heket of myrrh; 236 bull-cakes; 258 dressed-geese cakes; 24 obelisk-cakes;ᵉ 562 white-loaf cakes; ³⁴—————.

573. Restorationᶠ which the King of Upper and Lower Egypt, Zeserkheperure, Setepnere (Harmhab) made, for his father, Amon-Re, lord of Thebes, that he might be granted life through him like Re, forever.

BIOGRAPHY OF AMENEMHABᵍ

574. This inscription is an account of the services and adventures of an officer named Amenemhab on the Asiatic

---

ᵃBrugsch's text stops here.

ᵇThese lists contain many uncertain things which require special investigation; the following version is merely given for the sake of completeness.

ᶜApparently an unknown measure of bulk (see also § 159, l. 37).

ᵈThere is a "*two*" after "*fowl*" which is not clear, possibly "*pairs.*"

ᵉThese are cakes in the shape of the top of an obelisk; in the Berlin Kahun papyri occur pyramidion (*bnbn*) loaves of white bread. The other two varieties were doubtless also made in the shape indicated by the name.

ᶠThis refers to the re-insertion of Amon's name throughout the inscription by Harmhab, after its erasure by Amenhotep IV.

ᵍEngraved upon the walls of his tomb in the necropolis of Thebes, which was noted by Champollion (*Notices descriptives*, I, 505, Tomb 12; hence not "discovered" by Ebers, as he stated (*Zeitschrift der Deutschen Morgenländischen Gesellschaft*, 30, p. 391). Ebers, however, did discover and publish the text: first in *Zeitschrift für ägyptische Sprache*, 1873, 3–9 (corrections by Ebers and campaigns of Thutmose III (ll. 3–32), and his subsequent favor and service under Amenhotep II (§§ 807 ff., ll. 32–46). It forms a very important supplement to the Annals of Thutmose III, but unfortunately does not insert the dates of the campaigns nor follow a chronological order.

The old soldier seems to have narrated to some scribe, who recorded them, the more important incidents and adventures of his career as they occurred to him, without attempt at order, beyond the involuntary association of events that belong to the same campaign. This narrative he had engraved beside his own figure on the wall of his tomb, as he is represented standing in the presence of Amenhotep II, to whom this recital of his life is evidently directed.

575. Beginning with a battle in the Negeb (year 39), he proceeds to three battles in Naharin, and the capture of Senzar (year 33), followed by the capture of Kadesh (year 30). The name of the next country (———h^3) is mutilated, and this is followed by a battle in Tikhsi (probably year 35), and the elephant hunt at Niy (year 33); while the whole series concludes, as it should, with the siege of Kadesh on the last campaign of Thutmose III in the year 42. Arranged in chronological order, Amenemhab records the following campaigns:

SIXTH CAMPAIGN, YEAR 30—

Capture of Kadesh (§ 585).

Stern, *ibid.*, 63, 64); again by Chabas, *Mélanges égyptologiques*, III, Pls. XVI–XVII (from *Zeitschrift für ägyptische Sprache*, corrections by Stern, *ibid.*, 1875, 174). Again by Ebers more accurately in *Zeitschrift der Deutschen Morgenländischen Gesellschaft*, 30, 391–416 and 3 plates; *ibid.*, 31, 439 ff.; very incorrectly also by Virey, "Sept tombeaux Thebains de la XVIIIᵉ dynastie," in *Mémoires de la mission française au Caire*, V, 238–40; corrections by Sjöberg, *Sphinx*, I, 18–20. See also Piehl, *Inscriptions*, I, CIX, F–CXIII, G, and Pls. CXXV, O–CXXVII, P and pp. 87–92. I am indebted to the kindness of Mr. Newberry for a careful scale copy of the inscription, which adds some new readings.

EIGHTH CAMPAIGN, YEAR 33—
  Capture of Senzar; three battles in Naharin (§§ 581-84, and 588), and elephant hunt at Niy (§ 588).
TENTH CAMPAIGN, YEAR 35—
  Battle in Tikhsi (§ 587).
FOURTEENTH CAMPAIGN, YEAR 39—
  Battle in the Negeb (§ 580).
SEVENTEENTH CAMPAIGN, YEAR 42—
  Siege of Kadesh (§ 589).

Following the campaigning is a feast at Thebes, possibly that of the fourteenth of Pakhons, on Thutmose III's return from his first campaign (§ 550). The death of the old king is then narrated with the date, from which we may compute the exact length of his reign—fifty-three years, ten months, and twenty-six days.

576. This biography affords us fleeting glimpses of the arduous tasks which beset the remarkable campaigns of Thutmose III, of which the Annals offer us little or nothing. The first campaign in Naharin (year 33) brought three successive battles in which Amenemhab distinguished himself; of these the Annals mention only one, without referring to the place where it occurred.

577. These adventures of Amenemhab are, of course, typical of a host of others, which fell to the lot of the Egyptian soldier in Syria. Some of them found place in folk-tales, and one has survived in the story of the capture of Joppa by Thutiy, one of Thutmose III's generals,[a] whose

---
[a]Part of the reverse (the first three pages) of the British Museum papyrus, known as Harris 500. Text first published by Maspero, *Études égyptologiques*, I, Pls. I–III, with transliteration and notes, pp. 53–66; it had already been translated by Goodwin, *Transactions of the Society of Biblical Archæology*, III, 340–48; then by Maspero, *ibid.*, I, 53–66; paraphrase based on Maspero by Petrie, *Egyptian Tales*, II, 1–7.

reality is vouched for by his tomb and other contemporaneous monuments of his.[a] The manuscript of the story is about 200 years later.

578. Besides his biography, Amenemhab's tomb contained a series of scenes showing him in the exercise of certain of his functions as a deputy of the army, especially introducing the officers of the commissariat to the king to report (?) on the maintenance of the army.[b] His tomb also contains other references to his career, like those inserted among his titles:

Attendant of his lord on his expeditions in the countries of the south and north, not separated from the Lord of the Two Lands on the battlefield in the hour of repelling millions of men.[c]

He was evidently a favorite of Thutmose III, and may have owed his favor to his wife, who was the royal nurse, possibly of Thutmose III himself.

Introduction

579. The officer, Amenemhab; he says:

[1]"I was the very faithful one of the sovereign, L. P. H., the wise-hearted of the King of Upper Egypt, the excellent-hearted of the King of Lower Egypt. I followed [2]my lord on his expeditions in the northern and the southern country. He desired that I should be the companion of his feet, while he was [3]upon the battlefield[d] of his victories, while his valor fortified the heart."

---

[a]A list of them in Maspero, *Etudes égyptologiques*, I, 68 f. See also DeVéria, *Bibliothèque égyptologique*, IV, 35 ff. The tomb is now unknown, but must have been known to the natives early in the last century, when it was plundered.

[b]This scene is repeated in the tomb of Pehsukher, whose office was similar to that of Amenemhab (*Mémoires de la mission française au Caire*, V, 289).

[c]*Mémoires de la mission française au Caire*, V, 245.

[d]Restored from text in *Zeitschrift für ägyptische Sprache*, 1876, 100, l. 2. Piehl has preceded me in this restoration, *ibid.*, 1885, 61, where the particle *ty*, "*while*," introducing a nominal clause, was not yet understood (it has nothing to do with *mn*, "*remain*").

Battle in Negeb

580. "I fought hand to hand in the land of ⁴Negeb (N-g-b ᵓ).ª I brought off three men, Asiatics, as living prisoners."

Battle in Naharin

581. "When his majesty came to Naharin (N-h-r-n)ᵇ ⁵I brought off three men from the fight there; I set them before thy majesty as living prisoners."

Battle in Wan

582. ⁶"Again I fought hand to hand (on) that expedition in the land of 'The-Height-of-Wan' (W-ᶜ-n)ᶜ on the west of Aleppo (H ᵓ-r ᵓ-bw). I brought off ⁷13 Asiatics as living prisoners, 13 men; 70 living asses; 13 bronze ⌈spears⌉;ᵈ the bronze was wrought with gold — ⁸—."

Battle of Carchemish

583. "Again I fought (on) that expedition in the land of Carchemish (K ᵓ-ry-k ᵓ-my-ᶜ-$š$ ᵓ).ᵉ I brought off — ⁹— as living prisoners. I

ªThis is clearly the Hebrew Negeb="*south country*;" the fourteenth campaign of the Annals was against the Bedwin (Shasu) of this region.

ᵇThe following three battles all took place on a campaign in Naharin, probably that of year 33 (§§ 476–87), as he later mentions another in Naharin, which would correspond with that of year 35.

ᶜIdentified by Müller (*Asien und Europa*, 259 f.), with the heights (Mons Casius) on the south shore of the seaward stretch of the Orontes by Antioch. But *ts't* ("*height*") does not mean "Ufer," and Mons Casius could have been much more easily identified by the scribe by mentioning the Orontes, rather than the distant Aleppo. Evidently some height not far from Aleppo is meant, for which Gebel Simᶜan (2,700 feet high) answers admirably. It is but slightly north of west of Aleppo, but the Egyptian did not carry a compass, and any traveler of today would speak of it as west of Aleppo, and refer to his table of bearings for the exact direction. But there is a ruin by Dânâ directly west of Aleppo, on a height of nearly 1,100 feet, which will do equally well.

ᵈThe rendering of Brugsch (*Zeitschrift für ägyptische Sprache*, 1873, 144): "13 Wurfspiesse von Eisen und mit Gold ausgelegt," is entirely unjustifiable. The material (*hsmn*) precedes as usual; then follows the object made of it, viz., *ynb*, which is some article of which each of the thirteen captured men carried one. Bronze helmets are mentioned in Annals (year 35, l. 41), and perhaps it is not an accident that "*13 inlaid corselets and 13 bronze suits of armor*" are also mentioned in the Naharin campaign of year 35, l. 41 (§ 501).

ᵉThis was on the northern march described in the Annals (§ 479, l. 18).

crossed over the water of Naharin (N-h-r-n), while they were in my hand, to ᵃ— ¹⁰—; I [set] them before my lord. He rewarded me with a great reward; list thereof:ᵇ — ¹¹—."

Battle in Senzar

584. "I beheld the royal victories of the King Menkheperre (Thutmose III), given life, in the country of Senzar (Sn-$ḏ$ ᵓ-r ᵓ),ᶜ when he made a [great] sl[aughter] ¹²[among] them. I fought hand to hand before the king, I brought off a hand there. He gave to me the gold of honor; list thereof: — ¹³— two silver rings."

Capture of Kadesh

585. "Again I beheld his bravery, while I was among his followers. [He] captured [the city of] ¹⁴Kadesh ($Ḳd$-$šw$);ᵈ I was not absent from the place where he was; I brought off two men,ᵉ lords (m-r ᵓ-y-n ᵓ), as [living prisoners; I set them] ¹⁵before the king, the Lord of the Two Lands, Thutmose (III), living forever. He gave to me gold because of bravery, before the whole people — — —; ¹⁶list thereof: of the finest gold: a lion; 2 necklaces, 2 flies,ᶠ 4 arm rings."

Campaign in Unknown Country

586. "I saw my lord in — — — ¹⁷— — — in all his forms in the country of the endsᵍ of [ᵍthe earthᵓ] — — — ¹⁸Ha — ($Ḥ$ ᵓ —). Then I was raised to be the — —ᴵ— —ᴵ of the army, like — —."

ᵃAhmose, son of Ebana, had a similar adventure, see § 11.

ᵇRestored from l. 16.

ᶜZinzar of the *Amarna Letters*, it is the modern Kalᶜat Seidjar on the Orontes below Hamath; see Meyer (*Festschrift für Georg Ebers*, 71), Müller (*Asien und Europa*, 185, n. 3), and Maspero (*Struggle of the Nations*, 264). It was taken in the year 33, on the Naharin campaign.

ᵈThis occurred in the year 30 (see Annals, § 465).

ᵉApposition with "*lords.*"

ᶠSee Breasted, *Proceedings of the Society of Biblical Archæology*, March, 1900, 7 f. Ebers' corrected text (in *Zeitschrift der Deutschen Morgenländischen Gesell_ schaft*, 30, Taf. II, l. 16) has ᶜdj, an error for ᶜff, as in l. 21.

ᵍSee Annals, year 35, l. 38 (§ 498), and "Hymn of Victory" (§ 661, l. 20). This was probably on the march from the coast to Naharin, on the second campaign against that country.

Battle in Tikhsi

587. ¹⁹"Again I beheld his victory in the country of Tikhsi (*Ty-ḫ-sy*) the wretched, in the city of Mero— (*Mr-yw* —). ²⁰I fought hand to hand therein before the king. I brought off Asiatics, 3 men, as living prisoners. ²¹Then my lord gave to me the gold of honor; list thereof: 2 golden necklaces, 4 arm rings, 2 flies, a lion, a female slave, and a male slave."

Elephant Hunt in Niy

588. ²²"Again ⌜I beheld⌝ another excellent deed which the Lord of the Two Lands did in Niy (*Nyy*). He hunted 120 elephants, for the sake of their tusks and ⌜—⌝. ²³I engaged the largest which was among them, which fought against his majesty; I cut off his hand[a] while he was alive ²⁴[before] his majesty, while I stood in the water between two rocks.[b] Then my lord rewarded me with gold; ²⁵[he] gave — — — and 3 changes of clothing."

Siege of Kadesh

589. "The prince of Kadesh[c] sent forth a mare[d] ²⁶before ⌜the army⌝; in order to — ⌜them,⌝ she entered among the army. I pursued after her ²⁷on foot, with my sword, and I ripped open her belly; I cut off her tail, I set ²⁸it before[e] the king; while there was thanksgiving to god for it![f] He gave (me) joy, it filled my body, (⌜with⌝) rejoicing, he endued my limbs."

Assault on Kadesh

590. ²⁹"His majesty sent forth every valiant man of his army, in order to pierce the wall for the first time, which Kadesh had made.

---

[a]Doubtless the trunk is meant.

[b]He was perhaps pursued by the wounded elephant, and took refuge between the rocks.

[c]On the last campaign of Thutmose III in year 42 (§ 531) and the last mentioned by Amenemhab.

[d]For the purpose of exciting the stallions of the Egyptian chariotry and thus confusing their line of battle; but Amenemhab leaps down from his chariot, and, pursuing her "*on foot*," slays her. See Borchardt, *Zeitschrift für ägyptische Sprache*, 31, 62 f.

[e]The preposition is incomplete.

[f]The phrase occurs not infrequently, denoting the thanks of a king for the faithfulness of a servant; e. g., Amenemhet (I, 520, l. 14) The impersonal form merely indicates that it was the king who gave thanks.

I ³⁰was the one who pierced it, being the first of all the valiant; no other before me did (it). I went forth, I brought off ³¹² men,ᵃ (*m-r ʾ - y-n ʾ*) lords, as living prisoners. Again my lord rewarded me because of it, with ³²every good thing for satisfying the heart, of the king's-presence."

Feast at Thebes

591. "I made this capture while [I] was an officer of the navy ——— ³³I was the commander of ⌜—⌝ [⌜his vessel⌝] — I was the chief of his associates ³⁴on the voyage — — — at his beautiful Feastᵇ of Opet, when all the land was in acclamation."

Death of Thutmose III

592. ³⁵"Lo, the king completed his lifetime of many years, splendid in valor, in [migh]t, ³⁶and in triumph; from year 1 to year 54, third month of the second season, the last dayᶜ (of the month) under [the majesty of] ³⁷King Menkheperre (Thutmose III), triumphant. He mounted to heaven, [he] ᵈjoined the sun; the divine limbs mingling with him who begat him."

[Concluded §§ 807–809]

FRAGMENTS OF KARNAK PYLON VIIᵉ

593. From the data thus far given by Legrain, it is impossible to put together all the fragments heretofore found;

ᵃApposition.

ᵇThis is perhaps the celebration of the Feast of Southern Opet on the fourteenth of Paophi, after the return from the first campaign (§ 550), which Amenemhab here relates after the campaigns exactly as the inscription of Feasts and Offerings continues the Annals.

ᶜThat is the thirtieth of the seventh month (Phamenoth); as he was crowned on the fourth of the ninth month (Pakhons), he lacked one month and four days of concluding his fifty-fourth year, dying on the seventeenth of March, while his fifty-fourth year would have been completed on the nineteenth of the following April (his coronation day coming over thirteen days earlier than when he was crowned fifty-four years earlier). If born before his father's accession, as seems probable, he was at least eighty-four years old at his death.

ᵈThis phrase is rendered by Brugsch (*Zeitschrift für ägyptische Sprache*, 1873, 134): "es ging unter die Sonnenscheibe," for which he gives excellent reasons; but in Ineni (§ 46, l. 4), the pronoun "he" is expressed, rendering B's translation impossible. See also IV, 988 E and 988 G.

ᵉFragments of a great granite doorway some forty feet high through the center of Pylon VII (Baedeker's plan), the northernmost of the southern pylons, were

but even from the fragments the great historical value of the monument is evident. It contained a record of Thutmose III's military career as an explanation of the sources of the costly materials used on this pylon and other good works in the Karnak temple. It begins with his coronation, passes to the reign of Thutmose II, and furnishes our most important proof of Thurmose III's coregency with Thutmose II,[a] whom, as his predecessor, he officially calls his "*father*," as was customary on the monuments in referring to deceased Pharaohs. The record then proceeds to the first campaign, the battle of Megiddo, the siege of Megiddo, its capture, the prisoners, and the disposal of the prisoners and plunder in Karnak. Whether the succeeding campaigns were now taken up is uncertain. In any case, the record now included some account of the important eighth campaign, of the year 33, when Thutmose III first conquered the Euphrates country.

With some omissions of mutilated portions, necessitated by the exceedingly fragmentary character of some of the material, the fragments are as follows:

First Fragment[b]

594. Year 1, first month of the third season (ninth month), the fourth day,[c] occurred the coronation of the king's-son ———.

Second Fragment[d]

595. ——— ¹before me into the —. There was assigned to me the sovereignty of the Two Lands upon the throne of Keb, the office

---

found by Legrain in September-October, 1901, and published by him in the *Annales du Service*, II, 272–79, IV, Pl. III. The inscription is in vertical lines, of which there were at least fourteen, computed by Legrain to have had a combined length (if set end to end) of 200 meters. Of all this the surviving fragments contain but a small fraction.

[a]A lintel block, found by Petrie at Abydos in 1902 (*Abydos*, I, Pl. LXI, 2; LXIV, and p. 30), shows their two names together, as having been coregent during work on the Eighteenth Dynasty Abydos temple.

[b]Legrain's E. 279.   [c]See Annals, § 417.

[d]Legrain's combination of several fragments, 276, 277.

of Khepri by the side of my father, the Good God, King of Upper and Lower Egypt, Okhepernere (Thutmose II), given life forever ....
4........

Spoil of First Campaign

596. His majesty commanded to build stone ——— 5— it with electrum. The divine shadow was the likeness of a ram, whose name was made: "Menkheperre — — Monuments." It is the favorite place of the lord of the gods. .... All its vessels were of electrum, gold, [every] costly stone, ——— 6 [⌜captured when his majesty went to⌝] Retenu, to repel the northern countries, on his first victorious campaign, which Amon decreed to him.......... 7——— put in front of their wall, surrounding it with a firm rampart. My majesty besieged it[a] like a terrible lion. As for him who ⌜came⌝ upon it by night, ———8———. Lo, my majesty carried off the wives of that vanquished one, together with [⌜his⌝] children, and the wives of the chiefs who were [there, together with their] children. My majesty placed these women ——9—— the name of another. Their impost was brought into the temple of my father, Amon, as the dues of Retenu — — — — — these wives of the vanquished chief of Kadesh ——— 10——— of Egypt, extending the boundaries, forever. — — — My majesty made this equipment to overlay — — [a barge] of the "Beginning-of-the-River" (named): "Userhet,"[b] hewn [of cedar] ——— 11........ 12——— with all [products] of the northern countries, when my majesty returned from these countries.

Third Fragment[c]

597. ——— their horses ——— the great chiefs of this country who came to fight ——— their — into the temple of Amon. Then my majesty commanded ——— my [father] Amon dues as yearly impost. Lo, ——— Lo, my majesty furnished an example of might,

---

[a]Meaning, of course, Megiddo; the preceding being a reference to his siege works; compare Annals, § 433, ll. 9-11.

[b]For "*Userhetamon.*" Of course, we are to read $h^{\circ}t$ instead of Legrain's ^{c}t; see Lateran Obelisk (§§ 838).

[c]Legrain's, I, 274. According to Legrain, these sections of seven lines belong to ll. 8-14, presumably referring to his numbering of the second fragment; but they are too far separated from that fragment to be here placed in connection with it. They evidently refer to the king's prowess in some battle.

with my own sword, in the midst of ——— Bekhu (*Bḫw*).ᵃ None stood before [me] ——— anew for my father, Amon.

*Fourth Fragment*ᵇ

598. ——— of Ketne (*Ḳd-n*ᵓ) on the eighth victorious campaign, to repel ———.ᶜ

GREAT KARNAK BUILDING INSCRIPTIONᵈ

599. This inscription contained the record of Thutmose III's buildings, erected after the beginning of his wars.ᵉ In particular, it recounts the erection of one of his extensive additions to the east end of the great Karnak temple. The inscription is unfortunately badly mutilated, only the introductory lines being preserved, but we see that it recorded the erection of Thutmose III's splendid colonnaded halls and sanctuary, which form the eastern extension of the Karnak temple;ᶠ for it was a building so extensive that an old shrine of Nun had to be removed farther eastward.

600. There was a reason, hitherto overlooked, for the erection of these eastern halls by Thutmose III, which

---

ᵃWith a foreign determinative.

ᵇLegrain's G, 279.

ᶜThere are two more lines, of which the first seems to contain some reference to making bows.

ᵈA large granite stela, found by Mariette in the great Karnak temple, now in Cairo; fragments of only seventeen lines are preserved; text: Mariette, *Karnak*, 12.

ᵉThe record of his Theban buildings before his wars is contained in the great coronation inscription (§§ 131 ff.). Of his buildings elsewhere, he has left but slight record: a fragmentary dedication at El Kab (Lepsius, *Denkmäler*, Text, IV, 37); a similar fragment at Erment (*ibid.*, IV, 1); and a record of his share in the Pasht speos at Benihasan (Rougé, *Inscriptions hiéroglyphiques*, 149), which is chiefly of religious character. Further building records also in §§ 609–22; 637–43.

ᶠAccording to an altar found at Karnak, this building was called: "*Menkheperre-is-Glorious-in-Monuments*" (*Zeitschrift für ägyptische Sprache*, 1879, 137). An altar with the same inscription was reported at Salonichi (*ibid.*, 1868, 78 ff.), and is possibly identical with the first. See also § 560 for the only other occurrence of the name in Thutmose III's time. This name of Thutmose III's sanctuary was still in use in the reign of Takelot II, 650 years later (IV, 753).

must be noted here. The colonnaded hall built by Thutmose I between his two pylons (IV and V) formed the entrance-hall to the Karnak temple, and at this time was the largest hall in the building, the only one sufficiently large for a procession of the god, such as that which took place there when Thutmose III was installed as king by the priests. Now, this hall had been rendered unfit for use by Hatshepsut's strange insertion of her obelisks there (§ 304); it now stood roofless, with a small group of six columns at its northern end. Of these, four were the original cedar columns of Thutmose I, which Thutmose III now renews, recording the renewal on one of them, as follows:[a]

601. ¹He (Thutmose III) made (it) as his monument for his father, Amon-Re, erecting for him [4 columns] of sandstone set up[b] [in] the hypostyle, as [ʳa renewal of that whichʱ] his [ʳfather had madeʱ], the Good God, Lord of Offering (viz., Thutmose I), shaped of cedar.[c] My majesty [ʳaddedʱ][d] 4 columns to the two columns[e] in the north side, together 6; wrought with —, established with — — ²and that which was brought because of the fame of my majesty, being impost of all countries, which my father, Amon-Re, assigned to me, shaped[f] of sandstone. The height thereof was made 30 cubits,[g] on both sides of the great august portal,[h] — — throughout. They illuminated Karnak

---

[a]Published by Piehl, *Actes du 6ᵐᵉ congrès international des orientalistes tenu en 1883 à Leide, IVᵐᵉ* partie, section 3, pp. 203–19. The text is badly broken, and unessential fragments have been omitted.

[b]Read: *smn*.

[c]This reference is the first mention of wooden columns in an Egyptian temple, and shows that Thutmose I built his hall with cedar columns. (See my *New Chapter*, 31, note b).

[d]Piehl.

[e]That is, the two columns of stone already inserted by Thutmose I (§ 100 and note).

[f]Three passive participles agree with "*4 columns*," viz., "*wrought*," "*established*," and "*shaped*." This mention of the material is in contrast with "*shaped of cedar*" (l. 1), referring to the wooden predecessors of the four new stone columns.

[g]Over fifty-one feet.

[h]Northern portal; see plan, *New Chapter*, 13.

like — — — of sandstone, painted with figures of my father Amon, together with figures of my majesty, and figures of my father, the Good God (viz., Thutmose I). Behold, as for that which was found[a] going to ruin among them, my majesty established it with sandstone, in order that this temple might be established — ³— like the heavens, abiding upon their four pillars, as a monument, great, excellent and useful for the lord of eternity; of granite, ivory, of sandstone, — — — silver, of the Beautiful-faced (Ptah). I swear as [Re] loves me, [as my father, Amon, favors me,[b] I made it] anew in the north side, being an increase of that which my father had made.

602. Thus the north end of the hall, the end where Thutmose III had been stationed when he was proclaimed king, was repaired by him, but the south end was still without columns and roofless, and the obelisk-bases had usurped the room of eight columns, over a third of the entire colonnade. The hall could not be made fit for great ceremonials, with the obelisks preventing the replacement of over a third of the roof. Thutmose III therefore built a masonry sheathing around each of the obelisks, covering the inscriptions of Hatshepsut, and desisted[c] from any further attempt to restore the hall where he had been raised to the throne. But as such a great ceremonial hypostyle was of course indispensable, he built the splendid colonnaded halls still standing at the other or east end of the temple. On his return from the second[d] campaign, in the year 24, the building was begun, and on the thirtieth of Mekhir, that is, in the latter part of February, some two months before his departure for Syria on the third campaign, the brilliant

---

[a]Read: *gmy·t?*

[b]Restored from the common form of royal oath, e. g., Hatshepsut's obelisk inscription, § 318, l. 2.

[c]This is clear from the fact that his son Amenhotep II, erected the columns of the south end (§ 805).

[d]Not the first campaign, as I have incorrectly stated in *Zeitschrift für ägyptische Sprache*, 39, 61.

celebration of the foundation ceremonies took place. On his return from the third campaign, in the year 25, the building was sufficiently far advanced to record on the walls of one of its chambers, the plants and flowers which he brought from Syria[a] in that year (§§ 450 f.).

603. The architraves of the building bear the following dedications:[b]

[c]He made (it) as his monument for his father, Amon-Re, lord of Thebes, erecting for him an august central hypostyle[d] anew, of fine white sandstone (variant, fine limestone of Ayan).

Another form of this dedication is an epitheton attached to Thutmose III's name:

Establishing the house of his father, Amon-Re, of fine white limestone of Ayan.

604. Another dedication designates the hall[e] in the temple which was set apart by Thutmose III for the mortuary service of his ancestors. It is as follows:

[f]...... making for them a great dwelling of myriads of years, anew[g] of fine limestone of Ayan, shining like the horizon of heaven, established as an eternal work. His majesty commanded to record the names of his fathers, to increase their offerings, and to fashion statues ⌜— —⌝[h] to establish for them divine offerings anew, as increase of [what was formerly].

605. In one of the chambers to which this hall gave access, Thutmose had recorded on the walls a list[i] of the

---

[a]This is the earliest extract from his annals; the extracts around the sanctuary were, of course, made after the conclusion of his campaigns.

[b]Lepsius, *Denkmäler*, Text, III, 31; Champollion, *Notices descriptives*, II, 159 f., 162; and Brugsch, *Thesaurus*, VI, 1313.

[c]Preceded by the titulary of Thutmose III.

[d]Ḥry·t-yb.   [e]Z in Mariette's Plan (*Karnak*, Pl. V).

[f]Brugsch, *Thesaurus*, VI, 1313; Champollion, *Notices descriptives*, II, 168; Mariette, *Karnak*, 32, h; titulary and usual introduction are omitted.

[g]Or: "*for the first time.*"   [h]"*Of their bodies?*"

[i]Removed by Prisse to Paris, where it now is, in the Bibliothèque Nationale. This is the famous Karnak list of kings. See I, p. 197, note a.

Pharaohs, his ancestors who were worshiped in this temple, and whose statues were set up in it. It is to this list that the dedication inscription refers.

This ancestral character of the temple is also referred to in another inscription[a] of Thutmose III, which designates the temple as "*a monument for his father, the king of Upper and Lower Egypt, Thutmose I, and a monument of his fathers, the kings of Upper and Lower Egypt.*"

The architect in charge of these great additions was the first prophet of Amon, Menkheperreseneb, who briefly recounts his connection with them in his tomb inscriptions (§§ 772 ff.).

The great building inscription on our granite stela is as follows:

The Oracle

606. [1]......[b] The king himself commanded to put in [2]writing, according to the statement of the oracle,[c] to execute monuments before those who are on earth —. My majesty desired to make a monument to my father, Amon-Re, in Karnak, erecting a dwelling, beautifying the horizon, adorning for him Khaftet-hir-nebes, the favorite place of my father [3]from the beginning, Amon-Re, lord of Thebes. I made it for him upon this block of enduring stone,[d] exalting and magnifying greatly, since — — — water to the shrine[e] of Nun, on arriving at his seasons.

Old Buildings Removed

607. I built it for him according to (his) desire, I satisfied him by that which I made for him (as) at first, building [4]a shrine at the east of

---

[a]Brugsch, *Thesaurus*, VI, 1315.

[b]The usual titulary of Thutmose III complete.

[c]This is doubtless the same as the oracle in the Punt inscriptions (§ 285, l. 5, *nḏ·t-r* ᵓ) commanding the expedition. So also Thutmose III is building in response to an oracle.

[d]Mariette states that this tablet is of "granite gris" (Mariette, *Karnak*, Texte, 47); so that *rwd·t* cannot mean "*sandstone*" here.

[e]As Brugsch has supposed (*Egypt under the Pharaohs*, p. 180), this temple, or shrine of Nun, was in the way of enlarging the Amon-temple. It seems, therefore, to have been taken down and rebuilt farther eastward.

this temple. Behold, my majesty found the encircling wall of mud brick, — — [⌜I removed the wall of⌝] mud [brick,] in order to extend ᵃthis temple.ᵃ I cleansed it, I overthrew its ruinous (parts), and removed the inclosure, which was by its side, which went up ⁵[⌜to⌝] the house. I built this place where the encircling wall was, in order to erect this monument upon it — — — — — Karnak. I made (it) anew,ᵇ I fulfilled that which was prescribed, I did not appropriate the monument of another. My majesty spake this in truth for the information of ⁶every one, my great abomination is to speak lies, there is no fiction in — — — — — really. I know that he is pleased therewith.ᶜ

Foundation Ceremonies

608. My majesty ordered that the ᵈfoundation ceremonyᵈ should be prepared ⌜at the approach of⌝ the day of the Feast of the New Moon,ᵉ ⁷to extend the measuring-line upon this monument. In the year 24, second month of the second season, the last day (of the month), on the day of the tenth feast of Amon in ——————ᶠ the god rested (⌜on⌝) his great throne. After this, I proceeded ⌜after⌝ (my) father, ⁸Amon; the god proceeded at his going to celebrate this his beautiful feast. The majesty of this god marveled —————;ᵍ this god [⌜assum⌝]ed the station ⌜for⌝ the extension of the [measuring-line]. He set his majesty before him at this monument, which his majesty had exacted. ⁹The majesty of this god rejoiced in this monument —————ᶠ [the majesty] of this god proceeded; the beautiful feast was celebrated ⌜for⌝ my lord. Then I went to do the extending of the measuring-line upon that which —————ʰ ¹⁰before him. He led ⁱ[— — —]ⁱ the first feast of extending the line. Behold, the majesty of this revered god desired to do the extending of the line himself ¹¹—————ʲ [—————]ᵏ ¹²————— all that he made.

ᵃBy a slight emendation of the text.
ᵇOr: "*for the first time.*"   ᶜViz., with the truth; a common idea.
ᵈLit., "*the line extension,*" as in l. 7, following.
ᵉSee Brugsch (*Thesaurus*, VI, 1290 f.).
ᶠAbout one-third line.   ᵍLess than one-third line.
ʰOver one-half line. The remaining short ends of eight lines still have to do with this building, but offer nothing decisive by which to identify it.
ⁱPartially broken.   ʲNearly two-thirds line.
ᵏSee Brugsch (*Thesaurus*, VI, 1291); I do not understand the passage, and his explanation does not seem to me probable.

His majesty rejoiced exceedingly when he saw the great marvels which his father [Amon] had performed for him. ¹³————ᵃ My heart dilated at every beautiful approach to begin this monument, enduring ¹⁴————ᵇ all the names of the great gods who are in Karnak and of the gods and goddesses ¹⁵————ᵃ All the people made jubilee. After this ¹⁶————ᶜ electrum, which [my majesty] made for him ¹⁷————.ᵈ

BUILDING INSCRIPTION OF THE KARNAK PTAH-TEMPLEᵉ

609. This inscription records how Thutmose III found the Ptah-temple, just north of the great hypostyle in Karnak, built of brick, with wooden columns and doorposts, falling to ruin. The occasion of rebuilding, or at least of new offerings, was the return from the first campaign, and the inscription contains interesting references (§ 616) to the investment and capture of Megiddo on that campaign. From the plunder thus obtained the temple was also newly and richly furnished. As this temple was one of the stopping-places of Amon, when his processions moved out from the Karnak temple, on all feast days, offerings are provided for Amon on such occasions (§§ 615, 617). At such times also the lay priesthood was to receive an offering, as well as the royal statue which was carried in procession (§ 618); and the usual daily offering was made to Ptah (§ 619), increased by certain new offerings now established for the first time

---

ᵃOver two-thirds line.

ᵇAbout three-fourths line.   ᶜAbout four-fifths line.

ᵈThe remainder of the tablet must have contained at least as many more lines as the above.

ᵉLarge granite stela 1.50 m. high, 0.74 m. wide, and 0.32 m. thick, found in the Ptah-temple at Thebes; now in Cairo, thus far without number. It was published and translated by Maspero, *Comptes rendus de l'académie des inscriptions et belles-lettres*, 1900, Tome I, 113–23, with facsimile plate; and again by Legrain, *Annales*, III, 107–11. I had also a copy of the original, kindly loaned me by Schaefer.

(§ 620). These were further increased on the king's return from a subsequent campaign late in September (§ 621). With offerings for Mut-Hathor (§ 622), the inscription closes.

These offerings are all "*for the sake of life, prosperity, and health*" of the Pharaoh; that is, they are the official sacrifices in his behalf, which were begun as soon as a king was crowned (cf. § 57).

610. The stela was badly defaced, when the persecution of Ikhnaton caused the chiseling out of the entire relief and every occurrence of the names of other gods. This defacement is important as showing that the persecution of Ikhnaton was not confined to Amon. The restorers of Seti I at Thebes were so accustomed to inserting the name of Amon that they have here inserted it where the titles clearly show that Ptah was original.

611. The dedication inscription on the wall of the Ptah-temple also attributes the building to Thutmose III, of whom it says:[a]

[He made (it) as his monument][b] for his father, Ptah, the beautiful of face, lord of "Life of the Two Lands," presiding over the great seat; erecting for him the house of Ptah anew [of] fine white sandstone, doors of new cedar of the best of the terraces. It is more beautiful than it was before. Lo, my majesty found this house of brick — — — of the ancestors. His majesty commanded to make for him this temple of sandstone, established as an eternal work, made to flourish, an abiding monument — —,[c] which the Son of Re, Thutmose (III), makes for him.

612. Our stela inscription is surmounted by a relief,[d] down the middle of which is the following record of Seti I's restoration:

---

[a]Brugsch, *Thesaurus*, V, 1188 = Lepsius, *Denkmäler*, Text, III, 7 = Legrain, *Annales*, III, 98, 99.

[b]The restoration in Lepsius, *Denkmäler*, Text, is not correct; and that of Legrain is impossible.

[c]Name of Ptah erased by Ikhnaton; see Lepsius, *Denkmäler*, Text, III, 8.

[d]This entire relief was chiseled out by Ikhnaton.

Restoration of the monument, which King Menmare (Seti I) made, in the house of his father, Ptah.

On the right, Thutmose III offers wine to Ptah. Behind the king is the divine wife ($hm\cdot t\ ntr$) Sityoh ($S^{\,\flat}\cdot t\ y^{\,c}\ h$),[a] offering ointment. On the left, before the same god, Thutmose III, offering a libation of water, is followed by the same princess,[b] again offering ointment.

The inscription below the relief is as follows:

Introduction

613. [1]Live Horus .... Thutmose III, beloved of Ptah-South-of-His-Wall, in Thebes, given life forever.

Building the New Temple

614. [2]My[c] majesty commands that there be built the temple of Ptah-South-of-His-Wall, in Thebes, which is a station ($w^{\,\flat}\ hy\cdot t$) of my father, Amon-Re, lord of Thebes, wherein he [—][d] on the day of "Bringing-in-the-God," and all his feasts [3]during the year, when he proceeds to the treasury of the south ($tp\ rsy$). Lo, my majesty found this temple built of brick and wooden columns,[e] and its doorway of wood, beginning to go to ruin. [4]My majesty commands to stretch the cord upon this temple anew, erected of fine white sandstone, and the walls around it[f] of brick, as a work enduring for eternity. [5]My majesty erected for it doors of new cedar of the best of the terraces, mounted with Asiatic copper, ⌜corresponding to⌝ (hft) the house of Ptah anew, in the name of my majesty. [6]Never was done for him the like, before my majesty.

New Equipment of the Temple

615. My majesty made him rich, and I made him greater than before. I overlaid for him his great seat with electrum of the best of

---

[a] The name is perhaps wrongly restored, and Maspero affirms he has seen traces of the name Merytre; but of this Schaefer saw nothing.

[b] Her name is here original.

[c] The text has a Horus-hawk on the standard, used for the first person when the king speaks, in the rest of the inscription.

[d] We expect some verb like "rests" or "turns aside," but the text shows only the verb "*give*" and a very small lacuna.

[e] On wooden columns in a temple, see § 100.

[f] That is, the walls of the temple inclosure.

the countries. ⁷All vessels were of gold and silver, and every splendid, costly stone, clothing of fine linen, white linen, ointments of divine ingredients, to perform his pleasing ceremonies at the feasts of ⁸the beginnings of the seasons, which occur in this temple, when my majesty caused him to proceed, to assume his throne.

Offerings on Return from First Campaign

616. I filled his temple with every good thing, with oxen, geese, incense, wine, offerings of ⁹all sorts of fruit, at the return of my majesty from (ḥr) the country of Retenu (R*t*nw), on the first victorious campaign, which[a] my father, Amon, gave to me, when he gave to me all the allied countries of Zahi[b] (*D* ᵓ -*ḥy*), ¹⁰shut up in one city. The fear of my majesty entered their hearts, (they) fell,[c] (they) slunk back; when I reached them, there was not one left ¹¹who stirred (*wtwt*) among them. I snared them in one city, I built around them with a rampart of thick wall, to —[d] their nostrils of the breath of life, by the fame of ¹²my father, Amon, who guides me into a prosperous way by all his good designs, which he has wrought for my majesty. He has made great the victories of my majesty above (those of) any king who has been before.

New Offerings for Amon

617. ¹³My majesty commanded that his altar should be supplied with every good thing. My majesty commanded that offerings be added anew for my father, Amon, in Karnak, ¹⁴when he rested there: 12 ᵉ"heaps of offerings[e] supplied with everything," for the day of "Bringing-in-the-God" and every feast of Amon, being[f] an increase of what was before, for the sake of the life, prosperity, and health of my majesty —.[g]

---

[a]This relative clause (*rdyn ny yt·y*) is common. Maspero's rendering, "Je fis en effet ces dons à mon père, etc.," is possible only by overlooking one of the *n*'s.

[b]This shows the wide extent of Zahi, evidently far beyond the limits of Phœnicia.

[c]The text has been restored here, and may be corrupt; "*fell*" (*ḥr*) may be the particle "*then, so.*"

[d]Some verb like "deprive."

[e]This is a cultus term for a kind of oblation. See § 566.

[f]Emend after l. 19.

[g]Amon is here wrongly restored in an erasure extending over from the next line. The ancient restoration "*my majesty*" (*ḥn-y*) is quite right, as is shown by l. 19; Maspero (*Comptes rendus*, 1900, I, 115) corrects the restoration, and appeals to l. 19 as supporting his correction; but his quotation of l. 19 overlooks *ḥn*.

Offerings for the Priesthood and Royal Statue

618. Now, ¹⁵when the majesty of this august god is satisfied with his offering (*yḥ·t*), let one cause a "heap of offerings, supplied with everything" to be issued to the lay priests of the temple of my father, Amon, in Karnak; ¹⁶and 6 "heaps of offerings, supplied with everything"ᵃ and with bread ofᵇ the "Coming Forth" (to be issued) before the statue of millions of years of my majesty, which follows to this temple, which is in the domain of the majesty of ¹⁷this august god, for the sake of this offering, ᶜthe name of which is: "Menkheperre-is-Great-in-Offerings."

Offerings for Ptah

619. Now, when this statue is satisfied with this offering, there shall be issued for the temple of ¹⁸Ptah, lord of truth, South-of-His-Wall, in Thebes, according to the measure of the customaryᵈ offering, which is in this temple.

New Offerings for Ptah

620. My majesty has moreover commanded to found divine offerings anew for my father, ¹⁹ᵉPtah-South-of-His-Wall in Thebes, consisting of 60 various loaves, 2 jars (*ds*) of beer, —— vegetables, bread of the daily offering of every day, as an increase of that which was before, for the sake of the life, prosperity, and health of my majesty.

²⁰Now, when the god is satisfied with his offerings, let this ⌜offering⌝ be placed before [this] statue of my majesty, when the lay priesthood of the temple of Ptah-South-of-His-Wall, in Thebes, go forth. My majesty [⌜commands⌝]ᶠ ²¹to have executed every contract of the court, for his father, Ptah-South-of-His-Wall, in Thebes ——— Amon in Karnak.

ᵃThis is interpreting the loaf as determinative of the whole group; it is possible to separate it, as. Maspero does, and read "*six loaves from the bread of, etc.*"

ᵇOr: "*for the Coming Forth;*" in which case the parenthesis must be inserted after "*bread*," thus: ". . . . . *bread (to be issued) for the Coming Forth, etc.*"

ᶜThis relative clause, as the gender shows, does not belong to "*offering*," but to "*temple!*" The order of words above is as in the original, which is very confused. Such royal statues are depicted in reliefs "*following*" in procession to the temple.

ᵈFor another example of this use of this word (*mtt*), see § 798; and the Treaty, III, § 377, l. 14.

ᵉThe restorer has absurdly inserted Amon here before Ptah!

ᶠThe restoration has probably omitted this word.

Further Addition to Ptah's Offerings

621. First (month) of the first season (first month), twenty-sixth day.[a] My majesty hath founded for him: ²²a bull, —[b] jars (*mnw*) of wine, 2 geese, 4 great ⌜—⌝, 5 measures (*dny·t*) of fruit, grain for 6 white loaves, 2 [bundles of vegetables],[c] 20 (*ṯ᾽ b-*) jars and 10 (*ds-*) jars of beer, 5 table fowl, ²³200 various loaves of the divine offerings from the house (*pr*) of Amon, 4 measures of incense, — cakes, 20 white loaves, [d]for the sake of[d] the life, prosperity, and health of Pharaoh, fixed as annual dues, burned in the presence of this god ²⁴every day.

Offerings for Mut-Hathor

622. My [majesty commands] to have executed every contract of the court for Mut-Hathor, mistress of Thebes, on the day of the "Altar-of-the-Feast," which takes place[e] on the last day of the third month of the third season (eleventh month). ²⁵[My majesty] has [founded ⌜divine offerings of⌝] — jars of wine, 1 goose, 2 great ⌜—⌝, 4 measures (*dny·t*) of fruit, grain for four white loaves, 2 bundles of vegetables, 2 (*ṯ᾽ b-*)jars of beer. ²⁶5 table-fowl, 25 [various loaves of the divine][f] offerings, ⌜—⌝ of the garden, and every plant, burned[g] in the presence of this goddess, every day.

²⁷[It is] my [majesty] who does all the things to be done in this house in this good hour ⌜exactly⌝, in which is the burning. It is my majesty who makes anew ———.

---

[a]This is about the twenty-third of September and was, of course, the time of the king's return with the plunder from some campaign of the preceding summer (see §§ 409 ff.).

[b]The numeral has been corrupted in the restoration.

[c]To be restored from l. 25.

[d]Maspero restores: *nw* = "*of;*" but the context demands the usual connection, viz., "for the sake of (*ḥr-ḏ᾽ ḏ᾽*), etc.," which Schaefer read; and this is shown by the photograph to be correct.

[e]Maspero has "fête de faire être;" but the phrase "*cause to be*" is usual for the taking place of a feast. See *Zeitschrift für ägyptische Sprache*, 37, 124 f., where it occurs three times, and the Elephantine appendix to the Amâda stela, § 798.

[f]Restored from l. 23.

[g]A particiEple referring to the entire preceding series of offerings; the same above in l. 23.

OBELISKS

623. In celebration of the usual jubilee on the thirtieth anniversary of his being proclaimed crown prince, and on recurrences[a] of the same feast, Thutmose III erected a series of at least seven[b] obelisks, of which five were in Thebes and two in Heliopolis. The first of these feasts must have taken place in his thirtieth year as king, because his proclamation as crown prince was coincident with his coronation. He had no prospect of succeeding until he was crowned. These obelisks are chronologically important, and bear inscriptions, some of which possess great historical value.

I. KARNAK OBELISKS

624. If we exclude those of Hatshepsut, there are now no obelisks erected by Thutmose III remaining in Karnak; for that of Thutmose I which he appropriated was not erected by Thutmose III (see §§ 105, 86 ff.), but only inscribed by him. In the year 42, however, he had already erected in Karnak four obelisks, for which he decreed offerings (§§ 563, 572). Whether he later erected more, we cannot tell, but it can hardly be an accident that other sources also refer to four at Karnak, two being recorded by the king

---

[a] A record of the celebration of a jubilee on the second of Pauni in year 33 is found in a tablet at el-Bersheh (Sharpe, *Egyptian Inscriptions*, II, 47; again less accurately, II, 33). The monument is now destroyed.

[b] That is: Mentioned in texts at Karnak 4
(Includes Constantinople obelisk)
Lateran obelisk 1
Heliopolis obelisks 2
                                                    ―
Total 7

The Lateran obelisk was, of course, not completed by Thutmose III. There is a small obelisk of his at Sion house; see Birch, *History*, 102. A new obelisk of "Thotmes" (not stated which one) is mentioned in *Egypt Exploration Fund Archæological Report*, 98, 99, 22. See Breasted, "The Obelisks of Thutmose III and His Building Season in Egypt" (*Zeitschrift für ägyptische Sprache*, 39, 55–61). Legrain's recent discoveries at Karnak (*Annales*, V) arrived too late for use here.

himself and two mentioned in the tomb of Puemre (§§ 382 ff.) The former two are represented in a relief[a] where Thutmose III is presenting to Amon a magnificent array of costly gifts in gold and silver and the like. Among these appear two obelisks each inscribed with titles, etc., of Thutmose III, followed on the one by the words:

> He made (it) as his monument [for his father, Amon, lord of Thebes],[b] erecting for him two great and mighty obelisks of granite; the pyramidions (being) of electrum;[c] at the double façade of the temple.

As the inscription is different from that upon the obelisks in the tomb of Puemre, they must be a different pair.[d] The inscriptions in the tomb of Menkheperreseneb also refer to "*many obelisks and flagstaves*"[e] erected by him for Thutmose III at Thebes.

625. A scarab,[f] issued in celebration of the erection of obelisks in Karnak, bears the words:

> Thutmose III, whose obelisks abide in the house of Amon.

In addition to these four, for which we have chiefly inscriptional evidence, Thutmose III had at least one more

---

[a]In the corridor of the Annals in the great Karnak temple; published by Champollion, *Monuments*, IV, 316, 317; partially by Rosellini, *Monumenti Storici*, Text, III, 1, plate opposite p. 125; partially by Burton, *Excerpta hieroglyphica*, 29, and Brugsch, *Thesaurus*, V, 1185 ff.

[b]Brugsch and Rosellini represent this as erased, but Champollion has it in full, having doubtless inserted it from similar dedications.

[c]See Ineni (§ 103, l. 8); Lepsius says of the obelisk in tomb of Puemre: "das pyramidion ist gelb gemalt," of course representing electrum (Lepsius, *Denkmäler*, Text, III, 244). On the other obelisk the same inscription with the variant "*obelisks*" (for the dual).

[d]None of these can be the Lateran obelisk, for it was not one of a pair; but the Constantinople obelisk is one of the first pair above mentioned, for the position, of the representations and the wording of the inscriptions tally exactly (the only difference is the omission of $dsr-h^c w$ in the Golden Horus name in the Karnak relief). See *Zeitschrift für ägyptische Sprache*, 39, Tafel III, 1 and 2 (opp. p. 56), and p. 57.

[e]Virey, *Mémoires de la mission française au Caire*, V, 209, l. 15.

[f]Berlin, No 3530, *Ausführliches Verzeichniss des Berliner Museums*, 417.

obelisk in Karnak, which has itself survived, though far from its original site, viz., the Lateran Obelisk.

II. LATERAN OBELISK[a]

626. This obelisk has had an interesting history. It was intended by Thutmose III probably for the forecourt before his southern pylon (VIII) in Karnak.[b] But he apparently died after it had reached its site, but before it was erected or inscribed. There it lay for thirty-five years in "*the hands of the craftsmen*" until it was piously erected and properly inscribed with Thutmose III's dedication, etc., by his grandson, Thutmose IV, who adds also his own inscription with an account of the monument's history thus far. It is herein distinctly stated that this is the first time that a single obelisk was erected.[c] The next date of its history is that of its erection by Constantius in the Circus Maximus at Rome in 357 A. D. In 1587 it was discovered there broken into three pieces, and was set up on its present site in the next year by Pope Sixtus V.

The inscriptions of Thutmose III occupy the middle

---

[a]In the piazza of the Lateran in Rome; published in *Interpretatio Obeliscorum Urbis .... digesta per A. M. Ungarellium*, Romæ, MDCCCXLII, Tab. I; Birch, *Transactions of the Royal Society of Literature*, 2d ser., II, 228; de Horrack, *Revue Archéologique*, N. S., 1864, IX, 45 (incomplete); Marucchi, *Gli obelischi egiziani di Roma*, Tav. I and II.

[b]Thutmose III says it was set "*in the forecourt of the temple over against Karnak;*" Thutmose IV refers three times to its location: (1) when found it was lying "*on the south side of Karnak;*" (2) it was erected "*in Karnak;*" (3) it was erected "*at the upper portal of Karnak.*" Taken altogether, these data show that in No. 3 the southern entrance through Pylon VIII is meant, and there the obelisk stood. There is a reference to the same portal in the inscription of Beknekhonsu (III, 567, l. 5), where it is also called the "*upper portal.*" In both cases the same word (hr) is used for "*upper.*" It is unusual in this sense, viz., referring to the river, but occurs twice in the same way in the inscription of Zoser (Sehel, ll. 16 and 30).

[c]Hence it was not paired with the Constantinople obelisk, as Wiedemann states (*Aegyptische Geschichte*, 365).

lines, those of Thutmose IV the side lines.[a] All have suffered much from restoration by the papal architect at the last erection.

Dedication (South Side)

627. ....[b] Thutmose (III). He made (it) as his monument for his father, Amon-Re, lord of Thebes, erecting for him a single obelisk in the forecourt ($wb^{\,\flat}$) of the temple over against ($r\text{-}h^{\,\flat}\,w$) Karnak, as the first beginning of erecting a single obelisk in Thebes; that he might be given life.

North Side

.... (Thutmose III), son of Amon, of his body, whom Mut bore to him in Ishru, of the same limbs as he who fashioned him, Son of Re, Thutmose, Beautiful of Form, beloved of Amon-Re, lord of Thebes, given life, like Re.

East Side

628. .... (Thutmose III), rich in monuments in the house of Amon; making his monuments greater than that which the ancestors made, who were before; exceeding that which ever was, not resembling the likeness of anything that was made in the house of his father, Amon, that the son of Re, Thutmose, Ruler of Heliopolis, may be given life through him (nf).

West Side

.... (Thutmose III), who praises Amon, when he rises in Karnak. He sends Amon to rest in the house, "Bearer-of-Diadems," while his (Amon's) heart is glad at the monuments of his beloved son, "Enduring in Kingship."[c] Cause him to endure and to repeat for thee the celebration of this million of jubilees; Son of Re, Thutmose, Beautiful of Form, given life.

III. CONSTANTINOPLE OBELISK[d]

629. This obelisk was removed by the emperor Theodosius from Egypt to Constantinople.[e] It originally stood

---

[a]These latter will be found under his reign (§§ 830 ff.).
[b]Full five-name titulary, as in §§ 143 ff.
[c]Second name of Thutmose III.
[d]In Constantinople, published by Lepsius, *Denkmäler*, III, 60; Sharpe, *Egyptian Inscriptions*, II, 65. Only the upper portion is preserved.
[e]Wiedemann, *Aegyptische Geschichte*, 365.

somewhere in Karnak,[a] and is shown with its fellow in a relief there, in which the king offers the pair to Amon. The exact location of these obelisks, or of the pair erected by Puemre, is doubtless indicated by an inscription on a fragment of a sphinx found near Thutmose III's southern pylon (VII) at Karnak, which reads: "*He presented two obelisks of stone, one on each side of it*" (*Annales*, IV, 9), evidently meaning the door of the pylon. The inscriptions on the Constantinople obelisk[b] are as follows:

Dedication (South Side)

630. .... [c](Thutmose III); he made (it) as his monument for his father, Amon-Re, lord of Thebes; erecting [d][for him very great obelisks of red granite, the pyramidions of electrum; that he may be given life, like Re, forever].

North Side

.... (Thutmose III), whom Atum reared as a child, in the arms of Neit, Divine Mother, to be king; who has taken all lands, the extent of time; lord of jubilees (*ḥb-sd*) ———.

East Side

631. .... (Thutmose III), lord of victory, binder of every land, who makes his boundary as far as the Horns of the Earth, the marshes as far as Naharin (*N-h-r-n*) ———.

West Side

.... (Thutmose III), who crossed the "Great Bend" of Naharin (*N-h-r-n*)[e] with might and with victory at the head of his army, making a great slaughter [among them] ———.

---

[a]See § 624 and note.

[b]Petrie (*History of Egypt*, II, 131 ff.) has shown that this obelisk must have been very high. He would for this reason identify it with the great obelisks of Thutiy's inscription (§ 376), but those obelisks belonged to Hatshepsut, and, as we have seen, the Constantinople obelisk is certainly one of those shown in the Karnak relief (§ 624 and note).

[c]Full titulary except last fifth name.

[d]The Karnak relief (§ 543) furnishes the lost conclusion of this dedication.

[e]This is the campaign of the thirty-third year. See §§ 477 ff.

IV. LONDON OBELISK[a]

632. This obelisk, with its fellow, now in New York, stood in the temple of Heliopolis. Removed to Alexandria, they were erected before the temple of the Cæsars there, in 13–12 B. C.,[b] by the Roman[c] (?) architect Pontius, while Barbarus was prefect. The London obelisk, which had fallen early in the fourteenth century, was removed[d] thither in 1877 and landed in England in January, 1878. It is 68½ feet high (Petrie, *History of Egypt*, II, 127).

633. Its inscriptions[e] are not of great historical importance; the dedication is as follows:

.... Thutmose (III); he made (it) as his monument for his father, Harakhte, erecting for him two great obelisks; with pyramidion of electrum, at the fourth[f] occurrence of the jubilee (*ḥb-sd*), because he so much loved ⌈his father.⌉ May the Son of Re, Thutmose (III), be [given life] through him (*nf*).

---

[a]Stands on the Thames embankment in London; published in *Description, Antiquités*, V, 32, 33 (partially and badly); Champollion, *Monuments*, IV, 445, 446; Burton, *Excerpta hieroglyphica*, 51; phototype, Gorringe, *Egyptian Obelisks;* Brugsch, *Thesaurus*, V, 11, 30 (dedication only); King, *Cleopatra's Needle* (London, 1886).

[b]The current date, 22 B. C., is an error, to be corrected from the revised text of Merriam (*The Greek and Latin Inscriptions on the Obelisk-Crab*, by A. C. Merriam, New York, 1883) on the bronze crabs which were inserted under the obelisks at their re-erection. Those under the fallen London obelisk had, of course, disappeared; on a claw found under the other (New York) obelisk, and now in the Metropolitan Museum (New York), both the Greek and Latin versions are preserved. Merriam's copy reads:

L IH ΚΑΙΣΑΡΣ	A[N]NO XVIII CAESARIS
BAPBAPOΣ ΑΝΕΘΗΚΕ	BARBARUS PRAEF
ΑΡΧΙΤΕΚΤΟΝΟΥΝΤΟΣ	AEGYPTI POSUIT
ΠΟΝΤΙΟΥ	ARCHITECTANTE PONTIO

(Ligatures and missing portions of broken letters I have not indicated).

[c]If he be the same as the "Pontios" of the fountain in the garden of Mæcenas (Merriam, *Obelisk-Crab*, 47), he was an Athenian.

[d]See Gorringe.

[e]The middle lines are by Thutmose III; the side lines by Ramses II.

[f]On the Thames embankment, in 1901, I could see only three strokes of the numeral; nor (with an opera-glass) could I discern room for a fourth; but Brugsch read it when it was prostrate (*Thesaurus*, V, 1130) as four.

V. NEW YORK OBELISK[a]

634. It was removed to New York[b] with admirable skill and success by Lieutenant-Commander Gorringe,[c] landing in July, 1880. Unfortunately, the dedication inscription[d] is illegible, and the others contain only the conventional praise of the king. They are as follows:

East Side

635. Horus: Mighty Bull, Shining in Thebes; Favorite of the Two Goddesses; Enduring in Kingship like Re in Heaven; [e]Born of Atum, Lord of Heliopolis, Son of his body, whom Thoth fashioned;[e] whom they fashioned in the Great House in the beauty of their limbs, knowing that he would exercise a kingship enduring forever, King of Upper and Lower Egypt, Menkheperre (Thutmose III), beloved of Atum, the great god, and the divine ennead; given life, stability, and satisfaction, like Re, forever.

North Side

636. Horus: ⌈Taking⌉ the white crown; King of Upper and Lower Egypt, Menkheperre; Golden Horus: satisfied in smiting the rulers of the countries ⌈approaching⌉ him, according as his father, Re, has decreed for him victory[f] against every land, and might of the sword by his arms, in order to widen the boundaries of Egypt; Son of Re, Thutmose (III) — —.

---

[a]Central Park, New York. See introduction to London Obelisk; published in *Description, Antiquités*, V, 32, 33 (incomplete); Champollion, *Monuments*, IV, 444; Burton, *Excerpta hieroglyphica*, 52; Gorringe, *Egyptian Obelisks;* Moldenke, *The New York Obelisk* (New York, 1891).

[b]For its earlier history, see § 632.

[c]See his excellent account of the achievement in *Egyptian Obelisks*, by H. Gorringe (New York, 1882). It contains useful descriptions of the transport of the London, Paris, and other obelisks.

[d]The inscriptions of Thutmose III occupy the middle lines; the side lines are by Ramses II, as in London.

[e]This is all in one cartouche, and the words *ms* and Thoth, appearing together below, are perhaps intended to be joined as "Thutmose," although they belong to the two separate lines, "*Born* . . . . . . *fashioned*," above.

[f]See Lateran Obelisk, north side, right line (§ 831).

MEDINET HABU BUILDING INSCRIPTIONS[a]

637. The small Eighteenth Dynasty temple of Medinet Habu, on the west shore at Thebes, is so shut in by the larger buildings later erected around it that it is little noticed by the modern visitor. It was begun by Thutmose I. Although Hatshepsut certainly had a share in it, the dedication inscriptions attribute its erection to Thutmose III, but refer to an earlier temple on the spot, meaning the work of Thutmose I. They are as follows:

638. [b]......... He made (it) as his monument for his father, Amon-Re,[c] king of gods, making for him a great temple upon the ⌜——⌝ district of the West of Thutmose III (called): "Splendid-is-the-Seat-of-Amon;"[d] of fine white sandstone; that he might therefore be given life, forever.

639. .... He made (it) as his monument for his father, Amon, lord of Thebes, presider over "Splendor-of-the-West," erecting for him a splendid adytum of fine white sandstone, (⌜in⌝) his accustomed place of the first beginning. My majesty established it anew, that he might therefore be given life forever.

640. [e]......... erecting for him his splendid seat of the first beginning, establishing it as an eternal work, his majesty having found it beginning to fall to ruin; that he might be given life like Re, forever.

641. [f]......... making for him "Splendor-of-the-West," to shelter its lord and these lords of the district of Thamut ($T^{\jmath}$-$mw\cdot t$) ....

---

[a]See Brugsch, *Thesaurus*, VI, 1304-6.

[b]The following three texts are from Lepsius, *Denkmäler*, III, 38, c, and d. I have omitted in all the full fivefold titulary of Thutmose III.

[c]Chiseled out and restored.

[d]Or: "*Amon-is-Splendid-in-Throne*" (as to his throne), *Ymn-dsr-ys·t*. It is abbreviated as *dsr-ys·t*, and probably also as *Ymn-dsr* on a set of foundation deposit tools (Brugsch, *Thesaurus*, VI, 1298, 1299). Another name of the temple or district is "*Splendor-of-the-West*."

[e]Titulary and introduction are omitted. On this form see Lepsius, *Denkmäler*, Text, III, 156, as Lepsius, *Denkmäler*, III, 38, d, is wrongly reconstructed.

[f]Rougé, *Inscriptions hiéroglyphiques*, 130, and Dümichen, *Historische Inschriften*, II, xxxvi; titulary and introduction omitted as above. The other two are also from the same sources.

He made "Chamber-of-the-Cemetery" for his fathers, the lords of the splendid region..........

He made "Possessed-of-Eternity" for his father Ptah-Tatenen of "Lord-of-Life"..........[a]

HELIOPOLIS BUILDING INSCRIPTIONS

642. A round-topped stela[b] bears in the upper two-thirds a relief showing Thutmose III, offering an oblation to Harakhte. Below the relief is the following inscription:

Year 47, under the majesty of the King of Upper and Lower Egypt: Menkheperre; Son of Re: Thutmose (III), [living] forever.

His majesty commanded to encircle this temple with a thick wall of stone-work, for his father Re-Harakhte forever, when he cleansed Heliopolis, the house of Re — — — — —.[c]

643. A doorpost[d] in Cairo bears a dedication of Thutmose III, as follows:

He made (it) as his monument for his father Atum, lord of Heliopolis, making for him a doorway of benut ($bnw\cdot t$) stone, (called): "Pure-are-the-Offerings-of-Menkheperre-Beloved-of-the-Gods-of-Heliopolis."

NUBIAN WARS

644. The records of Thutmose III's conquests in Nubia are very meager; although he had evidently been early active there, as is shown by his building of the Semneh temple (§§ 167 ff.), yet the first mention of a Nubian campaign is in his fiftieth year, when in passing through the canal at the first cataract he was obliged to clear it of stones, as recorded in his inscription, cut there at the time (§§ 649 ff.).

---

[a]Two others add: "*for the father of his fathers, all the gods of the splendid region;*" and "*for his father, Amon-Re.*"

[b]Stela found by Lepsius at Heliopolis; limestone, 96 cm. high, now in Berlin, No. 1634. Published by Lepsius, *Denkmäler*, III, 29, b; I had also my own photograph of the original, and the copy for the Berlin dictionary.

[c]One line, and perhaps more, lacking.

[d]Sharpe, *Egyptian Inscriptions*, II, 34.

645. Besides this, the king commemorated his victories in Nubia by having engraved upon the front of each tower of one of his pylons[a] at Karnak a list[b] of seventeen names of towns and districts captured there. Over one list is a relief,[c] now in a very fragmentary state, representing the king sacrificing his Nubian foes before Amon. The scene is accompanied by the words:

—————— ⌜bringing⌝ the living prisoners to Egypt, all their herds being led to Egypt. He has filled the storehouse of his father, the lord of gods with —— —— of the chiefs ⌜whom⌝ he has ⌜conquered⌝. The kings have not done it (before) in this land. His name shall abide forever and ever.

Over the other list was a similar inscription, now too fragmentary for translation.

646. A further and much fuller list was placed by the king in duplicate, one on each of the two towers of the sixth Karnak pylon, a list which contains no less than 115[d] names of the towns and districts of the Nubian regions conquered.[e] One of these lists was surmounted by a relief showing the Nubian god Dedun leading and presenting to Thutmose III the towns, etc., enumerated in the list. Over both the lists is the following inscription:

List of these south[f] countries, the Nubian Troglodytes of Khenthennofer, whom his majesty overthrew, making a great[g] slaughter among them, (whose) number is unknown, and carrying away all their subjects as living captives to Thebes, in order to fill the storehouse of his father,

---

[a]Bouriant does not indicate clearly which pylon is meant, but says it is in front of the sanctuary.

[b]Daressy, *Recueil*, XI, 154, 155.

[c]South of door.   [d]Mariette's 116 is an error.

[e]Mariette, *Karnak*, 22, 23; Maspero, *Recueil*, VII, 99, 100; Golénischeff, *Zeitschrift für ägyptische Sprache*, 1882, 145–48, and Taf. VI; Dümichen, *Historische Inschriften*, II, 37; Brugsch, *Thesaurus*, VI, 1544–53.

[f]The duplicate has "*south and north!*" but as the two lists are duplicates, and the Nubian god Dedun presents them to the king, "*north*" is certainly an error.

[g]"*Great*" is from the duplicate.

Amon-Re, lord of Thebes. Lo, all lands are the subjects of his majesty, according as his father, Amon, has commanded.

647. Finally, on his southern pylon (VII) at Karnak, the king recorded a table of nearly, and possibly more than, 400 names of towns, districts, countries, etc., conquered in Nubia.[a] It was accompanied by the same inscription as that over the lists on Pylon VI. The geography of Nubia is too little known to determine the limits of the territory included in these lists, and it is uncertain how far up the Nile Thutmose III's conquests extended. As his son Amenhotep II reached the extreme southern limit at Napata, it is probable that Thutmose III's wars at least prepared the way thither, if they did not include Napata.

648. A short inscription[b] in the tomb of Ineni refers to captives and spoil from Nubia:

———— among the negroes, given from chiefs and living captives, ⌜—⌝ for divine offerings of Amon, when Kush, the wretched, was overthrown; together with the tribute of all countries, which his majesty gave to the temple of Amon as yearly dues, for the sake of the life, prosperity, and health of King Thutmose III.[c]

The above document is corroborated by a record of such offerings placed by the king in the Karnak temple (§§ 541 ff.).

I. CANAL INSCRIPTION[d]

649. On this expedition into Nubia, the king found the old Middle Kingdom canal of Sesostris III (I, 642 ff.)

---

[a]Mariette, *Karnak*, 24–26; Maspero, *Recueil*, VII, 97–99; Golénischeff, *Zeitschrift für ägyptische Sprache*, 1882, 145–48, and Taf. VI; Brugsch, *Thesaurus*, VI, 1544–53 (where material from this list is combined with others, especially the 115 names of Pylon VI).

[b]Piehl, *Inscriptions*, I, 129, Q–130, and p. 105.

[c]Piehl's copy has $Ḫpr-k\text{ʾ}-Rʿ$, which would be Sesostris I; but *mn* of *Mn-ḫpr-kʾ-Rʿ* has certainly fallen out, as offerings "*for the sake of the life, etc.*," were made only for living kings.

[d]Cut on the rock of the island of Sehel, at the first cataract. It was discovered by Mr. E. C. Wilbour in 1889, and published in *Recueil*, XIII, 202 f.; again, inaccurately, in de Morgan, *Catalogue des monuments*, 85, No. 18.

stopped up, although it had been cleared by his father, Thutmose I (§§ 74 ff.). He ordered it cleared, and was able to sail through without trouble on his return. He put up a record of the clearance, beside that of his father and in the identical language;[a] he also made the fishermen of Elephantine responsible for the yearly clearance of the passage in the future.

650. Year 50, first (month) of the third season (ninth month), day 22, under the majesty of the King of Upper and Lower Egypt, Menkheperre (Thutmose III), given life.

His majesty commanded to dig this canal, after he had found it[b] stopped up with stones, (so that) no ship sailed upon it. He sailed down-stream upon it, his heart glad, having slain his enemies.

The name of this canal is: "Opening-of-This-Way-in-the-Beauty[c]-of-Menkheperre-Living-Forever." The fishermen of Elephantine shall clear this canal each year.

II. INSCRIPTIONS OF NEHI, VICEROY OF KUSH

651. Nehi held the office of "*King's-son*," or viceroy of Kush, in the second half of the reign of Thutmose III (see § 61), beginning not later than the year 23, when he erected Thutmose III's record of victory at Wadi Halfa (§§ 411 ff.). He was evidently in charge of the alterations in the Semneh temple, later undertaken by Thutmose III. A mutilated inscription[d] of his in this temple speaks of "*bringing stone .... in restoring the monument — of eternity —*

---

[a]This probably indicates that we are not to understand literally the identical statements made by his father as to his actually sailing on the canal. Thutmose III was now an old man of eighty years at least, and it is impossible that he should have accompanied the expedition himself.

[b]Lit., "*after his finding* (infinitive) *it.*"

[c]It is, of course, the same as the Middle Kingdom canal, but is given a new name by each king.

[d]Outside, south wall, Lepsius, *Denkmäler*, III, 47, *u*, below, at the right of the door; the "*governor of the south countries*," whose name is lost on the left of the door, belongs to the Ramsessid period, as he is adoring Ramses III.

— — [*Governor of the*] *south* [*countries*], *Nehi* (*Nḥy*)." Another record[a] of his on the latest portion of the building, the northern addition,[b] is too fragmentary for translation.

652. The grotto at Ellesiyeh[c] dates from the fifty-second year[d] of Thutmose III, and contains the following inscription[e] of Nehi:

Bringing[f] the tribute of the south countries, consisting of gold, ivory, and ebony, [by] the hereditary prince, count, wearer of the royal seal, sole companion, satisfying the heart of the king at the Horns of the Earth,[g] having access to the king, pleasant to the divine limbs; companion, approaching the mighty sovereign, vigilant for the lord of the palace, king's-son, governor of the south countries, Nehi.

He saith: "I am a servant useful to his lord, filling his house with gold, giving tribute to —, consisting of the impost of the south countries; ⌜whose⌝ praise comes forth in the presence of his lord;[h] the king's-son, governor of the south countries, Nehi."[i]

Another inscription[j] of Nehi, containing only his name and titles, is on the island of Sai, one hundred miles above Semneh.

III. OFFERINGS FROM THE SOUTH COUNTRIES[k]

653. A relief shows Amon enthroned, and receiving from Thutmose III, who stands before him, a great array of offer-

---

[a]Lepsius, *Denkmäler*, III, 56, *a*.
[b]See Sethe, *Untersuchungen*, I, 21 f.
[c]Lepsius, *Denkmäler*, III, 45, *e*.
[d]See Sethe, *Untersuchungen*, I, 23, n. 1.
[e]Lepsius, *Denkmäler*, III, 46, *c* = Champollion, *Notices descriptives*, I, 80.
[f] The inscription of course accompanied a representation of the Nubians bringing the tribute before Nehi.
[g]See Index. [h]Read: *nb· f*.
[i] This inscription has been understood by Wiedemann as belonging to the tomb of Nehi; for he refers (*Aegyptische Geschichte*, 362) to this inscription to prove the statement that the Tomb of Nehi was at Silsileh (confusion with Ellesiyeh?). The tomb of Nehi is unknown, as far as I have been able to find.
[j]Lepsius, *Denkmäler*, III, 59, *b*.
[k]A relief with inscription in one of the rear rooms in Thutmose III's portion of the Karnak temple; Champollion, *Notices descriptives*, II, 165 f.

ings, including cattle, fowl, flowers, bread, all sorts of fruit, together with metal libation-vessels, necklaces, amulets, and pendants. The whole is accompanied by the following inscription:

654. Good God, Lord of the Two Lands, King of Upper and Lower Egypt, Menkheperre; he made (it) as his monument for his father, Amon-Re, lord of Thebes, [making] for him divine possessions, presenting to him all divine offerings, and very great feasts, which his majesty made for the first time as an increase of that which was before: giving an oblation of vessels of very plentiful ⌜fullness⌝; necklaces, amulets, and pendants of real[a] electrum, brought to his majesty from the south countries as their yearly impost; that he may live forever.

HYMN OF VICTORY[b]

655. At the top, occupying over one-fourth of the stela, are two scenes of worship, in each of which Thutmose III, accompanied by the goddess of the Theban necropolis, Khaftet-hir-nebes ($ḫft\cdot t$-$ḥr$-nbs), offers to Amon, with the usual superscriptions.[c]

The hymn itself in twenty-five lines occupying the remainder of the stela, is the best specimen of its class, and was later partly copied by scribes of Seti I for the wall of the great Karnak temple[d] in which this tablet was set up. The hymn is of sufficient historical importance to be included here; although due allowance must be made for its rhetorical style, it is a very helpful supplement to the Annals.

---

[a]Text has $m\ ɜ$, "*new.*"

[b]A black granite tablet 180 cm. in height, discovered by Mariette in a chamber northwest of the main sanctuary room of Karnak, now in Cairo. Text: Rougé, from a copy by Devéria, *Revue archéologique*, N. S., IV, 1861², opposite p. 196; Mariette, *Album photographique*, Pl. 32; Mariette, *Karnak*, Pl. 11. Mariette's text is very incorrect and must be compared with the photograph.

[c]The whole of both scenes was hammered out by Amenhotep IV, and has then been restored.

[d]Copied by Champollion, *Notices descriptives*, II, 96, republished by Maspero, *Du genre épistolaire*, 90, and Guieysse, *Recueil*, XI, 64, 65. See III, 117.

656. ¹Utterance of Amon-Re, lord of Thebes:
Thou comest to me, thou exultest, seeing my beauty,
O my son, my avenger, Menkheperre, living forever.
I shine for love of thee,
My heart ²is glad at thy beautiful comings into my temple;
(My) two hands furnish thy limbs with protection and life.
How pleasing is thy pleasantness toward my body.[a]
I have established ³thee in my dwelling,
I have worked a marvel for thee;
I have given to thee might and victory against all countries,
I have set thy fame (even) the fear of thee in all lands.
Thy terror as far as the ⁴four pillars of heaven;
I have magnified the dread of thee in all bodies,
I have put the roaring of thy majesty among the Nine Bows.
The chiefs of all countries are gathered in thy grasp,
⁵I myself have stretched out my two hands,
I have bound them for thee.
I have bound together the Nubian Troglodytes by tens of thousands and thousands,
The Northerners by hundreds of thousands as captives.
⁶I have felled thine enemies beneath thy sandals,
Thou hast smitten the ⌜hordes⌝ of rebels according as I commanded thee.
The earth in its length and breadth, Westerners and Easterners are subject[b] to thee,
⁷Thou tramplest all countries, thy heart glad;
None presents himself[c] before thy majesty,
While I am thy leader, so that thou mayest reach them.
Thou hast crossed the water of the Great Bend[d] of ⁸Naharin (*N-h-r-n*) with victory, with might.

---

[a]Referring to the king's adornment of the divine image as prescribed by the ritual.

[b]Lit., "*are under the place of thy face,*" an idiom for "*subject.*"

[c]Exactly the same phrase is found in Seti I's Syrian campaign (*Recueil*, XI, 59), III, 86; it is explained by the Tombos tablet, ll. 11, 12, § 73.

[d]Euphrates. On the obelisk of Thutmose III in Constantinople the same phrase is applied to him: "*who crossed the Great Bend of Naharin (N-h-r-n) with might and with victory*" (§ 631). This statement is therefore not merely poetic hyperbole, and coincides with the Annals, §§ 477 ff.

657. I have decreed for thee that they hear thy roarings and enter into caves;
I have deprived their nostrils of the breath of life.
⁹I have set the terrors of thy majesty in their hearts,
My serpent-diadem upon thy brow, it consumes them,
It makes[a] captive by the hair[b] the Kode-folk,
¹⁰It devours those who are in their marshes with its flame.
Cut down are the heads of the Asiatics (ʿ ʾ mw), there is not a remnant of them;[c]
Fallen are the children of their mighty ones.
¹¹I have caused thy victories to circulate among all lands,
My serpent-diadem gives light to thy dominion.
There is no rebel of thine as far as the circuit of heaven;
They come, bearing tribute upon their backs,
¹²Bowing down to thy majesty according to my command.
I have made powerless the invaders who came before thee;
Their hearts burned, their limbs trembling.
658. ¹³I have come, causing thee to smite the princes of Zahi (Ḏ ʾ h);
I have hurled them beneath thy feet among their highlands.
I have caused them to see thy majesty as lord of radiance,
So that thou hast shone in their faces like my image.
¹⁴I have come, causing thee to smite the Asiatics,[d]
Thou hast made captive the heads of the Asiatics[e] of Retenu.
I have caused them to see thy majesty equipped with thy adornment,
When thou takest the weapons of war in the chariot.
¹⁵I have come, causing thee to smite the eastern land,
Thou hast trampled those who are in the districts of God's-Land.
I have caused them to see thy majesty like a circling star,[f]
When it scatters its flame in fire, and gives forth its dew.
659. ¹⁶I have come, causing thee to smite the western land,
Keftyew (Kf-tyw) and Cyprus (Ysy) are in terror.
I have caused them to see thy majesty as a young bull,

---

[a] This phrase is explained in Annals, year 31, l. 10, § 470, note; for ys-ḥ ʾ k, see Sethe, *Verbum*, II, § 700.

[b] "*Hair*" is without determinative; it occurs with determinative on Tombos tablet, ll. 6, 7, § 71, q. v.

[c] Lit., "*their remnant is not.*"

[d] Ymyw-sṱ·t.   [e] ʿ ʾ mw.   [f] See I, 511, l. 2.

Firm of heart,[a] ready-horned, irresistible.
[17]I have come, causing thee to smite those who are in their marshes,
The lands of Mitanni (My-t-n) tremble under fear of thee.
I have caused them to see thy majesty as a crocodile,
Lord of fear in the water, unapproachable.

660. [18]I have come, causing thee to smite those who are in the isles;
Those who are in the midst of the Great Green (Sea) hear[b] thy roarings.
I have caused them to see thy majesty as an avenger ($nḏ·ty$)
Who rises upon the back of his slain victim.
[19]I have come, causing thee to smite the Tehenu (Libyans),
The isles of the Utentyew[c] are ⌜subject⌝ to the might of thy prowess.
I have caused them to see thy majesty as a fierce-eyed lion,
Thou makest them corpses in their valleys.

661. [20]I have come, causing thee to smite the uttermost ends of the lands,
The circuit[d] of the Great Circle (Okeanos) is inclosed in thy grasp.
I have caused them to see thy majesty as a lord of the wing,[e]
Who seizeth upon that which he seeth, as much as he desires.
[21]I have come, causing thee to smite those who are in front[f] of their land.
Thou hast smitten the Sand-dwellers as living captives.
I have caused them to see thy majesty as a southern jackal,
Lord of running, stealthy-going, who roves the Two Lands.
[22]I have come, causing thee to smite the Nubian Troglodytes,
As far as ⌜—⌝[g] (they) are in thy grasp.

---

[a]See a bead of Amenhotep II, bearing a bull, with the words: "*Firm of heart*" (Petrie, *Historical Scarabs*, XVIII, No. 1119); not uncommon.

[b]Lit., "*are under thy roarings.*"

[c]$Wįntyw$; unknown.

[d]Lit., "*That which the Great Circle encircles.*"

[e]A designation of the hawk.

[f]This is in contrast with the "*back-lands*" of l. 20; Maspero's rendering, "duars" = protected inclosures, is a conjecture which ignores the word "*land,*" written here with a single stroke, very easily to be overlooked. The text thus contrasts the nearest and the remotest Asiatic enemies of Egypt. Chabas (*Etudes sur l'antiquité historique*, 183) emends to read the same as the word for river- and harbor-mouths ($ḥ'wt$) under Ramses III.

[g]$Š'·t$, name of an uncertain Nubian country.

I have caused them to see thy majesty as thy two brothers,[a]
I have united their two arms for thee in ⌜v[ictory]⌝
662. ²³Thy two sisters,[b] I have set them as protection behind thee,
The arms of my majesty are above, warding off evil.
I have caused thee to reign, my beloved son,
Horus, Mighty Bull, Shining in Thebes, whom I have begotten, in [uprightness of heart][c].
²⁴Thutmose, living forever, who hast done for me all that my ka desired;
Thou hast erected my dwelling as an everlasting work,
Enlarging and extending (it) more than the past which had been.
The great doorway — — —.
²⁵Thou hast fêted the beauty of Amon-Re,
Thy monuments are greater than (those of) any king who has been.
When I commanded thee to do it, I was satisfied therewith;
I established thee upon the Horus-throne of millions of years;
Thou shalt continue life — — —.

TOMB OF REKHMIRE[d]

663. This tomb is the most important private monument of the Empire. The scenes and inscriptions on its walls depict and narrate the career of Rekhmire, who was prime minister, or vizier, of Egypt and governor of the residence

---

[a]Horus and Set.   [b]Isis and Nephthys.   [c]See § 138, l. 1.

[d]A cliff-tomb in the hill of Shekh Abd el-Kurna, on the west shore at Thebes; it attracted attention as early as 1819, when some scenes were copied by Cailliaud, and later published in "*Recherches sur les arts et métiers, les usages de la vie civile et domestique des anciens peuples de l'Egypte, de la Nubie et de l'Ethiopie*," par F. Cailliaud (Paris, 1831–37). Later Various scenes were published by Wilkinson, *Manners*, I, Pl. IV, etc.; Champollion, *Monuments*, 161, 164 ff.; Roṣellini, *Monumenti Civili*, 52–54; Hoskins, *Travels in Ethiopia* (London, 1835), 328; Lepsius, *Denkmäler*, III, 40, 41, and Text, III, 270 f.; Prisse, *Histoire de l'art égyptien*, 1863 (plates not numbered); Piehl, *Inscriptions hiéroglyphiques*, 113, 114, pp. 92, 93. The first attempt to publish the entire tomb was made by M. Ph. Virey. It was published by him in 1889 (*Mémoires de la mission française au Caire*, V, "*Le Tombeau de Rekhmara*"), but his work is so incomplete and incorrect, both in the drawings and the texts, that it is unusable; indeed, Virey himself translated from it the great inscription on the duties of the vizier backward! Thus this priceless monument steadily deteriorated during the last century, without a serious effort being made to preserve it in its entirety, until it was finally rescued by Mr.

during the latter half of the reign of Thutmose III, the period of Egypt's greatest power. He came of eminent family, having succeeded his uncle Woser in the vizierate,[a] and as his career brought him the highest post in the state during the most stirring years of Thutmose III's great conquests, he has put much of it in his tomb. We find in it the fullest known source for the study of the constitution of the state and the administration of the Pharaoh's government under the Empire, beside the best known representations in color of the peoples and products of Punt, Keftyew, Retenu, and Nubia.

664. Incidentally, Rekhmire also throws light upon the character of Thutmose III. After modestly remarking of himself that *"there was nothing of which he was ignorant in heaven, in earth, (or) in any quarter of the nether world;"*[b] and again: *"I was a noble, second to the king;"* he says of the king: *"Lo, his majesty knew that which occurred; there was nothing which he did not know —, he was Thoth in everything, there was no affair which he did not complete."*

I. APPOINTMENT OF REKHMIRE AS VIZIER[c]

665. The following inscription narrates Rekhmire's appointment to the highest office in the kingdom. The

---

Newberry, who published the first instalment of his complete copies in 1900 (*The Life of Rekhmara*, by Percy E. Newberry, London, 1900). From this careful work, for which we are much indebted, the following translations have been made; the plate numbers referred to are always those of Newberry's work.

[a]For a full account of his life, see Newberry, 13–20.

[b]He is, of course, referring to the affairs of his office, and to political matters. These extracts are all taken from a long inscription, too fragmentary for full translation (Pls. VII and VIII).

[c]Pls. IX and X. I had also the fragmentary copies of the same text in the tombs of Woser and Amenhotep (Newberry, 34), for which I am indebted to the kindness of Mr. Alan H. Gardiner. They fill up some lacunæ and furnish some corrections, cited as "Dupl.," but I have not added this remark merely to indicate the filling up of a lacuna. [Later: Mr. Gardiner has now published the text and duplicates, with an excellent rendering and commentary (*Recueil*, XXVI), from which I have incorporated a number of valuable points in the above.]

relief shows Thutmose III enthroned, before whom, in accordance with the statement of the inscription, Rekhmire appears for appointment.[a] The king then gives him instructions regarding the administration of his office. Unfortunately, these instructions, which occupy twenty long lines, are very fragmentary, and at the same time extremely obscure. The following version omits a number of passages which may not be safely rendered, and even so translates much more than can be understood, without a longer commentary than it is possible to offer here. It will be seen that the vizier is exhorted: to legal (l. 8), just (l. 8), and impartial (l. 15) decisions; not to be excessively forbidding, but still to keep himself aloof from the people (ll. 18, 19); finally, that his office is really to be administered according to the instructions given (l. 22). The instructions are remarkably humane in temper and show a surprisingly high appreciation of justice. As they present the fundamentals of Egyptian government, it is greatly to be regretted that they are so fragmentary and difficult. These were apparently the conventional instructions customarily delivered at the appointment of every vizier, for they were delivered to Woser, the uncle of Rekhmire, at his appointment, and also to Hapu, vizier under Thutmose IV.[b]

666. [1]Regulation laid upon the vizier, Rekhmire. [2]The officials were brought to the audience-hall, [his majesty] commanded that [3]the vizier, Rekhmire,[c] be presented [for] appointment for the first time.

[4]His majesty spake before him: ["Take heed] to thyself for the hall of the vizier; [5]be watchful over all that is done therein. Behold, it is a support[d] of the whole land; behold, as for the vizier, behold, he is not sweet, behold, bitter[d] is he, when he addresses —— [6]of copper is

---

[a]His figure has been intentionally erased.
[b]Newberry, *Rekhmara*, p. 34.
[c]Name intentionally erased from the wall.
[d]See Gardiner.

he, a wall of gold for the house of his —. Behold, he is not one setting his face toward the officials and councilors, neither one making [brethren] of all the people. Behold, — — — ⁷a man is in the dwelling of his lord, he [does] good for him; behold [he] does not — — for another.

667. Behold, the petitioner of the South, [the North] and the whole land, shall come, supplied — — — — —. ⁸Mayest thou see to it for thyself,ᵃ to do everything after that which is in accordance with law; to do everything according to the right thereof. Do not — — — that he may be just. Behold, as for an official, when he has reported ⁹water and wind of all his doings, behold, his deeds shall not be unknown — — — ⌜— — —⌝ — — —; he is not brought in because of the speech of the responsible officer, [⌜but⌝] it is known ¹⁰by the speech of his messengerᵇ as the one stating it;ᵇ he is by the side of the responsible officer as the speaker; he is not one lifting up the voice, a messenger petitioning — — — — — ¹¹or an official. Then one shall not be ignorant of his deeds; lo, it is the safetyᶜ of an official to do things according to the regulation, by doing that which is spoken by the petitioner. . . . . .ᵈ

668. ¹⁵It is an abomination of the god to show partiality. This is the teaching: thou shalt do the like, shalt regard him who is known to thee like him who is unknown to thee, and him who is near to — like him who is far ᵉ ———— ¹⁶an official who does like this, then shall he flourish greatly in the place. Do not ⌜avoid⌝ a petitioner, nor nod thy head when he speaks. As for him who draws near, who will approach to thee, do not — — — — ¹⁷the things which he saith in speaking. Thou shalt punish him when thou hast let him hear that on account of which thou punishest him. Lo, they will say, the petitioner loves him who nods the head ⌜— — —⌝ — —.

669. ¹⁸Be not enraged toward a man unjustly, but be thou enraged concerning that about which one should be enraged; show forth the fear of thee; let one be afraid of thee, (for) a prince is a prince of whom one is afraid. Lo, the true dread of a prince is to do ¹⁹justice. Behold, if a man show forth the fear of him a myriad of times, there is some-

---

ᵃAn ethical dative which might be omitted in the translation. Dupl. has *m᾽k nk*.

ᵇOr: "*Tell it not, (for) he is, etc.*"   ᶜLit., "*refuge.*"

ᵈIn l. 13 there is a reference to an unjust vizier Khety, but in what connection is uncertain.

ᵉFor a similar antithesis of *tkn*, "be near," and *w᾽ y*, "be far," see *Hierat. Papyrus aus den königlichen Museen zu Berlin*, II, 36, l. 8.

thing of violence in him. Be not known to the people; and they shall not say: "He is (only) a man."[a]

670. [20]He who speaks a lie shall go forth according to his docket,[b] Lo, ⌜—⌝ thou shalt do thy office, as thou doest justice. Lo, one shall desire to do justice .... [21] .... Lo, one shall say of the chief scribe of the vizier: "A scribe of justice," shall one say of him. Now, as for the hall, wherein thou holdest hearings there shall be a broad-hall therein ———. ⌜He who dispenses⌝ [22]justice before all the people, he is the vizier. Behold, a man shall be in his office, (as long as) he shall do things according to that which is given to him. Lo, a man is ⌜—⌝ when he shall act according to that which has been told him. Do not — thy — in — — [23]that thou knowest the law thereof. Lo, let one ⌜—⌝ to the proud-hearted;[c] the king loves the fearful more than the proud-hearted. Do thou according to ⌜that which is given⌝ to thee; lo, ——— [24] .... ———.

II. DUTIES OF THE VIZIER[d]

671. This, the most important inscription known on the organization of the state under the Eighteenth Dynasty, is unfortunately incomplete. Two duplicates[e] found by Newberry fill out many of the lacunæ, but the last fifth of the text is very fragmentary. This is especially unfortunate, as the latter part of the inscription is by far the most intelligible and deals with functions easily understood.

672. The inscription is an outline of the duties of the vizier, of the greatest interest. After prescribing the external arrangements for the vizier's daily sitting in his "*hall*," as his office is termed, the document proceeds to the daily conference of the vizier with the king, and, immediately

---

[a]This is the same advice given by Amenemhet I to his son Sesostris I (I, 479, ll. 3–5).

[b]See Duties of Vizier, § 683, l. 14.

[c]Lit., "*mighty-hearted.*"   [d]Pls. II and III.

[e]From the tomb of Woser, belonging to the early part of Thutmose III's reign; and the tomb of Amenemopet, belonging to Amenhotep II's reign (see Newberry, 25 f.).

subsequent to this, the daily reports of the chief treasurer and the vizier to each other, and of the chief officials to the vizier. These daily duties are now followed by a long list of exceedingly varied functions to be discharged by the vizier, making in all at least thirty. There seems to be no logical order in the enumeration, and the varied character of the list will be evident from a reading of the marginal heads, which may serve in lieu of a table of content here. It will be seen that the vizier is grand steward of all Egypt, and that all the activities of the state are under his control. He has general oversight of the treasury, and the chief treasurer reports to him; he is chief justice, or head of the judiciary; he is chief of police, both for the residence city and the kingdom; he is minister of war, both for army and navy; he is secretary of the interior and of agriculture, while all general executive functions of state, with many that may not be classified, are incumbent upon him. There is, indeed, no prime function of the state which does not operate through his office. He is a veritable Joseph, and it must be this office which the Hebrew writer has in mind in the story of Joseph. The only person other than the king to whom he owes any respect is the chief treasurer, to whom he seems to offer a daily statement that all is well with the royal possessions. Such power is, of course, possible only in a highly centralized state, and Egypt is shown by this inscription to be in the Empire simply a vast estate of the Pharaoh, of which the vizier is chief steward. The vizier's functions are distributed promiscuously throughout the document, as follows:

I. Judiciary (§§ 675, 681, 685–6, 688–91, 700, 704, 705).
II. Treasury (§§ 676, 680, 706, 708).
III. War { Army (§§ 693–95, 702).
           Navy (§§ 710, 687).

IV. Interior (§§ 677, 687, 697, 707).
V. Agriculture (§§ 698, 699).
VI. General Executive (§§ 692, 701, 703).
VII. Advisory and Unclassified (§§ 678, 679, 682, 684, 696, 709, 711).

673. It is impossible to discuss this inscription without raising the question of its origin and exact character. The fact that it is known to exist in two other tombs also, would suggest that it was not an informal enumeration of the vizier's duties drawn up by himself especially for his tomb, but a close examination of the document itself shows that it could not possibly have been a state document to the decrees of which the vizier was amenable. It was evidently no more than we have suggested, viz., a list of the vizier's duties, compiled by himself, for recording in his tomb. It must, of course, have been based upon the existent laws, from which it may, in places, contain extracts. In any case, it contains the purport of certain of the laws in force at the time, some of which, like those regulating the criminal docket, are very interesting and important. The only other surviving example of the laws of Egypt are in the Decree of Harmhab (III, 45 ff.), for of the "*40 skins,*" undoubtedly rolls containing "*this law which is in his hand*" mentioned by our inscription, nothing has ever been found. Such law was, of course, the codified fiat of the Pharaoh, as is evident in the Decree of Harmhab.

674. The language of the document is very difficult, and demonstrates how helpless our incomplete knowledge of the Egpytian dictionary leaves us as soon as we pass from the conventional language of the few classes of monuments familiar to us, to some untrodden path. Especially the legal enactments of the first half of the inscription abound in technical terms, most of which are totally unknown

to us. These render a final translation impossible, in many places.

External Arrangement of the Sitting

675. ¹Arrangement of the sitting[a] of the governor of the (residence) city, and vizier of the Southern City, (and) of the court, in the hall of the vizier. As for every act[b] of this official, the vizier while hearing in the hall of the vizier, he shall sit upon a chair,[c] with a rug upon the floor, and a dais upon it, a cushion[d] under his back, a cushion under his feet, a — upon it, ²and a baton at his hand; the 40 skins[e] shall be open before him. Then the magnates of the South[f] (shall stand) in the two aisles before him, while the master of the privy chamber is on his right, the ⌜receiver of income⌝ on his left, the scribes of the vizier at his (either) hand; one[g] ⌜corresponding⌝ to another, with each man at his proper place. One shall be heard after another, without allowing one who is behind to be heard before ³one who is in front. If one in front says: "There is none being heard at my hand," then he shall be taken by the messenger of the vizier.[h]

Intercourse of Palace with Outside World

676. There shall be reported to him the sealing of the sealed chambers up to (that) hour and the opening of them up to (that) hour. There shall be reported to him the affairs of the fortresses of the South and

---

[a]This is not the title of the entire document, but refers only to the opening paragraph.

[b]Lit., "*every doing*" (inf.!).

[c]Evidently a particular kind of chair called *phdw*, a word not occurring elsewhere.

[d]Erman; original has *šd*, "*a skin*," evidently meaning a leathern cushion so common on Egyptian furniture. "*Back*" is, of course, a euphemism.

[e]This word (*šsm*) is new; it has the determinative of leather. The 40 *šsm* are depicted in the accompanying scene lying on the floor before the vizier (§ 712). Erman suggests they may have been the leather cases in which the rolls of the papyrus were preserved; but such state documents were written on leather, e. g., the records of Thutmose III (§ 433).

[f]Only the magnates of the South, as the vizier with whom we are dealing is the southern vizier.

[g]"*One*" refers to the entire company before him; each shall occupy his proper place with reference to the other.

[h]Meaning that as soon as a petitioner in front sees no one before him ("*at his hand*"), he may say so, and be taken to the vizier by his messenger.

North. The going out of all that goes out ⁴of the king's-house shall be reported to him; and the coming in of all that comes into the king's-house shall be reported to him.[a] Now, as for everything going in (and) everything going out on the floor of the court, they shall go out (and) they shall go in through his messenger, who shall cause (them) to go in (and) go out.

Reports of Overseers

677. The overseers of hundreds and the overseers of ⌜—⌝[b] shall report to him their affairs.

Daily Report to Pharaoh

678. ⁵Furthermore, he shall go in to take counsel on the affairs of the king, L. P. H., and there shall be reported to him the affairs of the Two Lands in his house every day. He shall go in to Pharaoh, before the chief treasurer; he[c] shall wait at the northern flagstaff. Then the vizier shall come, proceeding from the gate of the great double façade.

Report of Treasurer and Vizier to Each Other

679. Then ⁶the chief treasurer, he shall come to meet him (the vizier) and shall report to him, saying: "All thy affairs are sound and prosperous; every responsible incumbent has reported to me, saying: 'All thy affairs are sound and prosperous, the king's-house is sound and prosperous.'" Then the vizier, he shall report to the chief treasurer, saying: ⁷"All thy affairs are sound and prosperous; every seat of the court is sound and prosperous.[d] There have been reported to me

---

[a]The "*king's-house*" is a whole, of which the "*court*" is but one part, in which the king lived. Entrance to the "*king's-house*" was only reported to the vizier, while entrance to the "*court*" could be gained only under conduct of his "*messenger*."

[b]*Mr-ḥrp*.

[c]The chief treasurer; the front of the palace was decorated, like the temple façades, with flagstaves, and near one of these the treasurer is to wait.

[d]On a fragment in the Louvre (without a number) is a relief showing a line of twelve priests: three of the "*first order*," three of the "*second order*," three of the "*third order*," and three of the "*fourth order*." Over their heads are fragments of two lines, as follows: "——— *in the temple of Amon, in 'Most-Splendid-of-Splendors'* (name of Der el-Bahri temple), *by the High Priest of Amon in 'Most-Splendid-of-Splendors,' Senu (Snw), triumphant* ——— *of Amon and of Hathor, Mistress of Thebes. They praise thee, they love thee, for all thy affairs are sound and prosperous in this temple.*" The High Priest of Hatshepsut's temple of Der el-Bahri is thus eulogized in the formal terms for a faithful officer's report. See the same words in the report of the lay priests at Illahun, *Zeitschrift für ägyptische Sprache*, 37, 97.

the sealing of the sealed chambers to this hour (and) the opening of them to (this) hour, by every responsible incumbent."ᵃ

Daily Opening of the King's-House

680. Now, after each has reported to the other, of the two officials, then the vizier shall send ⁸to open every gate of the king's-house, to cause to go in all that goes in, (and) ⌜to go out⌝ᵇ all that goes out likewise, by his messenger, who shall cause it to be put in writing.

Irregularities among the Princes

681. Let not any official be empowered to judge ⌜against a superior⌝ in his hall. If there be any assailantᶜ against ⁹any of these officials in his hall, then he shall cause that heᵈ be brought to the judgment-hall. It is the vizier who shall punish him, in order to expiate his fault. Let not any official have power to punish in his hall. There shall be reported ⌜to⌝ him every judgment which is against the hall, ⌜when he repairs thereto.⌝

Duties and Treatment of the Vizier's Messengers

682. As for every messenger ¹⁰whom the vizier sends with a message for an official, from the first official to the last, let him not be ⌜swerved⌝, and let him not be conducted; the official shall repeat his vizierial message while heᵉ stands before ¹¹the official, repeating his message and going forth to wait for him. His messenger shall seize the mayors and village sheiks for the judgment-hall; his messenger shall give the ⌜regulation⌝ ——— his messenger gives answer, saying: "I have been sent ¹²with a message for the official so and so; he caused that I be conducted, and

---

ᵃIt will be seen that the vizier reports on the "*court*," while the treasurer reports on the "*king's-house*." Now, the vizier possesses the reports concerning the "*king's-house*" (mentioned in ll. 3 and 4), by which he is enabled to control the report of the treasurer on the "*king's-house*." Similarly, if we possessed a list of the treasurer's duties, we should doubtless find that he received daily reports on the matters of the "*court*," by means of which he was enabled to control the vizier's report on the "*court*," which the vizier conducted directly by means of his messenger.

ᵇThe publication shows no lacuna, but the sense demands the inserted phrase.

ᶜ*Sk*.

ᵈThe confusion of pronouns is also in the original.

ᵉThe messenger.

he caused that something be entrusted to me.ᵃ Hear ⌜the affair⌝ of this official ———— expiate those things, about which there has been litigation by the vizier in ¹³his hall, in every ⌜crime⌝, with greaterᵇ punishment than by cutting off a limb.

Criminals

683. Now, as for every act of the vizier, while hearing in his hall; and as for every one who shall — — — — — [⌜he shall record⌝] everything concerning which he hears him. He who has not disproved the chargeᶜ at ¹⁴his hearing, which takes place ⌜—⌝, then it shall be entered in the criminal docket. He who is in the great prison,ᵈ not able to disprove the charge of hisᵉ messenger, likewise; when their case comes on another time, then one shall report and determine whether it is in the criminal docket, ¹⁵and there shall be ⌜executed⌝ the things concerning which entry was made, in order to expiate their offense.

Loan of Vizier's Records

684. As for any writing sent [⌜by the vizier⌝ to] any hall, being those which are not confidential,ᶠ it shall be taken to himᵍ together with the documents of the keepers ¹⁶thereof under seal of the (sḏm·w-) officers, and the scribes thereof after them; then he shall open it; then after he has seen it, it shall return to its place, sealed with the seal of the vizier. (But) if he furthermore ask for ¹⁷a confidential writing, then let it not be taken by the keepers thereof.

Summons of Petitioner

685. Now,ʰ as for every messenger whom the vizier sends on account of any petitioner, he shall cause that he go to him.

ᵃLit., "*put upon my neck.*" This message evidently furnishes the formula to be used by the messenger in reporting the replies of the officials to whom he has been sent.

ᵇErman; lit., "*with an increase upon punishment by, etc.*"

ᶜLit., "*warded off the evil.*"

ᵈOn our scanty knowledge of the prisons, see Spiegelberg, *Studien*, 64 ff.

ᵉOf the vizier.

ᶠLit., "*wrapped up.*"

ᵍThe official desiring to consult the document.

ʰOn this and the following paragraph, see Gardiner, *Inscription of Mes.* 37, 38.

Real Estate Cases

686. Now, as for every petitioner to the vizier concerning lands, he shall dispatch him (the messenger) to him, in addition to a hearing of ¹⁸the land-overseer and the local council[a] of the ⌈district.⌉[b] He shall decree a stay for him of two months for his lands in the South or North. As for his lands, however, which are near to the Southern City and to the court, he shall decree a stay for him of three days, being ¹⁹that which is according to law; (for) he shall[c] hear every petitioner according to this law which is in his hand.

Reports of District Officials

687. It is he who brings in the officials of the district; it is he who sends them out; they report [to] him the affairs of their districts.

Wills, Etc.

688. Every property-list[d] is brought to him; it is he who seals it.

Settlement of Registered Boundaries

689. ²⁰It is he who administers the ⌈gift⌉-lands[e] in all regions. As for every petitioner who shall say: "Our boundary is unsettled;" one shall examine whether it is under the seal of the official thereof; then he shall seize the seizures[f] of the local council who unsettled it.

Treatment of Unregistered Boundaries

690. Now, as for every remarkable case,[g] and everything pertaining thereto; do not look ²¹at anything therein.

---

[a] $\underline{D}\!\flat\underline{d}\!\flat\!\cdot\!t$. Whether this is a hearing before the vizier or a local hearing under the charge of "*messenger*," is not clear.

[b] $T\!m\flat$

[c] The verbal form (*sḏmtf*) seems to be incorrect.

[d] Such a property-list is frequently a will. A will, with the registration docket of the vizier's office upon it, is preserved to us; it reads: "(Date); *Done in the office* (lit., *hall*)*of the vizier in the presence of the governor of the city and vizier Khety, by the seal-scribe of the people's-bureau, Amenemhet-Ameny*." A remark, probably indicating the payment of the tax on the transfer, follows (Griffith, *Kahun Papyri*, Pl. XIII, ll. 9–12). The document is from the Middle Kingdom.

[e] These lands (*šd*) are thought by Moret to be the divisible lands held by tenantry as distinguished from indivisible tracts held by nobles (*Zeitschrift für ägyptische Sprache*, 39, 36).

[f] Meaning?

[g] Unregistered land? Erman.

Manner of Petition

691. One shall put every petition[a] in writing, not permitting that he petition orally.[b] Every petitioner to the king shall be reported to him,[c] after he puts (it) in writing.

Intercourse between Court and Local Authorities

692. It is he who dispatches every messenger of the king's-house, L. P. H., who is sent to the mayors and village sheiks. It is he who dispatches [22]every circuit messenger, every expedition of the king's-house. It is he who acts as the one who — — [in] the South and North, the Southern Frontier (*tp rsy*) and Abydos (*T ᴣ -wr*). They shall report to him all that happens among them, on the first day of every four-month season; they shall bring to him the writing thereof, in their hands, together with their local council.

Mustering King's Escort

693. [23]It is he who gathers the troops, moving in attendance upon the king, in journeying northward or southward.

Garrison of Residence City

694. It is he who stations the rest who remain in the Southern City, (and) in the court, according to the decision in the king's-house, L. P. H.

General Army Orders

695. The commandant of the ruler's table[d] is brought to him, to his hall, together with [24]the council of the army, in order to give to them the regulation of the army.

Advisory Functions

696. Let every office, from first to last,[e] proceed[f] to the hall of the vizier, to take counsel with him.

Felling Timber

697. It is he who dispatches to cut down trees according to the decision in the king's-house.

---

[a]Lit., "*petitioner*," strange as it seems; hence "*he*" in the next clause.
[b]Egyptian: "*by hearing.*"   [c]The vizier.
[d]A district commandant who delivered game and supplies for the prince's table. In the Middle Kingdom the nomarchs also had such officers.
[e]Lit., "*every first office to every last office.*"
[f]Only the determination of a verb of motion occupies the place where the verb should be.

Water-Supply

698. It is he who dispatches [25]the official staff, to attend to the water-supply[a] in the whole land.

Annual Plowing

699. It is he who dispatches the mayors and village sheiks to plow for harvest time.

Overseers of Labor?

700. It is he who ⌜appoints⌝ the overseers of hundreds in the hall of the king's-house.

Audience for Town Authorities

701. It is he who ⌜arranges⌝ the hearing of the mayors and village sheiks who go forth in his name, of South and North.

Administration of Fortresses

702. [26]Every matter is reported to him; there are reported to him the affairs of the southern fortress; and every arrest which is for seizing — — —.

Nome Administration, Boundaries, Etc.

703. It is he who makes the ⌜—⌝ of every nome; it is he who ' hears'" it. It is he who dispatches the ⌜district⌝ soldiers and scribes to carry out the ⌜administration⌝ of the king. [27]The records of the nome are in his hall. It is he who hears concerning all lands. It is he who makes the boundary of every nome, the field ⌜—⌝, all divine offerings[b] and every contract.

Record of Depositions, Etc.

704. It is he who takes every deposition; it is he who hears the rejoinder when a man comes for argument with his opponent.[c]

Appointment of Courts for Special Cases, Etc.

705. It is he who appoints every appointee [28]to the hall of judgment, when any litigant comes to him from the king's-house.[d] It is he who hears every edict.

---

[a]See I, 407, l. 6.   [b]Temple income.

[c]Lit., "*comes to words with his second.*" This evidently refers to argument of plaintiff and defendant before the Vizier. See Gardiner, *Inscription of Mes*, 36, 37.

[d]He appoints members of special courts for cases where a member of the king's household is concerned.

Sacred and Royal Revenues in Residence City and Court

706. It is he who hears concerning the "Great Beauty" of every divine offering. It is he[a] who levies all taxes of the income, and who gives it to him ⌜—⌝ ――― every — in the Southern City, (and) in the court. It is he who seals ²⁹it under his seal. It is he who hears every matter; it is he who makes the distribution of the tribute to the crown possessions. The great council shall report to him their dues ――― every — that is brought to ³⁰the judgment-hall, and every offering to the judgment-hall, he shall hear concerning it. It is he who opens the gold-house, together with the chief treasurer. It is he who inspects the tribute of [all] lands[b] ――― ³¹chief steward, together with the great council ($ḏ^ꜣḏ^{ꜣ\cdot}t\ wr^{\cdot}t$). It is he who makes the ⌜lists of⌝ all bulls, ⌜of⌝ which a ⌜list⌝ is made.

Canal Inspection (?) in Residence City

707. It is he who inspects the ⌜water-supply⌝ ($swr^{\cdot}t$)[c] on the first of every ten-day period ⌜—⌝ ――― ³²concerning every matter of the judgment-hall.

Revenues from Local Authorities

708. The mayors, village sheiks, and every man shall report to him, all their tribute. Every district supervisor, and every [⌜overseer of⌝] hundreds, they shall report to him every litigation ⌜—⌝ ――― ³³they shall report to him furthermore, monthly, in order to control the tribute. The treasurers and the ($kf^ꜣ\ yb$-) officials shall ―――.

Observation of Sirius and High Nile

709. ――― the rising of Sirius, and the ⌜—⌝ of the Nile. There shall be reported to him the high (Nile.)[d] ――― ⌜— — — —⌝ ³⁴—.

Administration of Navy

710. It is he who exacts the ships for every requisition made upon him. It is he who dispatches every messenger of the king's-house to ―――. When the king is with the army, it is he who makes report

---

[a]Read: ntf.

[b]This function of the vizier is depicted with great detail in a splendid series of wall scenes in this tomb (§§ 760 ff.).

[c]See Florence Stela, No. 1774.

[d]Similar duties are referred to in the tomb of Min (*Mémoires de la mission française au Caire*, V, 368), but the context is unfortunately broken. The following is visible: "――― *concerning the affairs of the king's-house, conducting the work — — — of the high Nile.*"

―――. ³⁵Report is made to him by all the officials of the head of the navy, from the highest to the lowest. It is he[a] who seals the edicts ――― ⌜―⌝ of the keeper of ⌜―⌝ who is dispatched with a message of the king's-house.

Method of Reporting to Vizier

711. Every report shall be reported to him by ³⁶the doorkeeper of the judgment-hall, who reports ⌜on his part⌝ all that he (the vizier) does while hearing in the hall of the vizier.

III. THE SITTING OF THE VIZIER[b]

Scene

712. The vizier sits enthroned at one end of the hall; before him are the "*Magnates of the South*" and the "*scribes of the vizier*," in two rows on each side of the central aisle; in this aisle, directly in front of the vizier, are the forty rolls of the law (see § 675, l. 2). Two deputies are leading petitioners down the aisle, and outside are other deputies or door-keepers receiving the petitioners as they arrive.

Inscription

713. Sitting, in order to hear the petitioners, in the hall of the vizier; by the hereditary prince, count, wearer of the royal seal, sole companion, (*mr· t-ntr-*) priest, chief of the six courts of justice, a mouth giving satisfaction in the whole land; (*sm-*) priest, ⌜master of every wardrobe⌝, judging justly, not showing partiality, sending two men forth satisfied, judging the weak and the powerful, not ⌜bringing sorrow⌝ to the one who petitioned him; satisfying the heart of the king before the Two Lands, prince before the people, companion approaching the sovereign, favorite of him who is in the palace.

IV. RECEPTION OF PETITIONS[c]

714. The following scene has unfortunately almost entirely disappeared; it portrayed the reception of petitions, from the people, regulated in the "Duties of the Vizier" (§§ 685 and 691).

[a]Text has *nf;* I emend to *ntf.*
[b]Pl. IV. See the description of the sitting in the first three lines of the preceding inscription (§ 675).
[c]Pl. XV.

Scene

Rekhmire stands leaning upon his staff, while scribes pass out among the people, where they receive and register complaints and petitions. Over Rekhmire is the following:

Inscription

715. Going forth over the land every morning to do the daily favors, to hear the matters of the people, the petitions of the South and the North; not preferring the great above the humble, rewarding the oppressed ⌈— —⌉, bringing the evil to him who committed it; by ——— [Rekhmire].

V. INSPECTION OF TAXES OF UPPER EGYPT

716. These important scenes,[a] representing the only tax-lists we possess, show the local officials of Upper Egypt paying their dues (*yp·w*) to the vizier. Just what part of the total revenues of Upper Egypt these dues formed, it is impossible to state; but that they were only a part is certain. For the inscription clearly indicates that they are only the dues exacted from the local officials (as a tax upon their offices), and not the taxes paid by the people, for which we find a different designation (*bk·w*), from that employed here. This tax (*yp·w*) upon the officials is the one remitted by Harmhab (III, 63). It was collected by the vizier, while the tax (*bk·w*) upon the people was, of course, collected by the chief treasurer. It is noticeable that the vizier has charge of these revenues (*yp·w*) only in Upper Egypt, showing clearly the extent of his fiscal jurisdiction. There was, of course, another vizier for Lower Egypt from below Assiut to the sea.[b]

Owing to the loss of a large portion of the lower rows, it is impossible to summarize and determine the total income

---

[a]Pls. V and VI. They are published for the first time by Newberry, having been passed over by all previous students of the tomb. We are therefore much indebted to him for their rescue.

[b]A relief at Berlin, for example, shows the two viziers (No. 12411); see additional references, Newberry, 17, n. 3, and a full statement, Gardiner, *Inscription of Mes*, 33. It is probable that the office was not divided before the Empire, and probably not before Thutmose III.

of the crown from this source in Upper Egypt. Gold, silver, cattle, and linen form the most valuable items; of the others many are uncertain, and have therefore only been transliterated. The list begins with the fortresses of Bigeh and Elephantine at the first cataract, and extends as far north as Assiut. Some of the place-names are unknown, and have been merely transliterated below. The list is divided into two parts: the first from the cataract to Thebes, and the second from Thebes to Assiut; that is, the first above, the second below Thebes.

A. ABOVE THEBES

Scene

717. Rekhmire, at the right, receives the local officials, who advance in four lines, bringing their dues.[a] Over their heads are inscribed their titles, the names of the towns or localities to which they belong, and the amounts of their dues.

Over Rekhmire

Inspection of the taxes ($yp\cdot w$) counted to[b] (the credit of) the hall of the vizier of the Southern City, and counted against the mayors, the town-rulers, the district officials, the recorders of the districts, their scribes, and their field-scribes, who are in the South ($Tp\text{-}rŝy$); beginning with Elephantine and the fortress of Bigeh; made according to the writings of ancient time, by the hereditary prince. . . . .[c] [Rekhmire].

	OFFICIAL AND PLACE	TAX
718.	Commandant of the fortress of Bigeh ($Sn\text{-}mw\cdot t$)	20 deben of gold 5 good hides apes; 10 bows 20 large staves of ⌜cedar⌝ wood

[a]There are thirty-one officials still preserved; of five of these the inscriptions with names and dues are lost. Besides this, at least three more, with their inscriptions, have been lost in the lower row; that is, nearly one-fourth of the officials with their dues are lost. How many names of localities are lost is uncertain.

[b]The two prepositions "*to*" or "*for*" (n) and "*against*" (r) are correlative, and antithetic, the first being the preposition of advantage, the second of disadvantage. This is precisely as in Arabic, where li and $ʿală(y)$ have the same relation; thus: li $dăynŭn$ = "A debt is (owing) to me" (lit., "to me is a debt") is opposed to: $ʿalăyyă$ $dăynŭn$ = "I owe a debt" (lit., "against me is a debt"). See Uni, l. 36 (I, 320) for the same use of yp n, "*count to.*"

[c]Omitted titles.

	Official and Place	Tax
719.	Commandant of the fortress of Elephantine	40 deben of gold, tribute weight; 1 chest of (*mt*-) linen ———
	Scribe of the recorder of Elephantine	6 deben of gold, in tribute weight; a pedet of raiment; a large ⌜bolt⌝
	Kenbeti of Elephantine	2 deben of gold; 2 pedet of raiment; a large ⌜bolt⌝; 1 chest of (*mt*-) linen
	Scribe of Elephantine	1 deben of gold; 2 oxen (*ng ꜣ· w*)
720.	Recorder of Ombos	2 deben of gold; ———
	Scribe of the Recorder of Ombos	1 deben of gold, in tribute weight; 3 large bolts; ———
		— deben of silver, in tribute weight
	Kenbeti of Ombos	4 deben of gold, in tribute weight; 1 ox; 1 two-year-old
721.	Mayor of Edfu	8 deben of gold, tribute weight; a great ⌜bolt⌝
	His scribe	
	Recorder of Edfu	gold (amount ?); 1 ox
	Town-Ruler of *Pr-mr-yw*[a]	1 deben of gold; 1 chest of (*mt*-) linen; 2 oxen
722.	Mayor of Nekhen	4 deben of gold; 3 deben of silver; 1 ox; 1 two-year-old
	Kenbeti of Nekhen	3 deben of gold, in tribute weight; 1 bead necklace [⌜of⌝ gold]; 2 oxen; 1 chest of (*mt*-) linen; 1 chest of (*dꜣ w*-) linen
	(Name lost, top row)	Garments, 2 (*pdt*-) bolts; (Linen) 1 great (*sm ꜣ·t*-) ⌜bolt⌝; gold (amount ?)
	(Name lost, top row)	1 (*wn-dw*-) ox, 2 yearlings; Gold, linen

[a] An uncertain town.

	Official and Place	Tax
723.	Town-Ruler of Esneh	— of silver 8 of gold 2 oxen; grain, linen
	Scribe of the Islands of Esneh	2 deben of gold ½ deben of silver 1 bead necklace ⌜of⌝ gold 1 (*wn-dw-*) ox, 1 yearling; linen
	Kenbeti of Esneh[a]	(*dꜣw-*) linen 2 chests of (*mt-*) linen grain 2 calves, 2 oxen (*sꜣ*)
724.	Recorder of Gebelen	1 deben of gold; ½ deben of silver
725.	Scribe of the District of ⌜—⌝	Gold, bead necklace, linen, yearlings; two-year-olds; (numbers lost)
726.	Scribe of the Islands which are in the South (*tp-rśy*)	2 deben of gold 30 pigeons ꜥ*nb-tm*ꜣ·*t* 2 oxen, 5 yearlings 1 chest of (*mt-*) linen
727.	Recorder of Hermonthis	3 deben of gold 10 ꜥ*nb-tm*ꜣ·*t* 1 chest of (*mt-*) linen
	Scribe of the Recorder of Hermonthis	Gold (amount lost) (*dꜣw-*) linen
	Scribe of — the District of Hermonthis	2 deben of gold 1 chest of (*mt-*) linen 40 pigeons 5 firstlings of the year 2 oxen, 5 yearlings Grain, honey
	Kenbeti of the District of Hermonthis	4 deben ⌜of⌝ gold 1 deben of silver 1 bead necklace ⌜of⌝ gold 1 chest of (*mt-*) linen (*dꜣw-*) linen
728.	Recorder of House of Hathor (*Pr-Ḥthr*)	(Lost)

---

[a] Only the end of the name is preserved. In the second row next to Esneh there is another Kenbeti, whose place-name is lost. He brings gold (amount?), 1 chest of (*mt-*) linen, 2 heket of grain, and 1 heket of grain (sic!).

B. BELOW THEBES

729. The scene is the same as before.[a]

Over Rekhmire

Inspection of the taxes (*yp·w*) counted to (the credit of) the hall of the vizier of the Southern City (and) counted against the mayors, the town-rulers, the district officials, the recorders of the districts, their scribes and the — of their fields, from above Koptos to below S[iut], by the hereditary prince . . . . [Rekhmire].

	OFFICIAL AND PLACE	TAX
730.	— in the midst of the City (Thebes)	1 deben of silver 3 deben of gold 1 chest of (*mt-*) linen 2 two-year-olds 3 yearlings
731.	Scribe of the District of *Rs-nj·t*	1 chest of (*mt-*) linen Honey 3 heket of grain 3 yearlings 3 two-year-olds 2 full-grown (oxen) gold (amount lost); bead necklace
732.	— of Cusae	3 deben of gold 1 bead necklace ⌜of⌝ gold ——— ———
	— of Cusae	— deben of gold — deben of silver ———

[a]The two lower rows have mostly disappeared; twenty-four figures of officials are visible, and the tribute of two more is partially preserved. Of these twenty-six, the dues of one are totally lost, while five more figures (at least) with their dues have also disappeared; thus the dues of about one-fifth of the officials have been lost; the number of place-names lost (if any) is uncertain.

	Official and Place	Tax
733.	Kenbeti of the District of of Coptos	1 deben of silver ½ deben of gold 10 measures of ($y^c\,h$-) grain 1 heket of grain 1 ($hbn\cdot t$-) jar of honey; calves
734.	Kenbeti of the District of Dendera	1 deben of gold — — of silver ($y^c\,h$-) grain 10 heket of grain 1 ($hbn\cdot t$-) jar of honey 5 calves — two-year-olds 1 ox
735.	Mayor of Haturt-Amenemhet ($Ht\text{-}wr\cdot t\text{-}Ymn\text{-}m\text{-}h^{\mathrm{o}}\cdot t$)	5 deben of gold 1 deben of silver, tribute weight 200 (kw-) loaves 1,000 (sht-) loaves -3 wdn 10 sacks of ⌜—⌝ 3 tm^{o} 5 calves 3 yearlings 3 two-year-olds 2 (full-grown) oxen 500 pigeons
736.	Recorder of $W^{\mathrm{o}}\,h\text{-}ys\cdot t$ Scribe of the Recorder of $W^{\mathrm{o}}\,h\text{-}ys\cdot t$	½ deben of gold 1 chest of (mt-) linen 1 ($hbn\cdot t$) jar of honey 1 two-year-old 1 bolt of ($d^{\mathrm{o}}\text{-}w$-) linen cattle
737.	Recorder of Diospolis Parva ($Ht\text{-}shm$) Scribe of the Recorder of Diospolis Parva	5 deben of gold 1 heket of (tb-) grain ($š^c$-) grain 1 measure of ($y^c\,h$-) grain 1 measure of ($sw\cdot t$-) grain 3 measures of southern grain 1 measure of southern grain pigeons, linen (many items lost) 3 deben of gold

	Official and Place	Tax
738.	Recorder of Abydos	1 deben of gold (*mt*-) linen (*d᾿w*-) linen 1 (*hbn·t*-) jar of honey 1 two-year-old
	His scribe	1 deben of gold 3 two-year-olds
	Scribe of the District of of Abydos	1 deben of gold 1 bead necklace ⌜of⌝ gold 1 heket of grain
	Kenbeti of Abydos	2 heket of southern grain oxen
739.	Mayor of Thinis	6 deben of gold ½ deben of silver (*y ͨ ḥ*-) bread, 20 (*ḳw*-) loaves 10 sacks of ⌜—⌝ 10 ͨ *nb-ỉm* ͨ·*t* 2 heket of grain 50 heket 10 heket of grain 1 (*hbn·t*-) jar of honey 5 calves 6 yearlings 3 two-year-olds 2 (full-grown) oxen
740.	Scribe[a] of the District of the city of Min (Akhmim)	2 deben of gold 1 deben of silver 2 bead necklaces ⌜of⌝ [gold] 200 ⌜—⌝ 2 heket of grain —1 calves — two-year-olds 1 (full-grown) ox
741.	Recorder of Itfit His scribe	3 heket of southern grain 1 measure of grain 1 (*hbn t*) jar of honey 2 (full-grown) oxen
742.	Mayor of *Pr-Ḥr*	1 heket of southern grain 10 measures of (*sw·t*-) grain 1 (*wn-dw*) ox 1 two-year-old (*šw*-) rolls

---

[a]Behind him was a figure now lost, with considerable tribute of grain, bread and cattle; the gold, if any, is lost. This may also belong to Akhmim.

	Official and Place	Tax
743.	Mayor —	1,000 (sḫt-) loaves (sw·t-) grain 3 measures of grain southern grain 2 heket of grain 10 (ḳw-) loaves 1 (hbn·t-) jar of honey ṭmꜥ·t 1 yearling 1 (full-grown) ox
744.	Scribe of the District of ꜥnṭ —	5 deben of gold 2 heket of grain 1 chest of (mt-) linen 1 chest of (ḏꜣw-) linen — [deben] of gold 1 chest of (mt-) linen 1 chest of (ḏꜣw-) linen
745.	Scribe of the Recorder of Siut[a] Kenbeti of Siut	Grain 1 (hbn·t-) jar of honey ———

VI. Reception of Dues to the Amon-Temple[b]

746. In this scene is represented the reception of the products of the field, including honey, due to the temple of Amon. The products of a Punt expedition and the annual tribute of North and South, so often recorded in the Annals, are mentioned.

Scene

747. Rekhmire, with his suite behind him, is enthroned at the right. Before him, in three registers, are officials and servants, presenting, storing, recording, and preparing

---

[a]There are two scribes, the name occurring with each.
[b]Pls. XII–XIV.

for use the products of Egypt and her tributary countries. Throughout this scene are distributed the following inscriptions:

Over Rekhmire

748. Reception of grain ($y^c ḥ$) and honey in the White House of the temple; sealing of all treasures in the [temple of Amon], by virtue of his office of master of secret things; by the hereditary prince, ... the vizier, Rekhmire.

Over Grain Scene

749. Reception of grain ($y^c ḥ$) in the [temple of Amon].

Over Trituration of Grain

Pounding grain ($y^c ḥ$) in the White House of the [temple of Amon], in order to make an oblation [at] every feast, which his majesty established anew.

Over Flour-Sifting

Servants of the date-storeroom. "Haste thee every matter ..... thou shalt cause that we be praised."

Over Bakers

Making ⌜loaves⌝ for the oblation of the divine offerings. Doing safely and well the baking of the cake.

Over Men Doing Reverence

750. Speech of the fleet-captains: "According to the desire of thy heart, O prince! ⌜Thy⌝ every matter is very good; the treasuries are overflowing with the tribute of all countries: oil, incense, wine, ... everything, all the products of Punt; bags and sacks bearing every good thing — — — in a myriad of hundred thousands, for King Menkheperre (Thutmose III), given life. May thy favor with his ka be every day.

Over Men Carrying Tribute

751. Introduction of wine into the storehouses ($wḏ$?) by the vizier, Rekhmire. Reception of the tribute of the South country, together with the tribute of the Northland before ...... Rekhmire.

On the Storehouses

Gold-houses of the temple. Storehouse ($wḏ$) of the temple. Double gold-house.

VII. INSPECTION OF DAILY OFFERINGS AND OF MONUMENTS[a]

Scene

752. Rekhmire, (figure erased) stands inspecting two lines of men with food-offerings, and two rows of statues of the king, behind which are weapons, temple furniture, and utensils.

Inscription over Rekhmire

Inspection of food of the divine offerings of every day; inspection of his —, and the beautiful monuments, which he executed for the Sovereign, the Good God, Lord of the Two Lands, Menkheperre (Thutmose III), given life forever, for the temple of Amon, and the temples which are in his —; by .... [Rekhmire].

VIII. INSPECTION OF CRAFTSMEN[b]

753. We here see Rekhmire inspecting the artificers, who are making for the temple of Amon various vessels, doors, furniture, etc., from the precious metals and other costly materials captured in Thutmose III's wars in Asia.

Scene

Rekhmire stands leaning on his staff; behind him are his suite, and before him are long lines of craftsmen in leather, wood, stone, and various metals, busily engaged at their work. Over them are the following inscriptions:

Over Rekhmire

754. Inspection of every craft ————,[c] in order to cause every man to know his duty according to the stipulation of every affair, by the hereditary prince, count, who gives the regulation to the prophets, who directs the priests to their duty, governor of the (residence) city, chief of the six courts of justice, Rekhmire.

---

[a]Pl. XXII.   [b]Pls. XVI-XVIII.

[c]The lacuna here and at the beginning of the following inscription would indicate that the name of Amon had been erased in both places.

Over Gold Weighing

⌜Reckoning⌝ of the gold ————, in order to fulfil all business of the daily stipulation. Their number is myriads of hundred-thousands; before the vizier . . . . Rekhmire.

Over Goldsmiths and Silversmiths

Making all vessels for the divine limbs; multiplying vases of gold and silver in every (style of) workmanship that endures forever.

Over Coppersmiths

755. Bringing the Asiatic copper which his majesty captured in the victories in Retenu, in order to ⌜cast⌝ the [two doors[a]] of the temple of Amon in Karnak. Its pavement was overlaid with gold like[b] the horizon of heaven; by the governor of the (residence) city, and vizier.

They say: "The king, beautiful in monuments, Menkheperre (Thutmose III), given life forever; (as) he is (so) they are forever. . . . . He repeats monuments in the house of his father."

Over Cabinet-makers

Making chests of ivory, ebony, carob wood, meru wood, and of cedar of the best of the terraces; by this official who gives the regulation, guiding the hands of his craftsmen.

IX. INSPECTION OF SCULPTORS AND BUILDERS[c]

756. The heavier works of the Amon-temple are here under inspection by Rekhmire. Of particular interest are the Semitic foreigners, who appear among the brickmakers, of the "*captivity which his majesty brought for the works of the temple of Amon.*" This is, of course, precisely what was afterward exacted of the Hebrews.

---

[a]These words are in Virey's copy (*Mémoires de la mission française au Caire*, V, Pl. XV), but had been lost before Newberry's was made.

[b]Lit., "*in likeness to*" (*m sn·t r*), a circumlocution not uncommonly used for the simple "*like*" (*my*).

[c]Pls. XX and XXI.

Scene

Rekhmire stands leaning on his staff, his suite behind him; and before him, at work, are stonecutters, sculptors, brickmakers, and builders. The inscriptions are as follows:

Over Rekhmire

757. Inspection of all works of divine offerings of Amon in Karnak; causing every man to know his way, by virtue of his office as chief of works; by the hereditary prince, count, who establishes laws in the temples of the gods of the South and North ..... ———— [Rekhmire].

By Bricklayers[a]

758. The layer of brick who brings the field,[b] the very numerous ⌜—⌝; building with ready fingers, skilled[c] in his duty, causing vigilance among the ⌜conquered⌝,[d] who hear the sayings of this official, skilful[e] in bui[lding] of works, giving regulation to their chiefs. [⌜They say⌝]: "He [⌜supplies⌝] us with bread, beer, and every good sort; he leads us, with a loving heart for the king, amiable — — — King Menkheperre (Thutmose III), who builds the sanctuary of [⌜the gods⌝]; may they grant to him a reward therefor with myriads of years.

The taskmaster,[f] he says to the builders: "The rod is in my hand; be not idle."

By Brickmakers[g]

759. Captivity which his majesty brought, for the works of the temple of Amon.

By Bricklayer

Laying the brick, in order to build the storehouse anew, [in the temple of Amon] of Karnak.

---

[a] Pl. XX. The beginning of the inscription is very difficult and a little doubtful.
[b] A similar reference to a "*clay-field*" in Ineni (§ 106, l. 12).
[c] *Wn-ḥr, wbʾ-ḥr*, and *šsʾ-ḥr* are not uncommon, meaning "*experienced, instructed, skilful.*"
[d] The captives of war shown in the same scene?
[e] The adjectives now refer to the prince.
[f] *Dy-rs-ḏʾḏʾ* = lit., "*he who causes to be vigilant.*"
[g] Some of these are clearly Semitic foreigners.

By Builders

Let your hands build, ye people. Let us do the pleasure of this official in restoring the monuments of his lord in the house of his father Amon. His name is upon them, abiding, permanent, for both æons of years. The overseer of works, he saith to those bringing stone: "Strengthen your hands, ye people. Let us lay [ᵗthe foundation⁾] of stone, of work [⸺] ⸺ ⸺."

X. RECEPTION OF FOREIGN TRIBUTE[a]

760. This is one of the most important scenes preserved in ancient Egypt. Similar scenes will be found in other Theban tombs, but none contains so elaborate, detailed, and extensive representations of the wealth of the Asiatic peoples, which was now flowing as tribute into the treasury of the Pharaohs. The pride of the Egyptian vizier, which led him to depict these official incidents in his career, has thus been the means of preserving to us much of the early civilization of Asia, which on its native soil has perished utterly.

Scene

761. At the right stands Rekhmire, while the foreigners, carrying their tribute, approach in five long lines from the left. At the head of each line is a scribe, who records their tribute as it is deposited in splendid profusion before him.

Inscription

Reception of the tribute of the south country, besides the tribute of Punt, the tribute of Retenu (*Rṯnw*), the tribute of Keftyew, besides the booty of all countries which the fame of his majesty, King

---

[a]This scene has not yet been published by Newberry; I had only Champollion, *Notices descriptives*, I, 505-10; Brugsch, *Thesaurus*, V, 1110-113 (whose description is taken bodily from Champollion); and the two plates in Wilkinson, *Manners and Customs*, I, Pl. II A and II B.

Menkheperre (Thutmose III), brought; by the hereditary prince ......[a] Rekhmire.[b]

A weighing scene[c] shows the reckoning of "*this great heap of electrum, which is (measured) by the heket, making 36,692[d] deben.*"

XI. ACCESSION OF AMENHOTEP II

762. This scene is not yet published, but Newberry describes it (*op. cit.*, 20) as showing Rekhmire after having sailed down-river to Hatsekhem to meet his new sovereign, presenting to him "the royal insignia."

STELA OF INTEF THE HERALD[e]

763. This splendid stela was erected by the "*royal herald*" of Thutmose III, whose important offices were the following:

Hereditary prince and count, companion, great in love, count of Thinis of the Thinite nome, lord of the entire oasis region, great herald of the king.

---

[a] Titles, etc., of Rekhmire.

[b] An inscription over each of the five rows begins in each case: "*Arrival in peace, of the chiefs of X*" (Punt, Retenu, etc., as the case may be). To Keftyew is added "*and of the isles in the midst of the sea,*" and to Retenu: "*all the northern countries of the ends of the earth.*" This introductory formula is followed by the conventional acclamations of the foreigners; but these inscriptions are not readable in Wilkinson's plates. Champollion gives only the introductory formula of each row, and Newberry's second volume containing these scenes has not yet appeared.

[c] Lepsius, *Denkmäler*, III, 39, d. [d] About 8,943 pounds (troy).

[e] Now in the Louvre (C. 26), being doubtless the finest stela in that great collection. It is nearly 6 feet high by nearly 4 feet in width, and of the finest workmanship (see de Rougé, *Notices des monuments*, 84–89). It was published by Gayet, *Stèles de la XII[e] dynastie*, Pl. XIX, and the long inscription (partially) by Brugsch (*Thesaurus*, VI, 1479–85). Owing simply to the name of its owner, "Intef," it has always been attributed to the early Middle Kingdom. It has long been evident, both from its language and content, however, that it belongs to the Eighteenth Dynasty. The discovery of Intef's tomb at Thebes by Newberry shows that this conclusion is correct, and that Intef lived in the reign of Thutmose III. The important conclusions regarding the oases in the Middle Kingdom, often drawn from this inscription (e. g., Maspero, *Dawn*, 432, n. 3, and *ibid.*, 459, n. 3), are therefore to be given up.

Or again:

Hereditary prince and count, wearer of the royal seal, sole companion, favorite of the Good God, excellent scribe of computation, first herald of the king.

Again:

First herald of the judgment-hall (ᶜrry·t).[a]

It would thus appear that the Oases, at least those of the Theban region, were dependents of the Thinite princes,[b] who have survived into the Eighteenth Dynasty and taken office at the court of the Pharaoh.

764. The stela contains, in a less formal list than the "Duties of the Vizier" (§§ 675 ff.), a similar statement of the duties of the *"royal herald"* (*whm-śtny*[c] = lit., *"royal reporter or repeater"*). This statement, far from being an extract from the government archives, is but a random rehearsal, in a boastful style, of the powers of the court herald. It is evident that his office is only partially expressed by our word herald, for the duties of the Egyptian herald show him to have been of ministerial power and importance; they were the following:

1. The management of the formalities and ceremonies of court and palace (ll. 4–7, only part of l. 5).

2. Communication of the messages of the people and affairs of the land to the king[d] (l. 5).

---

[a]All the above titles are from the head of the stela; others will be found in the following translation.

[b]For another Thinite prince, who was also lord of the oasis, see *Recueil*, X, 141.

[c]So in Ahmose-pen-Nekhbet (ll. 10 and 13), but in Intef's inscription "*whm-n-śtny*."

[d]Here he seems to cover the same ground as the vizier (Duties, 4, l. 5); but the vizier evidently reported larger affairs of state, while the herald communicated personal matters, of which we have an example in the brave deeds of Ahmose, which are regularly reported to the king by the *"royal herald"* (§§ 9 ff.).

3. Messenger of the judgment-hall (ʿry·t), or general administrative office of the Pharaoh (l. 6).

4. The communication to the people of all commissions laid on them by the Pharaoh (l. 7).

5. The communication, both to Egyptians and foreign countries, of the amount of their taxes, and verification of same (l. 8, and l. 27 end). This is but a specialization of 4.

6. To be in general the mouthpiece of the palace (l. 9).

7. To exercise a kind of police control, wherever the Pharaoh proceeded (ll. 10–12).

765. This unsystematic list of powers is followed by an enumeration of Intef's good qualities (ll. 13–20), to which is added, after an asseveration of its truth (ll. 20–22), a remarkable statement of the source of his success (ll. 22–24).

Finally, a rapid statement of the herald's duties abroad while accompanying the Pharaoh on his Syrian campaigns, completes the inscription (ll. 24–27). As the Pharaoh, in this instance, was Thutmose III, these brief references are of the greatest interest, showing the herald, as they do, preceding the great commander from town to town, and preparing his residence in the palaces of the Syrian princes.

Intef's Address to Passers-by

766. ²He says: "O ye that live upon earth, all people (rḫy·t), every priest, every scribe, every ritual priest, who shall enter into this tomb of the necropolis; if ye love life, and think not on death, if your native gods shall favor you, if ye would not taste the fear of another land, ³if ye would be buried in your tombs, if ye would bequeath your offices to your children; whether (ye be) one that readeth these words upon this stela, being a scribe; or one that heareth them, so shall ye say: 'An offering which the king gives, etc. . . . .'"

Intef's Duties

767. ⁴For the ka of the hereditary prince, count, wearer of the royal seal, sole companion, favorite of the king, as leader of his army, who levies

the official staffs and the soldiers, who counts the companions, who conducts the nobles, who makes the king's-confidants approach their places, leader of leaders, ⁵guide of millions of men, superior of advanced offices, advanced in place, excellent in the (royal) presence, who sends up the words of the people (*rḥy·t*), who reports the affairs of the Two Lands, who discourses concerning matters in the secret place, who enters with good things and comes out with favor, ⁶who places every man upon his father's seat, who makes glad the heart and favors the favorites, at whose words the great arise, who does the errands of the judgment-hall (ᶜ*ry·t*), who originates the regulations in the palace, L. P. H., who makes every man to know his duties, who gives the administration in the —, ⌈great⌉ ⁷in power in the great seat (i. e., the palace), who silences the voice, and originates honors, who guards the foot from the place of silence, the counterpoise of the balances of the Good God, who conducts the people to that which they do, who says: "Let it be done," and it is done on [the instant], ⁸like that which comes out of the mouth of a god; who lays commands on the people (*ḫnmm·t*), to number their work (impost) for the king, who fixes the ⌈reckoning⌉ of every country, who furnishes the ⌈supplies⌉ of their princes, great in affairs at the counting of the numbers, prepared — ⁹— — — to do, knowing that which is in the heart of the king, L. P. H., the speaking tongue of him who is in the palace (i. e., the king), the eyes of the king, the heart of the lord of the palace, the instruction of the whole land, who binds the rebellious, who quiets the —, ¹⁰— — from the hostile, strong-armed toward robbers, applying violence to them that apply violence, mighty-hearted against the mighty-hearted, who brings down the arm ¹¹of him whose — is high, who ⌈shortens⌉ the hour of the ⌈cruel-hearted⌉, who causes the evil-hearted to perform the regulation of the laws, although his heart is unwilling, great in terror among criminals, lord of fear among rebellious-¹²hearted, who binds the adversary, and repels the violent, the safety of the palace, the establisher of its laws, who quiets the multitude for their lord, the chief herald of the judgment-hall, count of Thinis of the Thinite nome, chief of all the oasis country, excellent scribe, solving writings, Intef, triumphant.

Intef's Qualities

768. ¹³The only wise, equipped with knowledge, the really safe one, distinguishing the simple from the wise, exalting the craftsman, turning his back upon the ignorant, ⌈—⌉ in mind, very ⌈complete⌉ in mind, giving attention to hear the man of truth, ¹⁴void of deceit, useful to his lords, accurate-minded, with no lie in him, experienced in every way, protector of the seemly, hearer of his prayer, gentle toward the cold-hot one, interceding for him, who does according to his plans, not — ¹⁵the truthful, understanding the heart,ᵃ knowing the thoughts, when nothing has come forth from the lips, speaking to wit: according to his thought; there is none, whom he hath not known, turning his face to him that speaks the truth, disregarding him that speaketh lies, who does ⌜—⌝ to — —, ¹⁶not mild toward the ⌜loquacious⌝, but opposing him by doing the truth, content with giving satisfaction, not exalting him that knew not above him that knew, going about after the truth, giving attention to hear petitions, judging — ¹⁷for him who is without offense and for the liar, free from partiality, justifying the just, chastising the guilty for his guilt, servant of the poor, father of the fatherless, — — ¹⁸of the orphan, mother of the fearful, ⌜dungeon⌝ of the turbulent, protector of the weak, advocate of him who has been deprived of his possessions by one stronger than he, husband of the widow, shelter of the orphan [⌜making⌝ the wee]¹⁹per rejoice, ⌜— — —⌝, who is praised on account of his character, for whom the worthy thank god, because of the greatness of his worth, for whom health and life are besought by all people ($r\d{h}y\cdot t$), great herald of the judgment-hall, ²⁰chief steward, overseer of the double granary, leader of all works of the king's L. P. H. estate, to whom all offices report, who counts the impost of the leaders, the mayors and the village sheiks of the South and the North excellent scribe, Intef, triumphant.

Intef's Asseveration

769. He says: "Those were my qualities, of which ²¹I have testified; there is no deceit therein; these were my excellencies in very truth, there is no exception therein. Nor was there any likening of words to boast for myself with lies, but that was my color, ²²which I showed; that was my office in the king's L. H. P. estate, that was my service at the court L. P. H., that was my ⌜duty⌝ in the judgment-hall.

Intef's Explanation of His Success

770. ᵇIt was my heart which caused that I should do it, by its leading of my affairs; it is — —²³an excellent witness, I did not violate its

---

ᵃOn this passage, cf. my article, *Zeitschrift für ägyptische Sprache*, 39, 47.

ᵇOn this remarkable passage, see my article, *Zeitschrift für ägyptische Sprache*, 39, 47.

speech, I feared to transgress its leading; I prospered on account of it exceedingly. I was excellent by reason of that which it caused that I should do, I was valuable by reason of its leading. 'Lo, — — —,' ²⁴said the people, 'it is an oracle of the gods, which is in every body. He is a counsellor, whom it has led to the goodly way of achievement.' Lo, thus I was.

Intef's Duties Abroad

771. I followed the King of the Two Lands, I struck into his tracks in the countries, — — ²⁵— the earth, I arrived at its end, being at the heels of his majesty, L. P. H., my valor was like the lords of strength, and I captured like his brave ones. Every palace in a country — — ²⁶— — before the troops, at the head of the army. When my lord arrived in safety where I was, I had prepared it (the palace), I had equipped it with everything that is desired in a foreign country, made better than the palaces of Egypt, ²⁷purified, cleansed, set apart, their mansions adorned, (each) chamber for its proper purpose, I made the king's heart satisfied with that which I did, — — —. I numbered the tribute of the rulers dwelling in every country, consisting of silver, gold, oil, incense, wine."

TOMB OF MENKHEPERRESENEB[a]

772. This tomb is one of the most interesting and important at Thebes. Menkheperreseneb, besides being High Priest[b] of Amon under Thutmose III, was also "*overseer of the gold-house and overseer of the silver-house,*" as well as chief architect in the temple of Amon, and "*chief of the overseers of craftsmen.*" As treasurer, he is depicted in his tomb receiving the tribute of Asia, and the treasure from the mines of Africa; while as architect and chief of the master-craftsmen, we find him in charge of Thutmose

---

[a]In the cliff of Shekh Abd-el-Kurna at Thebes, published by Piehl, *Inscriptions*, I, Pl. 127 P-129 and 102-5; Virey, *Mémoires de la mission française au Caire*, V, 197 ff. I had also a copy of the building inscription, kindly furnished me by Mr. Newberry.

[b]See his statue (*Annales*, IV, 8, 9) found at Karnak, according to which he was a son of Rekhmire.

III's great works in the Karnak temple, recounted in this king's building inscriptions (§§ 599 ff.).

Scene of Asiatic Tribute

773. Two lines of Asiatics bring forward splendid and richly chased vessels of gold, silver, etc. The Asiatics are designated as "*the chief of Keftyew, the chief of Kheta, the chief of Tunip (Tnpw), the chief of Kadesh.*" Before them is an inscription:

> Giving praise to the Lord of the Two Lands, obeisance to the Good God, by the chiefs of every land. They acclaim the victories of his majesty; their tribute is upon their backs, being every [product] of God's-Land: silver, gold, lapis lazuli, malachite, every splendid, costly stone . . . . .

A line of superscription contains the acclamations of the Asiatics; the bulk of it is lost:

> ——— the sea; thy fear is in all lands. Thou hast overthrown the lands of Mitanni ($My\text{-}tn$ —); thou hast hacked up their cities, their chiefs are in caves — —.

Reception of Gold

774. Another scene shows the deceased receiving shipments of gold, from the "*captain of the gendarmes of Coptos*" and the "*governor of the gold-country of Coptos:*"

> Reception of gold of the highland of Coptos, besides gold of Kush the wretched, being the yearly dues — —; by Menkheperreseneb.

Inspection of Workmen

775. Again we see the deceased inspecting the work of the craftsmen, accompanied by the words:

> Viewing the workshop of the temple of [Amon], the work of the craftsmen, in real lapis lazuli, and in real malachite, which his majesty made after the design of his heart,[a] to be ⌜monuments⌝ for his father,

---

[a]These very works are shown in the great relief depicting the presentation of monuments to Amon by Thutmose III at Karnak (§ 545), accompanied by the same words, showing that Thutmose III himself furnished the design to the craftsmen.

Amon, in [ʳthe house of Amonʳ], abiding, flourishing as eternal works; by the hereditary prince, count, pleasing the king as the establisher of his monuments, chief of the overseers of craftsmen, chief of works in the [ʳhouse ofʳ] Amon, first prophet of [Amon], Menkheperreseneb. He says:

A Shrine

"I inspected when the lord, King Thutmose III, erected [a shrine,] called 'Thutmose-III-is-the-Wearer-of-the-Diadem-of-Amon,' of enduring granite, in one block,ᵃ upon the ʳcanalʳ ——— ᵇwrought with electrum, the ʳhallʳ being of sandstone, wrought with gold of the best of the hills ——— wrought with gold."

A Second Shrine

776. "I inspected, when his majesty erected a greatᶜ shrine of electrum (called): 'Thutmose-III-is-Great-in-Love-in-the-House-of-Amon.'"

Colonnade

"I inspected when his majesty made a great colonnade,ᵈ [wrought] with electrum ———."

Obelisks and Flagstaves

"I inspected when his majesty erected obelisks and numerous flagstaves for his father, Amon. I pleased his majesty while conducting the work on his monuments. I did these things, without being unpleasant to the heart of ———."

STELA OF NIBAMONᵉ

777. This official lived at Thebes under the early Thutmosids, and finally became steward of Nebetu, one of

---

ᵃA monolithic chapel of granite, such as still exists, for example, at Edfu.

ᵇThe following is either a different building, the account of which began in the preceding lacuna, or the hall in which the shrine stood.

ᶜSo Piehl; Newberry, "*beautiful.*"

ᵈThis is doubtless the building at the east end of the Karnak temple; but may be the attempted restoration of the hall dismantled for Hatshepsut's obelisks.

ᵉStela in his tomb in the hill of Drah-abu-'n-Neggah, at Thebes; published by Bouriant, *Recueil,* IX, 95–97.

Thutmose III's wives, and chief captain of the king's fleet. His tomb stela is chiefly devoted to the usual mortuary prayers, in the midst of which he refers to his favor under the first three Thutmosids. The name of Thutmose I is evidently lost in one of the numerous lacunæ; but Nibamon seems to have received gifts of land and cattle from this king. He then says:

Favor under Thutmose II

778. [17]My lord, the King of Upper and Lower Egypt, Okhepernere (Thutmose II), triumphant, repeated favors to me; he appointed me overseer of the hall ($ẖ$?) of the king.

Favor under Thutmose III

779. My lord, the King of Upper and Lower Egypt, Menkheperre (Thutmose III), given life, repeated favors to me; he magnified [18]me until I was at the front; he appointed me as steward of the king's-wife, Nebetu ($Nb·t-w$), triumphant. My lord, the King of Upper and Lower Egypt, Menkheperre, [19]given life, repeated favors to me; he appointed me to be captain of all the ships of the king. There happened no oversight of mine, nor was there found any neglect of mine. I was not associated with [20]evil, but I attained a revered old age, being in the favor of the king's presence.

Then follows a final prayer, addressed to the living.

REIGN OF AMENHOTEP II

ASIATIC CAMPAIGN

780. Syria, of course, revolted on the death of Thutmose III, and already in his second year we find his energetic son, Amenhotep II, on the march into northern Syria to quell the rebellion. Doubtless the harbor cities had also rebelled, and hence the young king is forced to proceed by land. Leaving Egypt in April, as his father had done on the first campaign thirty-three years before, he had already in early May won a battle at Shemesh-Edom in northern Palestine. On the twelfth of May he crossed the Orontes, and gained a skirmish near the river. He celebrated a feast of thanksgiving to Amon there, and fourteen days later (May 26) he arrived at Niy, which opened its gates to him and received him with acclamation. June 5 he reached and punished the rebellious city of Ikathi, which was plotting against its Egyptian garrison. Somewhere in Naharin he set up his tablet of victory,[a] as his father and grandfather had done before him. Here the sources fail, and the further course of the campaign is unknown until the king's return to Egypt; but it is clear that the coalition against Egypt was crushed in Tikhsi, probably at the battle on the Orontes, for on his return in the autumn the king brought back with him to Thebes "*the seven princes who were in the district of Tikhsi,*" and sacrificed them himself before Amon. Early in the following July we find the king in Nubia, arranging the completion of his father's temples at Elephantine and Amâda. In both he set up a

---

[a]Turra inscription of Minhotep (§ 800).

tablet bearing the same inscription, recording the building and mentioning the seven princes, six of whom he says he hanged on the walls of Thebes, and the seventh on the walls of Napata. At Napata or above it he set up a tablet marking his southern boundary (§ 800). It is perhaps on his return from this last errand that he stops at Amâda for the foundation ceremonies of the temple.

The said Amâda and Elephantine stelæ, another at Karnak, and a Karnak chapel are the only sources for this campaign.[a]

I. KARNAK STELA[b]

781. Above is a relief in two parts, each showing the king offering to Amon-Re. Between the two parts is a vertical line of text recording the restoration of the monument by Seti I, just as on the Building Inscription of Amenhotep III.

Date and Introduction

782. ⌜[Year 2]⌝[c] ——— under the majesty of:
[d]Horus: Mighty Bull, Great of Strength; ——— Part of Atum;

---

[a]An inscription from a tomb at Shekh Abd-el-Kûrna probably refers to his campaigns in calling the deceased "*a follower of the king on his journeys on water, on land, and in every country; to whom has been given favors of the king's-presence, consisting of rings of electrum*" (Piehl, *Zeitschrift für ägyptische Sprache*, 1883, 135).

[b]A pink granite stela, found by Champollion against the second of the southern pylons at Karnak, in a deplorably fragmentary condition. Text: Champollion, *Notices descriptives*, II, 185, 186 (only ll. 1–10; l. 9 is not omitted as indicated); Maspero, *Zeitschrift für ägyptische Sprache*, XVII, 56, 57 (only ll. 3–10, copying Champollion); Rougé, *Inscriptions hiéroglyphiques*, 175, 176; Bouriant, *Recueil*, XIII, 160, 161; Wiedemann, *Proceedings of the Society of Biblical Archæology*, XI, 422, 423; a new fragment by Legrain, *Annales*, IV. The text is corrupt, being full of errors, like the omission of the determinative (important emendations by Erman, *Zeitschrift für ägyptische Sprache*, 1889, 39–41). The reason for these errors is the careless restoration of the text after its erasure by the emissaries of Ikhnaton. See Legrain, *Annales*, IV.

[c]The tablet of Amâda below (§§ 791 ff.), dated in year 3, speaks of an Asiatic campaign already completed; it can hardly refer to any other than this campaign to Niy. Hence the latter would have taken place in the year 1 or 2, more probably the latter. The lacuna at the beginning of each line is four or five words long.

[d]The complete titulary of Amenhotep II.

Favorite of the Two Goddesses: Mighty in Opulence, Who is Crowned in Thebes;
Golden Horus: Who Seizes by His Might in all Lands;
²[King of Upper and Lower Egypt] ———— Opet: Okheperure, Lord — of the Sword, Who Binds the Nine Bows;
Son of Re, of his Body, Lord of All Countries: Amenhotep (II), Divine Ruler of Heliopolis, Giver of Life, Forever, like Re.[a]

Battle of Shemesh-Edom

783. ³[His majesty was] in the city of Shemesh-Edom ($\check{S}$-m-$\check{s}w$-y-tw-my);[b] his majesty furnished an example of bravery there; his majesty himself fought hand to hand. Behold, he was like a fierce-eyed lion, smiting the countries of Lebanon ([R-m]-n-n)[c] ⁴⌈— —⌉ ———— -s-$ḫw$[d] was his name.

Booty

List of that which his majesty himself captured on this day: Asiatics, 18 living persons; 16 horses.[e]

Battle on the Orontes

784. First month of the third season (ninth month), day 26; his majesty crossed over the ford of the Orontes[f] on this day, caused to cross ⁵⌈———⌉ ———— ⌈— — —⌉ like the might of Montu of Thebes. His majesty raised his arm, in order to see the end of the

---

[a]The complete titulary of Amenhotep II.

[b]A town of northern Palestine, which occurs in the first of Thutmose III's town-lists as: $\check{S}$ ꜣ -my-$\check{s}$ ꜣ -y-t ꜣ -my (No. 51).

[c]The undoubtedly correct restoration of Erman, *Zeitschrift für ägyptische Sprache*, 1889, 39. Wiedemann's variants only show the decay of the stone since Champollion.

[d]Remnant of the name of a chief or a country.

[e]All the texts but de Rougé have "*oxen*," but "*horses*" is certainly confirmed by the context.

[f]Texts all have y-r ꜣ-s-t, but Brugsch read "Arinath," hence the wavy-lined n, which is straight in hieratic, has been transferred to the stone straight; it has been read as an s by all modern copyists but Brugsch. There is no question, therefore, concerning the emendation to n first made by Maspero. Geographically, the emendation is also convincing. From a northern Palestinian city the king marches northward to Lebanon; this course continued would bring him to the Orontes. Moreover, the identical phrase, "*crossed over the channel of the Orontes*," with the same rare word ($m\check{s}d\cdot t$) for "*channel*" (or "*ford?*") occurs in Ramses II's Kadesh campaign (III, 308, l. 12). The objections of Bissing (*Statistische Tafel*, 34) are not convincing. Petrie's identification with Harosheth on the

earth;[a] his majesty descried a few Asiatics (*Sttyw*) coming on horses ⁶⌈—⌉ coming at a ⌈gallop⌉ (*rkrk*). Behold, his majesty was equipped with his weapons of battle, his majesty conquered with[b] the might ⌈of Set⌉ in his hour. They retreated when his majesty looked at one ⁷of[c] them. Then his majesty himself overthrew their ⌈—⌉[d], with his spear ⌈— — — —⌉. Behold, he carried away this Asiatic ⌈—⌉, ⁸his horses,[e] his chariot, and all his weapons of battle. His majesty returned with joy of heart [to][f] his father, Amon; he (his majesty) gave to him a feast ⌈—⌉.

Booty

785. List of that which his majesty captured on this day:[g] ⁹his horses, 2; chariots, 1; a coat of mail; 2 bows; a quiver, full of arrows; a corselet; and ⌈—⌉.[h]

Arrival at Niy

786. Second month of the third season[i] (tenth month), day 10; passing ¹⁰southward toward Egypt, his majesty proceeded by horse to

---

Kishon (Petrie, *History of Egypt*, II, 155) is impossible, for the king is already in the Lebanon, and has left the Kishon far behind. The route by which Amenhotep advanced northward from Shemesh-Edom is not certain, but the crossing of the Orontes is doubtless the last one as he turned toward the Euphrates. This would be most naturally at Senzar. He would then march by way of Aleppo to Niy, which was about 175 miles from Senzar. That he reached Senzar is shown by his list in § 798A. This suits his marching speed also, as he would have made about 12½ miles a day from Senzar to Niy.

[a]There may be a reference here to the common designation of this remote region as the "*end of the earth*," but it more probably refers merely to the king's shading his eyes that he might scan the horizon.

[b]Lit., "*behind.*"

[c]Legrain's lacuna of 24 cm. is of course impossible; it is improbable also at the head of the next two lines.

[d]*ḫntw*. [e]Lit., "*his span*" (*ḥtry*).

[f]Restore *n*, "*to*," according to Amâda tablet, ll. 16, 17 (§ 797).

[g]There is no line omitted here, as Champollion indicates.

[h]The same word (*sḫntw*) applied to the corselet (*ḫ ꜣ nr*) is found in Thutmose III's first campaign, l. 23 (*shnw-ty?*).

[i]The texts of de Rougé, Bouriant, Wiedemann, and Brugsch's translations show "*month II*," not III, as usually read from Champollion. That Shemu (not 'akhet) is to be read here is clear from the determinative and the other dates (ll. 4 and 13; note, l. 13). Maspero now accepts this (Maspero, *Struggle of the Nations*, 291), although he formerly read 'akhet. Petrie's date (Petrie, *History of Egypt*, II, 155) is therefore about five months too late; for had this date been in another year, the year must have been added. The arrival at Niy is therefore fourteen days after the crossing of the Orontes.

the city of Niy. Behold, these Asiatics of this city, men as well as women, were upon their walls praising his majesty, [11]— — — to the Good God.

Revolt of Ikathi

787. Behold, his majesty heard saying, that some of those Asiatics (*St̊ tyw*) who were in the city of Ikathi (*Y-k ͻ -ty*) had ⌈plotted⌉ (*ngmgm*) to make a plan for casting out the infantry[a] of his majesty [12]⌈⌈who were⌉⌉ in the city, in order to overturn — — — — who were loyal to his majesty. Then [his] majesty put them in ⌈— — — — —⌉ in this city [13]— — he —[b] them immediately, and he pacified [this] city ——— against the entire country —.[c] Second month[d] of the third season (tenth month),[d] day 20 (+*x*). [14]— ⌈————⌉, made the city of Ikathi [*Y-k ͻ*]-*t ͻ* ———— [15]———— [16]————.

788. The remainder as far as l. 29 shows but a few scattered traces, of which the following are significant: "*of his children. Statement of that which [his majesty] captured*" (l. 21); "*his chariot*" (l. 26); "*list of captives*" (l. 27); "*[weapon]s of war without number*" (l. 28); "*his majesty was adorned with [his] regalia*" (l. 29). The record then becomes more connected:

Overthrow of Khatithana

789. [30]——— His majesty —[e] the tribe of Khatithana (*Ḫ ͻ -ty-t ͻ-n ͻ*) united [31]— —. Behold, the chief[f] — — — — — the city, for fear of his majesty. His chiefs, his wives, his children were carried captive, [32]and all his people likewise. Statement of that which his majesty himself captured — — — — his horses.

---

[a]Probably the Egyptian garrison of the town.

[b]Verb.

[c]Possibly the name of the country, containing *kh*.

[d]This date is very important, showing (1) that we must read Shemu (the third season, not ͻ *ḥ·t*, the first season) in l. 10 above, and (2) that we must read second month (in l. 10) with all the copies (except Champollion).

[e]Verb.

[f]The position of the introductory words (before the lacunæ) in ll. 31 and 32 is not certain.

Return to Egypt

790. ³³— — day 27; his majesty went forth from the house of the Beautiful-of-Face (Ptah)ᵃ and proceeded ⌈to⌉ — Memphis, bearing the plunder which he had taken in the country of Retenu. List of that which was taken:

Nobles (*my-r ʾ-y-n ʾ*) alive	³⁴550 (+x)
Their [wiv]es	240
⌈Vessels wrought⌉ of gold	6,800ᵇ deben
Copper	500,000ᶜ deben
Horses	210
Chariots	300

The whole land beheld the victories of his majesty.
³⁵By the Good God, Lord of the Two Lands, Lord of Offerings — — — —,ᵈ beloved of Amon, protector of him who is in Thebes, celebrator of the feasts of the house of Amon, lord of Thebes, ⌈— —⌉, Son of Re, Thutmose (⌈IV⌉),ᵉ given life [forever] and ever.

II. AMÂDAᶠ AND ELEPHANTINEᵍ STELÆ

791. Both are dedication tablets, the upper half of which is occupied by an oblation scene: at Amâda, Amenhotep II offering wine to Harakhte and Amon-Re, all in a sacred boat; at Elephantine, the king once with Amon and

---

ᵃOr: "*the beautiful house, proceeding*" (*ḥr wḏ ʾ*), etc.
ᵇ1,657½ pounds, troy.   Nearly 100,000 pounds.
ᵈRoyal name is lost.
ᵉIf this is correct, the stela was erected by Thutmose IV, son of Amenhotep II.
ᶠOn the interior of the back wall of the sanctuary of the temple of Amâda. Text: Champollion, *Notices descriptives*, I, 105-7 (very imperfectly and incorrectly copied); Lepsius, *Denkmäler*, III, 65, a; Brugsch, *Thesaurus*, 1280 (only ll. 12-20). I had also the Berlin lexicon copy, collated by Erman with the squeeze of Lepsius, and a collation of the original by Steindorff.
ᵍFrom a similar position in the Elephantine temple (now perished); the upper part with the relief and parts of thirteen lines of text is in Vienna (No. 141); the lower portion is in Cairo (No. 158). I had: my own photograph and von Bergmann's publication (*Recueil*, IV, 33 ff.) of the Vienna fragment; two copies of the Cairo fragment, one by Steindorff and one by Schaefer, which they kindly loaned me; and a photograph by Borchardt.

Anuket and once before Khnum, receiving "*life and stability.*" Both tablets were intended to mark the "*station of the king,*" both record similar buildings in the year 3 (material at Elephantine is better), and the same facts regarding the Asiatic princes. The differences in wording are almost nil. The Elephantine stela has an interesting addition from the year 4.

Date and Introduction

792. ¹Year 3, third month of the third season (eleventh month), day 15,[a] under the majesty of . . . .[b] Amenhotep[c] (II), beloved of Harakhte and Amon, lord of Thebes, ²Good God, creation of Re, sovereign who came forth from the body, mighty; likeness of Horus upon the throne of his father; great in strength, whose like does not exist; of whom a second is not found. He is a king very weighty of arm; there is not one who can draw his bow[d] among his army ³among the hill-country sheiks (or) among the princes of Retenu, because his strength is so much greater than (that of) any king who has ever existed; raging like a panther, when he courses through the battlefield; there is none fighting before him; an archer mighty in smiting; ⁴a wall protecting Egypt; firm of heart, ⌐—⌐ in the hour of ⌐conflict⌐; trampling down those who rebel against him; ⌐instantly⌐ prevailing against all the barbarians with people and horses,[e] when they came with myriads of men, while they knew not that Amon-Re was ⁵his ally, (nor) that he would be seen to ⌐approach⌐ instantly, strength in his limbs;[f] likeness of Min

---

[a]The date of the Elephantine tablet is lost; but it was earlier than the "*year 4,*" in which an addition was made to it.

[b]Full five-name titulary.

[c]Chiseled away and reinserted (Steindorff).

[d]This is the basis for the well-known legend of Herodotus (III, 21), which represents Cambyses as unable to draw the bow of the king of Ethiopia (Schaefer, *Zeitschrift für ägyptische Sprache*, 38, 66 f.). It is a not uncommon statement. Curiously enough, the bow of Amenhotep II was found in his tomb; it bears an inscription designating him as "*smiter of the Troglodytes, overthrower of Kush, hacking up [their] cities . . . . the great wall of Egypt, protector of his soldiers*" (Cairo, *Catalogue*, 24120).

[e]This is not a generality, but doubtless specifically refers to a battle with the Asiatics in the campaign of the previous year.

[f]The god's strength in the king's limbs.

in the year of terror. There is not one that saves himself from him; he makes a ⌜slaughter⌝ among his enemies, the Nine Bows likewise. All lands and all rebellious countries pay him impost, ⁶for he is a king ⌜————⌝. There is not one who makes a boundary with him;ª (but) they live by his breath. King of kings, ruler of rulers, who captures the boundaries ⁷of ⌜— —⌝; the only mighty one, whose fame is exaltedᵇ until Re in heaven knows it, (⌜and⌝) the one who faces him⌝ in the day of smiting. There is no boundary made for him toward all countries united, (or) toward all lands together; (but) they fall instantly because of his flaming crest, like ———— ⁸————. There is none among them that escapes from the overthrow, like the foes of Bastet on the road of Ir-Amon.ᶜ It is a happy chance for all those who know that he is his real son, who came forth from (his) limbs, one ⁹with him, in order to rule that which the sun encircles, all the lands, and countries which he knew, that he might seize them immediately with victory and power.

Buildings and Offerings

793. He is a king with heart favorable to the buildings of all gods, being one who builds their temples (and) fashions their statues. The divine offerings ¹⁰are established for the first time, loaves and beer in plenty and (ḫt-ꜥ ?) fowl in multitude as a daily offering every day, forever; large cattle and small cattle at their seasons, without ⌜—⌝.ᵈ He gave the house to its lord, supplied with everything, with oxen,¹¹ calves, young cattle, fowl [without] limit, this temple being supplied throughout with loaves and wine. He established ⌜revenues⌝ for the first time [for] (his) fathers, the gods,ᵉ to be seen of the people, ¹²to be known of all.

Completion of Temple

794. Behold, his majesty beautifiedᶠ the temple which his father, King of Upper and Lower Egypt, Menkheperre (Thutmose III), had

---

ªIt is all his own matter where a boundary shall be.
ᵇLit., "*of exalting his fame.*"
ᶜLit., "*begotten of Amon*" = the king (Erman).
ᵈSee long Khnumhotep inscription (I, 637, l. 201).
ᵉElephantine: "*Khnum.*"
ᶠ"*Beautified*" means here (as on the Lateran and Popolo obelisks) "*to supply with inscriptions*," the monument having been left uninscribed by Thutmose III.

made for (his) fathers, all the gods,[a] built of stone as an everlasting work. The walls around it are of brick,[b] the doors of [cedar of the best[c]] ¹³of the Terraces; the doorways are of sandstone,[b] in order that the great name of his father, the Son of Re, Thutmose (III), may remain in this temple forever and ever.

Foundation Ceremony

795. The majesty of this Good God, King of Upper and Lower Egypt, Lord of the Two Lands, Okheprure (Amenhotep II) extended the line and loosened the ⌜—⌝ for all the fathers,[d] [the gods] ¹⁴making for it[e] a great pylon of sandstone opposite[f] the hall of the ⌜sacred chamber⌝ in the august dwelling;[g] surrounded by columns of sandstone as an everlasting work; many tables[h] with vessels of silver and bronze, oblation-standards, ¹⁵altars, fire-pans, ⌜oblation-vessels⌝, oblation-tablets, ⌜—⌝.

Erection of the Tablet

796. Then his majesty caused that this tablet should be made and set up in this temple in the place of the Station of the King,[i] and engraved with the great name of the Lord of the Two Lands, ¹⁶the Son of Re, Amenhotep (II), Divine Ruler of Heliopolis in the house of the fathers, the gods,[j] after the return[k] of his majesty from Retenu the Upper, having overthrown all his enemies, extending the boundaries of Egypt, on the first victorious campaign.

---

[a]Elephantine: "*Khnum, lord of the cataract, his mother, Satet, mistress of Elephantine, and Anuket, presider over Nubia (T ꜣ pd·t)*."

[b]Elephantine: "*the doors of cedar, wrought with copper, the portals of enduring granite.*"

[c]Restored from Ineni, 1. 8. (§ 103).

[d]Elephantine: "*Khnum.*"   [e]The temple.

[f]Elephantine: *Ḥft-ḥr*. The first pylon and the colonnaded hall behind it are referred to; but these, with the exception of the back row of columns, were all inscribed by Thutmose IV, and must have been left unfinished by Amenhotep II.

[g]Elephantine: "*in the august colonnade.*"

[h]The account merges into a list of temple furniture given by the king without any syntactical connection with the preceding.

[i]His ceremonial position. See § 140, l. 7, and note.

[j]Elephantine: "*Khnum, lord of the cataract.*"

[k]If he arrived at about the time of Thutmose III's return from the first campaign (§ 409), the Amâda stela is then dated about nine and a half months later than his arrival; for it is impossible to suppose that this Shemu of the Asiatic campaign is the same as the Shemu of the Amâda stela, which would then be only twenty-five days later than the last date readable in the Asiatic campaign.

Sacrifice of Asiatic Princes

797. When his majesty returned ¹⁷with joy of heart to his father, Amon, he slew with his own weapon the seven princes,[a] who had been in the district of Tikhsi (*Ty-ḫ-sy*), and had been placed head downward at the prow of his majesty's barge, the name of which was: "Okheprure (Amenhotep II)-¹⁸is-the-Establisher-of-the-Two-Lands." One hanged the six men of those fallen ones, before the wall of Thebes; those hands likewise. Then the other fallen one was taken up-river to Nubia and hanged ⌜on⌝ the wall of ¹⁹Napata (*Npt*), in order to cause to be manifest the victories of his majesty, forever and ever in all lands and countries of the land of the Negro; since he had taken the Southerners and bound the Northerners, the back-lands of ²⁰the whole earth, upon which Re shines; that he might make his boundary as far as he desired, none opposing his hands, according to the command of his father Re, Amon-Re, lord of Thebes; in order that the Son of Re, of his body, his beloved, Amenhotep[b] (II), divine ruler of Heliopolis, might be given life, stability, satisfaction, joy of heart, through him, like Re, forever and ever.

798. The Elephantine stela[c] here adds enactments for the sacred feasts there, as follows:

Year 4. His majesty commanded to have the sails[d] made for the voyages of these gods dwelling in Elephantine; large sails, each one of 10 cubits, while they were (formerly) small sails of 3 cubits.

His majesty commanded to add one day for his mother, Anuket, to her feast of Nubia (*Pd·tt*), at her voyage of the "Beginning-of-the-River." The supplies are: bread, beer, oxen, geese, wine, incense, fruit, every good and pure thing, as dues each year, as an increase upon

---

[a]These unfortunate kings were sacrificed by the Pharaoh himself before the god, as so often represented in the temple reliefs.

[b]Chiseled away and reinserted (Steindorff).

[c]An obelisk of Amenhotep II was also found at Elephantine; it is now in the collection at Alnwick Castle, England. It bears the inscription: "*Amenhotep II; he made* (*it*) *as his monument for his father Khnum, making for him two obelisks of the altar of Re; that he might be given life forever.*" The pyramidion shows the king worshiping before "*Khnum, residing in Elephantine*" (Birch, *Catalogue Alnwick*, 345; Bonomi, *Transactions of the Royal Society of Literature*, New Ser., 1843, I, 170).

[d]The usual sign for linen fabric is used, so that anything of linen may be meant.

the 3 days of her customary[a] feast, in order to make her great feast of the first (month) of the third season (ninth month) of 4 days'[b] duration, to abide and to endure; that he may be given life forever.

III. KARNAK CHAPEL[c]

798A. This monument, of which only a few fragments have survived, bears a relief showing Amenhotep II leading seventy Asiatic prisoners to Amon. They are accompanied by the words:

List of those countries which his majesty smote in their valleys, overthrown in [their] blood ——— that he might be given life forever.

Twenty-four prisoners in two rows bear the names of the countries they represent. The following are still legible:

1. Retenu [the Upper]; 2. Retenu [the Low]er; 3. Kharu; 12. Kadesh; 13. Aleppo; 14. Niy; 15. Sezar[d] ($S^{\flat}$-$d^{\flat}$-$r^{\flat}$); 16. Thenew (Tnw); 17. Ketne.

TURRA INSCRIPTION[e]

799. Above is a relief showing the king before two rows of divinities, thirteen in number, for whose buildings the quarry-chambers have been opened. A dedication at the left side is as follows:

He made (it) as his monument for the gods and goddesses, for whose temples of a [million of years] the quarry-chamber was opened, in order to quarry fine limestone of Ayan.

---

[a]For a similar use of this rather rare word (mty), see § 619, l. 18, and III, 377, note.

[b]That is, one day has been added. Cf. the same formula in the feasts of victory (§§ 550–52).

[c]Found by Legrain near Pylon V at Karnak; published by him, *Annales*, V, 34, 35.

[d]The same as Senzar of § 584; see § 784, note, where it is shown that Senzar was a natural point of departure from the Orontes for Niy.

[e]Cut in the rock walls of the limestone quarry of Turra, south of Cairo. Published by Vyse, *Pyramids*, III, 95; less fully by Lepsius, *Denkmäler*, Text, I, 20.

800. Below the relief is the following record:

¹Year 4, under the majesty of the king, Okheprure, Son of Re [Amenhotep II], given life.

His majesty commanded [to open] the quarry-chambers anew, ²in order to quarry fine limestone of Ayan, in order to build his temples of a million of years; after his majesty found [the quarry-chambers which are in Troja]ᵃ ³beginning to go to ruin since the times that were before. It was my majesty who made (them) anew, that he might be given satisfying life, like Re, forever.

⁴Made under the hand of the hereditary prince, count, satisfying the king by maintaining his monuments; vigilant for the temples; who erected tablets ⁵in the land of Naharin (N-h-r-n)ᵇ and in the land of Karoy (K ᵓ-r ᵓ-y),ᶜ overseer of works in the temples of the gods of the South and North, king's-scribe, Min[hotep].

TOMB OF AMENKENᵈ

801. The tomb of Amenken,ᵉ a treasurer of Amenhotep II, whose name is everywhere erased, shows a remarkable scene representing the production before the king of the New Year's gifts intended for his favorites.ᶠ He sits enthroned at the right, and the gifts are brought before him in magnificent array for his inspection.

ᵃRestored from the inscription of Amenhotep III (§ 875).

ᵇThis was on the Asiatic campaign (§§ 780 ff.); and makes at least four such tablets in Naharin, one of Thutmose I, two of Thutmose III, and one of Amenhotep II.

ᶜRegion around Napata; see § 1020.

ᵈRelief scenes and inscriptions in a Theban tomb, at Shekh Abd-el-Kurna; published, Lepsius, *Denkmäler*, III, 63, 64, and Text, III, 274; Champollion, *Notices descriptives*, I, 500 f.; Rosellini, *Monumenti Civili*, 121; Mond, *Annales*, V, 97 ff.

ᵉThe name is not found in Lepsius, *Denkmäler*, but is given by Newberry, Benson and Gourlay, *The Temple of Mut in Asher*, 328, and Mond, *Annales*, V, 97 ff.

ᶠThey are not presents from the noblemen to the king, as Erman supposed (*Aegypten*, 177); one of the statues bears the words: "*Given as a favor of the king's-presence,*" the usual formula upon gifts from the king, e. g., Nebwawi (§ 186, l. 10) received as a gift from this same king, Amenhotep II, a statue of the king's father, Thutmose III, it being customary for the king to present such royal statues to his favorites.

Inscription before the King

¹First occasion of doing the pleasant deed in the great palace — —. ²Production of the New Year's gifts: ³chariots of silver ⁴and gold; statues of ivory ⁵and ebony; necklaces of every costly stone; weapons ⁶of warfare, works of all craftsmen . . . . . ⁹. . . . .[a]

802   The following are the gifts ranged before the king: 13 statues of the king;[b] 7 sphinx portraits of the king; 1 standing statue of his mother, Hatshepsut-Meretre; 8 necklaces; 7 shields, over the last three are the words: "*Leather of ⌐—⌐ 680;*" 10 quivers, the last three bearing the words: "*Leather — — 230;*" 6 battle axes, 2 coats scale armor; 6 (ḫpš-) swords, bearing the words: "*360 bronze (ḫpš-) swords;*" "*140 bronze daggers;*" 3 ebony staves tipped with silver and gold, marked: "*30 staves;*" 6 whips, bearing the words: "*220 gold, ivory, and ebony whips;*" 7 elaborate chests; sun shades, chairs, vases, and numerous small objects. Except in the case of the statues, it is not the number of times that an object is represented that is significant, but the accompanying numeral. Before the accompanying inscriptions the name of Amenhotep II appears.[c]

KARNAK BUILDING INSCRIPTION[d]

803.   After interesting references in the introduction to his conquests in Asia, particularly Mitanni, the king narrates the erection of the columns in the southern half of the

---

[a]Titles of the noblemen.

[b]One marked "*Thutmose I;*" eight standing, two sitting, three kneeling; for description, see Lepsius, *Denkmäler*, Text, III, 276 f.

[c]Lepsius, *Denkmäler*, Text, III, 277.

[d]On a column in the hypostyle of Thutmose I between pylons IV and V at Karnak; published Rougé, *Inscriptions hiéroglyphiques*, 157, 158; Piehl, *Actes du Congrès à Leyde*, 1883, IVᵐᵉ partie, section 3, 203-19; and Dümichen, *Historische Inschriften*, II, 38.

hypostyle of Thutmose I, pulled down by his mother Hatshepsut to introduce her obelisks (§ 304). The northern colonnade had already been restored by Thutmose III (§§ 600 ff.). A description of the king's wealth from his wars follows.ᵃ

Universal Sway

804. Live the Horus: Mighty Bull, Great in Strength; Favorite of the Two Goddesses: Mighty in Opulence; Made to Shine in Thebes; Golden Horus: Seizing by his Might in all Lands, Good God, Likeness of Re, Splendid Emanation of Atum, —ᵇ Son, whom he begat, whom he made to shine in Karnak. He appointed him to be king of the living, to do that which his ka did; his avenger, seeking excellent things; great in marvels, ²creative in knowledge, wise in execution, skilful-hearted like Ptah; king of kings, ruler of rulers, valiant, without his equal, lord of terror among the southern lands, great in fear at the end of the north. Every land comes to him bowing down; their chiefs bearing their offerings; King of Upper and Lower Egypt, Okheprure (Amenhotep II), given life; victorious lord, who takes every land, whom ⌜Horus⌝ has magnified because of his strength. The chiefs of Mitanni (*My-tn*) come to him, their tribute ³upon their backs, to beseech his majesty that there may [be given to them]ᶜ his sweet breath of life. A mighty occurrence, it has never been heard since the times of the gods. This country which knew not Egypt beseeches the Good God. ᵈ" It is my father Re who commands that I do it; ⌜he⌝ is the fashioner of my beauty. He appointed me to be protector of this land, (for) he knew that I would offer it to him. He assigned to me that which is with him, which the eye of his uraeus illuminates, ⁴all lands, all countries, every circuit, the Great Circle (Okeanos); they come to me in submission like every subject of my majesty; Son of Re, Amenhotep (II), Divine Ruler of Thebes, living forever, only vigilant one, begotten of the gods."

ᵃOf his other buildings the king has left us no narrative. His small temple between the two southernmost pylons at Karnak is without building inscription. His mortuary temple on the west shore at Thebes was just north of the Ramesseum and alongside that of his father, Thutmose III (see Baedeker, Map, 260), but it has utterly perished. See Spiegelberg, *Recueil*, XVI, 30, and XIX, 88, 89; also Petrie, *Six Temples*.

ᵇProbably the name of Amon is cut out here.

ᶜRestored after Naville, *Deir-el-Bahari*, III, 84, ll. 3, 4; *infra*, § 285, ll. 3, 4.

ᵈThe king speaks.

Dedication

805. He made (it) as his monument for his father [Amon], making for him the august columns of the southern hypostyle, wrought with electrum very plentifully, as an eternal work. I made for him a monument in ⌜—⌝. It was more beautiful than that which had been; I increased that which was before; I surpassed that which the ancestors made. He appointed me to be[a] lord of the people (*rḫy·t*), while I was a youth in the nest; he gave to me the two halves; he caused that my majesty should assume the throne, as one does a useful thing for his father. I rested upon his throne; he gave to me the land ⌜— —⌝. I have no enemies ⁶in all lands.

Temple Equipment

806. I made for him an adytum (*sḥm*) of gold; its floor was of silver. I made for him many vessels; they were more beautiful than the bodies of the stars. His silver-house, it inclosed treasures of the tribute of every country. His granaries were bursting with clean grain, rising upon the walls. I founded for him divine offerings. I restored the things of him that begat me, that the Son of Re [Amenhotep II], Divine Ruler of Heliopolis, might be given life, stability, satisfaction, like Re, forever.

BIOGRAPHY OF AMENEMHAB
[Concluded from § 592]

807. A scene[b] in the tomb shows Amenhotep II standing before the deceased Thutmose III enthroned as Osiris. This is in accord with the copy of the "Book of the Dead" found with Thutmose III's body, which also testifies to Amenhotep's piety; for it bears the title:[c] "*Amenhotep II,*[d] *he made (it) as his monument for his father, Thutmose III,*[d] *making for him a book of glorifying the soul.*" Behind

---

[a]Read: *dhn·n·f wy r nb*.
[b]*Mémoires de la mission française au Caire*, V, 245.
[c]Maspero, *Momies royales*, 548.
[d]Double name.

Amenhotep II appear Amenemhab and his wife bearing flowers and food. The biography continues, after the death of Thutmose III, as follows:

Accession of Amenhotep II

808. "When the morning brightened, ³⁸the sun arose, and the heavens shone, King Okheprure, Son of Re, Amenhotep (II), given life, ³⁹was established upon the throne of his father, he assumed the royal titulary. He ⌈— —⌉ all, he mingled with ⌈—⌉ᵃ in —, ⁴⁰the Red Land; he cut off the heads of their chiefs.ᵇ Diademed as Horus, son of Isis, [he] took ——————— ⁴¹——————— ⌈—⌉ᶜ the Kenemetyew (*Knm᎐ tyw*), every land, bowed down because of his fame; with their tribute upon their backs, ⁴²[that he might grant] to them the breath of life."

Favor Shown Amenemhab

809. ⁴² "His majesty noticed me rowing won[derfully] with him in ⁴³[his] vessel; 'Khammat' was its name. I was rowing ⌈with⌉ both hands at his beautiful feast of Luxor, likewise to the splendors ⁴⁴————. I was brought to the midst of the palace, one caused that I should stand before [the king, O]khepru[re] (Amenhotep II), — ⁴⁵— ⌈—⌉. I bowed down immediately before his majesty; he said to me, 'I know thy character; I was abiding in the nest, while thou wert in ⁴⁶the following of my father. I commission thee with office that thou shalt be deputy of the army as I have said, watch thou the élite troopsᵈ of the king.' The deputy, Mahu, executed (all) that his lord said."ᵉ

ᵃ*Ḳɜ᎐t*, with plural strokes and determinative of a prisoner or enemy. It is not Kehek with whom it was identified as formerly restored (Maspero, *Struggle of the Nations*, 290).

ᵇSee Piehl, *Zeitschrift für ägyptische Sprache*, 1888, 115, ıı. 3. Amenemhab doubtless refers to the sacrifice of the seven kings of Tikhsi.

ᶜ⌈*pⁿn wntyw*, Newberry; he also has *nb* instead of *k*, as the first sign of the following word.

ᵈThe élite troops as in l. 29; *k* is to be corrected to *nb* in Eber's copy, as in l. 29.

ᵉSo, after Newberry's copy, which unfortunately does not support Piehl's excellent suggestion (*Zeitschrift für ägyptische Sprache*, 1885, 61, 62).

REIGN OF THUTMOSE IV

SPHINX STELA[a]

810. This remarkable document purports to be a votive stela of Thutmose IV, recording how he had been raised to the throne by Harmakhis, the Sphinx, in recognition of his clearance of the great image from the encumbering sands, in response to the god's appeal to him as a young prince, to whom he appeared in a vision as the youth, weary with the chase, slept at noonday in his shadow. The form and content of the document are strikingly unlike the official or royal records of the Pharaohs. It is besides filled with errors and striking irregularities in orthography, and exhibits a number of suspicious peculiarities not to be expected in a monument of this class. It is therefore to be regarded as a late restoration,[b] and it is a great question to what extent it reproduces the content of the monument of which

---

[a] A huge red granite tablet, standing between the paws of the Great Sphinx, made from one of the architraves of the neighboring (so-called) Temple of the Sphinx. It is 11 feet 10 inches high, and 7 feet 2 inches wide. The lower third of the face has flaked off, so that over half the inscription is lost. It was uncovered by Caviglia in 1818, copied by Salt in 1820; his manuscript text is in the British Museum, *Memoirs on the Pyramids and the Great Sphinx*, fol. 1820; it was published from this manuscript in Young's *Hieroglyphics* (London, 1823), Pl. 80; again from the same manuscript inaccurately in Vyse Appendix to *Operations Carried on at the Pyramids of Gizeh* (London, 1842), III, 115; more accurately than any of these, but with further lacunæ, in Lepsius, *Denkmäler*, III, 68; repeated partially by Brugsch, *Zeitschrift für ägyptische Sprache*, 1876, 89–92. Finally a collation of all texts by Erman, *Sitzungsberichte Königlichen Akademie*, Berlin, VI, 428–37. I had collated all old publications and Berlin squeeze, and my readings have now been confirmed by Erman's text.

[b] Erman has now put together the reasons for the same conclusion, which he also has reached. He would date the document between the Twenty-first and Twenty-second Dynasty and Saitic times. Spiegelberg's objections to this conclusion (*Orientalistische Litteraturzeitung*, 1904) would explain the mistakes and peculiarities in the orthography as due to the erasure of the inscription under Ikhnaton

it is a restoration. Some such current incident during the youth of Thutmose IV may possibly have prompted it; but the form of the narrative as now on the monument is that of a folk-tale.

811. Moreover, a similar incident was narrated of a prince named Amenmose, son of Thutmose I. It was on a monument[a] by the Sphinx, of which the following fragments are preserved:

Year 4, under the majesty of Thutmose I, beloved of Harmakhis[b] [given life] like Re, forever.

——————[c] There went forth the eldest king's-son, commander in chief of the army of his father, Amenmose, living forever, to take a pleasure walk[d] ——————.

Evidently the priests were striving by such tales as these to enhance the reputation of the Sphinx.

The upper third of the Sphinx stela is occupied by an adoration scene in which Thutmose IV offers to Harmakhis in form of a sphinx. Below is the inscription, as follows:

Introduction

812. ¹Year 1, third month of the first season, day 19, under the majesty of Horus: Mighty - Bull - ⌈Begetting⌉- Radiance; Favorite of the Two Goddesses: Enduring - in - Kingship - like -Atum; Golden Horus: Mighty-of-Sword, Repelling-the-Nine-Bows; King of Upper and Lower Egypt; Menkheprure (Mn-$ḫpr[w]$-R^c), Son of Re: [Thutmose IV, Shining] in Diadems; beloved of —, given life, stability, satisfaction, like Re, forever. ²Live the Good God, son of Atum, Pro-

---

and the subsequent careless restoration, as in the Theban stelæ (e. g., §§ 878 ff.). That this objection cannot hold is evident; for the Sphinx is a sun-god, and the monuments of the sun-gods, especially of the Horuses, were respected by Ikhnaton, and not erased. It is impossible to conceive that Ikhnaton would erase the inscription to a god called "*Harmakhis-Khepri-Re-Atum*" (l. 9) in said inscription.

[a]A stone vessel in the Louvre, of which only a fragment, inscribed on two faces, survives. From my own copy of the original. See Erman, *ibid.*, 1063.

[b]The Sphinx.   [c]Other face.

[d]R *šwtwt ḥr šḏ' ḥr*, as on Sphinx stela.

tector of Harakhte, living image of the All-Lord; sovereign, begotten of Re; excellent heir of Khepri; beautiful of face like[a] his father; who came forth ⌜—⌝ equipped with the form of Horus upon him;[b] a king who — the gods; who — favor with the ennead of gods; who purifies Heliopolis, [3]who satisfies Re; who beautifies Memphis; who presents truth to Atum, who offers it to Him-Who-is-South-of-His-Wall (Ptah); who makes a monument by daily offering to Horus; who does all things, seeking benefits for the gods of South and North; who builds their houses of limestone; who endows all their offerings; son of Atum, of his body, Thutmose (IV), Shining in Diadems, like Re;[c] [4]heir of Horus upon his throne, Menkheprure, given life.[c]

Youth of Thutmose

813. When his majesty was a stripling like Horus, the youth in Khemmis, his beauty was like the [d]protector of his father,[d] he seemed[e] like the god himself. The army rejoiced because of love for him, the king's-children and all the nobles. Then his strength overflowed him, and he [5]repeated the circuit of his might like the son of Nut.[f]

Hunting Expedition

Behold, he did a thing that gave him pleasure[g] upon the highlands of the Memphite nome, upon its southern and northern road,[h] shooting at a target with copper[i] bolts, hunting lions and wild goats, coursing in his chariot, his horses being swifter [6]than the wind; together with two of his followers, while not a soul knew it.

Midday Rest

814. Now, when his hour came on for giving rest to his followers, (it was always) at the ⌜shoulder⌝ of Harmakhis, beside Sokar in Rosta,

---

[a]Read *my* for *my ḥk ꜣ*.

[b]He was born with the royal insignia upon him, as in Papyrus Westcar.

[c]The usual predicate is here cut in two, with half of it after each name; the two names are in inverted order also. This could only have happened from the scribe's use of an original in which the two names were in two vertical lines, with the predicate under them (Erman).

[d]Harendotes, a title of Horus.

[e]Passive of "see;" cf. *videri*.   [f]So also Erman.

[g]*Sḏ ꜣ* occurs also in the hunting inscription of Imunzeh (*Mémoires de la mission française au Caire*, V, 355).

[h]Or: "*side.*"   [i]Not bronze, as in all the versions.

Renutet in ⌜— —⌝ᵃ in heaven, Mut — — of the northern — the mistress of the Wall of the South, Sekhmet ⁷presider (fem.) over Khas ($Ḥ\ni s$) ⌜— —⌝ the splendid place of the ᵇbeginning of time, over against the lords of Khereha ($Ḥr$-$ʿḥʿ$), the sacred road of the gods to the necropolisᶜ west of On (Heliopolis). Now, the very great statueᵈ of Khepri, rests in this place;ᵉ the great in prowess, the splendid in strength; upon which the shadow of Re tarries. The quarters of Memphis and all the cities which are by him come to him, (raising)ᶠ their hands for him in praise to his face, ⁸bearing great oblations for his ka.

The Vision

815. One of those daysᵍ it came to pass that the king's-son, Thutmose, came, coursing at the time of midday, and he rested in the shadow of this great god.ʰ A ⌜vision⌝ of sleep seized him at the hour (when) the sun was in the zenith, ⁹and he found the majesty of this revered god speaking with his own mouth, as a father speaks with his son, saying: "Behold thou me! See thou me! my son Thutmose. I am thy father, Harmakhis-Khepri-Re-Atum, who will give to thee my kingdom ¹⁰on earth at the head of the living.ⁱ Thou shalt wear the white crown and the red crown upon the throne of Keb, the hereditary prince. The land shall be thine in its length and breadth, that which the eye of the All-Lord shines upon. The food of the Two Lands shall be thine, the great tribute of all countries, the duration of a long period of years. My face is thine, my desire is toward thee. Thou shalt be to me a protector ¹¹(for) my manner is as I were ailing in all my limbs ⌜—⌝. The sand of this desert upon which I am, has reached me; turn to me, to

---

ᵃThe first two words indicate grains, a meaning which suits Renutet, a harvest goddess. $T\ni$-mwt is also the name of a Theban region (Djēme); it occurs e. g., Lepsius, *Denkmäler*, Text, I, 11, 1).

ᵇLit., "*the first time.*"

ᶜLit., "*horizon.*" If Giseh was the necropolis of Heliopolis, it is probable that the Fourth Dynasty kings may have actually resided in Heliopolis.

ᵈThe Great Sphinx.

ᵉThis is a resumption of the object, which preceded in the foregoing clauses.

ᶠLit., "*give.*"

ᵍIt would seem that the preceding lines narrate the hunting expedition(s?) as customary, and on "*one of those days*" the following incident of the dream occurred.

ʰThe Sphinx. ⁱYoung: $tp\ t\ni\ ḫnt\ ʿnḫ\cdot w$.

have that done which I have desired, knowing that thou art my son, my protector; ⌜come hither⌝, behold, I am with thee, I am ¹²ᵃthy leader." When he had finished this speech, this king's-son ⌜awoke⌝ hearing thisᵃ —— —; he understood the words of this god, and he kept silent in his heart. ᵇHe said:ᵇ "Come, let us hasten to our house in the city; theyᶜ shall protect the oblations for this god ¹³ᵈwhich we bring for him: oxen ⌜—⌝ and all young vegetables; and we shall give praise [to] Wennofer,ᵈ —— —— Khaf[re],ᵉ the statue made for Atum-Harmakhis ₁₄————.ᶠ

ASIATIC CAMPAIGN

816. The records of Thutmose IV's Asiatic war or wars are scanty and scattered. It is clear, however, that he still maintained the empire at its former northern limits. Naharin paid tribute, although a campaign thither had been necessary.

817. The king left a record referring to the first war in Asia in a list of offerings from his victories, which he had made in Karnak,ᵍ in which nothing more concerning the campaign can be seen than that there were among these offerings, things "*which his majesty captured in Naharin*ʰ (————*n*ᵓ) *the wretched, on his first victorious campaign.*"

ᵃAll from Young.   ᵇBrugsch's text.

ᶜOr: "*we?*" "*that we may protect .... and that we may bring*" (so Erman).

ᵈAll from Young.

ᵉThis mention of King Khafre has been understood to indicate that the Sphinx was the work of this king—a conclusion which does not follow; Young has no trace of a cartouche.

ᶠYoung shows two fragments, each bearing a few words (from the middle of ll. 16 and 17 and ll. 18 and 19) which probably refer to further offerings.

ᵍFragmentary lower ends of ten vertical lines east side of the wall surrounding Hatshepsut's obelisk; published Mariette, *Karnak*, 33 = Rougé, *Inscriptions hiéroglyphiques*, 164; photograph by Borchardt.

ʰMariette read only the final '(aleph), but Rougé read *n* ᵇ at the end. This reading is also perfectly clear on the photograph. Brugsch's "Kheta" (*Geschichte*, 393) must therefore be given up. See also Müller, *Asien und Europa*, 321, n. 2.

818. This is corroborated by the inscription of Amenhotep, a bodyguardsman of Thutmose IV, whose tomb stela[a] calls him:

Attendant of the king on his expeditions in the south and north countries; going from Naharin (N-h-ry-n) to Karoy (K ᵓ -r-y) behind his majesty, while he was upon the battlefield; companion of the feet of the Lord of the Two Lands, chief of the stable of his majesty, high priest of Onouris, Amenhotep, triumphant.

819. In harmony with these data, we find depicted on the two following monuments the tribute of Naharin and Retenu; the first is in the tomb of Khamhet,[b] who was a powerful noble, and served as chief treasurer under Thutmose IV and Amenhotep III.[c] His tomb contains three scenes of historical importance, of which one[d] belongs to the reign of Thutmose IV. It shows the king seated in a "naos" at the left; before him are magnificent vessels of Asiatic workmanship in gold and silver, and quantities of these metals in large rings. Behind these are Asiatic princes bowing to the earth, over whom is the inscription:[e]

Bringing in the tribute of Naharin (N-h-ry-n ᵓ) by the princes of this country, in order to crave that the breath of life be granted to them. Obeisance to the great Lord of the Two Lands, when they come, bearing their tribute to the Lord of the Two Lands, (saying:) "Grant us breath, which thou givest, O mighty king."

---

[a]Sharpe, *Inscriptions*, I, 93.

[b]In the cliff of Abd el-Kurna (No. 120) at Thebes; published entire by Loret, *Mémoires de la mission française au Caire*, I, 113–32; partially, Prisse, *Histoire de l'Art*; Lepsius, *Denkmäler*, III, 76, 77; Champollion, *Monuments*, 160, 1; Champollion, *Notices descriptives*, 498 f., 839 f. The entire tomb is now being broken up by natives, part of the reliefs having reached Berlin (1899). A useful summary in Baedeker's *Egypt*, 1902, 282, where the tomb is inadvertently placed in the reign of Amenhotep IV.

[c]See §§ 870 ff.

[d]Champollion, *Monuments*, 160, 1; Champollion, *Notices descriptives*, 498 f., 839 f. It has been incorrectly attributed to Amenhotep III by Wiedemann (*Aegyptische Geschichte*, 381).

[e]Champollion, *Monuments*, 160, 1; the remainder from Champollion, *Notices descriptives*, I, 839 f.

820. A similar scene in the tomb of Thaneni is accompanied by the following inscription:[a]

Bringing in the tribute of Retenu, presentation of the northern countries; silver, gold, malachite, every costly stone of God's-Land; by the princes of all countries. They come, to [⌈make gifts⌉] to the Good God, to ask for breath for their nostrils; by the real king's-scribe, his beloved, commander of troops, scribe of recruits, Thaneni.

821. A tablet[b] of the king, erected in his mortuary temple at Thebes, records the settlement of Syrians in the temple inclosure:

Settlement of the "Fortress of Menkheprure," with Syrians ($Ḫ\ᵓ$ -rw), which his majesty captured in the city of $K\ᵓ$ -$\underline{d}\ᵓ$ — (⌈Gezer⌉).

822. Finally, on the Lateran Obelisk (§ 838), the king refers to the cedar which he cut in the land of Retenu; and on the stela of Semen (*Smn*) in the Louvre (C 202),[c] he is twice called the "*conqueror of Syria*" (*sksk $ḫ\ᵓ$ rw*), a title which must have been won in successful Syrian wars.

KONOSSO INSCRIPTION[d]

823. This inscription contained perhaps the most interesting record of all the many Nubian wars, and its content has never been historically employed; but it is so incorrectly published that it is difficult to follow. While engaged in the ceremonies of the Theban temple, on the second of Phamenoth, in the year 8, Thutmose IV receives a message

---

[a]Scheil, *Mémoires de la mission française au Caire*, V, 601.

[b]Petrie, *Six Temples*, I, 7.

[c]De Rougé, *Notice des monuments*, 153; and text, Brugsch, *Thesaurus*, VI, 1461, No. 113.

[d]Cut on the rocks of the peninsula (high-water island) of Konosso by Philæ. It was first very incorrectly published by Bouriant (*Recueil*, XV, 178, 179); again, still worse, in de Morgan, *Catalogue des monuments*, 66, 67. The inscription contained 40 lines, of which the latter portion is much destroyed; only 23 lines are published.

reporting a revolt in Wawat. The next morning the king solemnly proceeds to the temple to consult the god, and is granted an oracle promising success. The expedition now embarks and moves southward, stopping on the way at all the great temples, where the divinities come forth to meet the king, and gird him for battle.[a] The result of the battle,[b] fought doubtless somewhere in Wawat, is of course a foregone conclusion, and the enumeration of the spoil begins, as the published portion comes to an end.

824. The prisoners whom the king brought back on his return were settled in his mortuary temple at Thebes, and the quarter was marked with a tablet[c] bearing the words:

Colony of Kush the wretched, which his majesty brought back from his victories.

The Konosso inscription is as follows:

Introduction

825. [1]Live Horus: ....[d] the King of Upper and Lower Egypt: Menkhperure (Thutmose IV), who is given life, forever. [2]Year 8, third month of the second season, day 2.

Announcement of Nubian Rebellion

826. Behold, his majesty was in the Southern City, at the town of Karnak. His two hands were pure with the purity[e] of [3]a king, and he

---

[a] A tablet (Lepsius, *Denkmäler*, III, 69 e = Champollion, *Notices descriptives*, I, 164) on Konosso, dated year 7, on the eighth of the same month, shows the king before the god Dedun, smiting his enemies.

[b] There is a reference to the victory in the king's architrave inscription at Amâda (Lepsius, *Denkmäler*, III, 69, f. 5), and campaigning in Nubia (Karoy) is mentioned by the king's bodyguardsman, Amenhotep (§ 818).

[c] Found by Petrie in the temple inclosure; it is now in Haskell Oriental Museum, of the University of Chicago (*Six Temples*, I).

[d] Full titulary, lacking only s ꜣ -R ꜥ -name.

[e] He was ceremonially pure, for carrying out the temple ritual; the emendation is certain, cf. "*His majesty was pure with the purity of a god;*" on the construction, see Sethe, *Verbum*, II, § 725.

performed the pleasing ceremonies of his father Amon, because he had given to [him]ᵃ eternity as king, everlastingness while abiding upon the Horus-throne. One came to say to his majesty: "The Negro descends ⁴from above Wawat; he hath planned revolt against Egypt. He gathers to himself ⁵all the barbarians and the revolters of other countries."

Oracle of Amon

827. The king proceeded in peace to the temple at the time ⁶of morning, to cause that a great oblation be offered to his father, the fashioner of his beauty. ⌈Behold,⌉ his majesty, he himself petitioned in the presence of ⁷the ruler of the gods (Amon), that he might counsel him concerning the ⌈affair of his going⌉ — and inform concerning that which should happen to him; leading for him upon a goodly road ⁸to do that which his ka desired, as a father speaks to his son,ᵇ ⌈— — —⌉. He went forth from him, his heart ⁹rejoicing ⌈— —⌉ — — — (for) he sent him with might and victory.

Voyage Southward

828. After these things his majesty ¹⁰proceeded to overthrow the ⌈Negro⌉ in Nubia ($T^ɜ$-$pḏ·t$); mighty in his barge of ⌈—⌉ like Re when he shows himselfᶜ in the celestial barque ¹¹..........ᵈ His army ¹²of his victories, was with (him) on both banks, while the recruits were upon its (one) shore, and the ship was equipped with his attendants,ᵉ ¹³as the king proceeded up-stream like ⌈Orion.⌉ He illuminated the South with his beauty;ᶠ men shouted because of his kindness, ¹⁴women

---

ᵃOf course omitted by the copyist.

ᵇThe same phrase is used of the god's speaking to Thutmose IV, on the Sphinx Stela (l. 9, § 815).

ᶜA common phrase of the sun-hymns, e. g., Berlin Stela, No. 7316, *Ausführliches Verzeichniss des Berliner Museums*, 108.

ᵈAbout one-half line mere fragments. The other half is very uncertain. The subject is the embarkation, with the same obscure phrases used in the transportation of the el-Bersheh colossus (§ 698, ll. 7, 8), but "*horses*" appear here in the place of "*the youth*" there.

ᵉApparently we have here the disposition of troops as the king embarked; the veterans ("*of his victories*") on either bank, the young recruits on one bank, and the bodyguard in the royal barge.

ᶠCompare the southward advance of Sesostris I (I, 511, l. 2), also compared with a star in the same way.

danced at the message. Montu[a] was in Erment as the protection of [his] every limb; Irerti (*Yrrty*)[b] led before; every god of the South ¹⁵bore the ⌜—⌝ before him; Nekbet, the White, of El Kab, she[c] fastened the adornments of my majesty,[d] her two hands were behind ⌜me⌝, she bound for me the Nine Bows together ¹⁶..........[e] I stopped in the city of Edfu, the beautiful god come forth[f] like Montu in all his forms, ¹⁷girded with his arms and weapons, ⌜raging⌝[g] like Set of Kom Ombo .... ¹⁸..........

The Battle

829. His army came to him, ¹⁹numerous — with his mighty sword. The fear of him entered into every body; Re put the fear of him among the lands, like Sekhmet in the year of ²⁰the dew........... He coursed through the eastern highland, he traversed the ways like ²¹a jackal......... He found all [⌜his⌝] foes ⌜scattered⌝ in inaccessible valleys............

The remainder is published too badly for translation; one can make out a reference to "*their cattle* [⌜*their tribute*⌝][h] *upon their backs.*"

LATERAN OBELISK[i]

830. Although this obelisk belongs to Thutmose III (§§ 626 ff.), the inscriptions added by Thutmose IV as side columns are more interesting and important than the dedication in Thutmose III's name. They state that after

---

[a]There is no doubt of the emendation. The advance up-river is marked by references to the gods of the larger places passed. Hermonthis (Erment) is the first place south of Thebes; then follow El Kab, Edfu, and Kom Ombo in the proper order.

[b]Apparently a goddess.   [d]An abrupt change to the first person.

[c]Read *smn·n·s*.   [e]A reference to some feast.

[f]To meet the king; cf. the same occurrence at Abydos (I, 763).

[g]Read *nšn*?

[h]Of course, some such word is omitted in the publication.

[i]For bibliography, see § 626.

lying neglected and unfinished for thirty-five[a] years, the obelisk was found by Thutmose IV, erected and inscribed by him.

North Right

831. . . . .[b] (Thutmose IV) who seizes by his might, like the lord of Thebes; great in strength, like Montu; whom his father, Amon, has made victorious against all countries; to whom unknown lands come, his fear being in their bodies; Son of Re, Thutmose (IV), Shining in Diadems, beloved of Amon, Kamephis, given life.

North Left

832. King of Upper and Lower Egypt, beloved of the gods; whose excellence the ennead of gods praise; who sends Re to rest in the evening-barque; who praises Atum in the morning-barque; Lord of the Two Lands, Menkheprure (Thutmose IV), who beautifies Thebes, forever; who makes monuments in Karnak. The ennead of gods of the house of Amon is satisfied with that which he has done; Son of Atum, of his body, his heir upon his throne, Thutmose (IV), Shining in Diadems, beloved of Amon-Re.

South Left

833. . . . . Thutmose (IV), Begotten of Re, beloved of Amon. It was his majesty who beautified[c] the single, very great obelisk, being one which his father,[d] the King of Upper and Lower Egypt, Menkheperre (Thutmose III) had brought, after his majesty had found this obelisk, it having spent 35 years lying upon its side in the hands of the craftsmen, on the south side of Karnak. My father commanded that I should erect it for him, I, his son, his savior.

South Right

834. Son of Re, Thutmose (IV), Shining of Diadems. He erected it in Karnak, making its pyramidion of electrum, (so that) its beauty illu-

---

[a]Accepting Thutmose III's death as the probable cause of the unfinished condition of the monument, we should have an important chronological datum, if only Thutmose IV had given us the year of his own reign in which he found it. But as it is, the datum indicates only that Amenhotep II and Thutmose IV together reigned at least thirty-five years.

[b]Full titulary except last name, which comes at the end of this line.

[c]That is, finished and inscribed it.

[d]Really his grandfather, but any ancestor of a king may be called his father.

minated Thebes. It was graven with the name of his father, the Good God, Menkheperre (Thutmose III). The King of Upper and Lower Egypt, Lord of the Two Lands, Menkheprure (Thutmose IV), Beloved of Re, did this, in order to cause that the name of his father might abide and endure in the house of Amon-Re, that the Son of Re, Thutmose (IV), Shining in Diadems. may be given life through him (*nf*).

West Right

835. .... (Thutmose IV), whom Amon has chosen before the people [whom Mut] bore [to him], [whom] he [loves] more than any king, to see whose beauty he rejoices, because he has so fully set him in his heart; under whose authority he has placed the Southerners and the Northerners, doing obeisance to his fame. He made (it) as his monument for his father, Amon-Re, erecting for him a very great obelisk at the upper portal[a] of Karnak, over against Thebes, that the Son of Re, his beloved Thutmose (IV), Shining of Diadems, may be given life through him (*nf*).

West Left

836. .... Menkheprure, eldest son, useful to him who begat him; doing that which satisfies the lord of gods; (since) he knows the excellence of his plans. It is he who has led him to pleasant ways, and who hath bound for him the Nine Bows beneath his feet. Behold, his majesty was vigilant in beautifying the monument of his father. The king himself was the one who gave direction, being skilfully-minded like "Him-Who-is-South-of-His-Wall" (Ptah). He erected it ⌜at the completion of time⌝. He rejoiced the heart of the one who fashioned him; Son of Re, Thutmose (IV), Shining in Diadems, ——.

East Right

837. Good God, Mighty in Strength, Sovereign, seizing by his victories, who sets his terror among the Asiatics, and his roaring among the Nubian Troglodytes, whom his father, Amon, reared to exercise an enduring kingship, while the princes of all countries do obeisance to the fame of his majesty; who spoke with his mouth and executed with

---

[a]The entrance to the Karnak temenos on the south side, to which the four southern pylons lead. It is mentioned on the statue of Beknekhonsu (III, 567, l. 5), where it is also called "*upper portal*" (sb ꜣ-ḥry).

his hands. All that he commanded happened; King of Upper and Lower Egypt, Menkheprure (Thutmose IV), of abiding name in Karnak, given life.

East Left

838. ...... Menkheprure, who multiplied monuments in Karnak, of gold, lapis lazuli, malachite, every splendid costly stone; the great barge of the "Beginning-of-the-River"[a] (named): Userhet-Amon, shaped of new cedar, which his majesty cut[b] in the land of Retenu, wrought with gold throughout; all its adornments were fashioned for the first time, to receive the beauty of his father, Amon, on his voyage of the "Beginning-of-the-River." May the Son of Re, Thutmose (IV), Shining in Diadems, be given life through him.

STELA OF PE'AOKE[c]

839. The mortuary stela of the standard-bearer ($t^{\jmath}$-$sr\cdot t$) of the royal barge, Pe'aoke ($P^{\jmath\text{-}c\jmath\text{-}c}k$), after the usual prayers, records the arrival of a royal messenger at Abydos, to attend to the conveyance to Osiris of certain property of the people. The nature of these payments is not at all clear, and the purpose of their record is only incidental, being doubtless to explain the occasion on which Pe'aoke visited Abydos and executed his stela there. His reference to Ahmose shows that Thutmose IV increased his ancestor's mortuary endowment. A stela in the British Museum[d] mentions a "*palace ($h\cdot t$) of Thutmose IV, given life, in Abydos,*" which would indicate that he occasionally resided

---

[a]The same in Thutiy (l. 18, § 373). It was some feast on the river, perhaps that of the fourteenth of Paophi.

[b]The same statement by Amenhotep III (§ 888, ll. 16, 17).

[c]Stela in the Louvre, C 53; see de Rougé, *Notices des monuments*, 100. I had my own copy of the original.

[d]No. 148; it is the mortuary stela of Neferhet (N/r-$h^{\jmath}\cdot t$), the chief of works in the palace (from my own copy of the original).

there, and Pe'aoke's record of the gifts of cattle and lands would indicate great interest in Abydos on the part of Thutmose IV.

840. There came a royal messenger of King Menkheprure (Thutmose IV), who is given life, to his father, Osiris, lord of Abydos, to give to him all his property which was with all the people (*rḫy·t*), being bulls, oxen, wild cattle, fowl, and all his ⌜property⌝ which was therein.

Again one came to give the lands of Osiris to him,[a] which were [with] all the people (*rḫy·t*); the stat (*st꜄·t*) being 1,200.

Again came the like for the Good God, Nebpehtire (Ahmose I),[b] in order to give [to] him all the lands ⌜— —⌝.

---

[a]The order of words is unusual; the dative should precede the direct object.

[b]Referring to a mortuary endowment; but the form of expression is unusual for this idea.

REIGN OF AMENHOTEP III

BIRTH AND CORONATION[a]

841. The scenes and inscriptions representing Amenhotep III's supernatural birth and his coronation by the gods, which he had placed upon the walls in one of the chambers of his Amon-temple at Luxor, are taken from the same sources as those of Hatshepsut, and have already been treated under her reign (§§ 187–212, 215–42). For Ahmose, the mother of Hatshepsut there, one must here substitute Mutemuya, the mother of Amenhotep III; and for Hatshepsut, Amenhotep III.

NUBIAN WAR

842. In his fifth and sixth years, Amenhotep III found it necessary to invade Nubia as far as Karoy,[b] the district conquered by his grandfather, Amenhotep II (§§ 797), and his great-grandfather, Thutmose III, and probably much farther. He has left us a list of the Nubian regions

---

[a]In the Luxor temple of Amon in the first chamber on the east of the holy of holies, on the west wall. Partially published by Champollion, *Monuments*, IV, 339, No. 2–341); Rosellini (*Monumenti Storici*, 38–41), and Lepsius (*Denkmäler*, III, 74, *c*–75). First completely by Gayet, *Mémoires de la mission française au Caire*, XV, Pl. 62–68 and 75. Besides errors innumerable in the texts, every plate bears two numbers, and on these plates every figure bears two numbers; in each case only one is correct! The errors in the texts, evident everywhere, can be demonstrated easily by a comparison with the texts of the queen's interview with Amon, which have also been published by Bouriant (*Recueil*, IX, 84, 85).

[b]Karoy is not mentioned in the records of the campaign, but is referred to, as reached on the first campaign, in the building inscription (§ 889, l. 23).

subjugated, presumably on this campaign, on a colossal granite statue, now in the Louvre.ᵃ

I. STELA AT FIRST CATARACTᵇ

843. The upper third of the stela is occupied with a scene showing the king trampling down an Asiatic and smiting two Negroes; before him are Amon and Khnum; behind him, Ptah. The inscription of twelve lines is very fragmentary (having been mutilated by Amenhotep IV in erasing the name of Amon, which has afterward been restored), but shows clearly that, owing to a revolt in Nubia, Amenhotep III was obliged to invade the country, and crush the rebels in his fifth year.ᶜ

844. ¹Year 5, third month of the first season (third month), day 2, the coronation (day)ᵈ under the majesty of
Horus: Mighty Bull, Shining in Truth;
Favorite of the Two Goddesses: Establisher of Laws, ²Quieter of the Two Lands;
Golden Horus: Great in Strength, Smiter of the Asiatics, Good God, Ruler of Thebes, Lord of Strength, Mighty of Valor;
³King of Upper and Lower Egypt: Nibmare (*Nb-m ᵓ ᶜ ⋅ t-R ᶜ*)⋅

ᵃThis statue (A 18) was usurped by Amenhotep III; it belonged perhaps to a king of the Twelfth Dynasty. See Maspero, *Dawn*, 491, n. 6. I have verified this usurpation on the original. The list is published by Sharpe (*Inscriptions*, II, 26).

ᵇCut in the rock on the road from Assuan to Philæ. Text: Lepsius, *Denkmäler*, III, 81, g; de Rougé, *Inscriptions hiéroglyphiques*, 254; de Morgan, *Catalogue des monuments*, I, 4.

ᶜA second stela in the same locality, also relating to this war, is too fragmentary for translation (Lepsius, *Denkmäler*, III, 81, h; de Morgan, *Catalogue des monuments*, I, 5).

ᵈBased on an ostracon in London (No. 5637, Birch, *Inscriptions in the Hieratic and Demotic Character*, Pl. 15). His coronation is usually dated on the thirteenth of the eleventh month, see Brugsch, *Egypt under the Pharaohs*, 213. Sethe, however, has shown (*Untersuchungen*, I, 12, n. 1) that this ostracon does not specify which Amenhotep is meant, and rightly refers it to some one of the three other Amenhoteps.

Son of Re: Amenhotep (III), Ruler of Thebes; beloved of Amon-Re, King of Gods, and Khnum, Lord of the Cataract (*Ḳbḥ*), who giveth life.
⁴One came[a] to tell his majesty: "The foe of Kush the wretched, ⌜has planned⌝ rebellion in his heart."
⁵His majesty led on unto his victory, he completed it on his first victorious campaign.[b] His majesty went forth ⁶— like — Horus, like Montu (*Mnṭw*) ⌜— — —⌝ — ⌜————⌝ ⁷. . . . . .[c] ⁹He knew not this lion which was before him; Nibmare (Amenhotep III) was a ¹⁰fierce-eyed lion, he seized ⌜—⌝ Kush. ⌜All⌝ the chiefs were overthrown ¹¹in their valleys, cast down in their blood, one upon another — ¹². . . . .[d]

II. STELA OF KONOSSO[e]

845. A scene above shows Amon presenting four southern regions[f] to Amenhotep III. The inscription commemorates the same Nubian campaign as the preceding stela.

¹. . . . .[g] ⁵Year 5; his majesty returned, having triumphed on his first victorious campaign in the land ⁶of Kush the wretched; having made his boundary as far as he desired, as far as the four pillars which bear the heaven. He set up ⁷a tablet of victory as far as "Pool of Horus" (*Ḳbḥw-Ḥr*); there was no king of Egypt ⁸who did the like beside his majesty, the mighty, satisfied with victory, Nibmare (*Nb-m ᵓ ᶜ ˑ t-R ᶜ*, Amenhotep III) is he. . . . . . . .⁹. . . . .¹⁴. . . .[h]

---

[a]Compare a similar announcement of a revolt in Nubia, to Thutmose II on the Assuan stela (§ 121, ll. 9-11), and to Thutmose IV on the Konosso stela (§ 826).

[b]A rock inscription near Assuan shows an official doing homage to the names of Amenhotep III, and dates the event as occurring "*on his first victorious campaign in Kush*" (Lepsius, *Denkmäler*, Text, IV, 119; de Morgan, *Catalogue des monuments*, I, 28, No. 8).

[c]These two lines are very obscure and fragmentary, but refer to the king's valor and the overthrow of Kush.

[d]Titles and usual epitheta of the king.

[e]Cut on the rocks of the little island of Konosso at the north end of Philæ; text: Lepsius, *Denkmäler*, III, 82, a; Champollion, *Notices descriptives*, I, 164, 165; Brugsch, *Thesaurus*, V, 1218, 1219; de Morgan, *Catalogue des monuments*, I, 67, 68.

[f]These are: Kush (*Kš*), Irem (*Yr-m*), *Wrm* (?) and ᵓ *rk*.

[g]Full titulary of Amenhotep II.

[h]Contains only the usual conventional epithets; ll. 10-11 have: "*He (Amon) hath given to him the south* ¹¹*as well as north, west, and east.*"

III. BUBASTIS INSCRIPTION[a]

846. The fragment preserved to us belonged to an historical inscription of unusual interest, containing the account of an advance into Nubia, with descriptions of the battles and the stages of the advance in the same style as that of the Annals of Thutmose III. Indeed, it is not unlikely that the walls of the Bubastis temple contained annals of the wars of the Empire in Nubia, like those of the conquest of Syria on the walls of Karnak.

The fragment unfortunately contains no royal name, and has been conjecturally assigned to Sesostris III.[b] This is impossible, for the orthography[c] shows beyond doubt that the inscription dates from the Empire. Moreover, its content indicates a time when the Egyptian conquest extended far into the upper regions of Nubia, that is, from Amenhotep II on. A hitherto unnoticed reference to the coronation anniversary is here of great service. It is mentioned (l. 6) as occurring just after the first battle and before the advance to "*the height of Hua*" began. They reached this point in the third month of the first season (l. 11); the coronation anniversary therefore occurred not long before. Now, the coronation of Amenhotep III occurred in the third month of the first season on the second day; and the above inscriptions (§§ 844 ff.) show that he also celebrated a coronation festival on his Nubian campaign.[d] It is

---

[a]On a block of granite found at Bubastis; published by Naville (*Bubastis*, XXXIV, A). The block is from the middle of an inscription in vertical lines; not merely the beginning and end of the inscription are lost, but also the upper and lower portions of the lines, of which this block bears the middle portions.

[b]By Naville (*Bubastis*, 9).

[c]It contains the horizontal *m* which never occurs before the Eighteenth Dynasty; see Calice, *Zeitschrift für ägyptische Sprache*, 35, 170.

[d]Thutmose II also mentions a coronation festival in an inscription narrating his Nubian campaign, but this merely dates the arrival of the news of the revolt,

extremely probable, therefore, that this Bubastis fragment belongs to Amenhotep III, and describes the advance into Karoy, or the distant country beyond.

847. The expedition is very difficult to follow in the scanty fragment preserved to us, but its course was probably as follows:

Early in October, when the river is high, the army is already far up in Nubia. Before a battle the king makes a speech to his troops, after which the battle occurs, the king personally taking part in it (ll. 1–5). The expedition then started southward for the "*height of Hua*" on the coronation anniversary; reference is made to the first camp (l. 6). The king commanded that people (Nubians?) furnish certain things for the expedition[a] (l. 7), and reference is made to former troops; his majesty held a council (l. 8). A branch expedition of 124 men was sent out from the river to a certain well (l. 9); whether to destroy the well or attack the villages which would naturally be found near a well[b] is uncertain, but it was evidently the customary procedure to go out to these outlying wells, for in his expedition of the sixteenth year, Sesostris III "*went forth to their wells*"[b] (I, 658, l. 15); here also the purpose is not stated. The expedition then proceeded southward for "*the height of Hua*" (l. 10), taking captives and spoil on the way (l. 11). They were favored by a high north wind, and not more than a month after the coronation feast the desired "*height*

---

whereas Amenhotep III apparently actually celebrated the feast in Nubia (§ 844, l. 5). The question arises whether the cataract stela (§§ 843 ff.) represents the party as having actually arrived at the first cataract on the return from the campaign, on coronation day. If so, we then have two different expeditions of Amenhotep III. In attributing both inscriptions to the same expedition, I am assuming that the cataract inscription gives the date of the battle, which is coronation day in both.

[a]Compare the muster of Nubian troops by the viceroy Mermose (§ 852, ll. 1–4).

[b]Many villages in Nubia are unreached by the water of the Nile, and are supported by wells.

of Hua .... came forth," that is, rose from the horizon (1. 12). They passed to the southward of *"the height of Hua,"* and, having reached the land of Uneshek (⌈W⌉ nšk), they rested in a camp there (1. 13).

848. It would be of great importance to identify the countries mentioned and determine the southern limit of this expedition. Both Hua (hw^c) and the land of Khesekhet ($h^{\flat} sh \cdot t$) occur close together in the lists of the regions of Khenthennofor, placed on the Karnak walls by Thutmose III (see §§ 645 ff);[a] the occurrence of Punt along with these names, and the narrative of the expedition, would indicate that they denote localities in the extreme south beyond Karoy on the Nile (above the Atbara?).

849. ¹———— Negroes ———— ²———— this army, while their hearts were ⌈eager⌉ to fight quickly, beyond anything — came ————
³———— Ye [⌈see⌉] nothing has been done to you. Now, behold, as for your affair ⌈which my majesty mentions⌉ ———— ⁴———— ⌈—⌉ of the Negroes who fell, in order that my [majesty][b] might know, because ye do ⌈this⌉ ———— ⁵———— it was not commanded for them. His majesty smote them himself with the baton which was in [his] hand ———— ⁶———— the height of Hua (Hw^c) on the coronation day of the king, behind western Khesekhet.[c] Behold, the army was made to camp ———— ⁷———— all — very numerous beyond anything. His majesty issued a command to these people, to make them.[d] They

---

[a]⌈W⌉nšk (1. 13) I have not found in any of the lists. Hw^c occurs in the Karnak list as $Hw^{c \cdot t}$ (Mariette, *Karnak*, Pl. 22, No. 89); $H^{\flat} sh^{\cdot} t$ (*ibid.*, No. 95). $Hw^{c \cdot t}$ also occurs with Punt in the list of Ramses III (Lepsius, *Denkmäler*, III, 209).

[b]That which Naville has read as *t* with a lacuna over it is possibly the sign for *hn*, *"majesty;"* but the book-roll?

[c]The preceding last context perhaps contained some statement like: "[*The army departed for*] *the height of Hua*," etc. It cannot be the arrival, for that does not occur until 1. 12. The unknown land of Khesekhet ($H^{\flat} sh^{\cdot} t$) occurs in the southern lists of Thutmose III (Mariette, *Karnak*, Pl. 22, No. 95, and Pl. 25, No. 95), and is usually rendered simply *"barbarians."* It is however a proper name, having nothing to do with $h^{\flat} s^{\cdot} ty$, *"barbarian."*

[d]Lit., *"a command of making them."* Such a use of the genitive is common, especially in Papyrus Ebers receipts.

gave pra[ise ⌜to his majesty⌝] ———— 8 ———— infantry of the army which was of old, ⌜when⌝ they were brought up from the court. His majesty took counsel, ———— 9 ———— [the place] in which they were, doing everything.

850. His majesty commanded, that 124[a] men of the army be dispatched, going forth to the well which is in[b] ———— 10 ———— [c] southward to see the height of Hua, to make known the ways of sailing ———— 11 ———— living captives which they found among them: negroes, 113[d] cattle, male and female; 11 asses, male and female. Third month of the first season ———— 12 ———— the north wind, was very high for the coming forth of the height of Hua; the coming forth of this height was in safety, sailing ———— 13 ———— Uneshek (⌜Wnšk⌝)[e] was its name, south of the height of Hua, resting in the camp made there ————.

IV. SEMNEH INSCRIPTION[f]

851. The date of this inscription is lost, but it doubtless refers to the campaign in Nubia. A revolt having occurred in Ibhet, the viceroy, Mermose, levies an army in lower Nubia, marches into Ibhet, and quells the rebellion. The beginning of the inscription is lacking, but it apparently contained the announcement of the revolt.

---

[a]The rendering (*Bubastis*, 10) "123" is incorrect.

[b]The name of some land followed. See § 847.

[c]This lacuna probably contained some further remark that the expedition advanced "*southward*," etc. Evidently "*the height of Hua*" is the point by which the course of the ship was governed! The "*coming forth*" of the height indicates its rise into view on the horizon. The whole description sounds so much like a sea-voyage that, were it not for the mention of "*western Khesekhet*" (l. 6), one might see in it a voyage along the Red Sea coast to Punt.

[d]Naville's "203" (*ibid.*) is incorrect.

[e]Has the determinative of a foreign country, and of course indicates some region visited.

[f]Stela in British Museum, published by Birch, *Archæologia*, XXXIV, facing p. 388; see also *Archæological Journal*, VIII, 399. I collated Birch's text with the Berlin squeeze (No. 1097), and afterward with the original in the British Museum, and found a number of important corrections were necessary.

Muster of the Army

852. ¹————ᵃ ²———— occurred the reaping of the harvests of the ⌜foe⌝ of Ibhet (*Ybh·t*). Every man ⌜reported⌝ᵇ and one mustered ³[⌜an army of⌝] Pharaoh, L. P. H., which was under command of this king's-son. He made troops, commanded by commanders, each man withᶜ his village; ⁴from the fortress of Beki (*Bky*)ᵈ to the fortress of Taroy (*T ꜣ -r ꜣ -y*), making 52 iters (*ytr·w*) of sailing.

Defeat of Ibhet

853. ⁵The might of Nibmare took them in one day, in one hour, making a great slaughter ———— ⁶their cattle; not one of them escaped; each one of them was brought ———— fear. The might of Amenhotep took them; ⁷the barbarians among them, male as well as female, were not separated; by the plan of Horus, Lord of the Two Lands, King Nibmare, mighty bull, strong in might. Ibhet had been haughty,ᵉ ⁸great things were in their hearts, (⌜but⌝) the fierce-eyed lion, this ruler,ᶠ he slew them by command of Amon-Atum, his august father; it was he who led him ⁹in might and victory.

List of Prisoners and Killed

854. List of the captivity which his majesty took in the land of Ibbet, the wretched:

Living negroes	150 heads
Archers (*mygy*)	110 heads
Negresses	250 heads
¹⁰Servants (*sḏm- ꜥ š*) of the negroes	55 heads
Their children	175 heads
Total	740 living heads
Hands thereof	312
United ¹¹with the living heads	1,052

ᵃA few fragmentary words and signs can be discerned. Several lines before this have probably been lost.

ᵇLit., "*went down to his opposite, or opposite him*," which, in view of the connection, is perhaps a technical term for "*report for duty.*"

ᶜLit., "*opposite his village*," as above in preceding note.

ᵈNear Kubbân; Taroy is uncertain. See Griffith, *Proceedings of the Society of Biblical Archæology*, XIV, 408 f.; but accepting an iter as about 1.4 miles, the distance, some 75 miles, would put Taroy in the vicinity of Ibrim.

ᵉLit., "*was high-voiced.*"   ᶠIn a cartouche.

Words of the Viceroy

855. The king's-son, vigilant for his lord, favorite of the Good God, governor of the entire land of Kush, king's-scribe, Mermose. He saith: "Praise to thee! ¹²O Good God! Great is thy might against him that fronts[a] thee; thou causest them that are rebellious against thee to say: 'The fire that we have made rages against us.' Thou hast slain all thy enemies, overthrown beneath thy feet."

TABLET OF VICTORY[b]

856. This tablet was set up by Amenhotep III in his mortuary temple at Thebes, to commemorate his victories in the north and south. Above is a relief twice showing Amenhotep III before Amon. Both figures of Amon were cut out by Ikhnaton and restored by Seti I, with the usual legend:

Restoration of the monument, which the Son of Re, Seti-Merneptah, made for his father, Amon.

857. Below is a second relief, in which Amenhotep III appears twice in his chariot. On the right he drives over the fallen of Kush, with the chiefs bound upon his horses, over which is the legend:

The Good God ———[c] lord of the sword, mighty in dragging them (at his chariot), annihilating the heir of the wretched Kush, bringing their princes as living prisoners.

858. In the same way he drives over the Syrians on the left; above the princes bound on the horses, are the words:

The Good God, Golden [Horus], Shining in the chariot,[d] like the

---

[a]Lit., "*reaches thee*," meaning in battle.

[b]Limestone stela discovered by Petrie in the mortuary temple of Merneptah at Thebes, whither it had been carried by this king from the mortuary temple of Amenhotep III; text: Petrie, *Six Temples*, X.

[c]Traces of the cartouche.

[d]Text seems to show chariot and horses; possibly only horses!

rising of the sun; great in strength, strong in might, mighty-hearted like him who dwells in Thebes (Montu); smiting Naharin (N-h-r-ny, sic!) with his mighty sword.

A line of inscription runs across the bottom, as follows:

———— [every] country, all people ($rhyt$·), all populations ($hnmm$·t), Naharin (N-h-r-ny, sic!), the wretched Kush, Retenu the Upper and Retenu the Lower are at the feet of this Good God, like Re, forever.

859. A scarab published by Frazer (*Proceedings of the Society of Biblical Archæology*, XXI, Pl. III, facing p. 155), gives to Amenhotep III the epithet: "*Captor of Shinar*" (S ʾ-n-g-r). The Amarna Letters show that no significance is to be attached to this epithet. The decorations on the columns at Soleb show captive figures representing Shinar, Naharin, Hittites, Kadesh, Tunip, Ugarit, Keftyew, Carchemish, Asur, and Arrapachitis.[a] But such decorations are far from showing that Amenhotep III had conquered or maintained his conquest in these far-off regions.

THE COMMEMORATIVE SCARABS

860. On five different occasions, in commemoration of events in his personal history, Amenhotep IV issued a series of scarabs inscribed on the under side, recording the following matters:

I. Marriage with Tiy;
II. Wild Cattle Hunt;
III. Ten Years' Lion-Hunting;
IV. Marriage with Kirgipa;
V. Construction of Pleasure Lake.

---

[a]Lepsius, *Denkmäler*, III, 88. The above are all that can safely be identified. See also fragment of a list at Karnak (Lepsius, *Denkmäler*, Text, III, 9), containing also Naharin (?) and Shinar.

As far as we know, he was the only king who did this, although small scarabs referring in two or three words to great events were issued by other kings; e. g., Thutmose III thus refers to the erection of obelisks (§ 625) and the capture of Kadesh.

I. MARRIAGE WITH TIY[a]

861. This marriage took place before the year 2 when Tiy is already queen (see next scarab). The origin of the powerful Tiy is obscure; Maspero thinks her a native Egyptian,[b] and this is the most probable conclusion, but the persistent publication of the names of her untitled parents[c] on these and other scarabs is in that case remarkable, although paralleled by scarabs of the Thirteenth Dynasty. This difficulty is, however, not relieved by supposing her of foreign birth. It is incredible that anyone could identify her with Kirgipa,[d] on whose marriage scarab she already appears in the titulary as queen. She is the first queen who is thus recognized by the regular insertion of her name in the titulary. The innovation was continued by Amenhotep IV, who inserted his queen's name in the same way. His ephemeral successors show the same inclination, and the whole period from the time of Amenhotep III to the close of the Eighteenth Dynasty is characterized by the

---

[a]At least twelve of these scarabs are in the different collections of Europe; see list, Wiedemann, *Aegyptische Geschichte*, 393, n. 6; text: Mariette, *Album de Boulaq*, Pl. 36; Rosellini, *Monumenti Storici*, 44; Budge, *The Mummy*, 242, 234; Maspero, *Struggle of the Nations*, 315; translated from the last three.

[b]Maspero, *Struggle of the Nations*, 315, n. 1, where full bibliography is given.

[c]The tomb of these two people, Yuya and Thuya, was discovered this year (1905) in the Valley of the Kings' Tombs at Thebes by Mr. Theodore M. Davis of Newport. It was filled with the most magnificent mortuary furniture, and still contained the bodies of Yuya and Thuya.

[d]The absurd story of the king's meeting and falling in love with Tiy on a hunting expedition in Mesopotamia, which has been added to the English edition of Brugsch's *Egypt under the Pharaohs* (214), it is hardly necessary to say is totally without documentary foundation.

mention and prominent representation of the queens on all state occasions, in such a manner as is never found later.

862. Live . . . . .[a] King Amenhotep (III), who is given life, (and) the Great King's-Wife Tiy (Tyy), who liveth. The name of her father is Yuya (Ywy ⸱), the name of her mother is Thuya (Twy ⸱). She is the wife of a mighty king whose southern boundary is as far as Karoy (K ⸱ -r ⸱ -y) (and) northern as far as Naharin (N-h-ry-n ⸱).

II. WILD CATTLE HUNT[b]

863. This scarab records the first hunting achievements of the chase-loving Amenhotep III. Unfortunately, the region[c] where the hunt took place cannot be identified with certainty, but as it was reached in a night's voyage on the king's Nile barge, it was not some remote district like the scene of Thutmose III's elephant hunt in Naharin. As the voyage was northward, it is likely to have been some district in the Delta which could be reached in a night from Memphis. The method of hunting consisted in surrounding and driving the wild cattle into a huge encircling inclosure.[d] They thus inclosed 170 animals, of which the king killed not less than 75 on two different days.

864. Year 2 under the majesty of King Amenhotep (III)[e] given life, and the great king's-wife Tiy, living like Re.

---

[a]Full titulary.

[b]Only one specimen of this scarab is published; it is in the collection of Mr. G. W. Frazer, and was published by him (*Proceedings of the Society of Biblical Archæology*, XXI, Pl. III, opp. p. 155), with a good translation by Mr. Griffith (*ibid.*, 156); and again, *A Catalogue of the Scarabs Belonging to George Frazer* (London, 1900), frontispiece, Pl. XVI, and p. 56. Another specimen is said to be in the collection of Rev. W. MacGregor of Tamworth.

[c]It may be read either $\check{S}tp$ or $\check{S}t$ ⸱. The first determinative indicates a body of water, and the second the desert highlands. This would suit some spot in the Delta with its network of canals, near the margin of the desert.

[d]Such an inclosure, made with a net, may be seen at Benihasan (Newberry, *Beni Hasan*).

[e]Full titulary.

Marvel which happened to his majesty. One came to say to his majesty: "There are wild cattle upon the highlands, as far as the region[a] of ⌜Sheta⌝ (⌜Št⌝)." His majesty sailed down-stream in the royal barge, Khammat ($Ḥ ͨ-m-m ͻ ͨ ·t$) at the time of evening, beginning the goodly way, and arriving in safety at the region of ⌜Sheta⌝ (⌜Št⌝) at the time of morning.

His majesty appeared upon[b] a horse, his whole army being behind him. The commanders and the citizens[c] of all the army in its entirety and the children wit[h ⌜them were commanded⌝] to keep watch over the wild cattle. Behold, his majesty commanded to cause that these wild cattle be surrounded[d] by a wall with an inclosure.[d] His majesty commanded to count[e] all these wild cattle. Statement thereof: 170 wild cattle. Statement of [that which] his majesty [captured][f] in the hunt on this day: 56 wild cattle.

His majesty tarried 4 days —— to give fire[g] to his horses. His majesty appeared upon a horse [⌜a second time⌝. Statement] of these wild cattle, which he captured in the hunt: 20 (+x) wild cattle. [Total][h] 75 (+x) wild cattle.

III. TEN YEARS' LION-HUNTING[i]

865. In his tenth year, the king issued a large number of these scarabs, to commemorate his success in lion-hunting.

---

[a]Read $r w n$, as in l. 7; the t probably belongs to the $sm ·t$ in the preceding line.

[b]This is the strange preposition used when the king is in his chariot, for he did not ride horseback. See the Amarna Landmark Stelæ (§ 960, ll. 5–6). The hunting reliefs at Medinet Habu show that wild cattle were hunted from the chariot.

[c]See I, 681, ll. 3, 4, and note.

[d]The same words for "*surround*" (*yn*ḫ), "*wall*" (*sbty*), and "*inclosure*" (*šdy*) are used together in the same way in Thutmose III's description of the investiture of Megiddo (§ 433).

[e]Read ḥsb instead of r, which has customarily been read heretofore.

[f]Restored from lion-hunt scarab.

[g]This is literal; it perhaps means "*spirit*," as Griffith has rendered.

[h]This is the total from the two hunts; the sum of the two days is not less than 75, nor more than 85.

[i]At least thirty of these scarabs are in European museums, and three in the Art Institute of Chicago; they have been often published; e. g., Maspero, *Struggle of the Nations*, 298; *Biblical World*, June, 1896, 449 (with translation), Pierret, *Recueil d'Inscriptions*, I, 88; a list of them is in Wiedemann, *Aegyptische Geschichte*, 381, n. 6. The above translation is based on a comparison of several originals.

Live ....[a] Amenhotep (III), Ruler of Thebes, Given life, (and) the Great King's-Wife: Tiy, who liveth.

Statement of lions which his majesty brought down with his own arrows from year 1 to year 10: fierce lions, 102.[b]

IV. MARRIAGE WITH KIRGIPA[c]

866. This scarab records the marriage of the princess Kirgipa, daughter of Satirna, a king of Naharin, to Amenhotep III. When Brugsch published this scarab for the first time, in 1880, he expressed the hope[d] that the cuneiform literature might some time be able to throw some light on the origin of this princess. Curiously enough, the discovery of the Amarna correspondence in 1887 has done so.[e] In a letter[f] from Dushratta, king of Mitanni, she appears as his sister Gilukhipa; their father[g] was Shuttarna, king of Mitanni.[h] A mistranslation of Birch (*Records of the Past*,

---

[a]Full titulary.

[b]Some have 110 (e. g., Louvre, No. 580), an easy error for 102; Maspero's 112 (Maspero, *Struggle of the Nations*, 298) is not corroborated by his accompanying text.

[c]The specimens are in private hands. Mr. Frazer (*Proceedings of the Society of Biblical Archæology*, XXI, 155) speaks of "two or three;" first published by Brugsch, *Zeitschrift für ägyptische Sprache*, 1880, 81–87; then by Maspero, *Recueil*, XV, 200; finally Brugsch, *Thesaurus*, VI, 1413; another specimen, *Recueil*, XVI, 62.

[d]*Zeitschrift für ägyptische Sprache*, 1880, 86.

[e]Erman, *Zeitschrift für ägyptische Sprache*, 1890, 112; Evetts, *ibid.*, 113; Jensen and Winckler, *ibid.*, 114.

[f]Winckler, *Amarna Letters*, 16, 5, and 41, 42.   [g]*Ibid.*, 21, 18, 19.

[h]The marriages between this Asiatic family and the Pharaohs, as shown in the Amarna letters, are as follows:

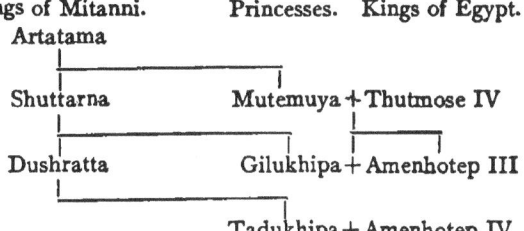

See Maspero, *Struggle of the Nations*, 281.

1st Series, XII, 39) has resulted in confusing Kirgipa with Tiy, who is quite another person (see § 861).

867. ¹Year 10 under the majesty of ²....⁵.....ᵃthe Son of Re, Amenhotep (III), Ruler of Thebes, who is granted life; (and) the Great King's-Wife, Tiy, who liveth; the name of whose father was Yuya (*Ywy*ᵃ), the name of whose mother was Thuya (*Twy*ᵃ).

Marvels brought to his majesty, L. P. H.:ᵇ Kirgipa (*Ky-r-gy-p*ᵃ), the daughter of the chief of Naharin (*N-h-r-n*ᵃ), Satirna (*S*ᵃ-*ty-r-n*ᵃ); (and) the chief of her harem-ladies, (viz.,) 317 persons.

V. CONSTRUCTION OF A PLEASURE LAKE ᶜ

868. This scarab records the construction of a pleasure lake by Amenhotep III, for his queen Tiy, in a town or a city quarter (*dmy*), called Zerukha (*ḏ ᶜr-wḫ* ᵃ), otherwise unknown. It is not unlikely that this is the lake of which the remains, called Birket Habu, are clearly visible south of Medinet Habu, beside the palace of Amenhotep III,ᵈ an exceedingly probable situation. But this lake varies considerably in dimensions from those given on the scarab.

The opening of the lake was doubtless in connection with the coronation anniversary, which fell on the next dayᵉ after orders for constructing the lake were given.

ᵃThe usual full titulary.

ᵇThis heads the list; we should expect the usual word "*statement*," as, e. g., in the lion-hunt scarabs.

ᶜFour copies of this scarab are known: (1) in the Vatican (Rosellini, *Monumenti Storici*, 44, No. 2 = Stern, *Zeitschrift für ägyptische Sprache*, 1877, 87, n. 2 = Marucchi, *Bessarione*, 1899, 122); (2) private collection of W. Golénischeff (privately distributed photographs); (3) collection in Alnwick Castle (Birch, *Catalogue*, No. 1030, 137); (4) fragment in University College, London (not published). The first three of the above were collated and published by Steindorff (*Zeitschrift für ägyptische Sprache*, 1901, 63).

ᵈCf. Steindorff, *Zeitschrift für ägyptische Sprache*, 1901, 64.

ᵉ§ 844, l. 1; Lieblein (*Sphinx*, VI, 113 ff.) has calculated the date of this opening in terms of our calendar as September 26, Julian, or November 5, Gregorian.

869. Year 11, third month of the first season, day 1, under the majesty of ....[a] Amenhotep III, given life; and the Great King's-Wife, Tiy, who liveth.

His majesty commanded to make a lake for the Great King's-Wife, Tiy, in her city of Zerukha ($D^c r\text{-}wḫ^{\,?}$).[b] Its length is 3,700 cubits; its width, 700[c] cubits. His majesty celebrated the feast of the opening of the ⌈lake⌉, in the third month of the first season, day 16,[d] when his majesty sailed thereon in the royal barge: "Aton-Gleams."[e]

JUBILEE CELEBRATIONS

870. Amenhotep III celebrated at least three royal jubilees: the first in the year 30; the second, although not recorded, probably like that of Ramses II, in the year 34; and the third in the year 36. The celebration of the first jubilee is recorded in the tomb of Khamhet,[f] in two remarkable reliefs.

871. The first shows the king enthroned in state at the right; before him is the inscription:[g]

---

[a]Full fivefold titulary.

[b]This name was long misread "Zaru," with which it has nothing to do (cf. Steindorff, *Zeitschrift für ägyptische Sprache*, 1901, 64; and Breasted, *ibid.*, 65, 66). The statements regarding the presentation of "Zaru" to Tiy, current in the histories, are all to be rejected.

[c]Vatican copy has 600, the others 700. Steindorff reads here "*upper arms*" (*rmn*) instead of "*cubits*" (*mḥy*). This distinction, although evident on the surviving cubit rods, is not carried through on the monuments. At Benihasan, the *rmn*-sign occurs in door dimensions, where it is clear that the cubit is meant; see my remarks (*Proceedings of the Society of Biblical Archæology*, March, 1900, 88–90).

[d]Thus the lake must have been completed in fifteen days!

[e]Cf. further examples by Spiegelberg (*Rechnungen*, Text, 81–86), who has compiled a very useful list of these barges, also Breasted, *Zeitschrift für ägyptische Sprache*, 1901, 66.

[f]Lepsius, *Denkmäler*, III, 76, 77, and Brugsch, *Thesaurus*, 1121–23; for full bibliography, see § 819, where also the inscriptions under the reign of Thutmose IV are given. For a scarab referring to the jubilees, see Brugsch (*Thesaurus*, VI, 1456).

[g]Among his titles both inscriptions add that of: "*Lord of the Jubilee.*"

Appearance of the king upon the great throne, to receive the report of the harvest of the South and North.

Before the king stands Khamhet reading to him a document; over Khamhet's head the following inscription in five vertical lines:

Communication of the report of the harvest of the year 30[a] in the presence of the king, consisting of the harvest of the great inundation of the jubilee [⌜which⌝] his majesty [⌜celebrated⌝]; by[b] the stewards of the ⌜estates⌝[c] of Pharaoh, L. P. H., together with the chiefs of the South and North, from this land of Kush the wretched, as far as the boundary of Naharin (N-h-ry-n).

Under the document are the words: *"Total: 33,333,300."*[d]

872. As a consequence of this favorable report, the treasury officials are now rewarded, as shown in the following scene.[e]

The king is seated in state in a splendid pavilion at the left; before him, the inscription:

Appearance of the king upon the great throne, to reward the chiefs of the South and North.

Before the king stands Khamhet with the inscription:

Hereditary prince, count, who satisfies the heart of the king in the whole land, the two eyes of the king in the cities of the South, his two ears in the nomes of the Northland, king's-scribe ——— (named), Khamhet.[f]

---

[a]So Brugsch, but Lepsius has a lacuna.

[b]To be connected with *"communication."*

[c]Or possibly better *"income;"* see Spiegelberg, *Studien*, 55 and note 227, who, however, does not refer to our passage.

[d]These are probably only plurals of the numeral signs.

[e]Lepsius, *Denkmäler*, III, 76.

[f]His titles are written more fully in Champollion, *Notices descriptives*, I, 840; "*Hereditary prince, count, who fills the heart of his lord, favorite of the Good God, to whom are told all the affairs of the* ⌜*palace* — —⌝ *companion of the feet of the Lord of the Two Lands in every place which he treads, chief of the archers of the Good God* ———"

Behind Khamhet are three lines of officials praising the king; the upper line is receiving rich gifts; inscription:

Reward of the stewards of the ⌜estates⌝ of Pharaoh, L. P. H., together with the chiefs of the South and the North after the statement[a] of the overseer of the granary concerning them: "They have increased the harvest of year 30."

873. The records of the second Jubilee have perished, but the third is mentioned in the tomb of Kheruf,[b] in the following heading:

"Year 36. Conducting the companions for presentation in the (royal) presence at the third ($ḥb$-sd) jubilee of his majesty.[c]

874. The ceremony of erecting the symbol of Osiris, the curious column, which is also the symbol of stability, was performed on the morning of the traditional royal jubilee feast day (first of Tybi). Amenhotep III is shown personally erecting this column on the morning of one of his jubilee days, in the reliefs in a Theban tomb.[d]

QUARRY AND MINE INSCRIPTIONS

875. New chambers in the Turra quarry were opened by the king in his first year,[e] and recorded in an inscription[f] identical in content with another[g] recording similar work

---

[a]Read $ḏd$ with Brugsch; not $ỉd$ as in Lepsius, *Denkmäler*.

[b]Brugsch, *Thesaurus*, 1120.

[c]That this is Amenhotep III is shown by the mention of Queen Tiy in the titulary.

[d]Brugsch, *Thesaurus*, V, 1190–96.

[e]The quarries at el-Bersheh were also opened in the "*year 1*," as recorded there in a mutilated inscription (*Proceedings of the Society of Biblical Archæology*, IX, 195); much better, Spiegelberg, *Recueil*, 26, 151, 152). It records the erection of a monument of uncertain character in the Thoth temple at Hermopolis.

[f]Cut on the walls of the limestone quarry at Turra; published Lepsius, *Denkmäler*, III, 71, *a–d*, and Vyse, *Pyramids*, III, 96, Nos. 3 and 4.

[g]This second inscription of the same content, Lepsius, *Denkmäler*, 71, *b*. Compare the similar inscription of Ahmose in the same quarry (§§ 26–28).

in the second year. The latter is surmounted by an offering scene, and is as follows:

¹Year 2, under the majesty of .... ².... ᵃ Amenhotep (III) ......; his majesty commanded to open the quarry-chambers anew, in order to quarry fine limestone of Ayan (ᶜn), in order to build his temples ³of a million of years, after his majesty found the quarry-chambers which are in Troja (R ᵓ - ᵓ wy), beginning to be very ruinous since the ⁴times which were before. It was my majesty who made (them) anew, in order that he might be given life, stability, satisfaction, health, like Re, forever.

876. The granite quarry at Assuan was visited by an official of this king, for the purpose of cutting out a colossal statue of his lord. This officer has had carved in relief[b] on the rock his own figure standing in homage before the names of Amenhotep III. Below are the words:

[Homage] to the Good God, when was made the great statue of his majesty (called): "Sun-of-Rulers."

Near by is an overturned, unfinished, colossal statue, to which the inscription doubtless refers.

877. A stela[c] of the year 36 in Sarbût-el-Khadem in Sinai, records an expedition thither in that year, in which the commanding official refers to the "*sea (the Great Green)*" in a connection[d] which would indicate that he crossed to Sinai by the sea route, but the inscription is too fragmentary for translation.

ᵃThe full titulary, but omitting the Golden Horus-name.

ᵇSharpe, *Egyptian Inscriptions*, II, 39; de Morgan, *Catalogue des monuments*, I, 63.

ᶜLepsius, *Denkmäler*, III, 71, c = *Ordnance Survey*, III, Pl. 14.

ᵈThe connection is broken by an interfering fragment of rock which the photographer of the *Ordnance Survey* failed to remove. Another stela of the year 36 shows Amenhotep III offering to Amon and Hathor (Lepsius, *Denkmäler*, III, 71, d; not in *Ordnance Survey*).

BUILDING INSCRIPTION[a]

878. This monument has had an interesting career. Erected by Amenhotep III in his temple behind the Memnon colossi, to record his buildings in honor of Amon, its inscription was almost totally obliterated by the reforming zeal of his son, Amenhotep IV.[b] It was restored by Seti I, who recorded his restoration thus: *"Restoration of the monument which the King of Upper and Lower Egypt, Menmare (Seti I), made for his father Amon-Re, King of all Gods."*[c] In restoring the monument, the sculptor of Seti found the old lines sufficiently traceable to be recut with tolerable certainty, not without some glaring errors, which cannot always be corrected. Four or five generations later, Merneptah demolished the splendid temple of Amenhotep III, containing this stela, and used the material, including the stela[d] in a building of his own, where it fell down and remained until taken out by Petrie in February, 1896.

879. The upper third is occupied by a scene twice showing Amenhotep III with the usual legends, offering a libation to Amon. The inscription of thirty-one lines records Amen-

---

[a]Discovered by Petrie in February, 1896, on a black granite stela lying in the ruins of the Theban mortuary temple of Merneptah; this stela is 10 feet 3 inches by 5 feet 4 inches, and 13 inches thick. See *Contemporary Review*, May, 1896, 619; *Century Magazine*, August, 1896, 501 (view of stela in situ). Text: Photographic reproduction and transcription with translation and excellent commentary by Spiegelberg, *Recueil*, XX, 37–54; finally in Petrie, *Six Temples*, Pl. XI, XII. I have used a photograph, kindly sent me by E. Brugsch-Bey shortly after the discovery of the monument, at which time I made the translation; later notes drawn from Spiegelberg I have carefully credited to him. Important suggestions in *Orientalistische Litteraturzeitung*, 1898, No. 5, 156, 157.

[b]One can clearly see in the photograph that the inscription has been hammered out, as far as the end of l. 22, including also parts of lines 23–28, leaving the last three lines untouched (see, e. g., photographs in *Recueil*, XX, and *Century Magazine*, August, 1896, 501). Excepting the two figures of the king, the scene at the top was also erased.

[c]Cut between the two figures of Amon at the top of the monument; similar restorations by Seti often, e. g., on the obelisk of Hatshepsut.

[d]He cut on the back of it the hymn of victory, mentioning Israel: see III, 602 ff.

hotep III's chief buildings and other pious works in honor of Amon:

1. Introduction, ll. 1–2 (§ 882).
2. Temple of the (Memnon) Colossi, ll. 2–10 (§§ 883–85).
3. Luxor Temple and Connected Buildings (§§ 886, 887).
4. Sacred Barge of Amon, ll. 16–20 (§ 888).
5. Third Pylon of Karnak, ll. 20–23 (§ 889).
6. Temple of Soleb, ll. 23–26 (§ 890).
7. Hymn of Amon to the King, ll. 26–31 (§§ 891, 892).

880. The architectural data given by the scribe are very important, but are as usual, very general and vague, showing great, if not total, lack of technical knowledge of the subject. The treatment of temple floors with silver (ll. 3, 11, and 22) and the walls with gold or electrum (ll. 3, 11), although very vaguely described, is important. The settlement of Syrians around the temple of the (Memnon) Colossi is historically of importance also. The king's selection of his Soleb temple in Nubia, to be mentioned in preference to his Egyptian temples outside of Thebes,[a] shows his strong interest in the region above the second cataract, where he was so active, and where he caused himself to be worshiped. It is furthermore noticeable that the king makes no reference to his other Theban buildings, the temple of Mut and the temple at the northern gate of the Karnak inclosure, of either of which very little now remains.[b]

---

[a]Thus he omits all reference to his Memphis temple, where he was evidently worshiped, for he appears with Ptah as one of the gods of Memphis (Papyrus Sallier, IV; Brugsch, *Thesaurus*, V, 961, No. 23); and his temple there was called "*House of Nibmare*" (Brugsch, *Thesaurus*, V, 963). A cultus statuette which he dedicated to himself as a god in this Memphis temple is in Alnwick collection; it bears the dedication: "*Nibmare (Amenhotep III); he made it as his monument for his living image in 'The House of Nibmare'*" (Birch, *Catalogue Alnwick Castle*, 56–58). The El Kab temple, which he is often stated to have built, was erected by Thutmose IV, his father, for whom he only decorated it, as the inscription states: "*Lo, the majesty of King Nibmare decorated this monument of his father, Thutmose IV, forever and ever*" (Lepsius, *Denkmäler*, III, 80, b = J. J. Tylor, *The Temple of Amenhotep III*, Pl. 10; again Pl, 8 = Lepsius, *Denkmäler*, Text, IV, 43).

[b]This is to be explained by the fact that the stela records only buildings of Amon.

Part of the dedicatory inscription of the latter is still preserved,[a] and contains data of importance. It is introduced by the king's titulary, to which is appended:

881. Who raises a monument in Karnak, a marvelous thing, unlimited in — of gold, plentiful in gold, unlimited in malachite and lazuli; a place of rest for the lord of gods, made like his throne that is in heaven, that he (the king) might be thereby given satisfying life like Re forever. ———[b] an inclosure made to flourish with monuments, made to shine with all flowers, filled with slaves ($mr\cdot t$) due from the ($ḥsb$-) officials, being children of the chiefs of all countries, coming in obeisance to his fame. The Son of Re, Amenhotep, ruler of Thebes, made it for the chosen of Re, because he loved his father, Amon, lord of Thebes, so much more than all the gods. He has been given life, stability, satisfaction, like Re, forever.

Of all this the great building stela makes no mention. It is as follows:

Introduction

882. ¹Live ....[c] Amenhotep (III), Ruler of Thebes; beloved of Amon, lord of Thebes, presider over Karnak; given life, joy of his heart, that he may rule the Two Lands like Re, forever; ²the Good God, possessor of joy, who is very vigilant for him that begat him, Amon, king of gods; who hath made great his (Amon's) house,[d] who hath satisfied his beauty[d] by doing that which his ka desires.

Temple of the Memnon Colossi[e]

883. Behold, the heart of his majesty was satisfied with making a very great[f] monument; never has happened the like since the beginning.

---

[a] Published by Bouriant, *Recueil*, XIII, 171–73.
[b] This section is covered by a Roman wall.
[c] Full five-name titulary.
[d] Not in Spiegelberg's transcription, *Recueil*, XX, 40.
[e] The colossi known as the Memnon colossi (cf. ll. 4, 5) still stand, but the temple, the entrance of which they flanked, has disappeared; see above, § 878. It was the mortuary temple of Amenhotep III, of which there is a further account inscribed on a huge stela now lying in the scanty ruins behind the colossi (§§ 904 ff.). For an account of the excavation around this temple, see Petrie, *Six Temples in Thebes;* the temple itself has never been excavated. View of the colossi, Mariette, *Voyage dans la haute Egypte*, II, 57, or my *Egypt through the Stereoscope*, No. 64.
[f] Although the adjective is plural, I translate singular, for in l. 4 it is also plural where it clearly should be singular.

He made (it) as ³his monument for his father, Amon, lord of Thebes, making for him an august temple[a] on the west of Thebes, an eternal, everlasting fortress[b] of fine white sandstone, wrought with gold throughout; its floor is adorned with silver, ⁴all its portals with electrum;[c] it is made very wide and large, and established forever; and adorned with this very great monument.[d] It is numerous in royal statues, of Elephantine granite, of costly gritstone, of every splendid costly stone, ⁵established as everlasting works.[e] Their stature shines more than the heavens, their rays are in the faces (of men) like the sun, when he shines early in the morning. It is supplied with a "Station of the King,"[f] wrought with gold and many costly stones. ⁶Flagstaves[g] are set up before it, wrought with electrum; it resembles the horizon in heaven when Re rises therein. Its lake is filled with the great Nile, lord of fish and fowl, pure in ⌜—⌝

Its Wealth

884. Its storehouse is filled with male and female slaves, ⁷with children of the princes of all the countries of the captivity of his majesty.

---

[a]Called "*House-of-Amon-on-the-West-of-Thebes*" in the inscription on a black granite statue of Amenhotep III at Erment, published by Daressy, *Recueil*, XIX, 14, and Spiegelberg, *Recueil*, XX, 49.

[b]The temple regarded as a stronghold; cf. remarks of Spiegelberg, *Recueil*, XX, 48.

[c]Just how the metals were used on floor, walls, and doorways is not clear from these vague data, but they materially augment our ideas of the splendor of the Egyptian temple.

[d]Probably the stela on which this text is cut.

[e]Spiegelberg (*Recueil*, XX, 49) calls attention to the fact that the French expedition found eighteen of these statues on the west shore still in situ, some of which are now in the museums: in the British Museum one of black granite (Arundale and Bonomi, *Gallery*, Pl. 35); two heads (*ibid.*, 107); also a black granite statue at Erment, first published by Daressy (*Recueil*, XIX, 14). Spiegelberg thinks it strange that the two Memnon colossi are not given separate mention, but they are clearly mentioned in the reference to "*costly gritstone*," which is the material of the colossi. Moreover, they are distinctly mentioned in the Dedication Inscription (l. 4, § 906). In further corroboration of the inscription, note the statement: "there were many of these statues which stood fronting the great colossi in the intervals of the front columns of the propylon" (Arundale and Bonomi, *Gallery*, 107), noted by Spiegelberg.

[f]The enormous stela lying overthrown behind the Memnon colossi (§ 904 ff.). The word "*station*" is here determined with a stela, showing that, as at Amâda (§ 796, l. 15), the "*station of the king*" was marked by the stela against the back wall of the holy of holies.

[g]Cf. similar staves in the inscription of Ineni, § 103.

Its storehouses contain all good things, whose number is not known. It is surrounded with settlements of Syrians ($Ḫ^ɔ$-rw), colonized with children of princes, its cattle ⁸are like the sand of the shore, they make up millions.

Western Pylon

885. The bow-rope of the Southland ⌈in it⌉ and the stern-rope of the Northland,[a] even his majesty revealed[b] himself like Ptah, was skilful-minded like Him-South-of-His-Wall (Ptah), searching out excellent things for his father, Amon-Re, King of Gods, making for him ⁹a very great pylon[c] over against Amon. Its beautiful name which his majesty made was: "Amon-Has-Received-His-Divine-Barque,"[d] a place of rest for the lord of the gods at his "Feast of the Valley" on the western voyage of Amon to behold the western gods, in order that he may endow ¹⁰his majesty with satisfying life.

Luxor Temple[e]

886. King of Upper and Lower Egypt, Lord of the Two Lands: Nibmare, Heir of Re; Son of Re, Lord of Diadems: Amenhotep (III), Ruler of Thebes, is satisfied with a building for his father Amon-Re,

---

[a]Inscription of Ineni (l. 17, § 341) has: "*the bow-rope of the South . . . . . . the stern-rope of the North is she*," as epithets of Hatshepsut. It seems to me that Spiegelberg (*Recueil*, XX, 50) has overlooked the determinative (a rope) in his rendering "Bug" and "Spiegel," "bow" and "stern." (Cf. Sethe, *Untersuchungen*, I, 52). In view of the Ineni passage, his rejection of the genitive signs seems to me impossible.

[b]Lit., "*opened himself;*" cf. *wb ᴅ sw*, a synonymous phrase (Lepsius, *Denkmäler*, III, 18, l. 3), which Müller renders "*sich zeigen*" (*Recueil*, IX, 162).

[c]This is probably the pylon which flanked the Memnon Colossi, but is now entirely gone.

[d]The literal meaning of the phrase used for the barque is: "*Bearer of his beauty;*" it was a portable shrine.

[e]The well-known temple at modern Luxor, of which the southern portion is due to Amenhotep III. The architrave inscriptions (Lepsius, *Denkmäler*, III, 73, and Text, III, 80, 81) offer a short account of the building: "*He made (it) as his monument for his father, Amon-Re, king of gods, again erecting for him Luxor anew, of fine white sandstone, made very, very high and wide, adorned with electrum throughout, and all splendid, costly stones; a rest for Amon, a place of rest for the lord of gods, made like unto his horizon in heaven. That he might be given life.*" Statements like: "*who built temples — — sculptured their statues; that which was of brick was (re)built of stone;*" or: "*who again erected Luxor anew,*" of course refer to the older Middle Empire temple which Amenhotep III enlarged or rebuilt. On the entire history of the Luxor temple, see Borchardt, *Zeitschrift für ägyptische Sprache*, 1896, 122–38.

lord of Thebes, in Southern Opet (Luxor), of fine white sandstone, made very wide and large ⁱⁱand its beauty increased. Its walls are of electrum, its floor[a] is of silver, all the portals are wrought with ⌜—⌝, its towers reach[b] heaven, and mingle with the stars. When the people see it, ¹²they give praise to his majesty.

It is the king Nibmare who hath satisfied[c] the heart of his father, Amon, lord of Thebes, who hath assigned to him every country, the Son of Re, Amenhotep (III), Ruler of Thebes, Brilliance of Re ⌜—⌝

Buildings Near Luxor

887. His majesty made another monument, for his father, Amon; making for him an ⌜inclosure⌝ as a divine offering over against Southern Opet; ¹³a salubrious place for my[d] father at his beautiful feast. I erected a great temple[e] in its midst[f] like Re when he rises in the horizon. It is planted with all flowers; how beautiful is Nun in his pool at every season; ¹⁴more is its wine[g] than water, like a full Nile, born of the lord of eternity. Many are the goods of the place, the impost of all countries is received, numerous tribute is brought before my father, being the offerings of all lands. He hath assigned to me the princes of the south countries; ¹⁵the Southerners are like the Northerners, and each one is[h] like his neighbor; their silver, their gold, their cattle, every splendid costly stone of their countries, by millions, hundred thousands, ten thousands, and thousands. I have done (it) for the one who begat me, in the uprightness[i] of my heart, according as ¹⁶he appointed me to be the sun of the Nine Bows.

---

[a]Corrected from l. 3, at the end. [c]Lit., "*washed.*"
[b]Restored from l. 22. [d]A sudden change to the first person.

[e]The only "*great temple*" of Amenhotep III which is "*over against*" Luxor is the temple of Mut, which could hardly be referred to here without some reference to the goddess. Hence there may be some undiscovered building of Amenhotep III in the unexplored ground between Luxor and Karnak, to which reference is here made.

[f]Spiegelberg, p. 41, n. 6.

[g]Lit., "*more to it is wine,*" a common phrase; text is corrupt, read: "*wr nj yrp.*"

[h]By an emendation drawn from a repetition of the very same phrase on the Luxor architrave (Lepsius, *Denkmäler*, III, 73, *d*, l. 3). This renders invalid the objections of Spiegelberg to the emendation (*Recueil*, XX, 51).

[i]Lit., "*correctness;*" Erman has treated the phrase (*Gespräch eines Lebensmüden*, 62).

Sacred Barge of Amon[b]

888. King of Upper and Lower Egypt: Nibmare, Part of Re; Son of Re: Amenhotep (III), Ruler of Thebes. I made another monument for him who begat me, Amon-Re, lord of Thebes, who established ⌜me⌝ upon his throne, making for him a great barge[a] for the "Beginning-of-the-River" (named): "Amon-Re-in-the-Sacred-Barge,"[b] of new cedar ¹⁷which his majesty cut in the countries[c] of God's-Land. It was dragged over the mountains of Retenu (*Rtnw*) by the princes of all countries. It was made very wide and large, there is no instance of doing the like. Its ⌜—⌝ is adorned with silver, wrought ¹⁸with gold throughout, the great shrine is of electrum so that it fills the land with its ⌜brightness⌝;[d] its bows,[e] they repeat the ⌜brightness⌝; they bear great crowns, whose serpents twine along its two sides; ⌜they exercise protection behind them.⌝ ¹⁹Flagstaves are set up before it[f] wrought with electrum, two great obelisks are between them; it is beautiful everywhere. The gods of Pe make jubilee to it; the gods of Nekhen praise it; the two Nile-gods of the South and the North, ²⁰they embrace its beauty, its bows[e] make Nun to shine[g] as when the sun rises in heaven, to make his beautiful voyage at his feast of Opet on his western voyage of a million of millions of years.

Third Karnak Pylon[h]

889. King of Upper and Lower Egypt: Nibmare, Son of Re: Amenhotep (III), Ruler of Thebes, ²¹who is vigilant to seek that which is

---

[a]A similar barge with details of measurements in the Harris Papyrus (*infra*, IV, 209).

[b]Egyptian Userhet, "*wsr-ḥ*ꜣ·*t*."

[c]The same statement by Thutmose IV on Lateran obelisk (§ 838).

[d]As it stands, the text is certainly corrupt; the rendering of Spiegelberg ("die ganze Erde") seems impossible, in view of the *m* for *r*. This *m* indicates the above rendering, which is a common idea in respect of monuments of electrum; cf. e. g., obelisk of Hatshepsut, base inscription, south side, l. 7 (§ 315). Since making the above remark, I find the same suggestion (by Müller?) in *Orientalistische Litteraturzeitung*, May, 1898, 158, n. 2, where I also find a good suggestion for the conclusion of the phrase.

[e]Plural, as often in English.

[f]The shrine, which was set up amidships; it is here regarded as a temple, and equipped therefore with flagstaves and obelisks.

[g]Referring to the reflection in the water, here called Nun, as above in l. 13; the same in the Abydos Stela of Thutmose I (§ 94) and Papyrus Harris (IV, § 189, Pl. 4, l. 3).

[h]This is the ruined pylon behind the great hall of columns, known as Pylon III.

useful, the king, who has erected another monument for Amon, making for him a very great portal over against Amon-Re, lord of Thebes, wrought with gold throughout. The Divine Shadow,[a] as a ram, is inlaid with real lazuli wrought with gold and many costly stones; there is no instance of doing the like. [22]Its floor is adorned with silver; ⌜towers⌝ (*sbḫ·t*) are over against it. Stelæ of lazuli are set up, one on each side. Its pylons reach heaven like the four pillars of heaven; its flagstaves shine more than the heavens, wrought [23]with electrum. His majesty brought gold for it in the land of Karoy ($K^{\jmath}\text{-}r^{\jmath}\text{-}y$) on the first victorious campaign,[b] slaying[c] the wretched Kush.[d]

Temple of Soleb

890. King of Upper and Lower Egypt: Nibmare, beloved of Amon-Re; Son of Re: Amenhotep (III), Ruler of Thebes. I made other monuments for Amon, [24]whose like hath not been. I built for thee thy[e] house of millions of years in the ⌜—⌝[f] of Amon-Re, lord of Thebes (named): Khammat ($Ḫ^{c}\text{-}m\text{-}m^{\jmath\,c\cdot}t$),[g] august in electrum, a resting-place for my father at all his feasts. It is finished with fine white sandstone; it is wrought [25]with gold throughout; its floor is adorned with

---

[a]The immaterial or intangible part of a god conceived as a shadow, a common conception both for gods and men (see Birch, *Transactions of the Society of Biblical Archæology*, VIII, 386–97; Maspero, *Dawn of Civilisation*, 108). The hieroglyph and symbol for this shadow is a sunshade, often figured in mortuary vignettes; it is this which is thus referred to in Ineni (§ 104, l. 9): "*its huge door was of Asiatic bronze, whereon was the Divine Shadow* (det. with ithyphallic Min) *inlaid with gold.*" In the above it is also connected with a door, but seems to be in the form of a ram; cf. also Spiegelberg, *Recueil*, XX, 53. Another similar reference to the "*shadow*" of the god is on one of the Soleb rams (Lepsius, *Denkmäler*, III, 89, *e*), but the context is broken off. A similar reference to the divine figure in connection with the door is found on the shrine of Saft: "*The doors upon it* (the shrine) *are of black copper, inlaid with gold, the image upon it is of —*" (Naville, *The Shrine of Saft-el-Henneh*, Pl. 6, l. 1).

[b]See the two stelæ of the Nubian War, §§ 844, 845, l. 5 in each; and scarab of marriage with Tiy, § 862.

[c]Lit., "*campaign . . . . of slaying.*"

[d]Text has *Kny*, which is, of course, an error.

[e]Emended.   [f]Same word ($s^{\jmath}ḥ$) in I, § 503, l. 16.

[g]This is the name of the Soleb temple in Nubia; it means: "*Shining (or rising) in (or as) Truth,*" which is also one of Amenhotep III's names, either in the full titulary, or alone, e. g., "*which his son Khammat made for him*" [east side of south tower, third pylon, Karnak (Mariette, *Karnak*, 34, l. 29)].

silver, all its portals are of gold. Two great obelisks[a] are erected, one on each side. When my father rises between them, I [b]am among his following. I have offered ²⁶to him thousands of oxen, ⌜limbs⌝ for the choicest of hind quarters.

Hymn of Amon

891. Utterance of Amon, king of gods:
My son, of my body, my beloved, Nibmare,
My living image, whom my limbs created,
Whom Mut, mistress of Ishru in Thebes, bore to me,
Mistress of the Nine Bows who brought thee up ²⁷as sole lord of the people.
My heart greatly rejoices when I see thy beauty,
I work a wonder for thy majesty, and thou renewest youth,
According as I have set thee as the Sun of the Two Lands.

When I turn my face to the south, I work a wonder for thee
I cause ²⁸the chiefs of Kush, the wretched, to turn to thee,
Bearing all their tribute upon their backs.
When I turn my face to the north, I work a wonder for thee;
I cause the countries of the ends of Asia to come to thee,
Bearing all their tribute upon their backs.
They present themselves to thee ²⁹with their children,
In order that thou mayest give to them the breath of life.

892. When I turn my face to the west, I work a wonder for thee;
I cause thee to seize the Tehenu (*Tyhnw*), (so that) there is no remnant of them.
(⌜They⌝) are building[c] in this fortress in the name of ³⁰my majesty;
Surrounded with a great wall reaching to heaven,
Settled with children of the chiefs of the Nubian Troglodytes.

When I turn my face to the orient,[d] I work a wonder for thee;
I cause to come to thee the countries of Punt,

---

[a]These obelisks are not shown on Lepsius' plan (Lepsius, *Denkmäler*, I, 117), but they are also mentioned in the ram inscriptions, § 894.

[b]The particle *ty*, introducing a nominal sentence; cf. Sethe, *Zeitschrift für ägyptische Sprache*, 36, p. 71, n. 3.

[c]As slaves?

[d]The usual word for east is not employed, but a term meaning "*sunrise*."

Bearing all the pleasant sweet woods ³¹of their countries,
To crave peace with him (sic!), and breath of thy giving.
King of Upper and Lower Egypt, Ruler of the Nine Bows, Lord of the Two Lands, Nibmare, Son of Re, his beloved Amenhotep (III), Ruler of Thebes, with whose monuments the heart of the gods is satisfied; that he may be given life, stability, satisfaction, health; that his heart may be joyful, like Re, forever.

BUILDING INSCRIPTIONS OF THE SOLEB TEMPLE

893. This Nubian temple, dedicated by Amenhotep III to the worship of himself, as well as of Amon, contains a number of building records. Among other things, they preserve the interesting name of the temple, which is not found in the account of the building given by the king in his great Theban building inscription (§ 890). The architrave dedications are not preserved, but only those upon the sculptures adorning the temple, the rams lining the avenue of approach, and the famous lions in the British Museum.

894. The inscriptions on the rams[a] are these:

[b]Live the Good God, Nibmare, Son of Re, Amenhotep (III). [He made] (it) as his monument for his image,[c] Nibmare, Lord of Nubia (T°-$pd\cdot t$), great god, lord of heaven; making for him an excellent fortress, surrounded with a great wall, whose battlements shine more than the heavens, like the great obelisks, which the king, Amenhotep (III), Ruler of Thebes, made for a million of million of years, forever and ever. Live the Good God ......[d] He made (it) as his monument for his father, Amon, lord of Thebes; making for him an august temple, made very wide and large, and its beauty increased. Its pylons reach heaven, and the flagstaves, the stars of heaven; it is seen (on) both sides of the river, illuminating the Two Lands.

---

[a]One now in Berlin (*Ausführliches Verzeichniss des Berliner Museums*, 23, 24). They were found by Lepsius at Gebel Barkal, whither they had been removed from Soleb by the Ethiopians; published, Lepsius, *Denkmäler*, III, 89, 90.

[b]Lepsius, *Denkmäler*, III, 89, a.

[c]See below.   [d]Continued as above.

895. On another ram,[a] the temple is said to be *"in the fortress Khammat ($ḫ^c$-m-$^ꜣc\cdot t$),"*[b] and is dedicated to Amon (as in the great Building Inscription, § 890), and the king's ka. Another ram inscription[c] thus describes the building:

Making for him an august temple of fine white sandstone; all its portals are of electrum, their radiance is in the faces (of men), the Divine Shadow —————."

896. The famous lions[d] contribute important historical data, from the state of their inscriptions. The dedications of Amenhotep III were cut out during the religious revolution of Ikhnaton, showing that the persecution of that king extended as far south as Soleb, and included even his own father as a god. They were restored by Tutenkhamon, who prefixed to the restored dedications a record of the restoration thus:

——— rest the gods, King of Upper and Lower Egypt, Lord of the Two Lands, Lord of Offering [Nebkheprure],[e] Son of Re, Lord of Diadems, Tutenkhamon, restorer of the monument of his father, the King of Upper and Lower Egypt, Lord of the Two Lands, Nibmare, Son of Re, Amenhotep (III), Ruler of Thebes. He made (it) as his

---

[a]Lepsius, *Denkmäler*, III, 89, *c*.

[b]On this name, see note, § 890. (Great Building Inscription, l. 24).

[c]Lepsius, *Denkmäler*, III, 89, *e*.

[d]These two magnificent animal figures were later carried away from Soleb and erected in Gebel Barkal (Napata) by the Ethiopians. That there should ever have been any doubt about this, especially in the minds of the British Museum authorities, (see Budge, *History*, IV, 112; VI, 100) is, to say the least, surprising. Not only do the above dedications show that the lions were originally erected at Soleb (Khammat), but the breast of one bears the inscription of the Ethiopian, stating that he removed it, as follows: *"Good God, Lion of Rulers, fierce-eyed Lion when he spies his foes treading his path —* (cartouche, name lost), *who brought it."* Below this, is the double name: *"King of Upper and Lower Egypt, Enekhneferibre* ($^c nḫ$-nfr-yb-R^c), *Son of Re, Amenisru (Ymn-ys-r-$w^ꜣ$)."* (Published Lepsius, *Auswahl der wichtigsten Urkunden*, XIII; I had also my own copies of the originals.) See a similar removal record, IV, 649.

[e]Cartouche with name erased. The name has been inserted by Lepsius (*Auswahl der wichtigsten Urkunden*, XIII), but is not discernible on the original.

monument for his father, Amon-Re, lord of Thebes, Atum, lord of Heliopolis, and Yoh[a] ($Y ^c ḥ$), that he might be given life, like Re, forever.

897. On the other lion, the original inscription of Amenhotep III is better preserved,[b] as only the name of the king (containing Amon) has been expunged, and later incorrectly restored, thus:

Horus, Mighty Bull ——— Nibmare, Son of Re, Nibmare[c] (sic!). He made (it) as his monument for ' His Living Image on Earth, Nibmare, Lord of Nubia in the Fortress of Khammat."[d]

898. Finally, a doorpost of the temple bears the following dedication:[e]

He made (it) as his monument for ' His Living Image upon Earth, Nibmare, Lord of [ʳKhenthen]nofer;"[d] making for him temples of fine white sandstone. All its portals are of electrum ——————.

GREAT INSCRIPTION OF THE THIRD KARNAK PYLON[f]

899. This pylon, now the rear wall of the great Karnak hypostyle, was erected by Amenhotep III before the obelisks of Thutmose I as the front of the temple, which it continued to be until the famous hypostyle hall was built in front of it by the Nineteenth Dynasty kings. It is referred to in

---

[a]Thoth, the moon-god.

[b]The inscription occurs twice on this lion, once in front and again behind. In front (facing the avenue) it has been completely hacked out, but behind the iconoclasts of Ikhnaton have hastily cut out only the royal names.

[c]Incorrect restoration by Tutenkhamon; it should be, of course, "*Amenhotep*."

[d]Cultus-name of the deified Amenhotep III.   [e]Lepsius, *Denkmäler*, III, 87, *u*.

[f] On the east face of the southern tower of the third pylon, in 71 vertical lines, of which only the lower ends have survived, the ends of the last 23 lines containing but two or three words each. It was seen and excerpted by Champollion (*Notices descriptives*, II, 126). The text was published by Mariette (*Karnak*, 34, 35) and by Dümichen (*Historische Inschriften*, II, 39); both number the lines backward, and are also excessively inaccurate; Dümichen even mixes up the lines, and evidently his papers were in confusion. I had excellent photographs of the original by Borchardt.

Amenhotep III's Building Inscription (§ 889), and its southern tower still bears the remnant of a long and magnificently cut inscription referring to the erection of the pylon. This inscription has the following content:

1. Laudation of the king (§ 900, ll. 1–24);
2. Offerings to Amon (§ 901, ll. 24–34).
3. Presents and Buildings (§ 902, ll. 24–39).
4. Third Pylon and Connected Monuments (§ 903, ll. 39–71).

The inscription is so fragmentary that much of it is unintelligible, but enough remains to show that the third pylon must have been a monument of the greatest richness and beauty.

Laudation of the King

900. ¹ᵃ——— luxuries and benefactions of the lord of eternity which he levied in God's-Land, abiding like the heavens, shining ⌈—⌉ ²——— ......ᵇ Amenhotep III ³——— in his beauty like him who created him; the hearts rejoice in the bodies at beholding him. ⁴——— their — with one ⌈accord⌉. He whom he hath chosen is prepared, exalted above millions to lead on the people forever. ⁵——— His eye is the sun, making brightness for all men. How prosperous is he who beholds him, his sun, rising ⁶——— of the sun forever. His two hands holdᶜ might, his word bears victory, in order to present to him (Amon) the whole earth, with the impost thereof ⁷——— whose path ⌈sends away⌉, whose name repels, whose ⌈word⌉ created him, ⌈—⌉ with his form to be the Sole Lord, whose doing hath led ⁸——— satisfied with victory, the leader of his soldiers, the first of millions. He is one who taketh thought, who maketh wise with knowledge ⁹——— his stride is swift, a star of electrum when he circles upon his horse, a victorious archer, shooting the ⌈target⌉ ¹⁰ ——— living captives, without his like, the good shepherd, vigilant

---

ᵃThis is l. 71 in Mariette's publication, as he numbered the lines backward, and this translation proceeds from l. 71 to l. 1, as numbered in his publication.

ᵇFull titulary of Amenhotep III.

ᶜLit., "*are in might.*"

for all people, whom the maker thereof has placed under his authority, lord of plenty, ⁱⁱ———— beholding benefactions is his satisfaction, ⌜doing that which occurs is⌝ his thriving forever; loving examples of truth, rejoicing in plans ¹²———— searching bodies, knowing that which is in the heart, whose fame apprehends the ⌜evil⌝ —, protector of the fearful, whose decree is the breath of life, prosperity, and health ¹³———— ⌜—⌝ in his body all his ⌜brightness⌝ to the form of the majesty of Re; his divine and beautiful emanation which he made for — ¹⁴———— like Thoth, who gives the Two Lands to the balances.[a] There are no rebels, (for) his strength is like the might of the son of Nut; there are no millions — ¹⁵———— protecting them, in order to do all that their ka's desire and to make Egypt flourish as in the beginning, by the plans of Truth, because she does ¹⁶———— adorning the splendid Great House of him who begat him, with monuments of beauty and splendor forever, which he decreed for his son ¹⁷———— the wealth of Ptah,[b] great in his form. He created him as his son, endowed with his beauty ¹⁸————. He gave to him the thought of every day as a benefaction, in ⌜magnifying⌝ the wonders of — — He rejoices in remembering ¹⁹———— joy of heart. He created me before him, while I was a youth therein. How beautiful is the ⌜—⌝ before the throne ²⁰———— it in the beginning. His accustomed splendid seat, wherein he alighted ⌜—⌝ ²¹———— him in his form in Thebes, they made rejoicing for love of him ²²———— ⌜— —⌝. I am his first born son ⌜— —⌝ ²³———— I — under his authority, I was endowed with his might, I was endued with his power ²⁴———— ⌜bringing⌝ all works ⌜from⌝ his temple.

Offerings to Amon

901. My majesty founded for him (Amon) very great divine offerings anew ²⁵———— in the land, true and pure in the (divine) presence in the great seat, which I have supplied with food ²⁶———— that he might multiply my years in joy of heart. I produced fulness of food and provision from my presence ²⁷———— my subjects under my feet by the might and victory which he decreed for me ²⁸———— food in thy house filled with supplies, which the ⌜—⌝ established in the horizon, the vessels of him who made the things that are ²⁹———— to him to be mighty in gifts to him, ⌜assigning⌝ them to him; the king,

---

[a]To be weighed as tribute.   [b]Read *rsy ynb·f*.

the unique one of the gods[a] so that they are satisfied every day ³⁰———— true, pure and flourishing with divine offerings of every day, abiding and fixed in his house forever. ³¹———— with millions, as a fierce-eyed lion, sated in the place ⌈—⌉ of the morning, taking captive ³²———— My face works terror — — ⌈when it fronts⌉ those who rebel against me, every time that occurs in ³³———— ⌈— — —⌉ my grasp. I reported my message to him that sent me; I presented it in the presence of my august father ³⁴———— him that begat him.

Presents and Buildings

902. He is divine in my heart at all times, that I may present flowers ³⁵———— according as he creates them, I bring to him silver, gold, genuine lapis lazuli, malachite ³⁶———— every costly stone, every splendid vessel of electrum without limit of number. ³⁷———— in his seat of truth. He hath made for himself splendid things which the maker made. He made me ³⁸———— his — in every august land, the good things of every land and the impost thereof together, that I may present ³⁹————

Third Pylon and Connected Monuments

903. ———— in the splendid place, in which he loves to be, wrought of sandstone ⁴⁰———— all flowers which he gathered, all food at all times. If there be the like ⁴¹———— all — in ⌈pleasing⌉ him, restored and established as he desires it. The weight of this monument:

⁴²ᵇ————

Malachite:	4,820 deben.
⌈—⌉ ($ḫnt$)[c]	3,623 deben.

⁴³————

———— flourishing and established, which his son, Khammat (Amenhotep III) made for him. The number of these things is: ⁴⁴———— flourishing in every garden, sweet in fragrance of all flowers, ⌈— — —⌉ ⁴⁵———— a great [pylon] over against the temple, [its door] made high and wide, of cedar of ⁴⁶———— it illuminates this whole

---

[a]The word "*gods*" was chiseled out in the time of Ikhnaton.

[b]Here follows a statement of the weight of some monument, above mentioned.

[c]This unknown substance appears as a basket of red kernels in the tomb of Rekhmire (Brugsch, *Thesaurus*, V, 1111, and Wilkinson, *Manners*, I, Pl. IIA).

land, its beauty seems like the horizon of heaven ⁴⁷————. He [ʳmade˥] wide for him its extent, an august judgment-hall of ⁴⁸————
an august — for this portal ⁽of the maker of his majesty as my father˥
⁴⁹———— desires them — — — monument for him who ⸱ raised
⁵⁰———— real lapis lazuli, 3,000 (+x) deben ⁵¹———— 3,631½ —
⁵²———— chiefs of all countries, monuments ⁵³———— great doorway of electrum ⁵⁴———— of the land that sees it, every land ʳ— —˥
⁵⁵———— as leader of them in ⁵⁶———— of new cedar of the royal domain ⁵⁷———— august — of electrum, obelisk[s]ᵃ ⁵⁸————
. . . . .ᵇ

DEDICATION STELAᶜ

904. This stela contained the dedication of the mortuary temple of Amenhotep III, which stood behind the (Memnon) Colossi at Thebes. It stood in the usual place, the "*Station of the King,*" which it marked, being erected, like the similar stelæ of Amenhotep II at Elephantine and Amâda (§ 791 ff.), against the inside of the rear wall of the holy of holies.ᵈ Here it proclaimed the king's gift of the temple to the god, on the spot where the king stood in officially absolving the ceremonies of the ritual.

The upper third of the stela is occupied by two conventional scenes, showing the king, Amenhotep III, and his

---

ᵃThese obelisks probably stood in front of this pylon (III); they must have been removed to build the great hypostyle; the only obelisks of Amenhotep III now known at Karnak are in the northern temple, but only fragments have survived (Lepsius, *Denkmäler*, Text, III, 2). Perhaps they stood on the two bases referred to in Baedeker's *Egypt*, 1902, 253.

ᵇLl. 59–71 contain only an incoherent word or two at the end; indeed, ll. 62 and 69–71 are entirely gone.

ᶜAn enormous sandstone stela about 30 feet high and 14 feet wide, still lying a few hundred feet behind the colossi of Amenhotep III at Thebes; text, Lepsius, *Denkmäler*, III, 72.

ᵈThe stela is directly referred to in another building inscription of Amenhotep III in this same temple (§ 883, l. 5), where it is called "*a station of the king, wrought with gold and many costly stones.*" The word "*station*" is here determined with a stela, and the text would indicate that it was overlaid and incrusted.

queen, Tiy, before "*Sokar-Osiris*" (on the left) and "*Amon-Re*" (on the right).

The text of twenty-four lines represents: (1) the king delivering the temple which stood behind the Colossi to Amon in a presentation address[a] (ll. 2-13); (2) Amon accepting it with words of praise to the king (ll. 14-20); (3) the "Divine Ennead" calling upon the god to enter his temple, while they praise him and the king (ll. 20-24).[b] The text is badly broken and certainly corrupt in a number of places.

I. SPEECH OF THE KING (LL. 1-13)

Temple

905. ¹Live .... [c] King Amenhotep (III). ²He saith: "Come thou, Amon-Re, lord of Thebes, presider over Karnak; thou hast seen thy house which I have made for thee in [d]the west of Thebes.[d] Its beauty mingles with Manu (M ꜣ $-nw$), when thou sailest over the heavens to set therein. ³When thou risest in the horizon of heaven, it shines[e] with the gold of thy face, (for) its face is toward the east ⌜———⌝[f] thou shinest in the morning every day; thy beauty is in its midst without ceasing. I made it ⁴in excellent work, of fine white sandstone.

Colossal Statues

906. My majesty filled it with monuments, with my [⌜statues⌝][g] from the mountain of gritstone. When they are seen (⌜in⌝) their place,

---

[a]The erection of the same temple is recorded in ll. 2-10 in the preceding building inscription, §§ 883, 884.

[b]It is therefore not merely a dialogue between the god and the king, as stated by Brugsch, *Egypt under the Pharaohs*, 207.

[c]The usual full titulary.

[d]$ys\cdot t\ wr\cdot t\ nt\ W$ ꜣ $s\cdot t$ probably designates "*the west of Thebes*," found in l. 3 of the preceding building inscription (ymy-$wr\cdot t\ nt\ w$ ꜣ $s\cdot t$).

[e]Though causative, this verb may be used intransitively, e. g., l. 24 below.

[f]The parallelism of "*because thou risest*" and "*because thou settest*" is all that can be made of this phrase.

[g]This restoration is probable, for the (Memnon) colossi before this temple are of gritstone.

there is great rejoicing because of their size.ᵃ I made ⁵likewise a
⌐——⌐ᵇ upon the stone; it is of alabaster, pink and black granite; my
majesty made a double pylon,ᶜ seeking excellent things for my father;
statues coming forth ⌐——⌐ they were shaped, ⁶—— throughout. Great
was that which I made, of gold, stone, and every splendid costly stone
without end. I gave to them the directions to do that which pleases
thy ka, ⌐——⌐ satisfied withᵈ an august dwelling like ⁷——————.

Offerings

907. I made for themᵉ offerings —————. My majesty hath
doneᶠ these things for millions (of years), and I know that they will
abide in the earth for my father ⁸——— all that was due him; I made
for thee a shadowᵍ for thy voyage across the heavens as Atum, coming
forth with all the [gods], while the divine ennead who are behind thee
and the Sacred Apes praise thy rising and thy appearing in ⁹— the
horizon. The divine ennead rejoice, they give exaltation to Khepri;
the Sacred Apes give praise to theeʰ when thou settest in Enekhⁱ in
the west.

Obelisks

908. I made ¹⁰obelisks there ⌐———⌐. Thou hast shown favor
forʲ all that my majesty made there in the likeness of a chapel of thy
majesty ⌐————⌐.ᵏ ¹¹Again I made for thee monuments on the

ᵃThe so-called Memnon colossi are about 58 feet high (Lepsius, *Denkmäler*,
Text, III, 141 ff.), but this height is reduced nearly 5 feet by the accumulated Nile
mud. They bear, or at least the southern statue bears, the dedication (Lepsius,
Denkmäler, Text, III, 144): "*He made (it) as his monument for his father Amon;
making for him a great statue of costly gritstone* . . . ." There is among
the titles of the king also a reference to the monument as "*brought from Northern
Heliopolis to Southern Heliopolis.*" The quarry of red gritstone, whence the
statues were taken, is at the Gebel el-Ahmar near Cairo (see I, 493, l. 15, note)
and Heliopolis; Southern Heliopolis is modern Erment, south of Thebes.

ᵇRead *ky*, "*form;*" the *b* as determinative?   ᵈOr: "*resting in.*"

ᶜTranslated from the determinative only.   ᵉFor the statues.

ᶠThere is a superfluous personal ending here.

ᵍThis is probably not the "*Divine Shadow,*" but a sunshade to protect the
god on festival processions, or, as the text has it, when he crosses the heavens.

ʰLit., "*to thy face,*" or before thee.

ⁱMeaning "*life,*" a euphemism for the place of the dead.

ʲLit., "*of.*"   ᵏA little over one-third line.

west of the Great [˹Sea˺]t˹˺;[a] I exacted all works ˹———˺[b] in order to furnish my impost by the [˹hand˺] of my army. I rejoiced [12]when I had done (it) for my father.

I [foun]ded for thee offerings every day at the beginning of the seasons and oblations at their times, d[˹ues for˺] thy temple; its prophets, its priests from the greatest and choicest of [13]the whole land......... Accept that which I have made, revered father, Amon, of the beginning of the world."

II. SPEECH OF AMON (LL. 14–20)

909. [14]Utterance by Amon-Re, ...:[c] "Come, my son Amenhotep,[d] [15]I hear what thou sayest; I have seen thy monument, I am thy [fath]er, creator of thy beauty........ [20]....[e] I accept the [monument] which thou hast made for me."

III. SPEECH OF THE DIVINE ENNEAD (LL. 20–24)

910. Utterance by the Divine Ennead: [f]........[f]: [21]"Come ——— into thy eternal temple. It is Nibmare, thy son, who has done this for thee.[g] .... [23]....[g] Thou art in heaven, [24]thou shinest for the earth; he (the king) is on earth, administering thy kingdom [g]......[g]

INSCRIPTIONS OF AMENHOTEP, SON OF HAPI

911. This famous official, who lived under Amenhotep III, was a descendant of an old noble family, the ancient nomarchs of Athribis, and still maintained the office of chief of the prophets of the temple at that place, which went with his ancient rank. He acquired a great reputation for

---

[a]The name of this temple was "*House-of-Amon-on-the-West-of-Thebes;*" see § 883, note.

[b]Five or six words.   [c]Half a line of titles.   [d]Both names.

[e]About one-fourth of the omitted portion is broken out, the remainder contains only the conventional praise of the king by the god.

[f]One-third line.

[g]Much broken, and contains only the conventional phrases of praise to Amon or the king.

wisdom. On the temple of Der el-Medineh at Thebes an inscription says of him: "*His name shall abide forever, his sayings shall not perish.*" These sayings were thought to be referred to in the papyrus of Heter at Gizeh,[a] but this has been clearly shown to be an error.[b] The attribution of a mortuary papyrus[c] to him is also very questionable.[d] The only wisdom unquestionably assigned to him, though it is probably a pseudepigraphon, is found in an eighteen-line Greek scrawl of the third century B. C., on a limestone ostracon belonging to the Egypt Exploration Fund.[e] It contains nine fragmentary sayings, of which Wilcken has found three also among the "Proverbs of the Seven Wise Men."[f] Amenhotep was long supposed to have built the original temple on the site of the present Der el-Medineh temple;[g] Sethe has shown the error of this supposition.[h] He was long ago pointed out by Brugsch, on the basis of his statue inscription, as the architect[i] of the Memnon colossi on the Theban plain—an error which a careful translation of the inscription immediately exposes.[j]

912. He lived to be at least eighty years old, when the king granted him a statue[k] in the Karnak temple of Amon with the following dedication:

---

[a]By Maspero, *Mémoire sur quelques papyri du Louvre*, 23.
[b]By Sethe, *Festschrift für Georg Ebers*, 113, 114.
[c]Mariette, *Papyri de Boulaq*, No. 5.   [d]Sethe, *ibid*.
[e]Published by Wilcken, *Festschrift für Georg Ebers*, 142–46. For other material which may be his, see Daressy, *Annales*, III, 43, 61, 62, where he appears as a god in the Ptah-temple of Karnak in the time of Tiberius.
[f]Wilcken, *Festschrift für Georg Ebers*, 144, 145.
[g]By Brugsch (*Zeitschrift für ägyptische Sprache*, 1875, 125–27) on the basis of the Mortuary Temple Edict below, §§ 921 ff.
[h]*Festschrift für Georg Ebers*, 110–12.
[i]*Zeitschrift für ägyptische Sprache*, 1876, 96 ff.   [j]See § 917.
[k]*Annales*, II, 272, 281–84; IV, Pl. V, IV. The long inscription has nothing of historical value. See another Karnak statue of him, *Recueil*, 19, 13, 14.

[Given as a favo]r of the king's-presence to the temple of Amon in Karnak, for the hereditary prince, count, sole companion, fan-bearer on the king's right hand, chief of the king's works even all the great monuments which are brought, of every excellent costly stone; steward of the king's-daughter of the king's-wife, Sitamon, who liveth; overseer of the cattle of Amon in the South and North, chief of the prophets of Horus, lord of Athribis, festival leader of Amon, Amenhotep, son of Hapi, born of the lady Yatu ($Y^{\supset}tw$), triumphant.

Having thus attained the age of eighty years, he prays (on this statue) for the usual 110 years. In later ages he gradually gained recognition as a god, for the first time probably under Ptolemy Euergetes II;[a] so that already in Manetho's time, this historian could say of him that he seemed to partake of the divine nature.[b]

I. STATUE INSCRIPTION[c]

913. This inscription is very difficult and obscure. The introduction (ll. 1–26) consists solely of eulogistic epithets and phrases applied to the deceased, and of mortuary texts, of no historical value. The remainder (ll. 26–43) contains his official career through three promotions, as follows:

Introduction, § 914, ll. 26–27.

First Promotion, to be Inferior Royal Scribe, § 915, ll. 27–29.

Second Promotion, to be Superior Royal Scribe, § 916, ll. 29–37.

Third Promotion, to be Minister of all Public Works, § 917, ll. 37–43.

---

[a]Sethe, *Festschrift für Georg Ebers*, 116.

[b]Josephus, *Contra Apion*, I, 26.

[c]The third statue of Amenhotep at Karnak; discovered there by Mariette. Published by Mariette, *Karnak*, 36, 37; Rougé, *Inscriptions hiéroglyphiques*, XXIII-XXVIII; Brugsch, *Thesaurus*, VI, 1292–98. I had also a copy of the original by Borchardt for the Berlin dictionary.

Introduction

914. ²⁶........ The king's-scribe, Amenhotep, triumphant; he saith: "I was great, at the head of the great, skilful in the divine words[a] in ²⁷the ⌈council⌉ of understanding, following the plans of the king; one whose ka the sovereign, L. P. H., advanced.

First Promotion

915. The Good God, King of Upper and Lower Egypt, Nibmare (Amenhotep III), firstborn son of Harakhte, praised me. I was appointed to be inferior king's-[b]scribe; ²⁸I was introduced into the divine book, I beheld the excellent things of Thoth; I was equipped with their secrets; I opened[c] all their ⌈passages⌉; one took counsel with me ²⁹on all their matters.

Second Promotion

916. My lord again showed favor to me; the King of Upper and Lower Egypt, Nibmare, he put all the people subject to me, and the listing of their number under my control, as superior king's-scribe[d] over recruits. ³⁰I levied the (military) classes of my lord, my pen reckoned the numbers of millions; I put them in ⌈classes⌉ in the place of their ⌈elders⌉; the staff of old age[e] as his beloved son. ³¹I taxed the houses with the numbers belonging thereto, I divided the troops (of workmen) and their houses, I filled out the subjects[f] with the best of the captivity, which his majesty had captured ³²on the battlefield. I appointed all their troops ($ts\cdot t$), I levied —— I placed troops at the heads of the way(s) to turn back the foreigners in their places. ³³The two regions were surrounded[g] with a watch scouting for the Sand-rangers. I did likewise at the heads of the river-mouths,[h] which were

---

[a]Term for hieroglyphics.   [b]$S\check{s}\text{-}\check{s}tny\text{-}hry\;d\;^\flat\;d\;^\flat$.

[c]The same phrase ($pg\;^\flat\;ny$) for opening sacred books in Neferhotep (I, 758).

[d]$S\check{s}\text{-}\check{s}tny\text{-}hry\text{-}d\;^\flat\;d\;^\flat$.

[e]Same phrase, I, 692. There is a reference here to the replacement of old by new levies, but the technical terms are not yet fully understood.

[f]The native-born Egyptians.

[g]Or: "*which surrounded the Two Lands.*"

[h]Lit., "*at the head(s) of the shore of the front mouths;*" the mouths of the Nile are indicated. The meaning "*river-mouths*" or "*harbor-mouths*" is clearly determined by the use of the word ($r\;^\flat\text{-}h\;^\flat\cdot wt$) in the wars of Ramses III (year 5,

closed under ³⁴my troops except to the troops of royal marines. I was the guide of their ways, they depended upon my command.

I was the chief at the head of ³⁵the mighty men, to smite the Nubians ⌜and the Asiatics⌝,ᵃ the plans of my lord were a refuge behind me; ⌜when I wandered⌝ his command surrounded me; his plans embraced all lands ³⁶and all foreigners who were by his side. I reckoned up the captivesᵇ of the victories of his majesty, being in charge of them. I did according to that which he (the king) said, I followed according to the things which he commanded ³⁷me, I found them excellent things for the future.

Third Promotion

917. My lord a third time showed favorᶜ to me; Son of Re, Amenhotep (III), Ruler of Thebes, the sun-god is he, to whom hath been given an eternity of his jubilees without end. ³⁸My lord made me chief of all works. I established the name of the king forever, I did not imitate that which had been done before. I fashioned for him a mountain of gritstone, for he is the heir of Atum.ᵈ ³⁹I did according to my desire, executing his likeness in this his great house,ᵉ with every precious stone, enduring like the heavens; there was not oneᶠ who had done it (the like) since the time of the founding of his Two Lands. ⁴⁰I con-

---

l. 53, IV, 44; year 8, l. 20, IV, 65). Maspero's "custom-houses erected at the mouths of the Nile" (Maspero, *Struggle of the Nations*, 299), while hardly derivable from this passage alone, are amply corroborated by the Amarna Letters, which show that there were custom-houses on the coast of the Delta (*Amarna Letters*, 29; 32 and 33).

ᵃPossibly "*the Nubians of the cataract region.*"

ᵇ$Ys-ḥ > k\cdot t$.   ᶜText has "*my favor.*"

ᵈSee note on l. 40, where the mountain is again connected with Atum, in whose district it was.

ᵉThe temple of Karnak where our nobleman's statue was found; hence the statue of the king here referred to must be in this temple, and cannot have been one of the Memnon colossi, as Piehl thinks possible (*Petites études*, 37). [Later: Since making the above note, I notice that Sethe has published the same remark (*Festschrift für Georg Ebers*, 109).] It is therefore clear that Brugsch is wrong in concluding from this inscription that Amenhotep, the son of Hapi, necessarily erected the Memnon colossi; as the passage refers clearly to a statue in the Karnak temple, where there actually still is a statue of Amenhotep III of the stone of Gebel el-Ahmar (cf. Sethe, *ibid.*, 109).

ᶠThe rendering, "*there was not a king, etc.,*" of Brugsch (*Zeitschrift für ägyptische Sprache*, 1876, 98) and Piehl (*Petites études*, 37), is due to the misreading of the particle *śwt* as *śtn(y)*, "*king;*" cf. Erman, *Aegyptische Grammatik*, § 320.

ducted the work of his statue,[a] immense in width, taller than his column, its beauty marred the pylon. Its length was 40[b] cubits in the august mountain[c] of gritstone at the side of Re-Atum. [41]I built an eight-vessel, I brought it (the statue) up-river;[d] it was set up in [this] great house, enduring as heaven. My witnesses are ye, ye who shall come [42]after us; the entire army was as one under my control, they wrought with joy, their hearts were glad, rejoicing and praising the Good God; [43]they landed at Thebes with rejoicing, the monuments rested in their places forever ─────.[e]

Service with the King

918. [3][f]───── I [saw] him[g] fighting hand to hand upon the battlefield, while he was like Min in the year of ⌜—⌝. I recorded the ⌜numbers⌝ of his ⌜captives⌝ as subjects of the temples ───── [4]───── while I was apportioner of ointment. I was versed in her art ⌜— — —⌝ and she knew (it), while I was in front with my lord, and I was great before him. I did that which men loved and gods praised ───── [5]─────.

Benefits for Athribis

919. Behold ye, I did excellent things; do (so) to me, and it shall be done (likewise) to you; for I am an heir who furnished his city, and expelled its ⌜—⌝ (*tw* ?) from every place. My lord[g] did benefactions for my god[h] ⌜—⌝ ───── [6]─────. My lord [⌜dug⌝] his southern lake

───────

[a]Text has plural, but the singular pronouns show the error.

[b]A statue of Amenhotep III of the Gebel el-Ahmar stone before Harmhab's pylon at Karnak was about 15 meters high, and is probably the one referred to; for it is not stated that the statue was 40 cubits high, but the block in the quarry was 40 cubits "*long*." A similar reference to the block in the mountain in I, 698, l. 6.

[c]The same as the "*Red Mountain*" of Mariette, *Karnak*, 15, 24 (I, 493, l. 15, note) near Cairo, and still called Red Mountain (Gebel el-Ahmar) cf. Baedeker's *Egypt*, 1902, 74. The phrase "*at the side of Re-Atum*" refers to its location near the Heliopolis sanctuary of Re. Sethe notes similar phrases on the Sphinx tablet, ll. 6 and 7 (§ 814).

[d]From the quarry near Cairo to Thebes.   [e]About one-half line.

[f]Another, shorter inscription on the same statue, Mariette, *Karnak*, 37, b. Ll. 1 and 2 have almost entirely disappeared.

[g]The king.

[h]The god of his city, Athribis. He calls on the people of the place to pray for him because he had used his influence with the king, to secure royal benefits for the local god and temple of Athribis.

and his northern lake, brightened with flowers upon their shores. I ⸺ their ⸺, and led them, because I was one ⌜— —⌝ his city. He made the house of my god, and my ⌜city⌝. How beautiful is ⸺⸺ 7 ⸺⸺ because of his daily offerings. My lord magnified my city greatly, and my family ⌜— —⌝ on earth.

Royal Favor

920. I buried my father, doing again that which "The-Son-Whom-He-Loves" did. I interred my mother ⸺⸺ 8 ⸺⸺. My lord — my necessities, causing me to receive bread ⌜after⌝ the feasts. Men said to me : "⌜— —⌝ it hath come to thee through the Lord of the Two Lands. There is no citizen ($šw^{\,?}$) to whom the like has been done." I executed truth ⸺⸺ 9 ⸺⸺ . . . .[a]

II. MORTUARY TEMPLE EDICT[b]

921. This document legally establishes in perpetuity an endowment for the maintenance of Amenhotep's mortuary cult. It was publicly read in his mortuary temple at Thebes to the more important officers of state assembled there in the king's presence, who are adjured to respect it, or suffer under the most dreadful curses. The surviving original is a late copy of the original of Amenhotep's day.

Date

922. ¹Year 31,[c] fourth month of the first season, sixth day, under the majesty of the King of Upper and Lower Egypt, the Lord of the Two Lands, Nibmare, L. P. H.; Son of Re, of his body, Lord of Diadems, Amenhotep (III), L. P. H.

---

[a]Two lines of self-praise.

[b]Hieratic text, being a copy of very late date, on a limestone stela in the British Museum, No. 138, published in transliteration by Birch (Chabas, *Mélanges égyptologiques*, II sér., 324–43); again by the same author in facsimile (*Inscriptions in the Hieratic and Demotic Character*, XXIX). I collated the original exhaustively and found the latter publication very inaccurate. It was translated by Brugsch, *Zeitschrift für ägyptische Sprache*, 1875, 125–27; Erman, *Life in Ancient Egypt*, 148 (*Aegypten*, 214, 215); the present translation is much indebted to Erman's version.

[c]Not 11, as Brugsch has it; even 41 is possible.

The Assembly

923. On this day, one (=the king) was in the ka-chapel[a] ²of the hereditary prince, count, king's-scribe, Amenhotep. There were brought in: the governor of the city, and vizier, Amenhotep; the overseer of the treasury, Meriptah, and the king's-scribes of the army.

Establishment of Chapel

924. One said to them in the presence of ³his majesty, L. P. H.: "Hear the command which is given, to furnish the ka-chapel of the hereditary prince, the royal scribe, Amenhotep, called Huy, Son of Hapu, whose excellence is ⌜extolled⌝,[b] ⁴in order to perpetuate his ka-chapel with slaves, male and female, forever; son to son, heir to heir; in order that none trespass upon it forever. It is commended to Amon-Re, king of gods, as long as it is upon earth; ⁵he is the king of eternity, he is the protector of the dead.

Curses on Violators

925. As for the general and scribe of the army who shall follow after me and shall find the ka-chapel beginning to decay, together with ⁶the male and female slaves who are cultivating (the field) for my endowment, and shall take away a man therefrom in order to put him (⌜to⌝) any business of Pharaoh, L. P. H., or any commission, may his body be ⌜accursed⌝.[c] ⁷Then if another trespasses upon them, and does not answer in their behalf, he shall suffer the destruction of Amon, lord of Thebes, he (the god) shall not permit them to be satisfied with the office of king's-scribe of the army, which they have received for me. ⁸He (Amon) shall deliver them into the flaming wrath of the king on the day of his anger; his serpent-diadem shall spit fire upon their heads, shall consume their limbs, shall devour their bodies, they shall become like Apophis on the morning of New Year's Day. They shall be engulfed in the sea, ⁹it shall hide their corpses. They shall not receive the mortuary ceremonies of the righteous; they shall not eat the food of them that dwell in Keret; the waters by the flood of the river shall not be poured out for them. Their sons shall not be put into their places,

---

[a]Not the "temple of Kak," as usually rendered; see Sethe, *Festschrift für Georg Ebers*, 111.

[b]Brugsch: "dessen Tugenden wohlbekannt sind;" but this is very doubtful.

[c]It is possible that this is the case of those who do respect the endowment; while the case of those who do not respect it begins with l. 7.

¹⁰their wives shall be violated while their eyes see it. The nobles shall not set foot in their houses as long as they are upon earth; the leaders of the two sides[a] shall not introduce them, nor shall they hear the words of the king in the hour of gladness. ¹¹They shall belong to the sword on the day of destruction, they shall be called enemies; when their bodies be consumed, they shall hunger, without bread, and their bodies shall die. If the vizier, overseer of the treasury, chief overseer of the estate, superintendent of the granary, ¹²high priests, divine fathers, and priests of Amon, to whom has been read this edict, issued for the ka-chapel of the hereditary prince, the king's-scribe, Amenhotep, son of Hapu, shall not show solicitude ¹³for his ka-chapel, the edict shall touch them, and them especially.

Blessings on Preservers of Chapel

926. But if they shall show solicitude for the ka-chapel, with the male and female slaves who are cultivating (the field) for my ¹⁴endowment, then all favor shall be shown them. Amon-Re, king of gods, shall reward them[b] with prosperous life.[c] The king of your day, shall ⌜reward⌝ you ¹⁵as he ⌜rewards⌝ —.[d] There shall be doubled for you office upon office, ye shall receive from son to son and heir to heir. They shall be sent on as messengers, and the king of their day will reward them. ⌜Their⌝ bodies shall (rest) ¹⁶in the West after (a life of) 110 years, doubled to you shall be the mortuary oblations likewise.

Warning to Gendarmes

927. As for the officers of the gendarmes, ⌜belonging to⌝ the district of the mayor of the west side, in Khaft(et)-hir-nebes, who ¹⁷shall not protect my endowment each day, and on my feast-days on the first of the month, the edict shall touch them, and their bodies shall not ⌜escape⌝. ¹⁸But if they shall hear all the edict, issued as a command, and they shall obey and shall not forsake it, good shall happen to them as (to) the just. ¹⁹They shall rest in the cemetery after years of old age.

Codicil. The mayor of the west side is he who ⌜—⌝ my servants during a single day.

---

[a]The people on the two sides of the central aisle in formal assemblies; the leaders (sšm·w) or ushers of such assemblies were the heralds (whm·w).
[b]Original shows a correction from "you" to "them."
[c]There is no lacuna here nor in the next line, as indicated in the publication.
[d]The text has omitted the object.

STATUE OF NEBNEFER[a]

928. This statue was probably dedicated in the chapel of Prince Wazmose; at least, there is a reference to this prince among the inscriptions which it bears. On the back, however, there is an historical inscription apparently recording the promotion of Nebnefer and the appointment of one Hui to his old place. The promotion was by special message of the king, which Nebnefer himself brought, and it was confirmed by a special formulary pronounced by the High Priest and witnessed by all four "*prophets*" for the temple, and one witness for the incumbent beside himself. The document thus furnishes us with interesting and important procedure in such temple appointments, which are as yet unknown in any other source.

Date

929. ¹Year 20, second month of the first season, under the majesty of King Amenhotep III, beloved of Amon ²....... .[b]

Royal Message

On this day, behold [his majesty ³was in the temple][c] of Ptah-South-of-His-Wall, lord of Life-of-the-Two-Lands. Message, concerning which the king's-scribe, the steward, Khampet, came to the chief treasurer, the High Priest of Amon, ⁴[Meriptah][d] ——— from the Pharaoh, L. P. H., (saying): "Let the chief measurer of the storehouse of divine offerings be ⌈brought —⌉ before his fathers; ⁵——— Hui being put into his place in the storehouse of divine offerings of Amon."

---

[a]Fragment of limestone sitting statue, now in the Museum of Brussels; published by Capart and Spiegelberg in *Annales de la Société d'Archéologie de Bruxelles*, Tome XVII, 1ʳᵉ et 2ᵐᵉ liv., 1903, 19–28.

[b]Double name of the king and conventional epithets.

[c]This was probably not Memphis, but the temple of Ptah at Karnak, which bore the same names as the Ptah-temple at Memphis.

[d]Supplied from l. 8; the middle three lines evidently extended higher up the plinth than the others, and were an uncertain amount longer.

Installation

930. Then it was done according to [all] that [his majesty] said
⁶———— [the High Priest of Amo]n, Meriptah, triumphant, to the king's-scribe, the steward Khampet: ᵃ"As for that which is done of thy father Amon, lord of Thebes, ⁷in all his commands, as heaven endures,ᵇ so shall that which he does endure, enduring and permanent forever."

Witnesses

931. Done in the presence of the chief treasurer, the High Priest of ⁸Amon, Meriptah; the second prophet, Enen (ᶜ *nn*); the third prophet, Amenemhet; the fourth prophet,ᶜ Simut; the king's-scribe, Khampet; the steward, Sebeknakht.

ᵃThe following is evidently the formulary of confirmation in office, pronounced by the High Priest to the incumbent.

ᵇThe phrase is common; hence the remark of the authors, "Le passage semble être fautif," is strange.

ᶜThe four prophets (the High Priest's title really reads "*first prophet*") represent the temple, and for the incumbent there are only himself and one more.

REIGN OF IKHNATON

QUARRY INSCRIPTION AT SILSILEH[a]

932. This inscription is among the earliest surviving documents of the great revolution under Ikhnaton. It records the opening of quarry-chambers at Silsileh to obtain stone for the king's first temple[b] to his new god, whose cult already seems to be in full development. Although Amon is not yet banished, Aton has his formal name, but not yet in the cartouches, in which it later always appears. The king is however, *"High Priest"* of his new god, whose sanctuary he is about to erect. Of this temple not one stone was left upon another by the king's enemies at his death. The materials have been found at Thebes, but scattered in various structures from Karnak to Erment, chiefly, however, in the Karnak pylons of Harmhab.[e] The name of this temple was: *"Aton-⌈is-Found⌉-in-the-House-of-Aton,"*[d]

---

[a]Tablet fourteen feet high, cut on the quarry wall at Silsileh; published by Lepsius, *Denkmäler*, III, 110, *i;* Legrain, *Annales*, III, 263.

[b]On the Aton-temples at Akhetaton (Amarna), see tomb of Hui (§§ 1016 ff.); and on the ones at Heliopolis, Hermonthis, and elsewhere, *ibid.* On the Aton-temples in general, see my remarks in *Zeitschrift für ägyptische Sprache*, 40, 110 ff.

[c]See Nestor l'Hôte, *Papiers inédits*, III, 80, 96, 97, 101, 104, 105 (not seen); Prisse, *Transactions of the Royal Society of Literature*, 2d Ser., I., 76–92, and again Prisse, *Monuments égyptiens*, V and XI; following Prisse, J. S. Perring, *Transactions of the Royal Society of Literature*, 2d Ser., I, 140 ff.; Brugsch, *Recueil de monuments*, Pl. 57, 2, *a–k*; Lepsius, *Denkmäler*, III, 110, *c* and *g*; Bouriant, *Recueil*, VI, 51 ff.; and a letter by Piehl (*Zeitschrift für ägyptische Sprache*, 1884, 41), which also refers to the names of Tutenkhamon and Eye as occurring in blocks rebuilt into this pylon. Blocks reused in repairs on the temple of Amenhotep II (Lepsius, *Denkmäler*, Text, III, 50); in Karnak (*ibid.*, 52); in town of Luxor (*ibid.*, 89).

[d]See tomb of Ramose, § 941, note.

and it must have been a large and imposing sanctuary.[a] It was erected early in the Aton schism, for the surviving fragments show a reference to Horus and Set. The name of Aton occurs without the cartouches,[b] and the king still bears his old name.[c] This last fact shows that the temple was built before the sixth year. It is also referred to in the tomb of Hatey ($ḥ\ni t-y\ni y$) at Thebes (Kurna), who was "*scribe, overseer of the granary in the house ($ḥ·t$) of the Aton,*"[d] at a time when the Amon cult was still unrepressed. Thebes as a whole was now apparently called "*City ($nw·t$)-of-the-Brightness-of-Aton,*" and the temple quarter was known as "*Brightness-of-Aton-the-Great.*"[e]

933. [f] The quarry inscription informs us that the highest officials of the court served in superintending the work of transportation. The date of the inscription must be very early in the king's reign, because the materials taken from the quarry were built into the temple, completed, and inscribed before the sixth year. The work in the quarry was therefore probably done in the first or second year. Over the inscrip-

---

[a]In the heart of Harmhab's pylon I found blocks of Ikhnaton's masonry of considerable dimensions; one cornice was 32 inches high. The king's leg, in a fragmentary relief, was 20 inches across at the lower edge of the apron; the k-vessel was 13 inches long; the dy-loaf was 12 inches high. The names of Aton and the king had been expunged before the destruction of the building.

[b]From my own copies of blocks deep in Harmhab's pylon. I found there also a date which might have settled this question, but unfortunately the year is lost, and only the season and the day remain. [Later: This date is now published in Lepsius, *Denkmäler*, Text, III, 52.]

[c]Lepsius, *Denkmäler*, III, 110, d. The old name, "*Amenhotep*," continued until the fifth year of his reign (Griffith, *Kahun Papyri*, Pl. 38 and pp. 91 and 92). In the sixth year we find the new name, "*Ikhnaton*," on the boundary stelæ at Amarna (§§ 949 ff.). The Theban temple must, therefore, have been built and sculptured before the sixth year.

[d]Daressy, *Annales*, II, 2–4; Legrain, *ibid.*, III, 265.

[e]On Canopics published by Legrain (*Annales*, IV, 17–19).

[f]Legrain's arguments for dating the temple, or a temple of Aton at Thebes, before Ikhnaton's reign are inconclusive (*Annales*, III, 265).

tion was a relief[a] showing the king worshiping before Amon, but it has been erased, probably by Ikhnaton himself. The inscription below is as follows:

934. [1]Live the Horus: Mighty Bull, Lofty of Plumes; Favorite of the Two Goddesses; Great in Kingship in [Karnak];[b] Golden Horus: Wearer of Diadems [2]in the Southern Heliopolis; King of Upper and Lower Egypt, High Priest of Harakhte-Rejoicing-in-the-Horizon, in His Name: "Heat-Which-is-in-Aton:" Neferkheprure[c]-Wanre; [3]Son of Re [Amenhotep,[d] Divine Ruler of Thebes], great in his duration, living forever and ever; [Amon]-[e] Re, lord of heaven, ruler of eternity.[f]

935. First occurrence of his majesty's giving command to — — [4]— — — to muster all the workmen[g] from Elephantine to Samhudet[h] (*Sm ꜣ -Ḥwḏ·t*), and the leaders of the army, [5]in order to make a great breach for cutting out sandstone, in order to make the great sanctuary (*bnbn*)[i] of Harakhte in his name: "Heat-Which-is-in-[6]Aton," in Karnak.

---

[a]Not shown on Lepsius' plate, but given by him in his notes (Lepsius, *Denkmäler*, Text, IV, 96, 97).

[b]Lepsius has incorrectly restored Akhetaton in this lacuna. This mention of the city in the first or second year had caused me much difficulty; but the publication of this stela by Legrain (*Annales*, III, 263) shows that "*Akhetaton*" is an error. We should restore "*Karnak*" as in the contemporary Zernik stela (*ibid.*, 260 f.). This fragmentary stela recorded similar quarry-work in the cliffs opposite and above Esneh. The king bears his old name, and the god's name also is as in the Silsileh stela; it is undated, but is clearly from the same time as the Silsileh stela, and the expedition recorded was carried out by Eye, afterward king. There is another stela beside Eye's, showing the "*chief of quarrymen, Neferronpet*," worshiping Amon (*ibid.*, 261 f.).

[c]This is the Napkhurya of the Amarna Letters; it means: "*Beautiful is the Being of Re.*" Wanre, the second part of the name, means, "*Unique One of Re.*"

[d]This old form of the king's name has been erased because it contained the name of Amon.

[e]Erased.

[f]The connection of the god's name is uncertain, but probably "*beloved of*" has been omitted before it (after it in original).

[g]The text has "*works*," but Brugsch has a similar example (*Hieroglyphisch-demotisches Wörterbuch, Supplement*, 1337), with "*the people*" as object of the verb, showing clearly what is meant here.

[h]Like the Hebrew "from Dan to Beersheba." On Samhudet, see Brugsch, *Dictionnaire géographique*, 704–6. Elephantine was, of course, at the first cataract, and Samhudet was in the Delta.

[i]Determined with an obelisk.

Behold, the officials, the companions, and the chiefs of the fan-bearers, were the chiefs of the quarry-service,[a] for the transportation of stone.

TOMB OF THE VIZIER RAMOSE[b]

936. This tomb contains reliefs and inscriptions which are among the most important documents of this reign, because among other facts they furnish contemporary and conclusive evidence of the identity of Amenhotep IV and Ikhnaton, the great religious revolutionary.

Ramose, the owner of the tomb, was an official high in the favor of the king and of exalted rank. He was:

"Governor of the (residence) city, vizier;" "hereditary prince, count ——— of Horus in his house; a doer of truth, a hater of deceit, ——— wearer of the royal seal, chief of works among the great monuments, chief of prophets of North and South, vizier, just judge; sole companion, approaching his lord, whom the Lord of the Two Lands loved because of his remarkable traits, who enters the palace, and comes forth with favor, with the utterances of whose mouth one (= the king) is satisfied;" "($mr\cdot t\text{-}ntr$-) priest, the mouth that makes content in the whole land, (sm-) priest, master of all wardrobes, entering into the secrets of heaven, of earth [and of the nether world];" "master of secret things of the palace;" "attached to Nekhen, prophet of Mat, chief justice."[c]

---

[a]See Hammamat Stela of Ramses IV, l. 14 (IV, 466); also Brugsch (*Aegyptologie*, 216 f., note). In Papyrus Hood there is a "*chief of the quarry-service of the whole land*" (p. 216).

[b]A cliff-tomb in the hill of Shekh Abd-el-Kurna on the west shore at Thebes, known as Stuart's Tomb, No. 108. It was discovered by one "Mustapha Noak" in 1860, and opened successively by Ebers in 1872 and Villiers Stuart in 1879 (see Wiedemann, *Recueil*, XVII, 9). It was inadequately published by Stuart in *The Funeral Tent of an Egyptian Queen*, 89 ff.; and *Egypt after the War*, Pl. 27, and pp. 386–88. Bouriant has some notes on the tomb in *Revue archéologique*, 1882, N. S., XXIII, 279–84. and *Recueil*, VI, 55, 56. Nearly all the inscriptions were published by Piehl with great accuracy in *Zeitschrift für ägyptische Sprache*, 1883, 127–30; 1887, 37–39. I excavated the unpublished inscriptions and recopied the whole in December, 1894. Some signs had been lost since Piehl made his copies. The accompanying translations are based upon a collation with Piehl, and upon my own copies alone, where Piehl had not copied.

[c]These are all the titles in the tomb, as found in my copies.

937. Ramose, as head of the religious, judicial, and administrative organization, must have been the most powerful official at the court of Ikhnaton. He had been vizier under the king's father, Amenhotep III;[a] he was early won over to the Aton faith, and the particular value of his tomb lies in the fact that we may trace in it this conversion of Ramose at a time when Ikhnaton still called himself Amenhotep, and still permitted references to Amon and "*the gods.*" This last term, as well as the name of Amon, has been expunged[b] at a later date. The materials in the tomb are as follows:

Relief Scene[c]

938. A king sits enthroned on the right, his face and figure executed in the usual conventional style; behind him the goddess Mat; before him, with upraised arms, Ramose.

---

[a]It must be the same Ramose who, in an inscription on the island of Sehel, is called: "*Hereditary prince, the two eyes of the king in the whole land, governor of the (residence) city and vizier, Ramose*" (Brugsch, *Thesaurus*, V, 1216, gg = de Morgan, *Catalogue des monuments*, I, 90, No. 79). See also Wiedemann, *Recueil*, 17, 9; Mariette, *Monuments divers*, 70, No. 21; *ibid.*, 72, No. 50; and Petrie, *Season in Egypt*, 13, No. 334.

[b]This expungement is very significant; for it is not the name of a particular god, but the word "*gods*," which is expunged. I have found this same erasure of the word "*gods*" at Karnak in the long offering inscription of Amenhotep III on Pylon III, and in the Coronation Inscription of Thutmose III; also on a number of Eighteenth Dynasty monuments in European museums. With this fact compare the erasure of the gods' names at Karnak as noted by Lepsius: "Auch hier [Temple of Ptah, northern Karnak] waren die Namen des Ptah und Amon wie auch der Hathor und ihre Figuren alle ausgekratzt; so auch auf dem Architrav der Thüre die Namen des Ptah. Ebenso sind sämmtliche Götter im Tempel zu Med. Habu und in dem hinteren Theile des grossen Tempels von Karnak ausgekratzt; die Götterverfolgung muss also nicht nur dem Amon gegolten haben, sondern viel allgemeiner gewesen sein."—Lepsius (*Denkmäler*, Text, III, 8; read also end of section), and see *ibid.*, 31. By comparing Leyden Stela, V, 26, and Vienna Stela, 53, it will be seen that the wife of a certain "*overseer of the cattle of Amon*" was a "*musician of Upwawet;*" but when her husband became "*overseer of the cattle of the house of Aton,*" she was obliged to drop her title (see Baillet, *Notice sur la collection égyptienne de l'Abbé Desnayers*, 40, and *Recueil*, 23, 144; also Bergmann, *Recueil*, IX, 42). The persecution therefore included all the gods. See Breasted, *Zeitschrift für ägyptische Sprache*, 40, 108–10.

[c]Inner wall, first chamber, left of door.

939. The accompanying inscriptions are:

Over the King[a]

King of Upper and Lower Egypt, Lord of the Two Lands, — re, given life, Son of Re, his beloved, Amenhotep, God, Ruler of Thebes, great in his duration.

Over Mat

Mat, daughter of Re, presider over the palace, mistress of heaven, ruler of the gods. She gives myriads of years.

Over Ramose[b]

940. Utterance of the governor of the (residence) city, the vizier, Ramose, triumphant, for the benefit of thy ka: "An adjuration to thy father, 'Harakhte-Rejoicing-in-the-Horizon, in his name: Heat-Which-is-[in]-Aton,'[c] that he may praise thee, that he may love thee, that he may establish thee, that he may give to thee myriads of years (so that) thy annals may be jubilees; that all lands may be under thy feet, that he may fell thy foes, dead or alive; that all joy may be with thee, all health with thee, all life with thee, and that thou mayest abide upon the throne of Re forever."

Relief Scene[d]

941. Under the radiating sun-disk stand a king and[e] queen, worshiping, all in the peculiar Amarna style. They are in a building, doubtless a part of the Theban Aton-temple. Outside are groups of bowing officials.

942. The inscriptions are these:

---

[a]In two lines; a third mutilated line is omitted above. Over the king's head is also the winged sun-disk, with its usual inscription: "*The Edfuan (Horus) great god, etc.*" This disappears entirely during the later Aton movement.

[b]This entire speech of Ramose to the king appears twice over his head, with slight variants.

[c]This and the mention in the Silsileh inscription are the earliest occurrences of Aton's name; it is not yet in the cartouche.

[d]Inner wall, first chamber, right of door.

[e]There are no children present as usual in such scenes so common at Amarna. This is perhaps another indication of the early date of this tomb in the reign.

By the Sun-Disk

ᵃ"Harakhte-Rejoicing-in-the-Horizon; in his name: Heat-Which-is-in-Aton," residing in "Aton-⌈is-Found⌉-in-the-House-of-Aton."ᵇ

By the King

Lord of the Two Lands, Nefer[khepru]re- —, given life, Lord of Diadems, Amenhotep, God, Ruler of Thebes, great in his duration.

Over the Queen

Great King's-wife, his beloved, Mistress of the Two Lands, — — living, flourishing.

943. These two reliefs show, first: that the Aton faith was in full swing under an Amenhotep whose prenomen begins like that of Ikhnaton; second, a king with the unmistakable features of Ikhnaton, worshiping the latter's peculiar god, appearing in public with his queen, as only Ikhnaton did, bears the name "Amenhotep." This is proof positive of the identity of Ikhnaton and Amenhotep IV.

944. The remaining reliefs illustrate the high favor of Ramose with the king.

Scene

The king stands at the left holding audience; before him in successive moments appears Ramose, kissing the earth, kneeling, standing decorated with gold, departing with servants bearing the gold collars just received from

---

ᵃThe god's two names are here in cartouches.

ᵇThis is the name of the Aton-temple at Thebes, in which the reliefs represent the king and queen as standing. The phrase "red image of Aton" (Bouriant, *Le Tombeau de Ramsès à Chêikh-abd-el-Gournah*, p. 7) is due to reading the bird here as the "red" bird ($d\check{s}r$), but even then the translation is impossible, for the word "image" is lacking. "*Gem-Aton*" is of uncertain meaning, but the name was also applied by Ikhnaton to a new city founded by him for the Aton-worship in Nubia, in the central cataract region. This Nubian city survived a thousand years under the name "Gem-Aton," and is mentioned several times on the Nastesen Stela (see my remarks, *Zeitschrift für ägyptische Sprache*, 40, 106 ff.).

the king, and finally issuing from the palace, when he is met by congratulating friends, rejoicing and carrying flowers.

Inscriptions

945. The inscriptions were very brief, and are now mostly too fragmentary for translation, but the speech of the king to Ramose contains interesting references to the origin of the Aton faith, unfortunately much broken. It is as follows:

"[a]The words of Re are before thee, ——— of my august father, who taught me their ⌜essence⌝, — — them to me. All that is, his — since he equipped the land ——— in order to ⌜exalt⌝ me since the time of the god. It was known in my heart, opened to my face, I understood — — — —."

946. The king is evidently referring to the revelation of the Aton faith directly to himself. To this Ramose makes the following remarkable reply:

"Thy monuments shall endure like the heavens, for thy duration is like Aton therein. The existence of thy monuments is like the existence of the heavens; thou art the Only One of [Aton], in possession of his designs. Thou hast led the mountains; their secret chambers, the terror of thee is in the midst of them, as the terror of thee is in the hearts of the people; they hearken to thee as the people hearken."[b]

947. An inscription in the doorway might indicate that Ramose was later buried in this tomb; it runs thus:

"I have arrived in peace at my tomb, possessed of the favor of the Good God. I did the pleasure of the king in my time; I did not disregard a regulation which he commanded, I practiced no deceit against the people, in order that I might gain my tomb (ḥr·t), upon the great West of Thebes."

---

[a]These accompanying inscriptions are directly below the upper row, depicting the decoration, and belong with a lower band connected with the same incident. They are only in ink and very faded; I believe my copy of them is the first made. They have never been published.

[b]See similar idea, Kubbân Stela, l. 6 (III, 285).

But doubtless this language is only conventional, for the tomb was never finished, and there is at Amarna the tomb[a] of a Ramose, perhaps the same man who has followed his king to the new capital.

948. This tomb at Thebes is in arrangement, style, and subject of reliefs exactly like those of Amarna, for which it doubtless served as a model. The rich gifts to Ramose which it depicts show how Ikhnaton gained his officials to his cause, while similar scenes upon the walls of almost every Amarna tomb show how he kept them faithful.

THE TELL EL-AMARNA LANDMARKS[b]

949. Having finally broken with the Theban priesthood of Amon, Ikhnaton abandoned Thebes as capital and royal residence, and determined to found a new city devoted exclusively to the service of Aton, the new solar god. The site selected for the new residence and holy city was about one hundred and sixty miles above modern Cairo, on the east bank of

---

[a]No. 11 in Daressy's list (*Recueil*, XV, 50); I copied the inscriptions in the tomb (doorway, thickness, right hand), and they give this Ramose the titles: "*Commander of the army of the Lord of the Two Lands,* ⌜*overseer of the White House*⌝ *of Amenhotep III*," which do not correspond with those of the Theban Ramose; but the rapid and sudden changes of the time may have transferred him to the head of the army. See also Wiedemann (*Recueil*, XVII, 9, 10) who opposes the identity.

[b]These fourteen landmarks are huge stelæ varying in size from K, which "is 5 feet wide and 8 feet 3 inches high," to U, which is "14½ feet wide and about 26 feet high." They are cut into the limestone cliffs, and the quality of the stone is such that they have suffered extremely from wind and weather. No one stela contains a completely preserved text, but by combining all those thus far published, a complete text of the second class of stelæ (the original six) was obtained. Professor Petrie has lettered all these stelæ on his map (*Tell el-Amarna*, Pl. XXXIV), and furnished the first complete account of them. I have followed his lettering. Of the fourteen stelæ (one more discovered since Petrie's map was made) I was able to secure copies of eight, as follows:

1. A (northwest corner); Prisse, *Monuments égyptiens*, XIV, ll. 20–25 (end); Daressy, *Recueil*, XV, 61.

2. B (middle, west side, Gebel Tûne); Lepsius, *Denkmäler*, III, 91, *a–f* (only

the Nile, at a point where the cliffs, suddenly retreating some three miles from the river, and as suddenly approaching it again, over five miles lower down, thus with the river inclose a roughly semicircular plain about three miles wide by five miles long. In this plain he built his new city,[a] called Akhetaton, "*Horizon of Aton*," but it was his design from the first to consecrate and devote to the city and its god's service a large domain around it.

950. For this purpose he established, above and below the two points where the cliffs leave the river, a northern and southern boundary line, the two being about eight miles apart, and running from cliff to cliff clear across the Nile valley, which here varies from twelve to seventeen and a half miles in width. The boundaries were then marked by fourteen splendid stelæ cut into the cliffs, some of them being as high as twenty-six feet. As the cliffs formed a natural boundary on the east and west, the northern and southern lines were of chief importance; hence the east and west ends of these two lines, where they struck the cliffs, were marked by four large stelæ cut in the rocks. But, probably owing to the irregularity of the cliff lines, another pair were placed opposite each other in the eastern and western cliffs, midway between the northern and south-

---

reliefs and accompanying names, date, etc.); Champollion, *Notices descriptives*, II, 321 f.

    3. F (southwest corner); hand copy by Petrie.
    4. J (southernmost on river front, east side); hand copy by Petrie.
    5. K (just north of J); Lepsius, *Denkmäler*, III, 110, *b*.
    6. S (southeast corner); best preserved of all; photograph and copy by Daressy, *Recueil*, XV, 52; Prisse, *Monuments égyptiens*, XIII.
    7. U (middle east side); Prisse, *ibid.*, XII, and hand copy by Petrie.
    8. X (close by Shekh Sa ᶜ ȋd, matching K on the south); recently discovered by Mr. N. de G. Davies, to whose kindness I am indebted for a squeeze.
    Professor Petrie kindly placed his copies of F, J, and U at my disposal.

    [a]The modern name, "Tell el-Amarna," now universally applied to the locality, is a corruption of "El Amarieh;" see Petrie, *Tell el-Amarna*, 2.

ern lines^a (U and B). Finally, the irregularity of the cliffs forced the erection of no less than eight more, all on the east side, chiefly where the cliffs are broken by incoming valleys, across which the new stelæ carry the line (total, fourteen). It is not improbable that there are others yet undiscovered.

951. In form these stelæ are practically all of one design, showing at the top a relief scene in which appear the king, queen, and either two or three daughters, standing before an altar and adoring Aton, whose rays, terminating in hands, extend to them the symbol of life. All, including the god, are accompanied by their names in cartouches, and their titles. The inscription, beginning in the relief-field with a few vertical lines, continues below in horizontal lines. On either side of the stelæ were often altars with statues of the king and his family.

The stelæ (called *"landmarks"* in the translation) fall, according to content, into two classes.

952. The first class is represented by two stelæ,[b] containing a detailed endowment of the god, probably not confined to the gift of Akhetaton. They were of great length, containing nearly eighty lines each, but are so fragmentary that only a few detached phrases in the first half can be discerned.

953. After the date,[c] the introduction, the account of the king's first visit to Akhetaton, and the oblation, all being identical with the beginning of the stelæ of the second class

---

[a]See conclusion of Stela A (§ 971), which is different from that of the others, and clearly defines the position of the original six stelæ.

[b]These two stelæ (K and X) occupy important positions: one at the north and the other at the south end of the semicircle, where the cliffs approach to the river-bank above and below the city on the east bank.

[c]The date is lost on X; in K, Lepsius, *Denkmäler*, has "*year 4*," with signs of weathering; but the month, which is the same as on all the second class of stelæ (which are all of year 4), shows that Lepsius, *Denkmäler*, has misread 6 as 4.

(§§ 959 ff.), these two stelæ proceed with a glorification of the king:

All [lands], all countries, the Haunebu [come to him] bearing their impost, their tribute upon their backs, [for] him who makes their life.

954. Then follows apparently the king's solemn asseveration, in which he proclaims the gift of Akhetaton to Aton:

His majesty raised his hand to heaven, to him who made him, even Aton, [⌈saying: "This is my testimony⌉], forever, and this is my witness forever, this landmark . . . . I have made Akhetaton for my father as a dwelling for —. I have [⌈demarked⌉] Akhetaton on its south, on its north, on its west, on its east. I shall not pass beyond the southern landmark of Akhetaton toward the south, nor shall I pass beyond the northern landmark of [Akhetaton toward the north].[a] . . . . He has made its circuit for his own —; he hath made his ⌈altar⌉ in its midst, whereon I make offering to him; this is it."

955. Then follows the statement that Akhetaton shall be a new capital, where he will hold audience for all the land (cf. III, 63, Harmhab):

"The whole land [⌈shall come hither⌉] for the beautiful seat of Akhetaton shall be another seat, and I will give them audience,[b] whether they be north, or south, or west, or east. . . . ."

956. After a short break, the text proceeds with the building of the temple:

"I have made Akhetaton in this [place] — — — — — that he may be satisfied therewith, forever and ever. I have made a temple of Aton for Aton, my father, in Akhetaton in this [place]. I have made — — [for Aton], my father, in Akhetaton in this place. I have made the 'Shadow-of-Re,' [for Aton, my father, in Akhetaton in this place] . . . ."[c]

---

[a]The only two stelæ bearing this text stand at the extreme north and south.

[b]Lit., "*hearing.*"

[c]Still another of these phrases follows here, but the object made is lost; possibly each refers to a different temple at Akhetaton, of which there were at least three called "*Shadow of Re*" (see §§ 1017 ff.).

957. From here on the text is in such fragmentary condition that little can be made out. It is probable that these thirty-seven lines contained the decree endowing Aton with lands and revenues outside of Akhetaton. This is practically certain in the following fragment:

"As for my ⌜ground⌝ in every town (⌜dmy⌝) of the north, of the south, of the west, or of the east, it is my — —; it shall be brought — my — for Akhetaton."

In l. 45 "*Kush*" is mentioned, and it may be that the decree here passes from the gift of lands in Egypt to those in Kush.

958. The second class of stelæ, of which there are twelve,[a] are not so long, but to them belong the original six, three on each side of the river, which were later increased to twelve. After the date and titulary they record the king's presence in Akhetaton on that day, on his first visit there (ll. 1-4), his exploration of the city, and oblation to Aton (ll. 5-8) in celebration of the foundation of the city, exactly as in the first class of stelæ (§§ 952 ff.). The king then proceeds to the southeastern stela (S), where, after a few words in praise of his queen and the princesses, his daughters, he declares the boundaries of his new city, marked by six stelæ, four at the eastern and western ends of the northern and southern boundary lines (§ 962 and § 964), and two more (§ 963), one in the eastern and one in the western cliffs, midway between the northern and southern boundary lines. The size of the inclosure is then indicated (§ 965),

---

[a]They occupy both sides of the river, three on the west and nine on the east bank. The three on the west are the three original stelæ, matching three original stelæ on the east side, which were later increased to nine on the east side. The northernmost of the original eastern three has never been found; X, at present the northernmost on the east side, belongs to the first class, and not to the second class, to which the original six belong. The six are: (1) on the west side: A, B, and F; (2) on the east side: S, U, and the northeast stela still undiscovered. A differs in its conclusion from the others (see §§ 970-72).

and the whole is solemnly conveyed as a permanent gift to Aton (§ 966), the other landmarks being appealed to as containing a similar record (§ 967), which will in all cases be renewed in case it has suffered defacement or erasure from any cause (§ 968). A later note (§ 969) in conclusion records an inspection by the king in the year 8.

Introduction

959. Year 6, fourth month of the second season, thirteenth day.

¹Live the Good God, satisfied with truth, lord of heaven, lord of Aton; live the great one who illuminates the Two Lands; live my father; live "Harakhte-Rejoicing-in-the-Horizon, in his name: Heat-Which-is-in-Aton," who is given life forever and ever.

Live Horus: Mighty-Bull, Beloved-of-Aton; Favorite of the Two Goddesses:[a] Great-in-Kingship-in-Akhetaton; Golden Horus: Bearer-of-the-Name-of-Aton; King of Upper and Lower Egypt, Living in Truth, Lord of the Two Lands: [Neferkhepru]re-Wanre;[b] Son of Re, Living in Truth, Lord of Diadems: Ikhnaton ($Y^\jmath\ \hbar\text{-}n\text{-}Ytn$), great in duration, ²given life forever and ever; Good God — whose beauty Aton created, the really good-hearted toward Irsu,[c] satisfying him with that which pleases his ka, doing that which is useful for him that begat him; ³offering the earth to him that placed him upon his throne, supplying his eternal house with millions and hundred-thousands of things, exalter of Aton, magnifier of his name; who causes that the earth should belong to Irsu, ⁴Ikhnaton.[d]

---

[a]In Egyptian one word *nb·ty*, a feminine dual noun, with an adjectival ending, so that the whole means "*he who belongs to, or is protégé of, the two goddesses,*" but the word for the latter is not as prominent as in English; hence Ikhnaton retained the old royal titulary without change, even including this somewhat compromising title, to preserve the old titulary complete. This is one of the few compromises with a traditional form by Ikhnaton. That he no longer retained a belief in the two goddesses is shown by the fact that the vulture, which regularly appears with wings outspread in protection over the heads of the other kings, is never found with Ikhnaton, but it is replaced by the sun-disk enveloping Ikhnaton in its rays.

[b]The first part is the Napkhurīya of the Amarna Letters; the whole means: "*Beautiful is the Being of Re; the Unique One of Re.*"

[c]*Yr-sw* = "*He that made him.*"

[d]Last two names of the titulary are repeated in full, as in l. 1.

Hereditary princess, great in the palace, lovely of face, beautiful in the double plume, lady of joy, abounding in favor, at the sound of whose voice there is rejoicing;[a] the Great King's-Wife, his beloved, the Mistress of the Two Lands, Nefernefruaton-Nofretete.

Founding of the City

960. ⁵On this day one was in Akhetaton in the pavilion of ⌈woven stuff⌉ which his majesty, L. P. H., made in Akhetaton, the name of which is: "Aton-is-Satisfied." His majesty, L. P. H., appeared upon a great chariot[b] ⁶of electrum, like Aton, when he rises in the horizon; he filled the Two Lands with his loveliness. On beginning the goodly way to Akhetaton, at the first exploration of it[c] which his majesty, L. P. H., made, in order to found it as a monument to Aton, according to the command ⁷of his father Aton,[d] who is given life forever and ever; in order to make for him a monument in its midst. One caused that a great oblation should be offered, consisting of bread, beer, oxen, calves, cattle, fowl, wine, ⌈gold⌉, incense, all beautiful flowers. On this day ⁸was founded Akhetaton for the living Aton, that favor and love might be received, on behalf of King Ikhnaton.[e]

King Goes to Southeastern Landmark

961. As one proceeded ⁹southward, his majesty halted in his chariot in the presence of his father Aton, upon the southeastern[f] mountain of Akhetaton, while the rays of ¹⁰Aton were upon him in satisfying life, making youthful his limbs every day. Vivat[g] which the king, Ikhnaton,

---

[a]Compare the description of Mutemuya (British Museum Boat, No. 43), "*Filling the hall with the fragrance of her dew.*" See also § 995.

[b]S has: "*upon a span of horses (and) upon a chariot, etc.*"

[c]Lit., "*at the first time of finding it.*"

[d]The full double name is used here and later.

[e]Under the orthodox régime offerings were officially made "*on behalf of*" ($hr\ \underline{d}\cdot\underline{d}\cdot$) the king (see § 57). We see here that their specific object was "*favor and love;*" of course, those of the god. It is this which is referred to in the stereotyped form of the royal oath: "*As Re loves me, as Amon favors me.*" Cf. IV, 958D.

[f]This stela (S), from which this translation is made, is at the southeast corner. The other stelæ vary the text to suit their respective locations.

[g]This rendering of the word ꜥnh here is made certain by the introduction to the second date (l. 25): "*Repetition of the vivat (ꜥ nh),*" followed by the date. The full vivat is the ꜥ nh, followed by the entire titulary of the god, as we have it at the beginning of the inscription; but to save space the second date is introduced merely by the words: "*Repetition of the vivat,*" which are thus a kind of abbreviation of the full introduction.

spake: "Live my father, ¹¹Aton, who is given life forever! My heart is joyous over the king's-wife and over her children, who bring long life for[a] the Great King's-Wife, Nofretete, living forever and ever, ¹²with the myriad of years. She is under the hand of the Pharaoh, L. P. H., who brings long life; the king's-daughter, Meretaton; the king's-daughter, Meketaton, her children, being under the hand of the King's-Wife, ¹³their mother, forever and ever. It is my oath by the truth, (namely), that which my heart shall speak; (and) that which I do not speak is falsity; forever and ever.[b]

East and West Ends of Southern Boundary Lines

962. ¹⁴As for the southern landmark, which is upon the eastern mountain of Akhetaton, it is the landmark of Akhetaton, as far as which I make a stand;[c] I shall not pass beyond it toward the south, forever and ever.[d] ¹⁵The southwestern landmark is made over against it, upon the [western] mountain of Akhetaton, opposite.

Middle of Eastern and Western Boundary Lines

963. As for the middle landmark which is upon the eastern mountain of Akhetaton, it is the landmark of Akhetaton, ¹⁶as far as which I make a stand,[c] upon the eastern mountain of Akhetaton; I shall not pass beyond it toward the east, forever and ever. The middle landmark which is upon the western mountain of Akhetaton is made over against it, opposite.

East and West Ends of Northern Boundary Line

964. As for the northeastern landmark of Akhetaton, as far as which I make a stand;[c] it is the northern landmark ¹⁷of Akhetaton;[e] I shall not pass beyond it toward the north, forever and ever. The northern landmark, which is upon the western mountain of Akhetaton is over against it, opposite.

---

[a]Lit., "*who cause that the great king's-wife N. should grow old*," in a good sense, meaning attain old age.

[b]The divergent conclusion of Stela A begins here (see § 970).

[c]Or a "*halt.*"

[d]This formula, repeated on all the stelæ of the second class (except A), may be either a traditional one taken from the legal form used in establishing boundaries; or it may be an extraordinary statement peculiar to this remarkable king, asserting that he will never pass beyond the boundaries of Akhetaton, but remain within his god's domain all his life.

[e]The order of phrases differs slightly from that in the preceding two clauses.

Area Contained

965. ¹⁸Now, as for Akhetaton, from the southern landmarks to the northern landmarks measured between landmark and landmark upon the eastern mountain of Akhetaton, it makes 6 iter, ¹⁹1 khet, 1 half-khet, 1 quarter-khet,[a] and 4 cubits. Likewise, from the southwestern landmark of Akhetaton to the [north]western landmark upon the western mountain of Akhetaton, it makes 6 iter, 1 khet, 1 half-khet, 1 quarter-khet, and 4 cubits; being the same on both sides.

Deed of Gift to Aton

966. ²⁰Now, as for the area within the four landmarks, from the [eastern] mountain [to the western mountain of[b]] Akhetaton opposite, it belongs to my father, Aton, who is given life, forever and and ever; whether mountains, ²¹or cliffs, or marshes, or ⌜—⌝[c] or uplands, or fields, or waters, or towns, or shores, or people, or cattle, or trees, or anything ²²which Aton, my father, has made, ... I have made it for Aton, my father, forever and ever.

Citation of the Other Landmarks

967. Moreover, ²³it is recorded upon the landmark of stone, at the southeastern limit, and at the northeastern limit of Akhetaton likewise. It is recorded upon the western landmark of stone, at the southwestern limit likewise — — ²⁴of Akhetaton.[d]

---

[a]The khet (ḫt) contained 100 cubits, but the iter varies in different localities; here it can be computed, for it is clear that these measurements concern only the original six stelæ, the only ones known to the maker of this text. There is no doubt regarding which stelæ are meant, as some have averred. The discovery of the northeastern stela, high above the river at Shekh Saᶜîd, by Mr. Davies, gives us the northern terminus on the east side for the first time. Previous calculations, starting at the next stela southward (V), have been based on too short a total measurement. The discovery of the Shekh Saᶜîd stela makes the east and west sides of Akhetaton of about the same length as the stela states they were, viz., some 45,830 feet, roughly, over 8¾ miles. This makes the iter here used equal some 4,400 cubits, or 7,587 feet = roughly, 1⅖ miles. This is longer than the iter as given by Griffith (*Proceedings of the Society of Biblical Archæology*, XV, 303–6), and Sethe (*Untersuchungen*, II, 3, 11) could now strike out his minimum of 1⅖ km. But these calculations antedate the discovery of the northeast stela, which was also unknown to Levy, *Recueil*, XVI, 162–72. See also Loret, *Sphinx*, VII, and Sethe, *Zeitschrift für ägyptische Sprache*, 41, 58–60.

[b]The word "*opposite*" renders the restoration practically certain.

[c]M ꜣ wt, a kind of land.

[d]For some reason, perhaps by oversight, the northwestern corner is omitted.

Permanence of the Record

968. It shall not be erased, it shall not be washed out, it shall not be abraded, it shall not be encumbered with detritus, [it] shall not be —. If it should disappear, if it should wear away, if [25]the stela upon which it is, should fall, I will restore it again anew in this place in which it is.

Inspection Two Years Later

969. Repetition of the vivat.[a] In the year 8, in the first month of the second season, the eighth day, [26]one (i. e., his majesty) was in Akhetaton; the Pharaoh, L. P. H., halted, shining in the great chariot of electrum, while inspecting these landmarks of Aton, which are in the eastern mountain, at the southeastern limit of Akhetaton, established forever and ever for the living Aton.

970. The stela at the northwest corner (A) follows the conventional text of all the other stelæ of the second class for thirteen lines,[a] but then proceeds with the position of the stelæ, the demarcation, etc., in a form quite different from all the others of the second class. It runs thus:

Landmarks and Boundaries

971. Said the King of Upper and Lower Egypt, [Neferkheprure-Wanre], Son of Re, living in truth, Ikhnaton, great in his duration, when setting up these landmarks [21]— — — (cartouche) given life, forever and ever: "As for these [6[c] landmarks] which I have set up at the boundaries of Akhetaton, the 3 landmarks upon the eastern mountain of Akhetaton, together with the 3 landmarks opposite them: [22][the southern landmark which is upon the eastern mountain of][d] Akhetaton as far as the [landmark upon] the western [mountain] of Akhetaton shall be for the southern boundary of Akhetaton; the northern land-

---

[a]See above note on l. 10, § 961.
[b]As numbered on Stela S.
[c]The numeral is broken away, except two strokes.
[d]The restoration is clear from the word "*likewise*" at the end of the definition of the northern boundary (l. 23); Daressy has not left room for it in his publication, but the length of other lines (like 24) shows that enough is lost for this restoration. The northernmost and southernmost eastern and western stelæ form the eastern and western termini of the northern and southern boundaries.

mark which is upon the eastern mountain of Akhetaton, [23]going to the landmark [upon] the western [mountain] of Akhetaton, shall be the northern boundary of Akhetaton likewise; the middle landmark which is upon the eastern mountain of Akhetaton, likewise the middle landmark which is opposite it upon the western mountain of Akhetaton."[a]

Deed to Aton

972. "Now, as for the width of Akhetaton, mountain to mountain [24]from its eastern horizon to its western horizon, it shall belong to my father, Aton,[b] given life, forever and ever; whether its mountains, or its cliffs, — — —, or its —, or all its people, or all its cattle, or anything which Aton causes to exist, upon which his rays shine, [25]or anything — — — of Akhetaton, they shall belong to my father, the living Aton, for the temple of Aton in Akhetaton, forever and ever. They shall be offered to his ka, the beautiful rays receiving them ————."

ASSUAN TABLET OF THE ARCHITECT BEK[c]

973. The presence of Ikhnaton's architect and master-sculptor at Assuan is, of course, to be explained by the fact of the quarries there, from which he was taking stone for the temples at Akhetaton.[d] It therefore bears the same relation to the Amarna temple as the Silsileh quarry inscription bears to the Theban Aton-temple. The expungement of Ikhnaton's figure from the relief shows that the persecution of his memory was extended as far south as the cataract,[e] and the fragments found at Memphis,[f] Heliopolis,[g] and

---

[a]This list gives the position of all the six stelæ and the limits thus marked; the territory thus inclosed is then taken up.

[b]Only the god's double cartouche is preserved.

[c]Cut on the rocks at Assuan; published by Mariette, *Monuments divers*, 26, u = de Morgan, *Catalogue des monuments*, I, 40, No. 174. Neither is accurate, and the relief faces opposite directions in the two publications.

[d]See tomb of Hui, §§ 1016 ff. [e]See also § 896.

[f]See "On Some Remains of the Disk Worshippers Discovered at Memphis," by Sir Charles Nicholson, *Transactions of the Royal Society of Literature* (Read, May 20, 1868); and *ibid.*, VIII, 308; also Bouriant, *Recueil*, VI, 52, 53.

[g]Bouriant, *Recueil*, VI, 53.

the Delta cities, show the northern limit of the persecution. The temple for which his Amarna architect labored has been razed to the ground, like all of Ikhnaton's buildings at Amarna, as well as elsewhere. The tablet is as follows:

Relief Scene

974. Before an altar, embraced by the hands terminating the rays of the sun which is above it, stands Bek at the right in gala costume, with a large bouquet of flowers. The space before Bek, on the left of the altar, contained the figure of Ikhnaton, as the inscription over Bek shows; but this figure has been obliterated[a] by the king's enemies. The scene is accompanied by the following inscriptions:

On Each Side of the Sun

975. [b]——— Living, great Aton, celebrator of jubilees, lord of heaven, lord of earth, lord of every circuit of Aton, lord of the house of Aton in Akhetaton.

Over Bek

Giving praise to the Lord of the Two Lands, obeisance to Wanre (Ikhnaton), by the chief of works in the Red Mountain,[c] the assistant ($ḥr$- [c]) whom his majesty himself taught, chief of sculptors on the great and mighty monuments of the king, in the house of Aton in Akhetaton, Bek (Bk), son of the chief of sculptors, Men (Mn), born of the matron, Royenet ($R^{ɔ}$-$yn·t$).

976. Beside this relief appears Bek's father, "*Men, chief of works in the Red Mountain, chief of sculptors on the great and mighty monuments of the king,*" presenting a food-offering to a statue of Amenhotep III,[d] under whom he, of

---

[a]The left half of the relief, which doubtless contained more inscriptions, and another figure is weathered off.

[b]Two cartouches, with content erased. They, of course, contained the god's two names.

[c]See I, 493, l. 15, note.

[d]This is not necessarily an apotheosis of Amenhotep III, as has been supposed, and is therefore not in conflict with the Aton cult.

course, held the offices which his son inherited. To the titles of these offices, when inherited by Bek, he added the necessary phrases to make them fit the new régime of Ikhnaton.

THE TELL EL-AMARNA TOMBS[a]

977. Like all ancient Egyptian cities, the life of Akhetaton, so much of it as has survived, must be sought rather in the city of the dead than in the city of the living; and far more of Akhetaton has survived in its cemetery than in its streets. The tombs are themselves the product of the king's bounty, and we find frequent statement of this in such remarks as this of a relative of the deceased official: *"We see the good things which the Good Ruler hath done for his table-scribe (Ani), commanding for him goodly burial in Akhetaton."*[b] The tombs are themselves therefore tangible evidence of the royal favor in claiming which, each of the owners of these tombs has used so much space on their walls.

---

[a]These tombs are cut into the limestone cliffs surrounding the plain of Amarna on the east side of the river. They are twenty-five in number, and fall into two groups, a northern (six) and a southern (nineteen). See Petrie's map, *Tell el-Amarna*, Pl. XXXV; and excellent description, Baedeker's *Egypt*, 1902, 195–99. The hymns here translated are usually engraved on the thickness or edge of the doorway (see Mariette, *Voyage dans la haute Egypte*, I, Pl. V); Davies, *Amarna*, I, 47, 48). The relief scenes occupy the walls of the chambers. Neither scenes nor inscriptions have ever been completely published. Lepsius published twenty-one plates of selected material (*Denkmäler*, III, 91–111), the first basis for study of Amenhotep IV's reign. The French Mission Archéologique au Caire spent a few days there and published some new material (Bouriant, *Mémoires de la mission française au Caire*, I, 1 ff.), but it is not reliable. Finally Daressy has furnished a useful sketch of the tombs with some new material (*Recueil*, XV, 36–50). Many scenes have also appeared in the old publications (see list in Davies, *Amarna*, I, 3 ff.). On the basis of the above publications I published a study of the hymns: *De Hymnis in Solem sub Rege Amenophide IV Conceptis* (Berlin, 1894). For the following translations, I had also my own copies of all the hymns at Amarna, made in the winter of 1894–95. A full and accurate publication of all the tombs has been begun by N. de G. Davies, for the Egyptian Exploration Fund, and two volumes have appeared.

[b]Tomb of Ani (*Recueil*, XV, 45). Such a practice is very old (see e. g. I, 242 ff.), but is nowhere so frequently mentioned as at Amarna.

978. But the walls also carry graphic evidence of that favor. Of the inscribed tombs at Amarna many show the owner standing before Ikhnaton and receiving rich decorations and gifts of gold. It is clear that Ikhnaton was holding all his great officials faithful to his reform, only by such means. These tombs contain, besides these scenes, many pictures from the life of the town, as illustrated in the functions of this or that official: the houses and gardens, the palaces and temples, even such a scene as that of the chief of the gendarmes bringing in prisoners.[a] All such scenes have been studied, and their inscriptions as far as possible, or useful, translated below.

979. The long inscriptions contain all that we know of the Aton faith, in the form of hymns. These hymns are of two classes: (1) those recited by the king; (2) those recited by his officials. The hymns of the first class are of chiefly religious interest, and contain almost exclusively praise of Aton. Those of the second class, besides praise of Aton, contain also encomiums of the king and queen, mingled with an account of the reciter's faithfulness and favor with the king, prayers for the king, as well as for prosperity and "*goodly burial*" for the reciter himself. Facts of historical importance are thus brought out. These hymns, therefore, have been included herein as historical documents; but the hymns of the first class, although they contain the religious ideas which characterized a great historical movement, have not been translated here.[b]

980. The following six hymns of the second class include all such hymns not too fragmentary for translation. Nu-

---

[a] Tomb of Mahu.
[b] The longer will be found in the author's *De Hymnis in Solem sub Rege Amenophide IV Conceptis*, with Latin translation, and thence translated by Griffith in Petrie, *History of Egypt*, II, 215–18, and in the author's *History of Egypt* (New York, 1905); and also in the section devoted to religion, which will later appear in this series.

merous short and mutilated hymns, not included here, have been studied and employed wherever applicable or useful. The relief scenes, wherever accompanied by historically important inscriptions, have likewise been employed.

Tomb of Merire II

981. One of the most important scenes[a] at Amarna, unaccompanied by inscriptions, is in the tomb of Merire II. It shows Ikhnaton, his queen, and six daughters, in a kiosk, or covered dais. The king and queen enthroned side by side have just stepped from their sedan chairs, which are set down before the dais. With trumpet sounding, Egyptian troops defile before them, and on either side of the military appear foreign embassies with their tribute: Nubians, Syrians, Libyans, and especially Hittites, who are here depicted for the first time on an Egyptian monument. They bear elaborately decorated vessels, undoubtedly of gold and silver.

TOMB OF MERIRE I[b]

982. The reliefs and inscriptions in this tomb are of unusual interest. The king, proceeding to the temple of Aton, is shown riding in his chariot, accompanied by four daughters, by soldiers and officials.[c] Before its door are the priests, who greet him with cries of *"Welcome!"* and one

---

[a]In tomb No. 2 (northern group), belonging to a certain Merire (not to be confused with Merire of tomb No. 4, who is earlier: Davies, *Amarna*, I), whom we call Merire II. Published from a sketch by Nestor l'Hôte, in Amélineau, *Histoire de la sépulture*, Pl. XCVI; and in Davies, *Amarna*, II, Pls. XXXVII–LX, 38–42.

[b]A cliff-tomb (No. 4) in the northern group of Amarna (Lepsius, No. 3); partially published by Lepsius, *Denkmäler*, III, 92–97, *d;* superb sketches by Nestor l'Hôte, in Amélineau's *Histoire de la sépulture*, II, Pl. 85, 92.; plans, also Prisse, *Histoire de l'art égyptien*, and often, e. g., Erman, *Life in Ancient Egypt*. The entire tomb has been published by Davies, *Rock Tombs of El Amarna*, Part I, "Tomb of Meryra" (London, 1903). I had also my own copies.

Davies, *Amarna*, I, Pls. X–XX.

may distinguish a reference to "*the first impost of Aton in the Aton-temple in Akhetaton.*" The occasion is, therefore, the celebration of the reception of the first dues of the god in the new capital; hence the temple[a] shows a richly crowded altar in the court and many chambers filled with food and drink. Such scenes are naturally depicted in the tomb of Merire, who was "*High Priest*" or "*great seer*" (*wr-m$^{\ni}$*), of Aton—a title adopted from the sun-temple of Heliopolis. His appointment to this exalted office is recorded in the tomb. The king, with the queen and daughters, is shown upon the balcony[b] of his palace before which appear Merire and his friends, acclaiming the praise of the king and queen:

983. "He trains[c] the youth and the generations;[d] the good ruler! As surely as the Aton rises, he shall be forever."

The "great seer" of the Aton in the Aton-temple in Akhetaton, Merire, triumphant, says: "How numerous are the things which the Aton is able to give, satisfying his heart."

984. A lady of the household of Merire, named Tenr, doubtless his wife, sings praise of Aton and the royal family:[e]

"Thy rising is beautiful, O [f]'Living-Sun, Horizon-Ruler, Rejoicing-in-the-Horizon,[f] [g]in his name: Heat-Which-is-in-Aton,'[g] who is given life, forever and ever. O living Aton, beside whom there is no other, who heals the eyes with his rays, the maker of all things that are. When

---

[a]For an account of these representations of the Aton-temple, see especially Erman, *Life in Ancient Egypt*, 285 ff.

[b]Lepsius, *Denkmäler*, III, 97, *b;* only the edge of the balcony is shown in Lepsius, *Denkmäler*, without the royal pair. The complete scene is published by Davies, *Amarna*, I, Pls. VI–VIII.

[c]*Š·ḫpr*, see III, 565.   [d]Or: "*classes*" (*ḏ·mw*); see IV, 402.

[e]Lepsius, *Denkmäler*, III, 97, *a;* Davies, *Amarna*, I, xxxvi: she does not belong to the company before the king, but her words well suit the occasion, especially her reference to the queen's presence beside the king. Her hymn or song was common property, for much of it appears also verbatim on the tomb doorposts of Ahmose (§§ 1004 ff.), and assists in correcting the errors in this tomb of Merire. I had also my own copy, but the inscription has been much mutilated since Lepsius' day.

[f]First cartouche.   [g]Second cartouche.

thou risest in the eastern horizon of heaven, to make live all that thou hast made, even men, cattle, them that fly and them that (only) flutter, and all reptiles that are in the earth, they live when they see thee, they sleep when thou settest. Grant thou thy beloved son, living in truth, Lord of the Two Lands, Neferkheprure-Wanre (Ikhnaton) that he may live with thee forever, that the Great King's-Wife, his beloved, Mistress of the Two Lands, Nefernefruaton-Nofretete, living forever and ever, may be by his side, doing that which pleases thy heart, seeing all that thou hast made every day. May he rejoice at the sight of thy beauty; grant to him eternity as king of the Two Lands."

The great favorite of the Mistress of the Two Lands, Tenr ($Ty\text{-}n\text{-}r^{\flat}$), triumphant; she says: "Praise to thee, O [⌈fashioner⌉] of years, creator of months, maker of days, reckoner of hours, lord of duration, by [whom] reckoning is made. [Grant] thou thy duration as Aton, to thy son, Wanre (Ikhnaton).''

985. The king proclaims from the balcony his appointment of Merire as High Priest ("*great seer*") of Aton thus:

King's Speech

[a]Said the king, living in truth, Lord of the Two Lands: Neferkheprure-Wanre, to the "great seer" of the Aton, Merire: "Behold, I am appointing thee for myself, to be 'great seer' of the Aton in the temple of Aton in Akhetaton, ⌈Irsu of thy beloved⌉[b], saying: "O my hearer of the call ($Sdm\ ^c\ š$), who hears the teaching. As for any commission with which thou art charged, my heart is satisfied therewith; I give to thee the office, saying: 'Thou shalt eat the food of Pharaoh, L. P. H., thy lord in the house of Aton.'"

986. In another scene[c] the reliefs depict further honors received from the king by Merire. Leaning on his staff as he stands before one of the richly filled magazines of the temple, and accompanied by the queen and his daughters,

---

[a]Lepsius, *Denkmäler*, III, 97, *b*; Davies, *Amarna*, I, VIII.

[b]"*Irsu*" (*Yr-sw*), or "*he that made him*," is a circumlocution for "*father*," often applied to a god; "*thy beloved*" is the king himself. The whole is therefore probably an epithet of the god meaning "*father of the king.*" "*Doing it for love of thee*" is an attractive rendering, but forbidden by the grammar.

[c]Lepsius, *Denkmäler*, 97, *e*; Davies, *Amarna*, I, xxv, xxix–xxxiii.

the king commands that Merire be decorated with gold. The fortunate official stands in the royal presence with arms upraised in praise, while attendants hang golden collars upon his neck, and four scribes record the gifts. The inscriptions furnish us with the words[a] of the king and his favorite:

Words of the King

987. [b]Speech of the King of Upper and Lower Egypt, living in truth, Lord of the Two Lands, Neferkheprure-Wanre, [to] the overseer of the silver-house, [concerning] the officer ($w^{?\cdot}w$), "great seer" of the Aton in Akhetaton, Merire: "Put gold at his throat and at his back, and gold on his legs, because of his hearing the teaching of Pharaoh, L. P. H., concerning every saying in[c] these beautiful seats which Pharaoh has made in the sanctuary[d] in the Aton-house of Aton in Akhetaton, filled with every good thing, with much corn and southern grain, the Aton[e]-offerings of the Aton."

Merire's Reply

988. "Great seer" of the Aton in the Aton-temple in Akhetaton, fan-bearer on the right of the king, favorite of the Lord of the Two Lands, Merire; he says: "Health —, the beautiful youthfulness of the Aton; grant that he may attain this age;[f] set him forever and ever.

TOMB OF EYE[g]

989. Eye, who afterward became king, has left a fine scene in his tomb, showing the royal family on the palace

---

[a]Lepsius, *Denkmäler, ibid.*; Davies, *ibid.*, xxx.
[b]Lepsius, *Denkmäler*, III, 97, *e;* Davies, *Amarna*, I, xxx.
[c]Possibly "*concerning*" (*ḥr*).   [d]$Ḥ\cdot t\text{-}bnbn$.
[e]The old word, "*god*" (*ntr*), is evidently avoided here, for in the old term, "*divine offerings*" (*ḥtp-ntr*), we have *ntr* replaced by Aton, thus: *ḥtp-Ytn*. There was thus an evident attempt to introduce the word Aton in place of the old word for "*god*" and "*divine;*" this accounts also for the term, "*Aton-house* (*pr-Ytn*) *of the Aton,*" where the old texts have *Ḥt-ntr* ("*god's-house*" = temple).
[f]Lit., "*make this age*," viz., the age of the god; that is, may he live as long a life as the god.
[g]Cliff-tomb (No. 25) at Amarna (No. 1) in the southern group; published by Lepsius, *Denkmäler*, III, 103–6, *a*, and 107, *a*–109. (These scenes [107, *d*–109] are

balcony, throwing down collars and vessels of gold to Eye and his wife Tiy. Unfortunately, the inscriptions such as we find in a similar scene in Merire's tomb (§§ 982 ff.) are here wanting. Only the comments of Eye's servants in the rear of his house have been recorded.[a] Eye had received a similar honor before his marriage with Tiy, and this is likewise depicted in his tomb, but without inscriptions. He was not an official of high rank, being only "*Fan-bearer on the right of the king, master of all the horses of his majesty, his truly beloved scribe, the divine father, Eye (ʾy)*." His favor was doubtless due to his zeal in the new faith and his marriage with Tiy, the "*great nurse, nourisher of the god, adorner of the king*," that is, she had been Ikhnaton's nurse in his childhood.

990. Further indications of his favor[b] are thus recorded:

I was one favored of his lord every day, great in favor from year to year, because of the exceeding greatness of my excellence in his opinion. He doubled for me my favors like the number of the sand; I was the first of the officials at the head of the people . . . . I am a ⌜true⌝ witness, devoid of evil; my name has penetrated into the palace, because of my usefulness to the king, because of my hearing his teaching. . . . .

O everyone that liveth upon earth, every generation that is to be, I will tell you the way of life. I bear you witness that I was praised for what I said, I was ⌜content⌝ by reason of what I did; I was truthful upon earth, making praise to the living Aton.

---

given by Lepsius as from a second tomb [No. 3] of the same man; this is an error which has been perpetuated in the modern histories. Eye had but one tomb at Amarna; it contains all the material given by Lepsius as from two tombs. See Breasted, *The Dial*, Chicago, May 1, 1897, 283.) The two long hymns were published by Bouriant, *Mémoires de la mission française au Caire*, I, 2–5, and Daressy, *Recueil*, XV, 46, 47; both are excessively incorrect. The following translation (of Daressy's hymn) is based on my own copy of the original. Unfortunately, I had not yet made these copies when I published my *De Hymnis in Solem sub Rege Amenophide IV Conceptis*.

[a]Erman gives an excellent description of the whole scene, *Life in Ancient Egypt*, 119–21.

[b]Lepsius, *Denkmäler*, III, 107, d.

Hymn to Aton and the King

991. [2a]Praise to thee! When thou risest in the horizon, O living Aton, lord of eternity. Obeisance to thy rising in heaven, to illuminate every land, with thy beauty. Thy rays are upon thy beloved son. Thy hand [3]has a myriad of jubilees for the King of Upper and Lower Egypt, Neferkheprure-Wanre, thy child who came forth from thy rays. Thou assignest to him thy lifetime and thy years. Thou hearest [4]for him that which is in his heart. He is thy beloved, thou makest him like Aton. When thou risest, eternity is given him; when thou settest, thou givest him everlastingness. Thou begettest him in the morning like thine own forms; thou formest him as thy emanation, [5]like Aton, ruler of truth, who came forth from eternity, son of Re, wearing his beauty, who offers to him the product of his rays; King of Upper and Lower Egypt, living in truth, Lord of the Two Lands, Neferkheprure-Wanre; the Great King's-Wife, Nefernefruaton-Nofretete; living forever and ever.

Hymn to Aton and the King

992. [6]The divine father, favorite of the Good God, fan-bearer at the right of the king, master of all the horses of his majesty, truly beloved scribe of the king, Eye. He saith: "Praise to thee! O living Aton, rising in heaven. He inundates the hearts, and all lands are in festivity because of his rising; their hearts [7]are happy with the joy of their lord, Irsu[b] who shineth upon them. Thy beloved son presents truth before thy beautiful face; thou rejoicest when thou seest him, (for) he came forth from thee; son of eternity, who came forth from [8]Aton, spirit of his spirit, gratifying the heart of Aton. When he rises in heaven, he rejoices in his son; he embraces him with his rays; he gives to him eternity as king, like the [9]Aton; Neferkheprure-Wanre, this god, who made me, who caused my ka to be. Grant that I may be satisfied with seeing thee without ceasing; this lord who forms like Aton; rich in possessions [10]a full Nile every day, making Egypt live. Silver and gold are like the sand of the shore; the land awakens to mighty rejoicing in his ka, the offspring of the Aton. Thou art eternal, Neferkheprure-Wanre; living and sound art thou, for he begat thee."

---

[a]L. 1 contains the usual title: "*Praise of Aton, the king and the queen,*" indicating the content of the hymn.

[b]See § 985.

Self-Praise

993. ¹¹The divine father, etc., Eye; he saith: "I am the truthful one of the king whom he created, the upright one of the Lord of the Two Lands, useful to his lord, following the ka of his majesty, like his favorite, who sees ¹²his beauty when he 'appears' in his palace. I am at the head of the princes, the companions of the king, the first of all the followers of his majesty. He put truth in my body, and my abomination is lying. I know that Wanre rejoices in it (truth), this lord, ¹³wise like Aton, knowing the truth. He doubles to me my favors in silver and gold; I am first of the officials, at the head of the people ($rḫy·t$). ⌜———⌝ ¹⁴the lord ⌜—⌝ me. I have carried out his teaching."

Prayer for Self

994. "May I live praising his ka, may I be satisfied following him; (for) my breath of life is in him, this north wind, this myriad of high Niles every day, Neferkheprure-Wanre. ¹⁵Grant me long life in thy favor. How prosperous is thy favorite, O son of the Aton! All that he does endures and prospers, and the ka of the Lord of the Two Lands is with him forever, so that he is satisfied with life, when he reaches ¹⁶old age. O lord, who forms the people, and creates duration, who performs the pleasant obligation to his favorite, (whose) heart is satisfied with truth, whose abomination is lying. How prosperous is he who hears thy teaching of life, of life; he is satisfied with seeing thee without ceasing, ¹⁷and his two eyes see Aton every day. Grant to me a good old age like thy favorite; grant to me goodly burial by thy command in my house, wherein thou commandest me to rest, in the mountain of Akhetaton, the place of the favorite. May I hear thy sweet voice ¹⁸in the sanctuary[a] when thou performest the pleasant ceremonies[b] of thy father, the living Aton."

Prayer for King and Queen

995. "May he set thee forever and ever; may he endow thee with jubilees like the numbers of the shore, when measured with an ipet-rod; like reckoning the sea when measured with ¹⁹zawets, (or) a statement of the numbering of the mountains when weighed in balances; (or) the feathers of the birds, ²⁰(or) the leaves of the trees, in jubilees for the king, Wanre (Ikhnaton), forever and ever as king; and ²¹for the Great

---

[a]$Ḥ·t$-$bnbn$.   [b]Lit., "*doest the pleasing things.*"

King's-Wife, his beloved, abounding in her beauty;[a] her who sends the Aton to rest[b] with ²²a sweet voice, and with her two beautiful hands, bearing ²³two sistrums, the Mistress of the Two Lands, Nefernefruaton-Nofretete, living forever and ever. May she be by the side of ²⁴Wanre (Ikhnaton) forever and ever as the heavens abide ²⁵under that which is in them. Thy father Aton rises in heaven, to protect thee ²⁶every day, for he begat thee."

Prayer for Self

996. Grant me to kiss the pure ground, to come forth in thy presence with ²⁷offerings for thy father, Aton, of that which thy ka gives. Grant that ²⁸my mortuary priest may abide and flourish for me, (as) for one who is on earth following thy ka, ²⁹⌜who has been exalted⌝ for ⌜my⌝ name's sake, to the place of the favorites, wherein thou makest one to rest. My mouth ³⁰is full of truth, my name is mentioned because of it, for thou hast commanded that I be like thy every favorite who follows thy ka. May I go on, enjoying thy favor after old age.

For the ka of Eye[c] the revered, who lives again.

TOMB OF MAI[d]

997. Mai was one of the most powerful officials at the Amarna court, as is shown by his titles:

Hereditary prince, count, wearer of the royal seal, sole companion, — — his Two Lands, commander of the army of the Lord of the Two Lands, overseer of the "House-of-Sending-Aton-to-Rest;" king's-attendant in his august barge, master of the suite behind the Lord of the Two Lands, chief of all works of the king.

---

[a]See § 959, l. 4.

[b]There was a "*house for sending Aton to rest*," at Amarna, of which Mai was overseer (*mr*). Here doubtless the vesper service in the daily ritual was held at sunset.

[c]His titles, as usual in the original, are omitted above.

[d]Cliff-tomb (No. 14) in the southern group at Amarna (not numbered by Lepsius); published by Daressy, *Recueil*, XV, 38-41, where the name of the owner of the tomb is stated to be illegible. I found his name twice; it is certainly Mai ($M ͗ y$). Daressy's copy is inaccurate; I have used my own for the translation. The tomb is unfinished, but it contains, besides the above hymn (left doorpost), an address by Mai (right doorpost), beginning: "*Hear ye my speech, all ye people,*" in five columns, very faint, and still unpublished; and two prayers published by Daressy, from which some of above titles of Mai are taken.

998. He has left a long hymn, containing some of the most interesting references to the king and his *"teaching"* which have survived to us.

Hymn to Aton

999. [3][a]Thy rising is beautiful in the horizon of heaven, O living Aton, beginning of life. When thou risest in the horizon, thou fillest the earth with thy beauty. Thou art beautiful, great, brilliant, high over every hand. Thy rays [4]embrace the lands, even all that thou hast made. Thou art Re, and thou takest them all captive; thou bindest them for thy beloved son.

Praise of the King and Akhetaton

1000. Thy rays are upon thy glorious emanation, the ruler of truth, who came forth from eternity. [5]Thou grantest to him thy lifetime and thy years; thou hearest for him that which is in his heart. He is thy beloved; thou makest him[b] like Aton; thy child, who came forth from thy rays, King of Upper and Lower Egypt, Neferkheprure-Wanre, who hath made for thee the mighty Akhetaton, [6]great in loveliness, mistress of pleasant ceremonies, rich in possessions, the offerings to Re in her midst; at the sight of her beauty there is rejoicing. She is lovely and beautiful; when one sees her, it is like a glimpse at heaven; her number cannot be calculated. When the Aton rises in her, he fills her with his rays, [7]and he embraces his beloved son, son of eternity who came forth from Aton, and offers the earth to him who placed him on his throne, causing the earth to belong to Irsu.[c]

Praise of Aton and King

1001. Every land is festive at his rising; they assemble, making oblations to his ka, to Aton, rising in the horizon every early morning. [8]Thy[d] son presents truth to thy beautiful face; thou rejoicest when thou seest him, (for) he came forth from thee. Thou settest ⌜him⌝ as king like the Aton, Neferkheprure-Wanre, living and sound, like the Aton.

---

[a]Ll. 1 and 2 contain the usual title (*"Praise of Aton, the king and queen"*), which characterizes the content; although this does not contain any praise of the queen, as in Eye (§§ 989 ff.).

[b]Read *sw*, as in Eye, § 991, l. 4.

[c]See § 985, note. [d]Original has *"his."*

Self-Praise

1002. Hereditary prince, count, wearer of the royal seal, sole companion, [9]— — his Two Lands, commander of the army of the Lord of the Two Lands, overseer of the house of sending [the Aton] to rest, [Mai ($M ^c y$)]; he saith:

"I am his servant, whom he created; upright for the Lord of the Two Lands, one useful to his lord, who put truth in my body; (my) abomination is lying. [10]I know that the son of the Aton, Neferkheprure-Wanre, rejoices because of it, (for) he hath doubled to me my favors like the numbers of the sand. I am the head of the officials at the head of the people ($rḥy·t$). [11]My lord has advanced me, (because) I have carried out his teaching, and I hear his word without ceasing. My eyes behold thy beauty every day."

Prayer for Self

1003. "O my lord, wise like Aton, satisfied with truth. How prosperous is [12]he who hears thy teaching of life! May he be satisfied with seeing thee, when he reaches old age. Grant me goodly burial, of that which thy ka gives, in the house wherein thou commandest me to rest, [in] the mountain of Akhetaton, [13]the place of the favorites. O thou Myriad of full Niles every day, Neferkheprure-Wanre, god, that madest me, through whose ka ⌈I⌉ live; grant that I may be satisfied with following thee without ceasing, O [14]child of the Aton. Thou art for eternity, O thou Myriad of — — beseeching Wanre (Ikhnaton). How prosperous is he [15]who follows thee! Grant him, that all that he does may abide forever. May his lord give him burial, (for) his mouth was full of truth."

TOMB OF AHMOSE[a]

1004. Ahmose was *"real king's-scribe, his beloved, fan-bearer on the right of the king, master of the judgment-hall, steward of the estate of Neferkheprure-Wanre (Ikhnaton)."*

---

[a]Cliff-tomb (No. 3) at Amarna, northern group (Lepsius, No. 4); the hymns are on the doorposts: left-hand, Sharpe, *Egyptian Inscriptions*, Pl. VII (very bad), and my own copy. I found this doorpost much mutilated since Sharpe's time, and could not check all he copied. Right-hand: Lepsius, *Denkmäler*, III, 98, *a*; this doorpost is now so mutilated that I made no attempt to copy, in view of the short time at my disposal.

He has left the usual composite hymn upon the doorposts of his tomb.

1005. The two portions of this hymn, one introduced by praise to the rising, the other by praise to the setting, sun, form really one hymn, of the usual character above described (§ 979). The introductory praise of the god, the king, and the queen, is verbatim identical with the hymn of Tenr (§ 984), to which the reader is referred for the translation. Ahmose's hymn then proceeds with a tribute to the universality of the king's power, as follows:

Praise of the King

1006. — — — ⌜the praise⌝ of all that thou hast encircled. ——— presenting them to thy ka.· ⁵Thy child whom thou thyself didst beget — — — —. The south, as well as the north, the west and the east, [and the isles] in the midst of the sea ⁶are in jubilation to his ka. His southern boundary is as far as the wind, and (his) northern as far as the shining of Aton. All their princes make supplication, whom his fame has cowed ⁷through his beautiful ka, who makes festive the Two Lands, who supplies the needs of the whole land. Place him with[a] thyself forever, according as he has loved to behold thee. ⁸Grant him very many jubilees of peaceful years. Grant him the love of thy heart, like the sands of the shore, like the scales of the ⁹fish in the river, (or) the hair ¹⁰of the cattle......... May I be a follower of the Good God until he assigns the burial which he gives.

Hymn to Aton

1007. ᵇThy setting is beautiful, O living Aton, lord of lords, ruler of the Two Lands, — — — in the peace of the Two Lands. The people are in rejoicing before thee, giving praise to him who formed them, doing obeisance [⌜to him who created⌝] them, ⌜—⌝ to thy beloved son, the King of Upper and Lower Egypt, living in truth, Neferkheprure-

---

[a]Read ḥnꜥ-k.

[b]The second portion (Lepsius, *Denkmäler*, III, 98, a, right doorpost) begins here. It is clearly the second half of one hymn, the first half containing the praise of god, king, and queen; the second chiefly the prayer of the deceased as usual.

Wanre (Ikhnaton). The whole land, every country in thy every circuit, at thy appearance shall make jubilee to thy rising and to thy setting likewise, O god, living in truth before the eyes. Thou art the maker of that which is not, the maker of all these things that come forth from thy mouth.

Prayer for Self

1008. Grant to me advancement before the king every day, without ceasing; goodly burial after old age, on the highland of Akhetaton, when I have finished life in prosperity. May I be a follower of the Good God, when he treads any place he desires; may I be the companion of his two feet, for he trained me, when I was a child, until [I] attained revered age in peace and joy, a follower of the ruler, when he was at the feast, every day.

TOMB OF TUTU[a]

1009. Tutu (Tw-tw) was an imi-khentit (ymy-$ḫnty·t$) in Akhetaton. He was decorated with gold, like most of his colleagues, and has recorded some remarkable statements concerning his king in the following hymn:

Hymn to Aton and the King

1010. [1]— — — —[b] O Aton, given life forever and ever. As for thy son, the king, living in truth, Lord of the Two Lands [Neferkheprure-Wa]nre, thy child, who came forth from thy rays, thou establishest him in thy office of King of Upper and Lower Egypt, as ruler of the circuit of Aton. Thou givest him eternity, as thou hast made thyself, (for) thy son is thy emanation; spending for ⌜thee⌝ thy lifetime; Son of Re, great in duration; Great King's-Wife [Nefernefru]aton-[Nofretete], living forever. [2]— — — forever, Lord of the Two Lands. Thy rays

---

[a]Cliff-tomb (No. 8) in the southern group at Amarna (Lepsius, No. 2); Lepsius, *Denkmäler*, III, 107, *a;* Lepsius' squeeze of the same text; and my own copies of the original. The tomb contains, besides the above hymn, also a long and magnificent text (too long to be copied in the time at my disposal) and the short form of the great hymn.

[b]This beginning is apparently not a title, as in the other hymns, but a direct address.

are upon thy beloved son; thy hand carries satisfying life. Thy love is great, immense, ⌜—⌝, by thy august skin, when thou floodest heaven and earth with thy beauty. (Then) thy son, who came forth from thy limbs, adores thee, thou hearest for him that which is in his heart, (and) thou doest according to that which comes forth from his mouth. He is thy beloved, thou makest him like Aton. Although thou art in heaven, thy rays are upon [earth].[a] ³As thou begettest thyself every day without ceasing, (so) thou hast formed him out of thine own rays to spend the lifetime of Aton. When thou sailest the heavens, his eye [sees] thy beauty, rejoicing with joy at beholding thee, O living Aton, (for) he is thy favorite. Those who are under the heavens, even all that see thy rays, — — —, for thou hast made them, that he might satisfy thy heart therewith. ⁴— — — — great in duration.

Hymn to Aton

1011. I come with praise to Aton, the living, the only god, lord of radiance, who makes light when he rises in heaven, who illuminates the Two Lands. When he made to live all that he created, he drove away the darkness. When he sends out his rays, every land is filled with his love. The herbage and the trees start up before thee; the denizens of the water spring up at thy shining; all people arise in their places. (When) [their limbs][b] are washed [they take][b] their clothing, [they do][b] all work, they make their products. Thou hast awakened the Two Lands, when thou risest in thy form of living Aton. Their mouths are filled with that which thou givest. All small cattle rest upon their herbage; thou expellest evil and hast given health. Every one lifts himself up because thou risest: they have seen their lord (when) he appears

Praise of the King

1012. As for thine only son who came forth from thy body, thou embracest him with thy beautiful rays. ⁶— — — — — — in thy form of Aton, every land trips to thy rising. Thy rays bear a myriad of jubilees for thy son, living in truth, King of Upper and Lower Egypt, Neferkheprure-Wanre, my god, my fashioner, and my creator.

---

[a]Restored from Eye's great hymn (see my *De Hymnis in Solem sub Rege Amenophide IV Conceptis*, 19, V. 11).

[b]*Ibid.*, 34 and 36.

Prayer and Self-Praise

1013. Grant me that my eye may see him, that [my] hands may adore him, that my ear may hear his voice, that his ka may be before me without ceasing. I am the favorite servant, who ⌈hears⌉ his teaching, and his marvelous things are in my body without ceasing. I will speak truth to his majesty, (for) I know that he lives therein ......
⁸...... I do not that which his majesty hates, (for) my abomination is lying in my body, ⌈— — —⌉. I have sent up truth to his majesty, (for) I know that he lives therein. Thou art Re, begetter of truth; thou hast given ⁹———. My voice was not [lifted up] in the king's house, nor was my step too broad in the palace. I took not the reward of lying, nor expelled the truth for the violent; but it was the truth ⌈which⌉ I executed by his (the king's) might before me; I was mighty through the ka of Wanre, I was honored with reward — — ¹⁰— —
...... I set not lying in my body .... He glorified my teachableness every day, because I so fully carried out his teaching, not transgressing by any evil thing ¹¹....... May I be one who may adore his majesty; may I be his follower. Grant that I may be satisfied with seeing thee .... and assign to me — burial ¹²after old age — — in the mountain of Akhetaton..........ᵃ

TOMB OF HUYᵇ

1014. In Huy we have the usual favorite of Ikhnaton. His offices were responsible and important ones; for he was "*Overseer of the royal harem, overseer of the White House, steward in the house of the* ⌈—⌉,ᶜ *great king's-wife, Tiy (Tyy).*" The events depicted in his tomb are naturally those connected with his offices. As "*overseer of the White House*" he had charge of incoming tribute. A sceneᵈ in the tomb shows the king on a splendid throne-chair, borne

---

ᵃLl. 12–15 are mere fragments, showing that the prayers usual in these hymns form the conclusion.

ᵇCliff-tomb (No. 1) at Amarna, in the northern group (No. 7); published by Lepsius, *Denkmäler*, III, 100–102; sketches by Nestor l'Hôte in Amélineau, *Histoire de la sépulture*, Pls. 100–103; and my own copies.

ᶜSee § 1017.   ᵈLepsius, *Denkmäler*, III, 100, b.

on the shoulders of eighteen soldiers, and accompanied by fan- and shade-bearers. The fragmentary inscription shows that he is going to inspect the incoming foreign tribute of the twelfth year.

1015. Year 12, second month of the second season, day 8. Live my father, [Aton],[a] given life forever and ever; [live] the King of Upper and Lower Egypt, [Ikhnaton] and the Great King's-Wife, Nefernefruaton-Nofretete, living forever, at the arrival — — — — the tribute of Kharu ($H^{\jmath}$ -rw) and Kush, the west and east — — united in one head, the isles [in the midst] of the sea — on the side —, the tribute — — — the great storehouse of Akhetaton for receiving the impost of —, [that he may give to] them the breath of life.

1016. As steward of the queen-mother Tiy, we see him in charge of a feast,[b] doubtless in her house, at which she entertains the king, his queen, and three daughters. On another occasion Huy stands in the door of a temple ushering into it the king, who is leading the queen-mother Tiy, followed by the princess Bekateton and the court. Before them are the words:

Conducting the great king's-wife, ⌜—⌝, Tiy, to show to her her "Shadow-of-Re."

1017. This sanctuary, called here *"Shadow-of-Re,"*[c] is the queen-mother's temple; for besides being called *"hers"* above, the titles of Aton in the same temple have twice appended to them the words:[d] *"in the 'Shadow-of-Re' of* ⌜—⌝,[e] *the Great King's-Wife, Tiy."* It is perhaps the smaller of the two temples[f] found by Petrie at Amarna. As the relief shows, it was magnificently equipped with colonnades, statues, and cultus materials. Another temple of Aton, erected by the king's-daughter Meretaton, is similarly

---

[a]Two cartouches, contents erased.   [b]Lepsius, *Denkmäler*, III, 100, c.
[c]See *Proceedings of the Society of Biblical Archæology*, XV, 213, 214.
[d]Lepsius, *Denkmäler*, III, 102.
[e]Uncertain title of the queen, also in the preceding inscription and in § 1014.
[f]Petrie, *Amarna*, 7 and Pl. XXXV.

referred to on an altar (?) block[a] dedicated by the princess. It refers to Aton *"in the 'Shadow-of-Re' of the king's-daughter .... Meretaton .... in the chamber (called): 'Rejoicing-of-the-Aton' in the Aton-temple in Akhetaton."*

1018. What was probably another sanctuary is referred to in an unpublished hymn[b] from the tomb of Merire:

The singers and musicians are rejoicing with joy in the broad-hall ($wsh \cdot t$) of the house: "Shadow-of-Re," thy temple in Akhetaton, the place wherein thou art pleased.

This is probably the king's own official sanctuary, and *"Shadow-of-Re"*[c] is thus not a proper name, but a designation of any Aton-temple.[d] The temple of Aton at Heliopolis was called *"Exaltation-of-Re-in-Heliopolis."*[e] This was perhaps the first of the Aton-temples. Another Aton-temple erected at Hermonthis,[f] was called: *"Horizon-of-Aton-($y^{\jmath} hw \cdot t$-n-ytn)-in-Hermonthis ($ynw šm^c$)."* Still another, in Memphis, was called simply: *"The-House-of-the-Aton."*[g]

---

[a]British Museum, 1000; from my own copy; published by Sharpe, *Egyptian Inscriptions*, II, 48; also *Transactions of the Royal Society of Literature*, 2d Ser., I, Pl. II; and *Proceedings of the Society of Biblical Archæology*, XV, 209–11.

[b]My own copy; this passage is also found in the tomb of Apy, which fact enabled me to correct the Merire passage, which is corrupt. The Apy passage uses "*h·t-bnbn*" in place of "*Shadow-of-Re*," as given in Merire's tomb. (Piehl, *Inscriptions*, 1st Ser., Pl. CXCI = Bouriant, *Mémoires de la mission française au Caire*, I, 11, 12, ll. 6 and 7.) These passages show clearly that "*Shadow-of-Re*" is the name of the Akhetaton temple, and not of the god's statue, as supposed by some.

[c]Temples called "*Shadow-of-Re*" were found in the sacred districts of all the divinities of Egypt in the Twentieth Dynasty (IV, 363). Such a temple is known under Ramses II and also in the Twenty-first Dynasty; see Spiegelberg (*Recueil*, 17, 159, 160), who thinks these later ones were in the necropolis.

[d]On the Aton-temples at Amarna and elsewhere, see my article in *Zeitschrift für ägyptische Sprache*, 40, 106 ff. [Later—too late for insertion above, I have received the discussion of Davies (*Amarna*, II, 20–28) on the Amarna temples.]

[e]Ts-R^c-m-Ynw, possibly also "*Re-is-Exalted-in-Heliopolis*" (*Recueil*, XVI, 123, CIX).

[f]*Recueil*, 23, 62.

[g]Spiegelberg, *Rechnungen*, Taf. XVI, l. 4; Mariette, *Monuments divers*, 56 = Rougé, *Inscriptions hiéroglyphiques*, 54; fragments of inscriptions from this temple are in Mariette, *ibid.*, 34, *e*.

REIGN OF TUTENKHAMON
TOMB OF HUY[a]

1019. So little is known of the immediate successors of Ikhnaton that the tomb of Huy, viceroy of Kush under Tutenkhamon, is of the greatest importance. We know that this king marked the transition from the Aton faith back to Amon, having changed his name from Tutenkh*aton* to Tutenkh*amon*;[b] but on returning to Thebes he extended the temple of Aton.[c] Nevertheless, he was forced by the priestly party to begin the restoration of the monuments defaced by Ikhnaton, and to recut the inscriptions and dedications to Amon, which they bore.[d] We might infer that the Egyptian power in Asia was not wholly broken by Ikhnaton's reform, in view of the rich tribute of Syria shown in the following document; but see the remarks below. That of Nubia naturally continued without interruption,[e] as the scenes in this tomb likewise indicate. These scenes fall into three series:
  I. Investiture of the Viceroy of Kush.
  II. Tribute of the North.
  III. Tribute of the South.

---

[a]Hewn into the cliff of Kurnet-Murrai on the west side at Thebes; published partially by Champollion, *Notices descriptives*, I, 477-80; by Lepsius, *Denkmäler*, III, 115-18; Lepsius, *Denkmäler*, Text, III, 301-6; Brugsch, *Thesaurus*, V, 1133-41; and Piehl, *Inscriptions*, Pls. 144, A-145; a good account of the scenes, Baedeker, *Egypt*, 288, 289. These scenes are among the most gorgeous and elaborate of the Empire.

[b]The old form, Tutenkhaton, occurs on a Berlin stela, No. 14197 (*Ausführliches Verzeichniss des Berliner Museums*, 128); see Erman, *Zeitschrift für ägyptische Sprache*, 38, 112.

[c]Fragments of his extension are now rebuilt in the pylon of Harmhab at Karnak, Lepsius, *Denkmäler*, III, a-b; Bouriant, *Recueil*, VI, 51 ff.; and Piehl, *Zeitschrift für ägyptische Sprache*, 1884, 41. The name of Eye is found on similar reused blocks also.

[d]See II, 896.   [e]See also II, 896.

I. INVESTITURE OF THE VICEROY OF KUSH[a]

1020. The interesting and important ceremony depicted in this series of scenes throws light on a number of obscure points in the administration of Kush by the Pharaohs. We here learn its limits, viz., from El Kab on the north to Napata on the south. For Napata appears (§ 1025) the important variant Karoy, thus locating this otherwise unknown region, designated by the Eighteenth Dynasty kings as their southern boundary.[b]

Scene

1021. King Tutenkhamon is enthroned at the left in a kiosk; before him are two lines of men in groups, representing successive incidents in the ceremony

Reception of Huy

1022. An officer standing with back to the king receives Huy as he advances, accompanied by several courtiers. The inscriptions are these:

Over the Officer

The overseer of the White House; he says: "This is the seal[c] from the Pharaoh, L. P. H., who assigns to thee (the territory) from Nekhen to Napata."

Over Huy

1023. King's-son of Kush ———.

Words of Courtiers

"Thou art the Son of Amon ———;[d] he causes that the chiefs of all countries come to thee, bearing every good and choice thing of their countries."

---

[a]Scenes and inscriptions copied by Erman, and published from his notes by Brugsch (*Thesaurus*, V, 1133-41).

[b]This had been already noticed by Erman (*Aegypten*, 666), and was not new, as I supposed when I called attention to it in *Zeitschrift für ägyptische Sprache*, 40, 108.

[c]Reading the *my*-sign as the usual determinative of ḫtm, "seal;" see Piehl (*Inscriptions*, I, 112, n. 5).

[d]Cartouche with name illegible.

Investiture of Huy

1024. Huy stands before an officer who holds a small object, perhaps an étui containing the seal, which is to be delivered to Huy. No inscriptions. Immediately beside this scene appears an official who extends to Huy the seal of office. The inscriptions are:

Over Official

1025. ['Take'] the seal of office, O king's-son of [Kush].

Over Huy

The office is assigned to the king's-son of Kush, Huy, from Nekhen to Karoy.

1026. Another scene shows Huy's reception by his family and officials (among whom are the *"inspectors"* (*rwd·w*)), as he issues from the palace.

Over Huy

The coming forth, favored, from the court, having been appointed in the presence of the Good God to be king's-son and governor of the southern countries, Huy. He accounts Khenthennofer, included under his authority, to offer it to the Lord of the Two Lands, like every subject of his majesty.

II. TRIBUTE OF THE NORTH

1027. It is evident in this series that the administration of Kush now requires two viceroys, for Huy's brother, Amenhotep, here appears as *"King's-son of Kush."* For reasons not evident in the inscriptions, these two viceroys of the South appear presenting to the king the tribute of the North. This circumstance looks suspicious. What should the viceroy of Kush have to do with the tribute of the North? Moreover, we know from the Amarna Letters that Egyptian power in Asia was at an end under Ikhnaton. One might be inclined to think, therefore, that the frequent representation of the tribute of the South and North in earlier Theban tombs of the Eighteenth Dynasty induced Huy to add the tribute of the North as a pendant to the tribute of the South which he actually collected. But it should not be forgotten that one of Ikhnaton's successors carried on war in Asia (III, 20), and this can hardly have been any other than Tutenkhamon. He may thus have been able to collect some northern tribute.

Scene

1028. King Tutenkhamon is enthroned at the left under a splendid kiosk. Before him bows the viceroy of Kush, Huy, behind whom comes a second viceroy of Kush, Huy's brother, Amenhotep, bearing gifts. These two officials are introducing four lines of Asiatics who bring a magnificent array of tribute, chiefly gold and silver vessels, costly stones, and horses.

1029. The following inscriptions accompany the scene:

Over Huy

King's-son of Kush, governor of the south countries, fan-bearer at the right of the king, Huy (Hwy), triumphant; he says: "May thy father, Amon, protect thee during myriads of jubilees (hb-sd). May he give to thee eternity as king of the Two Lands, everlastingness as ruler of the Nine Bows. Thou art Re, and thy emanation is his emanation. Thou art heaven,[a] abiding like its four pillars, the earth sits beneath thee, because of thy permanence, O good ruler."

With Amenhotep

1030. Bringing in all the tribute to the Lord of the Two Lands, the presents of Retenu ($Rtnw$) the wretched; by the king's-messenger to every country, the king's-son of Kush, governor of the southern countries, Amenhotep, triumphant.

---

[a]Meaning, as enduring as heaven.

With Vessels

1031. Vessels of all the choicest of the best of their countries, in silver, gold, lapis lazuli, malachite, every splendid costly stone.

With an Official Receiving Asiatics

1032. All the chiefs of the ⌜north⌝ countries ⌜— —⌝; they say: "How great is thy fame, O Good God! how mighty thy strength! there is none living in ignorance of thee."

The chiefs of [all countries] that knew not Egypt since the time of the god, are craving peace from his majesty that it may not be. "Give to us the breath which thou givest, etc., (as below)."

Over Asiatics

1033. The chiefs of Retenu (*Rtnw*) the Upper, who knew not Egypt since the time of the god, are craving peace from his majesty. They say: "Give to us the breath which thou givest, O ⌜lord⌝. Tell us[a] thy victories; and there shall be no revolters in thy time; but every land shall be in peace."

III. TRIBUTE OF THE SOUTH[b]

1034. In this series the two viceroys present to the king the tribute of the lands under them. This ceremony took place in the temple, from which Huy then goes forth to embark for Nubia, and is received on his dahabiyeh by his local officials, who have accompanied him to Thebes.

Scene

1035. King Tutenkhamon is enthroned as in the previous scene, with Huy before him. In the king's presence a magnificent array of tribute; chiefly commercial gold and silver, gold and silver vessels, a chariot, shields, and furniture.

---

[a]The two *n*'s (dative?) are probably an error for one, viz., "*that we may tell*, etc."

[b]See Lepsius, *Denkmäler*, Text, III, 301–6; where the inscriptions are much more accurate than in the folio of Lepsius.

A second part of the scene shows Huy receiving three lines of Negroes, and a line of Egyptians below. In the top line of Negroes are children of the Kushite chiefs, among them a princess in a chariot drawn by oxen. The negro chiefs wear Egyptian clothing;[a] they bring similar tribute, and also curiously decorated cattle. Behind all, we see six Nile boats landing. With the exception of the king's names, the inscriptions are confined to the second part of the scene.

Before Huy

1036. The arrival in peace — from the house of the hereditary prince, count, (*mry-nṯr-*) priest, king's-son of Kush, Huy ⌜having received⌝ the favor of the Lord of the Two Lands, ⌜who ordered⌝ gold [to be put] upon his neck and his arms. ⌜How many are the⌝ examples[b] of thy favor, O Nebkheprure (Tutenkhamon)! One mentions them (one) time (each) by its name; they are too numerous to put them into writing.

Over the Upper Line of Negroes

1037. The chief of Miam*ᶜ* (*My ᶜ m*), good ruler.[d] The chiefs of Wayet (*w ꜣ y· t*).[e] The children of the chiefs of all countries.

Over the Middle Line of Negroes

The chiefs of Kush, they say: "Hail to thee, O king of Egypt, Sun of the Nine Bows! Give to us the breath which thou givest. Men live by thy love."[f]

Over the Egyptians

1038. The coming forth of the people of the king's-son, to receive him, when he received the favor of the Lord of the Two Lands; (⌜from⌝)

---

[a]Under Thutmose III they still wore native costume; see tomb of Rekhmire.
[b]Lit., "*Examples upon very many examples, and great is thy favor, etc.*"
[c]Country around Ibrim; see tomb of Penno (IV, 474).
[d]The presence of these chiefs shows that the country was still under its native rulers, and that the Egyptian administrative officers were not in sole control.
[e]As in Champollion (*Notices descriptives*, I, 478).
[f]Very much the same inscription is over the lower row of Negroes (Lepsius, *Denkmäler*, Text, III, 303).

the house^a of the king's-son of Kush, king's-scribe, Amenhotep — — living again.

They say: "O ruler, L. P. H., good, mighty in creation, for whom the sun rises; many are the things ⌜which⌝ ⌜his two hands⌝ ⌜accomplish⌝."

Over the Boats

Arrival from Kush bearing this good tribute of all the choicest of the best of the south countries. Landing at the city of the South (Thebes) by the king's-son of Kush, Huy.

Scene

1039. Huy leans on his staff; behind him are the members of his family; before him a richly decorated dahabiyeh with sail spread, and another with sail furled, bearing a chariot and horses. On the boats approaching Huy, are four rows of officials under Huy, followed by sailors and women with tambourines. The inscriptions show that the presentation ceremonies depicted above have just been completed in the temple, and Huy is now doubtless embarking for his post. The inscriptions are these:

Over Huy

1040. The coming from the temple of Amon after the pleasing ceremonies before him, to offer this land to thee;^b by the hereditary prince, count, sole companion, great in [his office], great [in his ra]nk, great —, — king's-scribe, ——— Amenhotep — —.

Over Huy's Family

The inscriptions are nearly vanished, but the words: "*His son*" (twice); "*his mother*," and "*his sister*," may be distinguished.

---

^aThe door of the house from which they come is seen behind them; on it are the cartouches of Tutenkhamon.

^bThe change of person is difficult.

Over Officials

1041. 1. Deputy of Kush. 2. Mayor of Khammat (Soleb) 3. Overseer of cattle. 4. ─────. 5. Deputy of the fortres: (called): "Neb[khepr]ure[a]-Satisfier-of-the-Gods,"[b] Penno. 6. Mayor of "Satisfier-of-the-Gods." 7. His brother, ⌜prophet⌝ of —[c] ⌜in⌝ the fortress; "Satisfier-of-the-Gods," Mermose; 8. Priest of —,[c] residing in the fortress: "Satisfier-of-the-Gods." 9. ─────.

---

[a] Tutenkhamon's throne-name.
[b] $S\cdot ḥtp\text{-}ntr\cdot w$.
[c] Cartouche.

REIGN OF EYE

LANDMARK OF EYE[a]

1042. Documents of this king are rare. This stela shows the king, in relief at the top, offering flowers to "*Hathor, mistress of Hotep.*" The exclusive worship of Aton had therefore been abandoned by him at this date, year 3. The inscription records a gift of land by the king to one of his officials, whose name is no longer visible, and to the latter's wife, Mutnezmet.

1043. Year 3, third month of the third season (eleventh month), first day, of King Eye,[b] given life, while he was in Memphis.

His majesty commanded to endow him with lands, a reward for the king's- —, —,[c] and for his wife, Mutnezmet. It was laid out in the district called: "⌜Field⌝-of-the-Kheta," in the fields of the "House-of-Okheperkere (Thutmose I)" and the "House-of-Menkheprure (Thutmose IV)," a field of 154 stat.

The south is the "House-of-Menkheprure (Thutmose IV);" the north is the "House-of-Ptah" and the "House-of-Okheperkere (Thutmose I)," between his ⌜—⌝; the west is [⌜the "House-of-Okheperkere (Thutmose I)⌝¹"];[d] the east is the "House-of-Menkheprure (Thutmose IV)" between his ⌜—⌝.

There came[e] the chief king's-scribe, the steward, Ramose; the scribe, Merire; — Thay. Command was given to the — attendant, Re, to transfer it.[f]

---

[a]Stela now in Cairo; found by the Great Pyramid, in the chapel of Pesibkhenno; published by Daressy (*Recueil*, 16, 123) and from Daressy by Spiegelberg (*Rechnungen*, 36).

[b]Full fivefold titulary is used in the original.

[c]The lacuna contained the remainder of a royal official's title, and his name, which latter ended in *nf*.

[d]The land, as already stated, lay in the fields of the House-of-Thutmose I and the House-of-Thutmose IV; the southern and eastern boundaries were formed by the House-of-Thutmose IV, and the northern boundary by the House-of-Thutmose I. Hence it is probable that the western boundary was also formed by the House-of-Thutmose I, and that Daressy has overlooked it in his copy, owing to its identity with the preceding boundary.

[e]As witnesses? Spiegelberg renders "those who came," but the *nt* which he renders as the relative pronoun occurs above, with the first, "*his* ⌜—⌝ (*nwy*)," and must therefore belong to *nwy* here.

[f]The land.

www.ingramcontent.com/pod-product-compliance
Lightning Source LLC
Chambersburg PA
CBHW040338300426
44113CB00027B/2671